Josephus, the bible, and history

Josephus, the bible, and history

Edited by Louis H. Feldman and Gohei Hata

WAYNE STATE UNIVERSITY PRESS • DETROIT • 1989

Distributed in the United States and Canada by Wayne State University Press,
Detroit, Michigan. Distributed in other countries of the world by E.J. Brill, Leiden.

93 92 91 90 89   5 4 3 2 1

Library of Congress Cataloging-in-Publication Data
Josephus, the Bible, and history / edited by Louis Feldman and Gohei Hata.
   p. cm.
   Bibliography: p.
   Includes index.
   ISBN 0-8143-1982-3 (alk. paper). ISBN 0-8143-1983-1 (pbk : alk.
paper)
   1. Josephus, Flavius. 2. Jews—History—168 B.C.—135 A.D.—
Historiography. 3. Bible. O.T.—Criticism, interpretation, etc.,
Jewish. I. Feldman, Louis H. II. Hata, Gōhei, 1942–
DS115.9.J6J68   1989   88-10832
933′.0072024—dc19   CIP

To the memory of the parents of my wife, Miriam,
Moshe Yaakov and Rivkah Blum, Z"L, martyrs in the Holocaust,
whose devotion to the Jewish tradition is their greatest legacy.

Louis H. Feldman

Contents

Contributors

Shimon Applebaum, who received his doctorate from Oxford in 1952, is professor emeritus of classical archaeology and Jewish history at Tel Aviv University, Israel. He is the author of *Agrarian History of England and Wales—Roman Britain* (1972) and *Jews and Greeks in Ancient Cyrene* (1979).

Günther Baumbach, professor of New Testament in the Department of Theology of the Humboldt University in East Berlin, has written *Das Verständnis des Bösen in den synoptischen Evangelien* (1963), *Jesus von Nazareth im Lichte der jüdischen Gruppenbildung* (1971), and (with K. M. Fischer) *Das Neue Testament mit Erklärungen* (1986).

Louis H. Feldman, professor of classics at Yeshiva University, New York, is the editor of Books XVIII to XX of Josephus' *Antiquities* in the Loeb Classical Library (1965) and is the author of an extensive Prolegomenon to the reissue of M. R. James' version of *Pseudo-Philo's Biblical Antiquities* (1971), of *Josephus and Modern Scholarship* (1984), and of *Josephus: A Supplementary Bibliography* (1986). He is the coeditor (with Gohei Hata) of *Josephus, Judaism, and Christianity* (1987).

Isaiah M. Gafni is senior lecturer in Jewish history at the Hebrew University, Jerusalem. He is the author of *Babylonian Jewry and Its Institutions in the Period of the Talmud* [Hebrew] (1975). His doctoral dissertation at the Hebrew University (1978) was on *The Babylonian Yeshiva: Internal Structure, Spiritual and Social Functions within the Jewish Community in the Amoraic Period.*

Heinz Kreissig, late professor of ancient history and archaeology at the Akademie der Wissenschaften in East Berlin, is the author of *Die sozialen Zusammenhänge des Judäischen Krieges: Klassen und Klassenkampf in Palästina des l. Jahrhunderts v. u. Z.* 1970) and *Die sozialökonomische Situation in Juda zur Achämenidenzeit* (1973). He died in 1984.

Sid Z. Leiman received his doctorate from the University of Pennsylvania. After teaching at Yale University and after serving as dean of the Bernard Revel Graduate School of Yeshiva University and chairman of the Department of Judaic Studies at Brooklyn College of the City University of New York, he is now professor of Jewish history and literature at Brooklyn College. He is the author of *The Canonization of Hebrew Scripture* (1976) and the editor of *The Canon and Masorah of the Hebrew Bible* (1974).

Benjamin Mazar received his doctorate from the University of Giessen, Germany, in 1928. He has directed archaeological excavations at Beth Shearim, Tel Qasile, Ein Gedi, and the Old City of Jerusalem. Professor emeritus in archaeology at the Hebrew University, Jerusalem, he has also served the university as rector and president. He is the author of *Untersuchungen zur alten Geschichte und Ethnographie Syriens und Palästinas* (1930), *History of Palestine Exploration* (1935), *History of Palestine* (1937), *Israel in Biblical Times* (1941), *Beth Shearim* (1944), *Canaan and Israel* (1974), *The Mountain of the Lord* (1975), *Excavations and Discoveries in Israel* (1986), and *The First Biblical Period* (1986), among others.

Raymond R. Newell, who is currently completing his doctoral studies with a dissertation on *The Suicide Accounts in Josephus* at Vanderbilt University, teaches at Martin Methodist College in Pulaski, Tennessee.

Valentin Nikiprowetzky, who died in 1983, was professor of Hebrew and Jewish Studies at the University of Paris III, La Sorbonne Nouvelle. He was the editor and translator into French of Philo's *De Decalogo* (1965) and of *Les Oracles Sibyllins, Fragments, Livres III, IV et V*, in *La Bible*, vol. 3: *Les écrits intertestamentaires* (1987). His *magnum opus* is *Le Commentaire de l'Écriture chez Philon d'Alexandrie: Son caractère et sa portée. Observations philologiques* (1977).

André Pelletier, who died in 1985, received his doctorate in 1962 from the Sorbonne with a dissertation on *Flavius Josèphe adaptateur de la Lettre d'Aristée* and served as professor of biblical Greek at the Centre Sèvres. He is the author of *Lettre d'Aristée à Philocrate* (1962), *Philon d'Alexandrie, In Flaccum* (1967), *Legatio ad Gaium* (1972), *Flavius Josèphe, Guerre des Juifs* (4 vols., 1975–1987) and *Autobiographie* (1983).

Zeev Safrai, who received his doctorate from the Hebrew University, Jerusalem, is senior lecturer in the Department of Land of Israel Studies at Bar Ilan University in Israel. He is the author of *Boundaries and Administration in Eretz-Israel in the Mishnah-Talmud Period* [Hebrew] (1980).

Joseph Sievers received his doctorate from Columbia University in 1981 with a dissertation on *The Hasmoneans and Their Supporters from Mattathias to Hyrcanus I*. He has taught ancient history, Jewish studies, and biblical studies at the City University of New York, Seton Hall University, and Fordham University.

Clemens Thoma, after receiving his doctorate in 1966 from the University of Vienna with a dissertation on *Die Zerstörung des jerusalemischen Tempels im Jahre 70 n. Chr. Geistig-religiöse Bedeutung für Judentum und Christentum nach den Aussagen jüdischer und christlicher Primärliteratur*, has served as professor of biblical and Judaic studies at the Theological Faculty of Lucerne, Switzerland. He has written *Judentum und christlicher Glaube* (1965), *A Christian Theology of Judaism* (1980), and (with Simon Lauer) *Die Gleichnisse der Rabbinen. Erster Teil: Pesiqta deRav Kahana* (1986).

Eugene Ulrich, who received his doctorate in 1975 from Harvard University, has published his dissertation, *The Qumran Text of Samuel and Josephus* (1978). He is the editor of the *Bulletin of the International Organization for Septuagint and Cognate Studies* and is currently completing the editions of biblical scrolls for the multivolume *Discoveries in the Judean Desert*.

Ben Zion Wacholder, professor of Talmud and rabbinics at Hebrew Union College-Jewish Institute of Religion in Cincinnati, received his doctorate from the University of California at Los Angeles in 1960. He has written *Nicolaus of Damascus* (1962), *Eupolemus* (1974), and *The Dawn of Qumran* (1983).

Abbreviations

A	*Antiquitates Judaicae* (Josephus)
AA	*Acta Antiqua*
AAN	*Atti della Accademia di Scienze morali e politiche della Società nazionale*
AC	*Acta Classica*
AJP	*American Journal of Philology*
AJSR	*Association for Jewish Studies Review*
ALUOS	*Annual of the Leeds University Oriental Society*
ANET	*Ancient Near Eastern Texts Relating to the Old Testament,* James B. Pritchard, ed., 3d ed. (Princeton 1969)
ANRW	*Aufstieg und Niedergang der römischen Welt*
AOASH	*Acta Orientalia Academiae Scientiarum Hungaricae*
Ap	*Contra Apionem* (Josephus)
Ar.	*Letter of Aristeas*
ASE	*Annuario di Studi Ebraici*
ASNSP	*Annali della R. Scuola Normale Superiore di Pisa. Lettere, Storia e Filosofia*
ASTI	*Annual of the Swedish Theological Institute*
AT	*Antik Tanulmányok* (= *Studia Antiqua*)
AUSS	*Andrews University Seminary Studies*
B	Codex Vaticanus of the Septuagint
b.	Babylonian Talmud
BA	*Biblical Archaeologist*
BAGB	*Bulletin de l'Association Guillaume Budé*
BAR	*Biblical Archaeology Review*
BASOR	*Bulletin of the American Schools of Oriental Research*
BFCT	*Beiträge zur Förderung Christlicher Theologie*
BIDR	*Bollettino dell' Istituto di Dritto Romano*
BIOSCS	*Bulletin of the International Organization for Septuagint and Cognate Studies*
BJ	*Bellum Judaicum* (Josephus)
BJH	*Bible and Jewish History: Studies in Bible and Jewish History. Dedicated to the Memory of Jacob Liver* [Hebrew], Benjamin Uffenheimer, ed. (Tel-Aviv 1972)
BJPES	*Bulletin of the Jewish Palestine Exploration Society*
BK	*Bibel und Kirche*

BL	*Bibel und Liturgie*
BM	*Beth Mikra*
BZ	*Biblische Zeitschrift*
C	Chronicles
CAH	*Cambridge Ancient History*
CBQ	*Catholic Biblical Quarterly*
CCARJ	*Central Conference of American Rabbis Journal*
CD	*The Cairo Damascus Document*
CIL	*Corpus Inscriptionum Latinarum*
CM	*Clio Medica*
CP	*Collected Papers: Josephus Flavius: Historian of Eretz-Israel in the Hellenistic-Roman Period,* Uriel Rappaport, ed. (Jerusalem 1982)
CPh	*Classical Philology*
CPJ	*Corpus Papyrorum Judaicarum,* Victor A. Tcherikover, Alexander Fuks, Menahem Stern, eds., 3 vols. (Cambridge, Mass. 1957–1964)
CQ	*Classical Quarterly*
DHA	*Dialogues d'Histoire Ancienne*
DLZ	*Deutsche Literaturzeitung*
DTT	*Dansk Teologisk Tidsskrift*
EAZ	*Ethnographisch-Archaeologische Zeitschrift*
EB	*Estudios Biblicos*
EI	*Eretz-Israel*
EJ	*Encyclopaedia Judaica,* Cecil Roth et al., eds., 16 vols. (Jerusalem 1971–1972)
ET	*Evangelische Theologie*
ETL	*Ephemerides Theologicae Lovanienses*
FGrH	*Fragmente der Griechischen Historiker,* Felix Jacoby, ed. (Berlin and Leiden 1923–1958)
FHG	*Fragmenta Historicorum Graecorum,* Carolus Mueller, ed., 5 vols. (Paris 1841–1870)
FR	*Freiburger Rundbrief*
G	Septuagint
GCS	*Die Griechische Christlichen Schriftsteller der ersten drei Jahrhunderte*
GJV	Emil Schürer, *Geschichte des jüdischen Volkes im Zeitalter Jesu Christi,* 3 vols., 3rd–4th ed. (Leipzig 1901–1909)
GLAJJ	*Greek and Latin Authors on Jews and Judaism,* Menahem Stern, ed., 3 vols. (Jerusalem 1974–1984)
GRBS	*Greek, Roman and Byzantine Studies*
HERE	*Encyclopaedia of Religion and Ethics.* James Hastings, ed., 12 vols. (Edinburgh 1914)
HHS	*Historians and Historical Schools. Lectures Delivered at the Seventh Convention of the Historical Society of Israel,*

	December 1961 [Hebrew], Samuel Ettinger et al., eds. (Jerusalem 1962)
HJ	*Historia Judaica*
HSM	*Harvard Semitic Monographs*
HT	*History and Theory*
HTR	*Harvard Theological Review*
HUCA	*Hebrew Union College Annual*
HZ	*Historische Zeitschrift*
IEJ	*Israel Exploration Journal*
IGR	*Inscriptiones Graecae ad Res Romanas Pertinentes*
IM	*Israelitische Monatsschrift* (supplement to *Die Jüdische Presse*)
IOSCS	International Organization for Septuagint and Cognate Studies
J	Josephus
J.	Jerusalem Talmud
JAOS	*Journal of the American Oriental Society*
JBL	*Journal of Biblical Literature*
JC	*Jerusalem Cathedra*
JCP	*Jahrbücher für Classische Philologie*
JE	*Jewish Encyclopedia*, Isidore Singer, ed., 12 vols. (New York 1901–1906)
JEH	*Journal of Ecclesiastical History*
JHS	*Journal of Historical Studies*
JJS	*Journal of Jewish Studies*
JNES	*Journal of Near Eastern Studies*
JPFC	*The Jewish People in the First Century: Historical Geography, Political History, Social, Cultural, and Religious Life and Institutions*, Samuel Safrai and Menahem Stern, eds. (*Compendia Rerum Iudaicarum ad Novum Testamentum*, Sect. 1: Philadelphia 1974)
JQR	*Jewish Quarterly Review*
JR	*Journal of Religion*
JRS	*Journal of Roman Studies*
JS	*Jewish Spectator*
J-S	*Josephus-Studien: Untersuchungen zu Josephus, dem antiken Judentum und dem Neuen Testament, Otto Michel zum 70. Geburtstag gewidmet*, Otto Betz, Klaus Haacker, and Martin Hengel, eds. (Göttingen 1974)
JSeS	*Journal of Semitic Studies*
JSJ	*Journal for the Study of Judaism*
JSNT	*Journal for the Study of the New Testament*
JSOT	*Journal for the Study of the Old Testament*
JSS	*Jewish Social Studies*
JTS	*Journal of Theological Studies*
JWI	*Journal of the Warburg Institute*
L	Lucianic Biblical Text

LAB	*Liber Antiquitatum Biblicarum* by Pseudo-Philo
LCL	*Loeb Classical Library*
LQR	*Law Quarterly Review*
M	Mishnah
MGWJ	*Monatsschrift für Geschichte und Wissenschaft des Judenthums*
MWJ	*Magazin für die Wissenschaft des Judentums*
MT	Masoretic text
NH	*Nation and History: Studies in the History of the Jewish People* [Hebrew], Menahem Stern, ed. (Jerusalem 1983)
NJKA	*Neue Jahrbücher für das klassische Altertum, Geschichte und deutsche Literatur*
NRT	*Nouvelle Revue Theologique*
NT	*Novum Testamentum*
NTS	*New Testament Studies*
NYSJM	*New York State Journal of Medicine*
OG	Old Greek (the Septuagint)
OL	Old Latin (version of the Septuagint)
OLZ	*Orientalistische Literaturzeitung*
PAAJR	*Proceedings of the American Academy for Jewish Research*
PEFQS	*Palestine Exploration Fund Quarterly Statement*
PEJ	*Palestine Exploration Journal*
PEQ	*Palestine Exploration Quarterly*
PG	*Patrologia Graeca*, J. P. Migne, ed.
PJ	*Palästinajahrbuch*
PSWCJS	*Proceedings of the Sixth World Congress of Jewish Studies, 1973* (Jerusalem 1975)
Q	Qumran
1QD	*Damascus Document* (from Cave 1 at Qumran)
1QS	*Serek hayyahad* (*Rule of the Community, Manual of Discipline*)
1QSa	Appendix A (*Rule of the Congregation*) to *1QS*
1QSb	Appendix B (*Blessings*) to *1QS*
4Qfl	*Florilegium* (or *Eschatological Midrashim* from Qumran Cave 4)
R	Later Recension of the Proto-Theodotion type bringing the Greek text into conformity with the Masoretic text
RB	*Revue Biblique*
RBPH	*Revue Belge de Philologie et d'Histoire*
RE	*Realencyclopädie der klassischen Altertumswissenschaft*, August Pauly and Georg Wissowa, eds.
REJ	*Revue des Études juives*
RF	*Rivista di Filologia*
RH	*Revue Historique*
RHDFE	*Revue Historique du Droit Français et Étranger*
RhM	*Rheinisches Museum*
RHR	*Revue de l'Histoire des Religions*
RiBi	*Rivista Biblica*

RMI	*Rassegna mensile di Israel*
ROIELAO	*Revue de l'Organisation Internationale pour l'Étude des Langues Anciennes par Ordinateur*
RQ	*Revue de Qumran*
RSA	*Ricerche di storiographia antica*
RSR	*Recherches de Science Religieuse*
S	Peshitta
SBL	Society of Biblical Literature
SBLMS	*Society of Biblical Literature Monograph Series*
SC	*Sources Chrétiennes*
SCI	*Scripta Classica Israelica*
SE	*Studia Evangelica*
SH	*Scripta Hierosolymitana*
SHR	*Studies in the History of Religions*
SP	*Studia Patristica*
ST	*Studia Theologica*
T	Targum
TAPA	*Transactions of the American Philological Association*
TCAAS	*Transactions of the Connecticut Academy of Arts and Sciences*
ThWNT	*Theologisches Wörterbuch zum Neuen Testament,* Gerhard Kittel and Gerhard Friedrich, eds., 9 vols. (Stuttgart 1933–1973)
TLZ	*Theologische Literaturzeitung*
TU	*Texte und Untersuchungen zur Geschichte der altchristlichen Literatur*
TZ	*Theologische Zeitschrift*
V	*Vita* (Josephus)
VC	*Vigiliae Christianae*
WHJP	*World History of the Jewish People,* Benjamin Netanyahu et al., eds. (New Brunswick 1964–)
ZAW	*Zeitschrift für die alttestamentliche Wissenschaft*
ZDPV	*Zeitschrift des Deutschen Palästina-Vereins*
ZNW	*Zeitschrift für die neutestamentliche Wissenschaft*
ZPE	*Zeitschrift für Papyrologie und Epigraphik*
ZRGG	*Zeitschrift für Religions- und Geistesgeschichte*

Introduction

LOUIS H. FELDMAN

t is hard to imagine a more controversial major figure in the history of letters than Flavius Josephus. His mysterious elevation to the rank of general in the ill-fated revolution of the Jews against the Romans in the first century, followed so quickly by his surrender to the enemy under the most suspicious of circumstances and the numerous subsequent rewards that he received from them, has hardly endeared him to the Jewish people and to lovers of liberty. And yet, he is, certainly of ancient writers, the most passionate defender of his people against the charges of anti-Semites in what must be regarded as the most famous treatise refuting anti-Semitic canards ever written, *Against Apion.*

As a historian Josephus has been defended as a careful writer who approached his craft critically, as we see, for example, in his extensive treatment of Herod; and yet, here, too, are contradictions between what he says in his *Jewish War* and what he writes in his later *Antiquities.* It has been noted[1] that inasmuch as he spent at least a dozen years writing the *Antiquities,* living on an imperial pension and, so far as we know, without having any additional duties or responsibilities, he wrote an average of about ten lines of Greek a day and that one should, therefore, expect a careful piece of work. However, he has been reviled as a careless, self-serving, lying propagandist, no less in the events leading up to the war against the Romans than in his account of the war itself, in which he played such an ambiguous role.

Nevertheless, on one point there surely is and must be general agreement. Josephus is our most important extant source for the period from the end of the second century B.C.E. to the year 70, when the Second Temple was destroyed by the Romans. To appreciate this, one need only compare what we know of this period with what information we have for the centuries that followed, when we do not have a Josephus.

However, the importance of Josephus far transcends his role as a chronicler of the political and military events for these turbulent years. He is also a most important source of our knowledge of the biblical canon and text, since our earliest complete manuscripts of the Bible, at least in the Hebrew, are a millennium later; he is crucial for our understanding of Jewish law and lore, antedating the codification of the Mishnah by a century and the Midrashim by several centuries; he is indispensable for our understanding of the political, social, economic, and religious background of the rise of Christianity and of the other sects of the era, as well as of Jewry of the Diaspora; he is our most important literary guide to the geography, topography, and monuments of Palestine, so that the archaeologist must dig with a spade in one hand and a copy of Josephus in the other; and he is most important as a historian of the Graeco-Roman world who sheds crucial light on events of the last century of the Roman Republic and on the first century of the Roman Empire. No wonder that Josephus' influence on literature, music, and art, particularly because of his importance for Christians, who saw fit to preserve all of his works, has been so profound. This popularity was due not merely to the passages about Jesus (the so-called *Testimonium Flavianum*), John the Baptist, and James the brother of Jesus, but also to the fact that he wrote a work, the *Jewish War,* that has as its climax the destruction of the Temple, which, according to the Gospels, Jesus had predicted years earlier and the cause of which, according to one view of Christian theology, was the Jewish sin of deicide. Indeed, on the shelf of literate Christians, Josephus very often occupied a place of honor between the Jewish Scriptures and the New Testament.

The present collection of essays represents an attempt to assess some of the questions surrounding this important and enigmatic personality. Its genesis was an interest expressed by the Japanese firm of Yamamoto Shoten, after its publication of the translation of Josephus into Japanese by Gohei Hata, in presenting Japanese readers with an overview of the present state of Josephan scholarship on key questions, so that they might attain a better understanding of the Judaism and of the beginnings of Christianity of that period. The essays here included, all of them expressly commissioned by the editors and written for this collection, have been selected from that work; and it may be in order here to comment briefly on them.

Josephus' importance for our knowledge of the canon, the text, and the interpretation of the Bible is particularly great because our other sources, such as the Septuagint, are fraught with incredibly complex problems of their own; or they are sectarian, such as the texts of the Samaritans or the Dead Sea Scrolls; or they are later, such as the Talmud or the writings of the church fathers.

The definitive study of the canon by Professor Sid Leiman in his doctoral dissertation and in its published form[2] is here summarized and updated. He calls attention to the fact that Josephus' passage about the canon (*Ap* I, 37–

43) appears in an apologetic context, defending the accuracy of the biblical account from a historical point of view, as against the chronicles of the Greeks and other peoples. Amazingly enough, Josephus does not here, as he does elsewhere, refer to the biblical writings as sacred but rather stresses that they were written by prophets who were inspired and who, we may add, wrote clearly (*Ap.* I, 37) rather than ambiguously about ancient history—an attack, we may suggest, similar to that made by Thucydides (1.20) upon his predecessors, most notably (though unnamed) Herodotus.

As to Josephus' statement that the canon had long since been closed and that no Jew had ventured to modify even a syllable but, on the contrary, had been ready to die for these writings, this, we may suggest, is to be viewed together with his statement (*A* I, 5) that he will present the precise details of the Scriptures, neither adding nor omitting anything. Four possible interpretations of this may be here presented. (1) As Professor Leiman suggests, this is a commonplace in classical historiography, found, we may remark, in such writers as Dionysius of Halicarnassus, Lucian, and pseudo-Cornelius Nepos, and that need not be taken literally, in which case it is merely the historian's way of saying that his account is accurate. (2) Josephus may be depending upon the ignorance of his readers, knowing that they would find it difficult to secure manuscripts and to check the veracity of statements without benefit of reference volumes and indices; however, pseudo-Longinus' (9.9) paraphrase of the opening chapter of Genesis shows that the Septuagint was well known, and the large number of converts to Judaism could hardly have been made without wide dissemination of this translation. (3) Josephus may have understood the prohibition against modifying the tradition in a broader sense than we do, for he cites (*A* I, 10) the Septuagint as his precedent for presenting biblical history to Gentiles; and yet, despite the fact that tradition (*Letter of Aristeas* 306) ascribed divine inspiration to the translation and a curse was pronounced upon anyone who dared to alter it, the rabbis themselves (*Megillah* 9a) noted that the translators had made certain deliberate changes; moreover, the term *Scriptures* may include tradition, subsuming what is later incorporated in the midrashic works. (4) When Josephus says that nothing may be modified, he may be thinking of the commandment (Deuteronomy 4.2 and 12.32) that one may not add to or subtract from the commandments of the Torah; presumably this would leave latitude in incorporating nonlegal material, which constitutes the overwhelming bulk of the Torah, let alone of the other books of the Bible.

As to the canon itself, Professor Leiman has made a conclusive case for indicating that, as cited by Josephus, it is identical with that found in the Talmud and in the writings of the church fathers. In view of the fact, we may remark, that Josephus was born to a family of such high rank and that he apparently received such an excellent education in the Jewish tradition, we should not be surprised to find him in accord with rabbinic tradition here, as in so much else, as now Goldenberg[3] has so effectively shown.

My own essay, "Josephus' *Jewish Antiquities* and Pseudo-Philo's *Biblical Antiquities*," attempts, for the first time, to compare these two, apparently contemporaneous, works systematically in their versions of the Bible. Though Josephus is ostensibly writing a history, whereas Pseudo-Philo is closer to the genre of Midrash, there are many parallels, at least thirty of which are to be found in no work that has come down to us.[4] In their treatment of a number of individual episodes—the prediction that the universe will be destroyed at one time by a violent fire and at another time by a mighty deluge, the account of the Tower of Babel and Abraham's association with it, the connection of circumcision with God's convenant concerning the land of Israel, the sacrifice of Isaac, the account of the birth of Moses, the Balaam episode, the Samson narrative, and the account of Saul—we may see a basic similarity in their predilection for building their versions around great leaders. But they differ in that, whereas Pseudo-Philo is writing primarily for a Jewish audience, Josephus is addressing, above all, a critical, non-Jewish, intellectual audience; though in some episodes, such as in his treatment of Balaam, he is aiming at such Jewish concerns as intermarriage. Moreover, Pseudo-Philo is interested primarily in theological and pietistic matters, whereas Josephus' main focus is on political and military events. I have suggested[5] that Pseudo-Philo may be answering Jewish sectarians or heretics, who were particularly numerous in this era. Moreover, whereas Josephus only occasionally, as in his version of the Balaam incident, inveighs against intermarriage, this is a major theme for Pseudo-Philo. On the whole, Pseudo-Philo seems to occupy an intermediate position between Josephus and rabbinic tradition, though generally he is closer to the rabbinic tradition. One main difference between them is that Pseudo-Philo is totally unacquainted with the classical tradition, whereas Josephus is constantly seeking to expound biblical narrative in the light of the Greek authors whom he knew so well, notably Homer, Herodotus, Thucydides, the tragedians, and Plato. Josephus, we may add, withdrew from the madding throng both politically and militarily and retreated to his ivory tower in Rome, whereas Pseudo-Philo remained in Palestine during the chaotic period that followed the destruction of the Temple and was very much involved with current theological debates with regard to the sacrifices, the covenant, sin, providence, eschatology, and angelology. He was to his era what the leaders of the Dead Sea sect were to a previous generation, presenting Jewish history through an apocalypticlike prism and giving his generation hope that it, too, would find a leader such as Kenaz, whom he so greatly elevates.

As Professor Eugene Ulrich has indicated, Josephus' close paraphrase of the Bible in the *Antiquities* is of great interest and importance in helping us to determine what biblical text was extant in Palestine in the first century, inasmuch as our earliest surviving Hebrew text dates from almost a millennium later. The discovery of a fragmentary text of the books of Samuel among the Dead Sea documents enables us to see what the text was for those books, though, as he cautiously emphasizes, his findings do not necessarily hold true for other books of the Bible.

It seems surprising that no systematic study of Josephus' biblical source has been made, with the exception of Mez's study[6] for Joshua, Judges, and Samuel, the findings of which are now confirmed by Professor Ulrich. Assertions such as Tachauer's[7] that Josephus employed only a Hebrew text now are clearly disproven. What complicates the matter is that apparently at the time of Josephus there were a number of divergent Greek and Hebrew texts of the Bible, as we can see, for example, from Philo's biblical quotations as compared with Josephus', as well as from those of Pseudo-Philo's *Biblical Antiquities* and the Dead Sea manuscripts. The last may reflect a sectarian point of view, though this seems unlikely in the context of historical books such as those of Samuel.

For the Pentateuch, our only published study is that of biblical names in Genesis by Shutt,[8] who notes that Josephus follows the Hebrew text in only four cases, whereas in twenty-five instances he follows the Septuagint. This, however, we may remark, is not conclusive, inasmuch as Shutt does not systematically consider variant readings in the manuscripts or the fact that later copyists may have modified Josephus' text to conform with their own text of the Septuagint.

One would have expected Josephus to utilize the Hebrew text, inasmuch as he, by his own admission (*A* XX, 263) at any rate, far excelled his fellow Jews in Jewish learning (which surely means, in the initial instance, in the text and interpretation of the Bible). Moreover, Josephus' statement (*V,* 418) that after the fall of Jerusalem he received from Titus a gift of "sacred books" presumably is a reference to books of the Bible in Hebrew. In addition, if, as seems likely, the practice of reading the Haftarah (selections from the books of the Prophets of the Bible) in the synagogues antedates Josephus, he heard portions of the Books of Samuel on seven occasions during the course of the year. One would, moreover, a priori expect Josephus, who was so highly conscious of the demands of style that he employed assistants (*Ap* I, 50) to help him with the Greek of the *Jewish War,* to shy away from using the Septuagint because, despite the compliment paid to it by Pseudo-Longinus (*On the Sublime* 9.9), its style is definitely inferior to the classical writers, such as Herodotus, Thucydides, and Plato, or the later writers, such as Polybius, Strabo, and Nicolaus of Damascus, whom he favors.

Hence, Professor Ulrich's conclusion that Josephus used only the Greek version seems as surprising as it is convincing. Perhaps, we may suggest, the *Hebrew* text available to Josephus was different from ours, as we may infer from the fact that the *Letter of Aristeas* (30) seems to refer to corrupt Hebrew manuscripts of the Pentateuch (and if they were corrupt for the Pentateuch we would assume that they would be even more corrupt for the historical books of the Bible, since less care was taken in copying them because of their lower degree of sanctity). Perhaps, he used the Greek text of the Bible because his projected audience, as we can see from his preface (*A* I, 10–12), is the non-Jewish Greek world, who, presumably, had access to the Septuagint. The very fact that Josephus devotes so much space (*A* XII, 11–118) to his close para-phrase of the *Letter of Aristeas* would indicate how important this translation was in his eyes. Indeed, we may suggest that if he had ignored the Septuagint this might have been interpreted as an attempt to hide something. Of course, his agreement with the Septuagint is no guarantee that he had the text of the Septuagint before him, since such an agreement may be due to an exegetical tradition that he happened to know and that had been incorporated centuries earlier when the translation of the Septuagint was made. Another possibility is that Josephus had before him an Aramaic Targum; in this connection we may call attention to a little noticed passage in Philo (*De Vita Mosis* II, 5.26) that the Septuagint itself was translated from Chaldean, that is, Aramaic (though admittedly most scholars understand this to refer to Hebrew).

We may suggest that Josephus' recasting of the *Letter of Aristeas* (on which the late lamented Professor André Pelletier comments), as an indication of his method of working with his sources, is even more revealing than his paraphrase of the Bible, since we are not sure which text of the Bible he was using—the original Hebrew, an Aramaic paraphrase, or a Greek translation—and especially since, as the Dead Sea fragments show, we cannot be sure what the Hebrew or Greek texts said at any given point, whereas the text of the *Letter of Aristeas* is an established one. The changes that he makes are dic-tated not only by changes in vogue in grammar and style but also, we may add, by the question of the audience that each is addressing; the *Letter* is ad-dressed primarily to the Jewish community, whereas Josephus' version, as we can see from the proem to the *Antiquities* (I, 5), is directed primarily to the Gentile world, though it is hard to be sure that it would not find its way into the hands of the vast Greek-speaking Jewish audience of the Diaspora. The importance of the *Letter* for Josephus, we may add, may be seen not merely in the fact that he devotes so much space to retelling the story (*A* XII, 12–118), composing, as it does, almost one quarter of Book XII, but also in the fact that, strictly speaking, the incident is only tangentially relevant to the *political* history of the Jews. The explanation for this attention, we may suggest, may be deduced from the proem of the *Antiquities,* where Josephus cites (*A* I, 10–12) the Septuagint as a precedent for his own enterprise of setting forth the Bible to Gentiles, especially since the Jews were said to have "secret" books

(*A* I, 11; cf. Juvenal 14. 102), perhaps an allusion to the prohibition, as later codified in the Talmud (*Ḥagigah* 13a), of teaching the Torah to Gentiles.

Professor Pelletier calls attention to the interesting discrepancy in the number of translators. Whereas the *Letter of Aristeas* (39) speaks of six translators from each of the twelve tribes (an obvious anachronism, since after the destruction of the kingdom of Israel in 722–721 B.C.E. only two tribes remained) and proceeds (50) to give the names of the seventy-two translators, Josephus (*A* XII, 56), after initially adhering to the *Letter of Aristeas* in quoting the letter of the high priest Eleazar to King Ptolemy Philadelphus, in response to the latter's invitation, that he was sending him six elders from each tribe, then suddenly, in the very next paragraph (*A* XII, 57), speaks of only seventy elders. We may guess that the number *seventy* is, indeed, an error, since if there had been seventy Philo would probably have commented on its significance when he discusses the Septuagint (*De Vita Mosis* 2.5.25–2.7.44) at some length, inasmuch as he speaks (*De Migratione Abrahami* 31.169) of seventy as "the holy and perfect measure of seven multiplied tenfold." We may suggest that the discrepancy may have arisen in the rabbinic tradition, which states (*Megillah* 9a, *Soferim* 1.8) that the translators entered seventy-two cells. If the number seventy-two is written in letters, as numbers frequently are, the Hebrew for "in seventy-two cells" would be בע״ב בתים; and, as Müller[9] has suggested, dittography would explain how בע״ב בתים became בע״ב בתים (or, we may suggest, the reverse). In any case, in the tractate *Sefer Torah*, which, as Higger has shown, predates *Soferim*, the number of translators is seventy, with no variant readings, though here *Sefer Torah* is paralleling the passage in *Soferim* (1.7) that speaks of five translators. It would seem, we may add, that in referring to five translators, *Soferim* is referring to a different translation of the Torah, since in the following passage (1.8) it declares that "furthermore there is a story," and then mentions seventy-two translators. Perhaps, the explanation is that there were, indeed, two stages in the work of the elders sent by the high priest: first, the establishment of a correct Hebrew text, since *Aristeas* (30) states that the Hebrew text had been transmitted rather carelessly; and second, the translation into Greek. The fact that the Greek church fathers—Justin, Irenaeus, Clement, Eusebius, and Chrysostom—speak of seventy rather than seventy-two translators shows the influence of Josephus. It is interesting that the third-century Tertullian, who wrote in Latin, speaks of seventy-two, presumably because Josephus had not yet been translated into Latin. Furthermore, we may suggest that the origin of the number *seventy-two* may be that such a number was necessary in order to confirm their capacity as an official body for making the changes in the translation of which the Talmud (*Megillah* 9a–b, *Soferim* 1.8)[10] gives a number of examples. We may guess that originally the number of translators was seventy, since in the *Letter of Aristeas* (273) we read that when King Ptolemy asked questions of the translators he accepted the tenth main response on the sixth day with gracious favor and then had an eleventh session because there were two more than *the* seventy. The church, we suggest, welcomed the number seventy because it is the product of two sacred numbers, seven and ten, and correlates with the number of the nations of the world (Genesis 10), the number of the family of Jacob that went down to Egypt (Exodus 1.5), the number of elders that accompanied Moses (Exodus 24.9), and the number of weeks in the famous prophecy of Daniel (9.24 ff.). We may also note that the same alternation of the numbers seventy and seventy-two will be found in the manuscript tradition of the number of disciples appointed by Jesus, according to Luke (10.1), who, we may note, was clearly influenced by the *Letter of Aristeas* and who consciously imitates the language of the Septuagint.[11]

Professor Pelletier in his essay notes that the church fathers understood the term *Septuagint* to include not only the Torah but also the other books of the Jewish Scriptures, in contrast, we may say, to Josephus, who restricts it, as it should be strictly speaking, to the Pentateuch. The reason for this extension, we may suggest, is that for the Christians the prophetic books especially, as well as such books as Psalms and Daniel, took on special importance in terms of supplying "prooftexts" for the deeds and significance of Jesus. It is interesting to note that despite Josephus' influence on the church fathers generally and especially, as we see, with regard to traditions concerning the Septuagint, the fathers do not follow him in restricting the term, as strictly speaking it should be, to the translation of the Pentateuch into Greek.

As to Jerome's downgrading of the Septuagint, this emanates from his respect for the Hebrew version, which he often refers to as the *veritas Hebraica* (*Preface to the Books of Samuel and Kings, PL* 28.557–58). In his *Preface to Chronicles,* moreover, Jerome is aware that by his time the textual tradition of the Septuagint was so weak that no fewer than three major recensions, differing in major degree, were circulating.

As to Jerome's dismissal of the tale of the translators being in isolated booths and arriving at identical versions, this may reflect the fact that he found no such account in Josephus, whom he held in such high regard that he cites him ninety times and refers to him as a second Livy (*Epistula ad Eustochium* 22.25, *PL* 22.421).[12] As for the tradition (Epiphanius, *De Mensuris et Ponderibus* 3) that the translators worked in pairs, interestingly enough, Baab[13] has noted evidence that for the Book of Genesis in the Pentateuch, the vocabulary and spelling of the Septuagint are rather different, to judge from the frequency of common key words, such as οὐδείς vs. οὐθείς, ὃς ἄν vs. ὃς ἐάν, πάλιν vs. ἔτι καὶ ἐγένετο vs. ἐγένετο δέ, and names of God, in the second half of the book as against the first half.

It is significant also that Josephus follows the text of the *Letter of Aristeas* so slavishly with respect to the purpose of the translation, namely that Ptolemy Philadelphus wanted to have it for his great library. As a historian, we may suggest, Josephus might have indicated several additional reasons for the translation, notably that the Jews of Egypt (as indicated, we may note, by the almost universal presence of Greek in papyri and inscriptions within two generations after the establishment of a Jewish community in Alexandria) had ceased to use Hebrew and Aramaic; that the translation might have been used to combat the anti-Semitism so blatant in the work of the Egyptian priest Manetho, whose treatise apparently appeared at almost precisely the same time as the Septuagint; that the translation was used in missionary propaganda by Jews, which apparently began in earnest at about this time; and that the work was used to combat the claims of the Samaritans (who apparently had established a settlement in Egypt at the same time that the Jews did).

As to the translation itself, as Professor Pelletier remarks, it is not verbatim but exegetical. Indeed, when we examine the words that Josephus uses for *translate*, we find that they are all ambiguous and seem to include paraphrasing and amplifying. When he declares (*A* I, 5) that his own work, which is hardly a translation of the Bible, has been translated from the Hebrew records, he employs the word μεθερμηνεύω for *translate*. Josephus uses the same verb (*A* XII, 20 and 48) in speaking of the "translation" of the Pentateuch known as the Septuagint; but inasmuch as this was hardly a literal translation, as we have noted, and indeed took considerable liberties, it will hardly buttress the meaning of *translate* but rather seems to signify "interpret." Indeed, in one of these passages (*A* XII, 20) we hear that the translators of the Pentateuch not merely translated (μεταγράψαι, "transcribe") but also interpreted (μεθερμηνεῦσαι) the law for Ptolemy's pleasure. There would hardly be much point in transcribing the law for Ptolemy; there would be a point in translating and elucidating it, and this latter act would bring pleasure to Ptolemy; hence, the word μεθερμηνεύω seems to imply much more than mere translation.[14]

For the Maccabean period, we can be sure that Josephus' main source was I Maccabees, as Dr. Isaiah Gafni clearly demonstrates in his essay in this volume. Josephus' changes, to some degree, are stylistic, as we see in his paraphrase of the Bible and of the *Letter of Aristeas;* but Dr. Gafni has shown that the modifications are also in nuance, and especially in decreasing the role of God and focusing more upon the human characters of the drama—precisely what I have noted in numerous essays dealing with Josephus' treatment of such biblical figures as Noah, Abraham, Deborah, Samson, Saul, Solomon, and Esther.[15] Whereas the hortatory speeches to the Jewish fighters in I Maccabees put the emphasis on God and biblical precedent, Josephus is anthropocentric and stresses the attributes of the fighters themselves. In particular, Josephus introduces an element of martyrology, which is lacking in I

Maccabees and which is reminiscent, we may suggest, of a motif so frequently encountered in the Hebrew paraphrase of the *Jewish War,* Josippon. It is this passivity and readiness and even eagerness to be martyrs that we see, we may add, in Josephus' adaptation of the sacrifice of Isaac and in his account of the Jews' readiness to die rather than to introduce the statue of Caligula into the Temple (*BJ* II, 196–197; *A* XVIII, 269–271). Dr. Gafni stresses that these changes in nuance are in accord with Josephus' views on the justification of wars in general, namely to preserve the law even to the point of death; and, we may add, they accord also with his paraphrase of the Bible in the first half of the *Antiquities,* where his chief aim is apologetic, namely to defend the Jews against such charges as cowardice. This stress on the Jews' courage, indeed, agrees with his comment on the Essenes (*BJ* II, 151–153), where, we may add, Josephus, otherwise the lackey and admirer of the Romans, is forced to admit that the Romans tortured these innocent people in order to get them to violate the laws of the Torah but succeeded merely in bringing about their cheerful martyrdom. We may, however, question whether Dr. Gafni is justified in concluding that Josephus praised these qualities even in the Sicarii, since, in the passage he cites (*BJ* VII, 417–419), he speaks not of courage but of boldness ($\tau\acute{o}\lambda\mu\eta\varsigma$) and desperation or strength of purpose. The additions in Josephus' paraphrase of I Maccabees likewise highlight the major difference between the Maccabees and the revolutionaries of Josephus' own day, namely that only the Maccabees had God as their ally.

One major achievement of Dr. Gafni's study is to demonstrate that where Josephus departs from his major source it is not necessary or even desirable to postulate that he had access to another source. The changes often are due to Josephus' weltanschauung and aims in his history; and, indeed, we may add, the same is true in the modifications of his biblical narrative as well. This should put to rest once and for all the notion, so widely prevalent in the scholarship, especially in Germany in the earlier part of this century, that Josephus had no mind of his own and was merely copying or paraphrasing the source immediately before him.

It is surprising but true that no one has yet attempted to present a systematic examination of Josephus' attitude toward women. Dr. Joseph Sievers' evaluation of Hasmonean women is a major step toward such an appraisal. The increased importance of women during this dynasty reflects their heightened significance generally in ruling circles, especially among the Ptolemies in Egypt, during the Hellenistic period. We may venture to guess that the fact that the Jewish community in Egypt was so large (Alexandria itself may have had as many as 200,000 Jews, the largest Jewish community until the end of the ninteenth century) and so influential (four commanders-in-chief of the Ptolemaic armies were Jews) may have had an impact upon the Hasmoneans.

That Josephus would be less than generous in his appraisal of women, even of the Hasmonean family to which he belonged, may be gathered from the neglect of them in his autobiography—though he notes that his mother was descended from the royal house of the Hasmoneans, he does not give us even her name; nor, for that matter, does he mention the names of any of his wives, even that of the third, whom he praises (*V* 427) as having surpassed many women in character. The key to this attitude, we may suggest, is Josephus' snide reference to the woman who survived the mass suicide at Masada and whom he describes (*BJ* VII, 399) as "superior in sagacity and training to most women," as if women can be praised only in comparison with other women. We likewise may note that Josephus betrays his prejudice in his extra-biblical remark (*A* IV, 219) that women are not accepted as witnesses in Jewish law because of the levity and boldness of their sex; the rabbis (*Sifrei* 109b), we may remark, while also declaring women's evidence inadmissible, give no such reason. Likewise, Josephus (*A* V, 294) shows his misogyny in Samson's remark, apparently proverbial, that there is nothing "more deceitful than a woman who betrays your speech to you." Finally, we may add that in view of Josephus' lavish praise for the Essenes, it would seem that he saw merit in their disdain for marriage because "none of the sex keeps her plighted troth to one man" (*BJ* II, 121). In view of the fact that Josephus spent some time in his youth with the Essenes (*V* 10), we may conjecture that their attitude toward women may have influenced Josephus; or, alternatively, Josephus may have been influenced by the Greek and Roman attitudes toward women, as Drazin[16] conjectures.

Dr. Sievers focuses in particular upon Josephus' appraisal of Salome Alexandra. Here, too, Josephus betrays his misogyny when he disparages her (*BJ* I, 111–112) for listening to the Pharisees with too great deference and for allowing them to take advantage of her naiveté. This remark is particularly telling in view of the fact that Josephus identifies himself with these selfsame Pharisees (*V* 12) after having experimented with the other sects and in view of the fact that, in general, in the *War* the Pharisees are less prominent than in the *Antiquities*. This negative portrait of Salome, though it is contradicted by other judgments in Josephus, is in distinct contrast, we may add, to that found among the talmudic rabbis, who report (*Sifra Behuqotai* 1.1) that during her tenure as queen rain fell every Wednesday and Saturday evening, so that grain grew enormously. Indeed, even when he does praise her in his summary of her life (*A* XIII, 430), he does so grudgingly by comparing her only with other women, remarking that "she was a woman who showed none of the weakness of her sex."

The most dramatic of all the portraits of women is that of Mariamne, who quite clearly, we may suggest, is reminiscent of the famous Cleopatra in the independence with which she stood up to Herod. The fact, as pointed out by Josephus, that on one occasion (*A* XV, 216–17) she asked her husband to appoint a certain person to an administrative position leads us to think, we may remark, that she, like other Hellenistic queens, was more than a mere consort to Herod. Josephus' suppression of such data, we may suggest, is again due either to lack of information in his source, probably Nicolaus, or to his misogyny.

Professor Ben Zion Wacholder's study, "Josephus and Nicolaus of Damascus," casts important light on Josephus' use of sources. The most significant conclusion that emerges is that Josephus is no mere plagiarizer but a discerning critic. Though Josephus clearly had before him the most detailed history (in no fewer than 144 books) that we know of from antiquity, namely, that of Nicolaus (and Professor Wacholder makes a strong case for his use of this history not only for Herod, where it is particularly extensive, but also for the earlier portions, where he used it to supplement his biblical narrative), he exercises independent judgment at numerous points. In this connection, we may add that Josephus' use (A I, 73) of the word λάρναξ for Noah's ark, which is the very word used of the ark of Noah's equivalent in Greek mythology, Deucalion, by Apollodorus (1.7.2), Lucian (De Dea Syria 12), and Plutarch (2.968 f.), is clearly due to Nicolaus, whom he quotes (A I, 94–95), even to the point of giving the number of the book (96) where the passage occurs. Inasmuch as Josephus' main source for the Noah story is the Bible in the Septuagint translation, we would have expected the latter's word, κιβωτός (Gen. 6.14), or perhaps the word θίβις, used by the Septuagint for Moses' ark (Exod. 2.3). We may also suggest that the rough breathing in the name of Abraham (῎Αβραμος) would seem to be due to Nicolaus, who terms him ᾽Αβράμης (ap. Josephus, A I, 159), whereas the Septuagint apparently used a smooth breathing, ᾽Αβράμ. And yet, it would seem strange, we may remark, that Josephus would use a non-Jewish source for the biblical period, except, in the cases of Noah and Abraham, to confirm the historicity of details, since, apparently, anti-Semites suggested that these episodes had been fabricated. More important, it was Nicolaus, as Professor Wacholder suggests, who supplied Josephus with a model of how to dramatize and romanticize history; and the several studies that we and others have made of biblical episodes, such as those listed earlier, illustrate this technique.

And yet, Josephus at least occasionally shows his independence of Nicolaus, for example, when he charges Nicolaus (A XIV, 9) with falsifying the genealogy of Herod in order to purify him. That Josephus is not making this charge out of sheer spite seems likely from the support of him by the references in the talmudic literature. Nevertheless, despite, we may remark, the antagonism toward Herod that he, as a descendant of Herod's great enemies, the Hasmoneans, felt, Josephus sometimes, apparently, follows Nicolaus' account uncritically in glorifying Herod, notably in exaggerating Herod's achievement in connection with rebuilding the Temple. Likewise, Josephus stops short of condemning, in the strong terms that we would expect, Herod's violations of Jewish sensibilities, such as in his organizing barbaric spectacles in which animals were pitted against men. Moreover, we may add, Josephus' failure to condemn Herod for building theatres, despite the strong feeling of the rabbis and of the masses, since plays were dedicated to the pagan god Dionysus, may reflect either Josephus' modernism in seeking an accommodation of pagan and Jewish values or his fear of offending his pagan readers, who might well have regarded such criticism as indicative of obscurantism.

That Nicolaus was friendly to the Jews, we may remark, always comes as a surprise to those who assume, especially from the prevalent German scholarship of the late nineteenth and early twentieth centuries, that pagan intellectuals were anti-Semitic. Actually, a perusal of Stern's collection of the references to Jews in classical literature shows that a clear majority of these passages are either neutral or favorable. Indeed, according to my count, 111 (17 percent) are substantially favorable, 140 (22 percent) are substantially unfavorable, and the majority, 390 (61 percent) are more or less neutral, though we must note that the passages are of unequal length and importance.[17]

Of course, it is Nicolaus' treatment of Herod that is of the greatest interest. The very fact that such a disproportionate part of the *Antiquities* and even, we may add, of the *Jewish War* (where, strictly speaking, the account of his reign is only indirectly relevant) is devoted to his reign must be due to the wealth of detail that Josephus found in this, his main source for the period. It must have been an agonizing decision, we may add, for Josephus to resort to Nicolaus, inasmuch as his own sympathies clearly were with his own ancestors, the Hasmoneans, the bitter foes of Herod, whose court secretary and official biographer Nicolaus was. We may guess that in addition to the sheer length of Nicolaus' work, with its vast degree of detail, Josephus may have been led to use it by the fact that Nicolaus was a follower of Aristotle, whose interest in scientific investigation embraced every aspect of life not excluding biography; and Nicolaus himself, we may add, was the author of a biography of Augustus. This is the biographical approach to history that Josephus so strongly favored. Moreover, the schema of Aristotelian ethics was used as an instrument to classify the modes of conduct of individuals; and Josephus, especially in his portraits of biblical characters, as I have tried to show, follows such a pattern.[18]

And yet, despite his extensive use of Nicolaus' work, Josephus is blatantly unfair in his treatment of Herod. Thus, without for a moment justifying Herod's treatment of the rabbis and, indeed, of his own family, we must note that he did apparently admire the Essenes (*A* XV, 373–378) and respected their prophetic gifts (though perhaps this was because they did not meddle in politics); his coins, which bore the function of present-day postage stamps in advertising his kingdom, as it were, avoided offending Jewish sensibilities by eschewing human likenesses; when rebuilding the Temple he permitted only priests to participate, and he himself carefully avoided setting foot where only priests were allowed; he rooted out robber bands from his kingdom; he intervened several times on behalf of Jewish communities in the Diaspora; above all, he conferred upon his own land the astonishing and unprecedented phenomenon of peace for thirty years; he showed favor to the masses, not only by checking a famine in 25 B.C.E. but also by cutting taxes by one-third in 20 B.C.E. and by one-fourth in 14 B.C.E.; and he even achieved the popularity of being recognized by some as the Messiah (the sect of Herodians in the New Testament [Matthew 22:16, Mark 3:6, 12:13] may well reflect this admiration for him), according to the church father Epiphanius (*Heresies* 20). Finally, anyone who managed to win the approval and confidence of such excellent and diverse judges as Julius Caesar, Crassus, Antony, Agrippa, and Augustus must have had some positive qualities, at least from the point of view of the *Pax Romana*.

That Josephus made highly discriminating use of Nicolaus is clear particularly from his treatment of Herod, and especially in the *Antiquities,* where he was even more critical of Herod than in the *War.* Nevertheless, there are a few points, as noted by Professor Wacholder, where Josephus misread Nicolaus, though, so far as we can check him, Josephus seems to have made changes primarily in abbreviating portions and in balancing Nicolaus' pro-Herodian bias.

Professor Günther Baumbach's essay on "The Sadducees in Josephus" emphasizes the prejudice with which Josephus speaks of this group. Unfortunately, the other major sources for our knowledge of the Sadducees, the rabbinic corpus and the New Testament, likewise are very negatively disposed to them; and no writing has survived from their point of view, unless we regard the Dead Sea sect as an offshoot of them or follow those who classify Ben Sira as a Sadducee. As to the latter hypothesis, Ben Sira nowhere identifies himself as a Sadducee, and indeed, the view that everything is foreseen but that man has freedom of choice (15:15–17) is a characteristically Pharisaic view (*Avoth* 3.15). Moreover, when the Talmud (*Sanhedrin* 100b) decides that the book of Ben Sira should be excluded from the canon, it does not give what would seem to be an obvious reason, namely its Sadducean point of view, but rather states that it is because it contains what is regarded as nonsense, such views as that a thin-bearded man is very wise.[19]

As to the origin of the Sadducees, the fact that Josephus first mentions them in connection with the mid-second–century B.C.E. Jonathan the Hasmonean (*A* XIII, 171) hardly gives us the date when they arose, since he states that the three sects (Pharisees, Sadducees, and Essenes) existed (ἦσαν) at that time, rather than that they arose then. Moreover, elsewhere (*A* XVIII, 11), he says that the three sects existed from the most ancient times (ἦσαν ἐκ τοῦ πάνυ ἀρχαῖον). Inasmuch as the ancients ascribed so much importance to age of peoples and institutions, as we can see, for example, from the remark of the aged Egyptian priest (*ap*. Plato, *Timaeus* 22b) that the Greeks were children since they had no immemorial past, it hardly makes sense for Josephus to ascribe antiquity to such a despised group unless, indeed, such antiquity could not be denied. In point of fact, we may suggest, the cleavage between the Pharisees and the Sadducess was a continuation of the split between the prophets and the priests of the biblical period.

As to the name *Sadducees*, the most likely source, as Professor Baumbach suggests, is from the high priest of David's entourage, Sadoq. In this connection, we may note that the origin of other breakaway movements in Judaism seems to be, in part at least, connected with a difference of opinion with regard to the Temple or a split in the high priesthood. Thus, it may explain the origin of the Samaritans, who consequently established their temple on Mount Gerizim; it may also explain the origin of the Essenes, who, according to Josephus (*A* XVIII, 19), were barred from the precincts of the Temple, since they had a different ritual of purification. It may also explain the origin of the Dead Sea sect, who, like the Sadducees, were also known as Zadokites and who retreated to Damascus or to the Dead Sea caves because, we may suggest, they were displeased with the "Wicked Priest" and the Temple sacrifices in Jerusalem and perhaps, to judge from some bones found at Qumran, even sacrificed there.

In view of the etymology of the name *Sadducees* and especially in view of the statement in Acts 5.17, which identifies those who were with the high priest as the sect of the Sadducees, it seems strange that Josephus says nothing at all about their connection with the high priesthood and the Temple. In fact, as Professor Baumbach notes, he mentions only one high priest, Ananus (*A* XX, 199), as belonging to the Sadducees. A clue to this mystery perhaps may be found in the fact that Josephus, as a priest himself, felt embarrassed by the predominance of priests in the ranks of the Sadducees and hence played down this relationship. Another clue may be found in the fact that, when he discusses the same Ananus in his parallel account in the *War* (IV, 319–321), he omits all mention of his being a Sadducee. Perhaps, we may suggest, inasmuch as the *War* was written shortly after the Great War against the Romans, when the Sadducees still had some power and influence, Josephus did not feel it wise to attack them so openly. By the time that he wrote the *Antiquities*, about twenty years later, however, with the disappearance of their power base the Temple, the Sadducees had effectively disappeared from prominence and the Pharisees, to all intents and purposes, had taken over the role of leading party among the Jews of Palestine. As to why Josephus can speak such praise of John Hyrcanus, both in the *War* (I, 67–69) and in the *Antiquities* (XIII, 299–300), even though Hyrcanus had forsaken the Pharisees for the Sadducees (*A* XIII, 293–96), the answer may be that as a Hasmonean and thus as a descendant of the same family as Hyrcanus, Josephus may have been motivated by family loyalty.

We may also suggest that the two sects may have actually been less bitterly disposed toward one another than would appear to be the case from Josephus and the rabbinic writings. The very fact that we never hear in the Talmud of the excommunication of Sadducees, that, indeed, the Pharisees and the Sadducees seem to have managed to serve together in the Temple and in the Sanhedrin, and that they are not even mentioned by Philo, the Apocrypha, and the Pseudepigrapha would seem to indicate that the division was not as sharp as one would gather from Josephus. The strong language may simply be due to the tremendous influence of the training in rhetoric upon writers, especially historians (cf. Cicero's statement [*De Legibus* 1. 5] that history is an *opus . . . unum . . . oratorium maxime,* that is, "above all, an orator's work"). Josephus states (*V* 12) that the Pharisees hold views very similar to those of the Stoics but does not equate the Sadducees with the great opponents of the Stoics, the much hated and despised Epicureans, despite the fact that their disavowal of "providence" would stamp them as such, which may indicate that, after all, he did not harbor such feelings of disdain for them. Evidence that the two sects were not really so far apart may be found in Josephus' statement (*A* XVIII, 17) that the Sadducees "submit to the formulas of the Pharisees, since otherwise the masses would not tolerate them." Another such indication is the practice of the wives of the Sadducees (*Niddah* 33b) to submit questions concerning menstrual blood to the Pharisaic sages. Moreover, even in *Antiquities,* where, according to Smith,[20] one of Josephus' goals was to convince the Romans that Palestine is ungovernable without Pharisaic support, Josephus is critical of Salome Alexandra, who had favored the Pharisees, for being unduly influenced by them, since "they in no way differed from absolute rulers" (δεσποτῶν) (*A* XIII, 409; cf. *BJ* I, 111). But this may be due to misogyny on Josephus' part.

We may also ask why Josephus, in his various references to the Sadducees and to their views, mentions only once (*A* XIII, 297–298) what, according to the talmudic rabbis, is the crucial point of difference between them and the Pharisees, namely their nonacceptance of the oral law. One answer may be that, in the *Antiquities,* Josephus is writing for a non-Jewish intellectual audience. We can see this from his proem (*A* I, 10), where he cites as a precedent for his work the translation of the Torah into Greek for King Ptolemy Philadelphus, thus justifying his directing his work to Gentiles, inasmuch as he apparently held the talmudic view (*Ḥagigah* 13a, *Sanhedrin* 59a) prohibiting teaching the Torah to Gentiles. Indeed, Gentiles, well acquainted with the disputes between the two leading philosophical schools of the day, the Epicureans and the Stoics, would appreciate a distinction based on the attitude toward fate, whereas the implications of a concept of an oral law would be hard for them to understand. A second reason may be that the Sadducees actually had their own oral law, as embodied in a *sefer gezerot* ("book of decrees," *Megillat Ta'anith* 4); hence, this distinction was not as sharp as might be imagined.

We may also ask why Josephus omits mention of the Sadducees' nationalism, since, it would seem, the Hasmonean kings, John Hyrcanus (*A* XIII, 257–58), Aristobulus (*A* XIII, 318), and Alexander Jannaeus (*A* XIII, 395–97), all of them Sadducees, sought forcibly to convert to Judaism those whom they conquered because they felt that the land of Israel must not be defiled by idolatry. In answer, we may note that Josephus must have felt very uneasy about Jewish proselytizing activity, which had aroused such bitter opposition from the Romans that it had led apparently to expulsion of the Jews from Rome on three separate occasions (139 B.C.E., 19 C.E., and under Claudius).[21] In fact, he mentions proselytism favorably in the *Antiquities* only in connection with the conversion of the royal family of Adiabene, a kingdom which was part of the Parthian, not the Roman orbit, so that the proselytism would not be offensive to the Romans.

In his survey, "The High Priesthood in the Judgment of Josephus," Professor Clemens Thoma notes the importance of Josephus as a source of information, while noting his prejudices and inaccuracies. We may comment that critics tend to put excessive faith in Josephus' reports on the priesthood and the high priesthood because he was a priest, and a member of the first of the twenty-four courses of the priests at that. But we must bear in mind at least two caveats. First, he was of the family of the Hasmoneans and, therefore, he looked down upon priests of other families, such as Phanni (Phinehas) of Aphthia, the high priest who was chosen by lot by the revolutionaries at the beginning of the war against the Romans (*BJ* IV, 155). In this connection, we may note that the rabbis (Tosefta *Yoma* 1.6) offer a useful corrective to Josephus, since there Phinehas is mentioned as the son-in-law of the house of the *Nasi*, far from the obscure, ignorant farmer painted by Josephus (*BJ* IV, 155). Second, we may guess that Josephus himself may have been jealous as a fellow priest who, in view of the distinguished ancestry of which he boasts, may have been ambitious to be high priest.

In view of his priestly background, we may express surprise that Josephus is guilty of contradicting himself with regard to data concerning the high priesthood. We may note, in particular, the discrepancies between the list of high priests from the time of Herod found in the *Antiquities,* Books 15–20, and the recapitulation in the *Antiquities* XX, 224–51. Furthermore, though he mentions (*A* X, 152–153) seventeen priests who officiated in the Temple of Solomon, in the *Antiquities* XX, 231, he gives the names of eighteen (a number with which the Talmud, *Yoma* 9a, is in agreement). We may explain such disagreements by suggesting that Josephus had better sources, perhaps Nicolaus of Damascus. If one wonders why a non-Jew such as Nicolaus would have been interested in such details, the answer may be that he realized the importance of the Temple as not only the religious but also the political and economic center of the Jews and consequently saw the need to include such details in his account.

As to the contradiction between the critical depiction of the high priest Ananus (A XX, 199) and the laudatory portrait of Ananus (BJ IV, 319–321), we may conjecture that in the former passage we have a portrait of Ananus in the year 62, whereas in the latter he is older and wiser, in the year 68, or, very simply, de mortuis nihil nisi bonum. Josephus feels much sympathy for him when he mentions his murder by the Idumaeans because Josephus so despised the Idumaean revolutionaries and because Ananus was identified with the moderate party with which Josephus claims to be allied.[22]

As to the importance Josephus assigns the high priesthood of the Temple, we may suggest that in addition to being a high priest he was motivated by the great interest in the high priest that others exhibited in the very earliest works that mentioned the Jews, notably Hecataeus of Abdera (ca. 300 B.C.E.), who praises Moses (ap. Diodorus Siculus 40.3.4–5) for selecting men of most refinement (χαριεστάτους) and of the greatest ability (δυνησομένους) to head the nation, appointing them as priests and vesting authority as high priest over the people in whatever priest was regarded as superior to his colleagues in wisdom and virtue. As to the Temple, Polybius, in the second century B.C.E. (ap. Josephus A XII, 136), refers to its renown. We may also call attention to the distrust of Alexander and his successors—and the Romans who inherited their policies—for the secular aristocracy of those whom they conquered. They realized that the native clergy, who were deeply entrenched, could hardly be eliminated; and so they worked with them and, indeed, gave them honors and special privileges. In Hellenistic times, temple states, as Tarn and Griffith[23] have noted, were very numerous. In a work designed for pagan readers in particular, a depiction of the Jews' polity in such terms would be readily intelligible. Josephus may also have had apologetic reasons. Presumably, owing to their separatism, the Jews had been accused of hatred of mankind, to the point, according to Apion (ap. Josephus, Ap II, 91–96), that the Jews kept in the Temple a Greek whom they fattened up and sacrificed each year. Josephus, in reply (Ap II, 106), insists that "no unmentionable mysteries" took place in the Temple, perhaps, we may suggest, in reply to Philo, who had declared (De Cherubim 14.49) that he himself had been initiated into the greater mysteries of Judaism.

Moreover, in the case of the Jews, the priests were not only the spiritual but also the political and economic leaders of the people; thus, for example, the high priests were responsible for collecting taxes for the Ptolemies and, in any case, as treasurers of the vast sums sent yearly by Jews throughout the world to the Temple, they were extraordinarily wealthy and powerful. Indeed, they even served as physicians. Hence, when he conquered the land of Israel, King Antiochus IV of Syria, for example, relieved (*A* XIV, 142) the priests of various taxes.

In particular, whereas there is no indication in the Torah that the high priest had real power over his fellow priests, to Hecataeus (*ap.* Diodorus 40.3.5), viewing him as a pagan would, the high priest is the messenger to the people of God's commandments. Josephus continues to magnify the priests' importance; and even though he elsewhere avoids allegorical interpretation, he ascribes symbolic values (*A* III, 179–187) to the various parts of the Temple and the garments of the high priest, thus raising the discussion of the high priesthood to a philosophical level reminiscent of Philo and utterly unique in his own work.

Professor Valentin Nikiprowetzky, of blessed memory, in his survey, "Josephus and the Revolutionary Parties," in sharp contrast to the essays by Professors Applebaum and Kreissig, who stress the economic causes of the revolt against Rome, emphasizes the religious and cultural factors. In particular, he notes the connection between the ideology of the Hasidim in the days of the Maccabees in the second century B.C.E. and that of the revolutionary parties that led the revolt against Rome in 66–74. Farmer, following Jost,[24] linking the Maccabees and the revolutionary party of the Zealots, had argued that Josephus deliberately omitted the connection because he was descended from the Hasmoneans, the family of the Maccabees, who had been allies of Rome, and hence praised them, whereas he bitterly opposed the revolutionaries. Of course, we may note, there is a major difference between the Maccabees and the Zealots, namely that the former revolted because of the suppression of the Jewish religion, whereas the latter sought political liberty, which, to be sure, they viewed in religious terms as the sine qua non for Judaism itself. Moreover, the Zealots had a consuming drive to hasten the coming of the kingdom of God, which the Maccabees lacked. A connection between the Hasidim and the Zealots seems more likely, since both stressed the theological position that God alone was king.

Professor Nikiprowetzky notes that the revolutionaries believed that all depended upon heaven, and that when God allowed the Temple to be destroyed it was His way of punishing the Jews. We may then ask why if this was so, the revolutionary Sicarii continued to hold out at Masada for four more years. In answer we may suggest that inasmuch as one of the scrolls found at Masada by Yigael Yadin has the same calendar as the one found at Qumran, there may be a connection between the two groups; and if the sect at Qumran was the Essenes, we may recall Josephus' comment (*A* XVIII, 19) that the Essenes were barred from the Temple and performed their rites by themselves. Hence they would not be so directly affected by the burning of the Temple, though, to be sure, Eleazar, the leader of the Sicarii at Masada, does refer (*BJ* VII, 379) in his last speech to the destruction of the city and of the Temple.

Professor Nikiprowetzky's discussion of the Sicarii raises the question why Josephus condemns them in such extreme terms (*BJ* VII, 262) as "the first to set the example of this lawlessness and cruelty to their kinsmen, leaving no word unspoken to insult, no deed untried to ruin, the victims of their conspiracy," whereas in the same book (*BJ* VII, 417) he remarks that there was no one who was not amazed at the endurance (καρτερίαν, "fortitude") of those Sicarii who had escaped to Egypt. While, to be sure, he acknowledges their madness (ἀπόνοιαν), the fact that he uses the word καρτερίαν indicates admiration, as one can see from Josephus' use of the same word in connection with Pompey's admiration for the fortitude (καρτερίαν) of the Jews (*BJ* I, 148), in reference to the endurance of the Essenes during their novitiate (*BJ* II, 138), and in commenting on the bodily endurance of the army which he personally trained in Galilee (*BJ* II, 580). We may suggest that there is a parallel in the incredulity expressed by the Romans at the amazing daring of the Sicarii at Masada (*BJ* VII, 405). We may add that just as Caesar expresses admiration for some of his brave opponents fighting against him in Gaul, so Josephus, by noting the desperate courage of the revolutionaries, enhances the achievement of the Romans in conquering them. This also would serve to explain why it took the Romans so long before they were finally able to capture Masada.

As Professor Nikiprowetzky notes, the prototype of the revolutionaries is Phinehas (Numbers 25.1–15). One would think that Josephus would condemn such a zealot for taking the law into his own hands. How then, we may ask, can he praise Phinehas (*A* IV, 153), for his intrepidity of soul (τόλμη, the same root of the word [τολμήματος] which arouses the admiration of the Romans [*BJ* VII, 405] for the Sicarii at Masada) and courage of body? Here the explanation may be that, as a priest himself, Josephus identified with Phinehas, who was the son of the high priest. Still, we may note that Josephus omits the biblical statement that God showed His approval of this act by granting Phinehas His covenant of peace.

Professor Nikiprowetzky suggests that one of the causes of the friction leading to the revolution against the Romans was the reaction against the increasing Hellenization of the land of Israel. There is, of course, much evidence of commercial and linguistic influence, as we can see in tombstone inscriptions and artifacts, but the fact that Josephus is forced to admit (*A* XX, 263) that though he labored strenuously to acquire a thorough knowledge of Greek he was prevented from reaching his goal because of his habitual use of his native tongue (presumably Aramaic) indicates that a thorough knowledge of Greek was apparently not widespread. We may suggest that though there was not a single Greek urban community in Judea and though Hellenism did not become deeply rooted in Samaria or Idumaea, the tremendous increase in Jewish population created tension when Jews expanded into the Greek cities, particularly along the coast, such as Caesarea.

Professor Nikiprowetzky suggests that the Fourth Philosophy, which led the revolution against Rome, was not a sect or a highly structured party. We may comment that the very fact that Josephus calls it the "Fourth Philosophy" would seem to indicate this, inasmuch as all the other movements mentioned by Josephus have specific names. This would seem to refer to an "umbrella group" for various revolutionary parties.

In particular, Professor Nikiprowetzky emphasizes the messianic aspect of the revolt and notes that Josephus himself believed in a messianic hope. Indeed, we may comment that while it is true that there is no mention in the works of Josephus of a messiah (other than the references to Jesus [*A* XVIII, 63 and XX, 200], the former of which is probably interpolated), inasmuch as the belief in a messiah was a cardinal tenet of the Pharisees, with whom Josephus identified himself (*V* 12), it seems most likely that Josephus himself shared this view. Indeed, Josephus (*A* X, 210) does hint cryptically that the Roman Empire will be overthrown, presumably by a messiah. If Josephus suppresses the messianic ideals of the revolutionaries he apparently did so to avoid the wrath of the Romans, who would have recognized that a messiah was a political rebel against Rome. The fact is that Josephus in the last books of the *Antiquities* lists at least ten leaders who were probably regarded as messiahs by their adherents, though Josephus himself avoids calling them messiahs. The meaning of the term "messiah" was apparently flexible enough to accommodate their various careers. Inasmuch as the messianic background of the Bar Kochba rebellion (132–135) is unquestioned and inasmuch as the messianic character of the revolution led by Lukuas-Andreas (115–117) is likewise authenticated, we may suggest a messianic aspect to the revolt of 66–74, especially since Josephus presents Eleazar ben Dinai (*BJ* II, 235–236, 253; *A* XX, 121, 161) as a mere revolutionary, whereas the rabbis (*Midrash Song of Songs Rabbah* 2.18) note his messianic pretensions. Moreover, Menahem, the leader of the Sicarii (*BJ* II, 434), is described as returning to Jerusalem "like a veritable king" and as having been murdered while wearing royal robes (*BJ* II, 444), descriptions that are appropriate for a leader with messianic pretensions.

Professor Shimon Applebaum's essay, like that of Professor Kreissig, focusing on the economic causes of the great Jewish revolt against the Romans, stresses the strife between the owners of large estates and the landless people and, in particular, the growth of farmsteads into villages during the period just before the rebellion. This is confirmed by archaeological remains, especially field-towers, which enable us to trace the boundaries and area of each plot of some half dozen villages in Samaria, though, we may add, what was true of Samaria may not have been true in similar measure in Judea, inasmuch as Samaria was affected relatively little by the war. Ancient historians, he notes, have relatively little information about economic factors and, instead, we may remark, choose to stress political, military, and personal factors. Josephus, likewise, has relatively little on economic matters but, most interestingly, much more than non-Jewish historians; perhaps because the rabbis with whom he studied, presumably like the rabbis cited in tannaitic literature, placed such great emphasis on economics. As an example of Josephus' recognition of the importance of economic factors, Professor Applebaum cites the case (*A* XVIII, 272–74) of the Jews who, in protest against Caligula's intent to erect a statue of himself in the Temple, neglected their fields, though it was time to sow the seed; and thus, as the Jewish leaders pointed out to the Roman governor Petronius, they would not be able to meet the requirement of tribute to the Roman treasury. In particular, we may note the economic importance of the Temple, which collected vast sums of money each year from Jews throughout the world and was a veritable bank, supporting large projects and giving employment to large numbers of people. Indeed, that the economic factor is crucial may be seen from the fact that one of the earliest acts of the revolutionaries was to burn the records of debts (*BJ* III, 427). Moreover, Professor Applebaum notes the importance of the economic factor in the Maccabean revolt two centuries earlier; and if, as Farmer[25] has suggested, there is a link between the two revolts, this would add a further point of similarity.

That economic factors indeed are significant in explaining Jewish history may also be seen, we may add, in an examination of the factors leading to anti-Semitism. Here, too, our sources are almost completely silent; but the very fact that Cicero's client Flaccus seized the gold that the Jews of Asia Minor were about to ship to the Temple in Jerusalem is a case of *Sitz-in-Leben,* which illustrates how sensitive the Romans were to the charge that Jews were draining the state of money.

We may add to Professor Applebaum's analysis the hypothesis, now presented in an article by Martin Goodman,[26] that the discontent with the Romans was not restricted to the lower classes, as we see from the refusal of the aristocratic Jewish leaders (*BJ* II, 302–304) to identify the culprits who had insulted the procurator Florus by passing around a basket (*BJ* II, 295) and from the fact that Florus let loose his soldiers against the upper classes in particular (*BJ* II, 305–308), so that we may guess that the upper classes likewise were discontented.

Whether we should go as far as Professor Kreissig[27] in finding the economic factor as the major force leading to the rebellion is surely questionable, as Professor Applebaum realizes; and Professor Applebaum notes other important factors, notably overpopulation (we may remark that Josephus' statement that there were 204 villages in Galilee [V 235], the smallest of which had 15,000 inhabitants [BJ III, 587–88], giving a population of over 3 million, and his remark [BJ VI, 420] that the number of Jews killed in the war was 1.1 million, even if vastly exaggerated, gives some indication of the great growth of population) and the rise of proselytism. We may note that, if our figures are at all correct,[28] the number of Jews grew from approximately 150,000 at the time of return from Babylonian Captivity in 538 B.C.E. to anywhere from 2 to 12 million at the time of the destruction of the Second Temple in 70 C.E. Such success must have been frightening to the Romans, as we see from the bitter remarks of satirists such as Juvenal and the historian Tacitus and from the fact that two expulsions of Jews from Rome seem to have been occasioned by proselytizing activities by Jews.[29]

We may also add that a major factor in the revolt was the rise of messianism, a movement that Josephus passes over in silence, perhaps in order to conceal the popular hostility to the Romans, though, to be sure, there are hints of it in his account of the war. We may remark that even if we did not have Josephus' work we would have guessed that there was a messianic factor from the messianic nature of the other two great revolts against the Romans, those of Lukuas Andreas (115–117) and Bar Kochba (132–135). In particular, we may call attention to the depiction in Josephus (BJ II, 434) of Menahem, the leader of the Sicarii, as returning to Jerusalem "like a veritable king" and as having been murdered while wearing royal robes (BJ II, 444), a description that fits a messianic candidate (and, indeed, in the Talmud [Sanhedrin 94a] we hear of a messianic figure named Menahem ben Hezekiah).

Moreover, we may cite as an additional factor in bringing about the war the gradual assumption of political power in Rome by anti-Jewish freedmen of Greek origin and the aid and comfort that they gave to non-Jewish elements in Palestine in the latter's strife with Jews in such cities as Caesarea, where, indeed, the war first broke out.[30]

Finally, as Horsley[31] has pointed out, partly on the basis of comparison with similar conflicts in other societies, the rise of social banditry should be stressed as well as the relation between bandits and peasants.

Few readers will dispute that the most controversial essay in the present collection—including the very title, which was suggested to the author by the editors—is "A Marxist view of the Josephus' Account of the Jewish War," by the late lamented Professor Heinz Kreissig, in which he pleads for a correction in balance between those who undervalue and those who overestimate the social and economic factors.

Professor Kreissig makes much of the fact that Josephus came from a family of large landowners; but it is significant that, if it were not for a chance comment made only in passing in his *Life* (422), we would know nothing of this. The fact that Josephus declares that a Roman garrison was to be quartered in his family's home indicates the extensive size of the estate. The statement made by Professor Kreissig that Josephus' family sat in the Sanhedrin is merely a deduction based on the statement (*V* 7) that his father was among the most notable men in Jerusalem. That Josephus was probably his family's highest representative and a member of the *Gerousia* likewise is a deduction based on the statement (*V* 9) that when he was fourteen the chief priests and the leading men of the city of Jerusalem already used to come to him constantly for information on the laws; and when the war broke out, despite his youth (he was merely twenty-nine) and utter lack of military experience, he was chosen by the revolutionaries (*BJ* II, 568) to be general in Galilee, the most sensitive area in Palestine, since the Romans would be sure to invade it first from their headquarters in Syria. No doubt, as Professor Kreissig points out, Josephus, like the other priests living in Jerusalem, had an advantage over those who lived outside the city; though, inasmuch as there were twenty-four courses of priests, a given priest would serve for only approximately two weeks a year in the Temple.

There can be no doubt that economic oppression played a major role in the revolutionaries' burning and plundering of the houses of the high priest Ananus and the palaces of King Agrippa and Berenice, in the burning of the public archives, and especially the destruction of the moneylenders' bonds "to prevent the recovery of debts, in order to win over a host of grateful debtors and in causing a rising of the poor against the rich, sure of impunity" (*BJ* II, 426–427). That Josephus, who is so eager to paint the revolutionaries in black colors and to make them appear as utter madmen in their quest for national independence, would have even mentioned the economic factor is remarkable, especially when we consider that ancient historians, such as his much-admired Thucydides, seldom pay much attention to the economic factor in any analysis of the causes of war. And yet, Josephus must have been aware of the economic factor as the chief cause in the breakdown of the ideal state, since elsewhere (*Ap* II, 223–24, 256–57) he shows his acquaintance with Plato's *Republic,* where the shift from philosopher-kingship to timocracy, from timocracy to oligarchy, from oligarchy to democracy, and from democracy to tyranny takes place primarily for economic reasons. Yet he plays down such factors, either because he was convinced that they were not important or because he wished to convey the moral lesson that the downfall of the Jewish state was due to the selfishness and recklessness of the revolutionaries.

Professor Kreissig stresses the agrarian aspect of the revolt; and undoubtedly the tremendous increase in population of Jews, coupled with the increasing shortage of land, provided fuel for discontent. But, if any credence may be placed in Josephus' account, the revolt was urban in origin. Moreover, there is reason to believe that the economic situation of Judea had actually improved during the first century, certainly for the inhabitants of Jerusalem. If nothing else, the fact that so many Jews—according to Josephus, even if he exaggerates, the number in Jerusalem at the time of the outbreak of the war against the Romans (*BJ* VI, 425) was 2.7 million (actually 2,553,000, according to Josephus' own arithmetic)—came to Jerusalem for the three pilgrimage festivals and apparently stayed for considerable periods of time indicates a tremendous tourist trade. The outstanding success of Jewish proselytism meant vast sums of money coming in each year to the Temple to be spent on sacrifices, water supply, and other capital improvements.

But Josephus, we may remark, is not alone in painting the rebels as devils. The rabbis, too (*Gittin* 56a), depict the revolutionaries as terrorizing the population and even their very leaders and play down the economic factor. But their picture of the Sanhedrin is hardly one composed of high priests and large landowners, as Professor Kreissig hypothesizes, but rather of scholars. Moreover, the very fact that the Jewish people constantly appealed to the Roman Emperors, usually with success, when they felt oppressed, indicates that the vertical alliance of the Jews with the Roman government was fundamentally satisfactory.

But, of course, Professor Kreissig does not deny (even if he does not emphasize) that the economic factor was only one of the causes of the war. Surely, we should add other factors: the assumption of political power in Rome by anti-Jewish freedmen of Greek origin who had ambitions within the empire; the corrupt system of imperial administration; the struggle in the land of Israel in such cities as Caesarea, where the revolt originally broke out, between Jews and non-Jews; the corresponding increase in resentment caused by the highly successful Jewish proselytizing activities, which threatened to put an end to the whole Roman way of life; and the failure in the land of Israel of the policy of Hellenization.[32] In particular, we may point to the rise of messianic leaders of the type who led the other two great revolts against Rome— Lukuas-Andreas (115–117) and Bar Kochba (132–135). Tacitus (*Histories* 5.13), Suetonius (*Vespasian* 4), and Josephus (*BJ* II, 285–287) all mention a prophecy of a deliverer, thereby implying a messiah; and, indeed, the portrait of Menahem, the rebel commander, who returned "like a king" (*BJ* II, 434) to Jerusalem is surely reminiscent of the traditional picture of the anointed king-messiah as mentioned in the Hebrew prophets. Indeed, we should not underestimate the religious factors in the revolt, since the revolutionaries insisted that the very definition of the Jewish people required an independent state as a sine qua non. Moreover, there was growing disillusionment with Jewish religious leadership, notably that of the high priests, who were Roman government appointees and who often were apparently corrupt and self-seeking.

Rev. Raymond R. Newell, in "The Forms and Historical Value of Josephus' Suicide Accounts," attempts to apply form criticism, so successfully used in New Testament analysis, to Josephus and concludes that he uses three different forms for recording suicides, with varying historical value. What increases the historical probability is the mention of specific historical persons and the ability to trace the narrative to a trustworthy source, whether eyewitnesses or an official account.

As applied to the suicide of Josephus' own soldiers at Jotopata, there can be no doubt of Josephus' source, since he was present; and the very fact, we may add, that the whole episode, in all probability, was a cause of great embarrassment to Josephus, since the suicide of his men, even from Josephus' own account, seems more honorable than Josephus' act of surrender (and the suspicion that he saved himself by manipulating the lots), would argue for its authenticity, just as those episodes in the Gospels, such as Jesus' cursing of the fig tree (Mark 11.12–14; Matthew 21.18–19; Luke 13.6–9) or his showing disdain for the Syro-Phoenician woman (Mark 7.24–30; Matthew 15.21–28) or his justifying the pouring of ointment upon himself rather than having it expended for the poor (Mark 14.3–9; Matthew 26.6–13; Luke 7.36–38; John 12.1–8), or his asking why God had forsaken him (Mark 15.34; Matthew 27.46) are credible precisely because they are so embarrassing.

The case of Masada, which, as Rev. Newell remarks, has occasioned so much debate, is more complex. Yigael Yadin and his volunteers, we may note, dug up literally every inch of the site and found Josephus' description of the site and of the event to be substantially accurate, though we may note that Josephus had erred in some matters of detail.

As to the contention of Cohen[33] that the historicity is doubtful because Josephus' narrative follows the stock form of such narratives of mass suicides as found in other classical writers, Rev. Newell objects that we must make allowances for different forms of suicide narratives and consequently for different levels of credibility. We may add that the parallels cited by Cohen cover a huge expanse of time, that most of them involve barbarians, and that only two of them concern Greeks and Romans. Moreover, in several of them, the author is neutral about or even condemns the act of suicide.

It is Rev. Newell's contention that the speeches in suicide narratives will not help us to decide historicity, though he makes the interesting observation that Josephus is freer in adding details in the *Antiquities* (as we see, we may remark, in his version of Abraham's readiness to sacrifice his son Isaac) than he is in the *War*. In the case of Masada, we may note, the speeches are full of clichés taken especially from Plato. Even the fact that Eleazar ben Jair gives two speeches, with a distinct rhetorical relationship to each other, is an indication that Josephus is following literary precedent. But this does not impugn the historicity of the suicide itself, we must stress. As to the argument of those who assert that the defenders of Masada, as pious Jews, could not have committed suicide, since the talmudic decree enacted at Lydda (*Sanhedrin* 74a) forbids it except when one is required to murder someone, to worship idols, or to commit an illicit sexual act, this rule was not adopted until the time of the Bar Kochba rebellion (132–135), though it presumably represents an oral tradition antedating the enactment; and, in any case, the defenders of Masada were sectarian Sicarii, who may well have had a different view as to the circumstances under which suicide was justified. Moreover, there are a number of cases during the war, most notably at Gamala (*BJ* IV, 79–81), that did not involve sectarians.

If, indeed, the historicity of extended suicide narratives, into which form the Masada episode fits, is determined, at least in large part, by the reliability of the author's source, we would probably conclude that the narrative is historical, especially since, we may remark, Josephus may well have had at his disposal the account of the victor at Masada, Flavius Silva, a member of the family under whose patronage he wrote and whose family name he adopted. Moreover, we may add, despite Josephus' well-known misogyny, as noted earlier, he is forced to remark (*BJ* VII, 399) that the woman who told the story of the mass suicide and who was, we must guess, Josephus' ultimate source, was "superior in sagacity and training to most of her sex." It is hard to believe that Josephus would have fabricated the whole narrative when there were so many thousands of soldiers who had served at Masada (between 6,000 and 10,000 troops in the Tenth Legion, in addition to the between 10,000 and 15,000 Jewish prisoners who had carried supplies for the Romans at Masada) and when most of them presumably were still alive when Josephus' narrative was published. The very fact that the Romans express amazement at the nobility of the resolve and the contempt for death shown by the Sicarii at Masada (unless, of course, one wishes to argue that Josephus' portrayal of the defenders is intended to condemn their lack of self-control), despite the fact that he so despised them (*BJ* VII, 405–406) and despite the bitterness that the Romans must have felt after the lengthy war of the Jews, is further reason to believe Josephus' account. As to the suggestion that Josephus may be trying to cover up a Roman atrocity, this seems unlikely since elsewhere in the *War* Josephus recounts in horrifying detail Roman brutalities, even after a pledge of safety had been granted; for example, in the case of the rebels who had congregated at Tarichaeae (*BJ* III, 532–42). As to the contention that brave men do not commit suicide but fight to the very end,[34] the situation at Masada was militarily hopeless.[35] In any case, we are not dealing with rational people but with fanatics. If his purpose was to build up Silva by exaggerating the courage of the defenders, he would have achieved more, we may guess, by having the Sicarii fight desperately to the end. Finally, we may conclude, Josephus had so many enemies that it is hard to believe that he would have risked falsifying the account and thus laying himself open to their ridicule. However, we may add, as a postscript, that inasmuch as stylistically Book VII is so different from the rest of the *Jewish War*, Josephus may have written this episode under different circumstances; and just as there are contradictions, as noted by Rev. Newell, between the *Antiquities* and the *War*, so there may well be contradictions in attitude between the first six books of the *War* and the seventh book.

Dr. Zeev Safrai's essay, "The Description of the Land of Israel in Josephus' Works," presents numerous examples where Josephus is accurate as well as many where he contradicts himself or is inaccurate in his geographical descriptions and especially in his statement of the distances between places in the land of Israel. In particular, it is significant that even when Josephus is paraphrasing the Bible he is no mere copier but is reflecting either personal knowledge, since he was born in Palestine and must have traveled over a goodly portion of the land, or his knowledge of rabbinic tradition, with which he often accords (as, for example, in his descriptions of the divisions of Galilee and of the agriculture there). In particular, we would expect Josephus to be accurate in describing sites that he had fortified in Galilee. But, we may remark, as Bar-Kochva[36] has shown, Josephus' topographical descriptions, though precise, especially when it came to the sites that he himself had fortified, are unusually incomplete to judge from archaeological findings; and, in any case, Josephus tends to exaggerate measurements of height. We may also remark that in an important article, Stern[37] demonstrates that, in the relatively few places where there are differences between Josephus' version (*BJ* III, 54–58) and that of Pliny (*Natural History* 7.14.70) in their descriptions of the geography of the land of Israel, these are due to the fact that Pliny's source reflects the period of Herod, with some updating of details, whereas Josephus reflects the later period of the procurators. It is such "updating," we may remark, that one sees frequently in Josephus' description of the geography of biblical sites, with Hellenization in style and in order of details, based on patterns found in Greek historians, due to Josephus' desire to appeal to his Greek readers, most of whom presumably were not Jewish.

As to Josephus' inaccuracies in measurements of distance between cities or in such matters as the length of the Dead Sea, this would appear to be hard to explain if Josephus had access to Roman records of generals who had operated in Palestine during the war against the Jews and who presumably had the excellent engineers for which the Romans were so famous. The inaccuracies may be explained either by errors in the transmission of manuscripts, where numbers are very often confused by medieval copyists, who, of course, had no first-hand knowledge, or by the fact that Josephus' measure of the cubit, for example, is not accurate. As to the errors in the description of topography, to some extent, we may suggest, these may arise from Josephus' attempt to exaggerate the achievement of Agrippa I, at least so far as Jerusalem is concerned.

The picture that emerges is that Josephus is very uneven. Generally, he is reliable in his geographical descriptions, but his figures as to populations are apparently totally unreliable. Nor is he precise in his use of terms, such as "city" or "village," just as he is vague in his terminology concerning slavery[38] or concerning the titles of administrators. Though he is a sophisticated scholar, he is not above repeating old wives' tales, such as the "experiment" conducted by Philip, the tetrarch of Trachonitis (*BJ* III, 513), in which he threw chaff into a pool at Phiale and found it cast up in the spring of Panion (Paneas), or the report (*BJ* IV, 480) that the chunks of asphalt in the Dead Sea can be evaporated only through the use of menstrual blood, or the tradition (*BJ* VII, 97–99) of the river that rests six days of the week and flows on the seventh day. The explanation, we may suggest, is that Josephus sought to enliven his history by such wonderful tales, following in this a long-standing tradition going back to one of his favorite models, Herodotus, and continuing with the Isocratean school of historians to whom he is much indebted.[39]

Professor Benjamin Mazar focuses on the centrality of Jerusalem in Josephus' Jewish *War* and raises the interesting question whether the sixth book, which ends with the fall of Jerusalem, was not really the end of the work, at least in its first edition. We may note that Schwartz[40] has concluded that in the first part of the seventh book, down to Titus' return to Rome (119), he has introduced extraneous material with unusual crudeness and that the second part of the book is marred by what appears to be an irrelevant (at least in a Jewish historian) or unnecessarily long account of the Commagenic war and the invasion of Media by the Alani (219–251) and of the Sicarii at Alexandria (409–430) and at Cyrene (437–453). Moreover, whereas Books III–VI glorify Titus, Book VII glorifies Domitian. Schwartz thus contends that Book VII, as we have it, was composed in an earlier version under Titus and was revised first early in Domitian's reign and again under Nerva or early in Trajan's reign. We may add that Morton and Michaelson,[41] comparing the occurrence of crasis and elision, conclude that Book VII is definitely different in style from the other books of the *War*. We may also suggest that Josephus may have composed his work originally in six books and added a seventh only to make it parallel with another famous work about a war fought by rebels against the Romans, the *Bellum Gallicum,* written by one of the Jewish people's (and Josephus') great heroes, Julius Caesar.

Professor Mazar notes the surprising fact that in the *War* (VII, 438) Josephus presents Melchizedek as the first to build the Temple in Jerusalem, omitting totally Solomon's role. Here, we may remark, there is a distinct discrepancy between the *War* and the *Antiquities* (I, 180–181) in Josephus' account of Melchizedek; and, indeed, as Schwartz has noted, there are a number of places in the *War* where in his reference to biblical events Josephus is at variance with the Bible and with the *Antiquities* and where his goal seems to be to enhance the importance of the cult and the upper priesthood of Jerusalem, who ministered to it.

As to the degree of Josephus' accuracy in his description of Jerusalem, on the whole, as Professor Mazar has noted, archaeological excavations have confirmed his account, though, we may add, the city is far from being fully excavated. Inasmuch as Josephus was born in Jerusalem and is so proud of his distinguished Hasmonean ancestry on both sides, it is not surprising that he knows the city well. What is remarkable, however, is that he nods more than occasionally. Thus, we may call attention to his errors in mentioning three hills in the Lower City (*BJ* V, 136–138), in asserting (*BJ* V, 156) that the three towers in Jerusalem were square, whereas actually the Tower of David at any rate is rectangular, and in exaggerating the size of the blocks used in building them. Moreover, Josephus knew next to nothing about the history of the Hasmonean First Wall and is obscure, contradictory, and chaotic in his use of Greek terminology in his description of the wall of Agrippa I (*BJ* V, 147–155 and *A* XIX, 326–327), so that it is difficult to identify the wall described by Sukenik with that wall. In addition, we may add, in view of the tremendous detail that Josephus gives us in his description of Jerusalem, we may express surprise that he fails to mention the great southern wall built by Agrippa I on the crest of the Hinnom and Kidron valleys.

On the other hand, we may note, Josephus has been confirmed in most details, some of them extraordinarily minute. For example, as Avi-Yonah[42] has remarked, the measurements of the abandoned column in the Russian compound in Jerusalem correspond to those given by Josephus for the columns of the Temple portico and the royal basilica. Likewise, the contrast between the old and new work on the wall that has been found confirms Josephus' description. Moreover, we may add, whereas most scholars have been skeptical about Josephus' statement (*A* XII, 252) that the Akra was in the Lower City on the southeastern hill of Jerusalem and have assigned it to the Upper City because they felt it was a more suitable site overlooking the Temple, archaeology has shown that there were no major Hellenistic buildings in the latter area. Finally, the Herodian staircase that archaeologists have unearthed leading westward from the broad street that runs along the Western Wall toward the Upper City may well be the beginning of the stairs that Josephus mentions (*A* XV, 410).

In summary, if a single theme keeps running through most of these essays, it is the examination of the question of the reliability of Josephus as a historical source. Modern scholarship, as reflected in these essays, gives Josephus mixed grades: he is generally reliable in topography and geography of the land of Israel, for example, as on-the-spot observation and archaeology have shown, but he is far from infallible. Likewise, as a political and military historian, especially when he is not involved personally, he is generally reliable in the instances where we can check him against other sources; and he is, indeed, almost modern in giving greater attention to economic factors than other ancient historians. But he can be a propagandist, especially in his defense of Judaism, in his appeal to pagan intellectuals, and in his stance against revolutionaries who stood up against the mighty Roman Empire. Inasmuch as almost all of classical literature is lost and inasmuch as scientific archaeology is still a new discipline, it is seldom that we are able to verify or refute him in the mass of his details; but that is all the more reason for the interest in him and for his importance.

Notes

1. See Louis H. Feldman, "Josephus' Portrait of Saul," *HUCA* 53 (1982) 97.
2. Sid Z. Leiman, "The Talmudic and Midrashic Evidence for the Canonization of Hebrew Scripture (Ph.D. diss., University of Pennsylvania 1970); "The Canonization of Hebrew Scripture: The Talmudic and Midrashic Evidence," *TCAAS* 47 (February 1976): 1–234.
3. David Goldenberg, "The Halakhah in Josephus and in Tannaitic Literature: A Comparative Study (Ph.D. diss., Dropsie University 1978).
4. Louis H. Feldman, "Prolegomenon," *The Biblical Antiquities of Philo* by M. R. James (New York 1971) lviii–lx, and "Epilegomenon to Pseudo-Philo's *Liber Antiquitatum Biblicarum (LAB)*," *JJS* 25 (1974): 306–307.
5. Feldman, "Prolegomenon," *op. cit.*, xxxiv–xxxvi.
6. Adam Mez, *Die Bibel des Josephus untersucht für Buch V–VII der Archäologie* (Basel 1895).
7. Gustav Tachauer, *Das Verhältniss von Flavius Josephus zur Bibel und Tradition* (Erlangen 1871).
8. Robert J. H. Shutt, "Biblical Names and Their Meanings in Josephus, Jewish Antiquities, Books I and II, 1–200," *JSJ* 2 (1971) 167–182.
9. Joel Müller, ed., *Masechet Soferim* (Leipzig 1878) 13, n. 38.
10. Actually, the Sanhedrin had seventy-one members, but there was an additional member, called the *mufla*, who presided. Cf. M. *Zevaḥim* 11b: "I have a tradition from the mouth of the seventy-two elders on the day that Rabbi Eleazar was appointed to the academy."
11. See Sidney Jellicoe, "St. Luke and the Seventy(-two)," *NTS* 6 (1959–1960): 319–332, and "St. Luke and the Letter of Aristeas," *JBL* 80 (1961): 149–155.
12. See Louis H. Feldman, *Josephus and Modern Scholarship* (Berlin 1984) 850.
13. O. J. Baab, "A Theory of Two Translators for the Greek Genesis," *JBL* 52 (1933): 239–243.
14. Elsewhere (*A* I, 52 and VIII, 142), it seems to refer not to translation but to the etymology of words. In at least two instances (*BJ* V, 151 and *Ap* I, 167) the meaning is not "to translate" but "to signify." In one important passage (*Ap* I, 54), Josephus remarks that in his *Antiquities*, he has given a translation (or interpretation, μεθηρμήνευκα) of the Bible, being (γεγονώς) a priest and of priestly ancestry and being well versed (μετεσχηκώς) in the philosophy of those writings. Since the participles γεγονώς and μετεσχηκώς show that the clauses are directly connected with the first part of the sentence, it would appear that Josephus' qualifications as a "translator" were enhanced by the fact that he was a priest and by his knowledge of the philoso-

phy; that is, the scientific, systematic, and methodical study of the Bible. Clearly, to be a good "translator" required more than the mechanical knowledge of language. In fact, there is only one passage (*BJ* IV, 11) of the nine occurrences of this verb in Josephus where the meaning is unambiguously "to translate."

15. See Louis H. Feldman, "Abraham the Greek Philosopher in Josephus," *TAPA* 99 (1968): 143–156; "Abraham the General in Josephus," in Frederick E. Greenspahn, Earle Hilgert, and Burton L. Mack, eds., *Nourished with Peace: Studies in Hellenistic Judaism in Memory of Samuel Sandmel* (Chico 1984): 43–49; "Josephus as a Biblical Interpreter: The 'Aqedah," *JQR* 75 (1985): 212–252; "Josephus' Portrait of Deborah," in A. Caquot, M. Hadas-Lebel, and J. Riaud, eds., *Hellenica et Judaica: Hommage à Valentin Nikiprowetzky* (Leuven-Paris 1986) 115–128; "Josephus' Portrait of Samson," to appear in *JSJ;* "Josephus' Portrait of Saul," *HUCA* 53 (1982): 45–99; "Josephus as an Apologist to the Greco-Roman World: His Portrait of Solomon," in Elisabeth S. Fiorenza, ed., *Aspects of Religious Propaganda in Judaism and Early Christianity* (South Bend 1976) 69–98; and "Hellenizations in Josephus' Version of Esther," *TAPA* 101 (1970): 143–170.

16. Nathan Drazin, *History of Jewish Education from 515* B.C.E. *to 220* C.E. *(during the periods of the second commonwealth and the Tannaim)* (Baltimore 1940) 124–125. For further discussion of Josephus' demeaning attitude toward women see my "Josephus' Portrait of Deborah" (*op. cit.*, note 15), especially 115–120.

17. Menahem Stern, ed., *Greek and Latin Authors on Jews and Judaism,* 3 vols. (Jerusalem 1974–1984). For the 33 citations from the pre-Maccabean period, 9 (27 percent) are favorable, 6 (18 percent) are unfavorable, and 18 (55 percent) are neutral. For the 43 citations from the period from the Maccabees to 63 B.C.E., 12 (28 percent) are favorable, 14 (33 percent) are unfavorable, and 17 (39 percent) are neutral. For the 215 citations from 63 B.C.E. to 100 C.E., 27 (13 percent) are favorable, 60 (28 percent) are unfavorable, and 128 (59 percent) are neutral. For the 247 citations from the High Empire Period (100–300), 31 (13 percent) are favorable, 40 (16 percent) are unfavorable, and 176 (71 percent) are neutral. For the 103 citations from the Christian period (300–600), 32 (31 percent) are favorable, 20 (20 percent) are unfavorable, and 51 (49 percent) are neutral.

18. See my "Josephus' Portrait of Saul" (*op. cit.*, note 15), especially 46–49.

19. Our text of the Talmud (*Sanhedrin* 100b) specifically distinguishes the book of Ben Sira from those of the Sadducees, since it declares that one may not read the books of the Sadducees, whereupon Rabbi Joseph adds, "It is also forbidden to read the book of Ben Sira." But this is not conclusive, inasmuch as the word *Sadducees* may be due to a Christian censor who removed a word he thought referred to the Christians.

20. Morton Smith, "Palestinian Judaism in the First Century," in Moshe Davis, ed., *Israel: Its Role in Civilization* (New York 1956) 67–81. This view has been effectively challenged by Daniel R. Schwartz, "Josephus and Nicolaus on the Pharisees," *JSJ* 14 (1983): 157–171.

21. 139 B.C.E.: Valerius Maximus 1.3.3, in the epitome of Januarius Nepotianus. 19 C.E.: Josephus, *A* XVIII, 81–84; Tacitus, *Annals* 2.85; Suetonius, *Tiberius* 36; Dio Cassius 57.18.5a; Claudius: Suetonius, *Claudius* 25.4.

22. Most recently, Tessa Rajak, *Josephus: The Historian and His Society* (London 1983) 131, n. 73, argued that the passage about Ananus and James (*A* XX, 199–203) is a Christian interpolation because of its startling divergence from the account in the *War* (*BJ* IV, 319–321); but we may counter that a Christian probably would not have called James the brother of "the one called the Christ." A Christian, we may suggest, would have said "the one who was the Christ."

23. William Tarn and G. T. Griffith, *Hellenistic Civilization,* 3d ed. (London 1952) 138–140.

24. William R. Farmer, *Maccabees, Zealots, and Josephus: An Inquiry into Jewish Na-*

tionalism in the Greco-Roman Period (New York 1956); Isaac M. Jost, *Geschichte des Juden-thums und seine Sekten*, vol. 1 (Leipzig 1857), 327–328.

25. Farmer (*op. cit.*).

26. Martin Goodman, "A Bad Joke in Josephus," *JJS* 36 (1985): 195–199.

27. Heinz Kreissig, *Die sozialen Zusammenhänge des judäischen Krieges: Klassen und Klassenkampf in Palästina des 1. Jahrhunderts v. u. Z.* (Berlin 1970).

28. For a discussion of the evidence see Salo W. Baron, *A Social and Religious History of the Jews*, 2d ed., vol. 1 (New York and Philadelphia 1952): 370–372.

29. See the passages cited in note 21, and Stern (*op. cit.*, note 17) 1.358–360 and 2.68–72, 112–113, 365.

30. See Uriel Rappaport, "The Relations between Jews and Non-Jews and the Great War against Rome" [in Hebrew], *Tarbiz* 47 (1977–1978): 1–14.

31. Richard A. Horsley, "Ancient Jewish Banditry and the Revolt against Rome, A.D. 66–70," *CBQ* 43 (1981): 404–432.

32. See my "How Much Hellenism in Jewish Palestine?" *HUCA* 57 (1986):83–111.

33. Shaye J. D. Cohen, "Masada: Literary Traditions, Archaeological Remains, and the Credibility of Josephus," *JJS* 33 (1982): 385–405.

34. Trude Weiss-Rosmarin, "Masada, Josephus and Yadin," *JS* 32.8 (October 1967): 2–8, 30–32.

35. The late Yigael Yadin, who, as a former commander-in-chief of the armed forces of the state of Israel, was well qualified to comment on military matters, pointed out to me in a private letter that the very fact that the Romans had concentrated their battering rams, catapults, and archers at one spot rendered the other parts of the fort, with all its might, useless.

36. Bezalel Bar-Kochva, "Gamla in Gaulanitis," *ZDPV* 92 (1976): 54–71.

37. Menahem Stern, "The Description of Palestine by Pliny the Elder and the Administrative Division of Judea at the End of the Period of the Second Temple" [Hebrew], *Tarbiz* 37 (1967–1968): 215–229.

38. See John G. Gibbs and Louis H. Feldman, "Josephus' Vocabulary for Slavery," *JQR* 76 (1985–1986): 281–310.

39. Feldman, "Josephus' Portrait of Saul" (*op. cit.*, note 15) 46–52.

40. Seth Schwartz, "Josephus and Judaism from 70 to 100 of the Common Era" (Ph.D. diss., Columbia University 1985), Appendix I. See *HTR* 79 (1986): 373–386.

41. Andrew Q. Morton and Sidney Michaelson, "Elision as an Indicator of Authorship in Greek Writers," *ROIELAO* (1973, no. 3): 33–56.

42. Michael Avi-Yonah, "Zion, the Perfection of Beauty," *Ariel* 18 (Spring 1967): 25–44.

1 Josephus and the Canon of the Bible

SID Z. LEIMAN

The significance of Josephus for the history of the canonization of Hebrew Scripture rests largely with the fact that he is the first witness to a closed canon of Hebrew Scripture.[1] Since he is also the single most important source for the history of the Jews and Judaism in Palestine in the Graeco-Roman period, whatever he has to say about the Bible (relating to its content, text, interpretation, or theology) looms large in any serious discussion of what the Bible looked like and how it was understood in antiquity. Precisely because of his significance for the history of the canonization of the Bible, Josephus has been adduced with much confidence in support of a wide variety of contradictory views, most of which, had he been given the opportunity, he probably would have repudiated. The aim of this study will be to delineate Josephus' biblical canon and his attitude toward biblical books to the extent that the evidence permits. What remains uncertain—and much remains uncertain—will be so identified.

The Biblical Canon

In *Against Apion* I, 37–43, Josephus writes[2]

It therefore naturally, or rather necessarily, follows (seeing that with us it is not open to everybody to write the records, and that there is no discrepancy in what is written; seeing that, on the contrary, the prophets alone had this privilege, obtaining their knowledge of the most remote and ancient history through the inspiration which they owed to God, and committing to writing a clear account of the events of their time just as they occurred)—it follows, I say, that we do not possess myriads of inconsistent books, conflicting with each other. Our books, those which are justly accredited, are but two and twenty, and contain the record of all time.

Of these, five are the books of Moses, comprising the laws and the traditional history from the birth of man down to the death of the lawgiver. This period falls only a little short of three thousand years. From the death of Moses until Artaxerxes, who succeeded Xerxes as king of Persia, the prophets subsequent to Moses wrote the history of the events of their own times in thirteen books. The remaining four books contain hymns to God and precepts for the conduct of human life.

From Artaxerxes to our own time the complete history has been written, but has not been deemed worthy of equal credit with the earlier records, because of the failure of the exact succession of the prophets.

We have given practical proof of our reverence for our own Scriptures. For, although such long ages have now passed, no one has ventured either to add, or to remove, or to alter a syllable; and it is an instinct with every Jew, from the day of his birth, to regard them as the decrees of God, to abide by them, and, if need be, cheerfully to die for them. Time and again ere now the sight has been witnessed of prisoners enduring tortures and death in every form in the theaters, rather than utter a single word against the laws and the allied documents.

Josephus specifies that his canon consisted of twenty-two books, neither more nor less. These were "justly accredited" and apparently had been so for centuries ("although such long ages have now passed, no one has ventured either to add, or to remove, or to alter a syllable"). Since for Josephus the exact succession of the prophets had ceased with Artaxerxes son of Xerxes— elsewhere in his writings identified with Ahasuerus of the scroll of Esther[3]— it is no wonder that he assumed the biblical canon had been closed for centuries. Concerning the biblical books, Josephus informs us that they are historically accurate and consistent with each other, precisely because they were authored by prophets who were divinely inspired. The biblical books are authoritative for Jews, and revered by them, to the extent that some Jews suffered martyrdom rather than "utter a single word against the laws and the allied documents."

The claims of Josephus are clear enough, but they need to be viewed in the light of their immediate context in *Against Apion,* in the light of the attitudes toward biblical and nonbiblical books expressed elsewhere in the Josephan writings, and in the light of the modern scholarly consensus concerning the history of the canonization of Hebrew Scripture.

The Immediate Context

The immediate context of the *Against Apion* passage is a vigorous rebuttal by Josephus of those who would deny the antiquity of the Jews, and the accuracy of their ancient records. After pointing to various inconsistencies in the writings of the Greek historians, Josephus adduces evidence supporting the accuracy of the Jewish archives, first by pointing to the priestly genealogies recorded and preserved with great care for centuries in Jerusalem and second by pointing to the biblical canon as a collection of reliable historical sources. Note especially that in our passage Josephus does not describe the biblical books as "holy" or "sacred," though this is commonplace elsewhere in *Against Apion* and throughout Josephan literature.[4] The focus here is on the

Bible as reliable history, not as sacred literature. Some of the implications of this narrow, immediate context will become evident later.

The Attitudes Toward Biblical and Nonbiblical Books

The passage is entirely consistent with the attitudes toward biblical and nonbiblical books expressed elsewhere in the Josephan writings. Clearly, *Antiquities* is a retelling of biblical history. Although Josephus rarely refers to a specific biblical book and almost never cites biblical verses outside the Torah, he obviously is writing a narrative history based upon Genesis and including all the subsequent biblical books treating history, from Exodus through Ezra[5] and Chronicles. Josephus mentions specifically the books of Isaiah,[6] Jeremiah,[7] Ezekiel,[8] and Daniel.[9] There is a possible reference to Lamentations.[10] These and the other biblical books are often referred to as *sacred scripture* or *sacred writings* or *sacred books*.[11] Whether referred to by name or not, the biblical books more or less as we know them—those treating history—form the essence of Josephus' *Antiquities*. Only those historical books are sacred, and only those historical books are "justly accredited."[12]

Josephus' history, however, did not cease with the last of the biblical books. He traced Jewish history from the period of Artaxerxes through the first century of the common era, fully cognizant of the fact that he was relying on nonbiblical books. He relied heavily on such works as the Letter of Aristeas[13] and I Maccabees,[14] which, by Josephus' own definition, were excluded from the biblical canon. He also used I Esdras[15] and the Additions to Esther,[16] which, however, may have been included in his biblical canon. What this indicates is that, for Josephus, quotability is not proof of canonicity. When chosen judiciously, historical sources can be relied upon even if they are not inspired. However reliable the Letter of Aristeas and I Maccabees were for Josephus, he viewed them as historical sources not as sacred scripture.[17]

Modern Scholarly Consensus

When viewed in the light of the advances of modern biblical scholarship, Josephus' view is not without difficulty. One apparent difficulty, at least, can easily be dispensed with. Josephus writes: "We have given practical proof of our reverence for our own scriptures. For, although such long ages have now passed, no one has ventured to add, or to remove, or to alter a syllable." It is inconceivable that Josephus was unaware of the wide range of textual divergency that characterized the Hebrew, Greek, and Aramaic versions of Scripture current in first century Palestine. Several modern scholars, however, have noted that Josephus' rhetoric here is commonplace in classical historiography and need not be taken literally. When used by a classical historian to describe his own method, it simply reflects the author's assurance to the reader that he has remained faithful to the sources.[18] Given the apologetic context of our passage, it is quite understandable that Josephus would underscore the inviolability of the text of Scripture as well as his own fidelity to it. In a later period, Abraham Ibn Daud (d. 1180),[19] Maimonides (d. 1204),[20] and Joseph Albo (fifteenth century)[21] would make a similar claim regarding the biblical text, again for apologetic purposes, despite their keen awareness that textual divergencies among the Hebrew Bible manuscripts were commonplace in the medieval period. More difficult for modern biblical scholarship is Josephus' assumption that biblical books such as Daniel, Esther, Ezra (or Esdras), and Chronicles were all authored and published by the time of Artaxerxes, son of Xerxes, and, hence, eligible for inclusion in the biblical canon.[22] Indeed, this is precisely Josephus' view (who also records that the book of Daniel was shown by the Jews to Alexander the Great[23]—some 170 years before it was published, according to the modern consensus[24]), and it is generally considered to be anachronistic. While Josephus nowhere records a precise date for the closing of the biblical canon (he simply asserts that no book written after Artaxerxes could be included in it), it would appear that for Josephus the biblical canon had been closed for the longest time. For Josephus, perhaps, the date of the closing of the biblical canon could best be determined by identifying the last events recorded in the received Scriptures, namely those events that occurred during the reign of Artaxerxes, son of Xerxes.

Josephus' Twenty-Two Biblical Books

Except for the Five Books of Moses, Josephus does not identify the titles of the twenty-two biblical books by name in *Against Apion*. Scholars, thus, are forced to speculate as to the identity of the remaining seventeen books. Josephus' biblical canon probably consisted of the following books:

A. Five Books of Moses
B. Thirteen prophetic books
   1. Joshua
   2. Judges and Ruth
   3. Samuel
   4. Kings
   5. Isaiah
   6. Jeremiah and Lamentations
   7. Ezekiel
   8. Twelve Minor Prophets
   9. Job
  10. Daniel
  11. Ezra and Nehemiah
  12. Chronicles
  13. Esther

C. Four books of hymns and precepts
1. Psalms
2. Proverbs
3. Ecclesiastes
4. Song of Songs

The coupling of Judges-Ruth and Jeremiah-Lamentations, each unit counting as one book, is not unique to Josephus. Later Palestinian witnesses count twenty-two books precisely in this manner.[25] Noteworthy, too, is the fact that at *Antiquities* V, 318 ff. Josephus inserts the story of Ruth immediately after the death of Samson, which, in *Antiquities,* is the final episode drawn from the book of Judges. Note, too, that at *Antiquities* X, 78–79, the books of Jeremiah and Lamentations seem to be mentioned in the same breath. If the list presented earlier is correct, Josephus' twenty-two book canon corresponds exactly with the twenty-four-book canon of the Talmud. Some scholars, however, insist on keeping Judges-Ruth and Jeremiah-Lamentations separate, acknowledging thereby that Josephus' biblical canon consisted of two titles fewer than the biblical canon of the Talmud. Thus, H. Graetz[26] suggested that Song of Songs and Ecclesiastes were not included in Josephus' canon; so, too, L. B. Wolfenson.[27] S. Zeitlin[28] suggested that Esther and Ecclesiastes were not included in Josephus' canon. Still others excluded Chronicles, Ezra, and Esther from Josephus' canon.[29] The Palestinian witnesses to a twenty-two-book canon[30] (which included all twenty-four books of the talmudic canon) render Graetz' and Zeitlin's suggestions unnecessary but not impossible. Those who would exclude Esther from Josephus' canon seem not to have taken into account *Antiquities* XI, 184, where Josephus identified Ahasuerus with Artaxerxes. One suspects that Josephus reasoned that the exact succession of the prophets ceased soon after what is virtually the latest dated event in Scripture, namely the story of Esther. Note too that in *Antiquities,* the story of Purim (XI, 296) is almost immediately followed by Josephus' account of Alexander the Great (XI, 304). For Josephus, the biblical period ended with the close of the Persian period and the rise of Alexander the Great.

Josephus' Tripartite Canon

At first glance, it would appear from Josephus' statement in *Against Apion* that he recognized a tripartite canon, perhaps similar in its classification of books to the biblical canon of the Theraputae described by Philo,[31] but certainly different from the talmudic classification of biblical books.[32] Thus, for example, for Josephus the book of Daniel is included among the Prophets, whereas in the talmudic canon it is included among the Hagiographa. Specifically, Josephus notes five books by Moses, thirteen "historical" books by prophets, and four books of hymns and precepts. Aside from the ambiguities arising from the fact that Josephus does not identify which titles are included in the thirteen "historical" books, and which titles are included in the four books of hymns and precepts, much discussion has focused on how Josephus' tripartite canon relates to the tripartite canon of Ben Sira's grandson, the tripartite canon of the Talmud, and the topical arrangement of books in the Septuagint canon.[33] In fact, Josephus' arrangement, clearly a topical one, shows strong affinities to some Septuagint arrangements that are also topical. The key question that needs to be addressed is Does it make any difference whether a book is in the second or third division of a tripartite canon? For Josephus (in contrast to the rabbis) the answer appears to be no. Nowhere does Josephus make any distinction with regard to the degree of inspiration, sanctity, or authority of any of the twenty-two biblical books. Josephus would probably make a case for the uniqueness of the Five Books of Moses—notice that they form a separate category for him—due to the laws and covenants contained in them. But nowhere in the writings of Josephus are any substantive distinctions made between the prophetic books and the hymns and precepts. In light of this, R. Beckwith's suggestion that Josephus' arrangement of the biblical books is an ad hoc one designed specifically for the readers of *Against Apion* is persuasive indeed. Beckwith writes[34]

> Josephus is a historian, and is writing to defend not only the Scriptures but also his own history of the Jews, based on those Scriptures. . . . It would therefore be natural if he divided the canon for his purposes into historical and non-historical works, and this is in fact what he does in his passage about the canon, only subdividing the historical works into Mosaic and non-Mosaic, in deference to the well-established distinction between the Law of Moses and the rest. . . . From this it is quite clear that Josephus regards the first two sections of his canon as histories, and the third section as non-historical works. The distribution is therefore, in all probability, the historian's own. On the principle that all the biblical writers are, in one sense or another, prophets, and that historiography was in biblical times a prophetic prerogative, he has transferred the narrative books in the Hagiographa to join those in the Prophets, and has arranged the combined collection in chronological order. The only books which he has left in the Hagiographa are those which do not contain narrative material.

We would add only that Josephus' arrangement of the biblical books in *Against Apion* is consistent with *Antiquities* X, 35, which can only be understood as a reference to the (total of) thirteen "historical" books by the prophets.[35]

Canon and Prophecy

As is well known, Josephus did not restrict the phenomenon of prophecy to the First Temple period, or even to the period of Artaxerxes. Josephus allowed for the phenomenon of the prophecy throughout Second Temple times.[36] Thus, for example, Josephus describes John Hyrcanus (135–105 B.C.E.) as being blessed with the gift of prophecy.[37] Manaemus the Essene is presented as having "from God a foreknowledge of the future," which enabled him to predict that the lad Herod would one day reign as king.[38] Elsewhere,[39] Josephus describes a prophet of doom, reminiscent of Ezekiel, who in the year 62 C.E. predicted the fall of Jerusalem.[40] These samples suffice to raise the issue of why, from Josephus' perspective, literary prophecy ceased with the period of Artaxerxes? It would appear that a careful reading of the *Against Apion* passage, and an analysis of Josephan terminology for prophetic phenomena, provide some insight into Josephus' position on the matter. Josephus is quite clear in formulating a qualitative difference between prophecy prior to the period of Artaxerxes and prophecy following the period of Artaxerxes. So long as there was an exact succession of prophets, from Moses on, literary prophecy was possible. Once there was a break in the exact succession of the prophets, after the period of Artaxerxes, isolated instances of prophecy were possible but not literary prophecy.[41] Perhaps, for Josephus prophecy and history were integrally bound up with each other and linked to Moses, the greatest prophet and historian. The stress may well have been on the "historical" aspects of literary prophecy. Only a continuous history could be deemed inspired. Interrupted or sporadic histories are by definition incomplete and therefore inferior. Once the chain was broken, nothing new could be added to the biblical canon. This qualitative difference between pre- and post-Artaxerxes prophecy is also reflected in Josephan terminology. The term $\pi\rho o$-$\phi\dot\eta\tau\eta\varsigma$ is almost exclusively reserved for pre-Artaxerxes prophets. A post-Artaxerxes prophet is almost always called $\mu\dot\alpha\nu\tau\iota\varsigma$, or a related Greek term, but not $\pi\rho o\phi\dot\eta\tau\eta\varsigma$.[42]

It is no accident that the author of IV Ezra,[43] and the rabbis, too,[44] recognized that literary prophecy had ceased during the Persian period. Apparently, the author of I Maccabees, while nowhere providing a precise date for the cessation of prophecy, clearly recognized that prophecy had ceased prior to the Maccabean period.[45] This consensus seems to reflect the reality that there is no obvious reference in Scripture to a prophet who lived after the Persian period. It may also reflect the reality that Josephus, the early rabbis, and the authors of IV Ezra and I Maccabees inherited a fixed biblical canon that contained no books that seemed to date later than the Persian period. This required an explanation, the most obvious one being that either literary prophecy or the phenomenon of prophecy ceased with the close of the Persian period.[46]

Notes

1. The classical passage, discussed later, is drawn from *Against Apion*, which is generally dated to circa 95 C.E. See R. J. H. Shutt, *Studies in Josephus*, London, 1961, p. 43. A second witness to a closed biblical canon, IV Ezra 14:44 ff., is generally dated to circa 100 C.E. See J. H. Charlesworth, ed., *The Old Testament Pseudepigrapha*, New York, 1983, vol. 1, p. 520.

2. Loeb Classical Library translation by H. St. J. Thackeray.

3. See *A* XI, 184.

4. See, e.g., *Ap I*, 54 and 127; *A* X, 210; XIII, 167.

5. Josephus clearly used the Greek Esdras I rather than the Masoretic Hebrew version of Ezra or the Septuagint Greek version of Ezra-Nehemiah. See, e.g., J. M. Myers, *I and II Esdras*, New York, 1974, p. 8.

6. *A* X, 35; XI, 5.

7. *A* X, 79.

8. *Ibid.*

9. *A* X, 210, 267, and 276; XI, 337.

10. *A* X, 78–79 and Ralph Marcus' notes in the Loeb Classical Library edition, ad loc.

11. See note 4.

12. Also, four nonhistorical works are included in Josephus' biblical canon, for which see later.

13. *A* XII, 11 ff. Cf. the references cited by Ralph Marcus in the Loeb Classical Library edition, ad loc.

14. *A* XII, 240 ff. On Josephus' use of I Maccabees, see I. Gafni, "On the Use of I Maccabees by Josephus Flavius" [Hebrew], *Zion* 45 (1980):81–95.

15. See note 5.

16. *A* XI, 229 ff.

17. This is the clear implication of *Against Apion* I, 41.

18. See W. C. van Unnik, "De la regle Μήτε προσθεῖναι μήτε ἀφελεῖν dans l'histoire du canon," *VC* 3 (1949):1–36; *idem, Flavius Josephus als historischer Schriftsteller*, Heidelberg, 1978, pp. 26–40. Cf. H. W. Attridge, *The Interpretation of Biblical History in the AN-TIQUITATES JUDAICAE of Flavius Josephus*, Missoula, 1976, pp. 58–59 and notes; and S. J. D. Cohen, *Josephus in Galilee and Rome*, Leiden, 1979, pp. 28–29 and notes.

19. *Ha-Emunah ha-Ramah*, Frankfurt am Main, 1852 [reissued; Jerusalem, 1967], p. 80.

20. *Iggeret Teiman*, ed. A. S. Halkin, New York, 1952, pp. 39–41.

21. *Sefer ha-Ikkarim*, III, ed. I. Husik, Philadelphia, 1946, vol. 3, p. 199.

22. See the standard biblical introductions of Eissfeldt, Weisser, and Childs.

23. *A* XI, 337.

24. See, e.g., O. Eissfeldt, *The Old Testament: An Introduction*, New York, 1965, pp. 520–521.

25. So Origen, Epiphanius, Jerome, and probably Eusebius, Cyril, the anonymous Bryennios list, and others. See H. B. Swete, *An Introduction to the Old Testament in Greek*, Cambridge, 1914, pp. 203–213; cf. P. Katz, "The Old Testament Canon in Palestine and Alexandria," *ZNW* 47 (1956):196–197. For the Bryennios list, see S. Z. Leiman, *The Canonization of Hebrew Scripture: The Talmudic and Midrashic Evidence*, Hamden, 1976, pp. 43 and 161.

In the light of the early Palestinian witnesses to a twenty-two book canon that had the units Judges-Ruth and Jeremiah-Lamentations each counting as one book, the suggestion by H. M. Orlinsky, "The Canonization of the Bible and the Exclusion of the Apocrypha," in his *Essays in Biblical Culture and Bible Translation*, New York, 1974, p. 271, that the equation of the twenty-two- and twenty-four-book canons is "an essentially nineteenth century scholarly fiction," cannot be seriously entertained.

26. *Kohelet oder der Salomonische Prediger,* Leipzig, 1871, pp. 168–169.

27. L. B. Wolfenson, "Implications of the Place of the Book of Ruth in Editions, Manuscripts, and Canon of the Old Testament," *HUCA* 1 (1924):173–175.

28. "An Historical Study of the Canonization of the Hebrew Scriptures," *PAAJR* 3 (1931–1932):130.

29. See the sources cited by W. Fell, "Der Bibelkanon des Flavius Josephus," *BZ* 7 (1909):8, note 1.

30. See note 25.

31. *De Vita Contemplativa* 3.25, Loeb Classical Library, *Philo,* vol. 9, translated by F. H. Colson, p. 127. The passage in Philo is sufficiently ambiguous that almost any interpretation of it is conjectural. Cf. F. H. Colson's note, *op. cit.,* p. 520.

32. See S. Z. Leiman, (*op. cit.,* note 25), pp. 51–53 and notes. For an analysis of Josephus' biblical canon vis-à-vis the biblical canon of the rabbis, see R. Meyer, "Bemerkungen zum literargeschichtlichen Hintergrund des Kanontheorie des Josephus," in *J-S* (1974), pp. 285–99.

33. For a summary of the various views, see S. Z. Leiman, *op. cit.,* p. 150, note 135.

34. In his *The Old Testament Canon of the New Testament Church,* Grand Rapids, 1985, pp. 124–25.

35. See Ralph Marcus' note at *A* X, 35, Loeb Classical Library edition, pp. 176–177.

36. See, in general, J. Blenkinsopp, "Prophecy and Priesthood in Josephus," *JJS* 25 (1974):239–262.

37. *BJ* I, 68–69.

38. *A* XV, 373–379.

39. *BJ* VI, 300–309.

40. See M. Greenberg, "On Ezekiel's Dumbness," *JBL* 77 (1958):101–105. Cf. the discussion and references cited in his *Ezekiel 1–20,* New York, 1983, p. 121.

41. See W. C. van Unnik (*op. cit.,* note 18), pp. 41–54, especially pp. 47–48.

42. See J. Reiling, "The Use of ψευδοπροφήτης in the Septuagint, Philo and Josephus," *NT* 13 (1971):156; and cf. J. Blenkinsopp, *Prophecy and Canon,* Notre Dame, 1977, p. 182, note 59. I use the terms "almost exclusively" and "almost always" in deference to D. E. Aune, "The Use of προφήτης in Josephus," *BJL* 101 (1982):419–421. The evidence he adduces, however, does not change the picture in any substantive way.

43. See note 1. Cf. The Prayer of Azariah, verse 15 and C. E. Moore's comment in *Daniel, Esther and Jeremiah: The Additions,* New York, 1977, p. 58.

44. See the evidence adduced by E. E. Urbach, "When Did Prophecy Cease?" [Hebrew] *Tarbiẓ* 17 (1946):1–11. Urbach (p. 10) suggests that the rabbinic ascription of the cessation of prophecy to the Persian period was a Jewish response to the Christian argument that the cessation of prophecy among Jews was due to their rejection of Jesus. This seems highly unlikely, especially in the light of Josephus' ascription of the cessation of literary prophecy to the Persian period. Josephus most certainly was not responding to a Christian argument; nor, for that matter, was IV Ezra (see note 1). Similarly, I Maccabees, a pre-Christian work, recognized that prophecy had ceased prior to the Maccabean period (see the next note). Thus, views about the cessation of prophecy were not bound up with the advent of Christianity. For other suggestions as to why the rabbis ascribed the cessation of prophecy to the Persian period, see A. C. Sundberg, *The Old Testament of the Early Church,* Cambridge, 1964 [reissued New York, 1969], pp. 113–128.

45. See I Maccabees 4:46; 9:27; and 14:41. For the possible significance of I Maccabees 3:48 in this context, see S. Lieberman, *Hellenism in Jewish Palestine,* New York, 1962, pp. 194–199, especially p. 198, note 35.

46. For additional bibliography on Josephus and the biblical canon, see L. H. Feldman, *Josephus and Modern Scholarship (1937–1980),* New York, 1984, pp. 134–139.

2 *Josephus'* Jewish Antiquities and *Pseudo-Philo's* Biblical Antiquities

LOUIS H. FELDMAN

Habent sua fata libelli. As Terentianus Maurus so insightfully remarked, even books have their fates. This is well illustrated in the instance of the enigmatic work entitled *Biblical Antiquities* (*Liber Antiquitatum Biblicarum,* hereafter abbreviated *LAB*), ascribed to Philo, which presents a Midrashlike chronicle of biblical history from Adam to the death of Saul. This work, despite its intrinsic interest, was totally ignored by the church fathers and was almost completely unknown to modern scholars until its rediscovery by Cohn[1] at the end of the nineteenth century. Though it is one of the most significant links between early haggadah and rabbinic Midrash and though it is obviously an important example of Pseudepigrapha, it was completely overlooked in the collections and commentaries of Charles, Kautsch, Pfeiffer, and Strack-Billerbeck, among others. And yet, if the date arrived at by Cohn, James,[2] Kisch,[3] Bogaert,[4] and myself[5] is correct, *LAB* was composed in the latter half of the first century, making it somewhat older than Josephus' *Antiquities,* which was issued in 93/94, and thus is, with the exception of the Genesis Apocryphon (among the recently discovered Dead Sea Scrolls), our oldest substantive midrashic work.[6]

In content, *LAB* is a biblical history from Adam to the death of Saul. Its treatment, however, is very uneven. Thus, whereas the genealogies of Genesis (Chapters 5 and 10–11) are greatly embellished, most of the rest of Genesis is totally omitted. Again, whereas the account of the birth of Moses is developed at some length, most of the rest of Exodus is omitted. Similarly, aside from the story of Balaam and the farewell address and death of Moses, most of the rest of the Pentateuch has been passed by. The central focus of the work is on the period of the Judges, constituting approximately 40 percent of the work; and the brief biblical account of the first judge, Othniel, has been replaced by an extensive, unparalleled narrative of Kenaz (Cenez), his father, who is, in terms of the space devoted to him, second in importance only to Moses himself.

That *LAB* is not by Philo is clear from the facts that the language is everywhere redolent of Hebraisms, that its narrative abounds in apocryphal materials, and that there are a number of actual contradictions between it and Philo, notably in the chronology from Adam to the flood, in the attitude toward Balaam, and in its consonance with a Palestinian type of Hebrew biblical text in several places where Philo, as is his wont, agrees with the Septuagint.[7] Though it exists today only in Latin, it seems most likely that this is a translation from Greek, since it contains a number of Greek words. The Greek, in turn, appears to have been translated from a Hebrew original, since there are a number of Hebraisms, as we have noted, as well as a number of instances where the translator has misread or misunderstood his Hebrew original, in particular, since *LAB* often uses the Hebrew text rather than the Septuagint and since it also has close affinities with the Targumic tradition.[8] If, therefore, as seems likely, the original language of *LAB* was Hebrew, it is most probable that it was composed in Palestine, since we do not know of any works in Hebrew composed outside of Palestine during this period or for centuries thereafter and since *LAB* has some striking similarities with IV Esdras and with the Syriac Apocalypse of Baruch, which emanate from Palestine, notably in the author's theological concerns, particularly eschatology and angelology.[9]

The date of *LAB* is very much in doubt. I have suggested[10] that Pseudo-Philo's statement (22.8) that Joshua determined in the new sanctuary at Gilgal the sacrifices that were offered continually "even unto this day" (*usque in hodiernum diem*) indicates that the author would have us believe that the Temple was still standing, hence before 70 C.E. Perrot[11] argues for this date on the ground that such accounts, if composed after 70, would tend to become assimilated to targumlike writing. Harrington[12] contends that an examination of *LAB*'s biblical text leads to the conclusion that the work was composed before 100 C.E. Most recently, Zeron[13] has argued for a date after the second century, and possibly even after the fourth century, on the basis of *LAB*'s closeness to the midrashic traditions of the school of Rabbi Johanan of the third and fourth centuries and its similarity to the black magic of the Book of Raziel of the third to fifth centuries. He notes that since in most cases where there are differences between *LAB* and Josephus, the former appears to stand closer to the rabbinic tradition, *LAB* should be considered as originating at about the time of the rabbinic midrashim; but such a suggestion is unconvincing, since the rabbinic tradition itself is generally much older than the period at which it was reduced to writing.

The purpose of *LAB* has remained enigmatic. The work is marked particularly by extensive genealogies, fictitious speeches, original prayers and hymns, deathbed testimonies, and visions and dreams, the broad range of which is an indication that it is meant for the general rather than for the sectarian reader.

Thus, Cohn,[14] James,[15] and Kisch[16] concluded that the purpose was to interest and edify the reader and to strengthen his religious beliefs. Other theories,[17] however, have also been presented, namely that *LAB* was written to reinforce the Deuteronomic conception of Israel's history, to defend the Samaritans, to attack the Samaritans, to attack the Tobiads, to attack the worshippers of Mithra, to attack intermarriage, to show some connection with the Essenes or the Dead Sea sect or with some mystical, pehaps Gnostic, movement, to defend Judaism against heretics, or to show that the Idumeans were genuine Jews.[18] Most recently, Perrot[19] has suggested that it is a compilation of synagogal homilies, consisting of a corpus of haggadic traditions used by Targumists and preachers in connection with the Scriptural readings in the synagogue. However, there is no hard evidence to support such a theory, and the prominence given to the narrative of Kenaz, who plays no role in the Scriptural or Haftarah readings, whether in the annual or the triennial cycle, argues against it. In fact, *LAB* defies precise categorization. It is neither a targum nor a *pesher* commentary nor a Midrash nor an apocalypse nor a chronicle, although it has elements of all of these. We would like to suggest that a comparison of the way in which Pseudo-Philo and Josephus treat the same episodes may give us valuable clues as to the purposes of *LAB*, especially when these treatments are seen in the light of rabbinic parallels.

Prior to my Prolegomenon[20] and its supplement,[21] no one had discussed the relationship between Pseudo-Philo and his presumed contemporary,[22] Josephus. James,[23] to be sure, does comment that the title of Pseudo-Philo's work is probably due to the *Jewish Antiquities* of Josephus. He also notes[24] that the text of Josephus substitutes the name of Kenaz for Othniel, thus providing a slight parallel for the remarkably extensive discussion of Kenaz in Pseudo-Philo (Chapters 25–28).

However, there is a basic difference in method between Josephus and *LAB*, in that the former is a history, with Midrashlike tales introduced within that framework, whereas *LAB* is closer to Midrash in method, particularly in its propensity to quote verses from other portions of the Bible while expounding and expanding on a given passage. Yet, that there is a relationship between *LAB* and Josephus seems clear from the fact that I have noted thirty[25] parallels to be found in no other work that has come down to us and fifteen cases where Josephus is not alone in agreeing with *LAB* but where both may reflect a common tradition. But that the matter of the relationship between *LAB* and Josephus is not simple can be seen from the fact that I have noted thirty-six instances where *LAB* and Josephus disagree.[26] Our chief interest in this essay will be the relationship among *LAB*, Josephus, and the rabbinic writings where they seem to be parallel to one another.

The first instance of a parallel is the extrabiblical prediction by Adam (Josephus, *A* I, 70) that the universe will be destroyed at one time by a violent fire and at another time by a mighty deluge of water. To be sure, in *LAB* (3.9) it is not Adam but God who makes a promise rather than a prediction and who declares that He will judge mankind by famine or sword or fire or pestilence or earthquakes or by scattering them but not by flood.[27] In the Talmud (*Zebaḥim* 116a), as in *LAB*, it is God whose oath is recalled that He will not bring a flood of water upon mankind; and when the Torah is given to Israel, the heathen kings are seized with trembling and consult the pagan prophet Balaam because of the tumult. When he assures them of His oath, "Perhaps," they say, "He will not bring a flood of water, yet He will bring a flood of fire." Balaam then assures the kings that God has sworn that He will not destroy all flesh. We may see here that *LAB* is closer to Josephus in that a promise or prediction is mentioned in which fire and flood (or, in the case of *LAB*, additional alternatives) are referred to, whereas in the Talmud the promise of God is merely that He will not send another flood. On the other hand, *LAB* is closer to the Talmud in that it speaks of a promise by God rather than a prediction by Adam. The Talmud, finally, is closer to Josephus in that God's promise is quoted by a man, Balaam, just as in Josephus Adam presents the prophecy, whereas in *LAB* God makes the promise directly.[28] In sum, *LAB* seems to be somewhere between Josephus and rabbinic tradition in its treatment of detail.

In the account of the Tower of Babel, *LAB* likewise occupies an intermediate position between Josephus and rabbinic Midrash. On the one hand, *LAB* (6.14), Josephus (*A* I, 113–14), and the rabbis (*Pirke di-Rabbi Eliezer* 24)[29] all connect Nimrod[30] with the Tower of Babel. Like Josephus (*A* I, 116), *LAB* (7.2), apparently troubled by the biblical statement that God came down to see the Tower of Babel, softens the anthropomorphism by omitting God's descent and by saying merely that God saw the enterprise. Furthermore, Josephus, anticipating the question as to why, in view of the utter insolence of those who built the tower, God did not inflict a more severe penalty upon them, remarks that God decided not to exterminate them completely because not even the destruction of mankind in the deluge had taught their descendants to be moderate and that, therefore, He had chosen to create discord among them and thus to scatter them. *LAB* (7.3), on the other hand, in an apparently unique remark, has God declare that He will esteem them as a drop of water and liken them to spittle, and predicts that some will come to their end by water while others will die of thirst.

LAB is closer to the rabbis in connecting Abraham with the story of the Tower of Babel, though in a different way.[31] In *LAB* (6.3) Abram is one of the twelve men who refused to participate in the building of the Tower and who were subsequently imprisoned, and eleven of whom eventually managed to escape. Similarly, in rabbinic tradition (*Tanḥuma* B, 1.99–100, *Pirke di-*

Rabbi Eliezer 24, *Genesis Rabbah* 38.6), Abram attempts actively to dissuade those who were building the tower. Likewise, *LAB* (7.5), in a passage not paralleled in Josephus, agrees with rabbinic tradition[32] and 3 Baruch 3.4 in remarking that the builders were transformed into beasts.[33] *LAB*, however, departs from both Josephus (1.114) and the rabbis (*Genesis Rabbah* 38.1, 5, 7, 8)[34] in declaring that the purpose of the builders of the tower was to get renown for themselves and not, as in the rabbinic passages and in Josephus, to prevent their being drowned in a second flood.

Again, when mentioning circumcision (*A* I, 192), Josephus, most significantly, since he wishes to diminish the role of God in his narrative and since, as a Jew who spent the latter half of his life in the Diaspora, he seeks to reduce the centrality of the land of Israel,[35] omits the fact that it is a sign of the covenant between God and Abraham (Genesis 17.10–11) and instead declares that its purpose is to prevent Abraham's posterity from mixing with others. Pseudo-Philo, on the other hand, who dwells in the land of Israel, even though he has vastly abbreviated the whole narrative of Abraham, is closer to the biblical narrative and to that of the rabbis than is Josephus' account, for he twice (7.4 and 8.3) mentions and gives the terms of the covenant between God and Abraham, namely that God will give him and his descendants this land.

In the account of Abraham's readiness to sacrifice his son Isaac, we likewise may see Pseudo-Philo's position vis-à-vis Josephus and rabbinic Midrashim. At the beginning of the test of Abraham, whereas the Bible (Genesis 22.2) has God merely give an order to Abraham, Josephus (*A* I, 224), well aware that his readers would wonder at the seeming arbitrariness of such a command, has God build up to the order by first enumerating three major benefits that He had bestowed upon Abraham, namely victory over his enemies in war, happiness (presumably in material matters), and the birth of a son. Thus, the sacrifice is viewed, as in *LAB* (32.2), as a logical repayment to God for His benevolence. Rabbinic literature (*Tanḥuma Lekh Lekha* 13), on the other hand, saw no need to have God apologize, and so it is Abraham who justifies the sacrifice in his own mind as a repayment for God's great gifts to himself. Similarly, there is a close parallel between *LAB* (32.3), where Isaac asks, "What if I had not been born in the world to be offered a sacrifice unto Him that made me?" and Josephus (*A* I, 252), "He [Isaac] exclaimed that he deserved never to have been born at all, were he to reject the decision of God and of his father." Thus, both Josephus and Pseudo-Philo look upon the sacrifice as payment due to God. Moreover, both Josephus and *LAB* stress Isaac's joy in being sacrificed, his free and voluntary acceptance of his role, and the significance of the sacrifice for the destiny of Israel, namely that because Isaac did not resist, his offering (*LAB* 18.5) was acceptable to God and that God chose Israel because of his blood. In addition, whereas in the Bible (Genesis 22.11) an angel tells Abraham that his son's sacrifice is not required, in both

Josephus (*A* I, 233) and *LAB* (32.4) God Himself addresses him, presumably because the subject was too important to be left to God's deputies. Nevertheless, there is a difference in that Josephus' Isaac (*A* I, 321), through his sacrifice, according to Abraham, is to be a protector and stay of his old age by giving him God instead of himself, whereas *LAB*'s Isaac (32.3) asks quite logically how his father could tell him that he was to inherit a secure life for a duration of time that cannot be measured and yet simultaneously expect that he be sacrificed. Moreover, there is also a difference in that Pseudo-Philo omits the concept that for Isaac not to allow himself to be sacrificed would be to disobey his father. Indeed, in *LAB* the sacrifice is the fulfillment of a divine mission alone; for Josephus it is, in the first instance, the fulfillment of a human, that is a natural, mission and not only a divine mission. In short, Pseudo-Philo, like the rabbis (*Leviticus Rabbah* 2.11), emphasizes the theological consequences of Isaac's sacrifice, which, he says (32.3), will bring blessedness to all men; for all later generations will be instructed by his example.[36] Hence, he anticipates the Christian motif of Jesus' sacrifice.[37]

The fact that the incident of Judah and Tamar is mentioned only in retrospect in *LAB* (9.5), in the course of Amram's speech urging the Israelite elders not to sunder themselves from their wives, is an indication that the author of *LAB* felt that the incident was useful as a kind of prooftext. The whole point of the incident in the eyes of Pseudo-Philo is that Tamar justifies having relations with her father-in-law on the ground that it is better to die sinning with her father-in-law than to be joined with Gentiles. This detail is unique with *LAB* and is found nowhere in rabbinic literature or in Josephus, who omits the incident altogether, presumably for apologetic reasons, since it is too embarrassing to include. By alluding to it, *LAB* is in accord with the rabbis, who declare (*Megillah* 25a) that the incident should be both read and translated in the synagogue. Inasmuch as there are a number of places where *LAB* engages in polemic against mingling with foreigners (notably 18.13–14, 21.1, 44.7, 45.3, and 47.1), it is not surprising that this incident is here introduced as well. If, however, we ask why Josephus, who is similarly concerned, as we see from the emphasis that he puts on the incident of the Israelites' sin with the Midianite women,[38] omits the incident despite the moral that *LAB* derives from it, we may reply that the taboo of incest was so powerful that to have included it would have subjected the Jews to the greatest embarrassment. If we then ask why Josephus does include the account of the relations between Lot and his daughters (*A* I, 205), the answer is that he excuses this on the ground that they did so because they thought that the whole human race had perished.

There are a number of parallels among Josephus, Pseudo-Philo, and the rabbis in their accounts of Moses. In the first place, *LAB* (9.2) refers to the ordinance issued by the Israelite elders that men refrain from having relations with their wives because of Pharaoh's edict that female babies be kept by the

Egyptians, lest they grow up to serve idols. Amram, the father of Moses, objects, recalling God's pledge that the Israelites will be in bondage for four hundred years in Egypt but that thereafter they will be freed. In the Talmud, Amram also offers advice in connection with Pharaoh's edict; but there (*Sotah* 12a)[39] the advice given is the very opposite of that in *LAB*, for he divorces his wife and urges other husbands to do likewise. In Josephus (*A* II, 210), Amram is similarly concerned with Pharaoh's decree; but there his wife is already pregnant. God then appears (*A* II, 212) to him in a dream and exhorts him not to despair of the future. Whereas in Pseudo-Philo (9.2) the elders urge abstention from sexual relations "until we know what God will do," in Josephus God Himself (*A* II, 212) reassures Amram that He is watching over the welfare of the Israelites. In Josephus Amram has a dream in which (*A* II, 215–16) God tells him that the child yet to be born will deliver the Israelites from Egypt, whereas in *LAB* Maria (Miriam) has such a dream, in which she is told that Moses after being cast into the water would save the Israelites from water (of the Red Sea). Moreover, in both Josephus and *LAB* there are dreams foretelling the birth of Moses, but in Josephus the prediction is made once (*A* II, 205) by the Egyptian sacred scribes and once (*A* II, 215) by God in Amram's dream,[40] whereas in Pseudo-Philo (9.10), as in the Talmud (*Megillah* 14a), Miriam prophesies the birth of Moses, the vehicle being a dream in *LAB*, rather than pure prophecy, as in rabbinic literature, with the prediction itself being made by a man clad in a linen garment, presumably Gabriel, as I have indicated.[41] In addition, in *LAB* it is predicted that God will save His people through Moses; but there is no mention, as in Josephus (*A* II, 205), of the renown that he will enjoy. That Pseudo-Philo is closer to the Talmud than Josephus is seen, furthermore, in the fact that he (9.13), like the Talmud (*Sotah* 12a), mentions that Moses was born circumcised.

Gaster[42] has pointed to a Samaritan poem of the fourteenth century, which most likely is based on an earlier tradition, recounting how Amram has a vision at night in which an angel predicts that a child to be born to him will obtain renown and will be remembered forever. But the key phrase in Josephus, absent from the rabbinic accounts and from *LAB* and even from the Samaritan version, which otherwise is so similar, is that Moses is to remembered even by foreign peoples so long as the universe will endure (*A* II, 216). A glance at the *Contra Apionem* confirms Josephus' apologetic intention in citing Moses as the great example of a cultured Jew who had profound influence upon the statesmen and philosophers of other nations.

We may note that strangely both *LAB* (10.1) and Josephus (*A* II, 294–314), in enumerating the ten plagues, mention only nine, though each omits a different plague—boils (the sixth plague) in the case of *LAB* and the murrain on cattle (the fifth plague) in the case of Josephus. Furthermore, though Josephus generally agrees with the Septuagint as against the Hebrew Text, in the case of the fourth plague (Exodus 8.17 [21]) which, in the Septuagint is κυνόμυια "dog-fly," Josephus (*A* II, 303) speaks of wild beasts of every species and every kind, and similarly *LAB* speaks of *pammixia,* which here means all manner of animals. In this Josephus and *LAB* are in agreement with the prevalent rabbinic rendering.[43]

There are a number of similarities between Josephus and *LAB* in their treatment of the Balaam pericope. Thus, according to Josephus (*A* IV, 113) and Pseudo-Philo (18.10), Balaam offered the sacrifice, whereas according to the Septuagint and Philo (*De Vita Mosis* 1.277) Balak did so; and the Targum Onkelos and Targum Pseudo-Jonathan follow the Hebrew text (Numbers 23.2) in asserting that Balaam and Balak sacrificed together. In addition, Balaam's prediction that Israel will be spread over the entire world is found in Josephus (*A* IV, 115–17) and *LAB* (18.11), though it is, to be sure, paralleled also in Targum Onkelos on Numbers 23.9.[44] Moreover, in both Josephus (*A* IV, 119 ff.) and *LAB* (18.10 ff.), Balaam's four prophecies of Numbers 23.7 ff. are combined into one. The very language of Balaam's parting advice to Balak (*A* IV, 129), "Take of your daughters those who are comeliest" (εὐπρεπεῖς) is similar to *LAB* (18.13), "Choose out the most comely women (*speciosas*) that are among you."[45] Above all, we may note that whereas in rabbinic literature,[46] with few exceptions, Balaam is portrayed as the arch-villain, being guilty of greed, envy, and even beastiality, with a strong streak of anti-Semitism implicit in his acceptance of Balak's invitation to curse the Israelites, in Josephus and in *LAB* the picture is more balanced. We may remark, in particular, that in *LAB* Balaam gives the reply to God (18.4) that, according to the Midrash (*Numbers Rabbah* 20.6) he *ought* to have given: "Wherefore, Lord, dost Thou tempt the race of man? They, therefore, cannot sustain it, for Thou knewest, more than they, all that was in the world, before Thou foundedst it. And now enlighten Thy servant if it is right that I go with them." We may note, however, that whereas Josephus (*A* IV, 118), following the Septuagint and the Lucianic version (there is no corresponding Hebrew text), states that the divine spirit remained in Balaam, *LAB* (18.10) is alone in asserting the opposite, "The spirit of God abode not in him."

Josephus' portrayal of Balaam, on the other hand, is largely due to his apologetic goals and to his role as historian and is in line with his view (*A* IV, 140) that the lawlessness and corruption occasioned through the seduction of the Hebrew youth by the Midianite women that Balaam had advised as the means of overcoming the Israelites was far graver than the sedition (στάσις) introduced by Korah and for which (*A* IV, 12) Josephus asserts that he knows of no parallel, whether among the Greeks or the non-Greeks. In this respect, there is a similarity with *LAB,* since, like Josephus, Pseudo-Philo omits names such as Shittim and Ba'al Pe'or, thus making the story a generic tale that presumably has direct application to the situation in which the authors are writing, when Jews were likewise being seduced by the temptations of Hellenism. Hence, the emphasis on the conflict between Midian and Israel, from a political and military point of view,[47] whereas Pseudo-Philo, as a moralist, emphasizes the tragic elements in the narrative,[48] particularly in *LAB* 18.10. In this, *LAB* diverges from Josephus and is closer to the rabbinic tradition (*Numbers Rabbah* 20.19) in stressing Balaam's great discouragement rather than his prophecies.[49] In particular, we may cite Balaam's statement (18.11): "I am restrained in the speech of my voice, and I cannot express that which I see with mine eyes, for but little is left to me of the holy spirit which abideth in me, since I know that in that I was persuaded of Balak I have lost the days of my life."

In a similar moralist vein, in the farewell address that *LAB* (19.4) puts into the mouth of Moses, he speaks words of reproach, addressing the Israelites as "wicked," here following the rabbinic interpretation of Deuteronomy 1.1 (*Sifre*, quoted by Rashi's commentary ad loc.).[50] Josephus, on the other hand, as an apologist for the Jews, specifically (*A* IV, 189), in an extrabiblical addition, has Moses declare: "I say this with no intent to reproach you."

The most striking innovation in *LAB* is the great excursus on the judge Kenaz. Whereas the Bible (Judges 3.9–11) knows only of Othniel, who is the son of Kenaz and the first of the judges, Pseudo-Philo, like Josephus (*A* V, 182), does not mention Othniel and instead speaks of Kenaz. Both Josephus (*A* V, 182), in an extrabiblical addition, and *LAB* (25.5) indicate that Kenaz consulted an oracle (i.e., the Urim and the Thummim of the high priest), though for different purposes, with the oracle in Josephus serving a political purpose, namely (*A* V, 182) at great length telling Kenaz not to allow the Israelites to remain in such deep distress, and with the Urim and the Thummim in *LAB* serving a moral purpose, namely (25.5–26.15) advising Kenaz who of the Israelites had sinned.

Both Josephus (*A* V, 200) and *LAB* (30.4) add to the biblical account (Judges 4:3) in noting that the reason for the calamities of the Israelites after the death of Ehud (Zebul) was the contempt of the Israelites for the laws of the Torah. *LAB*, however, dramatizes this further by having the Israelites, even suckling children (30.4), made to fast seven days. It is only then that Deborah arises as a judge.

Both Josephus (*A* V, 235–39) and *LAB* (27.1–4) present Jotham's parable of the trees (Judges 9:7–15). Whereas in the Bible, however, the olive tree is approached first, then the fig tree, and finally the vine, in both Josephus and in Pseudo-Philo, the order is the fig tree, the vine, and the olive (in *LAB* the apple or myrtle takes the place of the olive). In the Bible and in Josephus, the three good trees—the olive, the fig, and the vine—refuse the kingship because they do not wish to exchange the esteem that their fruits bring them for mere power, but it is accepted by the fruitless bramble, which here is identified with Abimelech, Jotham's half-brother, the son of the judge Gideon by his Shechemite concubine whose hired assassins had killed seventy of seventy-one sons of Gideon. Nevertheless, in Josephus, the bramble is described as a symbol of tyranny (*A* V, 234) and Abimelech is specifically condemned after setting himself up to do whatever he pleased in defiance of the laws and after showing bitter animosity against the champions of justice, in line with Josephus' attacks elsewhere on tyranny, for example, where Cassius Chaerea, the hero of the plot against the tyrant Caligula, gives (*A* XIX, 186) "liberty" as the password of the conspiracy.[51] However, *LAB*, which is not politically minded as is Josephus, speaks of the bramble in terms of praise as a symbol of truth, noting (37.3), in an extrabiblical addition, that when the thorn was born, truth shone forth in the semblance of a thorn, and that when the truth enlightened Moses it enlightened him by a thorn bush. It is, therefore, the other trees that are chastised, and the bramble is vindicated.

In the account of the sacrifice of Jephthah's virgin daughter, both Josephus (*A* V, 265) and *LAB* (40.2), to the exclusion of other accounts, have her state that she cannot be sorrowful in her death because she sees her people delivered. But Josephus' version is much briefer than Pseudo-Philo's and makes no mention, as does the latter (40.2), of the obvious parallel with Abraham's intended sacrifice of Isaac and of the eagerness (40.3) of Jephthah's daughter, like Isaac, to offer herself willingly, lest her death be unacceptable. From *LAB*'s poignant account of her martyrdom while she was yet a virgin (a theme which is hardly mentioned by Josephus), we can perceive the degree of the lament. Here, too, we may see Pseudo-Philo's pious and theological orientation, in contrast to Josephus' merely political stress.

Another interesting insight into the difference between Josephus and *LAB* may be seen in the etymologies that they assign respectively to the name of Samson. On the one hand, Scripture gives no etymology for his name, while the rabbis (*Sotah* 10a and parallels) give the obvious etymology from the word *shemesh*, "sun," commenting that just as God (Psalms 84.12) is spoken of as a sun and a shield, so Samson shielded Israel during his generation. Josephus (V, 285), however, significantly emphasizes Samson's strength by postulating that his very name means "strong." Whatever the source of Josephus' etymology,[52] it is clear that Josephus thereby chose to stress Samson's fear-inspiring strength, as we see from a number of other extrabiblical details that he applies; for example (*A* V, 298), by contrasting Samson's courage and strength with the qualities of the tribe of Judah, who wish to hand him over to the Philistines. Pseudo-Philo (42.3), on the other hand, with his emphasis on the theological implications of the narrative, chooses to explain the etymology of the name as meaning "holy," though there is no Hebrew word meaning "holy" that in any way can be connected with the name of Samson.[53]

There are a number of parallels, moreover, between Josephus and *LAB* in their accounts of Samson that are found in no other sources. In the first place, both Josephus (*A* V, 276) and *LAB* (42.1) emphasize Samson's exalted origin. Then, Josephus presents the extrabiblical detail that Manoah, Samson's father, was one of the foremost among the Danites. Similarly, *LAB*, with typically midrashic concern for giving names (the name of Samson's mother, Eluma, is to be found nowhere else in Jewish literature), stresses her noble ancestry. In this respect *LAB* is closer to the view of the rabbis, who speak of the stature of Samson's mother, who, they say, came from the tribe of Judah (*Genesis Rabbah* 98.13 and *Numbers Rabbah* 10.5). Moreover, instead of listing Samson's ancestors, as does Pseudo-Philo, or making a statement, as does Josephus, about the prominence of Samson's ancestry, the rabbis (*Numbers Rabbah* 14.9) are concerned with connecting later biblical figures with the patriarchs, and thus point out that Jacob's blessing of Dan refers to Samson; he is identified (*Sotah* 9b) as the serpent in terms of which Jacob (Genesis 49.17) describes Dan. This would appear to raise the status of Samson; but the rabbis (*Numbers Rabbah* 23.5; *Mechilta,* ed. Friedmann, 55b; and *Tanhuma* on Numbers 34) are careful to note that Jacob, when shown the future figure of Samson, thought (*Genesis Rabbah* 98.14; *Midrash Hagadol* on Genesis 184a) that he was to be the Messiah, until he saw him dead, whereupon he realized that he was not. Moreover, we may note, the rabbis,[54] in line with their general criticism of Samson, omit all reference to his ancestry and instead condemn Manoah as an ignorant man—practically the most severe criticism that can be given by the rabbis. *LAB,* to be sure, sides with the Midrash (*Numbers Rabbah* 10.5 and parallels) and parts company with Josephus in stressing the strife between Manoah and his wife as to who is responsible for their childlessness, whereas Josephus (*A* V, 277), in line with his general tendency to highlight the erotic, stresses the jealous suspicion of Manoah. Indeed, Josephus (*A* V, 277) tells the reader—a detail not found in Judges 13.2, *LAB,* or the Midrashim—that Manoah was madly in love (μανιώδης ὑπ᾽ ἔρωτος) with his wife and hence inordinately (ἀκρατῶς, i.e., without command over himself or his passions, incontinently, immoderately, intemperately) jealous (ζηλότυπος). We may note, furthermore, that whereas in the Bible (Judges 13.6, 13.8) there is no indication that Manoah does not believe his wife's account of the words of the angel, and indeed, Manoah simply asks for additional instructions as to what to do with the child that he assumes will be born, in Josephus (*A* V, 279), Manoah, in his jealousy of the angel, is driven to the distraction that such passion arouses. The same distrust of his wife by Manoah is seen, to be sure, in Pseudo-Philo (42.5), who is even more explicit about it, "And Manue believed not his wife." Indeed, both *LAB* and Josephus note Manoah's grief at this report from his wife. But Pseudo-Philo has none of the details about the suspicion and jealousy of love that give such a distinct flavor to Josephus' narrative. And in Pseudo-Philo, unlike Josephus, the distrust is the occasion for feelings of shame and grief and leads him, in a manner typical of his ultra-pious attitude, to a prayer to God, "Lo, I am not worthy to hear the signs and wonders which God hath wrought in me, or to see the face of his messenger."

Furthermore, in Josephus (*A* V, 280) Manoah's wife, whose role he heightens for erotic reasons, entreats God to send the angel again that her husband may see him, whereas in *LAB* (42.5), as in the Bible (Judges 13.8) and in the Midrash, Manoah does so. In addition, *LAB* (42.7) is closer to Josephus (*A* V, 281) than to Scripture in asserting that Manoah had lingering doubts about the angel's promise; but, we may comment, Manoah's suspicion and the mysterious nature of the angel's errand are increased in Josephus when the angel refuses to repeat what he had revealed to Manoah's wife, whereas in the Bible (Judges 13.13–14) the angel repeats substantially what he had told Manoah's wife. Here, once again, *LAB* occupies something of a midway position between Josephus and the Midrash; for while, as in the Midrash, the angel does give directions to Manoah, he does so in a very much briefer form, "Go in unto thy wife and do quickly all these things."

Again, both Josephus (*A* V, 282) and *LAB* (42.8) avoid mentioning Manoah's ignorance, stressed by the Midrash, of the fact that it was an angel whom he had invited to dine with him; but *LAB* differs from both the Bible (Judges 13:16) and Josephus (*A* V, 282) in omitting the invitation to the angel. Furthermore, both Josephus (*A* V, 284) and *LAB* (42.9) add the statement (taken from an earlier passage in Judges 6.21) that the angel put forth his hand and touched Manoah's sacrifice with the end of his sceptre and that fire came forth out of the rock. Again, Josephus (*A* V, 286 ff.) elaborates on the erotic aspects of the episode at Timnah (Judges 14.1 ff.), whereas *LAB* (43.1) abbreviates it in two brief sentences. In addition, again stressing the erotic, Josephus (*A* V, 306) speaks of Delilah as a courtesan (ἑταιριζομένης), whereas Judges 16:1 and *LAB* 43.5 describe her as a harlot or prostitute (*fornicariam*). Josephus thus has a much more romantic picture of a courtesan, reminiscent of those for which the Greeks were famous. It seems most likely that this is another of Josephus' inventions calculated to give a Greek coloring to his narrative.

In its eagerness to impart tremendous faith in God, *LAB* (43.2–3), in its account of Samson's escape from the Philistine ambush at Gaza, puts into Samson's mouth a speech that shows utter contempt for the enemy and militant faith in God. Josephus' Samson (*A* V, 305), on the contrary, merely shows extreme contempt for the enemy. As I have stated elsewhere in my comment on this episode,[55] Josephus adds fury to Samson; but *LAB* makes him almost a kind of superman. Thus, for example, in the description of the incident when Samson brought down the Temple upon the Philistines at the end of his life, whereas the Bible (Judges 16.27) states that there were 3000 men and women upon the roof with an undetermined number elsewhere in the building, and Josephus (*A* V, 316) declares that the total slain was 3000, and the Septuagint more realistically reduces the number to 700, the Midrash (*Genesis Rabbah* 98.14) says that the number far exceeded 3000, while Pseudo-Philo (43.8) increases the number to 40,000.

Moreover, Pseudo-Philo (43.5), like the rabbinic Midrashim, compares Samson unfavorably with the earlier Hebrews. Thus, in attacking him for marrying Delilah, he ascribes to God an unscriptural speech berating Samson for not following the example of Joseph, who did not go astray, even though he was in a strange land. Consequently, Samson is to be punished, again as in rabbinic lore, measure for measure: "Behold, now Samson is led astray by his eyes. . . . Now, therefore, shall his concupiscence be a stumbling-block unto Samson, and his mingling shall be his destruction, and I will deliver him to his enemies and they shall blind him." But while Pseudo-Philo is here allied with the Midrashim in preaching against assimilation, he (43.6) and Josephus (*A* V, 309) are unique in indicating that Samson violated the Nazirite prohibition against drinking, thus emphasizing to their contemporaries that adoption of foreign ways leads to the debasement of one's own way of life.

Josephus' account is more romantic than that of the Bible in his omission of the payment of money by the Philistines to Delilah (Judges 16.18) and in his concentration instead on Delilah's learning of the secret and on her cutting off of Samson's hair (*A* V, 313). The rabbinic tradition (Tosefta-Targum on Judges 17.2) and *LAB* (44.2), on the other hand, speculate on what Delilah did with the money she received from the Philistines; and they conclude with emphasizing the danger of consorting with non-Jews, noting that she gave a part of it to her son Micah, who used it to make an idol for himself. Here again we see the relatively greater emphasis in *LAB* and in the rabbinic Midrashim than in Josephus on the fact that intermarriage leads to the greatest sin of all, idolatry.

A strong moralizing tendency, moreover, is to be seen in Samson's prayer (43.7) in *LAB*, stressing that God had given him the eyes that the Philistines had taken from him, with the clear implication that it is for God to obtain revenge for the affront to Him. His final words stress the theological dichotomy between body and soul: "Go forth, O my soul, and be not grieved. Die, O my body, and weep not for thyself." Here, once again, Pseudo-Philo is closer to the Midrash (*Genesis Rabbah* 66.3) than to Josephus, who has no such prayer (*A* V, 314 ff.).

A good clue to the difference in approach between *LAB* and Josephus may be seen in the treatment of the prayer of Hannah, who was to become the mother of Samuel. In Josephus (*A* V, 344–45), we are told simply that she went off to the tabernacle to beseech God to grant her offspring and that she lingered a long time over her prayers. In *LAB*, however, with its emphasis on piety, Hannah prays not once but twice, once (50.4–5) to ask that God enable her to bear a child, and once (51.3–6) in thanksgiving after the birth of her son Samuel. In particular, the second prayer is the occasion for Pseudo-Philo to express the pious sentiment that one should not hasten to talk proudly (51.4) and that it is God alone who kills with judgment and revives with mercy (51.5).

Finally, we may note a sharp contrast between Josephus and Pseudo-Philo in their portraits of Saul.[56] In the first place, Josephus devotes far more space to his reflections and encomium on Saul (*A* VI, 262–68, 343–50) than to any other biblical character, including Moses, since he apparently regarded Saul as his foremost paradigm in expressing the goals of his work, both in terms of the aims of Hellenistic historiography and in terms of his specific apologetic views, as I have noted.[57] In particular, he discerns and aggrandizes in him first the qualities of good birth and handsome stature, second the four cardinal virtues of character (wisdom, courage, temperance, and justice), and third the spiritual attribute of piety to God and family. As a historian, Josephus found in Saul a prime example to illustrate the changes in character caused by accession to power; and this is, indeed, the moral that he (*A* VI, 263–64) would have the reader learn about the character of men, "namely that so long as they are of private and humble stature, through inability to indulge their instincts or to dare all that they desire, they are kindly and moderate and pursue only what is right, . . . but when once they attain to power and sovereignty, then, stripping off all those qualities and laying aside their habits and ways as if they were stage masks, they assume in their place audacity, recklessness, contempt for things human and divine." As Josephus himself (*A* VI, 343) declares, his reflections on Saul's heroism are a subject profitable to city-states, peoples, and nations, and of interest to all good men. His depiction of Saul, he hopes (*A* VI, 343), will stimulate patriotism and courage. He especially stresses (*A* VI, 348) that despite the knowledge that he was destined to die, he went off to battle fearlessly.

On the other hand, unlike the Bible (I Samuel 9:1), which names Saul's ancestors for five generations, and unlike Josephus, who says that he was of good birth, Pseudo-Philo (56.4) declares merely that Saul's father was Kish, with no indication of Kish's ancestry. He furthermore (56.7) downgrades Saul by saying nothing about his being anointed (I Samuel 10.1) and thus presumably avoids the problem of how someone who had been officially anointed could have lost the kingship. Moreover, from the very beginning, the portrait of Saul's role is negative, since in contrast to the Bible (I Samuel 9.15–16), where we are told that God reveals to Samuel that He will send Saul, who will save the Israelites from the Philistines, and in contrast to Josephus (*A* VI, 49), who says merely that God had announced to Samuel that He would send him Saul without indicating his mission, *LAB* (56.3) adopts a negative stance toward Saul in that God declares that He will send to the Israelites a king who will lay them waste and He predicts that Saul himself thereafter will be laid waste. In addition, whereas in the Bible (I Samuel 9.17) and in Josephus (*A* VI, 50), when Saul arrives, God tells Samuel merely that this is the man who is to rule the Israelites, in *LAB* (56.5) Saul is important not for himself but as an instrument of prophecy of days to come; and we find the unparalleled, extrabiblical addition that Samuel declares that God "hath raised up thy ways (*erexit vias tuas*), and thy time shall be directed (*dirigetur tempus tuum*)." Then, in an editorial comment, Pseudo-Philo (56.6) compares Saul's humble reply to the words of the prophet Jeremiah (1.6).

Furthermore, Pseudo-Philo casts aspersions on Saul's motives for sparing Agag, the Amalekite king, by declaring (58.2) that he allowed him to live because Agag had promised to show him hidden treasures, whereas Josephus (*A* VI, 137) casts a much more favorable light upon Saul by stating that he was prompted by pity (οἴκτῳ); and, in an addition calculated to appeal to his Greek audience, he adds an aesthetic motive, namely that admiration for his beauty and stature had led him to conclude that he was worthy to be saved.

Above all, whereas in Josephus (*A* VI, 45) Saul is said to possess the spirited faculty (φρόνημα) that is characteristic of the warrior class in Plato's ideal state and whereas the Midrash (*Midrash Samuel* 11.78–79, *Midrash Psalms* 7.63) emphasizes the supernatural aspect of Saul's heroism, remarking that Saul was able to march sixty miles in order to rescue the tablets of the law from the Philistines and with the help of an angel to return on the same day, *LAB* presents Saul as a coward who (54.3–4), in an extrabiblical addition, flees before Goliath, while Eli's sons defend the ark at the cost of their lives. It is this cowardice of which Goliath (61.2) later reminds Saul[58] in a detail that is unique to *LAB*.

Even when, according to *LAB*, Saul performs the commendable act of expelling the sorcerers, in a detail found only in *LAB*, he ascribes this action to a selfish motive, namely so that he may be remembered for it after his death. The Midrashim (e.g., *Pirke di-Rabbi Eliezer* 33), likewise in a critical mood, note Saul's inconsistency in first expelling the sorcerers and then consulting with the witch of Endor. Josephus (*A* VI, 327), on the other hand, apparently seeking to avoid castigating Saul, merely reports the action of expelling the sorcerers without commenting at all on Saul's motives.

Finally, whereas in Josephus (*A* VI, 349) Saul's motive in meeting death at the hands of the Philistines is his desire for sheer glory and renown thereafter, reminiscent, as I have suggested,[59] of an Achilles or a Hector in Homer's *Iliad*, in *LAB* (64.8), as in rabbinic literature (*Pirke di-Rabbi Eliezer* 33), Saul's death is depicted as a repentance for his sins.

In summary, we may remark that both Josephus and *LAB* build their accounts primarily around great leaders.[60] But the basic difference between LAB and Josephus is that the former is a popular history intended for Jews, whereas the latter is writing a history for a primarily non-Jewish audience, with a strong streak of the apologetic, whose chief interest, as seen, for example, in his treatment of the Balaam episode, is the political and military side of events. Josephus himself (*A* I, 5) says that he undertook the *Antiquities* in the belief that "all the Greeks" would find it worthy of attention. The fact that (*A* I, 9) he asks whether there is a basis in Jewish tradition for imparting knowledge of Judaism to non-Jews and whether Greeks, indeed, are curious to learn about Jewish history and then proceeds to answer both questions in the affirmative is an indication that he sought to defend himself, presumably against Jewish critics, who looked askance at teaching Scripture to Gentiles. Josephus' apologetic stance toward "all the Greeks" is borne out by the fact that he omits such embarrassing episodes as the cunning of Jacob in connection with Laban's flock (Genesis 30.37–38), the Judah-Tamar episode (Genesis 38), Moses' slaying of the Egyptian (Exodus 2.12), Miriam's leprosy (Numbers 12), the story of Moses' striking the rock to bring forth water that speaks of his disgrace (Numbers 20.10–12), the story of the brazen serpent whereby Moses cures those who had been bitten by the fiery serpents (Numbers 21.4–9), and the building of the golden calf (Exodus 32). A similar apologetic motive toward his non-Jewish audience is to be seen in his additions to the biblical narrative: notably in his portrayal of Abraham as a philosopher, scientist, and general; his romanticizing of the story of Joseph and Potiphar's wife in the vein of the Hippolytus-Phaedra story; his depiction of Moses as a general, employed by the Egyptians against the Ethiopians, who marries the daughter of the Ethiopian king; his heightening of the erotic, heroic, and dramatic interest in his picture of Samson; his portrayal of Saul as a kind of Jewish Achilles; his presentation of Solomon as a kind of Jewish Oedipus; and his introduction into his Esther narrative of motifs found in Hellenistic novels.[61] In style, Josephus seldom quotes from the Bible, rather infrequently departs from his chronological format in paraphrasing the Bible, and only occasionally gives cross-references, so to speak, to other biblical episodes in the process of his exposition.

Pseudo-Philo, on the other hand, has written a narrative, closer in style to rabbinic Midrash, from the point of view of a moralist, with frequent quotations of biblical text and numerous citations of the Bible passages in the process of his exposition, precisely as we find in rabbinic Midrashim. To be sure, like Josephus, he fills in lacunae by giving details, such as names that are missing from the Bible, though far more often than Josephus. In this respect he may be answering Jewish sectarians or heretics.[62] Second, *LAB*, in preaching to Jews, inveighs strongly against intermarriage. This will explain why Pseudo-Philo introduces—and out of chronological order—the fact that Tamar's intention in having relations with Judah was to prevent her being joined with Gentiles. Whereas Josephus, writing for Gentiles, is too embarrassed to include this incident, Pseudo-Philo, addressing his fellow Jews, is saying, in effect, that it is preferable, under extraordinary circumstances, even to have incestuous relations than to marry outside of the Jewish faith. Similarly, the elaboration of the incident of Micah and the idol he made culminates in the statement (44.7) that as a result the Israelites "lusted after strange women." Likewise, *LAB* (45.3) adds the unique detail that the Levite's concubine of Judges 19.25 had transgressed against her husband by having relations with foreigners, the Amalekites, and thus attempts to justify the abuse that she suffered. Moreover, Pseudo-Philo (43.5), in an unparalleled addition to the Bible, attacks Samson for having married a non-Jewish woman, Delilah, and contrasts him with Joseph, who, though in a strange land, did not go astray. In addition, *LAB* avoids, as in the Samson pericope, erotic details that Josephus found of such interest for his Hellenistic readers and instead, in his ultrapious attitude, introduces prayers. Finally, *LAB* avoids political and favors moral issues, as we see, for example, in the case of Kenaz, who in Josephus consults an oracle for a political purpose, namely to seek a way how to extricate the Israelites from their duress; whereas in *LAB* he consults the Urim and Thummim for a moral purpose, namely to learn who had sinned. Most striking in this connection is Josephus' stance with regard to Jotham's parable, according to which the bramble is the symbol of political tyranny, whereas in Pseudo-Philo the bramble is praised as a symbol of truth and reminds the author of the thorn bush, no less, that had enlightened Moses. Again, Pseudo-Philo, the theologian and moralist, finds an obvious parallel between Abraham's intended sacrifice of Isaac and Jephthah's sacrifice of his daughter. Perhaps, we may summarize these divergences by noting the difference in etymologies of the name of Samson. For Josephus, the political historian, seeking to impress his non-Jewish readers with the fact that the biblical heroes possess the qualities of the great epic heroes of Greek literature, the name is derived from the word meaning "strong," thus conjuring up a picture of a Jewish Heracles. Pseudo-Philo, the theologian and moralist, on the other hand, derives the name from the word meaning "holy," a unique etymology unparalleled in rabbinic or other literature.

In its treatment of detail, as we have seen, *LAB* seems to occupy an intermediate position between Josephus and the rabbinic tradition in connection with the prediction that the universe will be destroyed by fire and water, the account of the Tower of Babel, the narrative of Abraham's readiness to sacrifice his son Isaac, the story of Amram and the background of the birth of Moses, the Balaam pericope, and various aspects of the Samson narrative. There are a number of pericopes, however, where *LAB* is closer to rabbinic tradition than to Josephus, notably in its connection of Abraham with the story of the Tower of Babel, the farewell address of Moses, Samson's prayer just before his death, and the portrait of Saul, who, far from being the kind of Achilles whom Josephus portrays, is a coward and betrays his mission for the sake of Amalek's treasure. In these instances, *LAB* joins the rabbis in stressing moralizing and prayer and, in general, the theological consequences of events.

However, the number of unique elements in *LAB* that differentiate it from both Josephus and rabbinic tradition and, indeed, from any other extant work is so large—I have counted 138[63] in a work containing only 4081 lines in Harrington's Latin text, that is, about 100 pages if there are approximately 40 lines to a page—that the work is hardly to be classified as either predominantly Josephan or rabbinic in its tendency. Of course, it is only fair to add, many of these apparently unique features would undoubtedly not be unique if we had all the midrashic and the other literature that has been lost. No fewer than fifty-three of these elements are names and numbers missing from the biblical text; and this would reinforce the view that one of *LAB*'s aims is, in accordance with the talmudic statement (*Baba Bathra* 91a), to supply such information in order to answer sectarians. But, as Perrot[64] has remarked, the aim of Pseudo-Philo is to write for the interest and edification of a large public. In this respect he is like Josephus, and like the latter, he seeks to touch the heart through painting a series of vivid pictures of eminent personages, though Josephus is more the historian, appealing to the critical, intellectual reader. Finally, we may note that in his style of narrative Pseudo-Philo is closer to Luke in the Book of Acts than to Josephus and emphasizes, more than does Josephus, the importance of prayer and of divine providence. In his approach, Pseudo-Philo, like the authors of the Apocalypse of Baruch and of IV Esdras and like Josephus, represents a Pharisaic outlook;[65] but he is more overt in stressing the current theological points of view of the rabbis, whether it be with regard to the Temple and the sacrificial laws, the covenant and the law, sin (especially idolatry, as seen in the emphasis given to it in Pseudo-Philo's version of the Ten Commandments, in the golden calf, and in the pericopes of Kenaz, Micah, Deborah, Aod, Gideon, and Jair), divine providence, eschatology, and angelology. Such interests, together with the stress on the fact that Israel has been subjugated by foreign oppressors as punishment for the egregious sins of the people, the emphasis on the great leaders that emerged during the days of the Judges precisely at the time when hopes seemed to reach a nadir, and the reiteration of God's promise that He will not allow Israel to be utterly destroyed (perhaps with reference to the contemporary political situation in which Israel found itself after the destruction of the Temple), may well suggest that *LAB* dates from the chaotic period just before or just after the destruction of the Temple, when, indeed, there was a dire need for an inspired leader such as Kenaz.[66]

Notes

1. Leopold Cohn, "An Apocryphal Work Ascribed to Philo of Alexandria," *JQR* (Old Series) 10 (1898):277–332.

2. M: R. James, *The Biblical Antiquities of Philo* (London, 1917; reissued New York, 1971), 29–33.

3. Guido Kisch, *Pseudo-Philo's Liber Antiquitatum Biblicarum* (Publications in Medieval Studies, the University of Notre Dame, vol. 10: South Bend, Indiana, 1949), 17.

4. Pierre-Maurice Bogaert, in Daniel J. Harrington, Jacques Cazeaux, Charles Perrot, Pierre-Maurice Bogaert, eds., *Pseudo-Philon: Les Antiquités Bibliques*, vol. 2 (Paris, 1976), 66–74. In volume 1, Harrington has presented us, for the first time, with a critical text, together with an extensive introduction and a careful stemma.

5. Louis H. Feldman, "Prolegomenon," in reissue of *The Biblical Antiquities of Philo* by M. R. James (New York, 1971), xxviii–xxxi.

6. See *ibid.*, ix–x.

7. See Daniel J. Harrington, "The Biblical Text of Pseudo-Philo's *Liber Antiquitatum Biblicarum*," *CBQ* 33 (1971):1–17.

8. See Feldman (*op. cit.*, note 5), xxv–xxvii.

9. See *ibid.*, xlviii–1 and A. J. Ferch, "The Two Aeons and the Messiah in Pseudo-Philo, 4 Ezra, and 2 Baruch," *AUSS* 15 (1977):135–151.

10. See Feldman (*op. cit.*, note 5), xxviii.

11. In Harrington, Cazeaux, Perrot, and Bogaert (*op. cit.*, note 4), vol. 2, 66–74.

12. In *ibid.*, vol. 2, 77–78.

13. Alexander Zeron, "Erwägungen zu Pseudo-Philos Quellen und Zeit," *JSS* 11 (1980): 38–52. Bernard J. Bamberger, "The Dating of Aggadic Materials," *JBL* 68 (1949):115–23, however, has shown that late Midrashim often reflect earlier traditions. Zeron in another article, "The Swansong of Edom," *JJS* 31 (1980):190, assigns *LAB* to the first century.

14. Cohn (*op. cit.*, note 1), 322.

15. James (*op. cit.*, note 2), 59.

16. Kisch, (*op. cit.*, note 3), 17.

17. See Feldman (*op. cit.*, note 5), xxxiii–xlvii.

18. So Zeron, "The Swansong of Edom," (*op. cit.*, note 13), 190–198.

19. In Harrington et al. (*op cit.*, note 4), vol. 2, 33–39.

20. *Op. cit.*, note 5, vii–clxix.

21. Louis H. Feldman, "Epilegomenon to Pseudo-Philo's *Liber Antiquitatum (LAB)*," *JJS* 25 (1974):305–312.

22. For the date of *LAB*, see my discussion in "Prolegomenon" (*op. cit.*, note 5), xxviii–xxxi.

23. James (*op. cit.*, note 2), 27.

24. *Ibid.*, 146, note on *LAB* 25.1.

25. Zeron, "Erwägungen" (*op. cit.*, note 13) 45, n. 43, has added another parallel: the connection of the name Peleg (from Greek πέλαγος) with the islands of the sea whither the builders of the Tower of Babel (*LAB* 4.3 and Josephus, *A* I, 120) were scattered.

26. See Feldman, "Prolegomenon" (*op. cit.*, note 5), lviii–lxiv; and "Epilegomenon" (*op. cit.*, note 21), 306–307.

27. Salomo Rappaport, *Agada und Exegese bei Flavius Josephus* (Wien, 1930), 88, n. 94a, is in doubt as to whether Josephus is referring to two catastrophes or whether he means that man will be destroyed partly by fire and partly by water. Abraham Schalit, in his translation of Josephus' *Antiquities* into Hebrew, vol. 2 (Jerusalem, 1944) 13, n. 45, concludes that two ca-

tastrophes are meant, since he notes that the *Vita Adae* 49–50, which speaks of two catastrophes, also, like Josephus, mentions two tablets. However, as I have argued, "Hellenizations in Josephus' Portrayal of Man's Decline," *Religions in Antiquity: Essays in Memory of Erwin Ramsdell Goodenough* (*Studies in the History of Religions,* 14, ed. Jacob Neusner), 351, n. 3, it seems more likely that Josephus is speaking of a single catastrophe, inasmuch as he says that in the one case (fire) a pillar of brick will survive, while in the other case (flood) a pillar of stone will survive. Cf. Levi (Louis) Ginzberg, "Flood of Fire" [in Hebrew], *Hagoren* 8 (1911–1912):35–51. A similar account, alluding to a catastrophe either by fire or by water and to inscriptions on marble and on bricks that would survive this disaster, is found in an anonymous Christian work, *Palaea Historica,* dating from perhaps the ninth century, where, however, Enoch rather than Adam makes the prediction. See David Flusser, "*Palaea Historica:* An Unknown Source of Biblical Legends," *SH* 22 (1971):50–52.

28. In form, as I (*op. cit.,* note 27), 352, have suggested, Josephus is closest to pagan Greek parallels, notably Plato (*Timaeus* 22 C 1–3), who remarks that there have been and will be many destructions of mankind, the greatest of them being caused by fire and water, and Ovid (*Metamorphoses* 1.253–261), who declares that Zeus was about to hurl his thunderbolts at the whole world but remembered that the fates had declared that some day sea, land, and sky would be destroyed by fire, and so thought it better to drown the world by a flood.

29. Cf. also *Ḥullin* 89a, *Avodah Zarah* 53b, *Pesaḥim* 94b, *Eruvin* 53a, and parallels cited by Louis Ginzberg, *The Legends of the Jews,* vol. 5 (Philadelphia, 1925), 201, n. 88.

30. There are, however, two totally divergent views of Nimrod in rabbinic literature. On the one hand, the prevalent view (*Pesaḥim* 94b and parallels cited by Ginzberg [*op. cit.,* note 29] vol. 5, 198, n. 77) agrees with *LAB* (4.7) in condemning Nimrod as a rebel against God. On the other hand, there is a view (Targum Yerushalmi 10.11) that Nimrod emigrated to Assyria so as to avoid participating in the building of the Tower of Babel.

31. Like Josephus (*A* I, 160), who knows the tradition of a site in the region of Damascus named after Abram, *LAB* (6.18) mentions a place called by the name of Abram and "in the tongue of the Chaldeans Deli, which is being interpreted, God." Perrot (*op. cit.,* note 4) vol. 2, 97–98, suggests that for *Deli* we should read *Beli,* in allusion to Belus, the builder of the Tower of Babel according to the anonymous Hellenistic writers cited by Eusebius (*Praeparatio Evangelica* 9.18.2).

32. Cf. Ginzberg (*op. cit.,* note 29) vol. 5, 203, n. 88.

33. *Ibid.,* vol. 5, 203, n. 88, argues that the transformations were into various complexions and features of the races of mankind; but I remark (*op. cit.,* note 5), lxxxix (*ad LAB* 7.5) that the fact that Baruch—with which, according to James (*op. cit.,* note 2), 46–54, *LAB* is closely related—understands it in the sense of transformation into beasts supports the view that this is the interpretation in *LAB* also.

34. Cf. parallels cited by Ginzberg (*op. cit.,* note 29) vol. 5, 202, n. 88.

35. See Betsy H. Amaru, "Land Theology in Josephus' *Jewish Antiquities,*" *JQR* 71 (1980–1981):201–229.

36. On Pseudo-Philo's view of the Aqedah see further Géza Vermès, *Scripture and Tradition in Judaism: Haggadic Studies* (Leiden, 1973), 199–202; Robert J. Daly, "The Soteriological Significance of the Sacrifice of Isaac," *CBQ* 39 (1977):59 ff.; and P. R. Davies and B. D. Chilton, "The Aqedah: A Revised Tradition History," *CBQ* 40 (1978):522 ff.

37. Daly (*op. cit.,* note 35), 58 concludes that the theology of the Aqedah had become accessible to Christian writers, through the treatments of Philo, Pseudo-Philo, and Josephus, by the beginning of the second century. We may comment, however, that it was not until the third century that extant church fathers refer to the Aqedah passage in Josephus, that they never refer to the passage in Pseudo-Philo, and that most likely they derived their theology of the Aqedah from a direct reading of the biblical passage itself.

38. Willem C. van Unnik, "Josephus' Account of the Story of Israel's Sin with Alien Women in the Country of Midian (Num. 25:1 ff.), *"Travels in the World of the Old Testament: Studies Presented to Professor M. A. Beek* (Assen, 1974), 241–261.

39. Cf. parallels cited by Ginzberg (*op. cit.*, note 29), vol. 5, 394, n. 27.

40. Cf. *Sotah* 12b–13a and parallels cited by Rappaport (*op. cit.*, note 27), 114, n. 129. On Miriam as a prophetess, see Roger LeDéaut, "Miryam, soeur de Moïse, et Marie, mère du Messie," *Biblica* 45 (1964):205–206, and Géza Vermès, "La Figure de Moïse au tournant des deux testamants," in Henri Cazelles et al., *Moïse l'Homme de l'Alliance* (Paris, 1955), 89.

41. See my "Prolegomenon" (*op. cit.*, note 5), xcii (*ad LAB* 9.10).

42. Moses Gaster, *The Samaritans: Their History, Doctrines, and Literature* (London, 1925), 73.

43. See Targum Yerushalmi on Exodus 8.17 and other passages cited by Ginzberg (*op. cit.*, note 29), vol. 5, 430, n. 188.

44. See Vermès (*op. cit.*, note 36), 146–147.

45. Targum Jonathan on Numbers 24:14, to be sure, has a similar statement of Balaam's advice to use seductive women, but the similarity in language between *LAB* and Josephus is more striking.

46. Cf. *Sanhedrin* 106b, where we find the statement of Mar bar Ravina, the fourth-century Babylonian amora, that in the case of all who are mentioned as having no portion in the world to come, one should not expound to their discredit the biblical passages pertaining to them, but when it comes to Balaam, one should expound such passages to his discredit. Even those passages that acknowledge Balaam's greatness as a prophet denigrate him so far as his morality is concerned. Cf. Ephraim E. Urbach, "Homilies of the Rabbis on the Prophets of the Nations and the Balaam Stories" [in Hebrew], *Tarbiẓ* 25 (1956):278, 283. In patristic literature, Balaam is viewed more positively but only because he was regarded as prophesying the coming of Jesus. See Jay Braverman, "Balaam in Rabbinic and Early Christian Traditions," *Joshua Finkel Festschrift*, eds. Sidney B. Hoenig and Leon D. Stitskin (New York, 1974), 41–50, and Judith R. Baskin, "Reflections of Attitudes Toward Gentiles in Jewish and Christian Exegesis of Jethro, Balaam, and Job" (Ph.D. diss., Yale University 1976), 171–197; publ.: *Pharaoh's Counsellors: Job, Jethro, and Balaam in Rabbinic and Patristic Tradition* (Chico, 1983).

47. Cf. van Unnik (*op. cit.*, note 38), 244–45, who notes that the words of the Midianite women, the behavior of Moses, and the audacious speech of Zambrias are unique to Josephus and (p. 259) that the last is an expression of what was thought by those of Josephus' contemporaries who deviated from the practice of Judaism.

48. Cf. Vermès (*op. cit.*, note 36), 174–77, who refers to Pseudo-Philo's Balaam as a "tragic hero."

49. So Vermès, *ibid.*, 145.

50. B. J. Malina, *The Palestinian Manna Tradition* (Leiden, 1968), 72, who cites the parallel between *LAB* and Josephus in their versions of Moses' address, fails to note that whereas in *LAB* Moses uses words of reproach, in Josephus he employs words of consolation.

51. Perrot, in Harrington et al. (*op. cit.*, note 4), vol. 2, 181, suggests that *LAB* is here commenting on the political scene of the first century and that from his reasons one can infer that he was not a fierce partisan of the Herodian family. But, we may remark, the praise accorded to the bramble hardly accords with such a view.

52. Eberhard Nestle, "Miscellen: Die Bibel des Josephus," *ZAW* 30 (1910):152, asks, in puzzlement, how Josephus arrived at this etymology; and Rappaport (*op. cit.*, note 27), xxxii, followed by Abraham Schalit, in his commentary on the *Antiquities* (Jerusalem, 1944), vol. 1, ad loc., suggests that Josephus was perhaps thinking of Judges 5:31, which speaks of the *sun* (*shemesh*) in his might. A possible source for Josephus' etymology is suggested by the Talmud's derivation (*Sotah* 10a; so also *Yalkut* 2.69 and *Yalkut ha-Machiri* on Psalms 2:31) of Samson's

name from *shemesh*, since the Talmud there quotes from Psalms 84:12: "For the Lord God is a sun (*shemesh*) and a shield." This juxtaposition of sun and shield may have led Josephus to stress Samson's strength as the explanation of his name. In his commentary on the talmudic passage, Rashi cites Isaiah 54:12, "And I will make thy pinnacles (*shimshotaikh*) as rubies" and explains *shemesh* here similarly as a wall. This, too, would emphasize the aspect of Samson's strength.

53. Pseudo-Philo may have had in mind a derivation from *shimesh*, "to minister," "to serve," in allusion to Samson's Nazirite status. Ginzberg (*op. cit.*, note 29), vol. 6, 205, n. 161, suggests that "holy unto the Lord" may be an inaccurate rendering of "anointed to the Lord," in allusion to *shemen*, "oil." Perhaps, we may add, this reflects the rabbinic Midrash (*Genesis Rabbah* 98.14 and 99.11) that Samson was shown to Jacob as the future messiah who would be an anointed king.

54. See *Numbers Rabbah* 10.5 and parallels cited by Ginzberg (*op. cit.*, note 29), vol. 6, 205, n. 11.

55. See my "Prolegomenon" (*op. cit.*, note 5), cxxvi, *ad LAB* 43.2–3.

56. See my "Josephus' Portrait of Saul," *HUCA* 53 (1982):45–99.

57. *Ibid.*, 52.

58. In identifying as Saul the nameless man of Benjamin (I Samuel 4.12) who ran to Shiloh with the news of the Israelite defeat, *LAB* agrees with rabbinic tradition (*Midrash Samuel* 11.78–79 and parallels noted by Ginzberg [*op. cit.*, note 29, vol. 6, 231, n. 48]), as I (*op. cit.*, note 5), cxxxiv–cxxxv, have remarked.

59. See my "Prolegomenon," *ibid.*, cxliv.

60. George W. E. Nickelsburg, "Good and Bad Leaders in Pseudo-Philo's *Liber Antiquitatum Biblicarum*," in John J. Collins and George W. E. Nickelsburg, eds., *Ideal Figures in Ancient Judaism: Profiles and Paradigms* (Chico, Calif., 1980), 49–65, notes this for *LAB* but nowhere cites the parallel motifs in Josephus. On Josephus' build-up of major biblical heroes see my "Josephus' Portrait of Saul" (*op. cit.*, note 56), 54–57.

61. See my "Josephus' Commentary on Genesis," *JQR* 72 (1981–1982):121–131; "Hellenizations in Josephus' Portrayal of Man's Decline" (*op. cit.*, note 27); "Abraham the Greek Philosopher in Josephus," *TAPA* 99 (1968):143–56; "Abraham the General in Josephus," in Frederick E. Greenspahn et al., eds., *Nourished with Peace: Studies in Hellenistic Judaism in Memory of Samuel Sandmel* (Chico, California, 1984) 43–50; "Josephus as a Biblical Interpreter: the *'Aqedah*," *JQR* 75 (1984–1985):212–252; "Josephus' Portrait of Saul" (*op. cit.*, note 56); "Josephus as an Apologist to the Greco-Roman World: His Portrait of Solomon," in Elisabeth S. Fiorenza, ed., *Aspects of Religious Propaganda in Judaism and Early Christianity* (Notre Dame, 1976), 69–98; "Hellenizations in Josephus' Version of Esther," *TAPA* 101 (1970):143–170.

62. The Talmud (*Baba Bathra* 91a), after giving the names of the mothers of Abraham, Haman, David, and Samson, and the sister of Samson, then asks of what importance such data are. It answers that such information may be needed to answer *minim*, i.e., heretics, perhaps Jewish Christians, who apparently were accustomed to ask why the names of these biblical women were omitted in the Bible and who could thus be answered from the oral tradition.

63. See my "Prolegomenon" (*op. cit.*, note 5), lxx–lxxvi; and "Epilegomenon" (*op. cit.*, note 21), 308.

64. Perrot, in Harrington, et al. (*op. cit.*, note 4), vol. 2, 29.

65. Cf. *ibid.*, vol. 2, 32–65.

66. So Nickelsburg (*op cit.*, note 60), 63–64. We may add that the fact that Kenaz, the ideal leader according to *LAB*, was chosen by lot (25.2) may be connected with the fact that during the revolt against the Romans the high priest Phanni was similarly chosen by lot (Josephus, *BJ* IV, 153–155) by the Zealots, a method and a choice that are ridiculed, of course, by Josephus, himself a priest.

3 Josephus' Biblical Text for the Books of Samuel

EUGENE ULRICH

Inquiry concerning the biblical text used as a source by Josephus for his monumental history, *The Jewish Antiquities,* can be doubly illuminating. It can shed light on the state of the biblical text in the first century C.E., and it can shed light on Josephus' method as a late first-century historian.

Josephus probably used scrolls of the scriptures that were copied in the first two-thirds of the first century of our era or perhaps even somewhat earlier. Shortly after the First Jewish Revolt against Rome and the destruction of the Temple in 70, he left for Rome with some copies of "sacred books" (*V,* 417–18). Thus, the more that is known about the specific biblical texts that Josephus used, the more we know about the specific form, or one of the specific forms, of the biblical text circulating in Judea during the late Second Temple period and during the formative stages of the literatures of the New Testament and the Mishnah. Similarly, the more we can determine about Josephus' biblical source, the more we can understand of his methods as a historiographer.[1] The emphasis in this study, however, will be on the biblical text used by Josephus.

The scope of this study will be limited to the Books of I–II Samuel.[2] In Septuagintal studies it is now common knowledge that the text type of one book is not necessarily that of another book and in fact is not necessarily the same within all parts of one book.[3] For books of the Masoretic Bible the same is true, though less attention is paid to this point. The biblical scrolls discovered in the area of the Dead Sea, dated from ca. 225 B.C.E. to 68 C.E., provide documentation for a measured variety in the texts of the different books. We should presume that, since the biblical books were copied on discrete scrolls, and since the text type of one scroll was not necessarily the same as that of another scroll, the relationship of Josephus' historical narrative to "the biblical text" will vary from book to book. Thus, for each biblical book, that relationship must be analyzed in detail. Since for this present study we will be concerned with the Books of Samuel,[4] our results may well hold true for other books but should be tested first.

The Content of Josephus' Bible

Josephus preserves narrative material that is or was "biblical" but that no longer appears in our contemporary Bibles. That is, when the text of Josephus is compared with contemporary Bibles, either vernacular translations or even the Hebrew or Greek text in critical editions, there are words, phrases, ideas, and even an entire passage that prima facie could seem classifiable as "nonbiblical" and that indeed have been noted by some scholars as "nonbiblical."[5] They were, however, biblical for Josephus, and he had actually derived them from a "biblical text."

4QSam[a](Q) gives us a new vantage point on this question. It is a biblical scroll of the Books of Samuel representing a text type at variance with the Masoretic textus receptus (MT) for Samuel.[6] It is interesting to compare Q and MT, and at the points of divergence to see with which text Josephus (J) agrees. Such a comparison highlights at least four readings in which the biblical scroll used by J agrees with Q against MT, but no readings emerge in which J agrees with MT against Q. The Septuagint (G) should also be compared,[7] since Josephus composed the *Antiquities* in Greek and since it has been claimed that Josephus' predominant biblical source was the Septuagint.[8] The four readings in which Josephus' biblical text differed from the textus receptus follow.

I Sam 11.1[init]   A VI, 68–69

Q [ונ]חֹש מלך בני עמון הוא לחץ את בני גד ואת בני ראובן בחזקה
ונקר להם כ]ול] \ [ע]ין ימין . . . בע]בר \ הירדן] . . .
ויהי כמו חדש ויעל נחש העמוני ויחן על יביש [גלעד] . . .

M   [11:1]ויעל נחש העמוני ויחן על יבש גלעד   ויהי כמחריש:

G Καὶ ἐγενήθη ὡς μετὰ μῆνα καὶ ἀνέβη Ναὰς ὁ Ἀμμανείτης καὶ
παρεμβάλλει ἐπὶ Ιαβις Γαλααδ·

J Μηνὶ δ' ὕστερον . . . Ναάσην . . . τὸν τῶν Ἀμμανιτῶν βασιλέα·
οὗτος γὰρ πολλὰ κακὰ τοὺς πέραν τοῦ Ἰορδάνου ποταμοῦ
κατῳκημένους τῶν Ἰουδαίων διατίθησι . . . , ἰσχύι μὲν καὶ βίᾳ
. . . τοὺς δεξιοὺς ὀφθαλμοὺς ἐξέκοπτεν.

4QSam[a] and Josephus share this extended passage absent from all other surviving biblical texts of Samuel.[9]

I Sam 1.22   *A* V, 347
Q   ]ונת[תֹיהו נזיר עד עולם
MT T S   om
G OL   om
J   ἀνατιθεῖσα τῷ θεῷ προφήτην

The epithet "*nazir*" applied to Samuel is a plus in 4QSam ᵃ attested in no other extant biblical manuscript, though reflected in Josephus. Josephus never uses ναζιραῖος for an individual, since his audience would not know the term; instead, he uses the more general term *prophet,* as he does, for example, in his description of the "nazir" Samson (*A* V, 285).[10]

I Sam 28.1ᶠⁱⁿ   *A* VI, 325
Q   למ[לחמה יזרעאֿל
M   om
G   om
J   εἰς τὸν πόλεμον εἰς ʹΡεγάν (or Ρελαν)[11]

Here 4QSam ᵃ probably has an addition, reflected by Josephus, but indirectly through the medium of a Greek *Vorlage.*[12]

II Sam 11.3ᶠⁱⁿ   (I Chr 20.1 om)   *A* VII, 131
Q   ]אוריה החתי נ[ושא כלי יואב
MT T S   אוריה החתי:
G   Οὐρείου τοῦ Χετταίου
J   τὸν ʹΙωάβου μὲν ὁπλοφόρον . . . Οὐρίαν

Josephus refers to Uriah as Joab's armor bearer, and 4QSam ᵃ is the only preserved biblical manuscript from which he could have derived that detail, here or elsewhere.[13]

Conclusion: There are at least four instances in which Josephus shows dependence on the contents of a biblical text at variance with all current Bibles. Since the content of his Bible was not necessarily identical with that of ours, Josephus should be studied to see if elements of his narrative that appear to be "nonbiblical" may occasionally point to a variant biblical text.

The Text Type of Josephus' Bible

The previous section showed that, at least for the Books of Samuel, Josephus' biblical text was somewhat different from our *textus receptus* represented in the Masoretic text, though it did agree with another biblical manuscript. This section will address the question Can we determine which particular text type Josephus used?

If the text of Josephus for his narrative of the content of I–II Samuel is compared with known biblical texts, such as MT, the Targum (T), the Greek of Samuel (G), and the Masoretic and Greek of Chronicles [C^{MT,G}] as well as with the new biblical manuscript discovered in 1952, 4QSam^a, one can get a reasonably clear picture of the type of text Josephus used as his source for the Samuel portion of the *Antiquities*. That clarity will not extend to all the individual readings; that is, we should not hope to know all the details of the precise manuscript that Josephus used, but it should reveal the general text type used.

Text Types in Samuel

Q and MT clearly and distinctly display variant text types for I–II Samuel. The differences between them are multiple and complex, however, and here it is possible to offer only a rough summary.[14] Q and MT are sufficiently close to consider it plausible that they both ultimately derived from a single textual tradition (which may have developed, or preserved, some very ancient variants). But at one early point, or through the course of time in an early period, an ancestor of MT suffered a number of haplographies that were never corrected in the MT tradition.[15] The remainder of the textual witnesses continued to preserve the text now lost in MT, and the Old Greek (OG) version was translated from a Hebrew text that also preserved those readings. Through the course of time, all witnesses developed in unique ways: through errors and other unintentional changes, and through deliberate changes such as expansions (some in MT, more in Q, others in G), omissions, and alterations for various reasons. Q is a longer text than MT for two reasons: (1) MT suffered a considerable number of losses of text, and (2) Q exhibits more secondary expansions or additions than MT, though MT also exhibits some other expansions. If one seeks the "preferable" text, one would follow Q and OG for the first category but MT and OG for the second. Thus, it emerged that Q is a longer text than MT for the two reasons just mentioned and that the OG translation (as opposed to simply the text of Vaticanus as printed in the Cambridge edition) agrees much more with the Q tradition rather than with the MT tradition.

Furthermore, comparison of the parallels in Chronicles with Q and MT of Samuel shows that C^{MT} also used as a source a text of Samuel significantly closer to Q than to MT.[16] Since C^{MT} demonstrates greater dependence upon the Q text type than upon the MT text type, and since the OG shows close and frequent affiliation with Q against MT, we must draw the conclusion that Q was not just some aberrant manuscript deviant from the widespread norm which was MT, but rather that it represented a text type influential in Judah during the fourth century B.C.E. (Chronicles), perhaps in Egypt around the end of the third century (the Old Greek translation), and again in Judah during the early (4QSamᶜ) and middle (4QSamᵃ) parts of the first century B.C.E. and the early centuries C.E. (the early, developed Greek texts used by Josephus and revised by Proto-Theodotion and Aquila).[17]

Thus, prior to the turn of the era the evidence indicates that MT was not the norm, not *the* text of Samuel, but rather that the text type exhibited in Q was, at least judging from the witnesses preserved, more influential.

Josephus' Affiliation with the Text Types

Josephus agrees in general with the Q G C tradition rather than the MT T Gᴿ tradition.[18] Mez in 1895 had already demonstrated that J used Gᴸ not M or Gᴮ.[19] Rahlfs attempted to counter the results of Mez,[20] but fresh analysis[21] sparked by the discovery of 4QSamᵃ, substantiated Mez' hypothesis in general, yielding four (or possibly five) readings in which J = Q alone ≠ MT G⁽ᴿ?⁾, already seen in the first section of this chapter. In thirty-four further readings Josephus showed agreement with Q G against MT, and in five more agreed with Q C against MT G. The results demonstrate that Josephus shows no dependence on MT specifically.[22]

Here we have space to present only a few examples to illustrate Josephus' dependence on the Q text type as opposed to that of MT.

II Sam 8.7ᶠⁱⁿ   (I Chr 18.7)   A VII, 104–105

Q	ירוש[לֹ]י[]ֹם גם []אותם [לקח... ב[עֲלוֹתו אל יר[ושלים] בימי רהבעם...
MT T S Cᴹᵀ,ᴳ	ירושלם:
G OL	εἰς Ἰερουσαλήμ· καὶ ἔλαβεν αὐτὰ Σουσακεὶμ . . . ἐν τῷ ἀναβῆναι αὐτὸν εἰς Ἰερουσαλὴμ ἐν ἡμέραις Ῥοβοάμ . . .
J	εἰς Ἱεροσόλυμα· ἃς ὕστερον . . . Σούσακος στρατεύσας ἐπὶ . . . Ῥοβόαμον ἔλαβε . . .

Josephus agrees with Q G OL against MT C for a plus in the Q G tradition (or possibly a haplography in MT); see *Qumran*, pages 45–48.

II Sam 13.21   A VII, 173

Q	[ולוא עצב את רוח אמנון בנו כי אה]בו כי בכור[ו הוא]
MT T S	om
G OL	καὶ οὐκ ἐλύπησεν τὸ πνεῦμα Ἀμνὼν τοῦ υἱοῦ αὐτοῦ, ὅτι ἠγάπα αὐτόν, ὅτι πρωτότοκος αὐτοῦ ἦν

J   φιλῶν δὲ τὸν Ἀμνῶνα σφόδρα, πρεσβύτατος γὰρ ἦν αὐτῷ υἱός, μὴ
         λυπεῖν αὐτὸν ἠναγκάζετο

Josephus agrees with Q G OL against MT (haplography in MT: ולא‎
ולא‎); see *Qumran,* pages 84–85.

II Sam 13.27[fin]   **A VII, 174**
Q   [ויעש אבשלום משתה כמשתה ה]מֹ[ל]ךֹ‎
MT T S   om
G OL   καὶ ἐποίησεν Ἀβεσσαλὼμ πότον κατὰ τὸν πότον τοῦ βασιλέως
J   ἐφ᾽ ἑστίασιν

Josephus agrees with Q G OL against MT (haplography in MT המלך‎
המלך‎); see *Qumran,* page 85.

II Sam 24.17   **I Chr 21.17**   **A VII, 328**
Q   [וא]נֹכי הרעֹה הרֹעתי‎
MT T S   העויתי   ואנכי‎
G[L] OL   καὶ ἐγὼ ὁ ποιμὴν ἐκακοποίησα
G[Btext]   ἠδίκησα
G[Bmargin]   καὶ ἐγώ εἰμι ὁ ποιμήν
G[MSS]   καὶ ἐγώ εἰμι (om Ax) ὁ ποιμὴν ἐκακοποίησα (καὶ ἠδίκησα a₂)
C[MT]   והרע הרעותי‎
C[G]   κακοποιῶν ἐκακοποίησα
J   αὐτὸς εἴη κολασθῆναι δίκαιος ὁ ποιμήν

    4QSam[a] probably has the original reading; G[L] represents the OG; ἐγώ
εἰμι for אנכי‎ shows that the G[MSS] are influenced by a later recension. Josephus
agrees with Q G OL against MT G[R] and against C[MT,G]; see *Qumran,* pages
86–87.

II Sam 6.2   **I Chr 13.6**   **A VII, 78**
Q   [בעלה היא קרי]ת יערים‎
MT T S   מבעלי‎
G   ἀπὸ τῶν ἀρχόντων . . . ἐν ἀναβάσει
C[MT]   בעלתה אל קרית יערים‎
C[G]   εἰς πόλιν Δαυειδ
C[L]   εἰς Καριαθιαρειμ
J   εἰς Καριαθιάριμα

Josephus agrees with Q C^{MT,L} against MT G C^G for a plus in Q (doublet in G); see *Qumran,* pages 179, 194, 230.

Conclusion: The first section displayed differences in the content of Josephus' biblical text compared with our current Bibles, and this second section has illuminated the cause of those differences: the affiliation of Josephus' biblical text with the text type found in 4QSam[a] and/or in the Septuagint, rather than with the text type found in the Masoretic text.

The Language of Josephus' Bible

This section will address the question: Can we determine the language— Hebrew, Aramaic, Greek, or a combination—in which Josephus' biblical text of Samuel was written? Since Josephus was writing his extensive history in Greek and since the Bible was one of the main sources, it stands to reason that his logical choice for a source text would be a Bible in Greek. Mez already in 1895, and Thackeray in 1927, had claimed that for the Books of Samuel Josephus used primarily a Greek text.[23]

Josephus' Use of a Bible in the Greek Language

We have already seen one example (in the first section: "Jezreel" = I Sam 28.1, *A* VI, 325) in which Josephus displays an error that betrays that he was using a Bible in the Greek language; he must have seen the *Greek* error, ΕΙΣΡ-, already in his source, because if it had been some recognizable form of "Jezreel," he would have added πόλις, and the Josephan manuscript tradition would display variants on "Jezreel" not on "Rela." It is important to note here that, as far as extant manuscripts can show, Josephus agrees with the *Hebrew* text 4QSam[a] alone; but his reading clearly demonstrates that he is dependent upon a *Greek* medium, a Greek text that had erred in interpreting a detail once found in a Greek manuscript but now lost from the manuscript tradition. A few further examples must suffice to illustrate Josephus' dependence on a Bible in the Greek, as opposed to Hebrew or Aramaic, language.

I Sam 25.3   *A* VI, 296
Q   והאיש כלבי
MT   והוא כלבו (qerê כלבי)
G   καὶ ὁ ἄνθρωπος κυνικός
J   κυνικῆς ἀσκήσεως

The Greek apparently did not recognize the gentilic "Calebite" and translated the root כלב "doglike." Josephus erroneously interprets κυνικός as meaning a

Cynic(!), his interpretation clearly based on a Greek text (see *Qumran*, pages 79, 184).

II Sam 6.13   I Chr 15.26   A VII, 85

Q   [om?]
MT   ששה צעדים
G   ἑπτὰ χοροὶ
C^MT,G   om
J   ἑπτὰ δὲ χορῶν

Josephus clearly based not only his content, found only in the Septuagint, but also his diction on the Greek words in the Septuagint (see *Qumran*, 182, 235).

II Sam 10.6   I Chr 19.6–7   A VII, 121

Q   [ומן ארם] . . . [וא]ישטוב
MT   . . . ואת ארם . . . ואיש טוב
G   τὸν Σύρον (G^L; τὴν Συρίαν G^B) . . . καὶ τὸν (G^L; om τὸν G^B) Εἰστώβ
C^MT,G   ומן ארם (. . . (ואיש טוב om
J   πρὸς Σύρον τὸν τῶν Μεσοποταμιτῶν βασιλέα . . . καὶ . . . Ἰστοβον ὄνομα

The text tradition of 4QSam^a and of the *Vorlage* of G contained [וא]ישטוב without word division, G erroneously interprets it as a proper name, and C^MT,G lack it. Josephus, following G, accordingly treats it as a proper name. He makes a second parallel error, interpreting Σύρον as king of the Mesopotamians! Josephus' *Vorlage* must have had the Greek masculine: Josephus could not have mistaken ארם for a person, named him Σύρος, and considered him to be 'king of the Mesopotamians'! Thus, again for this pair of readings Josephus' *Vorlage* must have been in Greek (see *Qumran*, 152–56, 184).

This selection from a larger number of examples suffices to demonstrate that at times Josephus used a Bible in the Greek language, producing readings that would be implausible or impossible had he consulted a Hebrew Bible. But, did he at other times use a supplementary Hebrew or Aramaic Bible? Does not the set of readings in which Josephus agrees with 4QSam^a alone, where no Greek text contains the material reflected by Josephus, substantiate the hypothesis that Josephus used a supplementary Hebrew Bible?

When the evidence is viewed comprehensively, we find, first, that the "Jezreel" reading shows that Josephus used a Greek text—a Greek medium linked intimately with the 4QSam^a tradition—which is no longer extant but which in his day contained the detail now extant only in 4QSam^a.[24] Second, there are eleven readings in which Josephus shows dependence upon G rather than 4QSam^a,[25] again because he is using a Greek Bible. And third, when the

Books of Samuel are studied systematically in comparison with the text of Josephus, it becomes quite clear that "for all the portions of the Samuel text for which 4QSam^a is extant, J shows no dependence on MT specifically or on a Vorlage in the Hebrew language." [26]

Contrary Evidence

Nonetheless, we find that in the notes to the Loeb edition Thackeray and Marcus indicate points in Josephus' recasting of the Samuel narrative where they allege that he is dependent upon a Hebrew or Aramaic source in contrast to a Greek source. We have seen, however, that Thackeray's conclusion with regard to the division of the Greek text of Samuel was generally accurate but required correction. [27] So also here his conclusion with regard to the language of Josephus' text of Samuel is generally accurate but requires correction. The results of my 1978 study confirmed the general hypothesis that Josephus used a Greek source continuously and predominantly. I went further, however, and examined all the evidence marshaled by Mez, Rahlfs, Thackeray, and Marcus that in their judgment indicated a Hebrew or Aramaic source. For the parts of I–II Samuel for which 4QSam^a is extant, not a single one of their arguments for a Hebrew or Aramaic source—primary or supplementary—turned out to be persuasive.

Mez listed, for the parts where 4QSam^a is extant, only one instance in which he discussed the possibility of specifically Hebrew influence on Josephus, [28] but he himself thought that that possibility deserved "kräftiges Misstrauen." [29]

Rahlfs discussed five of Mez' readings for which 4QSam^a is extant, but for three of them he agreed that Josephus' source was a Greek text. Of the other two, 4QSam^a shows that Mez was correct and Rahlfs incorrect. For the first, Rahlfs had claimed that Josephus had derived his reading from Chronicles not from Samuel, but now 4QSam^a provides us with a text of Samuel (from which text type Chronicles derived the details in question) containing those details; moreover, close inspection shows that Josephus must have gotten one of the details from a text necessarily in the Greek language. For the second reading as well, Josephus does err, but his error demonstrates dependence on a preexisting error in a specifically Greek source. [30] Thus, Mez and Rahlfs agree that in general Josephus is using a Greek text, and none of their suspicions of a supplementary Hebrew source survives scrutiny.

Thackeray and Marcus at thirty-four places in the notes to the Loeb edition draw conclusions concerning the *Vorlage* employed by Josephus, for portions of Samuel where 4QSam^a is extant. Of these, twenty-six agree that Josephus' *Vorlage* was in Greek, and five more, upon fuller consideration, also support that hypothesis. The remaining three are quite ambiguous: two involve proper names, the first resting on a dubious choice among the variant spellings in the manuscripts,[31] and the second involving the single difference between ג and כ in Hebrew manuscripts, both forms of which are reflected in Greek manuscripts especially in Chronicles.[32] The last of the three suspicions of a Hebrew or Aramaic source is due simply to failure to understand Josephus' style of paraphrasing his source, whether that source be biblical or non-biblical, and whether it be in Greek, Hebrew, or Aramaic.[33]

Thus, all agree that Josephus' main biblical source was a Greek Bible; but with regard to the question whether he used additional manuscripts in Hebrew or Aramaic as a supplementary source, when all the specific instances are examined for which Hebrew or Aramaic influence has been claimed, not one single example proves clear and persuasive.

Since 1978, only three scholars, to my knowledge, have taken issue with this conclusion. First, Jonas Greenfield, though agreeing that Josephus' "closeness to the 4QSam[a] text is clear," has argued that "the assumption that Josephus had no recourse to a Hebrew text seems to me to remain unproven. I find the viewpoint of Sebastian Brock . . . that Josephus made use of both the Greek and the Hebrew more logical, even if it is only an inference." [34]

Second, Louis Feldman has argued that it "seems hard to believe that [Josephus] would have stopped consulting the Hebrew text so suddenly,[35] especially since he must have heard in the synagogue portions from the historical and prophetical books in the form of *haftaroth,* the reading of which dates from at least the first century." [36]

Third, T. Muraoka, also acknowledging "Josephus' Greek source," [37] nonetheless pleads for more caution, finding at least one case where he concludes that "Josephus is evidently not dependent on the Greek, but if anything, is aware of one plausible interpretation of the Hebrew text." [38]

In response to Professors Greenfield and Feldman I would say that it may be logical to assume that Josephus used a Hebrew Bible as a supplementary source, but that assumption (1) is an assumption, (2) is based on unrevised findings from early in this century, prior to the significant reorientation of our textual knowledge by the discovery of the Qumran manuscripts, and (3) as yet lacks justification by a demonstration of evidence. I agree that the assumption is logical, and it was not my initial intention to set out to prove that Josephus was exempt from dependence upon a Hebrew manuscript; on the contrary, I was attempting to demonstrate his close relationship with the Hebrew manuscript 4QSam[a]. The conclusion, however, emerged from reexamination of the evidence: it happened to turn out that for the portions of I–II Samuel where 4QSam[a] is extant none of the readings used by earlier scholars to found the hypothesis of a supplementary Hebrew or Aramaic manuscript actually demonstrated that he did so. Thus, the assumption is logical, but it is also unproven. It seems questionable to rest with a general refusal to accept detailed conclusions, when those conclusions are based on detailed analysis of more than two hundred readings, without providing evidence to the contrary.[39]

I have suggested an alternate assumption, equally logical, equally unproven.[40] I can also imagine the possibility that, for portions of I–II Samuel not extant in 4QSam[a], one might find evidence of Hebrew influence that could withstand the counterclaim that the readings involved—like the readings illuminated by 4QSam[a]—are dependent upon a Greek manuscript of the 4QSam[a] tradition no longer extant.

In response to Professor Muraoka, I would like to commend his carefully detailed research on which his conclusions rest. As I also attempted to do, he has provided a general model for the kind of research needed to extend our knowledge of Josephus' biblical text to the remainder of the Books of Samuel and to the other books of the Bible.

At only one point, however, does a negative conclusion of his overlap with extant data from 4QSam[a]: II Sam 11:3 (the last example listed in the first section of this chapter). I should present his exact argument, since others may wish to compare the arguments in detail:

> Cf. Ulrich, *Qumran Text*, p. 173, where the addition in a 4Q Hebrew fragment at the end of the verse [3] of *nwś' kly yw'b* (= Josephus) is discussed. *Pace* Ulrich, the phrase can be more easily a later addition than a case of deliberate omission. See also Ulrich's discussion of *OL* at this point: Ulrich, "The Old Latin translation. . .", 126f. Given the appalling mode of publication of 4Q Hebrew materials, one cannot be sure that this "unscriptural detail" is to be considered to be part of verse 3, as Ulrich thinks. This does not appear to be the case in Josephus, though he adds the detail on the first mention of Uriah (*JA* 7.131). Finally, it must be pointed out that there is some doubt as to whether Josephus' source read οπλοφορος or αιρων σκευη, the latter rendition corresponding to Heb. *nośe' kelim* and sometimes replaced by him by οπλοφορος (1 Ki. xvi 21, xxxi 4), for Josephus (*JA* 7.132) reads παρεκοιμήθη τῷ βασιλεῖ σὺν τοῖς ἄλλοις ὁπλοφόροις, which is parallel to vs. 9 κοιμᾶται . . . μετὰ πάντων τῶν παίδων (Heb. *'abdê*) τοῦ κυρίου αὐτοῦ.[41]

(1) Concerning the "addition" vs. "omission," I am puzzled because I do explicitly call the phrase a "plus" and an "explanatory gloss" (*Qumran*, page 173) and judge that the MT is "the preferable, unexpanded text" to which 4QSam[a] and Josephus "add" ("Old Latin" [see my note 7 above], pages 126–127). His idea of "deliberate omission" may derive from my admittedly deductive explanation that *if* the phrase was present in Josephus' Greek source, it was subsequently "excised" (*Qumran*, page 173), because it no longer appears in any Greek biblical manuscripts. There are fairly clear examples of material excised from the Greek text because it did not correspond with the MT. Thus, concerning the "addition" we seem to be in agreement, and concerning the "omission" my conditional deductive argument remains

true. The "problem" that "there is no Greek witness to support Josephus" is not "especially acute" (Muraoka, page 57) in light of the other specifically Greek testimony adduced throughout I–II Samuel, unless one were to contend that it is legitimate to demand that the specific manuscript used by Josephus be actually present in one of our modern museums for collation in our critical editions.

(2) That this scriptural detail is part of verse 3 is virtually certain. My dissertation was explicitly not an edition, but an analysis, of 4QSam^a; but scholars may be confident of my reading in this individual case, confirmed by Professors F. M. Cross, P. W. Skehan (*New American Bible*), and P. K. Mc-Carter (Anchor Bible Commentary).

(3) Josephus adds the "armor-bearer" detail when he first mentions Uriah's name (*A*, VII, 171), just as 4QSam^a does. Once one understands Josephus' characteristic manner of composing his narratives, there is no reason at all to doubt that Josephus' biblical text had this detail at the end of verse 3. Nor is there a more likely place for it to occur.

(4) If Professor Muraoka refers to doubt concerning which of the two different possibilities, οπλοφορος vs. αιρων σκευη, was in Josephus' text, the answer does not matter, because, as he says, the latter is "sometimes replaced by [Josephus] by οπλοφορος." If he refers to doubt as to whether some other term (e.g., ʿebed, as he suggests from verse 9)—as opposed to either of the two equivalent possibilities, οπλοφορος or αιρων σκευη—was in the source, that seems implausible, especially in light of נ]ושא כלי in 4QSam^a. But in that unlikely event, he would then concur more closely with my thesis that Josephus used a Greek Bible; for if ʿebed were in Josephus' *Hebrew* Bible, there would have been no source other than a Greek (or Aramaic) Bible for the more specific οπλοφορος.

Finally, Professor Muraoka also concludes, discussing II Sam 11.8, that "Josephus is evidently not dependent on the Greek, but if anything, is aware of one plausible interpretation of the Hebrew text." [42] He is referring to the difficult משאת/ἄρσις/τῶν παρεστηκότων. But 4QSam^a is not extant for this word, nor does Muraoka sort out the complex stratigraphy of the recensional layers, but merely refers to the undifferentiated "*L* text." Thus, we do not know what Josephus' source had, regardless of whether that source were in Hebrew or Greek.

Conclusion: For the Books of Samuel the scholarly consensus that Josephus continuously and predominantly used a Greek Bible as the source for his narrative in *The Jewish Antiquities* is fully corroborated. The older view that he also used a supplementary Hebrew or Aramaic Bible is logical but, at least for those portions where the added control of 4QSam^a is available, lacks evidence produced to support it.

Conclusion

From a study of Josephus' recasting of the narrative of the Books of Samuel in *The Jewish Antiquities* compared with the major text of Samuel from Qumran, the Masoretic text of Samuel and Chronicles, and the Greek versions, we can sketch a fairly clear picture of the biblical text which he employed. He used a text intimately related to 4QSam[a]. His text was a biblical text in a tradition not aberrant but apparently more widely influential in the Second Temple period than that of the MT. It was a text of Samuel, not of Chronicles, though similarities in Chronicles indicate that the Chronicler also used as his source a text closer to 4QSam[a] than to the MT.

Josephus' biblical text was in the Greek, not Hebrew or Aramaic, language. Some scholars continue to hold that he used a Hebrew or Aramaic Bible as a supplementary source; this is a logical but unproven hypothesis which developed in an earlier period before we had wide documentation of Hebrew biblical manuscripts clearly at variance with the MT. Occasionally, especially in errors—where textual affiliation is often most easy to detect—he betrays that he is using a form of the text-tradition very closely allied to the 4QSam[a] text-tradition, but in the Greek language (the "proto-Lucianic text"). For the most part the readings of his Greek Bible are still preserved in our Greek manuscript tradition, but it is an ancient text-tradition a number of whose valuable readings succumbed to the knives of revisionists. These latter, part of a current whose culmination is well known in the recensions of (Proto-) Theodotion and Aquila, were intent upon bringing the old "Septuagint" into conformity with the *Hebraica veritas,* which they equated with the rabbinic Bible destined to be guarded by the Masoretes and thus to be handed down as our *textus receptus.* Our closest glimpse of Josephus' biblical text for the Books of Samuel comes through critical synoptic scrutiny of 4QSam[a] and the ancient Greek manuscript tradition.

Notes

1. See Harold W. Attridge, "Josephus and His Works," *Jewish Writings of the Second Temple Period* (ed. Michael E. Stone; *Compendia Rerum Iudaicarum ad Novum Testamentum,* Section Two, vol. 3; Assen: Van Gorcum, 1984) 185–232; *idem,* "Jewish Historiography," *Early Judaism and Its Modern Interpreters* (ed. Robert A. Kraft and George W. E. Nickelsburg; Atlanta: Scholars, 1986) 311–343; Louis H. Feldman, "Flavius Josephus Revisited: the Man, His Writings, and His Significance," *ANRW* II; Band 21/2 (ed. Hildegard Temporini and Wolfgang Haase, Berlin: Walter de Gruyter, 1984) 763–862; *idem,* "Josephus' Portrait of Saul," *HUCA* 53 (1982):45–99; *idem,* "Josephus as a Biblical Interpreter: The ʿ*Aqedah,*" *JQR* 75 (1985): 212–252.

2. Even more specifically, the research behind the present analysis was focused for consistency of results on those portions of the text of I–II Samuel where 4QSam[a] was extant and where one or more of the biblical texts (Q, MT, G, C[MT,G]) disagreed with another. Over two

hundred such readings were isolated, and the text of Josephus was compared with each of these. In order to balance the somewhat random character of that selection of readings, the analysis also included the continuous text of a complete chapter, II Sam 6. For this detailed analysis of the scroll and Josephus' relationship to it, see E. Ulrich, *The Qumran Text of Samuel and Josephus* (HSM 19; Missoula, MT: Scholars, 1978).

3. Thackeray (*The Septuagint and Jewish Worship* [London, 1921] 9–28) discerned the following divisions in the Greek text of Samuel-Kings: α (= I Sam), ββ (=II Sam 1:1–11:1), γγ (=I Kgs 2:12–21:29), βγ (=II Sam 11:2–I Kgs 2:11), γδ (=I Kgs 22:1–II Kgs 25:30). He assigned α, ββ, γγ to one "translator" and βγ, γδ to a second "translator." Barthélemy (*Les devanciers d'Aquila* [VTSup 10; Leiden: Brill, 1963] 34–41) refined Thackeray's results, showing that the second grouping was not due to another "translator" but to a recensionist, i.e., a reviser of the first translation bringing it into greater conformity with the Masoretic Text in word order, length of text, and choice of lexemes. Thus, the majority of the Greek texts of Samuel represents the Old Greek for part of the narrative and the "Proto-Theodotionic" recension for the remainder.

4. The specific texts used for comparison in this analysis are, for Josephus, the Loeb edition checked against Niese's edition; for the Hebrew Bible, the extensive fragments of the Qumran scroll 4QSam[a] (to be published by F. M. Cross in *Discoveries in the Judaean Desert;* provisionally see Cross, "A New Qumran Biblical Fragment Related to the Original Hebrew Underlying the Septuagint," *BASOR* 132 [1953]:15–26; and Ulrich, *Qumran* [see note 2]) and the Masoretic text of both Samuel and Chronicles as in *Biblia Hebraica Stuttgartensia;* for the Septuagint, the text and apparatus as in the Cambridge Septuagint, edited by Brooke, McLean, & Thackeray; and for the Vetus Latina, Fischer's revised edition of OL 115 (see B. Fischer with E. Ulrich and J. E. Sanderson, "Palimpsestus Vindobonensis: A Revised Edition of L 115 for Samuel-Kings," *BIOSCS* 16 [1983]:13–87; republished B. Fischer, *Beiträge zur Geschichte der lateinischen Bibeltexte* [Vetus Latina: Aus der Geschichte der lateinischen Bibel 12; Freiburg: Herder, 1986] 308–438), Sabatier's collection, and the critical apparatus of the Cambridge Septuagint.

5. See, e.g., Marcus in the Loeb edition, vol. V, p. 201 note c; pp. 330–331 note a; p. 425 note c; p. 433 note a; and *passim*.

6. For Samuel the Targum (T) and Peshitta (S) regularly agree with MT.

7. The Old Latin (OL), translated from early but somewhat developed forms of the Septuagint, is an important witness to the early Greek text before it suffered many of the intentional and unintentional variants exhibited in our extant manuscripts; see Ulrich, "The Old Latin Translation of the LXX and the Hebrew Scrolls from Qumran," *The Hebrew and Greek Texts of Samuel: 1980 Proceedings IOSCS—Vienna* (ed. E. Tov; Jerusalem: Academon, 1980), 121–165; idem, "Characteristics and Limitations of the Old Latin Translation of the Septuagint," *La Septuaginta en la investigación contemporánea (V Congreso de la IOSCS),* (Textos y estudios «Cardenal Cisneros» 34) (ed. N. Fernández Marcos; Madrid: Instituto «Arias Montano», 1985), 67–80; and Julio Trebolle, "Redaction, Recension, and Midrash in the Books of Kings," *BIOSCS* 15 (1982):12–35; idem, "From the 'Old Latin' through the 'Old Greek' to the 'Old Hebrew' (2 Kings 10:23–25)," *Textus* 11 (1984):17–36.

8. Adam Mez, *Die Bibel des Josephus untersucht für Buch V–VII der Archäologie* (Basel, 1895) 79–84; Thackeray, *Josephus: The Man and the Historian* (New York: Ktav, 1967) 81; Ulrich, *Qumran,* 223–259.

9. The line [גלעד] ויהי—יביש in 4QSam[a] is written supralinearly (*prima manu*). For discussion of the passage, see (Cross') note on 1 Sam 11:1 in *The New American Bible;* Cross, "The Evolution of a Theory of Local Texts," *Qumran and the History of the Biblical Text* (ed. F. M. Cross and S. Talmon; Cambridge, MA: Harvard University, 1975) 306–315, esp. p. 315; Ulrich, *Qumran,* 166–170; Cross, "The Ammonite Oppression of the Tribes of Gad and Reuben: Missing Verses from 1 Samuel 11 Found in 4QSam[a]," *The Hebrew and Greek Texts of Samuel*

[n. 7], 105–119. See further Terry L. Eves, "One Ammonite Invasion or Two? 1 Sam 10:27–11:2 in the Light of 4QSam^a," *WTJ* 44 (1982):308–326; Dominique Barthélemy, ed., *Critique textuelle de l'Ancien Testament 1: Josué, Juges, Ruth, Samuel, Rois, Chroniques, Esdras, Néhémie, Esther* (OBO 50/1; Fribourg: Editions Universitaires; Göttingen: Vandenhoeck & Ruprecht, 1982), 166–172; and Alexander Rofé, "The Acts of Nahash according to 4QSam^a," *IEJ* 32 (1982): 129–133.

10. See Cross, "A New Qumran" [n. 4], 18–19; Ulrich, *Qumran,* 165–166; cf. also 39–40.

11. The following variants occur in the Josephan manuscripts: Ρεγαν RE; Ριγαν O; Ρεγγαν MSP; *Rella* Lat. On the accuracy of the Latin text of Josephus, see Franz Blatt (ed.), *The Latin Josephus* (Copenhagen, 1958) 25. On the discovery of this reading, see Cross, "The History of the Biblical Text in the Light of Discoveries in the Judaean Desert," *HTR* 57 (1964):293.

12. See *Qumran,* 171–172: The Greek text used by Josephus "must have had approximately ΕΙΣ (ΤΟΝ) ΠΟΛΕΜΟΝ ΕΙΣΡ(Α)ΕΛ. . . . Josephus saw and reproduced Λ (and not Γ), for Λ is solidly in the text tradition. The double (Λ and Γ) text-tradition is not explainable if Γ was original. . . . Josephus himself . . . did not recognize that in his Vorlage Jezreel was meant (though something quite similar was present), because he habitually (VIII, 346, 355, 407; IX, 105; etc.) identifies it for his foreign readers by appending 'πόλις' to it, whereas here he does not append 'πόλις.' Thus the 4Q text type had יזרעאל correctly, G frequently errs on the name . . . , and Josephus' Vorlage contained a form quite close to ΙΕΣΡΑΕΛ but already corrupt. That 'corruption already in the Vorlage of J' is a specifically Greek language corruption: ‑זור > ΙΕΖΡ‑ (or ΙΕΣΡ‑) > ΕΙΣ Ρ‑."

13. See the text of *The New American Bible* at II Sam 11:3; *Qumran,* p. 173.

14. For fuller description, see F. M. Cross, "History" [n. 11], 281–299; Ulrich, *Qumran,* 194–207, 220–221, 257, and *passim;* for helpful critique of the latter, E. Tov, "The Textual Affiliations of 4QSam^a," *JSOT* 14 (1979):37–53; *idem,* "Determining the Relationship between the Qumran Scrolls and the LXX: Some Methodological Issues," *The Hebrew and Greek Texts of Samuel* [n. 7], 45–67; *idem, The Text-Critical Use of the Septuagint in Biblical Research* (Jerusalem: Simor, 1981), 260–271; *idem,* "A Modern Textual Outlook Based on the Qumran Scrolls," *HUCA* 53 (1982):11–27.

15. For a partially similar, partially different, assessment see *Critique textuelle* [n. 9], e.g., p. 270 (II Sam 14:30); and Stephen Pisano, *Additions or Omissions in the Books of Samuel: The Significant Pluses and Minuses in the Massoretic, LXX, and Qumran Texts* (Freiburg, Schweiz: Universitätsverlag; Göttingen: Vandenhoeck und Ruprecht, 1984), 283–285 and *passim.*

16. Cross, "History," 293; *Qumran,* 151–164, 193–221.

17. Cross, "History," 296.

18. Cross, "History," 292–297; Ulrich, *Qumran,* 220–221. Within the Greek manuscript tradition the following symbols are used: G^B = codex Vaticanus, G^L = the (Proto-)Lucianic text, and G^R = a later recension (of the Proto-Theodotion or καίγε type) bringing the earlier Greek text into conformity with MT.

19. Mez, *Die Bibel* [n.8], 80.

20. A. Rahlfs, *Lucians Rezension der Königsbücher: Septuaginta-Studien III* (2. Aufl.; Göttingen: Vandenhoeck und Ruprecht, 1911), 83–92.

21. *Qumran,* 22–27.

22. *Ibid.,* 190–191.

23. Mez, *Die Bibel* [n. 8], 79–84. Thackeray, "Note on the Evidence of Josephus," *The Old Testament in Greek* (ed. A. E. Brooke, N. McLean, and H. St J. Thackeray; vol. 2/1; Cambridge: Cambridge University, 1927), ix: "With the books of Samuel (more strictly from I S. viii onwards), Josephus becomes a witness of first-rate importance for the text of the Greek Bible.

Throughout the Octateuch he appears to have been mainly dependent for his Biblical matter upon a Semitic source, whether Hebrew or Aramaic (a Targum), and there has so far been little evidence of his use of the Alexandrian version. Throughout the later historical books, on the other hand, his main source is a Greek Bible containing a text closely allied to that of the 'Lucianic' group of MSS. . . . Besides this Greek Bible the historian still apparently employs a Semitic text as a collateral source. His use of a two-fold text renders his evidence somewhat uncertain. Instances where he agrees with the Masoretic text against all known Greek readings have been neglected in the apparatus to this volume, as presumably as derived from his Semitic source."

24. There are other examples where material which was originally in the ancient Greek text has demonstrably been excised in secondary recensional activity aimed at making the Greek text conform to the Masoretic *Hebraica veritas;* see, e.g., *Qumran,* 142.

25. *Ibid.*, 181–183, 191.

26. *Ibid.*, 191.

27. See note 3.

28. Mez, *Die Bibel,* p. 64 #XXXIV = I Sam 6:1 = A VI, 18.

29. *Ibid.*, 57 and 64.

30. For full discussion see *Qumran,* 25–26, 171–172, 250–252.

31. *Ibid.*, 81 and 188. Caution is warranted concerning proper names; Blatt, editor of *The Latin Josephus* [n. 11], 25, observed that in the Latin text of Josephus "Biblical names were given the form they had in the Vulgate," and thus the forms of names found there are witnesses to the Vulgate but not reliable witnesses to the original text of Josephus.

32. *Qumran,* 209 and 213.

33. *Ibid.*, 254.

34. Jonas C. Greenfield, review of *The Qumran Text of Samuel and Josephus* in *JNES* 42 (1983):67–68.

35. Feldman is referring to Thackeray's view that Josephus had primarily used a Hebrew source for the Octateuch; see note 23.

36. "Flavius Josephus Revisited" [note 1], 800.

37. T. Muraoka, "The Greek Text of 2 Samuel 11 in the Lucianic Manuscripts," *Abr-Nahrain* 20 (1981–1982):37–59, esp. p. 51. I wish to thank Professor Feldman for reminding me of this article which Professor Muraoka had kindly sent me several years ago.

38. Muraoka, p. 57.

39. In a private communication, Professor Feldman recently indicated that it would be appropriate to mention that he has revised his view.

40. *Qumran,* 223–224: "There are, admittedly, Josephan readings which cannot be accounted for, but this is true of every biblical manuscript and of every extended series of quotations from the Bible. In addition to the explanations of the human margin of error due to Josephus and of the vicissitudes of the bimillennial transmission of his text, otherwise unaccountable readings can be explained in part as marginal annotations made by Josephus himself in his Greek Bible intermittently during the decade and more which he spent composing the *Antiquities.* What scholar's much-used source book is not replete with corrections, additions, recordings of private judgments, etc., made throughout the years he or she has labored over the material?"

41. Muraoka, pp. 40–41.

42. Muraoka, p. 57.

4 Josephus, the Letter of Aristeas, and the Septuagint

ANDRÉ PELLETIER

U sing his position at the imperial court as an opportunity to acquaint the cultivated public with the history of his nation—which, after the fall of Jerusalem, was in peril of sinking into oblivion—Josephus composed a work in which he intended to present Judaism in the most favorable light: the *Jewish Antiquities*. For this purpose he made use of various collections of selected works all more or less directly concerned with his nation's relations with other peoples. Here we shall consider that portion of this work in which he had recourse successively to two texts with which he had extensive knowledge: the Bible and the *Letter of Aristeas*.

We know that after the fall of Jerusalem Josephus received from Titus copies of the "holy books," [1] that is, scrolls of the Torah and of the prophetic writings that had been carried off as plunder during the sack of Jerusalem. Thus, he had at his disposal at least these texts in Hebrew. Throughout the period when these books were serving him as written sources, he gave preference to the Hebrew over the Greek translation, first, by virtue of his familiarity from childhood with the Hebrew text, as is evidenced in his naive boast, "The High Priests and leaders of the city would come constantly to see me and hear my explanation of such and such a law." [2]

Furthermore, the first five books of the Hebrew Bible were those that every Jew heard most often read aloud, at the synagogue on the Sabbath.

With regard to the remainder of the history of his people, he has recourse more extensively to the Greek Bible, adopting its division into twenty-two books, as opposed to the traditional twenty-four of the Hebrew. [3]

Josephus and the Septuagint

What Josephus Says About the Septuagint

The High Priest of Jerusalem, responding to the desire of King Ptolemy Philadelphus, advises the latter that he is sending him a commission of translators chosen from among the twelve tribes of Israel, six from each tribe. Josephus adds, "I did not deem it necessary to cite the names of the Septuagint" (*A* XII, 56–57). H. G. Meecham[4] attributes this "error" to the common confusion between seventy and seventy-two in the manuscript tradition in both the Old and New Testaments. But this is a case of something quite different from a scribal mistake: we are dealing with a widely prevalent custom of using *Septuagint* to designate the translators of the Pentateuch. Josephus writes *Septuagint* because he has acquired the practice imposed on him by usage and for which he is merely the very first of several witnesses for us.

That this usage may be found in an utterly different milieu, the church fathers, confirms this explanation: Justin[5] at the beginning of the second century, Origen[6] after him, and so on down to the present day.

To whom should one ascribe this use of the term *Septuagint?* Assuredly to those milieus in which the text was the object of systematic study, in the mainstream of Judaism, for example, from the milieu of the first century, namely, the school of Rabban Johanan ben Zakkai and other predecessors of Akiba and Aquila. In Christian circles, too, it was employed by all those preachers who were engaged in converting Jews by means of the prophetic argument. That the Greek text became discredited in the eyes of the Jewish exegetes of the second century is the result of it, and in reaction a series of revisions were generated that came to be known under the names of Aquila, Theodotion, and Symmachus.

Among the Christians, who treated all books of the Jews as equally "inspired," we note in Eusebius[7] of Caesarea a new extension of the term *Septuagint*. No longer does it designate only the authors of the Greek translation of the Torah, but also the text of their version itself, augmented thereafter by the Greek text of the remainder of the Old Testament. Eusebius takes note of the absence of the expression διάψαλμα[8] in Psalm 2 in the version of Symmachus and Theodotion but of its presence in the Septuagint. "The word διάψαλμα is found here in the text of the Septuagint, but not in Theodotion or in Symmachus, who nevertheless continued [elsewhere] to use the term often, just as the Septuagint did." The three proper names cited—Septuagint, Symmachus, and Theodotion—refer not to persons but rather to the texts they wrote, respectively, and are the object of the comparison.

This passage from Eusebius is one of the oldest arguments we have for the use of our symbol *LXX* to designate the Greek translation of the entire Old Testament. In any event, Saint Augustine has only to affirm that at the close of the fourth century this usage has become constant: The translators "quorum interpretatio ut Septuaginta vocetur jam obtinet consuetudo"[9] ["whose interpretaton is now customarily called Septuagint"].

Historically, however, this extension of the term is aberrant. Saint Jerome[10] does not fail to comment on this. Yet, he himself most often adheres to the custom of designating as "Septuagint" the Greek text of everything in the Old Testament that has either been written in, or translated into, that language.

Our symbol *LXX* preserves this ambiguity, which is a source of confusion. For this reason, in the present study, unless there is contrary indication, I apply the term *Septuagint* to the text of the Torah alone translated into Greek. Thus, *Septuagint* will mean the Greek text of the Pentateuch.

Josephus, who was so intent upon his work of translating the Hebrew Bible in his *Antiquities,* dwells upon the Greek translation of the Torah as on no other event in the long drawn out period that his work encompasses. Nor should it be overlooked that in the *Letter of Aristeas* he had at his disposal a document truly worthy of receiving favorable treatment. But even more than that, I believe that the perspective of three centuries enabled him to assess the decisive importance for Judaism of Ptolemy's initiative in taking under his patronage, if not his actual responsibility, the translation of the Jewish "Law" into the vernacular of the day. Under these circumstances we can better appreciate the satisfaction Josephus derives from it: "Such were the honors and the glory that the Jews received from Ptolemy Philadelphus" (*A* XII, 118). This is not mere rhetoric. Josephus was well aware of the success this translation had obtained in the very heart of the most traditional Judaism. He could have realized that this same success had prompted the translation of other holy books and the composition in Greek of still other works, such as the *Book of Wisdom* (attributed to Solomon) and, in any event, the history of the Jews by Jason of Cyrene. In sum, he utilized the Greek Bible that was in existence in his day.

How Josephus Utilizes the Bible

From the point of view of the utilization of biblical narratives as a literary source, the *Jewish Antiquities* may be divided into two parts. In his account of the period from the Creation to the period of *Judges* (*A* I–V), Josephus is inspired by *Genesis,*[11] *Exodus, Leviticus, Numbers, Deuteronomy, Joshua, Judges,* and *Ruth.* From Samuel up to the Roman era, Josephus utilizes the biblical and other books of history, including *I Maccabees* (*A* VI–XIII).

As one might expect from his reports of his scholarly successes in his knowledge of the *Law* (*V* 7–9) and of his work as translator of the Hebrew text (*A* I, 5), for the first part (*A* I–V) he seems to have taken as his primary source the Hebrew, occasionally utilizing the Septuagint and certain Jewish traditions found in rabbinical literature, to which he added some rhetorical amplifications of his own, which are usually very clearly recognizable as such.

The Beginning of the Creation (A I, 27–33)

"In the beginning God created heaven and earth." In their intense preoccupation with the notion of artistic creation, the authors of the Septuagint had employed the verb ἐποίησεν as artists' signatures. Josephus prefers ἔκτισεν, as does Aquila, known for his tendency to hew to the literal translation of the Hebrew.

"Now the earth was without form, and void; and darkness was upon the face of the deep, and the Spirit of God hovered upon the waters. And God said, 'Let there be light,' and there was light." Josephus writes: "The latter [the earth] was not visible: it was hidden under the profound darkness, and a breath from on high moved upon its surface. God ordered that there be light." Throughout the whole account of the Creation, the Hebrew places emphasis on "God said: let there be . . . and there was." The Septuagint painstakingly reproduces this refrain. Josephus, on the contrary, discards this locution at the first opportunity, substituting the verb of the oral commandment, ἐκέλευσεν. This departure thus preserves the creative power of the divine word.

After the creation of light, Josephus continues (A I, 29): "And this day was to be the first, but Moses said 'Day One' (Μωυσῆς δ'αὐτὴν μίαν εἶπε). Why? I might explain at this point, but since I intend to examine all the causes in a special written work, I shall defer until that time the clarification of this point." The Septuagint likewise designated the initial day by the cardinal numeral. The fact that Josephus invokes it for the text of Moses suggests that he had compared the expression of the Septuagint with the Hebrew text. Elsewhere, Philo (De Opificio Mundi 3.15, 9.35) had already called attention to this anomaly to draw from it an allegorical commentary. Since there is no reason for Josephus to state that "as of this time" he has the key to it, his postponement betrays his embarrassment and shows that the word would remain, for the Jewish exegesis of the period, a difficult problem of interpretation.

The Seventh Day

The weekly cessation of all activity receives many explanations in the Torah. For Josephus, the sanctity of the Sabbath is not derived from a blessing or special consecration ritually conferred by God on the seventh day, but rather, more profoundly, from the sole fact that God put an end to His creative activity on that day. It is probable that this way of looking at it reflects the Pharisaic interpretation of his day (V 12).

Generally speaking, in any event, Josephus' borrowings from rabbinical exegesis are frequent throughout his paraphrases of the Pentateuch, and Reinach has cited a number of instances of them in Books I–VI of the Antiquities.[12]

Abraham's Sacrifice

Another procedure of Josephus consists of assigning a speech to various persons in the narrative. This was a convention in ancient historiography. Its drawback here is that certain amplifications are entirely out of place. An example is the episode in which Abraham goes forth to sacrifice his son Isaac (*A* I, 222–36).

A first supplement, "Isaac, according to the Scripture, is the son cherished by his father" (Gen. 22:2). Josephus (*A* I, 222–23) adds: "The child deserved this tenderness and made himself more and more beloved by his parents by practicing all the virtues and showing a very proper filial devotion and great zeal in the worship of God. Abraham staked all his happiness on leaving a son unscathed after his own days were ended."

To introduce the narrative, Genesis 22:1 simply states that God put Abraham to a test. Josephus develops by way of indirect discourse (*A* I, 223–24):

> Since God wanted to test Abraham's devotion to Him, He appeared to him, recounted all the blessings He had bestowed upon him, told him of the triumphs over his enemies that He had conferred upon him, [and reminded him] of his present happiness, which he owed to divine benevolence, and of the birth of his son Isaac; He asked him to offer this son as a sacrifice and victim . . . to make of him a burnt offering; only thus would he bear witness to his piety toward the Lord if the well-being of his son mattered less to him than the desire to please God.

The biblical account simply states that Abraham arose early in the morning (Gen. 22:3). Josephus tries to reconstruct the debate within his soul:

> Abraham, being of the opinion that nothing would justify disobedience to God and that he had to serve Him in every way since it was His providence that gives life to all whom He protects, concealed from his wife God's order, as well as his own intention to sacrifice his son; without revealing anything about it to anyone in his household, as they would have tried to prevent him from obeying God, he took Isaac with two servants and, having loaded his ass with the articles necessary for the sacrifice, he set out on the road toward the mountain. (*A* I, 225).

The idea that Abraham had hidden his project from Sarah and his household occurs in midrashic literature. According to the Bible, Abraham built the altar. Josephus assigns this role to Isaac, undoubtedly "to make it more tragic." [13] The Bible (Gen. 22:9) goes on to say: "Abraham bound Isaac, his son, and placed him on the altar above the wood." It is here that Josephus imagines a dialogue between father and son, which he intended to be edifying. A few extracts will bear this out:

> "Since it was the will of God which made me your father and since it now pleases Him that I should lose you, endure the sacrifice courageously: it is God to whom I give you up, God who wanted to have from me this testimony of veneration in return for the kindness with which He has shown Himself as my support and my defender. . . . He did not deem it proper that sickness or war-

fare or any of the scourges that naturally assail men should take away your life: it is in the midst of prayers and holy ceremonies that He will gather up your soul and will keep you close to Him: you will be for me a protector and you will take care of me in my old age. . . . but instead of you, it is God from whom I shall obtain support. Isaac—from such a father there could only be a brave-hearted son—receives these words with joy and exclaims that he would not have been worthy even to come into the world, had he wished to rebel against the decision of God and of his Father and not yield himself obediently to the will of both of them, seeing that were this the resolution of his father alone it would have been impious not to submit to it. He thus springs toward the altar and death.[14] . . . But God calls to Abraham and forbids him to sacrifice his son." (*A* I, 229–233)

There follows an explanation from God Himself in indirect discourse. It was not the desire for human blood, He says to Abraham, that had caused Him to command him to kill his own son, and He had not made him a father in order to take the son away from him; He simply wanted to put Abraham's feelings to a test and see if he would be obedient even to such commands. (There follow promises for the future inspired by the text of Genesis.) After having heard these magnificent promises, father and son embrace, then carry out the sacrifice of the ram that had "suddenly appeared." [15]

The text of Genesis remains a masterwork of sobriety that the Septuagint has faithfully reproduced, that still moves us when we read that the father— who said nothing—and the son—who might have wanted to know, but remained silent—"go forth together." [16] In contrast, the two "dramatic effects" of Josephus, neither the construction of the altar by Isaac nor the final embrace, makes any great impression on us.

Josephus and the Letter of Aristeas

Since the end of the seventh century B.C. the Jews had read their holy book, the Torah, in Hebrew, while in everyday life they spoke another tongue.[17] It stands to reason that translations of the Torah into that other language were improvised for homilies on the Sabbath, for the instruction of the young, and for the needs of discussion among exegetes. But to produce a written translation and recognize it as equivalent to the Hebrew text read in public in the synagogue would appear to many as a sacrilegious undertaking.

Under these circumstances, the existence of a translation into Greek predating Christianity leads one to assume that at one time or another subsequent to the Exile (86 B.C.) a decision was taken by a recognized authority to disregard this prejudice.

A Jewish tradition handed down in Greek, the *Letter of Aristeas* (*Ar.*), attempted to reconstitute the history of this translation. After the Bible, it is the document that Josephus cites most extensively. But after Aristeas, circumstances changed and the *koine* of the third and second centuries B.C. did not reflect the literary tastes of the early Roman Empire. Josephus therefore composed a paraphrase of it which takes into account the new situation.[18] A few examples will give an idea of how he goes about it.

Examples

The Decision to Cause the Law to Be Translated into Greek (Ar. 9–21; A XII, 12–27)

According to Aristeas, the initiative would have to have come from the court of the Ptolemies. Through a chance encounter with the keeper of the Royal Library in Alexandria, Ptolemy Philadelphus had learned that the holy books of the Jews were still wanting, for lack of a translation into Greek.[19] Josephus speaks of this library in the plural. Had he realized what prestige the expression *Royal Library* denoted in the eyes of Aristeas, he would have kept the term in the singular.

Asked by the King how many volumes the library contained, the librarian replies, "more than two hundred thousand." The direct style permits us to be present at this conversation, since Aristeas presumably was witness to it. Much later, Josephus, a simple narrator, speaks of it in indirect discourse, "Demetrius replied that there were about 200,000 volumes." One detail eluded Josephus: in the expression *the two hundred thousand* the article presumes that the King and the keeper of the library shared the common ambition of attaining that number; the reply reflects a certain satisfaction in having by that time already passed the goal; this fact will be confirmed by the official text of the King's request (*Ar.* 29a).

Aristeas (11) insists upon the difficulty the Greeks had in interpreting texts written in characters different from their own alphabet, and he cites by way of comparison the Egyptian script,[20] a normal observation in Alexandria. Josephus omits this comparison, which does not hold the same interest for Roman readers of the imperial era.

To accomplish the complete project, one wonders whether Aristeas or Josephus considered a simple transliteration of the Hebrew into Greek, in the manner of the second column of the Hexapla of Origen.[21] But such a labor would have left the Torah inaccessible to Greek-speaking persons having no knowledge of Hebrew. Josephus, in company with Aristeas, distinguishes the work of the translation from its written result, the Greek text.

With regard to the most technical aspect of the translation project, Josephus means by μεθερμηνεύειν (and the various synonyms for it which he uses on occasion), not a word-for-word translation such as we find in Aquila's work, but an exegetical translation, including an interpretation, which proceeds from the resolution of linguistic idioms to the clarification of local peculiarities. This is actually the way he considers the work of the Septuagint (*A*

XII, 12). In his estimation their essential merit is as the work of interpretation that permitted a significant written text to be established, thanks to which non-Jewish readers might thereafter "follow our scriptures" (*Ap* I, 218). This is what causes him to consider their work not as a copy but as a Greek text that presupposes a whole work of interpretation: οὐ μεταγράψαι μόνον ἀλλὰ καὶ μεθερμηνεῦσαι (*A* XII, 20). After all, are even our most literal translations anything other than this?

What Was the Material to Be Translated? (*Ar.* 30: "The Jewish Books of Law")

In the Septuagint this collection of books is always designated by νόμος in the singular. In the *Letter of Aristeas*, it is presented chiefly under three aspects: the moral and religious code (15, 31, 313), the literary work (15, 30, 32, 38, 39, 176, 309, 314), the text (Hebrew) to be translated (46). Νόμος is admitted for all these cases, νομοθεσία only for the first two: νόμιμα is employed only once, in the very general sense of "legislative text" (10), that which at the very beginning of the conversation with the king permits Demetrius to initiate his project. As things start to become more precise he passes over to νομοθεσία and finally to νόμος, a literal translation of the consecrated Hebraic expression, the Torah.

The Promulgation of the Septuagint (Ar. 310b; A XII, 108b)

At a period when various attempts at translation were circulating without any recognized authority, Aristeas became the promoter of a Greek text of the unique, official, "canonical" law. He took care to collect all the desirable guarantees and, in particular, to evoke in detail the historic day of its promulgation, which remained famous in the community of Alexandria and thereafter was commemorated every year. Josephus abridged the whole production. In his time, the principle of a translation of the Bible into Greek no longer posed a question, and the text itself had acquired official status among the Hellenized Jews. This difference in attitude makes it that much easier to establish how much closer to the event was the report of Aristeas.

The Trend of Josephus' Opinions

Lacking precise information on the Greek schools of rhetoric in Rome during the first century A.D., one cannot say which of them claimed Josephus as one of its representatives. It is out of the question, if we examine the paraphrase of the *Letter of Aristeas* and his other works, that Josephus could have been associated with a florid school of rhetoric, or even one that represented the easy abundance of a Dio Chrysostom. A master of rhetoric might try, strictly speaking, to form the public's taste. Josephus seeks merely to conform to that of the public.

This may be deduced from linguistic factors. What he has accomplished in vocabulary, grammar, literary composition, normalization and harmony of style has been offset by his gratuitous plagiarisms and a general weakening of the text. But, at the same time, one comes unexpectedly upon signs of much more profound characteristics, such as the didactic effort, the concern for Jewish apologetics reinforced by a concern for Pharisaic orthodoxy, and finally the influence of the historical conjunction with the prevailing literature and philosophy of the time.

Josephus at Work

Having pointed out Josephus' inclinations as he makes use of Aristeas' text, we can now imagine the Jewish historian at work.

Writing a history of the Jewish nation, he has now arrived at the period of the successors to Alexander. From his secular sources, he draws general information on the origin of the Ptolemaic monarchy, taking it as far as Philadelphus. He is particularly interested in the attitude of the sovereign towards the Jews, which, at the time that Aristeas wrote, was benevolent. The young King Ptolemy VI Philometor (180–145 B.C.) and his wife Cleopatra admitted Jews to the upper ranks of the army and the court.[22] So many were admitted that a tradition became current among the Jews that accorded Philadelphus a twofold merit, namely that he foresaw that the entire world would benefit from knowing the law of the Jews, and that, with this in mind, he took the initiative to produce a translation that would give the Books of Moses a place of authority in the universal language of cultivated people. This tradition is recorded in a Jewish work written in Greek and known to the literate public, because it derives as much from a Περὶ Βασιλείας under the form of a "banquet" as from the literary genre of the epistle.

It is thus an epistle that presents itself to Josephus at the moment when he is embarking on his project. His first concern is to omit the preamble, which has no meaning except in private correspondence. From there flow all the other omissions and modifications designed to transform the letter into impersonal history. But this did not imply necessarily the omission of the banquet, because the latter work belongs to the narrative genre, except that in the literary genre of the "banquet" the narrative element is merely a framework, an accessory. What is essential is the "subject" dealt with by the guests, here, a περὶ βασιλείας. Now, this type of treatment would have been politically inappropriate under the Flavians, especially as concerns the official historiography permitted by Vespasian and Titus. From that point the work of Josephus consists thus of extracting from Aristeas' short treatise the narrative element, to the exclusion of everything epistolary and of the περὶ βασιλείας altogether.

To the text thus limited, he applies a treatment that can be immediately grasped. His first concern is obviously to make the language of the document he is using conform to the model in classical Greek that was forged during its own epoch.

Now, it was no small task to adapt the koine of Aristeas to the correctness of that conventional Attic language. Vocabulary, the use of particles, constructions, clausulae, almost everything had to be redone. Thus, we may account for the greater part of the changes Josephus required his model to undergo. Other modifications, particularly in the vocabulary of the Ptolemaic institutions, are astonishing. Should not a historian conserve these essential terms for the sake of "local color"? But on this matter the ancients did not think as we do. In line with their custom, Josephus replaces these terms with more commonplace equivalents, which usually consist of attempts at explanation—a didactic tendency that gives the key to apparent falsifications.

The special interest that Josephus' paraphrase represents for us is that it shows, by way of plagiarisms from Aristeas, just what were in fact the literary preferences of the cultivated class of Rome at the end of the first century. The value of this testimony is all the more evident since one can compare this edition with the Hellenistic original. This is an exceptional opportunity in Graeco-Roman antiquity.

There is another area, a large one, where knowledge of Josephus' work processes can contribute to the establishment of a text that is still far from certain—that of the Septuagint. Josephus makes no secret of the liberties he has taken with it or with the Greek versions that he used as sources. This in itself is a valuable piece of information. It is even more useful to have been able to determine quickly, with respect to Aristeas, certain givens of his procedures in adapting the texts. Since it most often involves an element of vocabulary placed in question by the uncertainties of the manuscript tradition of the Septuagint, we guess that, the various procedures of plagiarism recognizable here having played a role, one must make certain each time that Josephus, in a given case, did not have some literary or ideological reason for resorting to it. One must undoubtedly reduce considerably the number of cases where the manuscript tradition of Josephus could be taken as arbiter on the variants of the biblical tradition. On the other hand, it happens more often that a term from the Antiquities or from the War, once recognized as a plagiarism, will indirectly support the lesson—apparently altogether different—of this tradition itself. Thus returned to its true role, the testimony of the contemporary Jewish historian of the first controversies between the synagogue and the Christian church will have its proper weight.

The Letter of Aristeas and the Septuagint

The Editing of the Septuagint

The *Letter of Aristeas* sets out to promote a Greek translation of the Torah as the only version having authority over other less careful attempts (30). Such a claim requires guarantees. Aristeas provided some that should have convinced the most exacting Jews. The translation had been undertaken under the high patronage of the most prestigious sovereign of the great monarchies of the period, Ptolemy Philadelphus, and at the behest of the most celebrated of the keepers of the Library of Alexandria, Demetrius of Phalerum, who was both scholar and statesman.[23] The juxtaposition of these two names is a chronological misplacement, but for Aristeas it could have inspired only confidence.

Furthermore, the new translation had been made from a Hebrew text originating in Jerusalem and sent from that city by the High Priest himself. In addition, it had been established by a commission of Jewish scholars also dispatched from Jerusalem by the same High Priest, who had recruited them according to the traditional rules of Israel on matters in which the whole nation should be represented.[24] The members of this commission had accomplished their work under the most ideal conditions, in silence and with freedom from all intellectual restraints (301, 307). After the ritual ablutions and their prayer to God (305), they would set to work according to a method of "confrontation." From the text that they would agree upon, Demetrius would cause an exact copy to be made (302). One final detail, which is indeed marvelous, is that the work was completed in seventy-two days "as if it had been done according to a premeditated design" (307).

Another token of the authority of this Greek text was the solemn proclamation (308) made in the presence of the whole assembly of Jews in Alexandria, acclaiming Demetrius and the translators. After a public reading, standing, the priests, senior members of the group of translators, and delegates of the community announced that the translation, which had been done correctly, with piety and rigorous exactitude, was to remain as it was without retouching. And a curse was pronounced against anyone who might alter the text, however slightly (310–311). This was the "canonization" of the Greek text of the Torah. This proclamation, evoking that of the Torah under Josiah (II Kings 23.1–2), was intended to assure acceptance of the Greek version as the equivalent of the Hebrew text.

With a translation thus authenticated, there was no mishap to be feared such as befell Theodectes, who, just at the point when he was about to borrow a passage written ἐν τῇ βίβλῳ (316) for a play, was stricken with cataracts over his eyes because the translation he was using did not carry the same guarantees as this latter, the only translation that would thereafter be called "The Book."

From the end of the second century B.C.,[25] the *Rule of the Community* of Qumran made use of the corresponding Hebrew expression (*Rule,* col. VI, lines 7 and 9): "Let the members of the Congregation keep watch together during a third of all the nights of the year in order to read 'The Book' [*hasefer*], to seek righteousness and bless God all together." The expression "The Book" to designate the Pentateuch is not biblical.[26] Its appearance in Aristeas undoubtedly reflects usage already established in the Judaism of his period; its parallel in Qumran confirms it, and it is continued in the rabbinical literature.[27] But the passage from Aristeas is for us the earliest testimony to the use of the expression "The Book" to designate the Torah.[28]

Certain guarantees were apparently aimed beyond the Jewish world, at the Hellenized pagans, proud of their culture, which at that time was synonymous with that of the civilized world. Would these Hellenists have paid any attention to a Greek text that did not present them the guarantees of being a critical edition conforming to the rules followed by the scholars of the Museum of Alexandria? That would represent no problem. The Greek Torah had been published under the high patronage of the king of Egypt, upon the demand of the most illustrious representative of culture, the keeper of the Royal Library of Alexander, assisted by a committee of experts (30).

The acquisition of this text appeared so important to the king that upon this occasion he freed more than a hundred thousand Jewish slaves (19–20) at the price of more than 660 talents (26–27). Whether this account has any basis in fact, the story underscores the role of the monarch in the decision.

The translators had been chosen in equal numbers from all the tribes of the Jewish nation,[29] from among the well-known persons possessing both Greek and Jewish culture; and we have the list of their names (47). The keeper of the Royal Library followed the progress of their labors day by day (302). As soon as the translation was completed, when the king heard the reading of the text, he displayed unbounded admiration for the genius of the lawgiver and marveled that historians and poets had never made mention of him (312); he prostrated himself before the books containing this precious text and gave orders to Demetrius that they should be preserved "religiously" (317).

As a matter of fact, if pagans of the Graeco-Roman period came to know or to utilize the Greek Bible, this would not seem to have been due to any guarantees that its editors had put forward with them in mind.

On the other hand, the Greek Bible enjoyed genuine success within the Jewish community, at least up to the end of the first century A.D., and among Christians for many years afterward.

The Development of the Legend

But in this latter milieu,[30] if the Septuagint served as a basis for Christian apologetics, during this period its disseminators witnessed the proliferation of its legend. This legend predates Aristeas, but the letter provides us the state in which it circulated in his time and which is for us the nearest to its pristine state. On reflection, the only element of the marvelous that may be gleaned from it is its observation that this whole endeavor had been accomplished by seventy-two translators in seventy-two days, "as if such a thing had been due to some premeditated design" (307).

At a time when the Septuagint was gaining favor among the Hellenized Jews, Philo testifies to an already more advanced state of the legend (*Life of Moses*, 2.26–44).

For Philo as for Aristeas, the initiative for the translation did not come from Jewish circles, but from the elite among the Hellenists; and for him this is primary evidence of divine action. But the decisive sign of the inspiration, in his eyes, was the miraculous accord among the translators.[31] The religious respect (προσκυνοῦσιν) that this translation inspired among connoisseurs prompts him to speak of them as men inspired of God, that is, His spokesmen (ἱεροφάντας καὶ προφήτας).[32] The institution of an annual celebration to commemorate the translation is a confirmation of the faith in the inspiration of the Greek version that prevailed among the Hellenized Jews of this period.

The fact is that the first apostles of the Christian message to the Jews quite naturally chose the Greek Bible as their source of knowledge and endeavored to stake their claim on the circumstances that guaranteed the miraculous character of the translation. The coincidence between the number of translators and the number of days it took them to accomplish this work as cited by Aristeas appeared from that time insufficient. More convincing was the agreement of the translators that Philo emphasizes. From that point on, the imagination was allowed to run on unimpeded.

According to Irenaeus (130–208), seeking to make sure that the translators did not agree among themselves to conceal any part of the Scriptures, Ptolemy separated them one from another and commanded them all to translate the same work. "Then, when they reconvened in Ptolemy's presence, each one undertook to compare his translation with that of the others . . . , all expressing the same passages by the same expressions and same words, from beginning to end, so that even the pagans who were present recognized that the Scriptures had been *translated under divine inspiration* (Irenaeus, *Adversus Haereses* 3.21.2, quoted by Eusebius, *Historia Ecclesiastica* 5.8.11–15; 21.4).

The "little cells" where the translators were sequestered appear in a document dating from the middle of the third century,[33] Pseudo-Justin's *Cohortatio ad Graecos* (*PG* 6.241–326). It was Ptolemy who wanted to separate the translators. And to better convince them, this author declared that the people in the place showed him "the ruins" of these locations.

Clement of Alexandria (150–211/16) sees in this translation "a design of

God adapted to Greek ears" (*Stromates* 1.148). Tertullian (150/60–240/50) (*Apologia* 18) declares that in his time, at the Serapeum in Alexandria, Ptolemy's Library was still being shown "with the Hebrew works themselves" (that is to say, the volumes that had served as models). According to his contemporary, Julius Africanus (240/250), the Septuagint translated from Hebrew into Greek "everything contained in the Old Testament" (*Epistula ad Origenem, PG* 11.45A).

Anatolius (last quarter of the third century), a Peripatetic who was Bishop of Laodicea in Syria, in *De Pascha canonibus,* in Eusebius, (*Historia Ecclesiastica* 7.32.10),[34] thought he had ascertained that Aristobulus had been one of the translators[35] and had dedicated some commentaries on the law of Moses to King Philadelphus and to the latter's father. Eusebius of Caesarea (265–340), in his *Praeparatio Evangelica* (8.1,7), quotes Aristeas as his authority because he considers the latter an eyewitness. In his *Demonstratio Evangelica* (*Proem* 35, p. 439, Gaisford) he further states that "recourse to this translation is a usage dear to the Church of Christ." Hilary of Poitiers (315–367/8) holds the position that by virtue of the fact that it antedates Christ, this version is a testimony of great value (*Treatise In II Psalm,* 3, p. 39.18 Jingerle; Wendland, p. 100).

If the identity of the translations done separately gives rise to the idea of an inspired translation, this inspired character seems to be motivated by expediency: from an inspired text comes an inspired translation. Thus, Cyril of Jerusalem (ca. 313–386) *Catecheses,* 4.34, *PG* 33.497; Wendland, p. 139) says that the translation of the divine Scriptures dictated by the Holy Spirit also emanated from the Holy Spirit. According to Ambrose (330/40–397) (*Hexaemeron* 3.5, 20, *PL* 14.165), we may state that the Septuagint made additions to the Hebrew text and highly appropriate (*non otiose*) supplementary remarks.

Epiphanius (310–405) (*De Mensuris et Ponderibus* 3, *PG* 43.242) is witness to the legend that had reached its latest development. He was familiar with its two states. Having a penchant for details, he takes from Aristeas the information on the origin and the names of the translators; but for the rest he prefers more detailed traditions, without a great deal of criticism. At least one element reveals a Christian influence, namely, the grouping of the seventy-two in pairs, after the manner of the seventy-two disciples whom Jesus sent out two by two to the locations to which He would come (*Luke* 10:1). As for the invention of a second letter of Ptolemy to demand not only texts but translators, it becomes more extravagant. For this great sovereign, it was not enough to want to accumulate precious volumes; he wanted, in addition, to enter their school of wisdom.

John Chrysostom (347–407) (*Homilies on Matthew* 5.2, *PG* 57.57) rejoices especially in the authority vested in the version of the Septuagint by its being anterior to Christ. But in that period, the only miraculous element of Aristeas' account is found amplified by exaggerations that finally brought on the reaction of Jerome.

The intervention of Jerome (347–419) was a dramatic turn of events. G. Bardy goes so far as to reproach him for having said that the Septuagint was worth nothing and did not represent "Hebraic truth." [36] However, there are at least a few texts from Jerome himself that allow him to state his position more precisely.

First, the term *Septuagint* should be reserved solely for the Greek Pentateuch, on the word of Aristeas, Josephus, and the rabbinical tradition. But Jerome himself most often adheres to the custom of using *Septuagint* to designate everything from the Old Testament that has been translated into Greek.

Second, the Septuagint, even in the broad sense of the word (cf. *Praefatio in Pentateucham, PL* 28.149), far from being something to be dismissed, presents a unique privilege: the help of the Holy Spirit ensuring it against any error. Are we that far from Irenaeus? [37]

Third, Jerome does not for a moment doubt the veracity of Aristeas' account. All that is "embroidered" beyond this authentic document written (in Jerome's view) by a contemporary to the events is to be rejected as an invention pure and simple. Such is the case of the famous little cells.

His contemporary Augustine (354–430), however, places more faith in the value of the Septuagint (*De Civitate Dei*, 18.42 and 15.11–13). In *De doctrina Christiana*, 2.15, 22, he writes: "In order to revise all the Latin translations one would have to have recourse to the Greeks. Among them, the version of the Septuagint, for the Old Testament, enjoys an unequalled authority." Augustine is therefore ready to admit that the unity of text of the Septuagint is the result of a concerted agreement of the translators that destroys all the embellishments of the legend. Even under these conditions he sees in their unanimity a "Divine disposition" before which one has to bow.

Cyril of Alexandria (ca. 390–444), in *Contra Julianum* (*PG* 76.521.D) points out that Ptolemy ordered that all the books of Moses and the holy prophets be sent. Justinian (482–565), in *Novella* 146, 1 (Wendland, p. 157), declares: "Separated as they were two by two and even though they had done their translations in different places, [the translators] nevertheless all produced a single version. Furthermore, who could fail to wonder that, even though antedating the redeeming appearance of the great Lord and Savior Jesus Christ, they nevertheless transmitted the sacred books as if they had already seen Him, under the action of a prophetic grace?"

Again, in the sixth century, Olympiodorus (*In Nicetae Serrani in Job Catena, PG* 93.16A) states: "It was by a disposition from God that the translation was made before the coming of the Lord . . . in order that no one could say that the Seventy translated as they did in order to please the Christians."

In the seventh century, the *Chronicon Paschale* (Wendland, p. 132) continues to pay its respects to the concordance of the translators, notwithstanding their separation. It reproduces, even word for word, the passage of Irenaeus cited earlier. In the eighth century, Nicetas (ca. 750–824), in *Catena in Psalmos, PG* 69. 700, professes to know that the Septuagint translated "all the Holy Scripture and even the Psalms." He finds a supernatural character in their concordance and declares that "the edition produced by these 72 persons was accomplished three hundred years before the coming of the Savior."

George the Syncellus (Wendland, p. 133) always speaks of the teams of two and of the divine inspiration. But the interest of his text is to teach us that it possesses these features from a collection of "Ptolemaica." Must we, along with Wendland (p. 133), identify this collection with the *Letter of Aristeas* itself or admit the existence of a sort of corpus of Graeco-Egyptian documents?

Agapius, an Arab Christian (tenth century), retains the thirty-six groups of two translators (*Patrologia Orientalis,* V, pp. 642 ff). In the eleventh century, George Cedrenus (1, p. 289, 17 Bekker, cited by Wendland, p. 135) appears to return to a more sober tradition. In the twelfth century, John Zonaras sums up the state of the tradition of his day by explicitly distinguishing two currents: on one side, an austere tradition, that of Josephus (and of Jerome); on the other, that which admits the separation of the translators into groups of two (Epiphanius).

What few soundings I have taken among the Orientals whose works have come down to us in languages other than Greek have left me with the impression that the legend did not undergo independent developments in their hands and that they were unaware of the reaction of Saint Jerome.

One should, however, cite Zacharias of Mytilene, in the sixth century: [38]

> Ptolemy Philadelphus, King of Egypt, as the Chronicle of Eusebius of Caesarea teaches, over 280 years before the birth of Our Lord, at the beginning of his reign ordered the freeing of the Jewish prisoners in Egypt and sent offerings to Jerusalem to Israel [sic], who was a priest at that time. He assembled 70 scribes of the Law and translated the Holy Scriptures from the Hebrew language into Greek. He gave them lodging and protection in his own quarters, because in this respect he had been impelled by God to prepare to summon the nations to attain knowledge in order to become true worshipers of the glorious Trinity, through the intervention of the Spirit.

Not only does Zacharias eliminate all the flourishes from the legend, like Jerome, but he brings to it an important theological reflection: the initiative of Philadelphus may be explained by a divine movement preparing well in advance the calling of pagans to the trinitarian faith.

If these traditions may be traced back well into the tannaitic period, we must recognize that the principal embellishment of the legend, the isolation of the translators, is of rabbinical origin (*Megillah* 9a). Starting from this point, the legend developed all its festoons down through the patristic literature, while on the Jewish side the disaffection for the Greek text of the Scriptures put a halt to every source of embellishment.

When Jerome resumes contact with the rabbinical tradition, he retains only one element, that the Septuagint translated only the Pentateuch. This he learned from Aristeas. With regard to the number of translators, there is no reason to suspect that he found any indication differing from Josephus and Aristeas; this would confirm Zeitlin's observation apropos of the alleged number five, which could only be a faulty reading of the article in the expression *ha-zekenim* ("the Ancients"),[39] where the definite article is the letter *he* ("five").

Massekhet Soferim 1.6–10 states:

> The Law ought not to be written in Hebrew [that is, archaic characters], nor in Aramaic, nor in the language of the Medes, nor in Greek. A copy written in any [foreign] language or characters other than for use in reading [in the synagogue] admits only one copy in Assyrian characters [that is, in 'square Hebrew']. It came to pass once upon a time that five (?) Elders wrote the law in Greek for King Ptolemy. That was an evil day for Israel, such as the day when Israel built the [Golden] Calf, because the Law could not be translated in conformity with all its requirements.

We are no longer among the enthusiasms of Philo.

It has been worthwhile to examine this long stream of testimony because there is undoubtedly no other legend the development of which we might trace so closely from its origins and follow down through the centuries. If it was suddenly unmasked by the critical spirit of a Saint Jerome, it would continue to prosper nonetheless in its most deceptive form in a large part of the Christian world at the height of the thirteenth century. In this respect, its development and its survival serve as an example.

—Translated by Katharine W. Carson

Notes

1. *V* 418. The verb ἔλαβον without a modifier leads one to assume that they were delivered by hand.
2. *V* 8–9.
3. *Ap* I, 38–41. The division into twenty-two books is also found in Melito, Origen, and Saint Jerome.
4. *The Oldest Version of the Bible* (1932), 168–170.
5. *Dialogue with Trypho* 137.3 (tr. Archambault; Collection Hemmer Lejay, *PG* 6.792 B).
6. *Homily* 12.5 on *Leviticus* 464.15, *GCS*, 6, p. 280; *SC* (Paris 1981), pp. 188–189; *PG* 12.542B.

7. *In Psalmos*, Psalm 2, *PG* 23.81. On the authenticity of this passage, cf. R. Devreesse, *Les anciens commentateurs grecs des Psaumes* (Rome 1970), 90.

8. The enigmatic *selah* of the Hebrew psalter, which is regarded as the indication of a "pause," with or without the intervention of an interlude of instrumental music.

9. *De Civitate Dei* 18.42; *PL* 41.603; *Bibliothèque augustinienne*, vol. 36, p. 632.

10. *Commentary on Ezekiel* 5.12; *PL* 25.57C.

11. On the whole of Genesis, Thomas W. Franxman, *Genesis and the Jewish Antiquities of Flavius Josephus* (Rome 1979) will be cited as Genesis.

12. Recently, regarding the portrait of Saul (I Samuel 9–11); cf. L. H. Feldman, "Josephus' Portrait of Saul," *HUCA* 53 (1982):45–99.

13. Cf. *ibid.*, 84. See now his "Josephus as a Biblical Interpreter: the ʿAqedah,ʾ" *JQR* 75 (1985):212–252.

14. Feldman, *ibid.* (regarding Jonathan, I Samuel 14.43) 78, 84.

15. The Hebrew Genesis 22:13 offers a faulty text, which may be read: "a ram behind him." The Septuagint reads "a ram." Josephus (*A* I, 236), κριὸν ἐκ τʾἀφανοῦς, literally, "a ram coming from one knows not where."

16. Gen. 22:8.

17. Jacob Levy, *Neuhebräisches und chaldäisches Wörterbuch über die Talmudim und Midraschim* II, s.v. *yavan* p. 230, carefully points out the distinction.

18. Cf. my study, *Flavius Josèphe adaptateur de la Lettre d'Aristée, Etudes et Commentaires* (Paris 1962).

19. This would lead to the assumption that the famous library possessed only Greek texts.

20. In this context, demotic writing rather than hieroglyphs.

21. On the ambiguity of the terms employed by Aristeas in this regard, see G. Zuntz, "Aristeas Studies II: Aristeas on the Translation of the Torah," *JSeS* 4 (1959):111–114.

22. Cf. *CPJ* I, 48–52.

23. Cf. my *Lettre d'Aristée à Philocrate* (Paris 1962), 66–67.

24. Cf. Numbers 11:16.

25. 110 or 95 B.C. cf. Gustave Lambert, S.J. *NRT* (April 1951):96; A. Dupont-Sommer, *Les écrits esséniens découverts près de la Mer Morte* (Paris 1959), 101.

26. The usage that is closest is in *Daniel* 9:2, but in the plural, since it there refers to a collection of "holy writings."

27. Jacob Levy, *Wörterbuch*, s.v. II, p. 576.

28. Through the intermediary of Latin it will become The Bible and will designate all the Old Testament, and finally the whole of the two testaments.

29. Six from each tribe (46).

30. The essential facts are provided by P. Wendland, *Aristeae ad Philocratem Epistula cum ceteris de origine versionis LXX interpretum testimoniis* (Leipzig 1900); H. St. J. Thackeray, *The Letter of Aristeas* (London 1918) (Appendix: "The Evidence of Some Ancient Jewish and Christian Writers on the Origin of the Septuagint Version," pp. 89–116); A. Pelletier (*op. cit.*, note 23), 78–98.

31. We mention in passing that he supposes that the translators dictated forms in shorthand. Naturally, this inspiration is of an order inferior to that of Moses.

32. E. R. Goodenough, *By Light, Light* (New Haven 1935), 77.

33. Robert M. Grant, "Studies in the Apologists," *HTR* 51 (1958):128–134.

34. *Dictionnaire d'Histoire et de Géographie écclésiastiques*, II, 1493.

35. Could this name fill in the lacuna of *Aristeas* 48 for the fourth tribe, where Wendland supplies Χηλκίας according to Epiphanius?

36. G. Bardy, *La question des langues dans l'Eglise ancienne* I (Beauchesne 1948), 266.

37. Cf. Paul Auvray, "Comment se pose le problème de l'inspiration des Septantes," *RB*, 59 (1952):321–336.

38. J. P. N. Land, *Anecdota Syriaca*, III (Leiden 1870), p. 327, lines 7–17. For the translation of this passage I am indebted to R. P. F. Graffin, S.J., Director of *Patrologia Orientalis*.

39. S. Zeitlin, cited by M. Hadas, ed. *Aristeas to Philocrates* (New York 1951), 81, note 109.

5 *Josephus and I Maccabees*

ISAIAH M. GAFNI

J osephus' description of the Hasmonean uprising, from the beginning of the revolt and until the days of Simon, relies primarily on I Maccabees. There can no longer remain any doubt on this issue,[1] and any comparison of *Antiquities* XII, 241 ff. with I Macc. 1.11 ff. leads to the irrefutable conclusion that, all the deviations and discrepancies notwithstanding, before us is essentially a "stylized paraphrase"[2] of I Maccabees.

Nevertheless, for over a century scholars have addressed themselves to the nature of Josephus' use of I Maccabees. The conclusions contribute to the understanding of a variety of issues: Josephus' use of sources in general while compiling his Jewish history; the nature of the original version of I Maccabees, its chronological scope, and the state of the text in Josephus' hands. When nineteenth century scholars[3] compared the two books, *Antiquities* and I Maccabees, they were struck not merely by the fact that Josephus was dependent on the earlier work, but that he availed himself of the Greek translation, rather than the original Hebrew version of I Maccabees.[4] To the extent that discrepancies existed between the two books, these were attributed to steps taken by Josephus, such as the deletion of hymns or speeches, and, as claimed by Bloch,[5] the tendency to render the contents of speeches in indirect speech.

Even before Bloch, Karl Grimm arrived at a similar conclusion. In his commentary to I Maccabees, Grimm carefully examined every discrepancy or addition in Josephus' work, as compared to his source. Grimm even categorized the different types of deviation in *Antiquities,* but nevertheless remained steadfast in his belief that Josephus had the Greek translation of I Maccabees before him. He went on to assert that Josephus by all means did not make use of II Maccabees.[6] The changes and adaptations inserted by Josephus were all attributed by Grimm to the historian's *willkurliche und leichtfertige Ueberar-*

beitung, and the one question that Grimm left unresolved relates to the final segment of I Maccabees, that portion devoted to Simon and which Josephus, for some reason, did not draw from, preferring instead another source for that time period. Was this portion in fact missing from the copy of I Maccabees before Josephus, thereby requiring him to turn elsewhere?[7]

As for the deviations and additions in Josephus' paraphrase of I Maccabees,[8] these continued to vex scholars. Various solutions were proposed in the late nineteenth and early twentieth centuries, frequently suggesting that it was not *our* version of I Maccabees that served as Josephus' source, but that before him (or, as suggested by Destinon, before the anonymous author whose work Josephus used) there existed an ancient and more complete version (save for the last three chapters) of I Maccabees, and this would explain the additions in Josephus' story.[9]

This idea was decisively refuted in a brilliant dissertation by Hans Drüner,[10] who clearly demonstrated that Josephus, throughout his works, did not hesitate to invent facts or even precise figures, all based solely on his own imagination or intuition, for the purpose of rendering his text more interesting and acceptable to his Greek audience.[11] Drüner adds, in this context, that Josephus considered it totally legitimate to add geographical information, such as the distance between two sites, as a means of assisting his readers, and for this type of interpolation no additional source was required, as Josephus could gather this information independently.[12] Another approach put forward to explain at least a portion of Josephus' deviations from the extant version of I Maccabees was to assume that Josephus did not possess only the Greek translation of the book, but also the original Hebrew version. This suggestion was raised over two hundred years ago,[13] and was repeated in modern times by E. Z. Melamed.[14] However, even if this theory could be proven conclusively, it is doubtful that all the additions in Josephus' rendition could be attributed only to a Hebrew original.

The crucial issue at hand, it appears, is to determine what criteria Josephus himself might have employed to justify a deviation from the Greek source before him. First and foremost, one must assume that Josephus was set on producing a polished, well-styled text. If indeed our Greek version of I Maccabees served as Josephus' source, he was thus confronted with an extremely literal translation of a Hebrew text, which frequently left the Greek reader himself bewildered and in doubt as to the true meaning of the text.[15] Pelletier's study on Josephus' adaptation of the *Letter of Aristeas*[16] presents a prime example of the historian's sensitivity to style, and his attempt to embellish the language of those sources incorporated into his text, adapting them to the atticism that was in vogue in the first century C.E.[17] Josephus himself states that the relation and recording of events that are unknown to most people because of their antiquity require charm of exposition, such as is imparted by the choice of words and their proper arrangement and by whatever else contributes elegance to the narrative, in order that readers may receive such information with a certain degree of gratification and pleasure. (A XIV, 2–3)[18]

And yet, a systematic comparison of *Antiquities* with I Maccabees leads to the irrefutable conclusion that before us emerges more than just a "stylized paraphrase," and that Josephus introduced changes in content[19] that cannot be explained merely as stylization or a wish to supply the reader with additional information. For a historian of Josephus' stature, the Hasmonean uprising was undoubtedly perceived as a major event in the Jewish history of the late Second Temple period, and Josephus' sensitivity to the implications of this development must have influenced his presentation of the events.

In fact, certain changes or deviations on Josephus' part from I Maccabees can almost certainly be attributed to the author's personal views. One illuminating and frequently discussed example touches on the question of prophecy in the Second Temple period. The author of I Maccabees was obviously convinced that prophecy had ceased to exist by his days,[20] and he makes this point at least three times.[21] To be sure, the third case refers to the days of Simon, for which Josephus no longer used I Maccabees as his main source, but the first two cases of Josephus' paraphrase present a clear-cut and conscious departure from the original:

I Maccabees 4.44–47	Antiquities XII, 318
They deliberated what to do about the altar of burnt offering which had been profaned. And they thought it best to tear it down, lest it bring reproach upon them, for the Gentiles had defiled it. So they tore down the altar and stored the stones in a convenient place on the Temple hill *until there should come a prophet* to tell what to do with them. Then they took unhewn stones, as the law directs, and built a new altar like the former one.	He [Judah] also pulled down the altar and built a new one of various stones which had not been hewn with iron.

While Josephus abbreviated the long description in I Maccabees regarding the question of the defiled altar, his short sentence preserved all the elements listed in his source: dismantling of the old altar, erection of a new one with stones meeting biblical standards, etc. The one element Josephus completely deletes is the reference to lack of a contemporary prophet. This tendency is even clearer in the following case:

I Maccabees 9.27	Antiquities XIII, 5
Thus there was great distress in Israel, such as had not been *since the time that prophets ceased to appear* among them.	After this calamity had fallen the Jews, which was greater than any they had experienced *since their return from* Babylon . . .

This departure introduced by Josephus is far from surprising, in view of the well-documented evidence that Josephus continued to believe in the existence of prophets and prophecy during the Second Temple period.[22] Consequently, he naturally was inclined to delete all references to the contrary in I Maccabees.

Yet another example of a clearly intentional and meaningful departure by Josephus from his source, relates to his treatment of one of the most tendentious statements made by the author of I Maccabees. In relating how two of Judah's generals, Joseph ben Zachariah and Azariah, were defeated in battle after not heeding the instructions of their commander, I Maccabees explains that their undoing was linked to the fact that "they did not belong to the family of those men through whom deliverance was given to Israel" (I Macc. 5.62). Josephus, who copied the fifth chapter of I Maccabees in a remarkably close paraphrase,[23] suddenly changes course and observes: "This reverse befell them because they disobeyed the instructions of Judah not to engage anyone in battle before his arrival; for in addition to the other instances of Judah's cleverness, one might well admire him also for having foreseen[24] that such a reverse would come to the men under Joseph and Azariah if they departed in any respect from the instructions given them" (*A* XII, 352).

Josephus thus moderates, and in effect erases, the dynastic tendency of I Maccabees, which is only fitting for a historian writing generations after the fall of the Hasmonean state and monarchy.[25]

Josephus, however, does not limit himself to the deletion of words or sentences while rewriting I Maccabees. He also systematically changes the contents of speeches made by the first leader of the revolt, Mattathias,[26] and by its first military commander, Judah. These departures frequently place into the mouths of those heroes ideas far removed from the atmosphere created by the author of I Maccabees, but these new tendencies correspond precisely to Josephus' attitudes towards wars in general and not only the Hasmonean uprising. In fact, they address head-on the issue of defining a justified war: under what conditions ought the people of Israel to embark on a military path, and what are the prerequisites for their achieving victory.

A clear example of such a change emerges from a comparison of I Maccabees 3.16–22 with *A* XII, 289–91. The scene is the speech delivered by Judah to his soldiers prior to the battle of Bet-Horon. It is noteworthy that in sections 287–89 of Antiquities, Josephus offers a close paraphrase of I Maccabees 3.10–15, and similarly *A* XII, 292 f. is a precise parallel to verses 23 f. in I Maccabees (including the same number, eight hundred, of fallen enemy soldiers). There is no reason, then, to assume, at least in this case, an additional source before Josephus.

I Maccabees 3.16–22	Antiquities XII, 289–91
When he approached the ascent of Bet-Horon, Judah went out to meet him with a small company. But when they saw the army coming to meet them, they said to Judah: How can we, few as we are, fight against so great and strong a multitude? And we are faint for we have eaten nothing today. Judah replied: It *is easy for many to be hemmed in by few, for in the sight of Heaven there is no difference between saving by many or by few.* It is not on the size of the army that victory in battle depends, but *strength comes from heaven.* They come against us in great pride and lawlessness to destroy us and our wives and our children, and to despoil us, but we fight for our lives and our laws. *He himself will crush them* before us; as for you, do not be afraid of them.	Having advanced as far as the village of Bet-Horon in Judaea, he encamped there. But Judah, meeting him there and intending to engage him, saw that his soldiers were shrinking from the battle because of their small number and lack of food—for they had fasted—and so he began to encourage them, saying that *victory and mastery over the enemy lay not in numbers, but in being pious toward the Deity.* And for this they had the clearest example in their forefathers, who *because of their righteousness* and their struggles on behalf of their own laws and children had many times defeated many tens of thousands; for, he said, *in doing no wrong there is a mighty force.*

Josephus has introduced a totally different nuance into Judah's speech. Whereas I Maccabees places all his trust in God, who can deliver the few from the multitude, for "strength comes from Heaven" and His aid is unconditional, Josephus transfers the focus of deliverance from God to the fighters. Victory is not solely in heaven's hands, but is also dependent on *piety* toward God, and thus the fathers were victorious "because of their righteousness" (διὰ δικαιοσύνην). To bring this point home, Josephus adds one line with no parallel at all in I Maccabees: "In doing no wrong there is a mighty force." [27]

This is not the only case where Josephus shifts the focal point from God's unconditional power of deliverance to a stress on the fighters' character and the goals for which they have taken up arms. Prior to the battle of Adasa against Nikanor, I Maccabees informs us that "Judah encamped in Adasa with three thousand men. Then Judah prayed and said: When the messengers of the King [of Assyria] spoke blasphemy [II Kings 19.35] thy angel went forth and struck down one hundred and eighty-five thousand of the Assyrians. *So also crush this army before us today*" (I Macc. 7.41–42).

Again, Judah beseeches God for His aid, while relying on historical precedent, whereas Josephus presents the picture as follows: "And Judah encamped at Adasa, another village thirty stades distant from Bet-Horon,[28] with two thousand[29] men in all. These he exhorted not to be overawed by the numbers of their adversaries nor to reflect how many they were about to contend against, but to bear in mind *who they were* and for *what prize* they were facing danger, and bravely encounter the enemy" (*A* XII, 408–409).

Josephus' anthropocentric tendency caused him to erase or distort portions of those speeches that cite precedents for God's intercession, where the character or righteousness of the delivered play no part. Just as Josephus ignored the allusions to God's intervention against the Syrian army (I Macc. 7.41), so he treats Judah's speech before the battle of Emmaus. I Maccabees has

> And they saw the camp of the gentiles, strong and fortified, with cavalry round about it; and these men were trained in war. But Judah said to the men who were with him: Do not fear their numbers or be afraid when they charge. Remember how our fathers were saved at the Red Sea, when Pharaoh with his forces pursued them. And now let us cry to Heaven, to see whether He will favor us and remember His covenant with our fathers, and crush this army before us today. (I Macc. 4.7–10)

Again, the salvation cited was not dependent on the character of the delivered, but solely on God's will. On the contrary, in the case of the parting of the waters of the Red Sea, if one takes into account the statements of the people there (Exodus 14.11–12), that deliverance ensued *despite* the lack of faith on the part of the people saved. In his paraphrase Josephus distorts this picture, again stressing the attributes of the fighters: "and when he saw that his foes were excellently protected and had shown great skill in taking up their position, he urged his own men on, saying that they must fight even if with unarmed bodies, and that the Deity had on other occasions in the past given the victory over more numerous and well-armed enemies to men in their condition *because He admired their courage*" (*A* XII, 307).

The character of the soldiers is only one of the elements introduced by Josephus into the speeches. In Judah's speech before the battle of Adasa, Josephus has the general cite two issues: the quality of the fighters and *the prize* for which they were fighting. Josephus in fact stresses elsewhere as well not only the condition that the fighters be worthy of deliverance, but also that the goal of this (the Hasmonean) war, was the restoration of the rule of Torah and the laws of the fathers, an element not always stressed in I Maccabees. Thus, for example, I Macc. 2.7–13 presents a lengthy lament by Mattathias over what has transpired in Judea and Jerusalem. It begins with the words, "Alas, why was I born to see this, the ruin of my people, the ruin of the holy city." The elegy goes on to describe the pillage of the Temple and murder of the population, and concludes with the words, "Why should we live any longer?" Josephus summarizes the lament in brief prose: "Now this Mattathias lamented to his sons over the state of things, the plundering of the city and the spoiling of the Temple, and the misfortunes of the people, and said *it was better for them to die for their country's laws* than to live so ingloriously" (*A* XII, 267). Thus, while Josephus presents the contents of the elegy in one brief sentence, he nevertheless adds a commentary to the last line, explaining that death was for "their country's laws."

This phenomenon is even more obvious in the amplification inserted into Judah's speech before the battle of Emmaus. After dividing the soldiers and dismissing those exempt according to biblical law, I Maccabees records: "And Judah said: Gird yourselves and be valiant. Be ready early in the morning to fight with these gentiles who have assembled against us to destroy us and our sanctuary. It is better for us to die in battle than to see the misfortunes of our nation and of the sanctuary. *But as His will in heaven may be, He will do*" (I Macc. 3.58–60). Josephus, however, lists more precisely the causes of the war, and the elements introduced by him are totally absent in I Maccabees:

> "If you now fight bravely, you may recover that liberty which is loved for its own sake by all men, but to you most of all happens to be desirable because it gives you the right to worship the Deity. Since therefore at the present moment it lies in your power either to recover this liberty and regain a happy and blessed life or to suffer the most shameful fate"—*by this he meant a life in accordance with the laws and customs of their fathers*—". . . exert yourselves accordingly, bearing in mind that death is the portion even of those who do not fight, and holding firmly to the belief that if you die for such precious causes as *liberty, country, laws and religion,* you will gain eternal glory." (*A* XII, 302–304)

What is striking here is not just the addition of "laws and customs of the fathers," but the fact that these take the place of the Temple, cited in I Maccabees. Another shift in nuance thus emerges. Whereas the "law" ($\nu \acute{o} \mu o \varsigma$) and its observance are stressed in I Maccabees, the maintenance of *strict Temple ritual* is the main expression of religious fidelity.[30] Josephus, however, places far greater stress on the keeping of "the laws,"[31] and even while describing the dedication of the Temple he takes care to add that the renewal of sacrificial worship was in accord with the laws:

I Maccabees 4.36	Antiquities XII, 316
Then said Judah and [or, to] his brothers: Behold our enemies are crushed, let us go up to cleanse the sanctuary and dedicate it.	and Judah assembled the people and said that after the many victories which God had given them, they ought to go up to Jerusalem and purify the Temple and offer the *customary* sacrifices.

The stress that the Hasmonean war was aimed primarily toward the restoration of the "Laws of the Fathers" is in fact one of the dominant additions in

Josephus' paraphrase. Thus, for example, we encounter the following two portrayals of Mattathias' deathbed scene:

I Maccabees 2.69–70	Antiquities XII, 285
Then he blessed them and was gathered to his fathers. He died in the one hundred and forty-sixth year, and was buried in the tomb of his fathers at Modi'in. And all Israel mourned for him with great lamentation.	Having addressed his sons in these words, he prayed to God to be their ally [32] and to *recover for the people its own way of life* once more; and not long afterwards he died and was buried in Modi'in, the entire people making great lamentation for him.

Immediately following this passage, I Maccabees lists the courageous deeds of Judah Maccabee in the form of a poem devoted entirely to the war and the fortitude of its leader:

> Like a giant he put on his breastplate,
> he girded on his armor of war and waged battles,
> protecting the host by his sword.
> He was like a lion in his deeds,
> like a lion's cub roaring for prey . . . (I Maccabees 3.3–4)

Josephus presents the poem's contents in brief prose, but his point is manifestly different: "Then Judah . . . drove the enemy out of the country, and made an end of those of his countrymen *who had violated their fathers' laws, and purified the land of all pollution*" (*A* XII, 286). The "purification of the land" is missing entirely in I Maccabees, and even "the Laws of the fathers" are not mentioned there explicitly.

As noted earlier, "freedom" in Josephus' eyes enables "life according to the laws and customs of the fathers" (*A* XII, 303), and therefore Josephus frequently inserts this term where it is lacking in I Maccabees. Whereas I Maccabees briefly eulogizes Judah, "How is the mighty fallen, the savior of Israel!" (I Macc. 9.21), Josephus elaborates, "Such was the end of Judah, who had been a valiant man and a great warrior,[33] and mindful of the injunctions of his father Mattathias, had had the fortitude to do and suffer all things *for the liberty of his fellow-citizens*" (*A* XII, 433).[34] Similarly, Josephus adds this element to his description of the battle of Bet-Zur:

I Maccabees 4.35	Antiquities XII, 314
When Lysias . . . observed the boldness which inspired those of Judah, and how ready they were either to live or to die nobly, he departed to Antioch.	When Lysias saw the spirit of the Jews, and that they were prepared to die *if they could not live as free men*, . . . he returned to Antioch.

In addition to these two aspects introduced by Josephus—the fact that the fighters must be *worthy* and *righteous,* and that the war be for a just cause, that is, the restoration of Patriarchal Law—a third element is also apparent: Josephus shifts the emphasis on bravery in I Maccabees to a *willingness to die.* We have already noted that Mattathias' statement in I Maccabees, "Why should we live any longer?" was presented by Josephus as "It was better for them to die for their country's laws than to live so ingloriously" (*A* XII, 267). Here, one might contend that Josephus is not departing radically from the original but merely elaborating. This, however, is not the case with his treatment of the rest of I Maccabees, Chapter 2. There, beginning with verse 48, Mattathias delivers a lengthy historical survey, aimed at stressing the initiative taken by the nation's patriarchs. All the examples cited by Mattathias [35] are of leaders who achieved glory and reward in their lifetime for their zeal. Not so by Josephus, and in one of the rare cases where he quotes a speech in the first person rather than by paraphrase, he completely overturns the intentions of I Maccabees' author:

> Since you are my sons, I wish you to remain constant as such and to be superior to all force and compulsion, being so prepared in spirit as *to die for the laws,* if need be, and bearing this in mind, that when the Deity sees you so disposed, He will not forget you, but in admiration of your heroism will give them [i.e., the laws] back to you again, and will restore to you *your liberty,* in which you shall live securely and in the enjoyment of your own customs. For though our bodies are mortal and subject to death, we can, through the memory of our deeds, attain the heights of immortality; it is this which I wish you to be in love with, and for its sake to pursue glory and undertake the greatest tasks and not shrink from *giving up your lives* for them. (*A* XII, 281–82) [36]

This martyrological element introduced by Josephus into I Maccabees can be found elsewhere as well. [37] To be sure, for example, Judah does not ignore the possibility of death in his speech before the battle of Emmaus, quoted earlier, but death is certainly not the main issue there: "Gird yourselves and be valiant. Be ready early in the morning to fight with these gentiles who have assembled against us to destroy us and our sanctuary. It is better for us to die in battle than to see the misfortunes of our nation and of the sanctuary. But as His will in heaven may be, so He will do" (I Macc. 3.58–60).

Again, Josephus enhances the speech, and concludes it thus: "Exert yourself accordingly, bearing in mind *that death is the portion even of those who do not fight,* and holding firmly to the belief that *if you die for such precious causes* as liberty, country, laws and religion, you will gain eternal glory" (*A* XII, 304). [38]

A similar shift in nuance, noted earlier, concerns Lysias' return to Antioch after the battle of Bet Zur. I Maccabees (4:35) claims that "he observed the boldness which inspired those of Judah, and how ready they were *either to live or die nobly,"* whereas Josephus describes how he "saw the spirit of the Jews, and that *they were prepared to die* if they could not live as free men" (*A* XII, 315). The same phenomenon recurs when the rebels appeal to Jonathan to assume leadership after Judah's death. I Maccabees records, "Since the death of your brother Judah there has been no one like him to go against our enemies. . . . So we now have chosen you as our ruler and leader, to fight our battle" (I Macc. 9.30). Josephus, however, puts it this way: "they went to his brother Jonathan, and begged him to imitate his brother, who in his concern for his countrymen *had died on behalf of the liberty of them all.* . . . Thereupon Jonathan said that he was *ready to die for them*" (*A* XIII, 5–6).[39]

What caused Josephus to introduce all these changes into his paraphrase of I Maccabees? A survey of his ideas on Jewish wars in general reveals that in essence Josephus was attributing to the Hasmonean uprising all those criteria that rendered a war justified and that, in his opinion, were apparently not stressed sufficiently in the version of I Maccabees serving as his source. In *Against Apion,* Josephus makes the following general comment on Jewish wars: "We have trained our courage not with a view to waging war for self-aggrandizment, but in order to preserve our laws. To defeat in any other form we patiently submit, but when pressure is put upon us to alter our statutes, then we deliberately fight even against tremendous odds, and hold out under reverses to the last extremity" (*Ap* II, 272).

The two elements singled out here—that wars were fought for the preservation of the law,[40] and the willingness to die for that law—are repeated more than once in Josephus' works. In *Against Apion* Josephus states that (1) "it is an instinct with every Jew from the day of his birth, to regard them [the laws] as the decrees of God, to abide by them, and if need be—*cheerfully to die for them*" (*Ap* I, 42); and (2) "to those who observe the laws and, *if they must needs die for them,* willingly meet death, God has granted a renewed existence and in the revolution of the ages the gift of a better life" (*Ap* II, 218).[41] Josephus' regard for martyrdom is reflected in his description of contemporary events as well. Thus, he relates the pathetic portrayal of the martyrdom of the Essenes (*BJ* II, 151–53) and even the brave stand of the Sicarii who fled to Egypt and were tortured there (*BJ* VII, 417–19), in spite of Josephus' well-known aversion to the policies of the Sicarii in general.

It is not inconceivable that by introducing into the Hasmonean war what he considered positive elements, Josephus attempted to solve what otherwise might have posed a delicate problem for him. The Hasmonean episode, in effect, was antithetical to the entire range of arguments voiced by Josephus against the Zealots and Sicarii of his day. What justification could there be, for example, in the speech of Agrippa II against the war, and especially the argument stressing "the might of the Roman empire and . . . your own weakness" (*BJ* II, 362) to a people raised on the exploits of the victorious Hasmo-

neans fighting against, and outnumbered by the Seleucid army? If I Maccabees speaks truth while stressing that "strength comes from Heaven" and that
"it is easy for many to be hemmed in by few," then the relative strength and
numbers of the opposing armies is rendered irrelevant!

Not so by Josephus. He too is aware that numbers alone are not decisive,
but in his eyes "victory . . . lay in *being pious* toward the Deity," for "in
doing no wrong there is a mighty force." God, then, doesn't automatically aid
the few and outnumbered, but those "worthy" of His assistance. Josephus had
no doubts that the fighters of *his* day did not fall into that category, for they
had defiled the name of God and in a sense had declared war on Him, and not
just the Romans (*BJ* V, 377–78). It was they who had polluted the Temple
(*BJ* V, 380), and in general the whole "fourth philosophy" of the Sicarii was
"an intrusive . . . school" (*A* XVIII, 9), an "innovation and reform in ancestral traditions" (*ibid.*). God's law had been trampled by them, "every dic-
tate of religion ridiculed" (*BJ* IV, 385).

It has been suggested that the freedom fighters of Josephus' day in fact
consciously saw themselves as carrying the torch of the Hasmoneans.[42] This
thesis, however, has yet to be substantiated conclusively.[43] And yet, even if the
Zealots did not wish to claim continuity with the Hasmoneans, it seems clear
that Josephus was doing his best to prove the opposite.[44] He went about this on
two levels: on one hand, by stressing the sins and revisionist laws of the Zealots; and on the other, by inserting into his description of the Hasmonean war
and particularly into the words of the two great leaders of that revolt, Mattathias and Judah, elements that totally justify their endeavor. By doing this,
Josephus could explain the success of the first revolt contrasted to the failure
of his contemporaries.

This tendency appears to emerge from an interesting addition to I Maccabees inserted by Josephus. Mattathias' death is reported in I Maccabees
(2.69) by the brief statement, "Then he blessed them and was gathered to his
fathers." Josephus, in developing this scene, delivers the *contents* of the
blessing as well: "Having addressed his sons in these words, he prayed to God
to be *their ally* (σύμμαχον αὐτοῖς γενέσθαι) and to recover for the people its
own way of life once more" (*A* XII, 285). Josephus contends that a sine qua
non for success in battle is God's position as ally to the soldiers. He therefore
castigates the Zealots of his day by declaring, "The only refuge, then, left to
you is *divine assistance* (λοιπὸν οὖν ἐπὶ τὴν τοῦ θεοῦ συμμαχίαν καταφευκ-
τέον), but even this is ranged on the side of the Romans' (*BJ* II, 390). This
term σύμμαχος, recurs in Josephus' own speech to the Zealots: "How mighty
an ally have you outraged" (*BJ* V, 377); Cyrus reestablished the worship of
"their Ally" (τὸν αὐτῶν σύμμαχον; *BJ* V, 389); and even the patriarch Abraham knew that although he commanded a boundless army, all these "count as
nothing *if unaided by God,* and uplifting pure hands . . . enlisted the invin-

cible Ally (τὸν . . . βοηθόν) on his side" (*BJ* V, 380). By adding the motif of God's allegiance with the Hasmoneans, Josephus identified in a stroke the root of their success, and at the same time drew a distinction between the Hasmoneans and the Zealots of his day.

These additions are solely the result of Josephus' tendentiousness, and need not be attributed to other sources available to him (although, in principle, the existence of such sources is also feasible). On the contrary, the departures from I Maccabees all point to the freedom Josephus allowed himself in rewriting his sources,[45] a common phenomenon in Hellenistic historiography. From the days of Thucydides, historians felt free to compose speeches that should have been delivered and to insert them into the proper hero's mouth.[46] Josephus broke no new ground here, nor did he commit any radical act by adding glosses and small bits of information to I Maccabees, intended as aids for his Greek audience. One such example are the Macedonian names for the various months that Josephus attaches to the Hebrew names.[47] Similarly, by introducing terms such as *freedom* (ἐλευθερία) *beloved by all people* (*A* XII, 302), Josephus probably had his Greek audience in mind and thereby may have wished to render the goals of the Hasmoneans closer to the hearts of the Greek readers.

Nevertheless, we must remember that Josephus did not *compose* speeches from the days of the revolt but *copied* existing ones from one major source before him. Thus, he was *changing* material,[48] and *these* changes cannot be explained merely as an attempt to provide additional information, but as a means of expressing his own ideas on the Hasmonean episode. This point is no less crucial in understanding his presentation of that war than the fact that the Hasmonean dynastic platform of I Maccabees[49] was by his time irrelevant. The fact that we possess Josephus' main source for his presentation provides us with an invaluable tool for appraising his work as an historian.

Notes

The author wishes to thank his colleague, Dr. Daniel Schwartz, for his advice and bibliographical references, which were most helpful in the preparation of this article.

1. Cf. the literature cited by H. W. Ettelson, *The Integrity of I Maccabees* (New Haven 1925), p. 255, n. 2; for the most recent critical discussions see S. J. D. Cohen, *Josephus in Galilee and Rome* (Leiden 1979), p. 44, n. 77; and L. H. Feldman, *Josephus and Modern Scholarship (1937–1980)* (Berlin-New York 1984), pp. 219–25, 916–917.

2. M. Stern, *The Documents on the History of the Hasmonean Revolt* [Hebrew] (Tel-Aviv 1965), p. 25; on the possibility of an additional source at Josephus' disposal, cf. Cohen (*op. cit.*, note 1), pp. 44–45.

3. E.g., H. Bloch, *Die Quellen des Flavius Josephus in seiner Archäologie* (Leipzig 1879), pp. 80–90.

4. Bloch, *ibid.*, p. 80.

5. Bloch, *ibid.*, pp. 86–87.

6. K. Grimm, *Kurzgeffastes exegetisches Handbuch zu den Apokryphen des Alten Testamentes, Das Erste Buch der Maccabäer* (Leipzig 1853); cf. the Introduction, pp. xxvii–xxx, for the issue under discussion here.

7. Grimm refrained from assuming that Josephus had access to another source, but it nevertheless appears that this was the case for the period beginning with Simon, and that this source was in fact Nicolaus of Damascus. Cf. J. C. Dancy, *I Maccabees, A Commentary* (Oxford 1954), p. 31; Stern (*op. cit.*, note 2), pp. 25–26; for Josephus' use of Nicolaus for the later Hasmonean period and the rule of Herod see M. Stern, "Nicolaus of Damascus as a Source of Jewish History in the Herodian and Hasmonean Age" [Hebrew], in B. Uffenheimer, ed., *Studies in Bible and Jewish History Dedicated to the Memory of Jacob Liver* (Tel-Aviv 1971), pp. 375 ff; M. Stern, *Greek and Latin Authors on Jews and Judaism*, vol. 1, (Jerusalem 1974), pp. 229 ff.

8. There are numerous examples of this, such as the number of Nikanor's soldiers (nine thousand) slain in battle according to Josephus (*A* XII 411), while no such number is cited in the parallel account in I Macc. 7:46. For other examples of Josephan additions cf. Feldman (*op. cit.*, note 1) p. 222.

9. J. von Destinon, *Die Quellen des Flavius Josephus* (Kiel 1882), pp. 60–91; other scholars also embraced the "anonymous author" theory, cf. Ettelson (*op. cit.*, note 1), p. 255 n. 1. Yet another theory singled out Alexander Polyhistor as the "mediator" between I Maccabees and Josephus, cf. G. Hölscher, *Die Quellen des Josephus* (Leipzig 1904), p. 52; Hölscher (pp. 43 ff.) discusses in general Josephus' use of Alexander Polyhistor, but cf. Stern, *Greek and Latin Authors* (*op. cit.*, note 7), vol. 1, p. 157.

10. H. Drüner, *Untersuchungen über Josephus* (Marburg 1896), pp. 35–50. Cf. also Schürer's critique of Destinon, *TLZ* 17 (1882):388–394; idem, *GJV* III, no. 4 (1909):196. See also the brief comments of H. St. J. Thackeray, *Josephus, The Man and The Historian* (New York 1929), pp. 62–64.

11. Drüner, *ibid.*, p. 39.

12. Drüner, *ibid.*, pp. 42–43.

13. J. D. Michaelis, *Deutsche Uebersetzung des ersten Buchs der Maccabäer*, (Göttingen & Leipzig 1778), p. xii; cf. also F. Perles, *Notes sur les Apocryphes et Pseudepigraphes, REJ* 73 (1921):179.

14. E. Z. Melamed, "Josephus and Maccabees I: A Comparison" [Hebrew], *Erez Israel* 1 (1951):122–30; cf. M. Schwabe and E. Melamed, "Zum Text der Seron episode in I Macc. und bei Josephus," *MGWJ* 72(1928):202–204. Drüner (*op. cit.*, note 10) also considered the possibility of Josephus' access to the Hebrew version, but nevertheless concluded that his main source was the Greek. See also Zeitlin's Introduction to *I Maccabees: The First Book of Maccabees*, ed. S. Tedesche and S. Zeitlin, (New York 1950), pp. 57–58, and most recently J. A. Goldstein, *I Maccabees*, (New York 1976), p. 14, n. 18.

15. P. Joüon, "Quelques Hebraismes de Syntaxe dans Le 1er Livre des Maccabées," *Biblica* 3(1922):204–206.

16. A. Pelletier, *Flavius Josèphe, Adaptateur de la Lettre D'Aristée, Une Reaction Atticisante Contre la Koinè* (Paris 1962).

17. H. W. Attridge, *The Interpretation of Biblical History in the Antiquitates Judaicae of Flavius Josephus* (Missoula 1976), p. 38.

18. Cf. M. Stern, "Josephus' Method of Writing History" [Hebrew], in *Historians and Historical Schools, Lectures Delivered at the Seventh Convention of the Historical Society of Israel—December 1961* (Jerusalem 1962), p. 24. Compare this to Josephus' pretension to refrain from either adding or deleting (*A* IV, 196), and see Attridge (*op. cit.*, note 17), p. 51.

19. M. Stern, *Encyclopaedia Biblica* [Hebrew] (Jerusalem 1968), p. 292.

20. Cf. Goldstein (*op. cit.*, note 14), pp. 12–13; B. Renaud, *RB*, 58 (1961):51–52.

21. I Macc. 4.46; 9.27; 14.41.

22. E. E. Urbach, "When Did Prophecy Cease?" [Hebrew], *Tarbiz* 17 (1946):3.

23. Cf. *A* XII, 327–351.

24. Josephus does not attribute "prophecy" to Judah; whereas Marcus translates ὅ συν-ῆκεν as "foreseen," the precise meaning of συνίημι is "to understand, realize." Cf. H. G. Liddell and R. Scott, *A Greek-English Lexicon* (Oxford, 1948), p. 1718.

25. Cf. Goldstein (*op. cit.*, note 14), p. 204; Zeitlin (*op. cit.*, note 14), p. 121, suggests that this line may not have been in Josephus' source, but this assumption is unnecessary. See also Goldstein, *ibid.*, p. 56, n. 9, and compare Cohen (*op. cit.*, note 1), p. 47, n. 83.

26. Cf. F. J. Foakes-Jackson, *Josephus and the Jews* (London 1930), p. 102, n. 1.

27. Goldstein (*op. cit.*, note 14), p. 247, notes this change but relates it to Josephus' admiration of martyrdom. The last sentence, he claims, "was a catch phrase of the quietists. . . . For the quietists so much power was there, one did not need to fight." As we shall see, Josephus indeed held martyrdom in great esteem, but this does not seem to be the issue here at all.

28. Note the addition of geographical information by Josephus; cf. Drüner (*op. cit.*, note 10) p. 42; see also Marcus' note, *Josephus, LCL,* vol. 7, p. 213, n. c.

29. The manuscripts of Josephus contain variants of this figure.

30. Cf. B. Renaud, "La Loi et les Lois dans les Livres des Maccabées," *RB* 78(1961):49.

31. Compare also *A* XII, 300, where Josephus deletes the clause in I Maccabees 3.43 that describes the war as a "fight for our people and our sanctuary."

32. The importance of this term added by Josephus is discussed later.

33. Up to this point, Josephus is closely paraphrasing I Maccabees.

34. Compare also *A* XIII, 5, where Judah is described as having died "on behalf of the liberty of them [i.e., his countrymen] all," which is lacking in I Maccabees 9.28–29.

35. Abraham, Joseph, Phineas, Caleb, David, Elijah, Hananiah, Mishael, Azariah, Daniel.

36. Section 280 in *Antiquities* is a paraphrase of verse 50 in I Maccabees, and section 283 closely follows verse 64. Marcus (*op. cit.*, note 28), p. 145, n. c, claims only that "Josephus converts into philosophical language what is in I Macc. a simple appeal by Mattathias to his sons to remember the heroism of the great national figures from Abraham to Daniel," but does not cite the basic difference between the two versions. Cf. Goldstein (*op. cit.*, note 14), p. 56, n. 9. On Mattathias' speech see also H. J. Cadbury, "The Greek and Jewish Traditions of Writing History," in F. J. Foakes-Jackson and K. Lake, eds., *The Beginnings of Christianity,* vol. 2 (London 1922), p. 27.

37. Compare also Josephus' portrayal (*BJ* II, 196–97) of the Jews in the days of Gaius Caligula, who "presented themselves, their wives and their children, ready for slaughter," with Philo's parallel description of those same Jews as prepared *to fight* (*Legatio ad Gaium* 208, 215), and cf. W. R. Farmer, *Maccabees, Zealots and Josephus* (New York 1956), p. 123, n. 84. P. Bilde, "The Roman Emperor Gaius Caligula's Attempt to Erect His Statue in the Temple in Jerusalem," *ST* 32(1978):79 misreads Josephus here as alluding to a Jewish threat to fight, whereas in fact Josephus stresses passive resistance. S. G. F. Brandon, *Jesus and the Zealots* (Manchester 1967), pp. 87–88, also notes that Josephus "depicts the Jews offering themselves as passive victims to Petronius rather than resort to war," but claims that he nevertheless "let slip the significant fact that Petronius had warned Gaius in his letter that the Jews were threatening to make war against his forces" (*A* XVIII, 302). In fact, Josephus stresses just the opposite, that is, that Gaius "wrongly concluded (καταδοξάσας) that the Jews were bent on revolt" (cf. Feldman, *LCL Josephus,* vol. IX, p. 175).

38. This idea, that death over the observance of the laws grants eternal glory, is found elsewhere in Josephus, in a passage reminiscent of that cited here. When two scholars in Jerusalem commanded their disciples to pull down the eagle erected by Herod over the gate to the Temple, they explained "that even if there should be some danger of their being doomed to death,

still to those about to die for the preservation and safeguarding of their fathers' way of life the virtue acquired by them in death would seem far more advantageous than the pleasures of living. For by winning eternal fame and glory for themselves etc." (*A* XVII, 152).

39. Goldstein (*op. cit.*, note 14), p. 52, notes the martyrological tendency in Josephus, but claims that Josephus found this idea in the work of Jason of Cyrene. Goldstein thus strives to show that Josephus had access to II Maccabees (cf. p. 56, n. 10), but other scholars have proven the contrary (cf. Stern, *Zion* 25 [1946]:11). The case before us, in fact, would tend to prove Josephus' lack of knowledge of a major portion of II Maccabees. His high regard for martyrdom, which we shall see further on transcended the Hasmonean episode, should have brought him to cite extensively the martyrs of II Maccabees, such as Eleazar, the Mother and her Seven Sons, and Razis. Strangely, Josephus omits any mention of all these, although he was aware in general terms of the martyrdom effected by the decrees of Antiochus (cf. *A* XII, 255–256; *BJ* I, 34–35). If, indeed, Josephus had Jason's work before him, it is inconceivable that these stories would not have been cited. Goldstein, *II Maccabees* (New York 1983), pp. 302–303, repeats his theory that Josephus wove his praise of martyrdom based on II Maccabees but claims that "inasmuch as the stories of Eleazar and the mother and her seven sons are anti-Hasmonean counterparts for the history of the deeds of Mattathias and his sons, it is not surprising that Josephus, despite his reverence for the martyrs of his people, only drew upon the stories and did not reproduce them." Inasmuch as I fail to note any anti-Hasmonean intentions in the martyrs' stories of II Maccabees, I find no reason to alter the premise suggested earlier, that is, that Josephus did not have II Maccabees before him as a source for the *Antiquities*.

40. Compare *Ap* II, 292.

41. Cf. *Ap* II, 235.

42. W. R. Farmer (*op. cit.*, note 37). Farmer attempts to prove not only that the memory of the Hasmoneans was kept alive throughout the Second Temple period, but that they became "influential prototypes for the Jewish nationalists in the Roman period" (p. 158). This leads him to search for common motifs in the Hasmonean war and Great Revolt.

43. It is not sufficient to show that in both cases the rebels were opposed to eating forbidden food, or adamant in their wish to keep the Sabbath and other laws, such as circumcision. These motifs, cited by Farmer, are in effect constant factors in Jewish history and do not necessarily point to a conscious link between the various rebel movements. Cf. S. Hoenig, "Maccabees, Zealots and Josephus—Second Commonwealth Parallelisms," *JQR* 49(1958/9):75–80; L. H. Feldman, *Scholarship on Philo and Josephus (1937–1962)* (New York 1963), p. 23; *idem*, (*op. cit.*, note 1), p. 353.

44. Farmer (*op. cit.*, note 37), p. 20, notes this distinction but maintains that it was an attempt by Josephus to defend the Jews of the Roman Empire by stressing that revolution is not an integral part of historic Judaism. This, he claims, was made manifest by the Hasmoneans, who were the loyal allies of Rome. Compare A. Schalit's Introduction to his translation of *Antiquities* [Hebrew] (Jerusalem–Tel Aviv 1967), p. xviii. For the suggestion that in Josephus' eyes the only good Judaism was that based on religion and the laws, even when dealing with rebels and motivation for revolution, cf. D. R. Schwartz, "Josephus and Nicolaus on the Pharisees," *JSJ* 14 (1983):157–171. Cf. also S. J. D. Cohen, "Josephus, Jeremiah and Polybius," *HT* 21(1982): 366–381, for a discussion of Josephus' justification of the victory of Titus over the Zealots (and note 40, for a comparison with his attitude toward the Maccabees).

45. Dancy's (*op. cit.*, note 7) statement, that "a single foreign detail inserted in a paraphrase of I Maccabees is probably his own invention, but anything over a sentence is more likely derived from another written source" (p. 31), cannot be applied to the type of changes analyzed in this article; cf. Cohen (*op. cit.*, note 1), p. 47.

46. Thucydides, 1.22. Much has been written on this, see for example E. Adcock,

Thucydides and His History (Cambridge 1963), pp. 27–42. It is interesting to note the opposition to this freedom in transmitting speeches, and see for example Polybius, *History* vol. 7, 25a.

47. *A* XII, 248 (compared to I Macc. 1.54); *A* XII, 319, 321 (I Macc. 4.52); *A* XII, 412 (I Macc. 7.43); cf. Zeitlin (*op. cit.*, note 14), pp. 56, 262–263.

48. Numerous examples exist for the introduction of major changes into existing speeches in Greek and Latin literature; such, for instance, was Livy's treatment of the speeches in Polybius' work. Cf. Cadbury (*op. cit.*, note 36), p. 13–14.

49. The dynastic legitimacy is stressed not only in I Maccabees 5.62 but throughout the book, and particularly in the enhanced roles of Mattathias and Simon, the first two links in the Hasmonean dynasty.

6   The Role of Women in the Hasmonean Dynasty

JOSEPH SIEVERS

I n my work on the history of the Hasmoneans I was struck by the fact
that our sources are completely silent about the female members of the family until the time of John Hyrcanus I,[1] but from then on mention quite a
number of prominent women. To be sure, with the exception of Herod's wife
Mariamme, these women are mentioned primarily when they are involved in
politics or in military operations, that is, in typically male activities. Many of
them are not even known by name, but only as mothers, wives, sisters, or
daughters of Hasmonean rulers. This is no mere accident, as Josephus in
many instances clearly avoided mentioning a woman's name.[2]

In this study, I have endeavored to examine all the evidence concerning
female members of the Hasmonean dynasty.[3] Such a study has, so far as
I know, never been undertaken. Swidler, in an otherwise very useful survey of the status of women in early Judaism, devotes only one paragraph
to Salome Alexandra.[4] However, there are many helpful studies on related
topics. Pomeroy's recent work on women in Hellenistic Egypt makes a first
attempt to conceptualize the role of Hellenistic queens.[5] Macurdy's two
books on queens in the Hellenistic period are still valuable.[6] Schalit in his
monumental study on Herod touches on almost every aspect of this paper, but
from a different angle.[7] For rabbinic literature, the works of Derenbourg,
Lichtenstein, and Neusner are fundamental.[8] Klausner and Schürer, Vermes,
and Millar are useful, particularly for Salome Alexandra.[9] Figure 6.1 shows
the Hasmonean genealogy.

A Nameless Heroine

The first two women—one the mother, the other the wife of John Hyrcanus—are known to us only because of the circumstances of their death. The
former was taken hostage by her own son-in-law, Ptolemy, the son of Abubus,

Hasmonean Genealogy

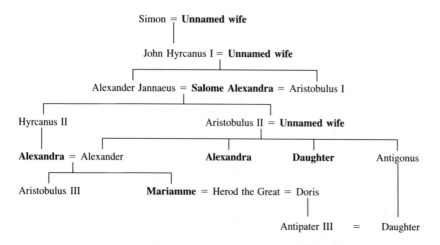

Simon = **Unnamed wife**

John Hyrcanus I = **Unnamed wife**

Alexander Jannaeus = **Salome Alexandra** = Aristobulus I

Hyrcanus II

Aristobulus II = **Unnamed wife**

Alexandra = Alexander   **Alexandra**   **Daughter**   Antigonus

Aristobulus III   **Mariamme** = Herod the Great = Doris

Antipater III   =   Daughter

Note: Women cited in boldface are discussed in this chapter.

after a banquet at which her husband, Simon Maccabeus, was slain. According to Josephus' dramatic account, she was held in the fortress of Dok near Jericho and was tortured on the wall of the fortress in full view of her son, John Hyrcanus I, who thereby was temporarily dissuaded from attacking it. She implored him not to be intimidated by her torment into relenting in his fight against Ptolemy. Hyrcanus, however, was long unable to conquer Dok, and Ptolemy finally put his mother-in-law to death (*BJ* I, 54–60; *A* XIII, 228–35). Significantly, the account of Hasmonean history in I Maccabees ends with the death of Simon and does not so much as mention his wife.

How much in Josephus' account is dramatization is hard to discern. This is one of a number of stories about the Hasmoneans that share features of popular legend, setting them off from their context. These stories do not appear in I Maccabees and are probably not derived from Nicolaus of Damascus.[10] The motif of a mother selflessly encouraging her sons, even though this may cause her death, is found in II Maccabees 7 and elsewhere in Hellenistic literature.

The Question of Royal Succession

The second Hasmonean woman about whom we learn in Josephus is the wife of John Hyrcanus. Josephus tells us that before he died, Hyrcanus had designated her as his successor and "mistress over everything."[11] She attempted to take control but was imprisoned and starved to death by her own son, Judas Aristobulus.

The fact that later Salome Alexandra, too, was designated as successor after the death of her husband has caused some scholars to think, without other justification, that this story may be a doublet.[12] The idea of such a mode of succession is not found anywhere in earlier Jewish history. The only queen who ruled in Judea in her own right before this time was Athaliah (c. 845–840 B.C.E.). She, however, was not Judean, was a devotee of Ba'al, and was notorious for seizing the throne upon the death of her son by destroying almost the entire royal family (II Kings 11.1–3). Evidently, she did not serve as a model for the Hasmoneans.

It is true that the mothers of Israelite kings had an important official position, but they could be demoted. King Asa "removed Ma'acah his mother from being queen mother because she had an abominable image made for Asherah" (I Kings 15.13).[13] Notwithstanding the prestigious position of queen mothers, it is doubtful that they had any right to royal succession.

In the major Hellenistic dynasties of Macedonian origin, several queens came to rule temporarily on their own: for example, Olympias, the mother of Alexander the Great, or Cleopatra Thea, a daughter of Cleopatra II, who became wife of three and mother of four Seleucid kings. But both Olympias and Cleopatra Thea made ample use of political murders in order to gain power and retain it.

Only among the Ptolemies, and only from the second century B.C.E. on, was it fairly well established that women have the right to govern.[14] It was not at issue in the many dynastic struggles that shook Egypt at the time. To be sure, the Ptolemaic queens usually had to share royalty, at least nominally, with a male, that is, a brother and/or husband or a son. But Cleopatra II, Cleopatra III, and, above all, Cleopatra VII were on the whole far more active and decisive influences in government than their male counterparts.

Relations between Egypt and Judea were fairly close at this time. Both Cleopatra II and Cleopatra III used Jewish commanders in their armies and Cleopatra III concluded a treaty with Alexander Jannaeus.[15] Even though we are not able to establish direct links between the succession of Ptolemaic and Hasmonean queens, the following factors make it plausible that the Hasmoneans actually followed the Ptolemaic model in this respect: the closeness in time and space, the comparable rarity of the phenomenon anywhere else, and the good relations between several Ptolemaic queens and Judea. It should be noted that, contrary to Ptolemaic practice, both Salome Alexandra and Hyrcanus' widow were, according to Josephus, designated to be sole rulers, without a coregent. It is clear, however, that their sons were to be high priests and, therefore, were to share at least nominally in power. In fact, if we have any coins minted by Salome Alexandra, they do not bear her name but the name of a high priest.[16]

It is sometimes claimed that Salome Alexandra was made queen as the result of a compromise with the Pharisees, so that kingship and priesthood would not be united in the same person.[17] A compromise with the Pharisees may have been necessary at the beginning of Salome Alexandra's reign, but no such need existed after the death of John Hyrcanus. Furthermore, the legendary account of Hyrcanus' break with the Pharisees includes a request that he give up the high priesthood and be content with governing the people (*A* XIII, 291). Thus, a queen was not the solution.

Salome Alexandra

Salome Alexandra Before 76 B.C.E.

Salome Alexandra first appears in Josephus as the wife of Judas Aristobulus I (104–103 B.C.E.). She allegedly was the driving force behind a plot to kill Antigonus, her brother-in-law (*BJ* I, 76; *A* XIII, 308). It is sometimes asserted that such a crime would be out of character for her. In fact, elsewhere Josephus speaks of her "utter lack of cruelty" (*BJ* I, 107). However, for her to have helped eliminate a possible rival would be nothing unusual. Both her husbands were willing to kill members of their immediate family in order to secure the throne, and Plutarch says "that brothers should put brothers to death was assumed [among the successors of Alexander the Great] like a mathematical axiom as the common and accepted principle of royal safety" (*Demetrius* 3.4).

When her first husband died of an illness, Salome Alexandra suddenly found herself in power. But her first act was to release her husband's surviving brothers from prison and to appoint one of them, Alexander Jannaeus, as king (*BJ* I, 85; *A* XIII, 320). Among other reasons, she is said to have chosen him because of his moderation (*metriotēs*). As Marcus has pointed out (LCL ad *A* XIII, 320), this term may also mean "knowing his place," indicating that Alexandra expected to dominate Jannaeus. Nothing is reported of any attempt on her part to do so, nor is there any reference to her marriage to him. Only after his death, twenty-seven years later, is his wife referred to as Alexandra (*BJ* I, 107 and passim). Nevertheless, there are no good reasons to doubt that this is the same Salome Alexandra.

There are some questions, however, concerning this marriage that are worth considering. Our sources are silent on whether or not Salome Alexandra was childless before she married Jannaeus and, consequently, we cannot determine whether theirs was a levirate marriage. Furthermore, a high priest was not permitted to marry a widow (Leviticus 21.14). Klausner points out that a priest was permitted to marry the widow of a priest (Ezekiel 44.22), but this verse in Ezekiel does not speak of a high priest.[18] There are three solutions: either Ezekiel 44.22 was interpreted as applying to a high priest as well; the marriage was concluded before Jannaeus became high priest (the question of a waiting period before Salome Alexandra's remarriage then would arise); or biblical law was interpreted or circumvented in some other way.

If we may take Josephus' indication of Salome's age seriously, she was Jannaeus' elder by fifteen years and was about thirty-seven years old when she married him (A XIII, 430; cf. XIII, 404). Klausner suggests that she may have been ten years younger, but there is no textual basis for such a change.[19]

During the reign of Alexander Jannaeus, Salome Alexandra does not appear at all in Josephus' account, except at her husband's deathbed. We know that during this period she gave birth to two sons, Hyrcanus II and Aristobulus II (BJ I, 109; A XIII, 407). Interestingly, we later hear that King Alexander (Jannaeus) *and his wife* appointed Herod's grandfather governor of the whole of Idumaea (A XIV, 10). This may indicate that, after all, Salome Alexandra did take an active role in matters of government. But Derenbourg goes beyond the evidence when he claims that during his military campaigns Jannaeus left internal affairs in the hands of Salome Alexandra.[20] Rabbinic literature mentions her on several occasions as an intermediary between her husband and Simon ben Shetach, who was, according to some rabbinic sources, her brother.[21] Neusner has shown convincingly that these stories are of little value for determining what Salome Alexandra actually did or what her position was.[22]

Salome's marriage to Jannaeus must not have been easy. Her husband was much involved in warfare, including prolonged and bloody civil war. He also kept a number of concubines and was a heavy drinker (A XIII, 380, 398). All this was quite common with Hellenistic kings, but not exactly the type of life one would expect of a high priest of Jerusalem.

His dramatic deathbed dialogue with his wife, reported in A XIII, 399–404, is primarily an attempt to prove the importance of the Pharisees, not a record of a private conversation between king and queen. In any event, the story of Jannaeus' posthumous reconciliation with the Pharisees is not very trustworthy. Perhaps, an enigmatic talmudic passage fits into this context. It reads "King Yannai said to his wife, 'Fear not the Pharisees and the non-Pharisees but the hypocrites who ape the Pharisees; because their deeds are the deeds of Zimri but they expect a reward like Phineas'" (b. Sota 22b).

According to the Scholion of *Megillath Ta'anith,* Salome Alexandra (here called *Shelaminon*) saved the lives of seventy elders who had been imprisoned and were supposed to be executed on the day of her husband's death. Before announcing his death, she freed them, and consequently the day of

Jannaeus' death was declared a holiday.[23] Besides being based on confusion between Salome Alexandra and Herod's sister Salome, this story is also contradicted by Josephus' account of the splendid funeral granted to Jannaeus by the Pharisees (*A* XIII, 406).

From Josephus and rabbinic literature, we learn that during the reigns of her husbands, Judas Aristobulus and Alexander Jannaeus, Salome Alexandra played some role in public affairs. This in itself is not much, but more than we can say of the wife of any earlier Hasmonean ruler.

Salome Alexandra as Ruler

Ancient opinions were divided about Salome Alexandra's rule. Perhaps, it is best first to outline briefly her actions before proceeding to an evaluation. In the essentials, both accounts of Josephus agree (*BJ* I, 107–119; *A* XIII, 405–432): Alexander Jannaeus had designated Salome as his successor. She took over without difficulty and appointed her older son, Hyrcanus II, high priest. To the younger son, Aristobulus II, she gave no public office. She recruited mercenaries and doubled the size of her army. When the Pharisees started to seek out and kill prominent citizens who had sided with Jannaeus, Salome, upon Aristobulus' intercession, granted them safety in the countryside.

Furthermore, she sent an army, under the command of her son Aristobulus (*A* XIII, 418), to the region of Damascus, against Ptolemy, son of Mennaeus, but without any success. When Tigranes besieged Cleopatra Selene in Ptolemais, Salome Alexandra sent envoys with gifts in order to avert a feared invasion of Judea. Tigranes accepted the gifts. He did not invade Judea because in the meantime the Romans had invaded his homeland, Armenia.

After a reign of nine years, Salome Alexandra fell ill. Her son Aristobulus tried to secure the throne for himself, gathered an army, and gained control of the Hasmonean fortresses. Alexandra, upon the entreaties of Hyrcanus and others, imprisoned Aristobulus' wife and children in Jerusalem. Before Salome Alexandra was able to take any further steps, she died, naming Hyrcanus her successor.

These basic facts are given in *The Jewish War* and repeated in the *Antiquities,* with the addition of a few details: Salome Alexandra kept the death of her husband secret until she had conquered the fortress of Ragaba, which he had been besieging (*A* XIII, 398, 405). She took hostages from neighboring rulers (XIII, 409). Those citizens who fled from the Pharisees were given control over the fortresses in the countryside, with the exception of Hyrcania, Alexandreion, and Machaerus, where she kept her most valuable possessions (417).

In addition, Josephus tells us in *The Jewish War* that "she was, indeed, the very strictest observer of the national traditions and would deprive of office any offenders against the sacred laws" (I, 108). According to the *Antiquities,* she restored "whatever regulations, introduced by the Pharisees in accordance with the tradition of their fathers, had been abolished by her father-in-law Hyrcanus" (XIII, 408).

Beyond this, both accounts speak of the Pharisees' power over her. In *The Jewish War,* Salome Alexandra out of piety listens too much to them and they,

> gradually taking advantage of an ingenuous woman, became at length the real administrators of the state, at liberty to banish and to recall, to loose and to bind, whom they would. In short, the enjoyments of royal authority were theirs, its expenses and troubles fell to Alexandra. She proved, however, to be a skillful administrator in larger affairs, . . . but if she ruled the nation, the Pharisees ruled her. (I, 111–12 *LCL*)

In the *Antiquities,* the picture is somewhat different. Here it is upon the advice of her dying husband that she entrusted to the Pharisees not only the arrangements for his funeral, but "the affairs of the kingdom" (*ta peri tēs basileias* XIII, 405). She permitted the Pharisees to do as they pleased in all matters and also commanded the people to obey them (408). Here we are not primarily concerned with how truthfully Josephus depicts the Pharisees,[24] but with the role of Salome Alexandra.

Few things can be said with certainty, and not all data of Josephus can be reconciled, but we may say that (on the advice of her husband or on her own) she made a dramatic change in policy and shifted from the support of one group, the Sadducees(?), to that of another, the Pharisees. There was some bloodshed in the process, but she helped to minimize it. Even at the end of the most derogatory statement about her, it is acknowledged that she kept the nation at peace (*A* XIII, 432). She was one of only a handful of Hasmoneans who lived to old age and died of natural causes, while over twenty-five members of the dynasty died a violent death. During her reign, the influence of the Pharisees certainly went beyond what we might call religious concerns, but their interests seem to have been focused on internal affairs. The initiative for armaments and military and diplomatic activity is credited entirely to her. Even during her final illness, the order to proceed against Aristobulus' revolt was expected from her.

Both accounts of Josephus stress that at the beginning of her rule, Salome Alexandra was very popular (*BJ* I, 107; *A* XIII, 407), in contrast to her late husband(s). Both report the tensions between her and her younger son Aristobulus. The *Antiquities* alone, however, uses this occasion to speak of her in the most unflattering terms: Aristobulus and his supporters were themselves to blame for "letting a woman gone mad in her lust for power rule unreasonably, even though her sons were in the prime of life" (XIII, 417). She "paid no attention to what was honorable or just" (431). Power was soon taken away from her house "because of her desire for things unbecoming a woman, and because she expressed the same opinions as did those who were hostile to her family [or, to their kin]. . . . And even after her death she caused the palace to be filled with misfortunes and disturbances which arose from the public measures taken during her lifetime" (431–432 *LCL*).

This contradiction with earlier judgments (and later ones as well, e.g., *A* XIV, 77) is hard to explain by any other means than by Josephus' careless juxtaposition of sources. Incidentally, whatever is said negatively about Salome Alexandra also touches her Pharisaic mentors and supporters. The hostility expressed here against her seems to be even more than what we might expect of Nicolaus of Damascus. He had no reason to be upset about the misfortunes of the later Hasmoneans, let alone to blame everything on her. That Josephus himself would have composed such attacks would seem unlikely, especially because of the negative characterization of her Pharisaic allies as "those who were hostile to her family [or, their kin]." We must remember, however, that Josephus had not always been on friendly terms with the Pharisees. While he served as a commander in Galilee, a predominantly Pharisaic delegation tried to arrest and kill him (*V* 197, 202, 302). Thus, a negative attitude toward the Pharisees may have been reflected in notes intended for *The Jewish War*, but used here in the *Antiquities* indiscriminately.

Although Josephus was capable of such careless use of material, it seems more plausible that we have here the vestige of a tradition of Aristobulus' circle, traditionally identified with the Sadducees. These people had been Alexandra's opponents and lost most in the ensuing power struggle. Thus, the absolute rejection of a woman as ruler expressed here may have had a very concrete reason: Salome Alexandra prevented her son Aristobulus from ruling, even though he was willing, able, and eager to take over the reins of government.

One rabbinic source also categorically objects to a woman having royal power.[25] It is uncertain whether this passage is related to the similar tradition in Josephus. Such objections are not widespread in rabbinic literature. On the contrary, miraculously bountiful harvests are credited to Salome Alexandra's piety.[26] We do not know whether she had anything to do with the ordinances attributed to Simon ben Shetach regarding the marriage *ketubah* and compulsory education. Therefore, we have no positive evidence that Salome took steps to improve the lot of women.

Modern opinion about Salome Alexandra has been generally favorable, especially in contrast to judgments about her husbands. Frequently, she is seen as a docile instrument of the Pharisees, and therefore completely opposed to everything Hellenistic. Tcherikover states that the Pharisees "finally, under Queen Salome Alexandra, victoriously put an end to the Hellenistic aspirations of the Hasmoneans."[27] Baron goes a step further and declares that "neither the Maccabees nor even the Herodians could reign as despots of the oriental or Hellenistic type."[28] Quite differently, Macurdy calls Salome Alexandra "a queen of the Hellenistic type" and observes that "the account of her character which Josephus gives might equally well describe many of the queens of the other Hellenistic dynasties."[29]

Perhaps, we have to describe her in more nuanced terms. On one hand, she certainly was devoted to Pharisaic Judaism. On the other hand, the very fact of her rule seems to have been influenced by Hellenistic customs. Also, the elimination of her brother-in-law, Antigonus, the recruitment of a mercenary force, and the taking of hostages to keep neighboring rulers on good behavior, though not uniquely Hellenistic actions, put her squarely in the world of the successors of Alexander the Great.

The Wife of Aristobulus II

Although Salome Alexandra remained the only Jewish queen to rule in her own right, there are a surprising number of other Hasmonean women who became active in politics. We have mentioned Salome Alexandra's daughter-in-law, the wife of Aristobulus II. She was the daughter of Absalom, probably a brother of Alexander Jannaeus (*A* XIV, 71; XIII, 323). If so, she was married to her first cousin. They had four children: Alexander, Mattathias Antigonus, Alexandra, and another daughter.[30]

According to Josephus, Aristobulus at first confided his plan to seize the throne only to his wife (*A* XIII, 424). When he started to implement it, she and her children were imprisoned by order of Salome Alexandra, and even held as hostages by Hyrcanus, until Aristobulus came to an agreement with him (*BJ* I, 121; *A* XIV, 5).

Later, in 63 B.C.E., her husband, two daughters, and one son were taken captive to Rome by Pompey. Her fourth child, Alexander, gathered an army to fight against the Romans but was forced to surrender his fortresses to Gabinius. In this situation, his mother went to Gabinius and suggested that he demolish the surrendered fortresses, to prevent their being used as bases of operations for another war. Josephus adds that she was on the side of the Romans because her husband and remaining children were in Roman captivity (*BJ* I, 168; *A* XIV, 90). Shortly afterward, her husband Aristobulus and her younger son, Mattathias Antigonus, escaped from Rome and gathered an army, but they were captured while trying to barricade themselves in the now defenseless fortress of Machaerus. Aristobulus was kept a prisoner, but his children were allowed to return to Judea; Gabinius had promised this favor to their mother in return for her earlier advice (*BJ* I, 174; *A* XIV, 97).

Once again we hear of this valiant nameless woman. After her husband and older son had been killed by Pompey's party, her other children, Mattathias Antigonus, Alexandra, and the remaining daughter, were taken (Josephus in *BJ* says "torn") from her and brought to the court of Ptolemy, son of Mennaeus, ruler of Chalcis in the Lebanon valley (*BJ* I, 186; *A* XIII, 126).

All our information about the wife of Aristobulus II is connected with her family, yet her world was not restricted to domestic matters. For the sake of her family, she acted boldly and even bargained with a Roman proconsul.

The Daughters of Aristobulus II

One of this woman's daughters, Alexandra by name, was taken in marriage by Philippion, the son of Ptolemy, son of Mennaeus. Soon, however, Ptolemy became jealous of his son and, according to Josephus, killed him in order to be able to marry Alexandra himself (*BJ* I, 186; *A* XIV, 126). We know nothing of her actions or her sufferings, but apparently Ptolemy treated her sister and her brother Antigonus well because of her. In the end, it was Ptolemy who brought Antigonus back to Judea with an army, "because of their kinship" (*BJ* I, 239; *A* XIV, 297).

The name of the sister of Alexandra and Antigonus is unknown, but the little of her life story that is known is significant. If she was born by 67 B.C.E., she was taken hostage that year by order of her grandmother Salome Alexandra and released only when her father and her uncle had settled their differences. In 63 B.C.E., she was taken to Rome as a prisoner by Pompey, along with her father, her sister Alexandra, and her brother Antigonus Mattathias (*BJ* I, 158; *A* XIV, 79). She was released in 56 B.C.E., through the intervention of her mother with Gabinius (*BJ* I, 174; *A* XIV, 97). She lost her father and oldest brother in 49 B.C.E. (*BJ* I, 184–185; *A* XIV, 124–125) and lived with her mother in Ascalon before she was forcibly taken away and brought to the court of Ptolemy, son of Mennaeus, the ruler of Chalcis (*BJ* I, 186; *A* XIV, 126). Presumably, she came back to Judea with her brother Antigonus in 40 B.C.E. (*BJ* I, 248; *A* XIV, 330 ff), but we hear nothing about her again until long after her brother's death. She was the last Hasmonean to stand up against Herod. Not too long before the battle of Actium (2 September 31 B.C.E.), Herod conquered the fortress of Hyrcania, which she had been holding. This occurred several years after the last male contender of the Hasmonean line, with the exception of the aged Hyrcanus II, had been killed.[31]

Unfortunately, we do not know more about this remarkable woman, whose extraordinary courage, skill, and ingenuity enabled her to resist Herod for several years.[32]

Alexandra the Daughter of Hyrcanus II

One of the Hasmonean women who tried hardest to influence the course of events was Alexandra, the daughter of Hyrcanus II and wife of her cousin Alexander, the son of Aristobulus II. Her early life is completely unknown, but before her husband was executed by the Romans in 49 B.C.E. she had borne him two children: Jonathan Aristobulus III, the future high priest, and Mariamme, who was to become Herod's wife.

Through her daughter, Alexandra became part of Herod's inner circle. She warned him not to trust the Parthians, and according to Josephus' *Antiquities,* Herod "trusted her as a very sensible woman." [33] When Herod had to flee from the Parthians, he took not only Mariamme, who was then betrothed to him, but also her mother Alexandra and brought them to safety in Masada (*BJ* I, 263–67; *A* XIV, 353–62).

The harmony between Herod and Alexandra did not last very long, however. When Herod appointed an undistinguished priest from Babylon to be high priest, Alexandra took it as an insult to her family, because being the daughter of the high priest Hyrcanus II, she expected her own son to follow in this office. Josephus tells of rather surprising machinations to achieve that goal: "Using the help of a certain musician to get the letter delivered, she wrote to Cleopatra [VII] asking her to request Antony to grant the high priesthood to her son" (*A* XV, 24). The letter did not bring any results, but a close associate of Antony, Quintus Dellius, came to Judea and is said to have persuaded Alexandra to have portraits of both Jonathan Aristobulus and Mariamme painted and sent to Antony (*A* XV, 26–27). This story has been regarded with suspicion because to make images of human beings would violate a biblical commandment (Exodus 20:4) and because in a similar passage (*BJ* I, 439) we hear of a *false* charge that Mariamme had sent her own portrait to Antony.[34]

In spite of these problems, such an incident is not implausible. If Alexandra had indeed ordered these paintings, a *false* rumor could easily be circulated later that Mariamme herself had commissioned the painting, exposing her to charges of unfaithfulness. Furthermore, Plutarch tells us that a few years earlier, in 41 B.C.E., Antony had sent the same Q. Dellius to summon Cleopatra VII and that Dellius advised her to go to see Antony (for the first time), dressed in her best finery (Plutarch, *Antony* 25). The results of that encounter are well known, though not always correctly interpreted. The consequences of Dellius' advice to Alexandra were not nearly as dramatic, but the story of the portrait paintings would not at all be out of character for Dellius.

Reportedly, Antony asked for Jonathan Aristobulus to be brought to him, but Herod, not wanting to let the young man leave the area under his control, decided to make him high priest, charging that Alexandra had secretly plotted with Cleopatra to remove him (Herod) from power. Josephus records a verbal exchange between Herod and Alexandra, after which all mutual suspicions seem to have been allayed (*A* XV, 31–38). But, after Jonathan Aristobulus became high priest, suspicions arose again on both sides. Alexandra was kept under constant surveillance so that she could not move freely. She wrote of her resentment about this situation to Cleopatra, who in turn suggested that she come secretly to Egypt with her son (*A* XV, 46). Alexandra planned to have herself and her son carried to a ship in coffins, but her plan was reported to Herod (*A* XV, 46–48). Again, a fake reconciliation took place. Herod apparently had great respect for, not to say fear of, Alexandra.

After the feast of Sukkoth (35 B.C.E.), Alexandra hosted a large party at the Hasmonean winter palace in Jericho. Herod, as well as the young high priest, participated. It is noteworthy that here, too, Herod could not simply take over. However, Alexandra certainly was no longer in full and complete control of the palace. Herod had brought enough of his confidants to be able to carry out the murder of the high priest with impunity, by drowning him in one of the swimming pools of the palace (*A* XV, 55–56).

After the murder of her son, Herod's suspicions arose again against Alexandra. It was a battle for survival, and apparently Alexandra knew it. She managed to act as if she had accepted that her son's murder was an accident, yet wrote for assistance to Cleopatra with whom she seems to have had close friendly relations (*A* XV, 58, 62–63).

Later she was accused of plotting to escape to the Roman camp (*A* XV, 71–73) and was kept in chains for allegedly causing trouble in the relations between Herod and Mariamme (*A* XV, 87). She was further accused of planning an escape or even a plot to overthrow Herod on behalf of her aged father, Hyrcanus II (*A* XV, 165–68), and was suspected of planning a popular revolt in Herod's absence (*A* XV, 183–86). She was condemned because allegedly she disavowed her daughter when the latter was led to her execution (*A* XV, 232–235). Finally, Alexandra herself was executed, in 28 B.C.E., on charges of having tried to seize control of the garrisons in Jerusalem at a time when Herod was ill (*A* XV, 247–251).

We cannot hope to find out the truth about these accusations and should be wary because Josephus' main source for this period was Nicolaus of Damascus, Herod's court historian and adviser. It is clear, however, that Alexandra was an unusually resourceful and capable person. In the literature, she is treated simply as one more woman in the life of Herod. Yet, she was one of the proudest Hasmoneans, who apparently used all possible means to save the cause of her family. In this endeavor, she was left almost completely to her own devices. She had been widowed at a young age and her father, Hyrcanus II, was not a man of initiative. If she failed, it was not because of lack of energy or ambition.

Mariamme

Mariamme is known primarily as the ill-fated second wife of Herod the Great. In spite of Josephus' very detailed account of Herod's infatuation with her, we learn very little about her actions. She was married to Herod in Samaria, while his troops were besieging her cousin Antigonus in Jerusalem (*BJ* I, 344; *A* XIV, 467). Schalit claims that Herod's love for her was the only reason for this marriage, but Josephus is certainly correct in stating that it was advantageous to him politically.[35]

Whether Mariamme got any satisfaction out of this marriage is impossible to determine. That question was seldom asked of a woman. In any case, it is evident that as time went on, especially after 35 B.C.E. when Herod killed her brother, she hated him with increasing intensity. Apparently, she was quite outspoken about her feelings, and that led to her downfall. It seems that until the end of her life, her mother remained a strong influence. Josephus tells us nothing of Mariamme beyond domestic affairs, except that on one occasion she asked her husband to appoint a certain Soemus to be a *meridarch* (district governor). Herod granted this request (*A* XV, 216–217), but Soemus was soon arrested and put to death because allegedly he had "gone too far in his intimacy with Mariamme" (*A* XV, 228–229). Because of these allegations and slanderous accusations that she had prepared love-potions and drugs for Herod, she was condemned to death.

Josephus gives a dramatic account of her last moments, emphasizing her greatness of spirit and her nobility (*A* XV, 232–236). But, as Schalit recognized, in this particular instance we are dealing more with a literary creation than a description of actual events.[36]

Conclusions

We have been able to sketch outlines of the lives of several Hasmonean women. In some instances we can detect specific Hellenistic influences, as in the case of succession to the throne, the taking of hostages, and the use of portrait paintings.

When we look at the life experiences of these women, we find that in many instances they were strongly influenced by captivity and by political and personal constraints. In general, however, we discover them as women who were ready, willing, and able to shape the world around them, to take risks, and often, to assume painful responsibilities.

When we ask what makes these women as a group so extraordinary, we can come up with two basic explanations:

First, if I Maccabees or a chronicle of its sort continued to be our main source, we would probably know very little about Hasmonean women, except Salome Alexandra. For that type of source, women's lives in general were not "newsworthy." The fact that we do have a record of these women seems to be due in part to Hellenistic standards of historiography. Second, more important, the recorded activities of these women all take place after they are widowed or separated from their husbands or have no man on whom they can rely. The Hasmoneans themselves eliminated the brothers of Aristobulus I and Alexander Jannaeus. Of the male descendants of Jannaeus, the Romans wiped out the line of Aristobulus II by killing him and his older son in 49 and the younger son in 37 B.C.E. Herod eliminated the line of Hyrcanus II by drowning his grandson and then killing Hyrcanus himself. Thus, increasingly, the remaining female members of the dynasty had an opportunity and a need to take their destiny and that of their family into their own hands—and a sizable number did so with great vigor and considerable skill.

Notes

This article was prepared, in part, during a 1983 Summer Seminar under the auspices of the National Endowment for the Humanities at Yeshiva University under the direction of Professor Louis H. Feldman. I should also like to thank Morton Smith, Sarah B. Pomeroy, Diana Delia, and Roberta Rubin-Dorsky for valuable suggestions. The responsibility for all remaining deficiencies, of course, is solely mine.

1. II Maccabees tells us that Judas Maccabeus married at Nicanor's urging (14:25). Through I Maccabees we know that Judas' brothers Jonathan and Simon had children but hear nothing of wives and daughters.

2. Concerning similar practices in Greek writers, see David Schaps, "The Woman Least Mentioned: Etiquette and Women's Names," *CQ* 27(1977):323–330. A study of Josephus' attitude toward women would be a very interesting undertaking. It would have to start from those texts in which he most clearly speaks his own mind, such as the *Vita*. For now see Evelyn Stagg and Frank Stagg, *Woman in the World of Jesus* (Philadelphia: Westminster, 1978), pp. 45–48.

3. For reasons of space, I have excluded the descendants of Mariamme and Herod. Their great-granddaughter Berenice II has been the subject of a detailed but somewhat uncritical popular monograph: Ruth Jordan, *Berenice* (New York: Barnes & Noble, 1974).

4. Leonard Swidler, *Women in Judaism. The Status of Women in Formative Judaism* (Metuchen, N.J.: Scarecrow Press, 1976), pp. 60–61.

5. Sarah B. Pomeroy, *Women in Hellenistic Egypt from Alexander to Cleopatra* (New York: Schocken, 1984).

6. Grace H. Macurdy, *Vassal-Queens and Some Contemporary Women in the Roman Empire* (The Johns Hopkins University Studies in Archaeology, No. 22; Baltimore: Johns Hopkins, 1937), esp. pp. 63–77; *idem. Hellenistic Queens* (The Johns Hopkins University Studies in Archaeology, No. 14; Baltimore: Johns Hopkins, 1932).

7. Abraham Schalit, *König Herodes* (*Studia Judaica*, Bd. 4; Berlin: De Gruyter, 1969).

8. Joseph Derenbourg, *Essai sur l'histoire et la géographie de la Palestine, d'après les Thalmuds et les autres sources rabbiniques. Première partie: Histoire de la Palestine depuis Cyrus jusqu'à Adrien* (Paris, 1867; republished 1971). Hans Lichtenstein, "Die Fastenrolle," *HUCA* 8/9 (1931–1932):257–371. Jacob Neusner, *The Rabbinic Traditions About the Pharisees Before 70* (3 vols.; Leiden: Brill, 1971).

9. Joseph Klausner, "Salome Alexandra," *WHJP* (vol. 6; New Brunswick, N.J.:

Rutgers, 1972). Emil Schürer, Geza Vermes, and Fergus Millar, *A History of the Jewish People in the Age of Jesus Christ* (vol. 1; Edinburgh: Clark, 1973).

10. See, e.g., *BJ* 1.36: The beginning of Mattathias' revolt; *A* XIII, 288–296, Hyrcanus' banquet and break with the Pharisees; *A* XIII, 301–317, the reign of Aristobulus I.

11. *BJ* I, 71; *A* XIII, 302.

12. Ralph Marcus, on *A* XIII, 301 (*LCL*).

13. N. E. A. Andreasen, "The Role of the Queen Mother in Israelite Society," *CBQ* 45(1983):179–194.

14. Pomeroy, (*op. cit.*, note 5), pp. 23–24.

15. *Ap* II, 49; *A* XIII, 284–87, 354–355. For contacts between Judea and Egypt at this time see II Macc. 1.1–10; *A* XIII, 74–79.

16. Although Madden and other scholars have assigned coins to Salome Alexander, none can be attributed to her with confidence; and none are listed in Hill, Reifenberg, Meshorer, or Kindler.

17. Salo W. Baron, *A Social and Religious History of the Jews*. 2d ed. (New York: Columbia University Press, vol. 1, 1952), p. 223.

18. *WHJP* vol. 6, p. 226.

19. *WHJP* vol. 6, p. 247.

20. Derenbourg (*op. cit.*, note 8), p. 96.

21. *Berakhoth* 48a; *Genesis Rabbah* 91.3; Derenbourg, *ibid.*, pp. 96–98.

22. Neusner (*op. cit.*, note 8), vol. 1, pp. 86–141.

23. Lichtenstein (*op. cit.*, note 8), pp. 343, 271.

24. For this question, see Morton Smith, "Palestinian Judaism in the First Century," *Israel: Its Role in Civilization* ed. Moshe Davis (New York: Harper & Row, 1956), pp. 74–81; Jacob Neusner, *From Politics to Piety* (Englewood Cliffs, N.J.: Prentice-Hall, 1973), pp. 45–66.

25. *Sifre Deuteronomy* 157. See Gedaliah Alon, *Jews, Judaism and the Classical World* (Jerusalem: Magnes, 1977), p. 4.

26. *Sifra Behuqotai* 1.1, ed. Weiss 110b; cf. *b. Ta'anith.* 23a; see Neusner, (*op. cit.*, note 8), vol. 1, pp. 89–90.

27. Victor Tcherikover, *Hellenistic Civilization and the Jews* (Philadelphia: Jewish Publication Society, 1959), p. 253.

28. Baron (*op. cit.*, note 17), vol. 1, p. 223.

29. Macurdy, *Vassal-Queens* (*op. cit.*, note 6), pp. 64–66.

30. *BJ* I, 158, 186; *A* XIV, 79, 126.

31. *BJ* I, 364. See, however, the passage about the sons of Baba (*A* XV, 260–266). It is not known in which way they were related to the Hasmonean dynasty.

32. Ben Zion Lurie, *Mi-Yannai ad Hordos* (Jerusalem: Kiryat-Sepher, 1974). Lurie devotes a whole chapter (pp. 242–251) to her and suggests that, in a talmudic story, the woman who is pursued by Herod and claims to be the last of the Hasmonean house may be identified as Antigonus' sister and not as Herod's wife Mariamme, as is commonly supposed (*b. Baba Bathra* 3b).

33. *A* XIV, 351. The parallel in *BJ* I, 262 attributes this advice mistakenly to Mariamme.

34. See Schalit (*op. cit.*, note 7), pp. 104–107.

35. *Ibid.*, pp. 61–66, emphasizes only that there were no legal advantages to Herod in this marriage. See, however, *BJ* I, 241; *A* XVII, 92. Herod's son Antipater, too, married a Hasmonean, a daughter of Antigonus (*A* XVII, 92).

36. Schalit, *ibid.*, pp. 585–588.

7 Josephus and Nicolaus of Damascus

BEN ZION WACHOLDER

Nicolaus of Damascus is important to the study of Josephus in three ways: (1) Josephus utilized not only Hebrew and Aramaic sources but also Greek writers, from Homer to Dionysius of Halicarnassus. He actually names fifty-five Greek writers, of whom half a dozen were presumably Jewish.[1] We may suppose that Nicolaus of Damascus is his most important pagan source, for Josephus drew on him not only for both the antediluvian and biblical periods, but Nicolaus' works became paramount for *Antiquities* XIII–XVII. (2) He served as a tutor for the children of Antony and Cleopatra, became a friend of Augustus and was Herod's chief advisor. He accompanied Herod on his journey through Greece in 14 B.C.E. and defended Herod's will before Augustus. As such, much of Nicolaus' personal experience was embedded in his accounts of Herod.[2] (3) In many ways, the life of Nicolaus resembles that of Josephus. Both served as diplomats for Jerusalem's ruling classes, both were influential in Rome on behalf of Jewish causes and both wrote extensively on history. Nicolaus, in addition, was a philosopher; and the *Treatise on Plants* of the Aristotelian corpus is usually ascribed to him. Aside from the world history of 144 books described later, Nicolaus also wrote a vita of Augustus.[3] Scattered fragments of his *Collection of Remarkable Customs* have been preserved by Joannes Stobias. Both he and Josephus wrote autobiographies, a genre of literature unknown before Nicolaus.

Aside from scattered fragments, Nicolaus' *Histories* have been preserved in Constantine VII Porphyrogenitus' tenth century *Excerpta de Virtutibus et Vitiis* and *Excerpta de Insidiis*. Strabo was the first to have drawn on Nicolaus' work but other writers such as Athenaeus, Stephanus of Byzantium, Socrates (the ecclesiastical historian), and most important, Josephus have preserved remnants of Nicolaus' writings.[4] Many ancient writers, now lost, have survived in Nicolaus' work, such as Xanthus of Lydia and Ctesias of Cnidos. For his Greek history Nicolaus used Hellanicus and Ephorus. Nicolaus, therefore, in part symbolizes the learned writer and polyhistor favored by kings and learned alike in the age of Augustus. The writing of Josephus in a way reflects a continuation of this cultural patrimony.

Nicolaus' *Histories,* containing, as it did, 144 books, was perhaps the most voluminous history written in Greek.[5] Its scope was equally impressive; beginning with mythology, it concluded with a full account of the author's own times. A brief outline of the contents of the fragments will show Nicolaus' scheme.

Books I and II (FF 1–6;82)

The History of Assyria, Babylonia and Media: Semiramis returning from India founds Babylon and foils a conspiracy by her son (F 1); Reign of Sardanapalus (F2); Arbaces, the Median, with the aid of the Babylonian Belesys, overthrows Sardanapalus (F 3); Nanarus, satrap of Babylon under Median King Artaeus, mutilates Parsondes, a Persian competitor for the satrapy (F 4); Stryangaeus, a general under Astybaros, commits suicide because of unrequited love (F 5); Origin of the Achaemenids (F 6).

Book III (FF 7–11; 83?; 84)

Hellas to the Trojan wars: Amphion and Zethus (F 7); Laius and Oedipus (F 8); Bellerophon (F 9); Pelops' overthrow of Oenomaus and marriage to Hippodamia (F 10); Argonauts (F 11; F12?); Heracles (F 13); Trojan wars (F 14).

Book IV (FF 15–36; 85; 86?)

The History of Lydia to the Heraclid Dynasty: Founding of Torrebus (F 15); King Moxus (F 16); Camblitas (F 22).

Digression into the History of Syria and Palestine: Founding of Nerabus (F 17); Ascalon (F 18); Abraham's reign in Damascus (F 19); King Adadus of Damascus (F 20).

Aeolian Migrations: The rape of Salmoneus' daughter by her father (F 21); settlement of the Peloponnesus (F 23); fame of the Amythaonidae (F 24); Orestes (F 25); Scamandrius and Andromache (F 26); foundation of Carnia? (F 27).

The Heraclids: Lacedaemon (FF 28–29); Argos (F 30); Messenia (FF 31–34); Corinth (FF 35–36).

Book V (FF 37–43)

Arcadia (FF 37–39); Aegaean Islands? (FF 40–42); Mesembria (F 43).

Book VI (FF 44–56)

History of Lydia: Lydian Heraclids: Cadys and Ardys, Sadyattes, Meles, Myrsus, Sadyattes (Tudo), Gyges (FF 44–47).

Athens: The kings Demophon (F 48); Hippomenes (F 49)

Cyrene and Ionian migrations: Cyrene (F 50);[6] Cyme (F 51); Miletus (FF 52–53).

The Heraclids of Thessaly: Pelias; Jason; Medea, Peleus, Acastus (FF 54–55).

Sparta: Lycurgus (F 56).

Book VII (FF 57–70)

Tyrants of Corinth and Sicyon: Cypselus (F 58); Periander (F 59); Cypselus or Psammetichus? (F 60); tyrants of Sicyon—Myron; Isodemus; Clisthenes (F 61).

History of Lydia: Gyges' campaign against Magnesians (F 62); Alyattes, Sadyattes (F 63); Alyattes (F 64); Croesus (F 65).

Rise of Persia: Rise and reign of Cyrus (FF 66–67); Cyrus and Croesus (F 68).

Early Rome(?):[7] Amulius; Numitor; Romulus and Remus (FF 69–70).

This table of contents shows that Nicolaus' *Histories* was a true universal history. Its scheme may properly be compared to the *Histories* of Ephorus, the first universal historian.[8] But Nicolaus' history was much wider in scope; it began properly, like the works of Herodotus and Ctesias, with the oriental empires, rather than with the conquest of the Peloponnesus used as the opening for Ephorus' work.[9] Nicolaus, following in the footsteps of Ctesias, gave an account of Semiramis' mythical conquest of India,[10] then he described the fates of Assyria, Media, and Babylonia, until the rise of Persia.[11] Unlike Ephorus, he included the mythological accounts of pre-Trojan Hellas.[12] The history of Lydia was divided into three parts, interwoven with the prehistory of the Hellenic states, both Dorian and Ionian.[13] Following Herodotus' method, the fall of Lydia, in turn, was subordinated to that of the rise of Persia, where the East and the West met. Even if we credit the broader vision of Nicolaus to the knowledge acquired since the days of Ephorus, the organization of the *Histories* is commendable. Here was neither a mere collection of national histories nor a synchronous account of generations.[14] The national histories were divided into parallel periods, each division being designed to coincide with an event of major import. The schemes charted by Herodotus and Ephorus were broadened in scope.[15]

As the work developed, it must have included more and more peoples, their histories becoming increasingly detailed.[16] Unfortunately, all that we have of the work, after Book VII, are a few incidents recorded in sundry fragments:[17] the landing of Noah's ark in Armenia, in Book XCVI (F 72); the Mithradates wars, in Books CIII–CIV (FF 73–74); Sulla, in Book CVII (F 75); Pompey's crossing of the Alps, in Book CVIII (F 76); Lucullus' triumph in 63 B.C.E., Book CX (FF 77–78); Crassus' defeat by the Parthians in

53 B.C.E., Book CXIV (F 79); Caesar's Gallic wars, in Book CXVI (F 80); Nicolaus' journey through Ionia in the company of Herod, in 14 B.C.E., in Books CXXIII–CXXIV (F 81). The remaining twenty-one fragments have no book number.[18] The last thirty or so books were devoted to the history of Israel and particularly Herod.[19]

Nicolaus' treatment of the history of ancient Israel becomes discernible in the following fragments.[20] After claiming that Berossus referred to Abraham without naming him, and that Hecataeus of Abdera wrote a work on Abraham,[21] Josephus cites the following from the fourth book of Nicolaus' *Histories:* "Habrames reigned [in Damascus] after having as an invader led an army from the country beyond Babylon called the land of the Chaldees. But soon thereafter he left this country together with his people for the land then called Canaan, now Judea, where his descendants multiplied. . . . The name of Abram is still celebrated in the region of Damascus, and a village is known that is called after him "Abram's abode." [22]

The tradition that made Abraham a Damascene king was also mentioned by Trogus (Timagenes?). But one would expect Nicolaus to have been better informed about the history of his place of birth, of which he was so proud. A Samaritan writer, Pseudo-Eupolemus, related that Abraham paid a visit to Hargarizin, where he was received with gifts by Melchizedek, the king and priest.[23] For it appears to have been the custom to make the Hebrew patriarch sojourn in places that were the author's favorites. Nicolaus' claim for Abraham, perhaps like that of Ascalon, may have been intended to express both pride in his own native city and flattery of the Judean king.[24] It did not weaken Herod's expansionist ambitions for that ancient city either.

Nicolaus' technique of intermingling Judean and Syrian prowess is still more clearly visible in *GLAJJ,* F 84. Both II Samuel 8:5–6 and I Chronicles 18.5–6 record David's conquest of Damascus upon his defeat of Hadad-ezer, king of Zobah, and his allies the Aramaeans of Damascus. According to Josephus, however, Nicolaus supplied the name of the Damascene king as Adadus, the founder of a Syrian dynasty of the same name. The war between David and Adadus, said Nicolaus, was long and bitter before the brave king of Damascus was finally defeated in a decisive battle at the Euphrates.[25] The Adadoi ruled over Syria for ten generations. Adadus the third was the most powerful of the dynasty. To avenge his grandfather's defeat, "he sacked the region which is now called the Samarite land." [26] Nicolaus undoubtedly expressed pride in the glorious past of Damascus, but there is nothing here which slighted the Jews;[27] quite the contrary. What Nicolaus attempted was to shed further light upon certain abbreviated passages of the Bible.

That this was not merely an incidental passage but part of the scheme of the *Histories* may be seen from an analysis of *A* I, 93–95. To confirm the Genesis account of Noah's ark, Josephus cites as witnesses certain Greek and barbarian historians: Berossus, Hieronymus the Egyptian, Mnaseas, and "many others."[28] Josephus then concludes with a quotation from the ninety-sixth book of Nicolaus' history: "Above the country of Minyas in Armenia there is a great mountain called Baris where many refugees saved themselves, so the story goes, during the flood, someone in an ark ran ashore on the summit, and the relics of the timber were preserved for a long time. This is perhaps the same of whom the Jewish law-giver Moses wrote."[29] It is worth noting that while many authors mentioned the flood, only Nicolaus, presumably, attempted to identify Noah with the popular tradition of the ark.

Did Josephus preserve some of Nicolaus' accounts of biblical history without acknowledging the source? Incontrovertible evidence is available only with reference to the nomenclature of the Damascene kings. The kings of Damascus are either unidentified[30] or referred to in the Masoretic text as Ben Hadad.[31] Josephus, probably following the usage of Nicolaus, calls them Adadus.[32] Does it follow that some of Josephus' frequent deviations from both the Masoretic and the Greek biblical nomenclature were based on Nicolaus' account of Jewish history? Nicolaus' Hellenization of the name Abraham may provide a supplementary clue: the Septuagint attempted to preserve the Hebrew forms of Ἀβράμ or Ἀβραάμ.[33] Josephus' form is Ἄβραμος, but the quotation from Nicolaus names him Ἀβράμης.[34] It is evident that Nicolaus, like Josephus, made the Hebrew name sound more Greek than did the Jewish translators of the Bible.

As to more substantial use of Nicolaus' account of biblical history by Josephus, we are forced to conjecture. Marcus is probably correct when he suggests that Nicolaus is the source for Josephus' statement that the Syrian kings, Adadus and his successor Azelus (Hebrew: Hazael; Septuagint: Azael), were worshipped in Damascus as gods.[35] But either Josephus or, as is more likely, Nicolaus is wrong in identifying this Adadus III as the ruler who made war against the king of Israel, Ahab.[36] For, if Nicolaus is correct in stating that all Damascene kings bore the same name for ten generations and that Adadus I flourished in the time of David, Adadus III could not have been a contemporary of Ahab.[37] The biblical account, however, confirms the statement that the Damascene king besieged Samaria in the days of Ahab.[38] An Assyrian inscription, it may be added, records that in 853 B.C. both Ahab and Adadidri, king of Damascus, fought Shalmaneser III at Qarqar, apparently checking the first Assyrian attempt to expand southward.[39] Be that as it may, the extrabiblical material in Nicolaus' account of the wars between Ahab and Adadus has probably been preserved in the *Jewish Antiquities*.[40]

What were Nicolaus' sources, in addition to the Bible, for his account of biblical history? A few more details supplied by Nicolaus resemble those of Trogus,[41] whose probable source was Timagenes.[42] In the absence of verifiable fragments of Nicolaus' treatment of ancient Jewish history, what is known of his method of assembling world history may offer some guide. In his treatment of Assyrian, Lydian, and Persian history, Nicolaus chose to copy or paraphrase highly dramatic incidents. The heroes are romanticized, and women, for good or evil, play an important role. It is likely that Nicolaus' account of the biblical heroes was given this same treatment. In many cases, these romantic stories already existed. Traces of such fictionalized accounts are preserved by Josephus, whose use of Nicolaus throughout his works is beyond doubt.[43]

Nicolaus' incidental references to Noah, Abraham, Moses, and David suggest that the author of the *Histories* gave full descriptions of the biblical heroes.[44] The references to the location of Noah's ark and to Abraham's reign in Damascus lead one to believe that Nicolaus made use of the Hellenized accounts that amplified and supplemented the biblical versions of the Hebrew heroes. Nicolaus' extensive borrowings from Ctesias, Xanthus, and Ephorus[45] to describe Semiramis, Arbacus, Lycurgus, and Cyrus[46] suggest that Moses may have received similar treatment. Moses' supposed campaign against the Ethiopians, preserved in the *Antiquities,* seems to suggest Nicolaus' pen.[47] When Ethiopian invaders threatened Memphis, Moses freed Egypt and seized the Ethiopian capital. The climax of the legend is Moses' marriage to the daughter of the Ethiopian king.[48] An early version of this story, it is true, is found in Artapanus, an author who flourished not later than the beginning of the first century B.C.E.[49] But the account found in the *Antiquities* suggests that Josephus was following a modified version of Artapanus.[50] An unknown historian, between the times of Artapanus and Josephus, had in all probability rewritten the legend, adding a romantic touch.[51] A. Schalit suggests that Alexander Polyhistor may have been the immediate source.[52] This is unlikely. Polyhistor was a dry copyist, never interested in romance.[53] Nicolaus would seem to be a more likely source, for the Moses legend in the *Antiquities* interweaves romance with warfare, an important characteristic of Nicolaus' technique.[54] The prominent role of women, the Egyptian conspiracy against Moses, and the anti-Egyptian bias are elements that strengthen the suspicion that we have here Nicolaus' version of the story of Moses. Certainly, it is unbelievable that Herod's court historian would have been satisfied with merely paraphrasing the version of Moses found in Exodus. Nicolaus was one of the Hellenistic historians who claimed to have more information than is found in the classical accounts of Herodotus or the Old Testament.[55]

Whereas Nicolaus' treatment of biblical history is of interest because it sheds light upon first century B.C.E. midrashic historiography, his treatment of Jewish history during the Hellenistic period is of greater significance. Except for I and II Maccabees and scattered references in the works of Hellenistic historians, Josephus is the primary source for Jewish history. The consensus of modern scholars is that Josephus, in his account of Hellenistic history, largely followed Nicolaus.[56] Here, however, one must review the evidence, not so much to find out Josephus' indebtedness to Nicolaus as to analyze Nicolaus' treatment of Jewish Hellenistic history. In his *Histories,* it has been assumed, Nicolaus frequently referred to Jewish events besides giving a connected account of ancient Israel. Did he follow the same procedure during the Hellenistic epoch?

To answer this question the safe method is to begin with an analysis of the ascertainable fragments. In his *Contra Apion,* Josephus cites a long list of Hellenistic historians who confirmed that Antiochus IV Epiphanes, in need of money, sacked the Temple at Jerusalem of gold; these historians include Polybius, Strabo, Nicolaus, Timagenes, Castor, and Apollodorus.[57] Few scholars would claim that Josephus himself collected all these witnesses;[58] he undoubtedly found the names in either Strabo or Nicolaus, or both.[59] As to the other historians, none of them is known to have given a connected account of Jewish history.[60] Antiochus' sacking of the Temple at Jerusalem was included in their accounts of the Seleucids. It is plausible, then, that the same remark of Nicolaus also occurred in that part of his history dealing primarily with the affairs of Antiochus, rather than with the Jews.

The next fragment, from the thirteenth book of the *Antiquities,* seems to confirm the impression that Josephus' citations from Nicolaus were derived from accounts that dealt with general, rather than Jewish, history.[61] Both *The Jewish War* and the *Antiquities* tell of Antiochus VII Sidetes' siege of Jerusalem in 129 B.C.E., whereupon John Hyrcanus bribed Antiochus to remove the blockade.[62] According to the *Antiquities,* however, Hyrcanus became Antiochus' ally. Josephus cites Nicolaus as witness for this statement: "Antiochus, after defeating the Parthian general Indates, set up a trophy at the Lycus river. He remained there in camp for two days at the request of the Jew Hyrcanus because there was a national festival during which the Jews were forbidden to march out."[63]

It is not clear whether the context of this passage in Nicolaus has to do with John Hyrcanus or Antiochus Sidetes. It is also possible that the fragment dealt with Parthia, a topic treated by Nicolaus in the 114th book of his *Histories.*[64] From Josephus, however, it would seem that the subject matter in Nicolaus was Antiochus Sidetes. For instead of continuing with his account of Hyrcanus, Josephus digresses to tell a chapter of Seleucid history. He describes Antiochus' death at the hands of the Parthian king Arsaces, whereupon Demetrius II ascended the Syrian throne. Demetrius, Josephus continues, was able to succeed Antiochus because Arsaces had released him from captivity when Antiochus was invading Parthia, "as has already been related elsewhere."[65] As Josephus never did retell this story, and had no reason to, it is the general consensus of modern scholars that Josephus copied the cross-reference from his source.[66] That the source was Nicolaus is evident from the fact that the Damascene is cited by Josephus immediately before his digression from Jewish history. Thus, it would seem that Josephus, while copying from Nicolaus the fact of Hyrcanus' presence in the Parthian campaign, followed his source in its description of Antiochus and Demetrius. The note "as had already been related elsewhere" fits well into the kind of work Nicolaus wrote. His topical treatment of history required cross-references. In this instance, the note probably referred to Nicolaus' account of Parthia, where more details of Antiochus' invasion were given.

Of greater interest is the fact that, while dealing with Antiochus Sidetes, Nicolaus recorded a relatively insignificant fact concerning Hyrcanus' request to remain in camp to celebrate the Jewish holiday.[67] Such a detail would have been of interest to Jewish readers only. At any rate, the parallel account in *The Jewish War*, which keeps to a minimum the general background of the period, omits Hyrcanus' campaign in Parthia.[68]

The evidence so far indicates that Nicolaus integrated Jewish history with that of the general Hellenistic monarchies. But the possibility that he gave a full description of the internal affairs of the Hasmoneans cannot be excluded, especially inasmuch as historians generally tended to become more detailed as they described the later times.[69] But it does not follow that Jewish history was treated apart from that of the Seleucids and the Ptolemies. This assumption would seem to run counter to the accepted view of modern scholarship. It is generally assumed that the *War* was more dependent on Nicolaus' history than the *Antiquities*. The basis for this hypothesis is that (1) the treatment of Herod in the *War* is more favorable than in the *Antiquities*; (2) in the *Antiquities*, Strabo is cited often; (3) the outlook of the *War* reflects that of a Hellenistic author writing in the days of Herod.[70] If we put aside for the moment Josephus' treatment of the Herodian period, this hypothesis leaves some questions unanswered. In his *Antiquities*, Josephus frequently strays from his account of the Hasmoneans to include subject matter which had no direct bearing on Jewish affairs; but the parallel account in the *War* is free from such extraneous material. It is only if we assume a Hellenistic source for the *Antiquities*, such as Nicolaus' *Histories*, whose interest was not limited to Jewish history, that the inclusion of the extraneous material in the *Antiquities* can be explained. A more compelling argument for the assumption that Josephus' account of the Hasmoneans in the *Antiquities* was based on the Damascene is the fact that it is interspersed with direct citations from the Damascene.[71] The hypothesis that the *War* followed Nicolaus, however, is founded on sheer guesswork. The evidence, then, points to a fuller dependence on Nicolaus in the *Antiquities* than in the *War*.

This is not to say that Nicolaus must be excluded as the source of the *War*. True, the *War*, unlike the *Antiquities*, deals primarily with internal affairs. But it is likely that Nicolaus included a detailed account of the Hasmoneans as background for the rise of Herod, an account that Josephus might have excerpted in the *War*.[72] In the *Antiquities*, however, Josephus, writing at a more leisurely pace, felt free to follow his source more closely.

The hypothesis that Josephus, in the *Antiquities*, supplemented his account of the *War* with citations from Nicolaus that dealt with general rather than Jewish history gains support from this statement for which Nicolaus and Strabo are cited as authorities: "Ptolemy Lathyrus overran Judea, commanding his soldiers to cut the throats of women and children, chop them up, boil and eat them."[73] Now Nicolaus and Strabo independently followed Timagenes, cited just previously by Josephus.[74] Timagenes, it is known, never gave a connected history of the Jews, although he made frequent references to them.[75] If Timagenes was here the source, as Jacoby assumes, it follows that Nicolaus may have simply paraphrased his source's account of Ptolemy Lathyrus. A check in the parallel account in the *War* shows that the author knew nothing of Ptolemy's atrocities in Judea.[76] And once again, the fragment concludes with the note "as we have shown elsewhere."[77]

These cross-references served a useful purpose. Having arranged his history topically, it is easy to imagine the difficulties Nicolaus encountered in his attempt to integrate a detailed history of the Jews with the complexities of Hellenistic history. For a Posidonius or a Timagenes, it was reasonable to subordinate accounts of the Jews to those of the period, adding some background on the peculiar development of the Jews.[78] But Nicolaus' history was much wider in scope. Wanting to include a detailed account of the Hasmonean rulers, he solved the problem by subordinating the internal to the external history and connecting the two with cross-references. Thus, Pompey's conquest of Jerusalem, as well as Crassus' campaign against Parthia and Caesar's conquest of Gaul, were treated consecutively under the general heading of the conflict between Pompey and Caesar.[79] This was a logical arrangement. For aside from petty border quarrels, the external history of the Jews must be viewed from the centers of power, rather than from the factional conflicts within Jerusalem.

Nevertheless, approaching the fall of the Hasmonean dynasty and the rise of Antipater, Nicolaus lost his sense of proportion. The description of the early Hasmoneans, while adequate, was never disproportionate to the general account of the *Histories*. But the struggle between Hyrcanus II and Aristobulus served to introduce the prominent role of Antipater and his son Herod.[80] Jacoby conjectures that *A* XIV, 8 (his fragment 96), which deals with Antipater's ancestry, was described in one of the books from 111 to 113.[81] This would mean that the last 30 books or more, out of the 144 of the entire universal history, dealt primarily with the rise and life of Herod. Unbelievable as this lack of proportion would seem, it may nevertheless be correct, for Nicolaus devoted a book or so (on the average) to each two years of Herod's life, from 14 to 4 B.C.E.[82] As Antipater rose to prominence in the early 70s B.C.E., the same proportion of a book per two years for the whole period is probable. If this is true, then Herod's reign was one of the most minutely described periods in Jewish history. And despite the loss of Nicolaus' work, it has remained so, thanks to Josephus' condensation of this period into nearly 4 books.[83]

Scholars since Destinon have attempted to probe more deeply into the nature of Nicolaus' treatment of Herod. The consensus is that Nicolaus' account may be reconstructed from those passages in Josephus favorable to the king.[84] As far as it goes, this seems a reasonable assumption. Its weakness, however, is that this hypothesis rests almost exclusively on Josephus' own quotations from Nicolaus.[85] The question still remains whether Josephus accurately reproduced Nicolaus' views. Fortunately, the remnants of Nicolaus' *Autobiography* furnish some evidence on this point.[86] To be sure, these fragments deal with relatively few incidents of the history of the period, and they do not come from the *Histories*. But unless there are special reasons why Nicolaus changed his views, it may be assumed that the description of the events in the *Histories* was essentially the same as in the *Autobiography,* although in a much abbreviated form.[87]

From *GLAJJ*, F96, we learn that Nicolaus described Herod's intellectual interests, something that Josephus failed to do. Nicolaus, as *GLAJJ*, F 97, shows, not only described fully Herod's benevolent acts on behalf of the Greek cities, but also "explained" his purpose: *philanthropia,* a point strongly belabored by the Damascene but omitted by Josephus, perhaps intentionally.[88] Nicolaus' journey to Rome in the company of Herod in 12 B.C.E., which was probably mentioned in the history, is not recorded in Josephus.[89] The same may be true of Nicolaus' visit to Antioch in 20 B.C.E., perhaps as an aide to the king.[90] By omitting these incidents Josephus probably eliminated some of the cruder aspects of Nicolaus' Herodian propaganda.

Nicolaus' second known journey to Rome in 8 B.C.E. was to bring about a reconciliation between Augustus and Herod. We reproduce the relevant fragment here because it is the most extensive remnant of the Damascene's writings. It is important to remember that, though similar, Josephus' account frequently differs from that of Nicolaus.

> Herod went on an expedition against Arabia without the approval of Caesar. In view of this the latter expressed his displeasure and was very angry with Herod, writing to him very harshly and dismissing his ambassadors with disrespect. Appearing before Caesar, Nicolaus not only exonerated Herod from the charges, but also turned Caesar's anger against the accusers. The Arab king had already died, and Caesar, being convinced by the accusation lodged by Nicolaus, condemned the Arabian minister, and later, finding him a very evil man, had him executed.

At the same time the court of Herod was thrown into confusion, since the eldest of his sons falsely accused the two next born of plotting against their father. These were indeed younger than he, but were his superiors in rank, because they were children of a queen, whereas his mother was a commoner. Before Nicolaus had returned from Rome, the young men were convicted by the council, and the father, having been much exasperated, was on the point of having them executed. After Nicolaus had sailed home, Herod informed him of what happened and asked his advice. Nicolaus suggested that they should be removed to one of the fortresses, in order to gain time for better consultation, and thus not appear to make a fatal decision concerning his nearest while actuated by anger. Antipater, perceiving this, looked on Nicolaus with suspicion, and suborning various persons, frightened his father into the belief that he was in danger of being immediately killed by his sons who had corrupted the whole army, as he maintained, and his service, and that his only safety lay in their quick execution. And Herod, being afraid for his life, took a quick but not a good decision. No more did he communicate about the matter with Nicolaus, but at night he secretly sent the executioners. Thus the sons died, and this constituted the beginning of all evil for Herod, while everything had gone well with him before. After Antipater had caused the death of his brothers, he thought Nicolaus to be his enemy, while he himself, in turn, was bitterly hated not only by the inhabitants of the realm, but also, by those of Syria and those living beyond. The tale of the events reached Rome as well, and none was to be found either great or small who did not hate the man both for the reason that he had caused the death of his brothers who were much his betters and because he had persuaded his father to be involved in such defilement and to dishonor his former goodwill. And since the later activities of Antipater were in line with his former misdeeds, and he formed a plot against his father, being eager to become king sooner, and bought poison from Egypt about which one of his accomplices confessed, Herod put his slaves to torture. These divulged everything, namely that he intended to kill his aunt and his other brothers as well as the children of his formerly executed brothers, in order that no heir would be left. He contrived also a plot against the house of Caesar that was much more dreadful than the transgressions he committed against his own house. When also Varus, the governor of Syria, and the other officials arrived, his father convened a tribunal; the poison as well as the confessions of the slaves under torture and the letters from Rome were publicly brought forth, and the king entrusted the delivery of the speech to Nicolaus. Thus, Nicolaus lodged the accusation, Antipater spoke in his defence, while Varus and his friends acted as judges. Antipater was convicted and handed over for execution. Even then Nicolaus proposed to send him to Caesar, since he had also committed an offence against him, and to do whatever Caesar would decide. But a letter coming from Caesar, who allowed the father to punish Antipater, reached them first; and he was executed, while Caesar also killed the freedwoman, who had been his accomplice. There was none who did not praise Nicolaus for his excellent arraignment of the parricide and murderer of his brothers.

After these events, when a short time passed, the king also died, and the nation rose against his children and against the Greeks. The last mentioned numbered more than ten thousand. In the battle which ensued the Greeks had the upper hand. And Archelaus, the heir, sailed away to Rome to deal with the whole question of his rule together with his brothers, and he exhorted Nicolaus, who had already been bent on retiring from public affairs since he was about 60 years old, to sail in his company. Thus he sailed in his company [to Rome] and he found that everywhere Archelaus' accusers were active. On the one hand, the younger brother laid claim to the crown, and, on the other hand, all the relatives levelled charges against him, though not working in the interest of the younger brother. Also the Greek cities subject to Herod sent emissaries petitioning Caesar to grant them freedom. The representatives of the whole Jewish nation accused Archelaus of the murder of three thousand men who fell in the battle, and above all asked to be subject to the rule of Caesar, and, if not, to that of the younger brother. So many trials having been announced, Nicolaus first fought for Archelaus in the contest against the relatives and then against his Jewish subjects, and won. But the contest against the Greek cities he did not think fit for him to undertake, and he also exhorted Archelaus not to oppose their striving for freedom, as the remaining dominion would be enough for him. For the same reason he did not choose to contend against his brother because of his friendship with their common father. Caesar settled the question of the whole inheritance, allotting to each of Herod's children a part of the realm, Archelaus' share amounting to a half of the whole. And Caesar honored Nicolaus and appointed Archelaus ethnarch. He promised that if he proved himself worthy, he would soon appoint him king. His younger brothers Philip and Antipas he appointed tetrarchs.[91]

Here the account in the *Antiquities* conforms to that related by Nicolaus.[92] According to the *Antiquities,* Augustus not only resumed his friendly relations with Herod but also condemned to death Herod's accuser, the Arab general Syllaeus.[93] Josephus, however, records that Syllaeus agitated against Herod in 4 B.C.E. in Rome.[94] But a check of Nicolaus may explain how Josephus came to make such a gross error. The relevant passage concludes, "And having been found *subsequently* very evil, he [Syllaeus] was condemned to death."[95] Nicolaus clearly referred to Syllaeus' misdeeds in 4 B.C.E., for which, as Strabo records, he was executed.[96] When paraphrasing Nicolaus, Josephus seems to have overlooked the word *subsequently.* Incidentally, the Syllaeus affair is not recorded in the *War,* which confirms the impression that the *Antiquities* was even more dependent on Nicolaus than Josephus' earlier work.

In the *Autobiography,* Nicolaus' account of the condemnation of Herod's sons parallels that of Josephus.[97] But Nicolaus, despite his brevity, adds details missing in Josephus: that Mariamne's sons were executed at night and that Antipater plotted to kill Salome, Herod's sister.[98] Nicolaus' version of the event following Herod's death contains facts missing in Josephus. He similarly records the number of the Jews massacred by Archelaus as three thousand, but only Nicolaus says that more than ten thousand participated in the revolt.[99] The line, however, is ambiguous. It may be that Nicolaus meant that there were ten thousand rebels or, as Stern suggests, that ten thousand Greeks suppressed the revolt.[100] Nicolaus alone records that the revolt of the Jews was directed against the "Hellenes," as it was against Archelaus.[101] As might be expected, Nicolaus is more accurate than his copyist.

Unlike Josephus, who describes two separate proceedings before Augustus dealing with the disposition of Herod's realm, Nicolaus, for the sake of brevity, combines them into one.[102] Otherwise, the superiority of Nicolaus's version to that of Josephus is again apparent. Nicolaus mentions the presence in Rome of a delegation from the Hellenistic cities to demand freedom and the fact that Archelaus, on the Damascene's advice, did not oppose their demand.[103] Josephus, although omitting the presence of the Hellenistic delegation, does say that the Greek cities of Gaza, Gadara, and Hippos were detached from Archelaus' ethnarchy and incorporated into the province of Syria.[104] The pleadings of the Jewish delegation are recorded more precisely in Nicolaus' account than that of Josephus. According to Josephus, the Jewish representatives pleaded for direct Roman rule; according to Nicolaus, they preferred Roman rule, but as second choice consented to be governed by Antipas,[105] Archelaus' younger brother. The Jewish opposition to the house of Herod was not as uncompromising as one would assume from Josephus. Nicolaus affirms that he deliberately refrained from attacking Antipas.[106] Josephus quotes Antipas' bitter attacks against Archelaus, but Nicolaus' response to these charges, as quoted by Josephus, is free from personal recriminations. Josephus thus indirectly confirms Nicolaus' account.[107]

The following may be deduced from fragments 94 to 97 in *GLAJJ*, assuming that Nicolaus' *Histories* contained the same information as his *Autobiography:* (1) Nicolaus described Herod's intellectual aspirations, including perhaps a philosophical justification of the king's reign;[108] (2) the relations between the Jews and the Hellenistic elements in Palestine were more clearly delineated than in Josephus;[109] (3) the prominence of Nicolaus was strongly emphasized;[110] (4) Nicolaus' account contained many details now lost;[111] (5) Josephus' dependence on Nicolaus, even more in the *Antiquities* than in the *War*, need not be questioned.[112] The loss of (1) and (2) is especially lamentable.

Concerning Nicolaus' description of contemporary Judaism, the fragments are not too informative. All we know directly is that Nicolaus praised the piety of the Jews, who continued to sacrifice at the Temple while Pompey's troops broke into Jerusalem.[113] The evidence that this may have reflected Nicolaus' personal opinion is somewhat weakened by Josephus, who besides Nicolaus also cites Strabo and Livy, men hardly in sympathy with Judaism.[114] But it is likely that Josephus found the friendly account of the Jews in Nicolaus and appended the names of Strabo and Livy, although these two gave only the bare facts. Among the most eloquent glorifications of Judaism are the words Josephus attributes to Nicolaus in his praise of Jewish religious practices in general and the Sabbath in particular.[115] But here again—assuming the speech to be that of Nicolaus—he was speaking as an advocate in defense of the rights of Ionian Jewry. However, the fact that Nicolaus apparently recorded it in his history, although its importance may have been exaggerated, would still indicate a favorable attitude to a much maligned Jewish custom.[116] At any rate, there is no reason to assume that Nicolaus would, on the one hand, describe his own acts, which were designed to strengthen the practice of Judaism in the Diaspora, and, on the other, disparage the same practices in Jerusalem.

Whether Nicolaus included an account of Jewish laws and customs in his *Collection* is a question worth asking. If he did, there is no trace of it in the fragments. But the fact that Nicolaus described the constitution and practices of both Hellenes and barbarians gives reason to assume that the customs of the Jews were not absent. Philo, in his description of the Therapeutae, a Jewish sect either similar to or identical with the Essenes, compares their communal living and their disdain of worldly goods to those of the Galactophagi mentioned in the *Iliad*.[117] It is perhaps no coincidence that both Philo's quotation from Homer and its interpretation, which diverges from the simple meaning, are found in Nicolaus.[118] Philo's reference to those who live on milk is rather brief; that of Nicolaus is lengthy. The Galactophagi, Nicolaus says, were a Scythian tribe, among whom "envy, hatred or fear had never been recorded because of their communal life and practice of justice."[119] In view of the ever-repeated theme of communal living among various peoples, one ventures to speculate that the *Collection of Remarkable Customs* may have contained a description of the Essenes.[120]

It is possible to go even further and to assume that both Philo's and Josephus' accounts of the Essenes were based on the account of Nicolaus.[121] Perceptive readers of Josephus have recognized that his description of the Essenes was based on some authority whose information was firsthand, but who was ignorant of the nicer distinctions of Jewish customs.[122] The Essenes alone, among Jewish sects, are treated favorably in Josephus' account of Herod, a version that was probably based on the one by Nicolaus.[123] Certainly Josephus, a Pharisee himself, cannot be regarded as the original author of the slurring remarks referring to a group with which he was identified with.[124] Philo's account of the Essenes, which is not too different from that of Josephus, also mentions that the Essenes were favored by kings, possibly a reference to Herod's sympathy with that sect.[125] In the *Antiquities,* the account of the Essenes concludes with a reference to the Dacians, another Scythian tribe.[126] This comparison seems to echo Nicolaus' description of the Galactophagi, whose Scythian way of life was said to have contained many elements comparable to those of the Essenes.[127] If Nicolaus, the author of several philosophical treatises, described the Jewish sects at all, he would have been likely to compare them with one or another of the Greek philosophical schools. To a non-Jew trained in the acrimonious metaphysical debates, the disputes in religious doctrines and practices among the Sadduccees, Pharisees, and Essenes may have assumed familiar philosophical connotations, which later Jewish apologists were glad to repeat.[128]

An evaluation of Nicolaus' work is necessarily connected with an appraisal of his activities as an agent of Herod. Having been urged by Herod to undertake the writing of a history, the tenor of Nicolaus' work was calculated to add to his master's glory.[129] The degeneration of the *Histories* into a description of Herodian rule has led some scholars to suspect that Nicolaus wrote a separate biography of Herod.[130] For this there is no evidence; the Nicolaean tradition does not mention such a work.[131] Whether Nicolaus subordinated the general period to his account of Herod, or whether he simply ignored events not directly connected with the Judean king, is not known. The latter is probable, however, if Josephus' account of this period is based on Nicolaus. The treatment of this period in both the *Antiquities* and *War* contains no trace of reference to the non-Jewish world. This is in sharp contrast to the treatment of the Hellenistic period in the *War* and the *Antiquities,* whose frequent references to the Seleucids betray a source that certainly dealt with non-Jewish history.[132] What greater monument to the king could there be than to begin with the exploits of Semiramis and end with the adventures of Herod?

The devotion of perhaps one-fifth of the *Histories* to Herod does not heighten our estimate of Nicolaus' historical perspective. Even so, we are grateful to Nicolaus for giving us an account of the world in which he was an active participant. One complaint against Strabo is that, in his *Geography,* he deals mostly with a world gone by.[133] Josephus maintained that the first duty of the historian was to describe the events that he knew best, instead of paraphrasing the accounts of others, a view perhaps widely held in antiquity.[134] Nicolaus is important precisely because, having become Herod's mouthpiece, he gave a full treatment of the contemporary scene that he knew intimately.

The reliability of Nicolaus as a faithful recorder of the contemporary scene is not high, however. The Augustan *Vita* has given its author a poor reputation. Plutarch cites Nicolaus as the authority for the statement, clearly false, that Porcia, upon hearing of the death of her husband, Brutus, ended her life by swallowing burning charcoal.[135] Was he, then, more reliable when describing his patron Herod? The king appears to have been depicted as representing the best of contemporary culture. According to Nicolaus, Herod was a cultured man interested in the arts and benevolent to both Jew and Greek.[136] The charge of *misanthropia* that was frequently hurled at the Jews did not apply to one who endowed Hellenistic cities and temples with lavish gifts.[137]

In the field of foreign policy, as one might expect, Nicolaus pointed out Herod's unconditional submission to Rome and his personal devotion to

Augustus. In his address before Agrippa, as quoted in the *Antiquities,* Nicolaus stressed that Herod's pro-Roman policies had been inaugurated by the king's father Antipater, who had fought on Caesar's behalf in Egypt.[138] Nicolaus' words here recall Josephus' dramatic account, probably based on Nicolaus, of Antipater's response to the charge of Antigonus that Hyrcanus II and Antipater had sided with Pompey: Antipater stripped off his clothes, exposing the numerous wounds he had suffered in Egypt.[139] Nicolaus' advice to Herod was to not make any important move, such as carrying out death sentences against his sons, without the expressed approval of Augustus.[140] It is not surprising, therefore, that when Herod did arouse Augustus' anger, Nicolaus was dispatched to heal the breach.[141] Nicolaus, accompanying Herod on his visit to Agrippa, also made trips through Ionia to spread Herod's fame.[142] These journeys, as well as Herod's participation in the Olympic games, suggest that Nicolaus was deeply involved in a grandiose plan of public relations.[143] The idea, it appears, was to spread the word that, excepting Augustus and Agrippa, Herod was the greatest benefactor of the Greek world.[144]

But in his detailed account of Herod, Nicolaus was compelled to allude to the less seemly aspects of the king's reign. It is not without irony that when Nicolaus was writing his major work in 14 B.C.E., Herod's reign was on the downgrade.[145] The king, it is true, was never without worries. His Greek subjects resented his rule.[146] More serious were the constant conflicts with the Nabataean kingdom, on whose territory Herod had attempted to encroach. In 12 B.C.E., while the king was accusing his sons of conspiracy before Augustus, his subjects in Trachonitis revolted.[147] Important segments of the Jewish population were never reconciled to the king's cosmopolitan outlook; they resented the presence of foreigners in his court, and they hated his oppressive methods. But the difficulties within his own family weakened Herod's position beyond repair. Nicolaus, according to the fragments of his *Autobiography,* regarded the struggle for succession among the royal sons as the beginning of the period of decline of Herod's reign.[148] Whether Nicolaus presented the same view in his *Histories* is not known, but Josephus' account seconds this opinion.[149] Nicolaus' work, then, although intended to glorify the Judean king, became more and more apologetic, and the story of Herod's benevolence became somewhat muted when Nicolaus had to defend the slaughter of the royal sons.[150] According to Josephus, Nicolaus upheld the legality of the execution of Mariamne and her two sons.[151] He himself prosecuted Antipater, Herod's oldest son.[152] It follows, perhaps, that Nicolaus in his history justified Herod's other wholesale killings, just as he defended the slaughter of three thousand Jews by Archelaus in 4 B.C.E.[153] Nicolaus accused Mariamne of ἀσέλγεια, or wanton behavior, a charge used by Nicolaus to incriminate Antipater also.[154] The story of Alexandra II, Mariamne's mother, who according to Josephus had sent paintings of Mariamne and Aristobulus to Antony to parade before him their comeliness, may also be based on Nicolaus.[155] After the king's death, incidentally, the Jewish leaders alleged that Herod had dishonored their virgin daughters.[156] In this instance, Nicolaus retorted that Herod was not on trial.[157] Licentious behavior was a stock charge to be hurled against anyone; even Nicolaus used it frequently to discredit the enemies of Herod.

One question still remains to be answered. Did Nicolaus believe in his apology for Herod? Nicolaus' curt retort to the Jewish deputies that Herod was not on trial would seem to indicate that he was not prepared to answer their charges.[158] But it is difficult to believe that a man of such wide experience as Nicolaus could be completely blinded by Herod's splendor. As noted, Nicolaus assumes in his *Autobiography* that Mariamne's sons were innocent, although in his history he had declared them guilty of conspiring against their father.[159] He had even hinted as much in his history when he advised Herod to postpone their execution.[160] Thus, Nicolaus seems to have been a court historian in the full sense of the word, writing as if someone were always looking over his shoulder.

Thus far, it has been shown that Nicolaus defended the legality of Herod's executions. He recorded that Mariamne had been convicted of wanton behavior and her sons of conspiracy, but he conveniently forgot to mention that they were perhaps innocent. Did he also invent facts to glorify Herod? Josephus censures Nicolaus for his failure to record Herod's desecration of the Davidic sepulchre in a search for gold, whereupon two guards were consumed by fire.[161] To atone for this sin, Herod built a monument in front of the royal shrines. Nicolaus, according to Josephus, mentioned the monument but failed to record Herod's violation of the shrine and the divine punishment.[162] Josephus weakens considerably his general indictment of Nicolaus' bias by building it around this incident.[163] In fact, Destinon has thereby attempted to show Josephus' unreasonableness vis-à-vis Nicolaus.[164] But even if we accept Josephus' premises, Nicolaus' sin once more consisted in glossing over important facts.

Only in one case does Josephus point to an outright invention by Nicolaus. Nicolaus wrote that Antipater, Herod's father, was a descendant of the Jewish aristocracy rather than an Idumaean.[165] Jacoby is correct in rejecting Hoelscher's view that a Jewish polemicist had invented this quotation to discredit Nicolaus' account.[166] Laqueur finds that Josephus in his *Antiquities* deliberately and ingeniously misinterpreted Nicolaus' reference to Antipater's distinguished "ancestry," as found in the *War,* to mean Jewish aristocratic ancestry.[167] There is no reason, however, to question the genuineness of Josephus' quotation.[168] The only issue would seem to be whether Nicolaus here was inventing something completely false or whether he was merely, as usual, overstating his point. Here, perhaps, the author of *Josippon* is correct in pointing out that Antipater had married an Idumaean, which according to Jewish law would have made his descendants Idumaeans.[169] The fact that only

Herod, among Antipater's sons, bore a Hellenistic name may indicate that the Idumaean family had been Judaized, perhaps by having intermarried with the native population.[170] It is not inconceivable that one of Herod's ancestors belonged to the Jewish aristocracy.[171] This, however, did not make Herod less of an "Idumaean," especially to those who hated him.[172] Josephus' indictment of Nicolaus must therefore stand: "For he [Nicolaus] lived in Herod's kingdom and was his favorite; he wrote as his servant, touching upon nothing but what tended to increase his glory, and apologizing for many of his clearly unjust acts and very diligently concealing others."[173]

This study has shown, as have many others, Josephus' use and expansion of the *Histories* of Nicolaus. On the other hand, it is necessary to stress that, by and large, the two writers represented a divergent picture of Jewish history. Josephus is the Jewish historian par excellence, even in passages that seem to the modern reader to be unsympathetic to the Jews. Nicolaus represents the Graeco-Syrian outlook on events. These divergent interests markedly affected the writings of each, and therefore the differences between what Nicolaus wrote and what Josephus drew from him were profound. What the Jewish historian has preserved is an interplay of these two traditions.

Notes

I express my deep gratitude to John Kampen, Jancy Jaslow, and John C. Reeves for their editorial assistance.

1. These are listed on the last page of *Flavii Iosephi Opera: edidit et apparatu critico instruxit*, ed. B. Niese, vol. 7 (Berlin, 1895). See his index for references.

2. Nicolaus' life and works are treated at greater length in my *Nicolaus of Damascus* (University of California Publications in History, 75; Berkeley/Los Angeles, 1962), pp. 14–36. See also R. J. H. Shutt, *Studies in Josephus* (London, 1961), pp. 79–91; and E. Schürer, *The History of the Jewish People in the Age of Jesus Christ (175 B.C.–A.D. 135)*, ed. G. Vermes et al., vol. 1 (Edinburgh, 1973), pp. 28–32.

3. This is considered his most important work by G. W. Bowersock, *Augustus and the Greek World* (Oxford, 1966).

4. The most complete collection of the preserved writings of Nicolaus is to be found in Felix Jacoby, *Die Fragmente der Griechischen Historiker*, IIA (Leiden, 1961), no. 90 (in this work cited as *FGrH*). References in this article to Nicolaus' preserved works, and to the works of many other Greek historians, are given from the *FGrH* unless noted otherwise. Where appropriate, they are cited from Menahem Stern, *Greek and Latin Authors on Jews and Judaism*, vol. 1 (Jerusalem, 1974) (hereafter cited as *GLAJJ*). The sections of Nicolaus' work relevant to Jewish history may be found in *GLAJJ*, FF 83–97. Stern's earlier and more complete study on Nicolaus as a source for Josephus is "Nicolaus of Damascus as a Source of Jewish History in the Herodian and Hasmonean Age," *Studies in Bible and Jewish History Dedicated to the Memory of Jacob Liver* [Hebrew], ed. E. Uffenheimer (Tel-Aviv, 1971), pp. 375–94. The various traditions that preserved Nicolaus' works are discussed in Wacholder (*op. cit.*, note 2), pp. 1–13.

5. Only Livy's *History of Rome*, with its 142 books, approached the length of Nicolaus' history; Ephorus' *Histories* (70 FF 7–221) contained 30; Diodorus' *Library*, 40; that of Timagenes

(*FGrH* 88), 44(?). See 90 T 11 = Athenaeus VI, 54, p. 249A, where Nicolaus' work is referred to as ἐν τῇ πολυβίβλῳ Ἱστορίαι.

6. Cyrene was in fact a Dorian settlement; see *FGrH*, IIC, 246, lines 41 ff.

7. Both Carolus Mueller, *Fragmenta Historicorum Graecorum*, vol. 3 (Paris 1849) (hereafter *FHG*, cited by volume and page), p. 409, F 69, and Jacoby (*FGrH* IIC, p. 253, lines 5 ff.) are probably correct in assuming that Constantine excerptors mistakenly credited to Nicolaus material (FF 69–70) taken from Dionysius of Halicarnassus, *Antiquitates Romanae*, I, 82, 3–84, 2 = *FHG*, F 69; II, 32, 1–34, 1 = *FGrH*, F 70. But it may be assumed that at this point Nicolaus began his account of Roman history (*FGrH*, IIC, p. 232, lines 31 ff.).

8. Ephorus (*FGrH*, 70) is classified by Jacoby as the first universal historian (*FGrH*, IIC, pp. 26 ff; see also Truesdell S. Brown, *Timaeus of Tauromenium* [Berkeley and Los Angeles, 1958], 13), although he does not regard him as a great historian.

9. *FGrH*, 90 FF 1–6; Ephorus, 70 TT 8; 10; Herodotus, I, 1ff.; Ctesias, IIIC, 688 FF 1 ff.

10. 90 F 1, p. 328, line 20.

11. 90 FF 1–6; Ctesias, IIIC, 688 FF 1 ff.

12. See Ephorus, 70 T 8 = Diodorus IV, 1, 2–3; T 10 = Diodorus XVI, 76, 5, for the reasons for Ephorus' exclusion of mythological history. But Jacoby (*FGrH*, IIC, pp. 25–26) denies that Ephorus was the first to distinguish between "heroic" and "human" history, an idea already present in Herodotus. The distinction is also present in Nicolaus, where the mythological accounts are frequently interspersed with rationalizations such as "they say," "it is said," etc. (F 38, p. 345, line 28; cf. IIC, p. 235, lines 1 ff.).

13. Lydia, in Books IV, VI, and VII (see listing in text). It is not known why this division was made, but as Book VII concludes with the meeting between Croesus and Cyrus, it follows that the other divisions likewise were based on historical epochs.

14. Aside from Ephorus' work, there remains only Diodorus' history, whose correlation of Roman and Greek history by archons and consuls helped to give him a low reputation. It would be of interest to know where Nicolaus placed his account of Egypt.

15. For Herodotus' scheme see Jacoby, *RE*, Supplement II, pp. 282, 330; on Ephorus, see Richard Laqueur, "Ephorus," *Hermes*, XLVI (1911):321 ff.; *FGrH*, IIC, pp. 25 ff.

16. This is standard in Greek and Roman historiography: Herodotus, Polybius, Ephorus, Livy, etc.

17. 90 F 71, dealing with the etymology of Thrace, is difficult to place (see 90 F 71, p. 376, line 1, and Apparatus). But see Wacholder, (*op. cit.*, note 2), 94, n.90, concerning its placement in Book XVIII of the *Histories*.

18. 90 FF 82–102; *GLAJJ* FF 87–93 (not all concern Jews or Judaism). See Jacoby's suggested placement of some of these fragments.

19. Wacholder, (*op. cit.*, note 2), 61–62.

20. *GLAJJ*, FF 83–84 = A I, 159–60; VII, 101–103.

21. A I, 158–59, where Josephus ascribes a book on Abraham to Hecataeus of Abdera, 264 T 8.

22. *GLAJJ*, F 83 = A I, 159.

23. Justin, *Pompei Trogi Fragmenta*, ed. Otto Seel (Leipzig, 1956), vol. 36, p. 2; Pseudo-Eupolemos, 724 F 1.

24. See 90 F 137, pp. 425, line 35 f. Although Nicolaus was following the same tradition found in Justin, he was undoubtedly better informed than Pompeius Trogus, and the likelihood of flattery thus cannot be excluded from Herod's aide.

25. According to II Samuel 8.3, David defeated Hadad-ezer at the Euphrates (I Chronicles 18.3, Hemat on the Euphrates). Damascus subsequently allied itself to Hadad-ezer, who also enlisted the aid of the Ammonites. David's decisive victory seems to have occurred near Helam

(II Sam. 8:3 ff.; 10.3 ff.) G. E. Wright and F. V. Filson, *The Westminster Historical Atlas to the Bible* (Philadelphia 1956), do not locate the place; M. Noth, *The History of Israel* (New York, 1958), p. 154, locates Helam "somewhere in the northernmost land east of Jordan." At any rate, Nicolaus ascribed much greater power to Damascus than the biblical narrator.

26. *GLAJJ*, F 84 = *A* VII, 103; I Kings 20:1 ff. According to the Assyrian inscription (James B. Pritchard, ed., *Ancient Near Eastern Texts Relating to the Old Testament*, 3d ed. [Princeton, 1969], hereafter *ANET*, pp. 278 f., 500 f; *Cambridge Ancient History* [Cambridge, 1923–1939] hereafter *CAH*, III, 22, n. 1), Ahab joined Ben Hadad's alliance, which succeeded in temporarily checking Shalmaneser III of Assyria in 853 B.C. See also M. F. Unger, *Israel and the Aramaeans of Damascus* (London, 1957), pp. 47 ff.

27. As claimed by Richard Laqueur, "Nicolaus," *RE* XVII, no. 20 (1936):363.

28. *GLAJJ*, F 85 = *A* I, 93 = Berossus, 680 F 4c = Hieronymus, 787 F 2.

29. *GLAJJ*, F 85 = *A* I, 95. *A* XX, 25, locates the ark in a region in Carrhes, Mesopotamia, remote from Ararat.

30. II Samuel 8.5; I Chronicles 18.5; II Samuel 10.6.

31. I Kings 15.18 ff.; II Chronicles 16.2, 4; I Kings 20.1 ff.; II Kings 6.24; 8.7. The Septuagint invariably renders Ben Hadad as υἱὸς ʼΑδὲρ.

32. *A* VII, 100; VII, 103; VIII, 363–80, 392, 401. Cf. J. Weill, in T. Reinach, *Oeuvres Complètes de Flavius Josèphe*, II (Paris, 1926), 99, n. 2; Marcus, *AJ*, VII, 100, Vol. V, p. 413, n. b.

33. ʼΑβράμ before Genesis 17.5; ʼΑβραάμ thereafter.

34. *GLAJJ*, F 83, line 2 = *A* I, 159.

35. *A* IX, 93–94 (Marcus, *A* VI, p. 50, n. b.[*LCL*]).

36. *GLAJJ*, F 84 = *A* VII, 103.

37. David flourished ca. 1000–961 B.C.E.; Ahab, ca. 869–850 B.C.E. W. Albright, "The Chronology of the Divided Monarchy of Israel," *BASOR* 100 (1945):16–22.

38. I Kings 20:1 ff.; cf. I Kings 22:1 ff., where Ahab is said to have died while fighting the Aramaeans. Some scholars have questioned whether I Kings 22 refers to Ahab, for Ahab is mentioned only once (verse 20), and verse 41 seems to assume a natural death (Noth [op. cit., note 25], p. 242, n. 1).

39. The references are given in note 26.

40. *A* contains details and additions not found in Kings: the assembly of kings as allies of Adadus "from beyond the Euphrates," *A* VIII, 363; Adadus' invasion of Samaria (*GLAJJ*, F 84 = *A* VII, 101–103) is described more fully in *A* VIII, 364–65 than in I Kings 20. Cf. also *A* IX, 93–94. At any rate, *GLAJJ*, F 84, makes it seem probable that Nicolaus gave a full account of the Damascene Adadoi. He probably utilized, with supplements from other sources, the descriptions found in the biblical books of Syrian prowess. For extrabiblical sources, see the "Zakir" inscription quoted in *ANET*, 655–56.

41. Like Nicolaus (*GLAJJ*, F 83 = *A* I, 159–60), Trogus (*GLAJJ*, F 137) = Justin, XXXVI, 2.3) made Abraham king of Damascus; cf. also *A* IX, 93–94, with Justin's statement concerning Hazael.

42. A. von Gutschmid, *Kleine Schriften*, V (Leipzig, 1889–1894), 218 ff; *FGrH*, IIC, pp. 220–21. For Nicolaus' use of Timagenes, see 88 F 6; 90 F 93; 91 F 12; *FGrH*, IIC, 293.

43. The Joseph-Potiphar drama in *A* II, 41–59 may well be an example of Nicolaus' romantic stories as preserved by Josephus. See Wacholder (*op. cit.*, note 2), p. 57.

44. *GLAJJ*, FF 83–85 = *A* I, 159–60; VII, 101–103; I, 93–95.

45. *FGrH*, IIC, p. 233, lines 26 ff.

46. 90 F 1–3; 56; 66–68.

47. This is disputed, perhaps correctly by J. G. Gager, *Moses in Greco-Roman Paganism* (*SBLMS*, 16; Nashville, 1972), pp. 20–21.

48. *A* II, 238–53.

49. Artapanus, 726 F3.

50. Artapanus, 726 F 3, like *A* II, 238 ff., makes Moses a great military leader and the founder of the Egyptian pantheon and worship; *Antiquities*, however, tells of the romance. For a detailed analysis of Artapanus, see J. Freudenthal, *Alexander Polyhistor* (Breslau, 1875), 143–74.

51. Freudenthal, *ibid.*, pp. 169–71; Thackeray, *A* II, 238, n. b. (*LCL*).

52. A. Schalit, *A* [*Kadmoniyoth ha-yehudim*, Hebrew (Jerusalem 1944–)], vol. 1, pp. xlviii–xlix.

53. Alexander Polyhistor seems to have been a faithful copyist rather than one who would change the ideological version of the story into a romantic affair. As to whether Josephus made extensive use of Alexander (273 F 102), see the literature cited in *FGrH*, IIIa, p. 269, lines 27 ff. Jacoby himself is rather skeptical on the point. As Alexander copied Artapanus' account, it is very unlikely that he is the author of the rewritten version.

54. See Wacholder (*op. cit.*, note 2), Chapter 5. Cf. 90 FF 1; 4; 5; 44, 2 ff; 66, p. 362, line 1; 102; 130, p. 398, line 1.

55. 90 FF 18–20; 72 = *GLAJJ*, FF 83–85 = *A* I, 159–60; VII, 101–103; 93–95; on Cyrus and Croesus, see 90, F 68, 8–9.

56. See Wacholder (*op. cit.*, note 2), Chapter 1, especially pp. 5–6, where differing views are also summarized. Aside from those works cited, scholars treating this period generally take it for granted that Josephus is largely reproducing Nicolaus' words. See, for example, E. Meyer, *Ursprung und Anfänge des Christentums* (Berlin, 1921), vol. 2, p. 164; E. Bickermann, *Der Gott der Makkabäer* (Berlin, 1937), p. 163; cf. V. Tcherikover, *Hellenistic Civilization and the Jews* (Philadelphia, 1960), p. 394.

57. *GLAJJ*, F 87 = *Ap* II, 83.

58. Apollodorus is cited nowhere else in the works of Josephus; Castor, only once more (*Ap* I, 184). *A* XII, 135–37; 358, does cite Polybius, but Josephus' direct use of him is doubtful, for the account frequently differs from that of Polybius; Josephus' use of Timagenes was indirect (*GLAJJ*, F 81 = *A* XIII, 319).

59. Nicolaus is a more likely source than Strabo (cf. *FGrH* II C, p. 294, lines 34ff.) For Nicolaus as a probable source for other historians, see *GLAJJ*, F 85 = *A* I, 93–95; 90 F 141 where, unlike *GLAJJ*, F 87 = *Ap*, II, 83–84, Nicolaus is listed last.

60. Neither Polybius, Apollodorus (244 F 1–356), nor Castor (250 FF 1–20) seem to have given a substantial account of Jewish affairs; for Timagenes, see *FGrH*, IIC, p. 226, lines 28 ff. See also *GLAJJ*, FF 31–33; 34; 77; 80–82.

61. *GLAJJ*, F 88 = *A* XIII, 250.

62. *A* XIII, 245–50; *BJ* I 61.

63. *GLAJJ*, F 88 = *A* XIII, 251.

64. 90 F 79 = Athenaeus VI, 61, p. 252D.

65. *A* XIII, 253.

66. Justus von Destinon, *Die Quellen des Flavius Josephus* (Kiel, 1882), p. 21 ff., was the first to point out that many of the cross-references in Josephus were taken bodily from his sources, especially in Books XIII–XIV of *A*, where he followed closely his Hellenistic sources. See also Reinach, *Oeuvres complètes* (Paris, 1900–1929), vol. 3, p. 171; Marcus, *A* VII, p. 203, n. g.(LCL), and *passim*. Another attempt to justify these references, H. Petersen, "Real and Alleged Literary Projects of Josephus," *AJP* LXXIX (1958):259–274, merely proves that the references belong to the author's sources. But see H. Drüner, *Untersuchungen über Josephus* (Marburg, 1896), p. 1 ff.

67. *GLAJJ*, F 88 = *A* XIII, 250–51.

68. *BJ* I, 62, likewise places Hyrcanus' attack upon the neighboring Syrian cities in 129 B.C.E., but *A* XIII, 254 ff. dates his conquest of these cities only some months later, after Antiochus' death (Marcus, *A* VII, 355, n. e [*LCL*]).

69. Cf. *FGrH*, IIC, p. 232, lines 39 ff.

70. G. Hoelscher, *Quellen des Josephus für die Zeit von Exil bis zum Jüdischen Kriege* (Leipzig, 1905), pp. 4 ff; *RE*, IX, 1946 ff.; and Otto, *RE*, Supplement II, pp. 10 ff., assume a "middle source" between Nicolaus and Josephus, but both grant that the *War* was more dependent on Nicolaus than was the *Antiquities*. See also Reinach (*op. cit.*, note 66), vol. 5, p. 9, n. 1; R. Laqueur, *Der jüdische Historiker Flavius Josephus: ein biographischer Versuch auf neuer quellenkritischer Grundlage* (Giessen, 1920), pp. 136 ff.

71. It is true that in *A*, unlike *BJ*, the sources are frequently cited. Yet the fact remains that the use of Nicolaus in the former is attested, while in the latter it is based on inference.

72. That *BJ* was based on an author writing in the time of Herod may be inferred from the frequent identifications of geographic locations by their older, as well as by their Herodian, names (*BJ* I, 87, 188); cf. Reinach (*op. cit.*, note 66), vol. 5, p. 9, n. 1.

73. *A* XIII, 345–47 = *GLAJJ*, F 89.

74. *A* XIII, 344 = *GLAJJ*, F 82; *FGrH*, IIC, p. 292, lines 9 ff.; p. 293, 15 ff. Jacoby, following Destinon (*op. cit.*, note 66), p. 40 and *passim*, assumes an anonymous source that made use of both Strabo and Nicolaus for *A* XIII, 345–47. For this there is no evidence; see 90 T 12, where Jacoby, *FGrH*, IIC, 230, questions W. Otto's (*RE*, Supplement II, p. 10) argument that ὡς ἔφην was taken from an anonymous source. T 12, as well as *A* XIV, 8–9; XVI, 179–185, leave no doubt that Josephus himself was the critic, rather than some hypothetical author, perhaps a priest or a friend of Agrippa II, who had written a history almost identical to Josephus'.

75. *FGrH*, IIC, p. 226, lines 28 ff.

76. *BJ* I, 86, knows nothing of Ptolemy Lathyrus' atrocities.

77. Stern, *GLAJJ*, F 89 has omitted (as have Jacoby, in F 93, and Mueller, *FGH*, III, 415) the final sentence of *A* XIII, 347: ἔλαβον δὲ καὶ τὴν Πτολεμαΐδα κατὰ κράτος, ὦ καὶ ἐν ἄλλοις φανερὸν πεποιήκαμεν. For a similar phrase used by Nicolaus in reference to Jewish history, see *A* I, 160 (*GLAJJ*, F 83).

78. Posidonius, *GLAJJ*, F 45; Timagenes, *FGrH*, IIC, p. 226, lines 14 ff.; cf. Justin (Trogus), XXXVI (*GLAJJ*, F 137).

79. 90 FF 79–80; 95–98; *FGrH*, IIA, p. 378, line 30; IIC, p. 254, lines 28 ff. FF 79–80 are from Athenaeus, VI, 61, p. 252D; IV, 54, p. 249A, who may be quoting out of context. Still this is what the evidence shows.

80. *GLAJJ*, F 90 = *A* XIV, 8.

81. *FGrH*, IIA, p. 381, lines 29–30.

82. *GLAJJ*, F 86 = *A* XII, 127; *FGrH*, IIC, p. 232, lines 40–41.

83. *A* XIV, 8–XVII, 323.

84. See Wacholder (*op. cit.*, note 2), Chapter 1.

85. See especially the following important studies on this subject. Destinon (*op. cit.*, note 66), pp. 10 ff., makes use of the fragments from the *Autobiography* to exonerate Nicolaus from Josephus' attacks (pp. 91 ff.). Otto, *RE*, Supplement II, pp. 7 ff. and *passim*, gives the most thorough analysis, but he is more interested in proving two anonymous middle sources between Nicolaus and Josephus (cf. note 70), than in an extrinsic evaluation of the evidence. Laqueur (*op. cit.*, note 70), pp. 136 ff., bases his study on extremely subtle differences between *BJ* and *A*; in the latter, Josephus imposed his nationalistic bias, a refutation of which may be found in Marcus' notes to *A*, VII, 384, n. b; 487, n. g; 490, n. a; 491, n. e; 500, n. a (*LCL*). Only Hoelscher, *RE*, IX, 1946 gives due weight to the fragments by finding verbal similarities between them and *BJ*. Otto, however, in a postscript, *RE*, IX, 2513, denies that anything may be deduced from the

similarities alleged by Hoelscher, except that the source of *BJ* was a Hellenistic writer, rather than a Jew. These studies, moreover, were directed primarily at Josephus rather than at Nicolaus.

86. *GLAJJ*, FF 96–97.

87. For a possibly intentional change by Nicolaus, see Wacholder (*op. cit.*, note 2), pp. 32–33.

88. *A* XVI, 26, devotes to this half a sentence, which *GLAJJ*, F 95, describes at length; but this incident, as well as the entire journey of Herod to Agrippa, is omitted in *BJ*.

89. *GLAJJ*, F 96, lines 12 ff.

90. 90 F 100; see Wacholder, (*op. cit.*, note 2), pp. 22–23, 24.

91. *GLAJJ*, F 97.

92. *A* XVI, 335–55 (Nicolaus' mission of reconciliation); cf. 271–99 (Herod's war against the Arabs); 300–34, 356 ff. (Herod's sons).

93. τὸ δὲ σύμπαν, ὁ μὲν Σύλλαιος ἀνεπέμπετο, τὰς δίκας καὶ τὰ χρέα τοῖς δεδανεικόσιν ἀποδώσων, εἶθ' οὕτω κολασθησό μενος (*A* XVI, 353).

94. *A* XVII, 54 ff.

95. *GLAJJ*, F 97, lines 7–8: ὕστερον εὑρὼν κάκιστον ἀπέκτεινεν.

96. Strabo, XVI, 4, 24, records the beheading of Syllaeus, for treacherously causing the death of the Roman general Gallus. For the date, see *CAH*, X, 254.

97. For the evidence, see Wacholder (*op. cit.*, note 2), pp. 32–34, 106–107.

98. *GLAJJ*, F 97, lines 24 ff, lines 37 ff.

99. *GLAJJ*, F 97, lines 61 ff., gives the number of the dead = *A* XVII, 218 = *BJ* II, 13. For the number of those in revolt, see lines 53–55.

100. *GLAJJ*, I, p. 260.

101. *GLAJJ*, F 97, lines 54 ff.

102. *BJ* II, 25–39, 80–100 = *A* XVII, 228–249, 301–323; *GLAJJ*, F 97, lines 55 ff.

103. *GLAJJ*, F 97, lines 55–70.

104. *BJ* II, 97 = *A* XVII, 320. This would seem to mean either that Strabo's Tower and Sebaste (Caesarea) were not Hellenistic cities, since they were retained by Archelaus, or that not all Hellenistic cities were granted autonomy.

105. The indictment of Herod and his family in *BJ* II, 84 ff. = 304 ff. is uncompromising; *GLAJJ*, F 97, lines 55 ff., would indicate that the anger of the Jews was directed primarily against Archelaus.

106. 90 F 136, 10, p. 424, lines 33–34; *GLAJJ*, F 97, lines 70–71.

107. *BJ* II, 26–36; *A* XVII, 230–47. See Otto, *RE*, Supplement II, 169; Reinach (*op. cit.*, note 66), IV, 113, n. 1.

108. *GLAJJ*, FF 94–96.

109. *GLAJJ*, F 97, lines 53–71; the account of the Jewish revolt having been directed against the Greeks is missing in Josephus.

110. *GLAJJ*, FF 94–96, 97, lines 40 ff.

111. See especially *GLAJJ*, FF 96, 97, lines 53–71.

112. In *GLAJJ*, F 97, lines 44–52, for example, Nicolaus tells of his advising that the evidence of Antipater's trial be dispatched to Rome, but not Antipater in person. *BJ* does not mention this; *A* XVII, 144–45, substantially reproduces this advice without mentioning Nicolaus.

113. *GLAJJ*, F 91 = *A* XIV, 66–68.

114. *GLAJJ*, F 91 = *A* XIV, 68 = Strabo, 91 F 14 = Livy, *periocha* 102.

115. 90 F 142 = *A* XVI, 31–57.

116. See Wacholder (*op. cit.*, note 2), Chapter 2.

117. Philo, *De Vita Contemplativa* 17, cites *Iliad* XIII, 5–6.

118. Both Philo and Nicolaus, 90 F 104, 5, interpret ἀβίων (*Iliad* XIII, 5) in the sense of

having no subsistence; Nicolaus explains that this was because the Galactophagi either did not till the land or possessed no houses, or that they lived by the chase only. It is generally agreed that 'Αβίων is a proper name (Liddell-Scott-Jones, *Greek-English Lexicon*, s.v. ἄβιος); this is at least the meaning in Nicolaus' probable source, Ephorus, 70 F 42 = Strabo, VII, 3, 9.

119. 90 F 104, 6.

120. For the tribes having a communal living that are cited in the *Collection*, see 90 F 103d, the Libyrnii; F 103p, the Dapsolibyes; F 104, Galactophagi; F 105, Iberians. It is probable, then, that Nicolaus treated the communal living of the Essenes likewise.

121. See A. Bauer, "Essener," *RE*, Supplement IV (1924), p. 408, who speculates, without giving proof, that Nicolaus was Philo's source for his account of the Essenes. Hoelscher (*op. cit.*, note 70), pp. 8, 14, 16, assumes the same for Josephus' treatment of this sect. His evidence is based on the unfavorable treatment of the Pharisees, in contrast with the favorable description of the Essenes, in Josephus' account of Herod.

122. See the comments of S. Lieberman (an authority on this subject) on *BJ* II, 128, 248, as quoted by M. Smith, "The Description of the Essenes in Josephus and the Philosophumena," *HUCA* 29 (1958):288, n. 55, "the reason alleged to explain them [the Essene practices of being careful with their excretion] probably reflects the misunderstanding of an outside [Gentile?] observer, wherefore it is not reliable evidence for Essene doctrine. He [Lieberman] finds similar misunderstanding in [Josephus'] account of Essene prayer 'to' the sun." Incidentally, Nicolaus' own dislike of slavery (90 F 139) echoes that ascribed to the Essenes (*A* XVIII, 21; Philo, *De Vita Contemplativa*, p. 70). Cf. J. Strugnell, "Flavius Josephus and the Essenes, *Antiquities*, XVIII, 18–22," *JBL* 77(1958):109–110. See also Wacholder (*op. cit.*, note 2), p. 49.

123. The sympathy for the Essenes may be seen in *A* XV, 371–379; XVIII, 18–22; contrasted with the unfavorable treatment of the Pharisees, *A* XIII, 288 ff. See the comments of Reinach (*op. cit.*, note 66), vol. 3, p. 177, n. 3; Marcus, VII, p. 373, n. d. [*LCL*], that the language and style of this passage look like those of Nicolaus; *A* XVII, 41–45. See also Hoelscher (*op. cit.*, note 70), pp. 8, 14, 16; E. Meyer (*op. cit.*, note 56), vol. 2, p. 286, n.

124. For Josephus' self-identification as a Pharisee, see *V* 12; for unfavorable references to this sect, see the preceding note.

125. Philo, *Hypothetica* 11, 1–18, see esp. end; Philo's reference to Herod's favoring of the Essenes is even more evident in *Quod Omnis Probus Liber Sit*, pp. 89–91.

126. *A* XVIII, 22.

127. 90 F 104, 6, describing the Scythian Galactophagi, lists almost the same virtues found in *A* XVIII, 20–21, concerning the Essenes (cf. also *BJ* II, 120 ff.). The Dacians are also mentioned by Nicolaus in F 125, 17, according to the readings of Mueller and Jacoby.

128. Philo, (*op. cit.*, note 121), pp. 75 ff.; *Hypothetica* 11 ff.; and Josephus, *A* XV, 371; *BJ* II, 156; *V* 12, all compare the Jewish sects with the Greek philosophical schools.

129. *GLAJJ*, F 96.

130. H. St. John Thackeray, *A* II, pp. xxii–xxiii (*LCL*); *idem, Josephus, the Man and the Historian* (New York, 1929), p. 40, speculates that Nicolaus had written "probably a separate life of Herod."

131. See 90 TT 1; 13; *GLAJJ*, F 86 = *A* XII, 127.

132. See *ibid.*, pp. 10–20; see also Wacholder (*op. cit.*, note 2), pp. 158–64.

133. Perhaps Strabo relied on his historical work (*FGrH* 91) to describe the contemporary scene.

134. *BJ* I, 13 ff.; *A* XIV, 2: ancient history requires elegance, but modern history calls for accuracy.

135. 90 F 99 = Plutarch, *Brutus*, p. 53. For the falsity of the account, see *FGrH*, IIC, p. 255, lines 20 ff.

136. See *GLAJJ*, FF 94–97, where Herod's interest in virtue, study, and benevolence is pointed out.

137. For Herod's benevolence, see *GLAJJ*, F 95. The charge that the Jews kept to themselves (ἀμιξία) is found in *A* XIII, 245, which Marcus (*LCL*) note c, attributes to Nicolaus' paraphrase of Posidonius, on the basis that Nicolaus is mentioned in 251. Marcus also cites Diodorus XXXIV, 1.

138. 90 F 142 = *A* XVI, 52 ff.

139. *BJ* I, 197–98 = *A* XIV, 141–142.

140. *GLAJJ*, F 97, lines 18–26 = *A* XVI, 371.

141. *GLAJJ*, F 97, lines 1–8; *A* XVI, 299.

142. *GLAJJ*, F 95.

143. In 12 B.C.E., Nicolaus accompanied Herod to Rome (*GLAJJ*, F 96; cf. *A* XVI, 90 ff.). For Herod's presiding over the Olympic games upon his return from Rome, see *BJ* I, 426–428.

144. Cf. *BJ* I, 400.

145. See *GLAJJ*, F 96, n. a, b, and c, which yields the date of Nicolaus' composition of the universal history.

146. See the request of the Gadaraeans to gain their freedom from Herod (*A* XV, 351); for the feeling among other Hellenistic cities, see *GLAJJ*, F 97, lines 53–71.

147. *A* XVI, 271 ff.; (cf. *GLAJJ*, F 97, lines 1–8).

148. *GLAJJ*, F 97, lines 9 ff.; cf. *BJ* I, 431 ff. The point is clear in both Nicolaus and Josephus: the king's domestic troubles constituted the major misfortune embittering the last decade of his rule.

149. See the preceding note. This view is also reflected in *A* XVI, 66 ff., where the struggle among the king's sons follows Herod's triumphal reception by Agrippa.

150. This, at least, is Nicolaus' presentation of the events in his *Autobiography: GLAJJ*, FF 94–96, show Herod at his best; F 97, dealing with last years of the reign, is extremely apologetical.

151. *GLAJJ*, F 93 = *A* XVI, 185.

152. *GLAJJ*, F 97, lines 44–52; 90 F 143; (T 7); *A* XVII, 96–99, 106 ff; *BJ* I, 629, 637–38.

153. *GLAJJ*, F 97, lines 53–70; *A* XVII, 315–316; *BJ* II, 92.

154. *GLAJJ*, F 93, lines 18–21 = *A* XVI, 185; XVII, 121; cf. *BJ*, I, 638. As noted in Wacholder (*op. cit.*, note 2), Chapter 2, Nicolaus seems to have been Josephus' source for Cleopatra's attempted seduction of Herod (*A* XV, 97–102).

155. *A* XV, 25–30. Julius Wellhausen, *Israelitische und jüdische Geschichte*, (Berlin, 1901), p. 318, n. 2, and Otto, *RE*, Supplement II, p. 37, find it hard to believe that a Jewess would have so clearly violated Jewish customs; Joseph Klausner, *Historiah shel ha-bayit ha-sheni*, vol. 4 (Jerusalem, 1954), p. 12, n. 15, however believes the story. The difficulty is not so much the paintings but the fantastic account of the attempted seduction of Antony.

156. *A* XVII, 309.

157. *A* XVII, 315. Nicolaus is said to have added that these people would never have dared to bring charges against Herod when he was alive.

158. *A* XVII, 315.

159. *GLAJJ*, F 97, lines 27 ff; lines 50–52; see also Wacholder (*op. cit.*, note 2), pp. 33–34.

160. 90 T 6 = *A* XVI, 370–372; F 136, 4.

161. *GLAJJ*, F 93, = *A* XVI, 179–182.

162. *GLAJJ*, F 93 = *A* XVI, 183.

163. It is in this connection that Josephus gives a general critique of Nicolaus' biography of Herod (*GLAJJ*, F 93 = *A* XVI, 179–185).

164. Destinon (*op. cit.*, note 66), p. 96. Destinon's generalization discrediting Josephus' other criticisms, however, is not justified.

165. *GLAJJ*, F 90 = *A* XIV, 8–9; cf. Ptolemy, 199 F1.

166. Hoelscher, *RE*, IX, 1945–1946; *FGrH*, IIC, p. 230; see Wacholder (*op. cit.*, note 2), Chapter 4.

167. Laqueur (*op. cit.*, note 70), p. 137. *BJ* I, 123, in the words of Nicolaus, describes Antipater as γένος δ' ἦν Ἰδουμαῖος, προγόνων τε ἕνεκα καὶ πλούτου καὶ τῆς ἄλλης ἰσχύος πρωτεύων τοῦ ἔθνους, which Laqueur renders: "*Um seiner Vorfahren, seines Reichtums und seiner sonstigen Kraft willen die erste Rolle in Volke gespielt.*" Josephus interpreted this to mean that Nicolaus ascribed to Antipater a distinguished Jewish ancestry. But if this sentence is from Nicolaus so also must be its beginning, which says outright that Antipater was an Idumaean. By ignoring this, Laqueur considerably weakens his thesis that Josephus, having turned nationalistic with the passage of time, rewrote the account of Herod given in *A* in accordance with his change of mind.

168. See the preceding note; Otto, *RE*, Suppl. II. 16; IX (Supplemental note, "Herodes," No. 14), 2513–5.

169. *Josippon*, ed. H. Hominer (Jerusalem, 1956), XXXVII, p. 129; see also Wacholder (*op. cit.*, note 2), p. 11.

170. The names of Herod's brothers were Phasael, Joseph, and Pheroras, and of his sister, Salome, all of Antipater and Cypros the "Arabian" (*BJ* I, 181; *A* XIV, 121). Whether Cypros was a Jewish name, see Immanuel Loew, *Die Flora der Juden*, vol. 2 (Vienna & Leipzig, 1924–1934), pp. 218–225; and Hugo Willrich, *Das Haus des Herodes zwischen Jerusalem und Rom* (Heidelberg, 1929), p. 172. F. Abel, *Histoire de la Palestine depuis de la conquête d'Alexandre jusqu'à l'invasion Arabe* (Paris, 1952), vol. 1, p. 314, n. 6, citing *Corpus Inscriptionum Semiticarum* II, 354 and *Recueil d'archéologie orientale*, shows that Phasael was a Semitic name, as its ending shows.

171. Agrippa II, though descended from Mariamne, was regarded by some Jews as "Idumaean" (*M Sotah* 7.8, *Sotah* 41b).

172. It may perhaps be assumed that, had Herod proved popular, his Idumaeum ancestry would not have been a great handicap (see the preceding note).

173. *GLAJJ*, F 93 = *A* XVI, 184.

Postscript to Notes: Further discussion of the relationship between Nicolaus of Damascus and Josephus can be found in Shaye J. D. Cohen, *Josephus in Galilee and Rome: His Vita and Development as a Historian* (Leiden: E. J. Brill, 1979), Tessa Rajak, *Josephus: The Historian and His Society* (Philadelphia: Fortress Press, 1984); and Louis H. Feldman, *Josephus and Modern Scholarship (1937–1980)* (Berlin & New York: Walter de Gruyter, 1984), pp. 402–406.

8 The Sadducees in Josephus

GÜNTHER BAUMBACH

To represent the view of the Sadducees in the writings of Josephus is particularly difficult because the term *Saddoukaioi* occurs in only a very few passages. Apart from the summarizing surveys of the three Jewish "sects" (*haereseis*) in *BJ* II, 119–66; *A* XIII, 171–73; XVIII, 11–22 (cf. *V* 10), *Saddoukaioi* appears only in *A* XIII 293–98 and XX, 199 f., so that their existence is directly attested only for the period of the Hasmoneans and for that of the procurators. Surprisingly, the word *Saddoukaios* does not occur in the parallel reports in *BJ* I, 67 f.; IV, 319–21. This meager attestation of the Sadducees and their different mention in the *War* and in the *Antiquities* prompts the suspicion that our author was by no means without prejudice as regards Sadduceeism. Our intention is so to proceed that first, by means of the summarizing surveys, we shall deal with the characteristics of the Sadducees according to Josephus. Then we shall turn to the question regarding the name *Saddoukaios* and the origin of the group thus designated. In an appendix, we shall attempt to reconstruct a history of the Sadducees. In this connection, we shall not avoid referring to other sources if a sufficiently clear picture is not forthcoming from the statements of Josephus. Unfortunately, these latter sources, too, are by no means "objective" but tendentious. Thus, in the rabbinic literature[1] we find a decidedly pro-Pharisee position, which has led to a polemical distortion of the Sadducees. In the New Testament, which, like the works of Josephus, was not produced until after the destruction of the Temple, the Sadducees occur relatively infrequently and are given such a one-sided characterization as rejectors of the concept of resurrection[2] that a polemical bias and a corresponding lack of precise knowledge about this group must be assumed. It is noteworthy that the word *Sadducees* does not occur in the Jewish Apocrypha, Pseudepigrapha, and Philo. Since the Qumran texts speak repeatedly of the "sons of Sadoq" (Sadoqids) (cf. *1 QS* V, 2.9; *1 QSa* I, 2.24; II, 3; *1 QSb* III, 22; *4 Qfl* I, 17; *CD* IV, 1.3; V, 5), the relationship of the

Sadoqids and the Sadducees is also to be considered. In viewing the presentation of the Sadducees in Josephus, we shall, in addition, have to ask about possible models and their reworking at the hands of our author. Above all, we shall attempt to clarify the tendencies that influenced Josephus in his presentation of the Sadducees and led to the deemphasizing of this group in the *Antiquities* and still more in the *War*.

I

Since the *War* was written about twenty years earlier than the *Antiquities*, we have the earliest mention of the Sadducees in *BJ* II, 119–66. Our author expressly refers to this passage in *A* XIII, 173 and 298 and *A* XVIII, 11 (cf. also *V* 10); in addition, this text is the basis of Hippolytus, *Refutatio omnium haeresium* 9.18–28,[3] where its importance is emphasized. In *BJ* II, the report on the three groups (τρία εἴδη) that "practice philosophy" among the Jews falls within a section that refers to the year 6 A.D., in which there appeared an ἰδία αἵρεσις that differed from the other Jewish groups. By this "sect of its own" is meant the party of the Sicarii founded by Judas the Galilaean; these were the nucleus of the Jewish resistance movement.[4] The reason for the insertion of this excursus on the Jewish groups, therefore, is the mention of the new party that arose in 6 A.D. With this representation, Josephus consciously invokes the period of the Roman procurators. For all four groups, he uses without difference in meaning the terms αἵρεσις (*BJ* II, 118, 122, 137, 142, 162; *A* XIII, 171, 288, 293; XX, 199; *V* 10, 12, 191, 197), γένος (*BJ* II, 119; VII, 268; *A* XIII, 172, 297; XV, 371), εἶδος (*BJ* II, 119, 254) and τάγμα (*BJ* II, 122, 125, 164); thereby, as φιλοσοφεῖται in *BJ* II, 119 shows, the groups are described and understood in the sense of philosophical schools. Accordingly, in characterizing these schools, the theoretical questions of dispute are emphasized. These abstractions are presented with a Greek reading public in mind.[5]

It is difficult to recognize the viewpoint that could have influenced Josephus in his arrangement of the parties. As a member of the order of the Pharisees (cf. *V* 12), it is understandable that he put this school in first place (*BJ* II, 119).[6] Yet, it is surprising that, with his individual presentations, he begins with the Essenes and describes their doctrine and life in forty-three paragraphs (119–61), thereafter devoting only two paragraphs each to the Pharisees (162 f.) and the Sadducees (164 f.), together with a single paragraph on both the Pharisees and the Sadducees together (166). The author's sympathy in this survey is so clearly with the Essenes that one can assume that here Josephus used a source that came from "a Greek-educated Jew who must have been well acquainted with a former adherent or novice of the sect or even had belonged to it for some time."[7] Josephus could have made such good use of the Essene source probably because the Essenes, described as "ministers of peace" (135), very conveniently served his purpose in the *War* of encouraging the Hellenistic Jews to seek peace and concord.[8] He consciously contrasts the terrifying example of the small, seditious Judas-group (118), which, according to the *War*, was guilty of the entire calamity of the Jewish War,[9] with the edifying picture of the peaceful Essenes, who, through their positive philosophical position, enhance the essence of Jewry in the Roman world. It probably also is because of this apologetic purpose that the Pharisees and the Sadducees are seen in 162–66 in only a philosophical aspect, namely in respect to their position on *heimarmene* ("fate").[10] The fact that Josephus here uses a *terminus technicus* of Stoic philosophy, for which there is no exact Hebrew equivalent,[11] is explained on the basis of this apologetic purpose. However, in ascribing to the Sadducees a disavowal of *heimarmene*, he in fact stamps them as atheists, that is, as Epicureans; for, according to *A* X, 278, they disavowed *pronoia*, ("providence")[12] which for Josephus is identical with *heimarmene*, and asserted that God had no concern for human affairs. To this extent a pronounced anti-Saducean tendency here makes itself felt. But it is worth noting that Josephus nowhere presumes an equation of the Sadducees with the Epicureans and never describes the Sadducees as atheists in the sense of Psalm 14:1, 53:2; therefore, he never questions their belonging to Jewry.[13]

Major doubts are also to be registered regarding Josephus' manner of presentation, according to which the question of predestination and free will formed the criterion for differentiation among the various Jewish groups. But, behind this formulation, there could be concealed a Jewish problem of a soteriological sort.[14] Possibly, the Sadducean doctrine wanted to remove God from the objection that he could stand in some relation with evil. If evil happens, it is uniquely and solely to be imputed to man, to his "choice" and therefore to his responsibility. With this emphasis on freedom of choice, the Sadducees would stand entirely in the tradition of Ben Sira, as Leszynsky[15] has already noticed. Especially close is the connection with Ben Sira 15; for here in verses 11–13 the attribution of sins to God is denied, and in verses 14–17 man's freedom to do God's will is emphasized. In addition, nowhere in Ben Sira do we find statements about resurrection; and accordingly divine retribution is there to be thought of as immanent, just as it is with the Sadducees, according to *BJ* II, 165.[16]

The already-mentioned deprecatory tendency of this presentation of the Sadducees, achieved through their being slighted, is especially clear in 166: the adherents of this group have unseemly forms of behavior toward their own people; i.e., they treat their comrades as foreigners, while, in contrast, the

Pharisees lead an exemplary social life. Behind such deprecatory statements concerning the Sadducees could lie Josephus' personal experiences, as we shall discuss later.

Somewhat different is the picture that Josephus gives of the Sadducees in the *Antiquities,* although in *A* XIII, 173, 298, and XVIII, 11 he expressly refers to *BJ* II, 119–66. The survey of the three Jewish parties in *A* XIII, 171–73 has the character of an insertion, precisely like that in *BJ* II, 119–66: it interrupts the description of the time of Jonathan in order to emphasize that "the Jews are also a distinguished cultural factor, since they have schools of philosophy." [17] At the same time, the transfer of John Hyrcanus from the Pharisees to the Sadducees, described in *A* XIII, 288–298, is foreshadowed through this insertion. Since this section is "much less colored by Judaism than the corresponding passage in the *War,* Josephus here would appear to be closely dependent upon Nicolaus." [18] To begin with, the arrangement of the three groups is precisely like that of *BJ* II, 119: the Pharisees occupy first place, and next come the Sadducees and the Essenes. But, in contrast to the *War,* the individual presentation begins with the Pharisees, and only afterwards deals with the Essenes and the Sadducees. In addition, the three descriptions in *Antiquities* XIII are of approximately the same length—in contrast to the overly long Essene chapter in *BJ* II, 119–61. At the time of the composition of the *Antiquities,* Josephus obviously had no further reason to extol the Essenes especially. As a whole, the presentation is objective. Characteristic of it is the lack of disparaging statements about the Sadducees. Instead of different "philosophies," the topic is now only of different "anthropologies" ($\pi\epsilon\rho i \ \tau\tilde{\omega}\nu \ \dot{\alpha}\nu\theta\rho\omega\pi i\nu\omega\nu \ \pi\rho\alpha\gamma\mu\dot{\alpha}\tau\omega\nu \ i\nu\omega\nu$ [171]), whereby it becomes patently obvious that a comprehensive characterization of the three Jewish parties is not intended, but that it is only a complex matter important for Greek readers, which is to be singled out. We can assume but not prove that Josephus, with the reference to *BJ* II, 119 ff. in 173, wanted, at least consciously, to express the idea that this "new composition" was "to correct the older" ones, for "the assessment had been displaced." [19]

With the individual presentation of the three groups, it is surprising that here the language is consciously nontheological: the Hellenistic concept of *heimarmene* is not paraphrased by *theos,* nor is it directly brought into connection with God. Since 173 presents a very factual formulation and no derogatory tendency can be discerned in it, Josephus probably took over his model without redactional change. [20] In *A* XVIII, 11–22 Josephus mentions first the Essenes, then the Sadducees, and third the Pharisees. In dealing with these three different "philosophies," he expressly refers to *BJ* II, 119–66, without regard to *A* XIII, 171–73. In his individual presentation of these "philosophical schools," he begins, as in *A* XIII, 171 ff., with the Pharisees and then deals with the Sadducees and the Essenes, respectively. The section on the Sadducees (16 f.) is the shortest, whereas those on the Pharisees (12–15) and the Essenes (18–22) are about equal in length, and each is more than twice as long as the description of the Sadducees (10 : 22 : 25 lines). As in *BJ* II, here, too, Josephus attaches the report on the three schools, which had existed among the Jews "from the most ancient times," to the mention of the Judas group. Nevertheless, here, in contrast to *BJ* II, the Judas group, is traced back to a "Pharisee Saddok," on the one hand, and is designated as the "fourth philosophical school" (9), on the other. In appending this presentation of the special nature of the "fourth philosophical school" (23–25), Josephus achieves an organic and seamless contextual juncture, whereby this report advantageously stands out against those previously treated. Not only as regards its logical connection with the context but also in regard to the content of the presentation, this section appears to be the most clearly conceived and the best composed. Here, the controversy of the Hellenistic philosophers concerning free will is conspicuously in the background. On the other hand, the ethico-religious behavior, as practiced by the individual groups, is given a relatively expansive treatment. Since, in addition, typically extra-Judeo-Hellenistic concepts, which were decisive in *A* XIII, 171–73, are here quite secondary—*heimarmene* occurs only in 13 and is completely absent in the treatment of the Sadducees and the Essenes—this report must go back to a Jew as composer, probably to Josephus himself.[21] Only thus is it understandable that here the Jewish character of the Sadducees appears most prominent, and the religious profile of this group is most clearly recognizable. In a similarly prominent fashion, the Sadducean denial of the resurrection of the dead is brought into association with the general adherence to the Torah. Obviously both are most intimately interconnected: precisely because the Sadducees totally adhere to the Torah, they deny the resurrection of the dead. This indicates that, since it is referred to as *nomos,* the Pentateuch must here be meant as the center of the written Torah; for in it is found no mention of a resurrection of the dead.[22] *A* XIII, 297 f. points clearly in the same direction: here the Sadducees reject the oral Torah of the Pharisees, the "transmission of the fathers," and rely exclusively on the written Torah.[23] The γάρ in 16 is surprising; for with it the prominent statement on the denial of the resurrection of the dead and the adherence to the written Torah is established by the following assertion: "in fact, they reckon it a virtue to dispute with the teachers of the path of wisdom that they pursue." It, therefore, follows, on the one hand, that here it is a question not of disputations on philosophical subjects but on correct biblical exegesis, and, on the other hand, that "this freedom of disputation presents the ground for the denial of every obligation which is not derived from the written Torah and therefore from the tradition."[24] Accordingly, 16 refers to the rejection of the Pharisees' principle of authority, which is connected with the constitutive meaning of the tradition of the fathers.[25] The mention of "wisdom" in this connection suggests that the Sadducean teachers knew that they were committed to the wisdom tradition of the Old Testament and of early Jewry and developed their own educational forms on this foundation.[26]

According to 17, this Sadducean wisdom doctrine found approval "with only a few men"; of course, here it is a question of very highly placed dignitaries, the aristocratic ruling class, who owed their position to their wealth or their noble ancestry.[27] Because, according to *Vita* 1, membership in the priestly class was considered by the Jewry of that time as the mark of pre-eminent ancestry,[28] the aristocratic ruling class should here be primarily understood as the priestly aristocracy.[29] Accordingly, in the case of the Sadducees, it must have been a question of an exclusively priestly ruling class, "the party of the highest priestly aristocracy,"[30] to which "obviously aristocratic laymen could have been attached without modifying its essence."[31]

After this statement about the high social status of the Sadducees, it is quite surprising to find that, in fact, they could achieve something only if they submitted to the guidelines of the Pharisees, "since otherwise the masses would not tolerate them." To elucidate this assertion one usually refers to *A* XIII, 288 and to *Yoma* 19b and *Niddah* 33b, because these passages likewise attest to the great influence of the Pharisees and emphasize that "normally the Sadducees who had attained positions had to submit to the Pharisaic precepts."[32] In view of the prevailing power structure, the biography of Josephus and the pro-Pharisaic character of rabbinic literature, such an anti-Sadducean assertion must fundamentally be called into question.[33]

In *Vita* 10, Josephus also refers to the three groups, which, as he explicitly indicates, he has "often" mentioned. This means that he presupposes knowledge of them on the part of his readers and, therefore, refrains from further details. In the first place, he mentions the Pharisees, as in *BJ* II, 119; *A* XIII, 171; in the second place, the Sadducees, as in *BJ* II, 119; *A* XIII, 171; XVIII, 11; and in the third place, the Essenes, as in *BJ* II, 119; *A* XIII, 171. Here, naturally, nothing is said about a fourth group, because Josephus for good reason guards against admitting any references to the Zealots' rebellious movement. From this passage, it becomes clear why Josephus put the Pharisees in first place: his goal lay in studying all three groups and ascertaining "the best," in order to associate himself with it. Since, according to 12, he began in his nineteenth year to conduct his life in accordance with Pharisaic rules, he obviously intends, with this reference, to proclaim the party of the Pharisees as "the best." Behind this, there is a definite apologetic purpose to be assumed, a purpose that may have also influenced his presentation of the Sadducees.

II

Now that we have dealt with the general statements of Josephus on the Sadducees, as they appear in the excursuses on the Jewish philosophical schools in the *War* and *Antiquities*, we must investigate what we can learn from Josephus about the name and the origin of this group. Unfortunately, our author fails us completely: neither does he address himself to the question of the meaning of the name of the Sadducees nor does he give information on the origin of this party. The chief difficulty with the meaning of Σαδδουκαῖοι lies in the fact "that we do not know with certitude the vocalization of this word in Semitic."[34] In view of *BJ* II, 451, 628 (Σαδούκι), *A* XVIII, 4 (Σάδδωκος) and *Avoth de-Rabbi Nathan* 5.26 (sadoqim), Σαδδουκαῖος ought to go back to the form Sadoq/Saddouq or to an obviously recent Hebrew linguistic form in the manner of what was originally or pertained to an adjective *ṣadduqi*.[35] Hence, it follows that the term Σαδδουκαῖος or *ṣadduqi* goes back to a proper name, Ṣadoq, Septuagint Σαδδούκ, and can, through the related term *ben ṣadoq*, "the son of Sadok," be restored as "Sadokid."[36] Accordingly, the Sadducees must have traced themselves back to some Sadoq and have stood in some connection with the Sadoqids of the Old Testament and the "sons of Sadoq" of the Qumran texts. There are primarily two possibilities of interpretation in regard to this Sadoq. The first appeals to *Avoth de-Rabbi Nathan* 5, according to which Antigonos of Soko is said to have had two students named Sadoq and Boethos. From this, G. F. Moore[37] concludes: "The possibility remains that the party, or sect, perpetuates the name of some [to us] unknown founder or leader." Since, however, the *Avoth de-Rabbi Nathan* exists in two different recensions and is very controversial, especially in respect to its reliability, it can afford no certain foundation on which to answer the question of the originator of the party of the Sadducees.[38] To that extent the division of this group, maintained by the *Avoth de-Rabbi Nathan*, into Sadducees and Boethusians, whereby the Sadducees are to be traced back to a Sadoq and the Boethusians to Boethos, must be regarded as artificial.[39] On the other hand, the reference to Sadoq as the founder of the Sadducees might contain a reliable historical recollection, yet scarcely in the sense of the aforementioned relation to his students. The majority of scholars trace the Sadoqids/Sadducees back to the high priest from David's entourage (see II Sam. 15:24 ff.; 17:15; 19:12).[40] The priestly character of this party corresponds to its priestly origin. The sons of Sadoq, who derive themselves from this Sadoq, emerged in the course of time at the head of the hierocracy of Jerusalem, from whom were appointed the high priests from time to time.[41]

The derivation of the Sadducees from the descendants of Sadoq, however, should not leave out of account the following surprising fact. On the one hand, the conservative Sadoqid clan of high priests emigrated with Onias III to Egypt, established a Jewish temple[42] in Leontopolis and, in addition, participated in the creation of the Qumran community, as the priestly designation "sons of Sadoq" shows.[43] On the other hand, the name *Sadducee* was claimed by the official Jerusalem hierocracy, as New Testament statements on the Sadducees show.[44] In this connection, we now turn to the first concrete mention of the Sadducees in the *Antiquities*, as it appears in *A* XIII, 288–96, in dealing with the description of the reign of John Hyrcanus (135–104 B.C.), who is said to have been at first a student of the Pharisees (289). During a feast, he was reproached by a Pharisee named Eleazar as being unworthy of the office of high priest because his mother was, so Eleazar maintained, a prisoner of war (292). Since John Hyrcanus assumed that Eleazar had made this slanderous charge with the support of all the Pharisees, he withdrew from them and attached himself to the Sadducees (296).

Inasmuch as a similar anecdote is reported in the Babylonian Talmud, *Qiddushin* 66a, but in connection with Alexander Jannaeus (103–76 B.C.) and without mention of the Sadducees, we must infer a common source.[45] Yet, what in this *Wanderlegende* can be used for historical reconstruction? It appears that with this legend an attempt was made to provide an answer to the question as to how the Maccabean-Hasmoneans, who in their religious connection originally stood far closer to the Pharisees than to the Sadducees,[46] attached themselves to the Sadducees. The reason for this change is probably to be sought in the need of the Hasmoneans to win the support of the powerful Jerusalem hierocracy, because of the objection raised against them by the Pharisaic side regarding the legitimacy of their holding the office of high priest. Accordingly, the "Sadducees" mentioned in *A* XIII, 296, cannot be the Sadoqids who emigrated to Leontopolis and Qumran but only the priestly majority who remained in the Temple of Jerusalem, that is, those who adopted the honorary title Sadoqids/Sadducees, ostensibly in order to validate their legal claim; for they controlled the administration of sacred justice and made use of the priestly Sadoqid halakhah.[47] Consequently, it follows that we must reckon with two flanks of the Sadoqid-Sadducean movement: (1) the "pure Sadoqids," who emphasized the legitimacy of their origin, validated their claims without compromise and therefore emigrated from Jerusalem to Leontopolis and Qumran; and (2) the "priestly majority," who remained in the Temple of Jerusalem.[48]

This division into two flanks and their constituting the priestly majority who remained in the Temple of Jerusalem as the αἵρεσις τῶν Σαδδουκαίων must have been completed in the time of Jonathan (ca. 160–143 B.C.), for "the reign of Jonathan was a period of crisis for the Sadducees. The High Priesthood had passed to a new family, and members of the Jerusalem aristocracy, who regarded themselves as unjustly deprived of their rights by the rise of *novi homines*, organized themselves as a conservative group under the slogan of the ancient theocratic authority."[49] Also supporting this is the fact that Josephus inserted the first survey of the three Jewish religious parties (A XIII, 171–173) into his description of the time of Jonathan (A XIII, 145–183). Consequently, it can be seen as somewhat probable that the three Jewish groups, which determined the appearance of Jewry at the beginning of the Christian Era, emerged for the first time in the middle of the second century B.C. as separate "parties," distinct from older movements. The separation of the Sadducees from the Sadoqids was so brought about that "sons of Sadoq," a designation of origin and family, now became a designation of class. From the middle of the second century B.C., therefore, we can speak of the Sadducees as the party of the class of priestly nobility of Jerusalem. It is precisely to this hierocratic class-party that A XVIII, 17 refers. According to this section, only the most prominent members of the population, that is, the priestly aristocracy, belonged to the Sadducees. Also, all the other statements found in Josephus concerning the Sadducees are to be referred to this "opportunistic wing" (J. Maier) or to this "normative Sadduceeism" (R. Eisenman).

Consequently, it follows that this flank of the Sadoqids thought in strongly conservative terms, rejected all Pharisaic innovation (the resurrection of the dead, the oral Torah, and high regard for scribes) and bound themselves closely to the letter of Scripture. This emphatic adherence to the written Torah found favor with a priestly party for economic reasons as well: "The Law of Moses granted the priestly class so many privileges that they might well prefer to content themselves with the Written Law rather than endanger their position by various interpretations, not all of which were invariably to their profit."[50] But this correct reference to the economic advantages for the priesthood, which resulted from the Saducean emphasis on writing, should not mislead us into assigning to them only a political motivation and not a religious one;[51] for a priestly aristocracy will always establish its prominence in priestly terms, that is, in religious terms, and will rely on old traditions that are sanctioned and made legitimate through their antiquity.[52] On the basis of such a statically established priestly way of thinking, the Sadducees rejected all innovations, including also the Pharisaic tradition of the fathers. This strongly priestly-conservative position joins the "Sadoqids" with the "Sadducees" and reveals both as the flanks of one movement.[53]

III

A presentation of the history of the Jewish group that Josephus designates as *Sadducees* must start with the period of the Hasmoneans, because this party is directly mentioned for the first time in connection with John Hyrcanus. The transference, described in A XIII, 288, of this high priest–regent to the side of the Sadducees surprisingly is not even allusively criticized by Josephus.

The Pharisaic reproach of the illegitimacy of the Hasmonean high priesthood consequently is not shared by him; for otherwise, he could not so unrestrictedly glorify John Hyrcanus in *A* XIII, 299f and see in him the embodiment of the office of high priest. Josephus totally avoids mentioning the fact that behind such a turning of the Hasmoneans to the Sadducees lay firm political and economic reasons.[54] The symbiosis of Hasmoneans and Sadducees he evaluates very positively, for he himself came from a Hasmonean family (cf. *V* 2). The fact that John Hyrcanus was the first Jewish leader to employ foreign mercenaries (cf. *A* XIII, 249), that he caused the destruction of the Samaritan central shrine on Mount Gerizim (cf. *A* XIII, 254 ff.), in order to eliminate every sign of a political and religious independence on the part of the Samaritans and to attach their land to Jerusalem as a political and religious center, and that he also wanted to convert the Idumaeans to Judaism through compulsory circumcision[55]—all this obviously met with the agreement of the Sadoqids/Sadducees and caused Josephus no problem.

The same observation can be made in the case of the description of the Judaizing policy of Alexander Jannaeus (103–76 B.C.), which was likewise of a cultic-national nature.[56]

While such a politico-militaristic expansion-aspiration was rejected by the Pharisees,[57] it certainly coincided with the theocratic interests of the Sadducees; for "Saducean or Sadoqid signifies a connection with the idea of a particular national temple-state that, in the sense of traditional eschatological expectations of salvation, forms the kernel for the expiation of the Holy Land."[58]

The close relation between Hasmoneans and Sadducees was dissolved under Salome Alexandra (76–67 B.C.). She restricted the Pharisees' privileges and demoted the Sadducees, who "perceived themselves as the pillars of the structure of the Hasmonean state."[59] She thus initiated the decline of the Hasmonean Jewish national state and is therefore not exactly sympathetically described by Josephus (cf. *A* XIII, 408 ff.; *BJ* I, 107–112).

The Roman period, which for Palestine began in the year 63 B.C., from the first is under an ill omen in Josephus: "The royal power which had formerly been bestowed on those who were high priests by birth became the privilege of commoners" (*A* XIV, 78). Therefore, Josephus can find no sympathy for Herod the Great (40–4 B.C.). For the Sadducees with their pro-Hasmonean orientation, a difficult time began in particular with the reign of Herod; for the king did not forget that it had been the Synhedrion, with its Hasmonean orientation, that had called him to account for his illegal murder of the Galilean rebels under Ezechias/Hiskia.[60] Since Herod, invested with the rank of *rex socius et amicus populi Romani,* also took over the administration of justice,[61] the tensions with the Synhedrion and also with the priestly nobility must have increased, since the nobility through its foremost representative, the high priest, controlled the highest offices of law, government, and religion.[62] Hence is explained the fact that Herod, after his storming of Jerusalem in 37 B.C., according to *A* XIV, 175, killed "all the members of the Synhedrion" with the exception of one Pharisee and, according to the less exaggerated and therefore more reliable report[63] in *A* XV, 6, had "forty-five of the leading men of Antigonus' party" killed. Both accounts clarify the king's desire to weaken the Sadducee-backed Synhedrion and the power base of the high priest.

If Josephus in his description of the period of Herod and that of the Roman procurators—with the exception of Ananus II (Hannas the Younger) in *A* XX, 199 ff.—never expressly mentions Sadducees, one should not therefore infer that they were insignificant or did not even exist, for Acts 5:17, 4:1, 23:6 mention that the priestly nobility in the first centuries before and after Christ had a Sadducean orientation.[64] Certainly, Herod was responsible for a significant interference in the history of the Sadducees; for "Herod abandoned the practice of appointing those of Asamonaean lineage as high priests, and, with the exception of Aristobulos alone, assigned the office to some insignificant persons who were merely of priestly descent" (*A* XX, 247). This pro-Hasmonean assertion of Josephus does not correspond to actuality. For, though Herod wanted to weaken the popular Hasmonean family, which of course displeased Josephus, he achieved this not by appointing insignificant priests but by adherence to old, pre-Hasmonean traditions. The first high priest whom Herod appointed after eliminating Antigonos was named Hananel and is said, according to *A* XV, 22, to have come from Babylon. Significantly, however, he appears in the *MParah* 3.5 as an "Egyptian," so that we can assume, along with R. Meyer, "that Herod, on grounds of legitimacy, appointed a priest from Leontopolis, who was qualified to be a bearer of the authentic Sadducean traditions, in order also to suppress ideologically the Hasmonean high priesthood."[65]

Of greatest significance for the following period was the high priest Simon, son of Boethos (*A* XV, 320 ff.), who is said to have attained to such a high honor only because he had a daughter (Mariamne II) who had the reputation of being the most beautiful woman of her time. In order to be able to contract a high-ranking marriage for her, her father, Simon, was elevated to the position of high priest. This reason shows only the frantic effort of Josephus to conceal the real causes of Herod's religious policies. Since the legitimacy of the house of Boethos is never questioned in rabbinic literature, it is thus to be reckoned that Boethos' family came from Leontopolis and was of purely Sadoqid origin.[66] Accordingly, Herod, with the bestowal of the rank of high priest on the family of Boethos, wanted to make a connection with old Sadoqid traditions and thus to show himself, imitating his prototype in Rome, as *restaurator morum majorum;* for "in the year 47, the Oniads were disloyal to Cleopatra and joined Caesar and . . . Herod. To take a representative of this cult to Jerusalem corresponded completely with the religious politics of Herod." [67]

After the time of Herod the Great, therefore, Sadduceeism can be designated as "Boethusian Sadduceeism" (E. Eisenman), except that one should not characterize these Sadducees so generally as "the corrupt Sadducee priesthood." [68] Rather, we should understand them as a hierocratic privileged party that came from Sadoqid tradition but thanks only to the favor of a "half-Jew" (A XIV, 403) attained to power and rank and, therefore, compromised itself. To that extent, under Herod a second transformation was effected within Sadduceeism, [69] which determined its history until the end of the Second Temple. Because in this period the family of Boethus showed itself as the most powerful priestly family, it is not surprising that in rabbinic literature the expressions Sadducees and Boethusians are used interchangeably [70] and that "toward the end of the first century A.D., Josephus and the rabbis joined together under 'Sadduceeism' and 'Boethusianism' concepts that no longer corresponded to the currently prevailing ideas in the synagogue." [71]

Eight priests in all were reckoned as belonging to the Boethos family in the Herodian and Roman period, and the same number to the Hannas family. [72] The behavior of these high priests, however, in no way confirms the often-advocated thesis that the Sadducees were basically "the party of collaboration." [73] The long tenure of Ananus I (Hannas the Elder, 6–15 A.D.) and that of Joseph Caiaphas (18–36/37 A.D.) certainly indicate a good relationship with the Romans, but most of the high priests in this period were removed from office by the Romans after only a short tenure. Thus Ismael son of Phiabi, Eleazar son of Hannas (Ananus), and Simon son of Kamithos were each in office for only about one year (15–18 A.D.; cf. A XVIII, 34), although Josephus does not tell us the reasons for their removal from office. It is tempting to assume that these high priests emphasized their Saducean ancestry too strongly and therefore became unbearable. Significantly, in A XVII, 339, Josephus reports that the high priest Joazar, who belonged to the Boethos family, made common cause with the rebels and therefore was removed from his position by Archelaos, the ethnarch of Judea (4 B.C.–6 A.D.). According to A XVIII, 3, on the other hand, he is said to have persuaded the Jews not to revolt against the census of Quirinius. According to A XVIII, 26, he became involved in a conflict with the populace and was deposed by Quirinius, who replaced him with Ananus II (Hannas the Elder). Yet, historically it probably is not correct to think that the Romans would have removed from office a high priest who is said to have furthered adherence to Roman measures, merely in order to please the Jews, who were disposed to be Rome's enemies. [74]

A high priest of the Roman period, Ananus II (Hannas the Younger, 62 A.D.) is designated by Josephus expressly as belonging to the group of the Sadducees (A XX, 199). This Ananus II arbitrarily convened the Synhedrion in order to accuse a few men, among them Jesus' brother James, of violating the law and to condemn them to be stoned to death (*A* XX, 200). He thereby embittered "the most zealous observers of the Law"—that is, the Pharisees (cf. *BJ* II, 162; *V* 191)—who complained about this action of the Sadducean high priest before the Jewish king Agrippa I and the Roman procurator Albinus and achieved his immediate removal from office (cf. *A* XX, 201–203). This episode, which happened in 62 A.D., is extraordinarily interesting for several reasons. First it indicates that in order to convene the Synhedrion the high priest always needed the agreement of the Roman procurator.[75] Second, it reveals the tension between Sadducees and Pharisees, in that the latter had no scruples about accusing the Sadducean high priest before the occupation authority. Therefore, we must regard as characteristically loyal to the Romans these "most zealous observers of the Law," for whom also the Roman rule came from God.[76] Third, this event shows how strongly national-particularistic the high priest was as the leading representative of the Sadducees and how little prepared the Sadducees accordingly were to allow themselves to be degraded into the willing tool of the Romans. Fourth, one can discern here that Sadduceeism was the mortal enemy of the new Christianity, because the latter critically opposed both the "national-particularistic eschatology of salvation"[77] and the rigid application of the law as practiced in Sadduceeism.[78]

How strongly determined by the national mood this high priest was is shown by his action reported in *BJ* II, 648 f. (cf. II, 563): In carrying out a commission given him by the populace to strengthen the city walls, he not only had them repaired but also saw to their refortification. As his motivating purpose, Josephus reports that he thereby wanted "to bend the malcontents and the infatuated so-called zealots to a more salutary policy" (*BJ* II, 651). This politically astute attempt to keep the malcontents from extreme and ill-considered actions nevertheless failed and was ultimately responsible for his murder.[79] Now, it is surprising that in *BJ* IV, 316–320, Josephus gives an extraordinarily positive evaluation of this high priest but is silent about his belonging to the Sadducees, while in *A* XX, 199 ff., he depicts him negatively and expressly designates him as a Sadducee. Both passages could be reconciled by the fact that for Josephus a positive characteristic was incompatible with the notion of "Sadducee," and he therefore had to present either a positive depiction without mentioning membership in the Sadducees or a negative characterization with emphasis on membership in the Sadducees. In any case, here we have a literary tendency that could be founded in the biography of our author.

The fact that a few members of the priestly aristocracy made common cause with the rebels and that the Sadducean high priest Ananus II made "preparations for the war" (*BJ* IV, 320) was based on the conservative national-particular position of the Sadducees, who in this area were associated with the priestly zealots.[80] The youth of the priestly nobility took part in the war against the Romans under the leadership of Eleazar, a son of the high priest Ananias,[81] and therefore could be designated as "zealous Sadducees."[82] In contrast to this revolutionary position, the older generation of the priestly nobility attempted to achieve the freedom of the Jewish temple-state, centered in cult around the Jerusalem sanctuary, through political means, adroit maneuvering, and utilization of their own power base. Therefore, they rejected all apocalyptic "zeal" and every form of radicalism that was eschatologically established, as being typical for the Zealots and Sicarii. For this reason, one of the most significant personalities of the Boethos family, the high priest Matthias, son of Boethos, supported even Simon Bar Giora but was later put to death by him, together with three of the priest's sons.[83] With the destruction of the Temple of Jerusalem in 70 A.D., the group of the Sadducees lost their historical significance and soon vanished from the scene.[84]

IV

In our attempt to represent the origin, history and essence of Sadduceeism through the writing of Josephus, it has been shown again and again how difficult such an undertaking is. On the one hand, Sadducees are mentioned relatively seldom, and there are few statements concerning their origin and the precise course of their historical development and their final phase. On the other hand, there is seen a varying mode of presentation and evaluation of the individual Jewish groups in the *War* and in the *Antiquities*. Ostensibly, Josephus, as a writer, in every case follows quite definite tendencies, which also influenced his depictions of the Sadducees. R. Laqueur[85] had already noticed that Josephus "in the various epochs of his life presents in totally different ways the events that he had lived through and the earlier history of the Jews and Romans, not on the basis of some new source but because he himself had arrived at a different view of matters. Where Josephus has a prejudice he is accustomed not to deal with the truth accurately." In the *War* our author's concern is "to present the deeds of the two Flavians in a clear light," whereby he answers "the difficult question as to those responsible for the great catastrophe, that neither the Romans nor the Jewish people as a whole can be blamed: only a small group of Jews are guilty. Josephus calls them 'tyrants' or also 'robbers.'"[86] By "tyrants" Josephus means the leaders of the rebellion,[87] and by the designation "robbers" "he wants to represent the Zealots as unjust rebels and lawless criminals from the Roman point of view."[88] This pro-Roman and anti-Zealot position may have been the reason for Josephus' avoiding in the *War* anything that could bring his own priestly class into the shade.

In *BJ* I, 3 he does indeed mention that he is a priest but is silent about his membership in the priestly class of Jehoiarib and about his descent from the Hasmoneans (cf. *V* 1f. and *Ap* 1, 54). Likewise, there is no reference to the fact that he, as a member of the priestly nobility of Jerusalem, was "close friends with the leading Sadducees." [89] Also the membership of leading priests in the party of the Sadducees is not mentioned. Since the only statement that Josephus makes in the *War* concerning the Sadducees has a clearly negative tone, we can assume, together with H. Rasp,[90] that Josephus "attaches to the Sadducees the qualities which the Greeks censured in the Jews" in order to take revenge on them as "his blood-related stock, before whom he had to defend himself in his conscience because of his repeated desertion." Regarding the historical question of the essence and the meaning of Sadduceeism, the *War* therefore makes no contribution. Somewhat more fruitful, in contrast, is the *Antiquities*, which was written about twenty years later than the *War*. Conditioned "by the greater distance of the author, who was dwelling in the house of the Emperor, and his pro-Jewish apologetic tendency there emerges in the *Antiquities* more strongly than in the *War* the legal Jewish position." [91] Understandably, Josephus, after the death of his Roman patron, wanted to reconcile himself with his Jewish countrymen and to rehabilitate himself by means of a decidedly pro-Jewish apologetic stance.[92] Since the Jewry that Josephus courted in the *Antiquities* and in the still later works (the *Life* and *Against Apion*) was of Pharisaic persuasion, he had to represent himself as pro-Pharisee. Therefore, in *V* 10–12 he emphasizes that his effort to find "the best" Jewish party has led him to attach himself to the Pharisees.[93] For the same reason in the *Antiquities* he begins his descriptions of the Jewish groups in each case with the Pharisees (*A* XIII, 171 ff.; XVIII, 12 ff.) and maintains in addition that even the Zealots and the Sadducees submitted to Pharisaic guidelines in order to be tolerated by the "people" (*A* XVIII, 23, 17). But the power relationships that existed in Judea under Roman rule—"the high priests were entrusted with the leadership of the nation" (*A* XX, 251)—and the Pharisaic criticism of the reckless power politics of the high priestly families of Boethos, Hannas, and Cantheras [94] make it very unlikely that the high priests depended on support from the Pharisees or were ready to make concessions to them. Rather, it is to be assumed that the high priestly ruling stratum, without regard to Pharisaic sensibilities, attempted, to the greatest degree possible, to push through their Sadducean principles without compromise. The frequent removal of high priests from their offices point clearly in this direction, in spite of Josephus' obfuscating tactics.

The real reason for Josephus' anti-Sadducean tendency perhaps is to be found in his Hasmonean descent, as reported in *V* 2. Only from this can we explain his prejudice. He does not criticize the transference of John Hyrcanus to the Sadducees. He disqualifies, of course "with the exception of Aristobulus alone" (*A* XX, 247) who was of Hasmonean lineage, the high priests whom

Herod appointed and who, in respect to a Sadoqid origin, were for the most part fully legitimate. He refers to them as δημοτικοὶ ἄνδρες (*A* XIV, 78) or as τινες ἄσημοι(*A* XX, 247). And, when the Zealots established as high priest Pinchas, son of Samuel from Aphthia (*BJ* IV, 155), who came from the branch of Jakim that belonged to the Sadoqid line,[95] Josephus sees in that act "the abrogation of the Law" (*BJ* IV, 154) and maintains that the Zealots, "abrogating the claims of those families from which in turn the high priests had always been drawn, appointed to that office ignoble and low-born individuals" (ἄσημοι καὶ ἀγενεῖς: *BJ* IV, 148). This hatred on the part of Josephus toward the Zealots and his outrage at the Sadducees come, therefore, from the same source: his pride in his royal and priestly descent from the Hasmonean family, which to him appears as the only one predestined for the office of high priest. This family was excluded by Herod from the high priesthood, and consequently, from Herod until the destruction of the Second Temple non-Hasmonean high priests held office. Therefore, the priestly privileged party of this period, the group of the Sadducees, is sharply criticized by Josephus and accordingly given a negative description. Thus, the writings of Josephus should not be used uncritically to elucidate the history and essence of Sadduceeism. Because, however, we lack reliable sources concerning the Sadducees, many of our statements must remain hypothetical; for "the vacuum that here must be filled by hypotheses is greater than in most other themes in the history of the Jewish and Christian religions."[96]

—Translated by Gerald M. Browne

Notes

1. Cf. the collection of rabbinic statements on the Sadducees in K. Kohler, "Sadducees," *The Jewish Encyclopedia* 10 (New York 1905), pp. 631f.; E. Schürer, G. Vermes, F. Millar, M. Black, *The History of the Jewish People in the Age of Jesus Christ*, vol. 2 (Edinburgh 1979), pp. 384–387; J. Le Moyne, *Les Sadducéens* (Paris 1972), pp. 95–120.

2. Cf. G. Baumbach, "Das Sadduzäerverständnis bei Josephus Flavius und im Neuen Testament," *Kairos* 13 (1971):17–37, esp. 28–35; J. Le Moyne, *op. cit.* note 1, pp. 121–136; R. Meyer, Σαδδουκαῖος *ThWNT* 7 (1960):35–54, esp. 51–54; K. Müller, "Jesus und die Sadduzäer," *Biblische Randbemerkungen, Schülerfestschrift R. Schnackenburg* (1974):3–24.

3. Cf. P. Wendland, *Hippolytus Werke* III, *GCS* 26 (1916):256–261; A. Adam, *Antike Berichte über die Essener* (*Lietzmanns Kleine Texte,* 182) (Berlin 1961), pp. 41–51; C. Burchard, "Zur Nebenüberlieferung von Josephus' Bericht über die Essener Bell 2, 119–161 bei Hippolyt, Porphyrius, Josippus, Niketas Choniates und anderen," in *J-S* (1974), pp. 77–96.

4. Cf. M. Hengel, *Die Zeloten* (Leiden 1961); D. M. Rhoads, *Israel in Revolution: 6–74 C.E.* (Philadelphia 1976); M. Stern, "Sicarii and Zealots," in M. Avi-Yonah, *WHJP*, vol. 8 (1977), pp. 263–301; G. Baumbach, "Einheit und Vielfalt der jüdischen Freiheitsbewegung im 1. Jh. n. Chr.," *ET* 45 (1985):93–107.

5. H. Rasp, "Flavius Josephus und die jüdischen Religionsparteien," *ZNW* 23 (1924):27–47, esp. 28.

6. So also in *A* XIII, 171, 172; XVIII, 12. The report of H. Rasp, *op. cit.*, note 5, p. 29, that the Pharisees were put in first place as the oldest group because of their age is not very convincing since the period when the individual groups arose is obscure and also since Josephus himself gives no information on this subject.

7. O. Michel, O. Bauernfeind, *Flavius Josephus De Bello Judaico*, vol. 1, 2nd ed., (Bad Homburg 1962), XXVIII; cf. G. Hölscher, "Josephus," *RE*, vol. 9 (1916) p. 1949, note 1, who separates this non-Josephan Essene report from 162–166: "Während die Pharisäer und Sadduzäer II, 162–166 in der üblichen Weise des Josephus gezeichnet werden, weicht der Essenerbericht II, 119–161 . . . stark ab."

8. Cf. O. Michel, O. Bauernfeind, *ibid.*, vol. 1, p. XXII.

9. Cf. M. Hengel, *op. cit.*, note 4, pp. 7–12.

10. Cf. G. F. Moore, "Fate and Free Will in the Jewish Philosophies according to Josephus," *HTR* 22 (1929):371–389; L. Wächter, "Die unterschiedliche Haltung der Pharisäer, Sadduzäer und Essener zur Heimarmene nach dem Bericht des Josephus," *ZRGG* 21 (1969): 97–114; G. Maier, *Mensch und freier Wille, Nach den jüdischen Religionsparteien zwischen Ben Sira und Paulus* (Tübingen 1971), pp. 116–164, 343–350; G. Stählin, "Das Schicksal im Neuen Testament und bei Josephus," in *J-S* (1974) pp. 319–343.

11. Cf. G. F. Moore, *ibid.*, p. 379.

12. Cf. L. Wächter, *op. cit.*, note 10, pp. 100–104.

13. Cf. R. Leszynsky, *Die Sadduzäer* (Berlin 1912), pp. 31f.; J. Le Moyne, *op. cit.*, note 1, p. 39; G. Maier, *op. cit.*, note 10, pp. 130f.; and L. Wächter, *ibid.*, p. 104.

14. Cf. G. Maier, *ibid.*, pp. 11ff., who wants to attribute this contention between Pharisees and Sadducees to the question "weshalb der Mensch als ein Gerechter oder Sünder handelt." To support this thesis, he refers to the phrase πράττειν τὰ δίκαια (163), which corresponds to עשׂה צדקה in the Old Testament and in the Qumran texts and which is rendered in the Psalms of Solomon and in the *NT* as ποιεῖν δικαιοσύνην (cf. 1QS I, 5; V, 3f; VIII, 2; Psalms of Solomon 9:4f.; Romans 10:5; Mark 6:1, etc.). To this extent a Jewish soteriological question could stand in the background. Paragraph 164 also points toward the fact that for Josephus "die Heimarmene der jüdischen Parteien dem Einen Gott untergeordnet ist . . . Demnach ist die Heimarmene der Juden die von Gott ausgehende Mittlerin des Geschicks der Menschen—ein wiederum für den Stoizismus unmöglicher Satz." Therefore, one should not conclude on the basis of 164 that the Sadducees are "die weniger Frommen" (so W. Lütgert, "Das Problem der Willensfreiheit in der vorchristlichen Synagoge," *BFCT* 10, no. 2 [1906]:177–212, esp. 193) or advocates of a "praktischen Atheismus, der von einem lebendigen Wirken Gottes nichts wissen will" (so G. Hölscher, *Der Sadduzäismus* [Leipzig 1906] p. 5; similarly also A. Schlatter, *Die Theologie des Judentums nach dem Bericht des Josefus* (*BFCT* 2, no. 26) [Gütersloh 1932]:180ff.; and R. Meyer, *op. cit.*, note 2, p. 46).

15. R. Leszynsky, *op. cit.*, note 13, p. 172.

16. Cf. J. Le Moyne, *op. cit.*, note 1, p. 69, who refers to Ben Sira 17.27f. In that the Sadducees stand in the tradition of Ben Sira, they show themselves to be advocates of an "orthodoxen Altjudentum" (R. Meyer, *Tradition und Neuschöpfung im antiken Judentum. Dargestellt an der Geschichte des Pharisäismus* [Berlin 1965], p. 76).

17. H. Rasp, *op. cit.*, note 5, p. 31.

18. G. Maier, *op. cit.*, note 10, p. 14, with reference to G. F. Moore, *op. cit.*, note 10, p. 383, and also to R. Marcus, *Josephus* (*LCL*) VII (London 1943), p. 311 note f.

19. H. Rasp, *op. cit.*, note 5, p. 31.

20. Thus, we disagree with the assumption of G Maier, *op. cit.*, note 10, "dass auch

hier Josephus in den Nikolausbericht eingegriffen hat, etwa indem er den Satzteil ὡς καὶ bis λαμβάνοντας einfügte." Of course, we do not dispute the fact *dass ein jüdisches Ohr* referred this phrase to *die irdische Vergeltung Gottes* and understood ἀβουλία as *Sünde* (G. Maier, *ibid.*).

21. Cf. G. Maier, *ibid.*, p. 8f. Whether Josephus thereby relied on Philo, as suggested by the context of the description of the Essenes in *A* XVIII, 18–22 with Philo, *Quod omnis probus liber sit*, 75–91, cannot be clearly determined; cf. G. Hölscher, *op. cit.*, note 14, p. 4; L. H. Feldman, *Josephus (LCL) IX* (London 1965), p. 14f., note d; G. Maier, *op. cit.*, note 10, pp. 9, 16f. The Jewish character of this description of the Essenes is shown especially clearly in comparison with *A* XIII, 172: instead of the *Heimarmene* mentioned here, to whose power everything is subordinate, *A* XVIII, 18 states that everything rests in God's hands.

22. Therefore, the Pharisees had to endeavor, through a sophistic exegesis, to prove to the Sadducees that the resurrection of the dead was already attested in the Pentateuch. According to *Sanhedrin* 90b, the Sadducean reading of Deuteronomy 31:16 is entirely correct: "You [i.e. Moses] will soon lie down with your ancestors. And this people will arise and depart." On the other hand, the Pharisees violated the intention of the text: "You [i.e., Moses] will soon lie down with your ancestors and will arise. And the people. . . ." In this way they wanted to base their resurrection doctrine on the Torah. Similarly artificial is the Pharisaic exegesis of Exodus 6:4, Deuteronomy 4:4, 11:9, and Numbers 15:30f. in *Sanhedrin* 90b. This frantic attempt on the part of the Pharisees to verify their resurrection dogma on the basis of the Torah underscores the fact that the decisive reason for the rejection of this innovation by the Sadducees was their strict adherence to the old, pre-Pharisaic viewpoint and thus their conservatism.

23. Cf. L. H. Feldman, *op. cit.*, note 21, p. 14, note a.; R. Leszynsky, *op. cit.*, note 13, p. 19; J. Jeremias, *Jerusalem zur Zeit Jesu*, 3rd ed. (Göttingen 1962) p. 262; S. W. Baron, *A Social and Religious History of the Jews*, 2nd ed., vol. 2 (New York 1962) p. 38; and J. Le Moyne, *op. cit.*, note 1, p. 42 ("Les Sadducéens sont donc les gens de l'Écriture").

24. G. Maier, *op. cit.*, note 10, p. 130.

25. With J. Le Moyne, *op. cit.*, note 1, p. 42, one should therefore make responsible for 16b neither a skepticism (*pace* M. L. Lagrange) nor Hellenistic influences (*pace* D. Daube).

26. Cf. J. Jeremias, *op. cit.* note 23, p. 263; G. Maier, *op. cit.*, note 10, p. 131f.; L. H. Feldman, *op. cit.*, note 21, p. 14, note a.: "The Sadducees . . . had their own traditions . . . , but these were *gezerot* (decrees) and not based on the oral Law," and G. W. E. Nickelsburg and M. E. Stone, *Faith and Piety in Early Judaism* (Philadelphia 1983) p. 30: "Surely the Sadducees did not just follow the literal word of Scripture with no exegesis. The difference with the Pharisees must have related to the extent of the development of the exegetical tradition and to the measure of authority attributed to it."

27. Cf. *A* IX, 3; *BJ* IV, 416; V, 439.

28. Cf. M. Stern, "Aspects of Jewish Society: The Priesthood and other Classes," in S. Safrai and M. Stern, *The Jewish People in the First Century*, vol. 2 (*Compendia Rerum Iudaicarum ad Novum Testamentum*, I) (Assen 1976) pp. 561–630, esp. 580: "The priesthood constituted the upper stratum of Jewish society in the Second Temple period. . . . The families whose influence was predominant in the Hellenistic period belonged to the priesthood"; cf. also J. Jeremias, *op. cit.* note 23, p. 167, and *Ap* II, 185.

29. Cf. G. Hölscher, *op. cit.*, note 14, p. 37 and G. Maier, *op. cit.* note 10, p. 133, against J. Jeremias, *op. cit.* note 23, p. 259 and note 5, who wants to refer this statement to "Angehörige des Laienadels" and as a foundation postulates "hellenistische Einflüsse" with the Sadducees, which are to refer "ebenfalls auf die wohlhabenden Kreise, da diese am stärksten mit der hellenistischen Kultur in Berührung kamen." But, significantly, the Sadducees are never reproached in the rabbinic texts with being "Hellenists"; cf. J. Le Moyne, *op. cit.*, note 1, p. 354f. The "relative Liberalismus" (J. Maier, *Geschichte der jüdischen Religion* [Berlin 1972] p. 47) of the Sadducees is based on their adherence to the written Torah, not on Hellenistic influences.

Likewise, the partisanship of the Sadducees, characterized in *A* XIII, 298 as "wohlhabende," must not be referred to the "Laienadel"; for "am wohlhabendsten" were the high priestly families in the Roman period, who derived profit from the Temple and its treasures and controlled large land-holdings. Cf. M. Stern, *op. cit.*, note 2č, p. 586f. and J. Jeremias, *op. cit.*, note 23, pp. 111–114, 221ff.

30. O. Michel and O. Bauernfeind, *op. cit.*, note 7, vol. 1, p. 440, note 89; similarly also G. Maier, *op. cit.*, note 10, p. 135, who designates them as the "aristokratische Priesterpartei."

31. G. Maier, *op. cit.*, note 10, p. 135.

32. *Ibid.*, p. 134; cf. also L. H. Feldman, *op. cit.*, note 21, p. 14, note c.

33. Cf. our discussion later in part IV.

34. J. Le Moyne, *op. cit.*, note 1, p. 155.

35. R. Meyer, *op. cit.*, note 2, p. 36, with reference to *Erubin* 6.2; Tosefta *Parah* 3.7.

36. *Ibid.*, p. 36; cf. also J. Wellhausen, *Die Pharisäer und die Sadducäer*, 2nd ed. (Greifswald 1924), p. 46: "Darüber kann . . . nicht der geringste Zweifel sein, dass çaddûqîm ein Gentilicum ist, abgeleitet von dem Eigennamen çaddûq"; similarly also E. Schürer et al., *op. cit.*, note 1, vol. 2, pp. 405f., as well as the authors cited in J. Le Moyne, p. 160. The derivation of *sedeq* as "just," first put forth by Epiphanius (*Haereses* 14.2f.: Σεδὲκ γὰρ ἑρμηνεύεται δικαιοσύνη), according to which the Sadducees are therefore said to be designated as the just (so also B. Reicke, *Neutestamentliche Zeitgeschichte*, 3rd ed. (Berlin 1982), p. 158; similarly also the view of R. Eisenman, *Maccabees, Zadokites, Christians and Qumran* (Leiden 1983), pp. 12ff. 42ff.), is scarcely possible on linguistic and factual grounds; cf. Le Moyne, p. 160, who speaks of an "impossibilité linguistique."

37. G. F. Moore, *Judaism in the First Centuries of the Christian Era*, vol. 1 (1962), p. 70; similarly also E. Baneth, *Ursprung der Sadokäer und Boethosäer* (Frankfurt 1882), p. 35, who assumes as founder a Sadoq from the period of Jose ben Joeser, i.e., the middle of the second century B.C.

38. Cf. J. Le Moyne, *op. cit.*, note 1, p. 161f.; R. Meyer, *op. cit.* note 2, pp. 41–43; E. Schürer et al., *op cit.*, note 1, vol. 2, p. 406.

39. J. Jeremias, *op. cit.* note 23, p. 261, n. 3.

40. Cf., in addition to the authors cited in R. Meyer, *op. cit.*, note 2, p. 36, note 9, L. Finkelstein, *The Pharisees: The Sociological Background of their Faith*, 3rd ed., vol. 2 (Philadelphia 1962), p. 765; J. Le Moyne, *op. cit.*, note 1, pp. 160, 163; V. Tcherikover, *Hellenistic Civilization and the Jews* (Philadelphia 1959), p. 493, note 40; A. Schalit, *König Herodes. Der Mann und sein Werk* (Berlin 1969), p. 520; K. Schubert, *Die jüdischen Religionsparteien in neutestamentlicher Zeit* (Stuttgart 1970), p. 16; and C. E. Hauer, Jr., "Who was Zadok?" *JBL* 82 (1963):89–94, esp. 94.

41. Cf. Ben Sira (Hebrew), 51:12; and J. Le Moyne, *op. cit.*, note 1; pp. 65ff., and R. Meyer, *op. cit.*, note 2, p. 37f.

42. Cf. *BJ* I, 33, VII, 456; *A* XII, 237, 387f., XIII, 62–73, XX, 236; and J. Jeremias, *op. cit.*, note 23, pp. 209–213.

43. Cf. *1QS* V, 2.9; *1QSa* I, 2.24, II, 3; *1QSb* III, 22; CD IV, 1.3, V, 5; *4QFl* I, 17; and E. Schürer et al., *op. cit.*, note 1, vol. 2, p. 587.

44. Cf. Acts 4:1ff., 5:17ff., and G. Baumbach, *op. cit.*, note 2, pp. 28–30; R. Meyer, *op. cit.*, note 2, pp. 52–54.

45. Cf. J. Le Moyne, *op. cit.*, note 1, pp. 51–60; R. Meyer, *op. cit.*, note 2, p. 43; E. Schürer, *Geschichte des jüdischen Volkes im Zeitalter Jesu Christi*, 4th ed., vol. 1 (Leipzig 1901), p. 272; and E. Bammel, "Sadduzäer und Sadokiden," *ETL* 55 (1979):107–115, esp. 110f.

46. E. Schürer, *ibid.*, vol. 1, p. 271, with reference to *A* XIII, 289; similarly also R. Meyer, *ibid.*, p. 43, who formulates the question as follows: "Wie es dazu kam, dass Johannes Hyrkanos I., dessen Haus letztlich den gesetzestreuen Widerstandskreisen sein Emporkommen

verdankte, an die Männer Anschluss fand, die in den Augen der 'Frommen' durch ihre Vergangenheit belastet waren." Against such a view is directed the polemic of R. Eisenman, *op. cit.*, note 36, p. 19, who wants to see question and answer as follows: "How then could John Hyrcanus have 'returned' to the Sadducee Party? He did so because this was the original party of Judas Maccabee, deserted by his family during the somewhat dubious machinations of his uncle Jonathan and father Simon to curry Seleucid favor for their claims to the high priesthood." Thus, R. Eisenman criticizes the widely held thesis (examples in Eisenman, 39, note 1) that the Maccabean families usurped the high priesthood from an earlier, purely Sadoqid line but did not themselves come from a Sadoqid clan and, to that extent, were illegitimate holders of the office of high priest. However, there is no reason to doubt the reproach directed, according to *A* XIII, 291, against John Hyrcanus regarding the illegitimacy of his office of high priest; the only problem lies in the reason for this given in 292, which has the character of a legend. The illegitimacy of the high priesthood of the Hasmoneans is probably based on the fact that, according to I Maccabees 2:1, 14:29, the Hasmoneans, of course, belonged to the priestly nobility because of the priestly arrangement of Jehoiarib, "aber diese Klasse . . . nicht zum Stamm der Tempelpriesterschaft [rechnete], da sie erst spät aus dem Exil zurückgekehrt ist, vgl. b. *Ta'anith* 27b Par, wo Jehoiarib als Anhängsel zu Jedaja erscheint" (R. Meyer, *op. cit.*, note 2, p. 38, note 23). Accordingly, it could be disputed whether the Hasmoneans legally belonged to the Jerusalem priesthood; cf. also E. Stauffer, "Probleme der Priester tradition," *TLZ* 81 (1956):135–150, esp. 140, and A. Schalit, *op. cit.*, note 40, p. 103, note 23.

47. Cf. A. Schalit, *op. cit.*, note 40, p. 520, esp. note 137; L. H. Feldman, *op. cit.*, note 21, p. 14, note a.

48. R. Meyer, *op. cit.*, note 2, p. 43. J. Maier, *op. cit.*, note 29, p. 44f., characterizes the first mentioned wing as "apokalyptischen Zadokismus," which under the "Lehrer der Gerechtigkeit" in the community of Qumran "seine bekannteste Ausprägung gewann"; the flank mentioned in second place he designates as the "opportunistischen Flügel," which "die angestammten Privilegien so weit als möglich zu erhalten suchte und dafür zum Kompromiss mit den Herrschenden bereit war" and which formed the "Kern der 'sadduzäischen' Partei"; it was thus a question of "zwei weltanschaulich völlig gegensätzlichen Flügel." Likewise, R. Eisenman, *op. cit.*, note 36, pp. 19f., 22, assumes two groups of Sadoqids/Sadducees: the "pietistic" or messianic," in which he includes Qumran and the Zealots, and the " 'Herodian' or normative Sadduceeism" or the "Boethusian Sadduceeism," whereby is meant "the corrupt Sadducee priesthood introduced under Herod and the procurators." Like Eisenman, E. Bammel, *op. cit.*, note 45, p. 110f., also wants to understand the normative Sadduceeism as arising first in the period of Herod, and he thus evaluates the reference to the Sadducees in *A* XIII, 293ff., as a "dem enttäuschten König aufgeklebtes Etikett." Now, it is certainly not to be disputed that this Sadduceeism found a typical representative in the person of Simon son of Boethos in the time of King Herod (cf. our discussion in part III) but it does not follow that this form of Sadduceeism did arise in the period of Herod.

49. V. Tcherikover, *op. cit.*, note 40, p. 491, note 30; cf. also R. Meyer, *op. cit.*, note 2, p. 46.

50. Tcherikover, *ibid.*, p. 494, note 44.

51. According to Tcherikover, *ibid.*, p. 263, with the transference of the Pharisees to the opposition against the Hasmoneans, the exegesis of the Torah must again have been taken over by the priests. Since, however, they were not in the position to do so, they could have countered the dilemma only by declaring that the Mosaic Law was "a legal code that required no interpretation, as all had been said in it and everything in it was clear." From this, Tcherikover concludes, "Hence the positive attitude of the Sadducees to the Mosaic Law rose, not from any special religious feeling, but from political opposition to the legislative activity of the Pharisees." But such a

purely political explanation for the denial of the oral Torah by the Sadducees, though thoroughly noteworthy, must not be taken absolutely and played out against the religious explanation.

52. Cf. *Ap* II, 156, 185, and especially 279, where we read: "Time is reckoned in all cases the surest test of worth"; also 280ff.

53. Cf. J. Le Moyne, *op. cit.*, note 1, p. 388: "La continuité historique entre les Sadocites de l'époque perse et grecque et les Sadducéens est en général affirmée par les historiens modernes."

54. In view of the Pharisaic opposition, the Hasmoneans needed a confederate who through his connection with the Temple and its resources represented a significant power (cf. V. Tcherikover, *op. cit.*, note 40, pp. 155ff.), who thanks to his tradition was in a position "von den Hasmonäern den Makel der Illegitimität zu nehmen" (R. Meyer, *op. cit.*, note 2, p. 43f.) and who, as a consequence of his strongly conservative position, could provide the religious foundation necessary for the politico-military expansion policy of the Hasmoneans. The ideal confederates for the Hasmoneans therefore were the Sadducees, who through this alliance had certainly become strongly politicized; cf. A. Schalit, *op. cit.*, note 40, p. 533.

55. Cf. *A* XIII, 257, XV, 254; and *BJ* I, 63.

56. Cf. *A* XIII, 320–404.

57. Cf. *A* XIII, 288, 372ff.; also *Sheqalim* V, 1.

58. R. Meyer, *op. cit.*, note 2, p. 44.

59. J. Wellhausen, *op. cit.*, note 36, p. 98f.; cf. *A* XIII, 408ff.; *BJ* I, 110ff.

60. Cf. *A* XIV, 159ff.; *BJ* I, 204ff.; cf. R. Meyer, *Der Prophet aus Galiläa* (Leipzig 1940), pp. 70–74.

61. Cf. *A* XIV, 385; *BJ* I, 282; and A. Schalit, *op. cit.*, note 40, p. 167ff.

62. Cf. J. Jeremias, *op. cit.*, note 23, pp. 167–181; E. Schürer et al., *op. cit.*, note 1, vol. 2, pp. 199–236.

63. Cf. A. Schalit, *op. cit.*, note 40, p. 99f., esp. n. 7.

64. Cf. J. Wellhausen, *op. cit.*, note 36, p. 107ff.; G. Hölscher, *op. cit.*, note 14, pp. 78ff.; E. Schürer, *op. cit.*, note 45, vol. 2, pp. 476, 488; R. Meyer, *op. cit.*, note 2, p. 45f.; J. Le Moyne, *op. cit.*, note 1, pp. 392ff.

65. R. Meyer, *ibid.*, p. 45; cf. also J. Jeremias, *op. cit.*, note 23, p. 218, especially note 1. Carefully balanced is A. Schalit, *op. cit.*, note 40, pp. 693–695.

66. Cf. A. Schlatter, *Geschichte Israels von Alexander dem Grossen bis Hadrian* (Stuttgart 1925), p. 231; R. Meyer, *ibid.*, pp. 42, 45; and E. Bammel, *op. cit.*, note 45, p. 109f., against A. Schalit, *ibid.*, p. 588.

67. Bammel, *ibid.*, p. 109f.; cf. also J. Jeremias, *op. cit.*, note 23, pp. 217f.

68. R. Eisenman, *op. cit.*, note 36, pp. 20, 22.

69. Cf. M. Stern, *op. cit.*, note 28, p. 570.

70. Cf. J. Jeremias, *op. cit.*, note 23, p. 219ff.; and J. Le Moyne, *op. cit.*, note 1, pp. 177–198, 332–340.

71. R. Meyer, *op. cit.*, note 2, p. 45; cf. also M. Stern, *op. cit.*, note 28, p. 604: "The term Boethusians became famous in Jewish tradition as a synonym for Sadduceans. The house of Boethus belonged to the new second élite that came to the fore with the Herodian house."

72. Cf. J. Jeremias, *op. cit.*, note 23, p. 219.

73. W. R. Farmer, *Maccabees, Zealots, and Josephus* (New York 1956), p. 189; similarly O. Cullmann, *Der Staat im Neuen Testament* (Tübingen 1956), p. 6; and V. Aptowitzer, *Parteipolitik der Hasmonäerzeit im rabbinischen und pseudoepigraphischen Schrifttum* (Wien 1927), p. ix.

74. Similarly contradictory is Josephus' description of the fate of the high priest Jonathan (son of Ananus I, 36/37), who was deposed again after three months, without a reason being given. Astoundingly, Agrippa I then wanted again to make him high priest, but he refused. From

A XX, 161–164, it then emerges that he spoke fearlessly against the Roman procurator M. Antonius Felix (52–60) and had to pay for his courage with his life. Significantly, in *BJ* II, 256, Felix's responsibility for his murder is passed over in silence, since such an admission could not be reconciled with the goal of *BJ*.

75. Cf. P. Winter, *On the Trial of Jesus* (Berlin 1961), p. 18. Hannas had used for his own purposes the favorable opportunity that arose through the death of Festus and the period before the establishment of the new procurator Albinus; cf. *A* XX, 200.

76. Cf. *Avodah Zarah* 18a; *Berakhoth* 58a; *Avoth* 3.2; *BJ* II, 140; and R. Eisenman, *op. cit.*, note 36, p. 55, note 83; C. Thoma, "Der Pharisäismus," in J. Maier and J. Schreiner, *Literatur und Religion des Frühjudentums* (Würzburg-Gütersloh 1973), pp. 254–272, esp. 271; G. Baumbach, *Jesus von Nazareth im Lichte der jüdischen Gruppenbildung* (Berlin 1971), pp. 72ff.

77. R. Meyer, *op. cit.*, note 2, p. 45.

78. Cf. *A* XX, 199, and XIII, 294. According to *Megillath Ta'anith* 4 they understood Exodus 21:24 ("an eye for an eye, a tooth for a tooth") literally; this strictness was based on their consistent adherence to the letter of the Torah. Cf. J. Le Moyne, *op. cit.*, note 1, pp. 43f. 239–243; E. Schürer et al., *op. cit.*, note 1, vol. 2, pp. 408–411.

79. Cf. *BJ* II, 653f. and IV, 316.

80. Cf. the literature cited in note 4.

81. Cf. *BJ* II, 409ff.

82. So R. Meyer, *op. cit.*, note 16, p. 69. Similarly also K. Schubert in *Kairos* 25 (1983):109, who designates the Zealots as "sozusagen radikalisierte Sadduzäer." Yet, one must certainly not bring the Sicarii into connection with the Sadducees, as H. Rasp, *op. cit.*, note 5, p. 38, does: "Die Sadduzäer hatten im Grunde dieselbe geistige Struktur wie die Sikarier."

83. Cf. *BJ* V, 527ff., IV, 574, and VI, 114; also M. Stern, *op. cit.*, note 28, p. 605f., especially p. 605, note 4; and O. Michel and O. Bauernfeind, *op. cit.*, note 7, vol. 2, pp. 272, note 207, 233, note 194.

84. Cf. J. Le Moyne, *op. cit.*, note 1, p. 399; unfortunately, as regards our part III, there is validity in what R. Meyer, *op. cit.*, note 2, p. 43, has determined: "Die Geschichte jener politisch handelnden Gruppe, die Josephus und die rabbinische Tradition als Sadduzäer im engen Zusammenhang mit dem Geschick des Tempelstaates von Jerusalem bezeichnen, lässt sich mangels geeigneter Quellen nicht vollständig schreiben."

85. R. Laqueur, *Der jüdische Historiker Flavius Josephus* (Giessen 1920), p. 246.

86. O. Michel and O. Bauernfeind, *op. cit.*, note 7, vol. 1, pp. xx–xxi.

87. Cf. *ibid.*, p. 403, note 6.

88. M. Hengel, *op. cit.*, note 4, p. 46.

89. *Ibid.*, p. 6, with reference to *V* 204.

90. H. Rasp, *op. cit.*, note 5, p. 45; cf. also H.-F. Weiss, "Pharisäismus und Hellenismus," *OLZ* 74, no. 5 (1979):421–433, esp. 424.

91. M. Hengel, *op. cit.*, note 4, p. 15; cf. R. Laqueur, *op. cit.*, note 85, pp. 258–261, and S. J. D. Cohen, *Josephus in Galilee and Rome* (Leiden 1979), pp. 84ff., 236ff.

92. Cf. H. St. J. Thackeray, *Josephus (LCL)* IV (London 1930), p. VIII.

93. The statement that Josephus had already entered the Pharisaic order when he was nineteen (as he maintains in *V* 12) must be doubted. It is more reasonable to assume, with M. Hengel, *op. cit.*, note 4, p. 378, n. 3, that not until after 70 A.D. he "sich der einzig überlebenden pharisäischen Partei anschloss"; cf. also H. Lindner, *Die Geschichtsauffassung des Flavius Josephus im Bellum Judaicum* (Leiden 1972), p. 146, especially note 2; J. Neusner, "Josephus' Pharisees," in *Ex Orbe Religionum, Studia Geo Widengren*, vol. 1 (*Studies in the History of Religions*, 21) (Leiden 1972), pp. 224–244, esp. p. 232: "Nothing . . . suggests he was a Pharisee, as he later claimed in his autobiography"; and O. Michel, "Die Rettung Israels

und die Rolle Roms nach den Reden im 'Bellum Judaicum,'" *ANRW* II, 21, no. 2 (1984):945–976, esp. p. 974: Josephus "schlechthin 'pharisäisch' zu nennen, hat seine Bedenken."

94. Cf. Baraitha *Pesaḥim* 57a, which, according to J. Jeremias, *op. cit.*, note 23, p. 221, contains "ausgezeichnetes geschichtliches Material" and goes back to Abba Schaul (ca. 70 A.D.).

95. Cf. I Chronicles 24:12 and J. Jeremias, *ibid.*, p. 216f.

96. G. Maier, *op. cit.*, note 10, p. 116; cf. also H. R. Moehring, "Joseph ben Matthia and Flavius Josephus: The Jewish Prophet and Roman Historian," *ANRW* II, 21, no. 2 (1984): 864–944, esp. p. 867: Our knowledge of the Jewish groups "is too fragmentary and far too inconsistent to permit any definitive statements or classification of people."

9 The High Priesthood in the Judgment of Josephus

CLEMENS THOMA

The high priesthood, according to Josephus Flavius' judgment, was the most important institution of Early Judaism with regard to cult, prophecy, salvation, and worldly policy. In his opinion, the weal and woe of the Jewish people, and partially also of the non-Jewish powers and nations, depended on the sacral and political activities of these prominent office holders.

Josephus described this office and its holders from the standpoint of his own status as an aristocratic chief priest, theologian of salvation, and ambitious politician (*BJ* I, 3; *V* I, 2–4). Most of his records are colored by his pride as a priest, aristocratic theologian, and prophet. In consequence of this personal background, he was highly interested in the rituals, in the various proceedings in the cult, and in the functions of the Jewish priesthood in its manifold hierarchical forms. In his mind, the priestly hierarchy and the worship of God in the Temple were realities that could never be separated from the destiny of the Jewish people. However, cult, hierarchy, and people not only represented religious life but were of an eminently political nature. Eventually, he was concerned about the question of how cult and priesthood could be integrated into the governmental powers and institutions within Jewry, and also how they might be accepted by the Graeco-Roman world power.

In view of this, it is important to follow up, at first, those motives that reveal the personal religious engagement of Josephus with regard to high priesthood and cult. Subsequently, Josephus as politician in religious matters and his theories about political systems will be taken into consideration. Finally, the manner in which Josephus describes the various high priests with their values and failures will show his historical and apologetic thinking.

We refrain from comparisons between reminiscences of Josephus and those of the rabbis. Inconsiderate comparisons with the rabbinic literature and endeavors will run into the danger of undervaluing Josephus in his independence. Besides, reliable investigations are available that throw light on the connections of Josephus' statements in matters of priesthood and cult with rabbinic statements.[1]

Josephus' Personal Religious Engagement in Connection with the High Priesthood

Josephus speaks mainly to the external world: to the Romans, in whose service and good graces he is standing; and, on the other hand, to Jews, who are opposed to him. However, where he stands up for his own affairs as a passionate speaker (for instance, in speeches devised as if they had been delivered by various Jewish personalities during the Jewish War against Rome) or where he reveals intimate, clandestine convictions of Jewish faith, his personal engagement as a man of Jewish faith comes suddenly to light.

We start from a seemingly insignificant religious symbol, namely from the term αὐγή, "sheen" or "glamor of light." In *Antiquities* III, 184, Josephus speaks of gold, interwoven in the garment of the high priest. This gold is a token, "I imagine, of the all-pervading sunlight." In the same sense, according to Josephus, the golden crown on the head of the high priest has that glamor of light "in which the Deity most delights" (*A* III, 187). We may speak of a theology of the high priest's garment, a theology to which Josephus attaches great importance, which he also extends to the office itself and the cult. At the head of this theology is the statement of the absolute sovereignty of God:

> For Moses left no possible opening for the malpractices of prophets, should there, in fact, be any capable of abusing the divine prerogative, but left to God supreme authority whether to attend the sacred rites, when it so pleased Him, or to absent Himself; and this he wished to be made manifest not to Hebrews only but also to any strangers who chanced to be present. Well, of those stones which, as I said before, the high priest wore upon his shoulders—they were sardonyxes, and I deem it superfluous to indicate the nature of jewels familiar to all—it came about, whenever God assisted at the sacred ceremonies, that the one that was buckled on the right shoulder began to shine, a light glancing from it, visible to the most distant, of which the stone had before betrayed no trace. That alone should be marvel enough for such as have not cultivated a superior wisdom to disparage all religious things; but I have yet a greater marvel to record. By means of the twelve stones, which the high priest wore upon his breast, stitched into the breast shield, God foreshowed victory to those on the eve of battle. For so brilliant a light flashed out from them, while the army was yet in motion, that it was evident to the whole host that God had come to their aid. Hence it is that those Greeks who revere our practices, because they can in no way gainsay them, call it an "oracle." Nevertheless, the breast shield and

sardonyx alike ceased to shine two hundred years before I composed this work, because of God's displeasure at the transgression of the laws. (A III, 214–218).

In the background of all these statements Exodus 3.14 ("I will be who I will be") appears, which Josephus considers as the guide to the very core of the biblical message. Josephus believed that the God of Israel, free from any manipulation, now and then reveals Himself to His people in suggestions as helper and victor, provided that His people are faithful to the law. The "sheen" is the continuation of the "shining cloud" that in former times appeared as Israel's aid (Exodus 34:5; 40:34; Numbers 10:34–35, etc.). For the time being, the "sheen" on the high priest's garment has disappeared, because of the sins of the Jewish people. In Josephus' eyes, the garment and the office of the high priest established a kind of earthly crystallike focus of the unobtainable, yet helpful God. The high priest heralds, by virtue of his office, the forthcoming events of his people's salvation.

From time to time, the voice of God happens to be revealed in the high priest's words (A XIII, 282, where it happened to the high priest John Hyrcanus I). In other words, the gift of prophecy will be bestowed upon him.[2] In the cult, which is the high priest's duty and is to be performed to God's satisfaction, His merciful condescension will also occur as a help. This condescension will be meaningful not only to Israel alone but to the whole world. Josephus' interpretation of King Solomon's prayer (see I Kings 8:27–53; II Chronicles 6:14–40) reads accordingly:

> And if Thy people Israel have sinned against Thee and because of their sin are smitten by some evil from Thee, by unfruitfulness of the soil or a destructive pestilence or any such affliction with which Thou visitest those who transgress any of the sacred laws, and if they all gather to take refuge in the Temple, entreating Thee and praying to be saved, then do Thou hearken to them as though Thou wert within, and pity them and deliver them from their misfortunes. And this help I ask of Thee not alone for the Hebrews who may fall into error, but also if any come even from the ends of the earth or from wherever it may be and turn to Thee, imploring to receive some kindness, do Thou hearken and give it them. For so would all men know that Thou Thyself didst desire that this house should be built for Thee in our land, and also that we are not inhuman by nature ($\dot{\alpha}\pi\dot{\alpha}\nu\theta\rho\omega\pi o\iota \tau\dot{\eta}\nu \phi\dot{\upsilon}\sigma\iota\nu$), nor unfriendly to those who are not of our country, but wish that all men equally should receive aid from Thee and enjoy Thy blessings." (A VIII, 115–17)[3]

The Temple office and therewith also the high priest himself represents to Josephus "those ceremonies of world-wide religious worship" ($\kappa o\sigma\mu\iota\kappa\dot{\eta}\varsigma$ $\theta\rho\eta\sigma\kappa\varepsilon i\alpha\varsigma$) (BJ IV, 324; A XI, 85), in the sense that by them also the anti-Semitism, that basic evil between the peoples of the world and the Jews, might be dissolved. However, the Jews must not turn the Temple services and the high priesthood into a mystery. This would merely nourish anti-Jewish prejudices. "No unmentionable mysteries took place" in the Temple, Josephus reports in *Apion* II, 106. The main sin of the priestly Zealots had been that they separated themselves from the external world; that is, that they had refused to accept gifts and sacrifices from the Roman world power (*BJ* II, 409). In an anti-Zealotic assembly, in 66 A.D., Josephus quotes a speaker as saying that the Zealots themselves "were provoking the arms of the Romans and courting a war with them, introducing a strange innovation into their religion, and, besides endangering the city, laying it open to the charge of impiety, if Jews henceforth were to be the only people to allow no alien the right of sacrifice or worship" (*BJ* II, 414).

In this respect, quite a number of personal concerns and hopes of Josephus become visible. The very Jewish existence is the near, "gracious God," whose appeals can be felt in the course of history. Those who do not submit to the authority of this God destroy themselves and likewise the Jewish people. They would also impair the forthcoming universal peace among the people of the world (*A* IV, 180–83: Moses exhorts his people before his death). Josephus is suffering from the fact that in his generation the sheen of God is hardly perceptible any more.

In Josephus' mind, the very place of this sheen of God's presence is not only the garment of the high priest nor the pious performance of the cult in the Temple but, in reality, the entire nature. His witnesses are the Essenes. For them, even the discharge of excrements, certainly a natural function, must "not offend the rays of the deity" (*BJ* II, 148), so that when discharging their excrements, they are bound to dig a trench with a mattock and to wrap their mantle about them.

As a synonym to the term αὐγή, Josephus also uses the term ἐπιφάνεια (τοῦ) θεοῦ: manifestation of God (*A* II, 339; III, 310, etc.). These are always cases where God manifests Himself as helpful in times of distress of his people.

According to Josephus (and also to the Essenes) the αὐγή and ἐπιφάεια of God do not imply a static binding to the cult and the high priest. Josephus emphasizes that "heaven, although concealed, be not closed" (*BJ* V, 208).[4] Everywhere, in times of distress or where God is worshipped, a sheen may descend from heaven. Therefore, Josephus understands αὐγή and ἐπιφάνεια almost the same way as the rabbis, who, after the destruction of the Temple in the year 70 A.D., used the expression *shekhinah,* in the sense of "God's special, dynamic presence amidst his people." An often-used rabbinical expression is "sheen (*zîv*) of the *shekhinah.*" Like the rabbis, Josephus recognized in God's suggestive appearance on earth the central hope of the Jews. To express this deep-rooted hope was one of his motives for establishing his great historical and apologetic work.

Josephus as a Priestly Religious Politician and Theorist of State Affairs

Josephus is not only a *homo religiosus* but also a *homo politicus*. His work deals to a great extent with political problems and religious strategy. But, in his personal view, all the holy and venerable tradition should be a help for coping with the hard religio-political problems of his own time. In consequence and unintentionally, Josephus thus became a theoretical thinker about religious and state affairs. Again, the office of the high priest turned out to him as the most important reference to theory and religious and political practice. For him the high priestly office was not only an honor (τιμή) but also a power (δύναμις; ἀρχή) (*A* XI, 309–310).

Religious and Worldly Power

According to *Ap* II, 194 the high priest "with his colleagues will sacrifice to God, guard the laws, adjudicate in cases of dispute, punish those convicted of crime." Any who disobey him will pay the penalty as if they had committed a crime against God Himself. Therefore, the primary religious power of the high priest has "direct political consequences."[5] In paraphrasing the halakhah for the king, as mentioned in Deuteronomy (17.14–20), Josephus calls the form of government that is under the guidance of the high priest and that reaches into all other political affairs, "aristocracy." In ancient times, Moses already had declared:

> Aristocracy, with the life that is lived thereunder, is indeed the best; let no craving possess you for another polity, but be content with this, having the laws for your masters and governing all your actions by them; for God suffices for your ruler. But should you become desirous of a king, let him be of your own race and let him have a perpetual care for justice and virtue in every other form. Let him concede to the laws and to God the possession of superior wisdom, and let him do nothing without the high priest and the counsel of his elders." (*A* IV, 223–224)

It can be seen therefrom that Josephus, together with a broad Jewish tradition, shares a strong mistrust of an absolutist kingdom in Israel. The old scriptures demand that the king transcribe the law himself or have it copied for him, so that he acquires a thorough knowledge of God's law (Deuteronomy 17.18; possibly Psalms 1.2; Temple Scroll 36. 20–21). Josephus extends this rule further, probably in the sense of the Pharisees, by demanding that the king must not issue laws unless he is in accordance with the high priest and the Sanhedrin. In this way, he places the king not only under the written Torah (*torah shebiktav*), but also under the oral Torah (*torah shebeʿalpe*). It is obvious that Josephus has his strong reserves against a constitutional monarchy. In accordance with the Pharisaic halakhah, Josephus shows a tendency "to prefer the absolute rule of the Sanhedrin to that of 'the constitutional monarchy.'"[6]

In consequence of his thinking, he declines the division of government power between two persons, the high priest and the king. When Pompey was besieging Jerusalem in 63 B.C., as Josephus records in *Antiquities* XIV, 41, the leaders of the Jews came to Pompey, claiming that they were tired of the quarrel between the two brothers, Hyrcanus II and Aristobulus II, the latter being in charge of the king's office, while the first was high priest. However, the leaders brought forward their case by "saying that it was the custom of their country to obey the priests of the God, who was venerated by them, but that these two, who were descended from the priests, were seeking to change their form of government in order that they might become a nation of slaves."[7] Since Josephus was in favor of the high priest's office dominating the king's office, he was against the division of the powers of the high priest and of the king between two different office holders who were both of priestly descent.

Josephus evades the question how much political power might be conceded to the high priest. Decisive for him is merely the fact that the high priest shall be granted an ἀρχή; that is, judicial and political power as such. He is well aware that in history the high priest was not in the position to insist upon his powers all the time to the same degree. From the Babylonian exile up to the time of the Hasmonean high priest–prince and high priest–kings, the high priest had been able to exercise his political power in a far more independent and elastic manner. Before the Hasmonean period, the form of government was "aristocratic and at the same time oligarchic. For the high priests were at the head of affairs until the descendants of the Hasmonean family came to rule as kings" (*A* XI, 111). Aristobulus I, in the year 103 B.C., had transformed the ἀρχή into a monarchy. From the time of the high priest Hyrcanus II (i.e., from 63 B.C. onward), the Romans had ordered a new form of government: "After this Gabinius reinstated Hyrcanus in Jerusalem and committed to him the custody of the Temple. The civil administration he reconstituted under the form of an aristocracy" (*BJ* I, 169). At last, at the time of the first Jewish revolt against Rome (66–70 A.D.), there had been a kind of "unofficial duumvirate" of the former high priest Ananus ben Ananus (only a few months in office as a high priest in 63 A.D.) and of the leader of the Pharisees, Simon ben Gamliel, both in charge of defensive actions at that time.[8] This very last arrangement of a sovereignty of the high priest, priests and scribes had then sinfully been destroyed by the radical rebels in the year 68 A.D., namely by drawing lots for the election of the last high priest Pinchas from Chafta (*BJ* IV, 147–157). Josephus never objects to any extensions of high priestly power, except for the case of Pinchas from Chafta. This is the more remarkable, as he is well aware of the objections from the Pharisees and surely from Qumran against the occupancy of the high priestly office and the kingship by the same person (*A* XIII, 290–299).

Dignity of Earthly, Cosmic, and Heavenly Dimensions

According to Josephus, the cult in the Temple and the high priest reach mysteriously into the realm of God: "We have but one Temple for the one God, . . . common to all as God is common to all. The priests are continuously engaged in His worship, under the leadership of the one who for the time is head of the line" (*Ap* II, 193; see *A* IV, 201). The triad of God, Temple, and High Priest, as indicated here, is related to the Greek thinking in correlations and analogies. This is not understood by Josephus in a naïve, trivial manner. He knows that God had not been cunningly made by the Jews but is prerequisite: "God is His own work" (*A* VIII, 280). God's very essence can be indicated only by negative attributes: Moses "represented Him as one, uncreated and immutable to all eternity; in beauty surpassing all mortal thought, made known to us by His power, although the nature of His real being surpasses essentially (κατ' οὐσίαν) human knowledge" (*Ap* II, 167). Therefore, according to Josephus, it is not the very nature of God that becomes transparent in the Temple and through the high priesthood but rather God's mightiness and—as Josephus often declares—His providence (πρόνοια) and His planning (διάνοια). In this sense, in *Ap* II, 185, he calls God the "head (ἡγεμόνα) of the universe" and the high priestly office "the head-office (ἡγεμονία) of the whole body of priests." In some respects, God and the high priest form, in a kind of heavenly-earthly accord of united hegemony, the commander, guide, and leader of the Jewish people.

Besides the triad of God, Temple, and High Priest, according to Josephus, there still exists the descending triad: high priest, priest, and people. The high priest and his priestly colleagues are backed up by those of the Jewish people who are faithful to the law. Josephus reports several critical situations where the high priest and the people of Jerusalem had stood side by side, and thus had been able to change the conquerer's mind to mildness, or had united in common efforts of a reasonable and disciplined defense. When Alexander the Great (332 B.C.) was standing before Jerusalem, the high priest Jaddus, who had every reason to fear for himself and his city, had ordered the gates of the city to be opened and the people in white garments and the priests in their robes to go toward Alexander in submission. This gesture had moved Alexander to mercy to Jerusalem, and had led him to offer a sacrifice in the Temple, in accordance with the law under the direction of the high priest, and to grant the Jews certain privileges (*A* XI, 317–47). At the beginning of the rebellion (66 A.D.), the high priests—with that plural form Josephus often means the high priest in office and his predecessors—as well as the leading men, that is, the Sanhedrin, assembled the people of Jerusalem, in order to warn them of the war. They implored the people to submit to the superior Romans, so that these would not make use of their arms (*BJ* II, 316–342). In the same way, under the guidance of the former high priest Ananus ben Ananus, they exhorted the populace for support against the radical priestly Zealots, as these "persuaded those who officiated in the Temple services to accept no gift or sacrifice from a foreigner" (*BJ* II, 409–414). Some time later, the same Ananus ben Ananus, together with his high priestly colleague Jesus, called together an assembly (ἐκκλησία) and enlisted and marshalled recruits to fight the Zealots (*BJ* IV, 160–215). Josephus considers Ananus ben Ananus, according to *BJ* IV, 320–321, as a man "unique in his love for liberty and an enthusiast for democracy" (δημοκρατία) and as "an effective speaker, whose words carried weight with the people." He is of a similar opinion with regard to the high priest Matthias ben Theophilus (65–67 A.D.), the son of Boëthus, who "had won the special confidence and esteem of the people" (*BJ* V, 528). The fact that Josephus revised these judgments in individual cases (e.g., in the case of Ananus ben Ananus; see *A* XX, 197–203) is not, in principle, a contradiction to the high value Josephus attributes to the unity of people, priests, and high priests. These three groups, holding together, will keep or restore peace for the Jewish people. Since the most important place of a meeting between high priests, priests, and people is the Temple, Josephus can describe the Jews as a community of those who preserve their "religious rules from contamination" (*BJ* II, 391, 394), or "as the guardians of His shrine" (*BJ* V, 383, 389).[9] The expression *Jewish Temple State*,[10] often quoted in scholarship, is, indeed, in accordance with Josephus' opinion.

Not only the Temple cult and the high priest reach into the realm of God but also the whole priesthood and the Jewish people, as far as it is obedient to the laws of the fathers. "God owns all things united in Him," Josephus says in *Ap* II, 190. The consequence of this concept of God is the understanding of the cosmic-transcosmic dimension of the Jewish cult, of the high priesthood, and of the people. The priestly offices of the Jews and the law-abiding people are of universal relevance in a negative and a positive view. As a negative example, Josephus mentions the high priest Johanan, who some time before the invasion of Alexander the Great killed his own brother in the Temple. Josephus comments: "That Johanan should have committed so impious a deed against his brother while serving as priest was terrible enough, but the more terrible is that neither among Greeks nor barbarians had such a savage and impious deed ever been committed. The Deity, however, was not indifferent to it, and it was for this reason that the people were made slaves and the Temple was defiled by the Persians" (*A* XI, 299–300). Hence, if high priests commit a crime in the Temple, it will have bad consequences for the Jewish people, and further consequence will be the increase in power of the pagan suppressors. However, the high priestly office stands in a positive correlation to the cosmos as well. In the same sense as the Temple (*BJ* V, 184–228), the official vestment of the high priest has a symbolic-cosmic meaning:

> The high priest's tunic likewise signifies the earth, being of linen, and its blue the arch of heaven, while it recalls the lightnings by its pomegranates, the thunder by the sound of its bells. His upper garment, too, denotes universal nature, which it pleased God to make of four elements. . . . The breast shield, again, he set in the midst of this garment, after the manner of the earth, which occupies the midmost place; and by the girdle, wherewith he encompassed it, he signified the ocean, which holds the whole in its embrace. Sun and moon are indicated by the two sardonyxes wherewith he pinned the high priest's robe . . . (*A* III, 184–185).

Josephus is very much in favor of the religious symbolism. To his mind this is the very means to represent the transcendent dimension of the Jews. Unfortunately, Josephus does not explain whether this dimension has a sacramental character as well, in other words, whether it influences the whole world from its inner core. However, this statement is sufficiently clear when speaking of "those ceremonies of world-wide significance, . . . reverenced by visitors to the city from every quarter of the earth" (*BJ* IV, 324), which thus includes the entire cosmos and, therefore, implies the consequence that the Jews must not refuse any gifts and sacrifices from the Hellenistic-Roman world power. Since the Zealots had done so, they had upset the order of the cosmos and were guilty of the destruction of the Temple and the universal symbolism of the high priesthood, of the downfall of the Jewish state, and of the renewed dispersion of the Jewish people.

Portrayals of Several High Priests

Actualization in Various Degrees

Josephus portrays some of the high priests in all their peculiarities, thereby heroizing, disqualifying, and typifying them. His ideological-historical view becomes particularly evident in his descriptions of the high priests John Hyrcanus I, Hyrcanus II, Ananus ben Ananus (Ananus II), and Pinchas from Chafta.[11] Before dealing more closely with these high priests, some general remarks will explain the manner in which Josephus portrayed these high priests of the past to his contemporaries.

For evaluating the historical prominence of the high priests, as reported by Josephus, it is necessary to distinguish between two periods, the first from the time of the First Temple until some time after the reign of the last Davidic descendant, Zerubbabel, who, in cooperation with the high priest Joshua/Jesus, completed the erection of the Second Temple (about 940–500/450 B.C.), and the second from the time of the invasion of Judea by Alexander the

Great until the destruction of the Second Temple (332 B.C.–70 A.D.). Until the time of the worldly-spiritual dual reign, Zerubbabel and Joshua, Josephus offers hardly more about the high priests than vague, schematic records, made up like annals. In *A* X, 149–153 he mentions seventeen high priests who had presided at the performance of the cult in the First Temple; in *A* XX, 231 he mentions eighteen high priests in the same period of the First Temple. With these lists, he deviates considerably from the records of the Masoretic text and Septuagint, notably with regard to the names, as well as to the rank of the respective religious dignitaries. For example, in *A* X, 149, he quotes Šeraya, who is mentioned in II Kings 25:18 as *kohen ha-rōš* (i.e., chief priest), as being a high priest, whereas in the Septuagint the very same is not mentioned as a high priest but merely as "first priest." In the case of Zerubbabel and Joshua, Josephus does not make any references concerning the higher position of the high priest over the layman; rather, in his records, Zerubbabel comes first, before the high priest Joshua, and Joshua himself before the chiefs of the Israelite families (*A* XI, 86). After having reported all that he knows about Zerubbabel, Josephus continues: "For the high priests were at the head of affairs" (*A* XI, 111). Presumably, he did not dare to subordinate Zerubbabel, being a Davidic descendant (see Haggai 2:20–23; Zechariah 4), under the high priest Joshua. Jews of messianic hopes would have resented it. After the disappearance of Zerubbabel, there was no longer any Davidic descendant with authority. In consequence, Josephus now had a free hand to advocate his evident ideology, namely that the high priest should be the primary dignitary in religious and worldly matters (as for instance also in Ben Sira 45.17). Further, he was now in the position to attribute the gift of prophecy to those high priests whom he preferred in particular (see *BJ* I, 68–69). He was interested in the union of high priesthood with the gift of prophecy. He saw Israel's strength and consistency in the combination of both dignities and charismata. In this sense, Josephus declares in *Ap* I, 29 that the Jewish forefathers had taken greater care in the keeping of their genuine records than had the Egyptians and Babylonians:

> Our forefathers assigned the keeping of their records to their chief priests and prophets. And down to our own times these records have been and, if I may venture to say so, will continue to be preserved with scrupulous accuracy (ἀκριβείας). From the very beginning our ancestors had not only entrusted this task to men of the highest character, who were devoted to the service of God, but they also took precautions that the succession of priestly generations be kept unadultered and pure.

The most convincing proof of the genuiness of the high priesthood, as Josephus declares, "is that our records contain the names of our high priests, with the succession from father to son for the last two thousand years. And whoever violates any of the above rules is forbidden to minister at the altars or to take any other part in divine worship" (*Ap* I, 36). In consequence, the priest Josephus can also present himself as a reliable commentator. He had been able to write his two great works, the *Jewish War* and the *Antiquities,* because, "being a priest and of priestly ancestry, I am well versed in the philosophy of those writings" (*Ap* I, 54). A Hellenistic-minded priest himself, he takes himself as inspired by prophecy, able to interpret the sacred books of the Jews (*BJ* III, 352; VI, 312), and to foretell the impending fate and destiny (*BJ* III, 352–353).

From the time of Alexander the Great onward, that is, the time of the Greek-Roman Hellenism, various high priests are described in all details. To Josephus, they are mirrors that show to his own contemporaries what should have been done in the years of the revolt in 66 to 73 A.D. and how the Jews might have reverted to a new beginning. These high priests are the prototypes for his own time, that is, the dignitaries of a supreme office, by means of which the salvation of the Jewish people had been tried and might be tried once more, even after the destruction of the Second Temple. The Jewish people might return again to its former glory and its religious-political order if it would take to heart the teachings that derive from the high priestly office and its dignitaries. *BJ* V, 19 refers to that hope, where Josephus speaks rhetorically to Jerusalem: "Yet might there be hopes for an amelioration of thy lot, if ever thou wouldst propitiate God who devastated thee!" (also *BJ* VI, 267; *A* X, 37; *Ap* I, 29–30).[12]

The high priest Jaddus, who was in office at the time of the invasion of Alexander the Great, is the first prototype, whose religious and political attitude is shown by Josephus as an example of Jewish attitude in the face of assault of superior enemies. The manner in which Jaddus, together with the priests and the people, had met Alexander and his army is for Josephus the most conceivable contrast to the senseless hostility against the Romans by the revolting Zealots of his days (*A* XI, 317–347). If in the years 66–70 A.D., the peace-loving Jewish party had gained acceptance as at the time of Alexander's march toward Jerusalem, the city would not have been destroyed and not so many would have been slaughtered.

The second high priestly prototype with a righteous religious and political attitude for Josephus is the high priest Eleazar, who lived in the time of Ptolemy II (283–246 B.C.). His merits are to bring about a religious communication with the Greek world power by enabling the translation of the Holy Scriptures of the Jews into Greek. Already, in his introduction to the *Antiquities,* Josephus speaks highly of Eleazar in words that aim distinctively at his own time:

> Eleazar, who yielded in virtue to none of our high priests, did not scruple to grant the monarch [i.e., Ptolemy II] the enjoyment of a benefit in the use of

these books, which he would certainly have refused, had it not been our traditional custom not to turn anything good and useful into a secret. Accordingly, I consider that the high priest's magnanimity should be imitated, and I hope that there are still today many lovers of learning like the king. (*A* I, 11–12)

In *A* XII, 11–118 Josephus comes again to speak of the Septuagint translation, accomplished under Eleazar and Ptolemy II, praising it as a religious and political act of peace between the Greeks and the Jews. The high priest, whose duties are to care for the welfare of the Jews, according to Josephus, is also bound to repress the hostilities of the people of the world against the Jews. It is Eleazar's merit to have given, together with the peaceful and studious king Ptolemy, an example of fruitful religious and cultural interchange between Jews and pagans. Both of them had finally given testimony that Greeks and Jews worship the same God (*A* XII, 22).[13] In this representation of the Septuagint translation Josephus is dependent upon the *Letter of Aristeas* (150–100 B.C.).

John Hyrcanus I (134–104 B.C.)

Whereas in *A* XII, 419 Judas Maccabaeus appears as the first Hasmonean high priest (although, in reality, he probably did not hold this office), the first Hasmonean high priest mentioned in the *Jewish War* by name and described in all details is John Hyrcanus. The first sentence of Josephus' report in the *Jewish War* already shows Josephus' point of view: "Hyrcanus, having gained the high priestly office held by his father before him, offered sacrifice to God and then started in haste after Ptolemy to bring aid to his mother and brothers" (*BJ* I, 56). Here Josephus is entirely guided by the attitude of the author of I Maccabees, where the legitimacy of the high priest is accepted pragmatically. Although the Hasmoneans had formerly been simple village priests, their rise to the high priestly office is justified on the ground that they proved themselves efficient defenders and saviors of the Jews (see I Maccabees 2:7–13, 49–69, 10:17–20, 13:3–6; similarly in the same sense in *A* XIII, 197–199). High priestly genealogical trees as such never suffice for justifying a candidacy for the high priestly office.[14]

Already, with the first mention of John Hyrcanus, Josephus recognizes that Hyrcanus had to deal with cultic and political affairs. He also knows that Hyrcanus was involved in enterprises, the consequences of which had been problematic throughout. Hyrcanus I destroyed the Temple of the Samaritans and "opened the tomb of David and took out three thousand talents of silver and, drawing on this sum, became the first Jewish king to support foreign troops. He also made a friendly alliance with Antiochus and, admitting him into the city, lavishly and generously supplied his army with all they needed. And when Antiochus undertook an expedition against the Parthians, Hyrcanus set out with him" (*A* XIII, 240–250). The most incomprehensible attitude of

Josephus is his obvious consent to Hyrcanus' dissension with the Pharisees (*A* XIII, 290–299). At a feast given by Hyrcanus, a man named Eleazar ben Poira frankly addressed the absolutistic-minded Hyrcanus: "Since you have asked to be told the truth, if you wish to be righteous, give up the high priest-hood and be content with governing the people" (*A* XIII, 291). Behind this sentence, there were strong concerns of the Pharisees (and of the Qumran priests) about the legitimacy of the Hasmonean high priests. With regard to their descent, they were not entitled to occupy the high priestly office (see Leviticus 21:13–15; cf. *A* XIII, 292, 372). Besides, according to Pharisaic doctrine, the combination of the highest cultic office with worldly, military activity is not in accordance with biblical tradition. Presumably, they regarded the Hasmoneans as usurpers with respect to Davidic-messianic privilege as well as to high priestly dignity. They understood the frankness of Eleazar not as "blasphemy" (*A* XIII, 294) but only as "slander" (λοιδορία). Although they did not dare to declare it on that occasion, they actually understood it as an act of legitimate and necessary contradiction to the Hasmonean usurpation. This episode shows that the attitude of Josephus, who was in accord with Hyr-canus, was not Pharisaic, that Pharisaic spirituality was irrelevant to him in some respects, although in his youth Josephus had conducted his life accord-ing to the rules of the Pharisees (*V* 7–12). Contrary to the Pharisees, he had no understanding for the disapproval of the double function of high priest and king held by the same person. Therefore, he had no scruples to conclude with the following glorification of John Hyrcanus: "He was truly a blessed individ-ual . . . , for he was the only man to unite in his person three of the highest privileges: the supreme command of the nation, the high priesthood, and the gift of prophecy. For he was so closely in touch with the Deity (ὡμίλει αὐτῷ), that he was never ignorant of the future" (*BJ* I, 68–69; similarly *A* XIII, 299–300). In Josephus' mind, the high priestly office had reached its highest possible manifestation in John Hyrcanus. In its ideal state, this office com-bined the three functions: political government, high priesthood, and proph-ecy. The same idea was later applied to Jesus and to the pope (*tria munera*). In consequence, Josephus is in the position to interpret the high priestly office as the origin of all Jewish offices, dignities, future developments, and merits. Therefore, he contradicts the opinion of his time that prophecy has expired (Psalms 74:9, Daniel 3:38, Septuagint, I Maccabees 4:46, 14:41; later also Talmud, *Sanhedrin* 11a). Moreover, he is firmly convinced—this is shown in no other case so distinctly as with John Hyrcanus—that the high priests must be prepared to make all possible concessions to the non-Jewish nations, even if this would result in uncertain expectations of meeting the non-Jewish pow-ers halfway. The high priest should behave like a diplomat in office in order to negotiate between Jews and non-Jews.

Hyrcanus II (76–67, 63–40, Died 30 B.C.)

Hyrcanus II was the elder son (besides Aristobolus II) of the high priest and king Alexander Jannaeus (103–76 B.C.) and queen Salome Alexandra (76–67 B.C.). He was the high priest, king, ethnarch, and delegate of the Romans, whose power and reputation were subjected most frequently to ups and downs and provocations. Nevertheless, he was successful enough to accomplish the longest time in office as high priest and sovereign (as king or prince) above all the other high priests of the Second Temple, though, on the other hand, he had to spend most of those years in utmost danger. In *A* XV, 179–182, after a detailed illustration of his previous career full of intrigues that had led to his unjust execution through Herod I in the year 30 B.C., his life is summarized as follows:

> This, then, was the way in which Hyrcanus was fated to end his life after experiencing a lifetime of diverse and varied fortunes. At the very beginning of the reign of his mother Alexandra he was appointed high priest of the Jewish nation and held this office for nine years. After taking the throne on the death of his mother, he held it for three months, but was driven from it by his brother Aristobulus. When he was restored to it later by Pompey, he received back all his honors and continued to enjoy them for forty years more. But he was deprived of them a second time by Antigonus, mutilated in body, and taken prisoner by the Parthians. From their country he returned to his own land some time later because of the hopes held out to him by Herod, but none of these was fulfilled in accordance with his expectations, after he had experienced much suffering in his lifetime. But what was most painful of all . . . , was that in his old age he came to an unworthy end.

Hyrcanus II grew old to an age above eighty. He was allegedly born about 112 B.C. These data taken from *A* XV, 179–181, however, do not correspond with the historical facts. The alleged forty years of office after his restoration as high priest by Pompey, if submitted to a close examination, will shrink to twenty-three years at the most. In the last ten years of his life, he could no longer have held the office of a high priest.

Originally, Hyrcanus was appointed as high priest by his mother Salome Alexandra, especially because of his lack of energy and proficiency in practical matters (*A* XIII, 408). After the death of Salome Alexandra, quarrels broke out between the Pharisaic-oriented Hyrcanus II and his Sadducean, nationalistically disposed brother Aristobulus II, in which Hyrcanus always was the loser, at first and up to the time of the invasion of the Roman commander Pompey (63 B.C.). From then on, more and more he turned out as a cautiously operating politician with a good feeling for the realities of power. Hyrcanus II opened the gates of Jerusalem and of the Temple to Pompey (*A* XIV, 66, 72). As a reward, he was allowed to keep the high priestly office; and, in addition, as a functionary of the conquerer, political power was bestowed on him in

Judea, Perea, and Galilee.[15] He turned out to be very clever in surviving politically when the ascent of Antipater and after him of his son Herod began to take shape. Since he was well aware of his political and administrative shortcomings, he made Antipater his adviser. Josephus considers this a prudent action: "When Caesar, after his victory over Pompey and the latter's death, was fighting in Egypt, Antipater, the governor of the Jews, under orders from Hyrcanus proved himself useful to Caesar in many ways" (*A* XIV, 127). Antipater had come to Caesar's aid with three thousand Jewish soldiers when Caesar, on his passage from Egypt to Syria, had met difficulties at Ascalon. Further, he had been able to persuade the Egyptian Jews, by showing them a letter from the high priest Hyrcanus, to be hospitable to Caesar and his army (*A* XIV, 128–132). Caesar had shown his gratitude by raising the political status of Hyrcanus II in the year 47 B.C. through appointing him an ethnarch.

The situation grew far more difficult for Hyrcanus when Herod began to play his role full of intrigues in an unrestrained manner (especially after 43 B.C.); and, at the same time, the power politics in Rome became unfathomable. During this time, Aristobulus II was able to make himself king for a short time. Hyrcanus, mutilated ritually by having his ears cut off, was taken prisoner by the Parthians and brought to Babylon. After being released from captivity by the Parthians, he was highly honored as high priest by the Jews who settled in the area of Euphrates (*A* XV, 11–15). In spite of the warnings of the Babylonian Jews, he returned to Jerusalem because of the hopes held out to him by Herod, but later, in the year 30 B.C., was liquidated by him as the last male descendant of the Hasmonean family. Some time earlier, his grandson, Aristobulus III, had been murdered by Herod, who ordered his servants to drown him while he was swimming with them in a pool (*A* XV, 50–56).

No other high priest is mentioned as often as Hyrcanus II. This derives only partially from the fact that Josephus had very good source-material at his disposal, for instance "the Memoirs of King Herod" (*A* XV, 174). Josephus' main purpose was to present Hyrcanus II to his contemporaries as a tragic and yet most prudent high priestly hero. Hyrcanus had lived in a politically most confused and dangerous time, and nevertheless had tried to fulfill his duties with all his might and abilities, so that the Jewish people would not perish, become hostile to foreigners, or give themselves up. In the case of Hyrcanus, it can be seen how dangerous and vulnerable the life of a high priest can be. Moreover, Hyrcanus had remained high priest in spite of his dismissals and expulsions, even in spite of the ritual mutilation of his body (*A* XV, 181).

Josephus never shows himself indignant about the *appointment* to the high priest office by foreign sovereigns or by Herod. However, he is very much opposed to the *deprivation* of this office by those potentates or by the high priestly rivals. In the case of the disrespectfully described high priest Ananel (37/36 B.C., then again from 34 B.C.), Josephus calls the high-handed dismissal by Herod an "unlawful" act (παράνομα ποιῶν; A XV, 40), in spite of his depreciatory remarks about Ananel. In the case of the high priest Jason/Jesus (175–172 B.C.), he calls Antiochus IV Epiphanes a "liquidator of the Law" (ἔλυσε τὸν νόμον; A XV, 41). In the same context, he passes such a judgment on Aristobulus II, who deprived Hyrcanus II of his high priestly office. In Josephus' opinion, the high priestly office is of an indelible character.[16] Notwithstanding that Hyrcanus II was impaired in the fulfillment of his office by being deprived of his honors and mutilated in his body, he remained high priest until his death! The indelible character of this office is a symbol of Israel's continuity.

Ananus ben Ananus (Ananus II)

Ananus ben Ananus held his office as high priest in 62 A.D. for only a few months. He was the son of Ananus I (Hanas, Anas), who was high priest in 6–15 A.D., and until his death in 35 A.D. possessed an undisputed leadership in the Sanhedrin. Ananus I reorganized the Sanhedrin to the effect that from then on the high priest, contrary to the time of the Hasmoneans, no longer had the air of a "priestly prince" but was an "aristocratic chairman," who was acknowledged as a decisive "president" or "princeps" of the Sanhedrin, and definitely dominated the latter.[17] According to Josephus (A XX, 198), "Ananus I was extremely fortunate. For he had five sons, all of whom, after he himself had previously enjoyed the office for a very long period, became high priests of God." These five high priestly sons were: Caiphas (18–37 A.D.; son-in-law), Jonathan (37 A.D.), Theophilus (37–40 A.D.?), Matthias (40 A.D.?), and Ananus II (62 A.D.). Just as previously in the high priestly Boëthus family, so the Ananus family kept to the rule that the brother (not, at first, the son) followed in succession as high priest. The "brother-succession" in the high priestly office was a characteristic feature during the first century before and the first century after Christ.[18]

Ananus II was the last representative of the Ananus family who received high priestly dignity. In the history of the high priests, he is especially remarkable because, in the first two years of the Jewish War, he was an energetic defender of Jerusalem, further because he sentenced to death the "brother of Jesus who was called the Christ," and because he is an example of how Josephus corrected himself in his historical work.

According to BJ II, 563, the former high priests Ananus II and (the less important) Jesus ben Damnaeus (high priest in 62/63 A.D.) were elected to supreme control of affairs in the city with unlimited authority (αὐτοκράτορες). "They were also given special charge to raise the height of the walls." Josephus points out that Ananus was one of the leading men "who were not pro-Romans." He had performed his duties with circumspection. Unfortunately he was not successful in "gradually abandoning these warlike preparations and bending the malcontents and the infatuated so-called Zealots to a more salutary policy" (*BJ* II, 648–651). Nevertheless, he was a capable leader of the people, who in all his actions was always concerned about popular consent. In the year 67 A.D., after the Zealots had illegally appointed Pinchas from Chafta their high priest, Ananus and Jesus "vehemently upbraided the people for their apathy and incited them against the Zealots" (*BJ* IV, 160–64). In a general assembly, Ananus was successful in convincing the people not to allow affairs to remain in such confusion. The Zealots, hearing of these proceedings, however, attacked the assembly. The supporters of Ananus pushed the invaders back into the Temple at last. However, while Ananus was endeavoring to avoid any fighting in this sacred place, in the end a unit of rebellious Idumaeans killed him and also Jesus, his successor in office.

The importance Josephus attaches to the death of Ananus is significant:

> I should not be wrong in saying that the capture of the city began with the death of Ananus; and that the overthrow of the walls and the downfall of the Jewish state dated from the day on which the Jews beheld their high priest, the captain of their salvation, butchered in the heart of Jerusalem. A man on every ground revered and of highest integrity, Ananus, with all distinction of his birth, his rank, and the honors to which he had attained, yet delighted to treat the very humblest as his equals. . . . On all occasions, he put the public welfare above his private interests. To maintain peace was his supreme object. He knew that the Roman power was irresistible, but, when driven to provide for a state of war, he endeavored to secure that, if the Jews would not come to terms, the struggle should at least be skilfully conducted. In a word, had Ananus lived, they would undoubtedly either have arranged terms . . . or else, had hostilities continued, they would have greatly retarded the victory of the Romans under such a general. . . . But it was, I suppose, because God had, for its pollutions, condemned the city to destruction and desired to purge the sanctuary by fire, that He thus cut off those who clung to them with such tender affection. So they, who but lately had worn the sacred vestments, had led those ceremonies of world-wide significance and had been reverenced by visitors to the city from every quarter of the earth, were now seen cast out naked, to be devoured by dogs and beasts of prey. (*BJ* IV, 318–24)

Here, we are confronted with the typical scheme of Josephus' view. The high priest Ananus II is a righteous man, an able military leader, a democrat, diplomat, and eager to preserve peace. If the people had followed him, the disaster would never have struck the city and the Temple, or at least not so devastatingly.

In *A* XX, 197–203, Josephus corrects this ideal description of Ananus II. There he describes him as a fervent, patriotic Sadducean high priest, who, being left to his own discretion during the four-months interregnum between the government of the Roman procurator Porcius Festus (60–62 A.D.) and his successor Albinus (62–64 A.D.), unscrupulously delivered up James, the brother of Jesus the Christ, to be stoned. He had been "rash in his temper," and "those of the inhabitants of the city who were considered the most fair-minded and who were strict in observance of the law [probably, the Pharisees] were offended at this," claiming that Ananus had no authority to convene the Sanhedrin on his own. These citizens had urged king Agrippa II to depose Ananus from the high priesthood.

Perhaps Josephus might not have heard of the unlawful death sentence of James before he had written his *Antiquities* in Rome. Perhaps this was the reason to abstain now in the *Antiquities* from any glorification of Ananus. In any case, the aged Josephus showed here his quality as a historian who was prepared to correct his historical judgment on certain points.

Pinchas from Chafta (Aphthia) (67–70 A.D.)

This last high priest of the Second Temple is of particular religious, historic, and theological significance because he is associated with a "change" in the high priest office [see Hebrews 7] and the radical Jewish eschatological expectations. The aristocratic, conservative priest Josephus showed no sympathy toward that uneducated stonemason from a village, who was elected by the Zealots during the rebellion. In *BJ* IV, 147–157, Josephus speaks of the "madness" of the Zealots, abrogating the claims of those families from which, in turn, the high priest had always been drawn in a certain order. He continues:

> For, to test the abject submission of the populace and make trial of their own strength, they essayed to appoint the high priests by lot, although, as we have stated, the succession was hereditary. As pretext for this scheme they adduced ancient custom, asserting that in olden days the high priesthood had been determined by lot; but in reality their action was the abrogation of established practice and a trick to make themselves supreme by getting these appointments into their own hands. They accordingly summoned one of the high priestly clans, called Eniachin, and cast lots for a high priest. By chance the lot fell to one who proved a signal illustration of their depravity; he was an individual named Pinchas, son of Samuel, of the village of Chafta, a man who not only was not descended from high priests, but was such a clown that he scarcely knew what the high priesthood meant. At any rate they dragged their reluctant victim out of the country and, dressing him up for his assumed part, as on the stage, put the sacred vestments upon him and instructed him how to act in keeping with the occasion.

This description betrays Josephus' personal anger and utmost moral indignation. The proceedings of the proponents of Pinchas, to him, are a dissolution of the law or unlawfulness, even if he has to admit that "they adduced ancient custom" (154). He suppresses the importance of the proceedings by much defamation. In reality, Eniachin was not a common high priestly family (155), rather a first-rank clan, descended from the "Sons of Sadoq" (see I Chronicles 24:12). The "Sons of Sadoq" had produced high priests until

172 B.C. (Jason) in Jerusalem, and since then in Leontopolis. However, in the first century B.C./A.D. the clan lived in the country. The Zealots wanted to put an end to the "Hasmonean outrage" and appointed again a high priest out of the clan of the "Sons of Sadoq." Thereby, they wanted to establish a procedure in the name of God. They could be sure of the consent of all those countrymen who, since 172 B.C., could not put up with the high priestly families in office. "Descent all the time counted more in the Orient than power, because descent was created by God." [19]

That Josephus defamed the election of Pinchas from Chafta, against his better knowledge, comes to light in *A* III, 188–92; IV, 57–58, where the election of the arch-high priest Aaron (according to Exodus 28; Leviticus 8; Numbers 14–16) is mentioned. However, after questioning Aaron's appointment by the horde of Korah and its final confirmation by a token from God, Josephus comments as follows: "Aaron was no longer believed to owe his high priesthood to the favor of Moses, but to the judgment of God" (*A* IV, 58).

What was right in the time of Aaron should also be fair in the case of Pinchas from Chafta! However, Josephus was neither willing nor able to consider the legitimacy of the Jewish high priest in connection with the rise of the Hasmoneans to the high priesthood. Already in the case of Ananel, "Son of Sadoq" (37–36 B.C., and again from 34 B.C.),[20] he showed his disapproval of acknowledging the high priestly descent. Pinchas from Chafta did not correspond to the pro-Hasmonean historiography of Josephus. Therefore, there is no mention of any hopes with regard to Pinchas' election and later fate (he presumably was murdered in 70 A.D.). It is likely that Josephus' silence in this respect was caused by his disapproval of the messianic-eschatological expectations that the Zealots had connected with the election of Pinchas. In any case, Josephus is the most important historian of the Jewish high priests. His prejudices and resentments, however, have to be taken into account and, in some respect, are responsible for shortcomings and inaccuracies in his works.

Notes

1. E.g., Paul Billerbeck, "Ein Tempelgottesdienst in Jesu Tagen," *ZNW* 55(1964): 1–17; Joachim Jeremias, *Jerusalem zur Zeit Jesu. Eine kulturgeschichtliche Untersuchung zur neutestamentlichen Zeitgeschichte* (Göttingen 1962).

2. Cf. Jeremias, *ibid.*, pp. 168 f.

3. Cf. Willem Cornelis van Unnik, "Eine merkwürdige liturgische Aussage bei Josephus (Jos Ant 8, 111–113)," *J-S* (Göttingen 1974), pp. 362–369.

4. Cf. Roland Bergmeier, "Miszellen zu Flavius Josephus Bell 5, 208.236," *ZNW* 54(1963):268–271.

5. Hans Conzelmann, *Heiden—Juden—Christen. Auseinandersetzungen in der Literatur der hellenistisch-römischen Zeit* (Tübingen 1981), p. 208.

6. Gedalyahu Alon, *Jews, Judaism and the Classical World. Studies in Jewish History in the Times of the Second Temple and Talmud* (Jerusalem 1977), p. 31.

7. Cf. Jürgen C. H. Lebram, "Der Idealstaat der Juden," *J-S* (Göttingen 1974), pp. 233–253.

8. This is the way Cecil Roth, "The Pharisees in the Jewish Revolution of 66–73," *JSeS* 7(1962), pp. 67 f., interprets the kind of Jewish government during the first Jewish Revolt against Rome.

9. Cf. Helgo Lindner, *Die Geschichtsauffassung des Flavius Josephus im Bellum Judaicum. Gleichzeitig ein Beitrag zur Quellenfrage* (Leiden 1972), p. 142.

10. Martin Hengel, *Judentum und Hellenismus* (Tübingen 1969), pp. 42–55.

11. For the whole history of the priesthood of the Second Temple cf. Bo Reicke, *Neutestamentliche Zeitgeschichte* (Berlin 1965).

12. Cf. Clemens Thoma, "Die Weltanschauung des Josephus Flavius. Dargestellt anhand seiner Schilderung des jüdischen Aufstandes gegen Rom (66–73 n. Chr.)," *Kairos* 11(1969): 39–52, esp. p. 49.

13. Concerning the equation of Zeus and the God of Israel, cf. Adolf Schlatter, *Die Theologie des Judentums nach dem Bericht des Josefus* (Gütersloh 1932), pp. 237–51; reprinted in Abraham Schalit, *Zur Josephus Forschung* (Darmstadt 1973), 190–204, esp. p. 197.

14. Cf. Clemens Thoma, "Religionsgeschichtliche und theologische Bedeutsamkeit der jüdischen Hohenpriester von 175 bis 37 v. Chr.," *BL* 45(1972):4–22.

15. Cf. Bo Reicke (*op. cit.*, note 11), p. 62.

16. For the indelible character of the Jewish high priest, cf. the excerpt of (Pseudo-) Hecataeus in *Ap* I, 183–204.

17. Cf. Bo Reicke, (*op. cit.*, note 11), pp. 106–113.

18. Cf. Ernst Bammel, "Die Bruderfolge im Hohenpriestertum der herodianisch-römischen Zeit," *ZDPV* 70(1954):147–153.

19. Joachim Jeremias (*op. cit.*, note 1), p. 218.

20. Cf. Abraham Schalit, *König Herodes. Der Mann und sein Werk*, (Berlin 1969), p. 308; and esp. *A* XV, 22, 39 f.

10 Josephus and the Revolutionary Parties

VALENTIN NIKIPROWETZKY

Zealousness for God and the Spirit of Zeal

In spite of what historians such as K. Kohler, W. R. Farmer, and others have affirmed, even if it is impossible to find material proof of connections between the religious ideology of the Hasidim during the Maccabean wars and the ideology that inspired some or all of the revolutionary parties who led the great revolt against the Romans in the first century of our era, the relationship is indisputable.

As a foreword to the ideology of rebel parties in the revolt of 66–74, it is therefore impossible not to mention, even if in a very condensed way, the guiding principles underlying the action of fighters in their struggle against Hellenism at the time of the Maccabeans.

The nature of the "zealous" or "jealous" state of mind and behavior that is man's reaction to the overdemanding exclusiveness of God is symbolized most clearly and dramatically in an episode related in Numbers 25.

One may recall that whereas Zimri in Shittim

> brought a Midianite woman to his brothers, before the eyes of Moses and the entire community of the sons of Israel, and whereas the latter were content to weep at the entrance of the Tent of the Presence, Phinehas, son of Eleazar son of Aaron the priest, stood up in the midst of the community, took up a spear in his hand, went into the inner room and transfixed both of them, the man of Israel and the woman through the lower abdomen: the plague ceased to weigh on the sons of Israel. . . . Yahweh spoke to Moses, saying "Phinehas son of Eleazar, son of Aaron the priest, has turned my wrath away from the Israelites; he displayed among them the same jealous anger that moved me, and therefore in my jealousy I did not exterminate the Israelites. Tell him that I hereby grant him my covenant of security of tenure. He and his descendants after him shall enjoy the priesthood under a covenant for all time, because he showed his zeal for God and made expiation for the Israelites."

This narrative brings to the fore a legal contradiction. On the one hand, according to Israelite law, no man, however obvious his guilt may seem, may be put to death without a trial. On the other, Phinehas' merit that gained divine alliance and peace, an alliance of everlasting priesthood for Aaron's grandson and his race, was that he had transcended the prevailing passivity by resorting to spontaneous violence in the service of God.

Those zealous for God cannot bear to witness any particularly serious violation of the law or offense against God without reacting: they instinctively take vengeance.

The vocation of Mattathias of Modin and his five sons in I Maccabees 2:19–28 is recounted in terms which irresistibly remind us of this episode in Numbers to which, moreover, it makes explicit reference. On their arrival at Modin, the king's envoys wanted to force the neighboring Jews to participate in sacrifices ordered by the king. Many Israelites submitted.

> Mattathias, the first to be summoned, replied in a ringing tone. "Though all the nations within the king's dominions obey him and forsake their ancestral worship, though they have chosen to submit to his commands, yet I and my sons and brothers will follow the covenant of our fathers. Heaven forbid we should ever abandon the law and its statutes. We will not obey the command of the king, nor will we deviate one step from our forms of worship."

As soon as he had finished, a Jew stepped forward in full view of all to offer sacrifice on the pagan altar at Modin, in obedience to the royal command. The sight stirred Mattathias to indignation; he shook with passion and in a fury of righteous anger rushed forward and slaughtered the traitor on the very altar. At the same time he killed the officer sent by the king to enforce sacrifice, and pulled the pagan altar down. Thus, Mattathias showed his fervent zeal for the law, just as Phinehas had done by killing Zimri, son of Salu. " 'Follow me,' he shouted through the town, 'every one of you who is zealous for the law and strives to maintain the covenant.' He and his sons took to the hills, leaving all their belongings behind in the town."

This narrative highlights features of religious mentality that we shall come across later, which lie at the base of the activity of most of the revolutionary parties involved in the great revolt against the Romans. According to the "zealous of God," religious faith and devotion to the commandments cannot exist without active involvement that puts man's entire being in jeopardy. God responds and grants his blessing and aid only to the man who has made the first step and put his life in danger in the service of the law. So here we are confronted with a sort of synergism.

Furthermore, in addition to this religious aspect, there is a traditional complement that, in this case, is none other than an apparently negative expression of the almighty power of God.

The fighters were convinced that they were in no way responsible for the victories they had won. They were merely the instruments of God, to whom all glory is due and who granted them triumph in recompense for the blind trust they continued to show in his favor, even in the most terrifying and desperate circumstances from the human point of view. Similarly, Hananiah, Mishael, and Azariah were saved from the blazing furnace because they never ceased to have faith (I Macc. 2:59).

Man, in order to serve God, has despised everything and put himself in such a situation that only divine intervention can save him from death. This assurance gives him a sort of sui generis serenity, a kind of quietism that is the basis of activist behavior apparently just the reverse.

Judas Maccabee's speech before Bethoron drew conclusions with perfect clarity:

> When his followers saw the host coming against them, they said to Judas, "How can so few of us fight against so many? Besides, we have had nothing to eat all day and we are exhausted." Judas replied: "Many can easily be overpowered by a few; *it makes no difference to Heaven to save through many or through few. Victory does not depend on numbers; strength comes from Heaven alone.* Our enemies come filled with insolence and lawlessness to plunder and kill us and our wives and children. *We are fighting for our lives and our religion. Heaven will crush them before our eyes.*" *(I Macc. 3:17–22)*

The corollary and consequence of this exclusive confidence in God is a symmetrical distrust of fear that a creature of flesh and blood claims to inspire. The glory of the ungodly is destined to the dung-hill and the worms. Today he will be exalted and tomorrow he will not exist, as he will have returned to dust and his intentions brought to nil (I Macc. 2:62ff.). His powerlessness is glaringly apparent, even when he thinks he wields thunder and inflicts death. God will render to the martyr, and to him alone, this body that the tyrant thinks he tortures beyond hope, this breath of life he thinks he destroys forever. Consequently, physical suffering appears to have no hold over the victim. He dies proclaiming his veneration for God and the law; his face shows incomprehensible joy as he taunts or menaces his persecutors. The young men distinguish themselves with almost inhuman determination.

On this point, the account of the seven Maccabean brothers and their mother is quite eloquent: " 'Fiend though you are,' cries the second Maccabean brother addressing Antiochus IV Epiphanes, organizer and witness of their torments, 'you are setting us free from this present life; and, since we die for his laws, the King of the Universe will raise us up to a life everlastingly made new.' "

The third brother heroically exclaims, boldly holding out his hands:

> "The God of Heaven gave me these. His law means far more to me than they do, and it is from him that I trust to receive them back." When they heard this, the king and his followers were amazed at the young man's spirit and his utter disregard for suffering. The fourth, at the point of death, says: "Better to be killed by men and cherish God's promise to raise us again. There will be no resurrection to life for you!"

As for the mother, she was altogether admirable and worthy of a glorious memory, since she, who had put her hopes in the Lord, watched her seven sons all die in the space of a single day. She encouraged each, in turn, in her native language. Filled with noble resolution, her woman's thoughts fired by a manly spirit, she said to them:

> You appeared in my womb I know not how; it was not I who gave you life and breath and set in order your bodily frame. It is the Creator of the universe who molds man at his birth and plans the origin of all things. Therefore he, in his mercy, will give you back *life and breath again, since now you put his law above all thought of self.* (II Macc. 7 passim)

It is striking to find this state of mind expressed with the same determination and éclat after Masada, when the six hundred Sicarii were captured and martyred in Egypt.

> Nor was there a person who was not amazed at the endurance—[relates Josephus]—call it what you will—desperation or strength of purpose, displayed by these victims. For under every form of torture and laceration of body, devised for the sole object of making them acknowledge Caesar as lord, not one submitted nor was brought to the verse of utterance; but all kept their resolve, triumphant over constraint, meeting the tortures and the fire with bodies that seemed insensible of pain and souls that wellnigh exulted in it. *But most of all were the spectators struck by the children of tender age, not one of whom could be prevailed upon to call Caesar lord. So far did the strength of courage rise superior to the weakness of their frames.* (BJ VII, 417–419)

In our opinion, such madness or strength of soul cannot be explained in terms of political or national fanaticism. It lies embedded in the deepest layers of man's being, by which we mean in religious mentality. Contemporary history provides us with similar examples.

Sometimes, forestalling the executioner, the martyr would take his own life; Razis' suicide (II Macc. 14:37–46) was prompted by religious devotion and the conviction that his voluntary death would bring him the martyr's crown; that is, resurrection and eternal life—the prerogative of martyrs. He died praying the Master of life to restore it to him one day.

Josephus has noted the sort of indifference or rather *joy* that the insurgents showed on seeing the city burn after the capture of Jerusalem, as the Roman troops slowly pushed them back to the Temple; right up to the end they hoped God would intervene.

Mentality and Cause of the War

The preceding pages constitute an indispensable introduction to our study. They set out to provide a theology or description of popular mentality that, grafted onto a traditional religious background, set other historical factors in motion and transformed them into active or explosive agents.

Anatole France expressed his sympathy for patriots who believed they had died for their country when, in fact, they had died for arms manufacturers. The fact is as true as, if I may say, it is inevitable. No one, in fact, would consent to die for prosaic or mercenary reasons. If all fighters were to become aware of the logic and moral infrastructure of war, there would be very few left to lead.

Consequently, the preceding description is no more than an outline, in many respects incomplete, of the wars of zeal in Palestine in late antiquity. This theology had become traditional in some Jewish circles. It takes into account motivation for zeal while leaving the deep-seated material causes or unforeseeable consequences of the conflict unexplained. Theological causes or mentality cannot themselves claim precedence over facts; they merely function as a detonator and apparently lie at the heart of the conflict because they set fire to the whole and provoke the conflagration. Moreover, in the case of an author such as Josephus, his search for an energetic and even sensational means of expression forced him to multiply hyperboles tending to assign to each important and fateful event a decisive role in the ruin of the Jewish nation; so much so, that the result is a list of multiple causes of the war, each presented as having played an instrumental, decisive, and unique role. To accept such qualifications uncritically leads to historical misjudgment, the result of erroneous stylistic appreciation. The best illustration of this phenomenon is to be found in P. Bilde's study in the *Journal for the Study of Judaism*, 10, no. 2 (1979):189–202.

Theology provides the principle that links apparently dissimilar factors together and gives them an external coherence. We shall give only a few examples.

It is often said, and the fact seems quite undisputed, that, at the outset, the war between the Jews and the Romans was basically a conflict between Jews and Hellenistic or Greek inhabitants of Palestine. Yet, the disagreement between the Jews and non-Jews of coastal Caesarea (*BJ* II, 266–267) cannot possibly be regarded as the starting point.

The same could be said about an incident that Josephus relates a few paragraphs later, when Nero decided in favor of the Greeks and granted them the right to govern Caesarea as a Hellenistic city, a city that had been founded by Herod the Great and whose possession was contested by the Jews for that very reason.

> Meanwhile, the Greeks of Caesarea had won their case at Caesar's tribunal, and obtained from him the government of that city; they brought back with them the text of the decision; and it was now that the war opened. . . . The ostensible pretext for war was out of proportion to the magnitude of the disasters to which it led. The Jews in Caesarea had a synagogue adjoining a plot of ground owned by a Greek of that city; this site they had frequently endeavored to purchase,

offering a price far exceeding its true value. The proprietor, disdaining their so-licitations, by way of insult further proceeded to build upon the site and erect workshops, leaving the Jews only a narrow and extremely awkward passage. . . . On the following day, which was a Sabbath, when the Jews assembled at the synagogue, they found that one of the Caesarean mischief-makers had placed beside the entrance a pot, turned bottom upwards, upon which he was sacrificing birds. This spectacle of what they considered an outrage upon their laws and a desecration of the spot enraged the Jews beyond endurance. (*BJ* II, 284–290)

It is clear that the incident in the synagogue at Caesarea *desecrated by pagan sacrifices* was only for effect when compared with the conflict between the Jews and Greeks of Caesarea. But this conflict, in turn, was no more than an inconsequential episode in an infinitely wider and deep-rooted unrest in Palestine since the Maccabean movement.

In this instance we refer, of course, to the Maccabean reaction itself. It is certain that the ideology behind the Maccabean revolt was far from prevailing undisputed in Palestine in the second century B.C.E, because many Jews were supporters of Hellenization. We should even point out that the Hasmonean successors of the Maccabeans themselves made some concessions and show features reminiscent of Herod the Great.

Here, we shall consider, as we said earlier, only *the theology of the zeal-ous for their faith*. From this point of view, it is not inexact to say that the rise of this theology implied a return to an ancestral and even quite archaic reli-gious mentality. Historians have noted the sacralization of Palestine during the last two centuries of antiquity. Palestine was the gem of the earth; it sheltered Jerusalem and the Temple. It derived from the latter the same degree of holi-ness measured with utmost precision. The holiness of Yahweh tended to radi-ate out from Jerusalem to encompass all Palestine, which was becoming known, significantly, as the Holy Land. Similarly, part of the Temple was for-bidden to Gentiles, even pacifists, on pain of death. And some fanatical groups considered the presence of uncircumcised men a dishonor to the Holy Land. Divine wrath might be aroused at the sight of this spectacle; and this largely explained the misfortunes of Israel. This determination to purify the Holy Land is perceptible in a passage such as I Macc. 2:45ff.: "Mattathias and his friends then swept through the country, pulling down pagan altars, and *forcibly circumcising all the uncircumcised boys* found within the frontiers of Israel" (our italics).

Once Judas Maccabaeus had an organized troop, notes the author of II Maccabeans 8:5, "he proved invincible to the Gentiles, for the Lord's anger had changed to mercy." After celebrating the Sabbath after the victory, Judas Maccabaeus and his companions made a public supplication to the merciful Lord, praying him to be fully reconciled with his servants (II Macc. 8:29).

All these accounts of conquests and battles cannot be explained in the last resort by clearly defined rational reasons that are intellectually satisfying. In the final analysis, they refer to obscure areas of mentality.

The Maccabean movement and the war against Rome are episodes where Judaism felt it was placed in a situation of mortal danger, where it struggled for survival by resorting to a war of extermination (*ḥerem*). Both the war against the Diadochi and the conflict with Rome refer to a pattern that remained alive in the national consciousness of Israel.

It is more than likely that the war against Alexander's successors, symbolized in the eyes of the Jews by the antichrist Antiochus IV Epiphanes, and the struggle against Rome included an implicit common reference to the first conquest of Canaan that the Hebrews, for reasons they believed identical, had dreamed about and attempted to achieve without reaching a successful conclusion. This reference comes out clearly in some identical features. In any case, it was a senseless struggle where no clemency was given, where the end in sight was not the appropriation of the wealth of the adversary by violence but their complete and utter annihilation.

This violence is perceptible in the account of the sacred murder related in II Macc. 12:13ff.:

> Judas' partisans invoked the world's great Sovereign, who, *in the days of Joshua, threw down the walls of Jericho* without battering rams or siege engines. They attacked the wall fiercely and, by the will of God, captured the town. The carnage was indescribable; the adjacent lake, a quarter of a mile wide, appeared to be overflowing with blood.

As a contemporary historian has pointed out,[1] the expansion of the Hasmonean dynasty—some of whose sovereigns, though remaining Jews, had compromised with some aspects of Hellenistic civilization to a greater extent than either Mattathias, John, Jonathan, or Simon—was characterized by total condemnation of Hellenistic civilization. André Paul writes:

> Greek civilization had to be annihilated, not only its achievements but also its opposition. Judaism or death, this expression might qualify the political program of the great Hasmonean leaders. Furthermore, many towns whose economic and cultural role was important, not only for Palestine, but for other territories as well, were destroyed. This was the fate in particular of the great prosperous Hellenistic coastal cities and towns established to the east of the river Jordan.

It goes without saying that this policy was materially and economically disastrous. It led to the immediate ruin of Palestine by depriving it of human resources and wealth. It clearly brought out the desire for profit that is sometimes seen in the practice of banditry. The struggle for power and high priesthood was pale in comparison with the deep and widespread commotion caused by the impression that *Judaism was faced with an implacable enemy whose one and only desire was the annihilation of Judaism and its practices.* A. Paul's severity needs to be seriously corrected. If the ban on Greek cities certainly does not merit favorable judgment, impartiality requires that it should not be forgotten that the first blows—and frightening blows at that—came not from Israel towards Hellenistic civilization, but from Antiochus at the instigation of the pro-Greek Jewish party.[2]

As our analysis shows, a Marxist explanation of the war as a war against Rome merely leads, at the price of persistent distortion, to the most banal, superficial, and unrepresentative appreciation of the facts. Our study, therefore, is firmly set in the perspective of the history of mentalities.

The Maccabean Uprising and the War Against Rome: Herod the Great

On his deathbed, Mattathias entreated his sons to keep intact their zeal for the law. What does the war against Rome have in common with the Maccabean uprising? At first sight, the situation is apparently entirely different and the differences outweigh the similarities.

Rome did not interfere materially with the free practice of Judaism, as has been constantly stressed. It is true that a reading of *The Jewish War* forces us to tone down this favorable opinion. Both in Palestine and the Roman Empire generally, Judaism was without doubt an authorized religion. But Palestine was a territory in the hands of occupied military forces, commanded by a leader whose views were not always as enlightened, benevolent, and generous as those of the legislators. *The Jewish War* gives a very detailed account of petty acts of violence perpetrated against the Jewish people or their religion, acts whose underhanded, trivial, provocative nature, often entirely unsolicited, must have been particularly unbearable for an emotional and tense population that was its target. However, it must be said, there is nothing there of the mortal gravity of measures taken by Antiochus against Judaism.

Unlike Antiochus, Herod the Great was not an exalted champion of Hellenism and an exterminating angel of a barbarous minority religion. Herod was half-Jewish in descent and much more respectful or considerate towards Judaism than is usually admitted. He was an enlightened sovereign. So powerful was the zeitgeist that some Hasmonean dynasties themselves bore its marks. For Herod the Great, the situation was much more complex.

There is no doubt he was a Jewish king whose main preoccupations were the fate of his subjects, governed with an iron hand, and their administration, not their exploitation. This monarch reigned over a national territory larger even than he who had the responsibility of undivided monarchy. He built a temple more beautiful than that of Solomon, thus perhaps revealing messianic pretensions and his concern with *Jewish glory* to a high degree. But Herod had another side to his nature; for he was a lover of Hellenic and Hellenistic civilization, which he considered not as an unavoidable evil with which Judaism had to come to terms and imitate but as the moral and intellectual flowering of humanity. He gloried in seeking immortality, which, for a man of the classical world, was procured by the founding of cities, respect for great heroes and famous poets of Hellenism, the erection of temples and the maintenance of the Olympic Games. He conducted himself like a benefactor and patron of Greek civilization, all the while taking precautions to avoid offending the religious sensibilities of his subjects. It is certain he aimed at a modus vivendi with the religious factions of Judaism. Thus, he made the marriage of his sister Salome to Syllaeus, minister to the king of Nabatene, conditional upon the latter's conversion to Judaism (*A* XVI, 225).

Nevertheless, in the eyes of his subjects, the Jewish side of Herod was much less apparent and obvious than the Hellenistic side, whereby he apparently pursued the aims of Antiochus IV Epiphanes with increased power and efficiency. However, Herod was dangerous not only because he was a much more equivocal figure than Antiochus Epiphanes but also because he achieved his aims in a sure but insidious way. He had supplanted the Hasmonean dynasty that the Jews had come to love and accept as the legitimate heir of national kings and installed his reign over Palestine by force like a bloody usurper. He had the active support of Rome, of whom he was considered a tool—so much so that Edom, the region where Herod's family originated as well as Herod himself, came to signify imperial power. Herod, who wanted to bring his Jewish kingdom into the universal civilization of the classical world, had come to represent an object of hate, rather like the last shah of Iran.

Moreover, the dramas and dissoluteness of his private life and the appalling illness that assailed him toward the end of his life, in popular imagination, transformed the figure of the king into an apocalyptic monster, even more terrifying than Antiochus Epiphanes.

Herod became the tyrant of the last days whose tragic terror could be only a prelude to the advent of the Messiah of Israel. He was spontaneously portrayed as a new pharaoh who, sometimes using similar methods, opposed the liberation of Israel. The Christian legend of the Massacre of the Innocents from which the child Jesus escaped, just as the infant Moses escaped from drowning in the Nile, retained one of these apocalyptic transpositions. In any case, it is significant that the return of the holy family to Palestine should be expressed in terms similar to those used in Exodus to announce to Moses that he could return to Egypt after his assassination of the Egyptian. This reference in no way implies the messianic character of the child Jesus because, in Matthew 2:19, 21 these words were addressed to Joseph. In our opinion, the comparison apparently refers to Herod and Pharaoh. Let us compare them. "The time came that Herod died; and an angel of the Lord appeared in a dream to

Joseph in Egypt and said to him, 'Rise up, take the child and his mother, and go with them to the land of Israel, for *the men who threatened the child's life are dead.'*" And "the Lord spoke to Moses in Midian and said to him, 'Go back to Egypt, for *all those who wished to kill you are dead.*' So Moses took his wife and children, mounted them on an ass and set out for Egypt" (Exodus 4:19–20). The account in Exodus is perhaps more natural than that of the Gospel. Pharaoh heard about the murder of the Egyptian and sought to have Moses killed (Exodus 4); possibly the victim's parents or avengers wanted his death, too. And this explains the plural "all those." The same expression was used after the death of Herod, who alone wanted to have the infant Messiah put to death. This is where, in our opinion, the suggested parallel refers to Pharaoh and Herod.

Belief in the appearance of the Messiah after Herod's death was the motive behind the plot where the Pharisees, much more actively involved than their attitude during the 66–67 war might imply, succeeded in involving the king's eunuch Bagoas. The same eschatological expectations are discernible in "the plot of the golden eagle" the year the king died.

Messianic Agitation

Herod's death was followed by an extraordinary messianic outburst. The disorders in Jerusalem were fomented by the partisans of two scholars whom Herod had put to death because of the affair of the Temple eagle (*BJ* II, 6ff.).

Various insurrectionary movements led by competing royal pretenders broke out all over the country. For instance, in Idumea, two thousand veterans of Herod rose up and attacked the royal troops commanded by Achiab, cousin to the late king. At Sepphoris in Galilee, Judas son of Ezechias is considered by many historians to be Judas the Galilean. If this is true it would make Judas the Galilean the son of the Ezechias, "leader of the bandits," whom Herod had captured and hastily executed when he was governor of Galilee. It would establish, moreover, the existence of material connections between certain hostile currents against Antipater and his sons and the Fourth Philosophy of Judaism (*BJ* I, 204, 256). We may also mention the insurrection in Perea by Simon, former slave and civil servant to Herod, or the activities of the shepherd Athronges and his four brothers (*BJ* II, 55–65).

They all culminated in Varus' war, which enflamed the Holy Land, bathed Jerusalem and the Temple in blood, and ended in extremely harsh repression by the Romans. This is an almost exact replica, except for its scale, of the events that were to follow Archelaus' deposition without respite from the year 6 C.E. to the capture of Masada by Flavius Silva in 74 (*BJ* II, 66–79).

Agitation continued in various and more systematic forms from the end of Archelaus' reign (6 C.E.) and the installation of the first procurator. The reduction of the states governed by Archelaus to a Roman province was confirmed by the census of the possessions of the tetrarchy. This undertaking, the administration's sign of the integration of a territory into the Roman Empire, was always awkward to execute. It was usually accompanied by an oath of allegiance to the emperor. In the case of the Jews, it amounted to a de jure renunciation of the dogma of divine kingship that made God the only legitimate king of Israel. It is not surprising that the Pharisees, outside any revolutionary context, refused to swear an oath of allegiance to Herod and to the emperor (A XVII, 41–46).

The operation of 6 C.E., which poses difficult questions for historians, was led jointly by Coponius, first procurator of the new province and responsible for military order, and P. Sulpicius Quirinius, in charge of the census that was to remain known in history as Quirinius' census.

The Jews, at first very shocked at the idea of this census, finally accepted the idea under pressure from the high priest Joazar son of Boethus (A XVIII, 3). Two leaders, Judas the Galilean or Judas of Gamala, aided by Saddok the Pharisee, preached rebellion against imperial order. They pointed out that consent to the census amounted to handing themselves over to complete slavery. They assured the people that heaven was on the side of those who do not fear to give their life for the sacred cause of freedom. The public was ready to listen to them, and the partisans increased so much in numbers that the masses were in a state of tumult (A XVIII, 6–7).

Josephus emphasized that Judas of Galilee's school, which was moreover associated with a Pharisee, differed from the Pharisaic sect (A XVIII, 23) only in their intractable determination to grant the title of Master to no one other than God himself. We have encountered this feature in substance in the Maccabean Hasidim. The refusal to swear to Herod and Augustus, a stand which the Pharisees sometimes took in peril of their lives, shows that the attitude of Judas the Galilean and Saddok the Pharisee was not a radical innovation in religious life in Israel. If, however, Josephus emphasized that nothing equivalent was to be found in other sects, we think it concerns more the style of doctrines and behavior than the basis of theological thought itself. The Maccabees and Essenes had no alternative when their persecutors claimed to make them consume prohibited food to the detriment of the faith of their fathers. In this case, the Jews obeyed their conscience and proclaimed that there was only one master, the Master they feared and obeyed. Judas the Galilean made a crime out of the proclamation that Jews have a master other than God. To prevent confessing to royal divinity, he did not hesitate to resort to violence and armed struggle.

Though Josephus notes that Judas the Galilean and his companions sowed the seeds of all the misfortunes that were to overwhelm the nation, it is far from certain that all future revolutionary parties were just offshoots of Judas' movement. More likely, he had spread a sort of activitist charisma that inspired each of the various parties struggling for the political and mystical freedom of Israel in turn; and they were the first to set an example.

The way in which Josephus presents the movement of Judas the Galilean and Saddok the Pharisee makes it difficult to see it as a sect or highly structured party. We prefer to group it as one of the messianic parties—the most important, of course—that was to come to prominence after the installation of the first Roman procurators in Israel.

Besides the teachers, Judas the Galilean and Saddok the Pharisee, we should also mention the messianic prophets who led to the desert crowds comparable to those who, according to the Gospels, followed Jesus and to whom they promised to show prodigious signs that would authenticate their mission. These were the forerunners of the supernatural liberation that they would surely procure before exercising sovereignty over Israel in the name of God. Among those "magicians," which, in Josephus' terminology, means "prophetic impostors," we may mention figures such as the "Samaritan prophet" who led his followers to Mount Gerizim, promising to show them the sacred vases from the Temple that Moses had deposited and that were buried there during the fire of 587. Ten years later, Theudas assured his supporters that the waters of the River Jordan would open up at his command as if he were a new Joshua or Elijah. In 47, Tiberius Alexander had James and Simon son of Judas the Galilean crucified. From then on, the action of the insurgents and that of the "magicians" were to run parallel or converge. In 56, the episode of the Egyptian pseudo-prophet who led some Jews to the Mount of Olives took place; he claimed he would make the walls of Jerusalem fall down at his command and procure the supernatural liberation of the Holy City.

Josephus also mentions, after the Egyptian's death, the combined action of some "magicians" and "brigands" who exhorted the people to shake off the Roman yoke and threatened to kill those who continued to accept such shameful servitude. In the preceding example, we recognize the doctrine of Judas the Galilean's party or that of the group who adopted his teaching, proof of the spread of the doctrine of "revolutionary, political, religious and mystical liberty" amongst Jews.

Josephus also mentions an anonymous impostor who led a large crowd into the desert with the promise of procuring them "sabbath," that is eschatological liberation.

In 66, Menahem, son (or grandson) of Judas the Galilean, attired like a king and accompanied by armed followers, made his entry into Jerusalem. He finally succumbed to the onslaught of the supporters of Eleazar son of Ananias. It is highly likely that the "tyrants" of Jerusalem, John of Gischala and Simon son of Gioras, also had "messianic pretensions." After the destruction of Palestine, one Jonathan, who had taken refuge in Cyrenaica, attempted to restart the agitation from there. He persuaded a fairly large crowd of poor folk to follow him and led them out into the desert, promising to reveal divine signs and apparitions.

This unrest was apparently encouraged by the interpretation of several scriptural oracles, in particular that of Balaam (Numbers 24:19), which predicted the rise of a ruler from the line of Jacob who was to destroy the survivors of the city; they could be interpreted as the remnants of the vanquished Roman army. And the seventy weeks oracle in Daniel 9:24–27, as ambiguous an oracle as could be wished for, seemed to announce a messianic liberator.

As the role of antichrist or an eschatological tyrant had been transferred from Herod the Great to the Roman Emperor himself, the accomplishment of prophecies as in Daniel 2:31–35 was expected in the near future (the statue broken into pieces by a rock falling from the mountain); Daniel 7, the eternal reign granted to saints after God's judgment against the Fourth Empire.

The Attitude of Jewish Sects and Josephus' Attitude Toward the Revolution

It is naturally difficult to make an accurate evaluation of the attitude of Jewish sects toward the struggle against the Romans. Most of the time, we must be satisfied with remarks of a general nature.

We have had occasion to observe that before 70, the Pharisees, experts on ancestral laws, were not just disinterested theologians set apart from the world. They were involved in state politics in the name of religious interests, sometimes in a very active and almost violent or even in an entirely violent way. It would therefore be unacceptable to see them as separated from the other revolutionary parties as if by a gulf. We have ascertained that, even according to Josephus himself, doctrinal differences separated the movement of Judas the Galilean and Saddok the Pharisee from the Pharisaic sect. However, the presence of Saddok beside Judas even seems to indicate that the movement originated from the sect.

The Pharisees, like all other Jewish sects, believed in the final destruction of the empire of evil represented by Rome. But they believed this destruction would take place in a far-distant future that God alone would decide. Man had only one means for precipitating the moment of God's liberating intervention, and that was to return wholeheartedly to the law of Moses by repentance and by a strict, exemplary observance of the law.

Josephus never saw Vespasian as the Messiah of Israel, as is too often said. Some cautious but highly significant allusions make it possible to ascertain that the historian had never renounced the messianic hopes of his people and that, like all Jews, he believed in the ultimate ruin of the Roman Empire. But he also situated this cataclysm in a far-distant future and thought that, in the meantime, the justification and survival of Israel required a realistic attitude and the establishment of a modus vivendi with the imperial city which, without any doubt, obeyed the laws of providence and whose reign, for one reason or another, was in conformity with the will of God, eager to punish the crimes of humanity and Israel's infidelity in particular. The liberation of Israel would come at the hour preordained by divine will, and the desire to precipitate the event, "to hurry up the end," according to the technical theological expression then in use, was a basically impious attitude. Hostility toward Rome and over-flamboyant patriotism constituted, in fact, just another impious act toward the divine being itself.

It is difficult to have any clear opinion about the Sadducees, who still remain the least known and most discredited sect in Israel's religious history. However, their preoccupation with a meticulous application of the rules of the Torah should have drawn their religious ideal closer to that of zeal for the law and God. Similarly, the ideal of zeal and jealousy originated in an overall concern with wholeheartedly submitting to God's commandments and the Torah. And it is this feeling that links the piety of violent groups, such as the Sicarii and the perfectionism of the Zealots, to an ancient traditional theme in Jewish piety in a sometimes unconscious but certain way.

The position of the Essenes in relation to activism and the revolution has given rise to many discussions that have still to reach firm conclusions. Ancient heresiologists, such as Bishop Hippolytus of Rome, sometimes connected the Essenes with the Zealot movement. Whatever the case may be, the Essenes had accepted the prophetic revelation of a great eschatological conflict that, at the *end of time,* would oppose the children of Light (the incarnation of Israel and the forces of Good) with the children of Darkness (the henchmen of Evil). This Manichean and final conflagration would see the ultimate triumph of the Torah and the God of Israel, the definitive elimination of evil, and the beginning of a new eon. The Essenes, in common with the Pharisees, believed in the duty of patience. God alone would designate the time of the ultimate tempest of liberation. However, they apparently ended up by falling into line with the Zealots as the group of Jews who saw the oracle in Daniel 9 as the announcement of the messianic liberator and who situated prophecies such as those in Daniel 2:31–35 and Daniel 7 in the near future. In short, all sects believed in the apocalyptical climax of history. They differed from one another only as to how and when the apocalypse would take place.

The Events of the Revolution
The Jewish revolt should be divided into several stages. Apart from the revolt itself, we can distinguish five stages.

The first stage is a long period of incubation that started in the year 6 C.E.

with the foundation of the Fourth Philosophy by Judas the Galilean and Saddok the Pharisee (*BJ* II, 117–118; *A* XVIII, 4–9) and ended in July–August 66.

The second stage runs from July–August 66 to the end of October 66. The excesses of the procurator Gessius Florus against the inhabitants of Jerusalem were the pretext for their anger; they revolted, as did the Temple priests led by Eleazar son of Ananias, prefect of the Temple priests. The clergy decided not to accept any more offerings from foreigners and, in particular, to refuse to celebrate the sacrifice offered to the emperor twice daily in the Temple. This courageous decision was an insult to the Roman Emperor and constituted a serious declaration of hostility toward Rome. The ranks of the clergy, under the leadership of the prefect of the priests (*segan hakkôhanîm*), were increased by many Sicarii (*BJ* II, 408–410, 414, 422, 425, 432).

Menahem son (or grandson) of Judas the Galilean seized Masada, then, accompanied by his armed "zealots," forced his way into Jerusalem like a messianic king. The insurgents crushed the moderates, the cavaliers dispatched by King Agrippa II, whom they allowed to leave Jerusalem alive. They treacherously massacred the Roman cohort with the exception of its leader, Metilius, who had promised to convert to Judaism and accept circumcision. However, Menahem was assassinated at the instigation of Eleazar son of Ananias, jealous of his claims and authority. The remnants of Menahem's army took refuge in Masada, which they were to leave only to participate in the war against the Romans (*BJ* II, 433–448).

The third stage runs from the end of October 66 to the spring of 67. The insurgents of Jerusalem won a spectacular victory over the twelfth Roman legion commanded by Cestius Gallus at Bethoron. The moderates then joined in the war against Rome. In fact, they took control of the insurgent party, which had been weakened by the elimination of Menahem's group. Joseph son of Gorion and the high priest Ananus, dictators in Jerusalem, organized the war and nominated the generals. Eleazar son of Ananias, assigned to a provincial command, was consequently exiled from the metropolis, while the priest Eleazar son of Simon and Simon son of Gioras, who had played an important role in the battle of Bethoron, were expelled from power.

The fourth stage runs from the spring of 67 to the end of 67. After the Jewish disasters of Ascalon and Galilee, the moderates were accused of treason. They were overthrown and crushed by rebellious priests headed by Eleazar son of Simon and Zacharias son of Amphicalleus, who were joined by the Galileans under John of Gishala and the Idumaeans, whom the insurgents helped enter Jerusalem.

The fifth, and final, stage for Jerusalem runs from 68 to 70. The siege of the metropolis was resisted by four great factions, who probably did not represent all the revolutionary parties involved in the Jewish war, and disseminated across the country, even excluding the Sicarii entrenched at Masada and no longer active in Jerusalem. Josephus differentiated among and identified five groups: (1) The Zealots were mainly rebellious priests who occupied the Temple under the leadership of Eleazar son of Simon (*BJ* IV, 135, 224). (2) John of Gischala and his Galilean followers (*BJ* IV, 258, 259), who joined forces with the Zealots at first by choice and then by necessity, afterward comprised the Zealots in the widest sense or John's army. This last name could be restricted to the Galileans alone (*BJ* IV, 566, 577; V, 98–105). (3) The Idumeans at first allied with John, then they seceded and rallied round Simon son of Gioras, whom they helped to force his way into Jerusalem (*BJ* IV, 566–584). (4) Simon's companions (*BJ* V, 248–250), along with the Idumeans composed "Simon's army." (5) After Masada (74), Josephus relates the suppression of the Sicarii movement in Alexandria and Cyrene (*BJ* VII, 410ff. and 437ff.).

Problems Relating to the Various Revolutionary Parties

Josephus' Terminology

Josephus used the term *bandits* (*lēistai*) in the first place (the earliest reference occurs in the *Jewish War*) to describe, as it were, all outlaws without distinction. This term does not however cover a homogenous social group. As Horsley[3] has pointed out, Jewish bandits must have been partly what they were in many other nations, socially desperate groups, estranged from normal society, interested only in personal profit, who practiced rape and pillage exclusively for their own benefit. Such characters may have wormed their way into the ranks of genuine revolutionary parties, as has been the case elsewhere.

But it is highly doubtful that this description is applicable to other "brigands" described by Josephus. Just to give one example, it was used to describe the Jews who took refuge with their families and possessions in a grotto in Galilee, like the Jews who fled persecution under Antiochus Epiphanes (I Macc. 2:29ff.). In any case, similar details occur frequently in Josephus' account.

> Herod's soldiers, lowered down in cradles to the entrance of the otherwise inaccessible grotto, "*massacred the brigands and their families . . . Herod was anxious to save some of them.* . . . Many of them preferred death to captivity: It was then that one old man, the father of seven children, being asked by them and their mother permission to leave under Herod's pledge, killed them in the following manner. Ordering them to come forward one by one, he stood at the entrance and slew each son as he advanced. *Herod, watching this spectacle from a conspicuous spot, was profoundly affected* and, extending his hand to the old man, implored him to spare his children; but, he unmoved by any word of

Herod, and even upbraiding him as a low-born upstart, followed up the slaughter of his sons by that of his wife, and, having flung their corpses over the precipice, finally threw himself after them." (*BJ* I, 311–313)

This "martyr" reminds one irresistibly of other great scenes at the time of the Maccabees; and this group of people, crouching in the grottoes with their families and their possessions, were disarmed. It was a group of refugees who followed the genuine cave-dwelling brigands" (*BJ* I, 304) that we see in conflict with Herod's army and who, more than likely, constituted the partisans of the national king Antigonus (*BJ* I, 303).

The word *Sicarii* means "assassins" in Latin. It refers to any criminal armed with a *sica*, a dagger or short-bladed sword. The term owed its expansion to the practice of Latin-speaking occupants and tended to replace *lēistēs*, without, however, succeeding in eliminating it completely. It designated any man living outside the law and had an extremely pejorative connotation. Its usage raises complicated historical problems. If one is to believe Josephus' summary (*BJ* II, 254–257), the Sicarii constituted a new category of *lēistai* who arose during Felix's procuratorship in the 50s C.E. However, if we refer to the speech made by Eleazar son of Jair before the end of Masada, we read: "For as we were the first of all to revolt, so we are the last in arms against them" (*BJ* VII, 324). However, Eleazar son of Jair was related to Judas the Galilean, and the expression *the first* refers to his movement.

It seems therefore that the term *sicarius*, first used by the Romans then in common usage, habitually designated the most abject of assassins. The word became a proper noun as people became aware of the existence of this politically oriented "secret society" formed by a group of *assassins* (*BJ* VII, 254). As for the Sicarii who arose in Felix's time, what was perhaps most striking and novel about them was their audacious and unheard-of strategy for committing assassinations. This said, it should be pointed out that the term *sicarius* itself has retained a certain vagueness in usage in Josephus' account and elsewhere, even after the appearance of the Sicarii "secret society."

According to Josephus' account, we are forced to conclude that not all the Sicarii took refuge in the fortress of Masada. In fact, the Sicarii must have been just as numerous outside Masada, if not more so, as within the fortress, as the movements in Egypt and Cyrenaica prove. This fact is rather surprising and quite unexpected. If the six hundred Sicarii who led the agitation in Egypt after the destruction of Palestine behave exactly like Sicarii, though freed from the authority of an historical leader, it is more difficult to attest the same of Jews who followed the weaver Jonathan into the Cyrenean wilderness. None of the partisans, consisting of poor folk, were armed. So Catullus, prefect of Libya, had no difficulty in *overpowering the unarmed crowd* (*BJ* VII, 440).

The account in the *Antiquities* (XX, 168–172) makes the same remark about the Egyptian prophet and his companions that we have already mentioned. Neither of them merit the name of Sicarii, it is true, but no doubt the margin between any prediction of political liberty for Israel and armed revolt was so narrow at a time when the methods of the Sicarii must have particularly impressed the public that it became, once again, a sort of generic term. For example, in Acts 21:38, the tribune of the cohort could quite naturally ask Paul: "Then you are not the Egyptian who started a revolt some time ago and led a force of four thousand Sicarii out into the wilds?"

The meaning of the name *Zealots* is clear. They are the *zealous* of God and his law, whose ideal we dated back to the episode of Phinehas and whose greatest models were figures like the prophet Elijah and later the priest Mattathias of Modin. This sort of piety is illustrated in particular by priestly heroes. The meaning of *Zealot* underwent specialization comparable to that of the name of *Sicarii*. Initially, it designated any Jew of extreme sensitivity on points concerning respect for God and the honor of his law. The *Mishnah Sanhedrin* 9.6 mentions the presence of individual Zealots in the temple, young priests grouped as avengers seeking instantaneous justice. But it is clear that Jews other than priests could be zealous for the law, like those mentioned in the Acts of the Apostles 21:20 or Simon the Zealot, mentioned in Luke 6 and Acts 1.13.

Only in 66–67 and especially 68 did the Zealots become a small revolutionary party whose aim was purification in the service of the Temple. They did not constitute a closed group and welcomed Jews from other horizons, such as John of Gischala and his Galileans, or refugee peasants from Judea; but the inner circle of the Zealots were mainly priests. John and his companions forced them to fuse with his forces when they let him infiltrate in 70, when the Temple was opened to the public eager to celebrate the Passover.

Portrayal of Persons

John of Gischala was a leading citizen of Galilee, whom Josephus often presents in a contradictory manner. Apparently connected with the Jewish conservative milieu in power at Jerusalem in the beginning, he took refuge in the religious metropolis when his homeland, Gischala, was about to fall into the hands of Titus. It seemed to him more important to defend Jerusalem, a city placed under the direct protection of God, than a small Galilean town.

It is difficult to describe John as purely ambitious, interested only in his personal ends. He was a religious man, as some remarks he made when he took refuge in Jerusalem show: "But even if the Romans had wings," he remarked (*BJ* IV, 127) "*they would never surmount the walls of Jerusalem.*" This is more than just a hyperbole about the strength of the metropolis' ramparts, because later on (*BJ* VI, 98), when Josephus came to exhort him to give himself up, he cried that he "could never fear capture, since Jerusalem was under God's protection."

As for the impiety of which Josephus accused him, it stems to some extent from the fact that John, like many others, gave a favorable interpretation to the Scriptural prophecies, whereas Josephus saw them as foretelling the ruin of Jerusalem. On the other hand, shut up in the Temple with his companions, John did not hesitate to use the wine and oil the priests kept for holocausts. He considered that this case did not constitute a sacrilege because the food was consumed by the defenders of the Temple. For Josephus, his behavior was a sufficient impiety to make Jerusalem merit the fate of Sodom (*BJ* V, 564–566). He would have been more inspired to refer to the episode related in 1 Samuel 21:1–6. The priest Ahimelech offered the famished David consecrated loaves that only the priests are allowed to consume inside the sanctuary. The priest of Nob authorized David to take them away and share them with his companions if they were in a state of Levitical piety. The Gospel according to Matthew (12:1–5) concerning Jesus, recalled that episode and concluded with the thought, "Have you not read in the Law that on the Sabbath the priests in the Temple break the Sabbath and it is not held against them?"

Whatever his piety, it did not prevent John of Gischala from nourishing strong ambitions, probably of a messianic reign. At first allied with the moderate government, whom he was not slow to distrust, John then entered into discussions with the Zealots, whom he finally openly supported. He exercised political terror in Jerusalem with them or in their name. Afraid of being unable to prevent the moderates from surrendering Jerusalem to the Romans and ending the war, he helped the group of Idumaeans infiltrate the city. They were to overthrow the moderate government, whose leader, the high priest Ananus, they put to death. However, John's "tyrannical" nature caused a rupture between himself and the Zealots, who sought to impose his authority at all costs. On the other hand, a number of Idumeans, disgusted by the terror Zealots imposed, freed two thousand people imprisoned by the Zealots and returned to Idumea with them. Those who stayed behind in Jerusalem mutinied against John and invited Simon son of Gioras to come in and restore order.

It is difficult to advance any consideration whatsoever about the political or religious concepts of the group of fighters raised by the Idumeans and sent to defend Jerusalem. At that time, they behaved like loyal Jews, eager to participate in a war that, according to them, was perhaps an eschatological conflict leading to the messianic royalty of Israel. Josephus describes them as differing from the moderates by their unflinching and belligerent determination. Nor were they bloodthirsty fanatics. The terror exercised by the Zealots and John incited them to move progressively away from the Zealots and subsequently John. Their love of justice or a certain tendency for order led some of them, as we have seen, to abandon the struggle. The others endeavored to submit to the orders of a leader who appeared to them more worthy of obedience than John. They finally sided with the high priest's party, which they had fought against initially.

They recognized their leader in Simon son of Gioras, a man of war who had distinguished himself at Bethoron at the start of the war against the Romans. Josephus presents him as leader of a band whose first recruits were slaves and outlaws, on whom he imposed respect and discipline that gave him undisputed authority. His success, his maintenance of strict military discipline, and probably his charismatic qualities as well, attracted free men to the ranks of his army who "were subservient to his command as to a king" (*BJ* IV, 510).

After a series of successful military operations, Simon turned to Jerusalem and forced his way in spite of the aggressive hostility of the Zealots; and his entry was acclaimed both by the high priests and the remnants of the Idumean contingent. Simon succeeded in imposing himself militarily without useless cruelty. He became the leader of the Jews in Jerusalem under siege and, with reason, the main adversary of the Romans, who were to execute him in Rome after the triumph of Titus over the *Judaea Capta.*

As a figure, Simon is a traditional leader in the history of ancient Israel. It would be presumptuous on our part to assume his democratic or social ideas on the basis of the social distribution of his first recruits. The proof is that he had no difficulty in incorporating *two thousand young noblemen,* survivors from Zealot excesses, into his powerful army. King David himself served as Simon's model and archetype. David started his life as a bandit when he fled from Saul, and he committed acts of banditry insidiously at the expense of the Philistines. The Bible clearly states that "Men in any kind of distress or in debt or with a grievance gathered around him, about four hundred in number, and he became their chief" (I Sam. 22:2). The Scriptures had noted the same feature when Jephthah became a fugitive: "So Jephthah, to escape his brothers, went away and settled in the land of Tob and swept up a number of idle men who followed him." (Judges 11:3).

In a much more recent past the emancipation of slaves and the abolition of debts constituted a means of recruiting soldiers that princes—such as Aristonicus, in his struggle against Rome (second century B.C.E.), or Mithridates, King of Pontus (first century B.C.E.)—did not hesitate to use, though this policy did not imply, on the part of its authors, adherence to utopian or revolutionary ideology.

Concerning Simon's pretensions to royalty over Israel, they come out strongly in a detail Josephus gives when the Jewish general was captured. Simon, with some companions, had tried in vain to escape from Jerusalem via an underground passage to reach the desert, where, in all likelihood, the struggle would continue. He emerged wearing a white tunic, which some saw as the robe of the martyr in atonement for his people, over which he had fastened a *purple cloak* (*BJ* VII, 29).

Conclusion

This is a very summary and incomplete description of the main problems on the question of Josephus and the revolutionary parties in the great war of the Jews against the Romans. This study highlights more probabilities than certainties, and it is more than likely that many of the problems are destined to remain hidden in an inscrutable shadow for some time or forever. However, this should not discourage research but, on the contrary provide a neverceasing stimulus.

—Translated by Angela Armstrong

Notes

Note: It is not possible here to give a bibliography on the subject, which is enormous and ongoing. We shall just refer the reader to the monumental work by Louis H. Feldman, *Josephus and Modern Scholarship (1937–1980)* (Berlin-New York: De Gruyter, 1984).

1. Cf. André Paul, *Le monde des Juifs à l'heure de Jésus. Histoire politique* (Paris: Desclée, 1981), pp. 174–176.

2. Similarly, it should not be forgotten that Jewish treatment of proselytes was without reproach. They reserved special treatment from the historical and eschatological period onward for nations who had never set foot in Israel. They spared the inhabitants of Scythopolis (II Macc. 12:30ff.) who had shown kindness towards the Jews and supported them. Their action was guided by human kindness or with other aims in mind, as in the case of Metilius, commander of the Roman cohort in Jerusalem. He promised to embrace Judaism and accept circumcision and, for this reason, was the only one to escape death. Jews certainly considered it a crime to kill religious proselytes.

3. Richard A. Horsley, "Josephus and the Bandits," *JSJ* 10(1979):37–63.

11 Josephus and the Economic Causes of the Jewish War

SHIMON APPLEBAUM

"The combination of causes of phenomena is beyond the grasp of the human intellect. But the impulse to seek causes is innate in the soul of man. And the human intellect, with no inkling of the immense variety and complexity of circumstances conditioning a phenomenon, any one of which may be separately conceived of as the cause of it, snatches at the first and most easily understood approximation, and says, Here is the cause."

Tolstoy

Tolstoy's own conceptions of warfare and politics were unique and controversial, but his observation in relation to history-writing was correct, and he lived in an age when social and economic history were making their first steps. The economy of antiquity, in any case, is the despair of historians;[1] ancient sources speak little of it, and archaeology often needs the sources to interpret its discoveries. Interpretation in either field, therefore, necessitates a degree of guided conjecture, but, to quote Max Weber, "an ingenious error is more fruitful for science than stupid accuracy."

Josephus had his own fish to fry when he wrote the *Jewish War*, the *Antiquities*, and his *Vita*. He was too personally involved to be objective and, in his position, he was bound to suppress or pervert information. To point out an instance that has economic implications, he both betrays and conceals the fact that when Cestius Gallus and later Vespasian were compelled to destroy the villages of the territory of Antipatris, in the course of suppressing the Jewish insurgents, they were depriving the city's inhabitants of their food supply.[2] Our task, then, must be to examine the material Josephus does furnish that may enable us to understand the economic aspects of the revolt of 66–74 and to compare such material with information of a similar nature derived from other sources. It may be said in advance that when Josephus does vouchsafe economic information, it is often indirect.

But first, some general remarks are necessary to set the matter in proportion. The economic factor was only one among several that generated the revolt. It is important to emphasize that similar factors were at work in other provinces of the Roman empire, and it was the reaction of an important part of the Jewish population that made the difference between the Jews of Judea and other peoples under Roman rule. Second, Jewish religion was profoundly involved in the problems of life, including its economic aspects. The notion of social justice was deeply rooted in the commandments and the oral law as they had developed over 1200 years, whatever might be the differences of interpretation among the Jews, differences that tended to derive from the class origin of the interpreters. Examples are the inalienability of the ancestral agricultural holding, the restrictions on slavery, and the prohibition of interest on loans. The revolutionary movement of which the Sicarii were the originators and prototype was a logical, organic product of Jewish ethical conceptions, and not merely an anarchic spontaneous outburst. It follows that whatever economic factors influenced the rising of 66, they were inseparable from and inherent in the Jewish outlook. Looked at from this angle, Josephus may be found sorely wanting, but he could not ignore the basic principle from which the revolution proceeded, namely, the refusal to equate any human sovereign with the Deity, and the conclusion that the monotheism from which that principle stemmed also implied the equality of man. Here it may be worth recalling Rabbi Yoḥanan ben Zakkai's words that anyone rejecting idolatry was a Jew, also the statement of *Pirqei Avoth* (4.10) that the ʿ*Am ha-aretz* believed in common property.

In order to understand the economic roots of the revolt against Rome, it is necessary to survey briefly the situation that preceded Roman rule in Judea, because it did much to mold the attitude of a large section of the Jewish community in its own land, chiefly the peasantry, in a direction that determined the activist reaction born with the initiation of direct Roman rule and continuing down to the revolt of 66 and probably beyond it.

The leadership of Nehemiah and Ezra in the period of the return from Babylon had secured for the Jewish cultivator the right to keep his ancestral holding in all circumstances. The three fundamental acts that guaranteed this right were the cancellation of current debts, the prohibition to sell into slavery members of families who were in debt, and the enforcement of the legislation that cancelled indebtedness in every seventh year.[3] In a source of the third century B.C.E., written after Judea had become a Ptolemaic possession, we read of the growth of a group of large Jerusalem landowners who worked their estates with slaves and also maintained contacts, evidently commercial, overseas.[4] Probably the Tobiad family belonged to this group, which became deeply involved as tax collectors on behalf of the Ptolemaic administration after they had transferred the right of collection in Judea from the high priest to themselves. The members of this group suffered a defeat when the Seleucids annexed Judea at the end of the century, but the lineal perpetuators of the same commercial group, now called Hellenizers, set themselves to regain their commercial and financial monopoly by obtaining for Jerusalem the status of a Greek city. Archaeological evidence suggests that under the Ptolemies at least half the territory of Judea had been state domain;[5] further, the opinion has been expressed that substantial concessions of land were made by the Seleucids to the wealthy Jerusalem group.[6] It is certain that confiscated lands were sold to Hellenizers after Antiochus Epiphanes' first suppression of Jewish disorders in Jerusalem;[7] further, that the followers of Mattathias and his son Judah the Maccabee, in their offensive against the Hellenizers, seized the group's estates and divided them up among themselves.[8] Ben Sira, writing about 200 B.C.E., had testified to the growing rift in Judea between rich and poor.[9] Therefore, in its earlier stages, the Maccabean revolt bore a pronouncedly agrarian and social aspect.

As the Jewish struggle developed and succeeded, the need for supplies to support the armed forces and the colonization of reacquired areas led to the growth of domain land controlled by the Maccabees and worked by tenants producing food to meet the needs of war and settlement.[10] Tracts awarded to military settlers on the Seleucid model, moreover, seem to have remained legally in the hands of the Maccabean administration.[11] At a later stage, as Jewish conquest turned northward, and the Maccabean family was granted both priestly and secular power, the conquest of Samaria required commanders and administrators to govern the new areas. These men received estates in return for their services to the high priests, and crystalized as the Sadducee faction.[12] *Pari passu*, the royal domains continued to expand. The result was the growth of tenancy and the rise of Sadducee estate owners, who exported produce (chiefly wine and oil) in their own ships[13] and engaged in the slave trade. These trends, combined with the growing weight of taxation resulting from the continuous wars of Jannaeus Alexander, led to the armed conflict between Jannaeus and the Pharisees in 88 B.C.E. Jannaeus' widow, Salome Alexandra, initiated an alliance with the Pharisees and a peace policy, but the conflict that broke out after her death (67 B.C.E.) between Hyrcanus II and Aristobulus revealed the same lines of social and economic cleavage.[14] The advent of Pompey decided the issue. Roman rule until Augustus initiated successive mulctings of the country in the interests of civil war and introduced the rule of Herod.

Herod's rule was autocratic, ruthless, pro-Roman, and Hellenistic in the negative sense. He confiscated the estates of his Sadducean opponents[15] and apparently failed to solve the problem of landlessness created by the expulsion of Jewish cultivators from the coastal plain when the Greek cities were rehabilitated.[16] It is, nevertheless, evident that not all the Jewish communities were evicted; there is evidence that Jews remained in Yavneh, Jaffa, and Antipatris. Events following Herod's death cast light on the situation: the revolt outside Jerusalem was centered on the royal estates of the Perea, and one of its leaders was an exslave, Simon, who attacked the country houses of the wealthy.[17] In Judea the uprising was led by Athronges, a shepherd.[18] In Idumaea, Herod's own troops rose in mutiny.[19] Not all the causes of the insurrection were economic, but in the countryside, the small cultivators and shepherds who took up arms.

The first crystalization of an ideological revolutionary movement was enounced ten years later, but it would be reasonable to conclude that the thinking that brought about the enunciation was impelled by the events following Herod's death. The previous resistance to Herod derived to a considerable extent from loyalty to the Hasmoneans, combining both the survivors of the Sadducean aristocracy and the cultivators, who doubtless included a large element descended from families settled by the Hasmoneans; the new opposition created a broader ideology dependent on a different type of leadership.

Nevertheless, to understand this movement better, we shall trace the preceding expressions of protest against economic oppression and social injustice in the later Second Temple period. Even if the dates of some of the Apocryphal sources concerned are still disputed, they contain a volume of criticism whose persistence implies considerable social discontent. Thus, the *Book of Enoch*, ascribable to the earlier phase of the Maccabean revolt, attacks those "who build [their] houses with iniquity" and predicts that "they who acquire silver and gold shall be destroyed by judgement." The book also threatens those who trample on the poor and who sin "by sea and land." Later, the author renews the attack on those who accumulate wealth and property unjustly: "and many are the ploughmen in [their] houses." [20] The *Book of Jubilees,* written, I believe, in the reign of Jannaeus Alexander, follows a tirade against the continuous warfare of the ruling group by impugning those who sell the populations of captured towns into slavery.[21] (The involvement of the Sadducees in sea-borne commerce is clear, and more than one group levied the charge of piracy, always closely associated with the slave trade, against them.) The *Testament of the Twelve Patriarchs,* composed much at the same time or perhaps a little before Jannaeus, at one point warns against love of money.[22] In this, it is joined by some of the writers associated with the Qumran literature. The *Damascus Covenant* warns that the three nets of Belial are prostitution, wealth, and the contamination of the Temple; and later refers to "the wealth of the wicked." [23] The *Habbaquq Commentary* accuses the priesthood of amassing wealth and gain.[24] Most striking are the lines of the third book of the *Sibylline Oracles,* written some time after 27 B.C.E. and describing the ideal Jewish community, proclaiming that the citizens shall be free of greed for wealth, "which breeds ten thousand evils for mortal men, war and insufferable famine" (lines 235–236), and they shall "fulfil the word of the great God; for the Heavenly One made the earth for all." [25] *The Assumption of Moses,* which belongs to the first half of the first century C.E., and, therefore, brings us close to the time of the great rebellion itself, fulminates against the evil and corrupt who pretend to be just but are men of deceit and falsehood, gluttons and drunkards and movers of boundary stones.[26]

Apart from the hatred of wealth unjustly acquired, which is common to nearly all the extracts cited, three phrases are worth stressing: (1) the reference to those who "sin by sea and land"; (2) the statement, in reference to those criticized, that "many are the ploughmen in our houses"; and (3) the reference to the "movers of boundary stones." The first would appear to relate to the maritime commerce and slave trade of the landowners; the second relates to the expansion of agricultural estates and possibly to the increase of tenants and wage laborers; the third to one of the unscrupulous methods that enabled such expansion to be achieved.

Bearing this literature of protest in mind, we may now turn to the new revolutionary movement that emerged in the year 6 c.e., when Judea became a province under direct Roman rule. It was normal Roman practice to initiate a new province with a census of heads and property in order to assess taxation. Such a practice may not have been invariable, but in this case it was applied; the census and land tax were Roman innovations instituted when Judea became a Roman province. There is disagreement among scholars as to whether Roman taxes were imposed on Judea during Herod's reign. Samaria and Idumaea certainly paid; Judea, I believe, also paid.[27] I have endeavored elsewhere to show that Herod's revenue was larger than can be calculated on the basis of the reports given by Josephus and others,[28] since the calculable tax payment per capita on the basis of an estimated population of three million and compared with the payments of the Egyptian fellahin produces too low a payment in Judea. That it was too low is probable in view of Herod's enormous expenditure on the foundation or rehabilitation of cities and fortresses, and on the maintenance of an expensive bureaucratic administration and an army and navy, to say nothing of the profuse gifts and aid rendered by him to Greek cities outside the country. In addition, he appears to have rebuilt the Temple of Jerusalem at his own expense,[29] and defrayed tribute to Rome for Samaria and Idumaea, probably also for Judea.

It is not surprising, therefore, that in 25 B.C.E. Herod's treasury was empty, yet five years later, we are told, he remitted taxation by a third.[30] How true was either imputation and what he did to recoup his revenue in the five years following 25 B.C.E., is an interesting problem. Prima facie, the tax reduction could be interpreted to mean that it succeeded five years of greatly increased taxation. Immediately after Herod's demise,[31] a Jewish delegation to Augustus complained that the king had "afflicted not only the bodies of his subjects but the cities also. He had crippled his own country and adorned the lands of aliens by lavishing Jewish blood on extraneous peoples. In place of their prosperity and national laws he had filled the nation with poverty and extreme lawlessness." Elsewhere with regard to the same delegation Josephus writes: "In addition to the collecting of taxes imposed on all annually, additional payments had to be made to him, his household and friends and the slaves sent to collect, because there was no restraint on violence except by bribery."[32] In a general assessment of Herod's character, Josephus writes: "Since he was involved in expenses greater than his means, he was compelled to be harsh towards his subjects. . . . And though he was aware of being hated because of the wrongs that he had done to his subjects, he decided that it would not be easy to mend his evil ways—that would have been unprofitable in respect of revenue—and instead, countered their opposition by seizing upon their ill will as an opportunity of satisfying his wants." [33]

Whatever the degree of exaggeration in these sources, the hatred of Herod's rule is clear, and it can hardly be doubted that he had confiscated the estates of the Sadducean aristocracy,[34] which had led the resistance prior to the year 38 B.C.E.

This aspect leads us back to the new revolutionary movement born with the inauguration of direct Roman rule in Judea. The new ideology found its formulation in two leaders, Judah of Gamala (or Galilee) and Zaddok,[35] a Pharisee, evidently a member of the "left" wing of that party. Briefly, it enounced that the payment of the Roman land tax (*tributum soli*) was an acknowledgment of slavery and a breach of the law, according to which the land belonged to God.[36] Nor could the Roman census be tolerated, since the law forbade the counting of the people. Further, no human ruler could be accepted, only the kingship of God could be acknowledged. Finally, Judah and his followers took direct action against those of their fellow countrymen who were collaborating with the Roman administration,[37] in accordance with the voluntarist principle that "God helps those that help themselves." [38] Their action took the form of attacking and burning the farms of the collaborators and appropriating their livestock.[39]

Irrespective of the roots of their ideology in Jewish law and tradition, we may acquire additional understanding of the reaction of the Jewish peasant to the census and the land tax from a more recent analogy. In a book on Africa, we find the following description of the native African attitude to the government hut tax.

> One of the root principles of African law is that the thing you pay anyone a regular fee for is a thing that is not your own—it is a thing belonging to whom you pay the fee—therefore if you have to pay the government a regular and recurring fee for your hut, it is the property of the government, and the fact that the government has neither taken the hut from you in war, bought it from you or had it given as a gift by you, vexes you too much, and makes you, if you are any sort of man, get a gun.
> The African understands and accepts taxes on trade, but taxing a man's individual possession is a violation of his idea of property.[40]

This reaction was doubtless experienced also by the Jewish peasant. But the question arises Why should the activist movement originate just at this time, in view of the fact that Judea had known rigorous taxation even under the Hasmoneans, certainly in the first period of Roman rule, and even more so under Herod? Much may have depended on the compelling character of Judah of Galilee and the clarity of his program. Also, the reaction may have been evoked by a "last straw" situation. But there may be an additional explanation. The agreement between Julius Caesar and Hyrcanus II had included a clause exempting Judea from tribute in the seventh year;[41] we do not know if this exemption continued to hold good under Herod, but it is possible. If it was ignored or abolished when Judea became a Roman province in 6 C.E., it would have been sufficient to arouse widespread opposition, for it was precisely the sabbatical year which emphasized that the soil belonged not to man but to God. This is a hypothesis, but it certainly fits the situation.

Nevertheless, the particular activism of the Sicarii, as the followers of Judah of Galilee came to be called, arose in a broader economic and social situation that requires description. It is fairly clear that the last two centuries before the current era had beheld a rise in the Jewish population of the country, expressed in the rapid growth of the Diaspora in the eastern Mediterranean. The second part of the Maccabean rebellion had become a demographic struggle between the Jewish and non-Jewish population of Judea (more especially the Greek cities), on the issue of to which of them the country should belong.[42] In this struggle the Hasmoneans prevailed but Pompey reversed the situation.

Two episodes will add to our understanding of the nature of the conflict. In 47 B.C.E., when Herod was governor of Galilee, he captured and slew one Hezeqiah, who with his following had been harrying the villages in the territory of Tyre.[43] The significance of Hezeqiah's action is made clear by the fact that five years later Mark Antony is found restoring to Hyrcanus II villages seized during the civil war by the Tyrians. During the disorders of 4 B.C.E., Hezeqiah's son Judah seized Sepphoris.[44] It is probable—though not all scholars agree on the point—that this was Judah of Gamala who, with Zaddok, founded the Sicarian movement. Over sixty years later, we find John of Gush Ḥalav (Gischala), who became the leader of one of the three main activist groups defending Jerusalem, heading the people of his townlet (which consisted chiefly of cultivators), and leading a group of activitists, refugees from Jewish villages in the territory of Tyre, against the Tyrians.[45] Additionally, Gush Ḥalav itself was in a state of continual strife with the strong Tyrian townlet of Qeddesh to its east.[46] The fact that nearly identical situations are found recurring despite an interval of over a century and that both incidents had a close connection with insurgent movements is significant.

Other incidents recorded by Josephus may belong to the same category. Thus, in 44 C.E., a boundary dispute broke out between the Jews of Perea and the city of Philadelphia (Amman).[47] Josephus furnishes no information on the reason for the clash, but one of the Jewish leaders, Amaram (Hebrew: Omram) is described by a talmudic Midrash[48] as one who had taken premature action to bring about the messianic advent or, in more recent terms, as one who was an activist and an extremist. Josephus reports for the same period the attacks of one Ptolemy, a "bandit chief," upon Idumaea and Arabia. His raids were suppressed by the Roman governor of Judea, Cuspius Fadus (44–?46).[49] We do not know if Ptolemy was a Jew, but the facts that he attacked non-Jewish territory, and that his operations are bracketed by Josephus with the boundary clash between Perea and Philadelphia suggest that he was Jewish and that the circumstances behind his attacks resembled the circumstances that impelled Hezeqiah and John of Gush Halav to take up arms—namely, the struggle for cultivable land, which inevitably asserted itself most markedly in marginal areas, where Jews and non-Jews met. Also, inevitably, the struggle was intensified by the new Sicarian movement, which maintained its existence as a force continuously from the beginning, since probably the penalty for nonpayment of taxes was the confiscation of the property of those convicted,[50] who, enlarging the number of landless men, thus became committed to the freedom movement.

What, in fact, were the processes at work in the agrarian society of the period? It has been stated by some historians that large estates were not numerous in Judea in this period. Rostovtzeff thought differently: he read the texts as pointing to a country "studded with hundreds of villages inhabited by peasants, above whom stands a native aristocracy of large landowners, who are patrons of the villages. . . . These men are . . . capitalists and merchants on a big scale."[51] He adds to the category of large proprietors the royal family, court officials, and the Roman emperor and his family. A study of the synoptic Gospels leads to the same conclusion, at least where the existence of large estates is concerned. Of the twenty references to landowners or cultivators that I have discovered in the three books (most of them in the parables of Jesus), only three refer to cultivators who are not described as big proprietors;[52] the rest most decidedly are. One wealthy man employs an estate manager, and is owed a hundred *kurim* of wheat, which was the equivalent of something like 220 hectares of arable land, without reckoning fallow land or plantations; he is further owed a hundred *bath* of oil, which on a rough calculation would imply approximately 300 olive trees.[53] Another proprietor, an aristocrat, before leaving the country on a journey, entrusts money to certain slaves for investment in profitable enterprises and rewards two of them, who have succeeded, with authority over ten and five "towns" (πόλεις) respectively.[54] The word *town* is in fact a translation of the Hebrew 'ir, which in the Second Temple period meant a farm estate.[55] Even allowing for possible hyperbole, we are bound to see here a large estate incorporating a number of individual farms and are obliged to believe that Jesus chose for his parable a phenomenon familiar to his audience. Mark[56] describes a vineyard owned by an absentee landlord and cultivated by tenants. The account is paralleled in the Gospel of Matthew,[57] and the dénouement is illuminating. The tenants refuse to hand over the landlord's share of the produce, killing the men sent to take it and finally his son, who has come to claim it. The tenants then expropriate the vineyard for their own use.[58] In Matthew we hear of a "king" (a common talmudic synonym for a wealthy man) who is owed ten thousand talents;[59] elsewhere of a young man of property "with great possessions,"[60] the son of a man of property;[61] and of a rich man who decides "to pull down his barns and build greater";[62] elsewhere of another absentee landowner.[63]

The picture is plain. The big landowner bulked large in the consciousness of the common people, and if the three synoptic Gospels were written after the destruction of the Temple, they nevertheless reflect conditions prevailing before that event.

The confiscation by Herod of the possessions of the Sadducean opposition—there are reasons for thinking that most of these estates were concentrated in Samaria—would have added to the royal domains, but how far they remained so is difficult to tell. The numerous villages credited by talmudic sources to Eleazar ben Ḥarsom in the so-called "King's Mountain Country" in the first half of the first century C.E. appear to have been in Samaria,[64] which would suggest that at least part of such properties passed into the hands of private but influential individuals. Part doubtless remained in royal hands and would have become lands of the reigning emperors, probably restored temporarily to Agrippa I and Agrippa II insofar as these respective sovereigns ruled territories where such tracts existed—but they also held some estates outside them. Thus, Berenice, sister of Agrippa II, owned domains in the western Plain of Esdraelon,[65] also in southwestern Samaria and in the Golan;[66] the eastern part of Esdraelon probably continued in the hands of the imperial house. Antipas, son of Herod, held land in the eastern Ḥepher Plain (between Netanyah and Ḥaderah), also in northwestern Samaria,[67] and archaeological evidence shows that the former estate was annexed by the emperors on his death.

Yavneh had been Hasmonean state land, given to Herod's sister Salome and bequeathed by her to Livia, Augustus' wife; ultimately, it was absorbed into the properties of the emperors.[68] The three sections of Perea east of Jordan, directly administered by Herod, appear to have remained state land to the end of Byzantine rule, to judge from the fact that their administrative centers never became cities and that these units were still termed *regiones* by the Byzantine geographers.[69] The profitable plain of Jericho, famous for its dates and its medicinal plants, was held by Herod and inherited by the emperors.[70] There were certainly Herodian domains also in Bashan and Hauran that were absorbed into imperial ownership; this we learn from an inscription found at Um e-Zeitun (near Shobḥa).[71] Herod further retained considerable estates between Nablus (Shechem) and Ramatayyim, south of the border between Judea and Samaria. This is evident from various place names[72] and from the fact that

Herod's minister Ptolemy of Rhodes received an estate at Ḥaris in the tract.[73] The western part of this belt was granted to Berenice, whose name is still borne by a considerable area from Qalqilia along the Wadi Qana.

We know very little about the administration of royal and imperial Roman lands in Judea and nothing of the conditions there. We have only a hint from one quarter concerning the lands held by the Hasmoneans round Lydda.[74] In Hadrian's time a contractor general of imperial land was resident in the town and is named in talmudic sources[75] in such a way as to leave no doubt that he was the equivalent of the official called in Asia Minor ὁ μισθωτής,[76] who was responsible for collecting the revenues from the *coloni* (subtenants) of imperial lands. As he was a friend of Rabbi ʿAqiva and one of a group interested in religious questions, he was probably a man of conscience. How far this related to agents responsible to the government for revenue collected from the *coloni* of other royal or imperial estates in Judea, we cannot say. But the fact that the centers of revolt after Herod's death included Jericho and the Perean areas suggests that the administrators of these tracts were unpopular if not oppressive. Some of these areas are referred to by Josephus. As to private land, the sale of the property of Archelaus by order of Augustus in 6 C.E. must have included considerable landed estate, and it may be assumed that most of these passed into the hands of families who possessed the means to buy them. They may have included the Herodian estates between Shechem and Ramatayyim.

Privately owned estates are further mentioned by Josephus. His own property lay near Jerusalem.[77] One Crispus of Tiberias held estates beyond the River Jordan.[78] An Idumaean, Costobarus, possessed farms, apparently in Idumaea,[79] and Herod rented Negev pasture lands to the Nabataeans,[80] whereas Agrippa I possessed an estate at Malḥata (Malatha or Tel el-Milik) in the northern Negev.[81] Philip, son of Iacimus and grandson of the Babylonian Zamaris whom Herod settled in the Golan and impinging territories, possessed villages in the neighborhood of Gamala.[82] These presumably were cultivated either by Jews settled there by Herod or by the indigenous inhabitants. The great wealth of such priests as Ananias, son of Nedbai, must have been founded at least in part on landed property.[83] As already mentioned, the Talmud records that Eleazar (ben) Ḥarsom inherited from his father a thousand villages (!) in the "King's Mountain Country," probably in western Samaria.[84]

We therefore may conclude from the evidence at our disposal that a considerable part of the country was composed of large estates and that another part, far from negligible, consisted of royal or imperial domain. Either category meant that the cultivators were tenants, with all that the status implies. But we also read of slave labor and of day laborers, and some of the latter are unemployed.[85] The fact that the Mishnah records two forms of tenancy and the

Talmud a third, which had probably existed at an earlier period, is sufficient indication of the widespread existence of this class of cultivators.

Two events demonstrate strikingly the phenomenon of indebtedness among the cultivators of Judea. The first is the decision of Hillel, who lived in Herod's time, to restrict the cancellation of debts in the seventh year (the *proz-bul*),[86] thus facilitating the advancement of loans to men of slender means. The other event is recorded by Josephus, who tells us that on the outbreak of the revolution against Rome, during the attack on the palaces of Agrippa and Berenice, the insurgents set fire to the archives "eager to destroy the debt contracts and to eliminate distraint for debt, so that they could win over the debtors and with confidence raise the poor against the rich."[87]

Other information from Jewish scholarly sources of the period indicates a period of social agrarian change in the rural economy of the country. An illuminating observation is found in Mishnah *'Eruvin* 5:6. The Mishnah was redacted in the last decades of the second century, but the halakhah concerned can hardly relate to a period later than the second Jewish revolt in Hadrian's time. The document refers "to the farmstead (*'ir*) of one owner that becomes the property of many . . . and the *'ir* that becomes the property of one man." The two phenomena discussed there relate respectively to the growth of a single farmstead into a village and to the village that becomes one man's property, because it has been absorbed into a large estate and its inhabitants transformed into dependents, probably tenants, of the estate owner. Both processes are represented among the ancient settlements of western Samaria, as revealed by a detailed archaeological survey conducted between the years 1974 and 1980.[88] From a certain point of view, there may have been differences between the Samaritan countryside and that of Judea in the period preceding the great rebellion, since the former enjoyed a certain favor on the part of Herod, but fundamentally the agrarian structure of Samaria resembled that experienced by the Jewish population, which certainly constituted an important component of the villages of Samaria down to the Second Revolt,[89] while the Samarian countryside was clearly in a state of ferment during the rebellion of 66–74 C.E.

First, several farmsteads of the Second Temple period are found to have outgrown their original built-up limits and to have become small villages or even townlets. But before showing how these changes can be traced in the archaeological record, it is necessary to specify one of the principal features encountered in the survey of Samaria, the ancient field tower. There are said to be over 1,200 field towers in the area, concentrated around the ancient villages and intimately connected with agriculture. A close study of these has shown that some were built in the Persian period but most belong to the Hellenistic period and a number were probably in use down to the Second

Revolt in Hadrian's time.[90] Clearly, each tower represents an individual holding, and it has been possible to trace the boundaries and area of each plot, thereby mapping the entire cultivated area and individual holdings of half a dozen ancient villages.[91] An examination of two such villages may illustrate the position of the average cultivator in western Samaria, and probably elsewhere, in the Second Temple period.

Ḥirbet Sheḥadah,[92] northwest of Qarwat ben Ḥassan, was an individual farm that became a village. Beginning in the Hellenistic period as a fortified farm whose land was shared, initially or subsequently, by forty-four field towers in its vicinity, it expanded and came under centralized management in the Roman period. On the analogy of what is known of other field towers in western Samaria, it may be assumed that those near Ḥirbet Sheḥadah went out of use at the latest in the third decade of the second century C.E., but not a few such towers in Samaria were abandoned in the reign of Herod. Thus, at Deir Sama'an,[93] two and a half kilometers east of Deir Balut, an area occupied by five field towers was abandoned not later than the second century C.E., possibly earlier, and replaced somewhat later by a courtyard "villa."

The settlement of Ḥirbet Ḥamid, north of Kefr Bruqin, evolved from a fortified "acropolis" of the Hellenistic and Herodian periods, apparently as a corn-growing estate under centralized management, to a village, then declined in the Roman period and probably became the property of one individual.[94]

Ḥirbet Karqush, not far east of Ḥirbet Ḥamid, originating in Early Iron Age II, became an agricultural townlet in the Hellenistic period and flourished especially under Hasmonean and Herodian rule.[95] Tombs of the Second Temple period here were certainly Jewish, but a complete absence of Roman pottery on the site suggests that the inhabitants were evicted by the Roman government and replaced by pagan settlers, who cut a niche for a statue into the front of one of the Jewish hypogea.

In northwestern Samaria, the prosperous Hellenistic farm of e-Lejja near Um e-Riḥan was abandoned in the early Roman period, which could mean at any time between Herod's death and the years 66–74 or 131–135.[96]

Ḥirbet Najjar, three kilometers east of Kefr Qasem, was a well-planned agricultural townlet, adorned with public buildings, a public square, comfortable houses, and strong fortifications.[97] Its cultivated area (150–200 hectares) contained field towers, each indicative of a family holding in the Hasmonean and Herodian periods; but these were abandoned, apparently with the Roman advent, and then or later a new field system was instituted. The replacement of comfortable small-holders by settlers of a higher class seems probable here.

The trends of the Herodian and earlier Roman periods are reflected most clearly in the archaeology of Qarwat bene Ḥassan.[98] The earliest known settlement here, established in Iron Age II, lay northeast of the present village, at the foot of a defensible hill (Ḥirbet Faradis). In the Hellenistic period, this became a large fortified enclosure containing storehouses and administrative buildings, evidently a supply depot where corn and other produce collected by the government were concentrated. Herod built a strong bastille in the present village to the south of the early settlement, and the entire area round it was studded with field towers to the number of 175, each representing a settler's plot. The towers extended over a cultivated area of some 8000 dunams (eight square kilometers). It may be reasonably supposed that these were the plots of Hasmonean military settlers. Only one of the towers here was examined archaeologically, but the surface pottery of the cultivated area ran from Early Iron Age II to Herodian times, with relatively few sherds of the first and second centuries C.E. In the later Second Temple period, an expensive ornamental tomb, Deir el-Darab, was quarried to the east of the village, and evidently some influential family had taken over the land entirely or in part. As the next village to east, Ḥaris, had been presented to Ptolemy of Rhodes by Herod,[99] it is a fair conjecture that the Qarwat bene Ḥassan land had also been royal domain and was granted to some similar beneficiary. Northwest of the present village, a large circular structure of Roman build has been described as a granary, but it may well have been the mausoleum of yet another incumbent who took over the estate after the First or Second Revolt. Other important buildings are known to lie in and around the village mosque. The evacuation of the field towers, therefore, is likely to have been linked with the arrival of a new proprietor, and it may be noted that his family tomb, the Deir el-Darab, was later adorned with a statue niche indicating the appearance of a pagan, who presumably displaced the wealthy Jewish or Samaritan family.

The area nearest the village of Ḥirbet Tzir,[100] lying eight kilometers east of Qalqilia, is equally instructive. An area south of Ḥirbet Tzir is studded with thirty field towers situated among the remains of ancient roadways, terraces, stone fences, and stone-clearance cairns. One of the towers here, when investigated with the spade, was found to have been in use from the middle third of the second century B.C.E. to the early Roman period. The surface pottery ran from Early Iron Age II to early Roman.[101] Two phenomena in this area were worthy of note. The stone-clearance cairns scattered among the towers fell into two types: small accumulations that could be described as the work of single families and huge monumental accumulations that must have been the result of gang labor. The second notable phenomenon was a considerable dike composed of large field stones that closed off the area on the south and east but did not enclose the entire cultivated tract. This structure gave the impression that it was a boundary drawn some time after the towers were built. Considered together, the two phenomena suggest that the greater part of the tract had been taken over in consolidated form by one proprietor, who fenced off his new property and had forced or corvée labor at his disposal.

Finally, we may mention the numerous field towers surrounding ʿAzun.[102]

ʿAzun is a nodal point on a crossroads, and the center of the village is an isolated mesa with a splendid command in all directions. The pottery from the tower area is Hellenistic and Herodian, and here, too, apparently, the cultivators were evacuated when the Roman province of Judea was established. The strategic hill was certainly occupied by a Roman fort at some period, for the funerary inscription of a Roman soldier who died in the third century was found at its foot.[103]

It therefore is clear that the period between the end of Hasmonean rule and the revolt of 66–74 witnessed various changes in the life of the rural population of western Samaria. These changes involved both change of status and, sometimes, displacement. Several isolated farmsteads became villages, indicating a growth of population, and in several, cultivators were displaced, their lands becoming the property of landlords. The population of one prosperous Jewish village was probably evicted completely in favor of pagan settlers. The smallholders of Qarwat bene Ḥassan were subjected to—probably displaced by—a wealthy proprietor in the Herodian period. At Ḥaris, Herod's beneficiary probably converted the inhabitants, already tenants of royal domain, into his own tenants. Something similar may have happened at Ḥirbet Tzir. The ʿAzun smallholders appear to have been evacuated by the Roman army. It follows that however Samaria may have been favored by Herod, the cultivators of the area—and not least the Jewish cultivators settled there since the Hasmonean conquest—had small cause to be contented.

It would be natural to suppose that one cause of discontent and probably of indebtedness among smallholders lay in the restrictedness of the farm unit or in a general land shortage, exacerbated by the displacement of various peasant communities or by their transfer to tenant status. The problem of the peasant land unit is one to which the survey of western Samaria may furnish an answer. At Qarwat bene Ḥassan, where the individual holdings, identifiable by their field towers, apparently ceased to be worked in the reign of Herod, of 175 traceable plots, 60 percent covered not more than ten dunams (two and one-half acres) in area; only 7.4 percent exceeded twenty dunams (two hectares or five acres). On the other hand, Dr. Dar, taking into account a number of plots without towers, which he regarded as having been cultivated jointly by the tower owners for grain, olives, and vines, calculated that the average total area held by each smallholder was 39.7 to 45.6 dunams (3.9–4.5 hectares).[104] Further, he regarded it as probable that the tower plots, which were generally used as vineyards, were intercultivated with grain crops, while it is clear that cattle and sheep were grazed in the open pastures around the village. With these added factors, basing his estimates on more recent cereal yields achieved by Arabs in the same areas, with improved varieties and seed selection but still working in the traditional fashion, Dar concludes that the ancient Jewish or Samaritan cultivator could support himself comfortably on his crops of olives, grapes, grain, and his livestock, leaving a reasonable surplus for taxes and the market. However, Dar states that his assessment has not taken account of the areas annually left fallow, and we cannot know whether the conjecturally communal plots worked for cereals and other crops were shared on a basis of strict equality or according to the size of each tower unit.

The individual tower plots at Shufah, southeast of Tul Karem, comprised 18 percent varying from 5 to 19 dunams each, 45 percent between 20 and 28 dunams, 18 percent between 31 and 39 dunams, and 18 percent between 50 and 98 dunams.[105] At Ḥirbet Buraq, however, the size of the average plot was only half the average of Qarwat bene Ḥassan.[106] The well-preserved houses of the ancient village indicate a comfortable standard of living but the towers belonged to the Hellenistic period, and we do not know how far the habitations represent the early as well as the later Roman and Byzantine epochs.

Our conclusions, therefore, cannot be unqualified or final. But, if we are permitted to judge from the tower plots alone, there was considerable inequality of possession among the cultivators; and the owners of smaller plots at Qarwat bene Ḥassan and Shufah comprised 60 percent and 63 percent, respectively. For the time being, nevertheless, it would seem that eviction and the growth of large properties that converted freeholders into tenants were the factors breeding discontent and ferment. To these may be added overpopulation, the loss of areas incurred by Pompey's "new order," and confiscation following the refusal of activists to pay the land tax. Land shortage, then, was a secondary phenomenon, arising from political and social factors.

We hear little or nothing from Josephus concerning events in Samaria during the great revolt, but one sentence indicates what the situation was: "The whole district of Samaria was already occupied by garrisons"—further reinforced by the fifth legion "Macedonica" and six hundred cavalry.[107] The presence in Samaria of a Jewish population, part of which survived till after the Second Revolt against Hadrian, no doubt led to complications before the year 66, but the general picture can have differed little in Judea proper. During the great rebellion, Simon bar Giora, a native of the village of Geresh in southeastern Samaria, attacked the country houses of the wealthy and freed the slaves. His main base was in 'Aqraba (Acrabbatene), which had been Jewish since the reign of John Hyrcanus.

The phenomenon of indebtedness has been referred to and there can be little doubt that it was most prevalent among the country's cultivators. One reason contributing to the situation may have been the Roman policy in relation to currency, and this will be discussed briefly later. More important was the burden of taxes and religious dues imposed by the cult. The free peasant with a plot of forty dunams at such villages as Qarwat bene Ḥassan and Shufah, if he left half his arable fallow annually, in an average year, after deducting for seed grain, family consumption, and wastage, would have been left with about fifty-one bushels with which to cover his religious dues and his taxes, before he sold the remainder.[108] In a poor year, he would have had less. He received additional income from his vines and olives, but his margin may have been a narrow one. The situation of a tenant clearly was worse. Tenant indebtedness was a chronic disease in Roman Italy, even when owners were inclined to avoid pressing those in arrears.[109] In Judea, the tenant paid a fixed rent or a share of the crop. Under the latter arrangement, the tenant fared better than his counterpart under the former if times were bad, but the owner's share probably was exorbitant.[110] In bad years, the tenant needed loans in seed or money, and these circumstances produced the situation described by Jesus according to Mark, where the sharecropper tenants of the vineyard decide to expropriate the expropriators. The loans were often furnished by the landlord, and this doubtless was a primary factor in the eviction of peasants from the land. Kreissig has advanced the theory that the landowner could undersell his tenants and the independent smallholder because of the superior quality of his grain.[111] It is questionable, however, how far the proprietor was interested in lowering prices, since it must be remembered that the greater part of his stock often came from his own tenants. The theory, moreover, involves the assumption of a modern countrywide market, which hardly existed in first-century Judea. Only the most important towns could afford to import grain in bulk, and even Antioch drew most of its grain from its own territory.[112] Such economic influence as the big landlord wielded, therefore, would have been confined, generally, to his own locality.

Two other economic factors affected not only the Jewish cultivators but also the inhabitants of town and country alike, and one of them may also have influenced the actions of the Roman government in relation to Judea. I refer to the system of currency introduced by the Roman conquest and to the Temple of Jerusalem.

The coinage of Judea under Roman rule favored the cities and the wealthy. It was a notable characteristic of the currencies of the tetrarchs succeeding Herod that they issued only bronze denominations and these are found to have been geographically restricted to the areas of their issue.[113] This would have made sales, purchases, and other limited transactions extremely difficult outside the relevant territories, and this apart from the ubiquitous network of customs levied at the borders of provinces, tetrarchies, imperial estates,[114] and city territories. Hence, bulk produce had to be paid chiefly with Roman gold and silver currency, and so would have favored the owners of capital,[115] and the same would have applied if the city treasuries issued money in the larger denominations. Under the empire, silver coins were struck by some prominent cities, but this was subject to the control of the provincial governments and the privilege was abolished early.[116] Generally, the Roman policy of favoring the denarius and the aureus seriously hampered trade and exchange.[117] As to customs, we may learn what the cultivator had to pay at a provincial or other boundary from the Zarai inscription, on the frontier between Africa Vetus and Numidia.[118] This tariff list was set up in the early third century of the Common Era when tariffs were higher, but the main point is that most of the wares were agricultural produce, chiefly livestock, skins, and wine. Some of these items, however, were exempted from customs on market days, but it was not until the third century C.E. that Jews began to attend Gentile fairs.[119]

The second factor was the Temple. The Temple concentrated within itself a very considerable accumulation of coins and treasure derived from the obligatory dues and voluntary gifts of Jews in Judea and throughout the world. The flow from outside the empire, more particularly from the Parthian kingdom, formed a notable part of the income. Although a number of pagan temples, such as Delphi and Ba'albek (Heliopolis), doubtless received comparable revenues from many quarters, the Temple of Jerusalem probably was unequalled in the geographical extent from which its revenue was derived. The payment of this revenue (the didrachma or half-sheqel) tended, on the one hand, to cause undue loss of currency to individual Greek cities but also guaranteed the empire a steady influx of hard currency from countries outside Roman territory. And there is good evidence that Parthia provided the highest percentage of gold and silver coins among those contributed by Jews within or without the imperial frontiers.[120]

Rome seems to have suffered from an adverse trade balance and loss of currency, at least in its dealings with the external orient, owing to its large consumption of luxury imports.[121] Whether the revenue of the Jerusalem Temple helped to modify the situation depended on the extent to which its income was ploughed back into the active economy. Part of it was; the Temple bore the expenses of maintaining the priestly watches and the monthly delegations (the *ma'amadot*), the bakers and incense makers, the Levites who performed various practical duties, the cost of public sacrifices, social aid, the salaries of judges, and the financing of the municipal services of the city of Jerusalem.[122] Surplus commodities, moreover, were resold on the free market. Although Herod financed the remodeling of the Temple at his own expense— the original source of the income employed is another question[123]—Agrippa II drew on Temple funds to prevent unemployment in Jerusalem, but he had been invested with the office of supervisor of the Temple by Claudius.[124] On the whole, however, while sober governors may have understood the advantages of a steady flow of gold and silver from beyond the imperial frontiers, the accumulation of untouchable capital in the Temple treasury aroused the cupidity of some Roman governors. It was no coincidence that Gessius Florus' demand for seventeen talents from the sacred funds was one of the incidents that brought about the explosive rising of the year 66. The loss of Jewish revenue from outside the empire was almost certainly realized by Vespasian and probably was a major reason for the imposition of the notorious Jewish tax after the Jewish War, but I doubt if it could have compensated for the lost extra-imperial revenue.

Factors inherent in the state of the Temple establishment in the period immediately before the rising impelled a number of the priests and Levites to revolt. Politically, the incumbents of the high priesthood were the appointees of the Roman government and, with few exceptions, subservient to it. The incumbents of the years immediately prior to the revolt were self-seeking, covetous, corrupt, and acquisitive and prone to violence in their frequent altercations with opposed factions.[125]

The Levites, whose traditional right to the tithes had long been appropriated by the priests,[126] suffered from discrimination in status and habiliment. The latter discrimination was remedied by Agrippa II shortly before the great revolt, but the measure may have been "too little and too late." [127] Further, as the revolutionary situation developed and the payment of tithes decreased owing to the growing numbers of the landless and the outlawed, the high priests began to send their slaves to commandeer the tithes from the threshing floors.[128] Nor should it be concluded that the agricultural population was indifferent to these abuses. Kreissig, in an interesting but biased study of social conditions prior to the rebellion, claims that the peasantry was not interested in religion. There certainly were elements who were indifferent both to halakhic regulations and to the demands of the Jewish establishment, but they were not confined to the rural sector or to one class.[129] The sensitivity of the cultivators to Jewish sanctities and ethics may be illustrated by two occurrences, both related by Josephus. One was the active protest roused by Gaius Caligula's order to erect his image in the Temple of Jerusalem. Of this, the historian writes that a mass of peasants neglected their fields at the time of sowing to demonstrate against the decision, while the leaders of the community warned Petronius that if the sowing continued to be neglected, taxes could not be paid and banditry would be the result.[130] The other incident was the Jewish reaction when a village scroll of the Law was torn up by a Roman soldier. The outcry was such that the offender was summarily executed.[131] It would be nearly superfluous to add that the revolutionary movement, which began in 6 C.E. and burst forth in full force in 66, is itself the most convincing evidence of the sensitivity of the rural population in respect to its own values.

The city governments of Judea consisted largely of landowners from the city-territories. This would have applied especially to Jerusalem, but also to Tzippori (Sepphoris), Tiberias, and Flavia Neapolis (Shechem). The tendency therefore would have been to see the city councillors as the enemies of the rural laborer, the smallholder, and the tenant. The social gulf and the resulting hostility between city and country in the classical period have been emphasized more than once.[132] An examination of Josephus' account of the rebellion of 66–74 discloses that, in nearly all the urban centers involved, there existed a section opposed to the revolt or indifferent to it. A very considerable number of the revolutionaries came from the villages and the lesser centers. But, even here, the cleavage must not be exaggerated. A high proportion of the city populations, and this applies equally to Jerusalem, cultivated holdings, often small, outside the city.[133] The violent reaction of the common people of Jerusalem to the procurator Gessius Florus shows plainly enough that there were militant elements amongst them, while the Levites and the lesser priesthood included radical activists who furnished leadership as the revolt developed. It is reasonable to suppose that the craftsmen and manual workers of Jerusalem also added a considerable factor. There is no written evidence of this so far as I am aware, but the importance of the craftsman in the city in this period is amply recorded by the scholarly sources;[134] and Josephus noted the active and radical character of Jewish craftsmen in the Diaspora.[135] The activism of the fishermen of Tiberias and Migdal during the revolt should be remembered in this context.[136]

Two further lines of approach may prove fruitful for our consideration of the degree to which economic factors caused or intensified the movement that became the revolt of 66. One is to examine the known factors in the light of what occurred in other provinces of the Roman Empire during the first century C.E.; the other is to scrutinize some other relatively recent movements whose circumstances and features are close enough to the rising of 66 to suggest that they might throw further light on the Jewish revolt.

The patterns of revolt in the Roman Empire have been studied by S. L. Dyson,[137] who holds that most of them resulted from extreme tensions imposed on a native society in the process of rapid acculturation, which involved a transition to a money economy, to a more complex administrative structure, and to more rigorous taxes with their various abuses. This is largely a psycho-sociological approach that takes economic factors into account. Certain of these factors, however, are not applicable to the Jewish situation.

The population of Judea had long known ancient Oriental and Hellenistic civilizations, and had absorbed various elements belonging to them. Much of their material culture was already Hellenistic, and their organization as well as their culture had been influenced by Greek language and civilization.[138] They had been subjected to taxation both by foreign rulers and their own at various periods, and had known the use of coins since the Persian occupation. Not the application of taxation as such had disturbed their equilibrium but its degree and frequency and its collision with their ethical concepts. A large part of the Jewish population lived in its own close framework of practice and prohibition, and these people claimed the right to sift, reject, or accept all that they encountered in the life and rule of other peoples.

It is nevertheless interesting that a revolt that took place in Gaul in 12

B.C.E. came as a reaction to the first Roman census,[139] thus presenting a parallel in reaction if not in situation. It therefore would seem that it was not so much the impact of a new form of administration, currency, or culture that governed the Jewish reaction as the humiliation caused by those who administered these processes and by the way it was done. Rome used Herod and a largely non-Jewish personnel to administer the country and doubtless continued to do so under the procurators. However, the basic problem of moral values and practices that the Jewish people had evolved over the centuries, and their close union of morality and common identity produced a national consciousness that far exceeded that of its neighbors in solidarity and roots. An important part of Jewish legislation, moreover, regulated such vital matters as local government, slavery, land ownership, cultivation, Sabbath, debt, and contributions to the central shrine—all of which had economic implications. An additional factor was the bitter enmity engendered by the presence in Judea of two peoples vastly differing in culture and religion, each of which regarded the country as its own. This element was absent in most of the other provinces, and only occasionally was the religious factor in evidence. Dyson cites cases in Gaul, Macedonia, and Thrace, but the evidence in Gaul is too tenuous to justify conclusions.[140] The Thracian incident, however, involving a charismatic prophet figure and a three-year war, is closer to the mark. The overpopulation problem that caused conflict in Judea, on the other hand, is referred to only once in Dyson's work in relation to other provinces, namely in Gaul,[141] where the colonization of the trans-Rhenane *Agri decumates*[142] makes the issue clear; yet, here again, Gaul possessed enormous undeveloped land tracts and the problem almost certainly was transient.

Dyson further notes the factor of the "permeable" frontier;[143] that is, the factor of kindred, often seminomadic, populations close to but outside the frontier, who offered aid and asylum to provincial dissidents and were also apt to engage in warfare against Rome because fixed frontiers restricted free movement to and from pastoral areas. In this context, we may note that the Idumaeans sent aid to Jerusalem, but they had been assimilated to their Jewish neighbors. Generally, the peoples bordering on Judea were hostile[144] and sometimes active on behalf of Rome, and the conflict between nomadic pasture and permanent agriculture remained chronic in Middle Eastern regions. Although the Parthians were almost permanently hostile to Rome, they offered no assistance to the Jews of Judea in the years of the great rebellion.

The important fact is that the first Jewish revolt was a complex and composite phenomenon; it was simultaneously a rising against Rome, a head-on collision between the Jewish and non-Jewish populations of the country, and an internal social revolution. It is improbable that any analogous movement could be traced elsewhere within the Roman Empire. Hence, it is not surprising that Dyson omits to discuss Judea in his work, perhaps recognizing that in insurrection, as in many other things, the Jews failed to conform to theories applicable elsewhere. But one basic fact cannot be overstressed. Unlike the Gauls or Berbers, the Jews fostered a proselytizing faith; their communities had spread throughout the Mediterranean and beyond the eastern frontier, too. They believed they had a way of life that the world should adopt, and they were nearer to the conception of nationhood, as it was later to be conceived, than any other people of the empire. It is well to note that the organized resistance that became the driving force of the Jewish revolution of 66–74 was generated by a strongly religious and ethical conception—that the earth belonged to the Divinity—the first protestant declaration of faith. This faith evoked resistance to an unjust economic situation, and the resistance intensified the confiscation and eviction and the growth of the landless, which composed the greater part of the active resistance movements.

If we turn to more modern movements that exhibit a certain resemblance to the Jewish rising, we find several parallels in the so-called Contestado rebellion of 1912–1916. This took place in southern Brazil. It was a preponderantly peasant movement, inspired by a messianic belief and caused, apparently, by the impact of new economic forces upon a longstanding traditional social system.[145] This system was built round the regime of "colonels," mainly large landowners, who procured political votes in the state elections by dispensing employment, loans, credit, and other favors, and further influenced both the law courts and the police. The expansion of the cattle industry and the growing of maté in the area began the building of the railway (1895) that created unlimited employment under entirely new conditions. On the conclusion of the work, however, no provision was made for the now redundant labor. Immigrant labor was introduced to operate the newly founded lumber industry, and no less than 6 million acres of land were cleared by eviction in order to settle new colonists. These new problems, quite naturally, were beyond the power or the will of the old regime of "colonels" to solve.

In the latter part of the nineteenth century a belief had developed among the peasantry that a certain monk, João Maria, who had worked in a nonrevolutionary fashion to improve the lot of the peasants, had returned to aid them. In 1912, José Maria, who claimed to be João's brother, organized the peasants, establishing his center on the Fazenda do Irani, the estate of an absentee landlord whose land was cultivated by sharecroppers (cf. Mark 12:1–11; Matthew 21:30–40). The sharecroppers joined the new movement. The government forces sent to suppress it were repulsed but at the cost of the death of José Maria, whereupon the rebels returned northward to São Catarina, where they founded a holy city based on the anticipation of the coming return of the Messiah, the belief in whom was said to have possessed monarchical tendencies. As it developed, the movement became a struggle for peasant rights to the soil. It was joined by numerous outlaws and bandits, who began to attack railway settlements and maté estates. A suicidal conflict developed between aspirants to the leadership of the rebellion. Ultimately, the rising was liquidated by the federal forces, who deprived the rebels of their resources by seizing their lands.

The analogies with the Jewish revolt inherent in the Contestado rebellion are as prominent as the differences distinguishing them. Clearly, the Jewish movement was not the product of any economic revolution comparable to the building of railways or drastic agricultural changes in the form of new commercialized branches. But a functional similarity might well be suggested between the influence of powerful landowners and the "colonels" of Brazil and Argentina. In both risings, the eviction of peasants from their lands was a factor, although the conversion of smallholders to tenants was probably a more prominent feature among the forces leading to the Jewish rebellion. On the other hand, the similarity of the incident of the sharecroppers of the Fazenda do Irani with the Gospel account is striking. Finally, the messianic and monarchical tendencies of the Contestado movement find their parallels in the rebellion of 66–74, as does the internecine strife between the claimants to leadership in the later phases of the insurrection. The utility of the Contestado revolt, however, lies not so much in the analogies it offers with the Jewish revolt, as in its demonstration that a profoundly religious peasantry could take up arms against formidable enemies and, inspired by the messianic concept, strive toward a new utopia.

What then is Josephus' contribution to our understanding of the economic causes of the great revolt? We have already expressed the opinion that the Roman historians whose works have come down to us do not furnish us with much explicit information on economic matters. A detailed survey of Tacitus on this point would be rewarding, but I cannot submit such a survey to the reader. Nevertheless, I have the impression that classical historians yield few reliable data *directly* related to economics, and that much of the evidence is to be derived from the implications of statements not directly concerning economic matters. Too often, archaeology (in which I include papyrology and epigraphy) furnishes more concrete information. However many literary citations Rostovtzeff could utilize, probably most of his conclusions are heavily indebted to inscriptions, papyri, and archaeological material. An examination of Dyson's two papers on the causes of provincial revolts in the Roman empire shows that, within the limits of his subject, he can quote only half a dozen statements from Tacitus' *Annals* and *Histories* that relate directly to economics. Dyson's first paper, it is true, restricts itself to an analysis of six major revolts, but his second surveys the great majority of such uprisings excluding those that occurred in the eastern provinces.

Josephus presents a strikingly different picture. I have counted twenty-four statements in the *War*, the *Antiquities*, and the *Vita* that bear directly on economic affairs in the period between Pompey's advent and the great revolt. I am certain that others can be found. However, when I survey those statements in Josephus' writings from which indirect economic implications can reasonably be drawn, I can record over sixty without pretending that the survey has been exhaustive. This does not mean that the Jewish historian was a step ahead of non-Jewish scholars in his awareness of the importance of economics or that he had formulated a scientific approach to the subject. It should be pointed out that the Mishnah and the Talmud furnish a much broader body of data relating to the ancient Jewish economy, and the existence of the rabbinical rulings concerning that sphere may well have influenced Josephus. Unfortunately, the Mishnah was not redacted before the last decades of the second century C.E., and it is not always easy to determine which economic rulings were in existence before the destruction of the Temple. Some forty rabbinical scholars, however, are known to have been active before 80 C.E. But Josephus was living in a small country, where problems of land and livelihood were all too familiar and pressing. He entered his brief but most intensive period of involvement precisely when the national and social crisis had reached its fullness. His silences are tantalizing, but his half-awareness that economic problems had joined hands with spiritual revolt was with him when he wrote.

Notes

1. Cf. M. Finley, *The Ancient Economy*, London 1973, especially p. 21.
2. *BJ* II, 513–514, IV, 443.
3. Nehemiah 5:9–12, 10:32; Exodus 23:10–11; Leviticus 25:1–9. Cf. Hecataeus, *ap.* Diodorus XL, 3, 7.
4. *Ecclesiastes* 2:4–9; S. Applebaum, *SCI* 5 (1979–1980):159–160.
5. P. Lapp, *BASOR* 172 (1963):22ff.; cf. Applebaum, *ibid.*, pp. 164–165.
6. Cf. A. H. M. Jones, *The Greek City*, Oxford 1940, p. 44.
7. Daniel 11:39.
8. I Maccabees 6:24.
9. Ecclesiasticus 13:15–20, 21–25.
10. See my research analysis, in *Man and His Land*, Jerusalem 1986, pp. 75–79 (Hebrew, with English resume).
11. This follows from the fact that 'Eqron, ceded by Balas to Jonathan (148 B.C.E.) specifically for settlement (I Maccabees 10:89), bordered on Yavneh, which is stated by Strabo (*Geography* XVI, 2.28) to have been occupied by a Jewish population able to raise forty thousand men. Yavneh was state land under Herod and passed through his sister Salome to Livia and then to the imperial family. Its imperial procurator is recorded by Josephus (*A* XVIII, 158); cf. H. G. Pflaum, *Les carrières procuratoriennes équestres sous le haut empire*, vol. 1, Paris 1960, p. 21, no. 9.
12. A Schalit, in *The World History of the Jewish People*, vol. 6, Jerusalem 1972, p. 284.

13. Cf. *A* XIV, 43; Strabo XVI, 738, 763; S. Safrai and M. Stern, eds., *The Jewish People in the First Century*, vol. 1.2, Assen-Amsterdam 1976, p. 677, note 41. Olive oil and wine: evidence of the archaeological survey of western Samaria, see below, note 88. Ships: I Maccabees 13:29; *'Atiqot* 4, 1964, plates x, 1–2, xi, 1, and the Maccabean coinage.

14. *A* XIV, 20, 24, 43–47; cf. *BJ* I, 150, and J. *Ta'anith* 66d–67a. But in *BJ* I, 153, Josephus says that the rural population was for Aristobulus.

15. *A* XVI, 155, XVII, 305–307, and especially τῶν τε ευπατριδῶν ὁπότε κτείνειεν αὐτοὺς ἐπ' ἀλόγοις αἰτίαις τὰς οὐτίας ἀποφερόμενον κτλ.

16. Cf. A. Schalit, *König Herodes, der Mann and sein Werk*, Berlin 1969, pp. 323, 732–759.

17. *BJ* II, 57–59.

18. *BJ* II, 60–65.

19. *BJ* II, 55.

20. *Enoch* 1:94, 96.5, 97.9.

21. *Jubilees* 10:1, 2 (pp. 245–246, Kahana). For a dispute between the Sadducees and the Pharisees on the status of slaves see M. *Yadaim* 4:7 (discussed by Zeitlin, *JQR* 53 [1962–1963]:209). The Sadducees claimed that the slave was an object, and hence could bear no responsibility. The Pharisees held that he could be responsible because he was a man.

22. *Testament of the Twelve Patriarchs*, Judah 17.

23. *CD* 4:15–18, 8:5 (Rabin).

24. M. Burrows, *The Dead Sea Scrolls*, London 1956, p. 368, chapter 2: 5, 7.

25. *Sibylline Oracles* 3.235–236, 246, 247.

26. *Assumption of Moses* 5.4–5, 7.1–3, 7.

27. As regards the payment of tribute, Professor Emilio Gabba, at a recent conference in Israel, stated with considerable force that Herod did not pay *tributum* after he had become king of Judea.

28. *ANRW* 2.8, Berlin-New York 1977, pp. 375–377.

29. *A* XV, 380: (Herod) ἐπεβάλετο τὸν νεὼν τοῦ θεοῦ δι' αὐτοῦ κατασκευάσασθαι. δι' αὐτοῦ = "at his own expense." Cf. II Maccabees 14:44.

30. *A* XV, 365.

31. *BJ* II, 85.

32. *A* XVII, 308.

33. *A* XVI, 154.

34. See note 15.

35. *A* XVIII, 4.

36. Leviticus 25:23: "And the land shall not be sold in perpetuity, for the land is mine."

37. *BJ* VII, 254.

38. *A* XVIII, 5.

39. *BJ* II, 63, VII, 254. This activity was renewed under the rule of Felix (52–60 C.E.): *BJ* II, 265.

40. R. Glynn, *Mary Kingsley in Africa*, London 1956, p. 135.

41. *A* XIV, 202.

42. Best brought out by E. Galili, "Against Whom Did the Maccabees Fight?" [Hebrew], *Molad* 218 (1968):168ff.

43. *BJ* I, 204; *A* XIV, 159.

44. *A* XVII, 271; *BJ* II, 56.

45. *BJ* II, 588.

46. *BJ* IV, 84, 105.

47. *A* XX, 2.

48. *Midrash Song of Songs Rabbah* II, 7.

49. *A* XX, 5. The results of Ptolemy's depredations are perhaps reflected at ʿAvedat, Muhilah, and elsewhere.

50. Penalties provided by the *Lex Cornelia de sicariis et venificis* (Justinian, *Institutiones* IV, 18.5) would have applied to Sicarii and activists refusing to pay *tributum soli;* for confiscation of lands of those convicted, *Digest* XLVIII, 8.3.5.

51. M. Rostovtzeff, *Social and Economic History of the Roman Empire*, 2nd ed., vol. 1, Oxford 1957, p. 270.

52. Mark 3:27; Luke 11:21–24. Of these, only two (Mark 3:24–25; Luke 11:21–24) were ἰσχυροί (Hebrew *baʿalei zeroʾa*, i.e. "strong men" [cf. English "yeomen"])—both liable to be plundered by brigands, according to the Gospel texts cited.

53. Luke 16:1–8. D. J. Herz, "Grundbesitz im Palästina in Zeitalter Jesu," *PJ*, 1928, p. 100, calculates 160 trees; he seems to have overestimated the average oil-yields.

54. Luke 19:12–26.

55. Cf. M. *Baba Bathra* 4:7.

56. Mark 12:1–10.

57. For the position of these sharecroppers see note 110.

58. Matthew 21:33–40 repeats this parable.

59. Matthew 18:24–26.

60. Matthew 19:21–22.

61. Luke 15:11–12.

62. Luke 12:16.

63. Luke 12:42ff. For a discussion of the Gospel material see Herz, *op. cit.* (note 53), pp. 99ff.

64. *Midrash Lamentations Rabbah* II, 5 (19) (Buber).

65. *V* 118–119.

66. A. Alt, *Kleine Schriften zur Geschichte des Volkes Israel*, vol. 2, Munich 1953, p. 386, note. 3.

67. S. Applebaum, "The Burial Place of Rabbi 'Aqiva," *Proceedings of the Seventh World Congress of Jewish Studies in the Talmud*, Jerusalem, 1981, pp. 37–47. Plain of Hepher: in northwest Samaria—Um Riḥan and Wadi Malik. The land around the former townlet was later centuriated, indicating that the area under Roman rule was government land.

68. See note 11.

69. Georgius Cyprius, *Descriptio*, p. 1017.

70. Pliny, *Historia Naturalis* XII, 113; Strabo XVI, 763. Salome received Phasaelis in this area (*A* XVII, 189, 321). A recently discovered inscription (R. Hachlili, *BASOR* 130, 1979, p. 33) shows that Agrippina (presumably the mother of the emperor Gaius) also possessed an estate in the Jericho region. M. *Pesahim* 4:8 further seems to suggest that there were also cultivators of arable land and plantations in the area, perhaps leasing royal domain.

71. W. H. Waddington, *Receuils des inscriptions grecques et latines de la Syrie*, vol. 1, Paris 1870, no. 2547.

72. For the evidence see Shimon Dar, *Landscape and Pattern: Western Samaria, 800 B.C.E.–636 C.E.* (British Archaeological Reports, International Series, 308 [ii]), Oxford 1986, p. 236.

73. *A* XVII, 289; *BJ* II, 69.

74. Cf. *A* XIV, 208.

75. *Sifrei Deuteronomy* 10.41, 85, p. 272; S. Klein, *Krauss Jubilee Volume* [Hebrew], Jerusalem 1936, p. 72; cf. *idem*, "Die Beschlüsse zu Lod," *Jeschurun* 5 (1918): 525–529; M. Finley, in *Studies in Roman Property*, Cambridge 1976, p. 50.

76. *IGR* IV, no. 927.

77. *V* 76.

78. *V* 33.

79. *A* XV, 264.

80. *A* XVI, 291.

81. *A* XVIII, 147. Possibly the entire area east and west of Beersheba was a royal estate, forming a security zone against Nabataea. Cf. the Saltus Constantiniaces and Gerariticus in the Byzantine period. (Georgius Cyprius 28, 29).

82. *V* 47.

83. Cf. *A* XX, 205–206; cf. XX, 181.

84. J. *Ta'anith* 4. 8.69a.

85. Matthew 20: 1–15.

86. M. *Shevi'ith* 10:3–4.

87. *BJ* II, 427.

88. The following is drawn, with permission, from the archaeological survey of western Samaria of 1974–1980, headed by Dr. Shimon Dar, the present author acting as adviser and participating in much of the survey. Dr. Dar carried out a number of trial excavations in the course of his work; his report is embodied in *Landscape and Pattern: Western Samaria* (see note 72).

89. J. *Demai* 6.25 a–b; J. *Yevamoth* 8.9d.

90. This is evident from the fact that all *halakhoth* dealing with the field towers are mishnaic, and all later discussion on that subject is derived from them. I am grateful to Dr. Z. Safrai for this information.

91. This was the work of Dr. Dar, who thus initiated a new epoch in the exploration of the country's ancient agriculture.

92. Dar, *Landscape and Pattern* (*op cit.*, note 72), pp. 18–21.

93. Dar, *op. cit.*, pp. 26–32.

94. *Op. cit.*, pp. 238–42.

95. *Op. cit.*, pp. 42–47.

96. Information from Dr. Dar.

97. Dar, *op. cit.*, pp. 46–51.

98. *Op. cit.*, pp. 236–48.

99. See note 73.

100. *ANRW* 2.8, p. 364; *PEQ* 110, 1978:91–100.

101. Dar, *op. cit.*, 2, fig. 83.

102. Dar, *op. cit.*, pp. 135–137.

103. R. J. Bull, *PEQ* 98, 1966–1967, p. 163f.

104. Dar, *op. cit.*, pp. 245–46.

105. *Op. cit.*, p. 51ff.

106. *Op. cit.*, pp. 95, 99.

107. *BJ* III, 309.

108. This calculation is based on an average yield of seventeen bushels per acre (two hectolitres per dunam), the present average yield, following improvements of seed quality and selection (Dar. [*op. cit.*, note 72], p. 197). For calculation of seed sown see Y. Felix, *Agriculture in Palestine in the Period of the Mishnah and the Talmud* [Hebrew], Tel Aviv 1963, p. 163. For rations of wheat per head, on Greek estimates, see A. Jardé, *Les céréales dans l'antiquité grecque*, Paris 1925, p. 133.

109. See M. Finley, in M. Finley, ed., *Studies* (*op. cit.*, note 75), pp. 109–112.

110. Rents in kind amounted to a quarter, a third and a half of the crop. See H. L. Strack and P. Billerbeck, *Kommentar zum Neuen Testament aus Talmud und Midrasch*, vol. 1, Munich 1926, p. 869.

111. H. Kreissig, *Die sociale Zusammenhänge des Jüdischen Krieges, Schriften zur Geschichte und Kultur der Antike*, vol. 1, Berlin 1970, pp. 38–39.

112. Libanius, *Orationes* XI, 250; cf. Julian, *Misopogon*, 368; J. H. W. G. Liebeschuetz, *Antioch*, Oxford 1972, p. 96; G. Downey, *A History of Antioch*, Princeton 1961, p. 389.

113. Y. Meshorer, *The Coins of the Jews in the Second Temple Period*, Tel Aviv 1966, pp. 41, 46.

114. See G. Alföldy, *Noricum*, London 1974, p. 100, for customs levied on the borders of imperial estates.

115. See S. Applebaum, in S. Safrai and M. Stern, eds. (op. cit., note 13), pp. 686ff.

116. Cf. G. F. Hill, *A Handbook of Greek and Roman Coins*, London 1899, pp. 89–92.

117. F. Heichelheim, *An Ancient Economic History*, Leiden 1970, III, p. 213.

118. *CIL* VIII, 4508.

119. Cf. M. *Avodah Zarah* 1:1–5.

120. Tosefta, *Sheqalim* 2:3–4 (Zuckermandel, p. 175).

121. Pliny, *Historia Naturalis* VI, 101; cf. Tacitus, *Annals* III, 53; Dio Chrysostom, 79.

122. S. Applebaum, "Economic Life in Palestine," in Safrai and Stern, eds. (*op. cit.*, note 13), p. 678.

123. *A* XV, 380; see note 29.

124. *A* XX, 222.

125. See generally H. Graetz, *History of the Jews*, vol. 2, Philadelphia 1893, p. 236; J. Klausner, *History of the Second Temple*, vol. 5, pp. 21, 22, 24–26; E. M. Smallwood, "High Priests and Politics in Roman Palestine," *JTS* 13, 1962, p. 14ff. Sources: *A* XX, 179, 204–207, 213; b. *Kerithoth* 28b; *Pesaḥim* 57a; Tosefta, *Menaḥoth* 13.21 (Zuckermandel, p. 533); b. *Yoma* 35b; Tosefta, *Yoma* 1.

126. *A* XX, 216–217.

127. Nehemiah 10:38–40; cf. Judith 11:13.

128. *A* XX, 206–207.

129. G. Alon, *History of the Jews of Eretz Yisrael in the Period of the Mishnah and the Talmud* [Hebrew], vol. 2, Tel Aviv 1955, pp. 80–81.

130. *A* XVIII, 274.

131. *A* XX, 113–117.

132. A. H. M. Jones, *The Greek City*, Oxford 1940, pp. 268, 275–276; M. Rostovtzeff, *Social and Economic History* (*op. cit.*, note 51), vol. 2, pp. 663–664, note 32, with special reference to Judea, and generally p. 802, Index, s.v. "peasants," "antagonism towards cities." For further discussion with regard to Judea see S. Applebaum, in Safrai and Stern (op. cit., note 13), pp. 663ff.

133. H. Kreissig (*op. cit.*, note 111), p. 29. Cf. Acts 5:1.

134. See Safrai and Stern (*op. cit.*, note 13), pp. 683–684.

135. *A* XVIII, 314–315; cf. *BJ* VII, 437; *V* 424.

136. *V* 66, 151.

137. *Historia* 20, 1971, pp. 239–274; *ANRW* 2.3, Berlin 1975, pp. 138ff.

138. Morton Smith, in *Israel, Its Role in Civilization*, ed. M. Davis, New York 1956, pp. 67–81; S. Applebaum, "Jewish Urban Communities and Greek Influences," *SCI* 5, 1979–1980, pp. 158ff., especially pp. 173–174; M. Hengel, *Judaism and Hellenism*, 2nd ed., Philadelphia 1974, *passim*.

139. Livy, *Periochae*, 139.

140. Yet cf. Dyson in *Historia* 20, 1971, pp. 265–266, where he outlines in a convincing manner the case for Civilis' use of native religion.

141. *ANRW* 2.3, p. 161.

142. Tacitus, *Germania* 29.

143. *ANRW* 2.3, p. 162.

144. E.g., *A* XV, 111–120; *BJ* II, 69–70.

145. B. J. Siegel, "The Contestado Rebellion 1912–1916: A Case Study in Brazilian Messianism and Regional Dynamics," *Journal of Anthropological Research* (New Mexico) 3, 1977, pp. 202ff. The present brief account of the movement is derived from this article.

12 A Marxist View of Josephus' Account of the Jewish War

HEINZ KREISSIG

should like to stress that the title of this article comes from the editors. I would never have thought of such a formulation myself. But I must concede that it has certainly stimulated me to take up the offer to contribute to the studies on Josephus, and I therefore allow it to stand unaltered.

Elsewhere,[1] I have already established the fact that today serious historical writing is not possible unless the writer has a clear point of view regarding the basic question of historical research, namely its relation to dialectical (historical) materialism, speculative (mechanical) materialism, dialectical (objective) idealism, and positivistic (subjective) idealism. Whoever regards himself as standing outside or above these historico-philosophical modes and does not raise the question of the relation between being and thinking can be certain that he possesses no ideology. Without an ideology, however, one cannot write history, since the reporting of facts is not history. Of these historico-philosophical modes, only dialectical materialism treats the course of movement in nature and society as forms of reality as it actually is, unbroken by expressions of belief. It is therefore the only conceptual model that is a priori free of dogma and thus the only method for historical research that is a priori free of dogma, while dogmatic alienation is inherent in metaphysical materialism as well as in the various forms of idealism. This does not mean that special applications of dialectical materialism, including historical research, cannot be "dogmatically" distorted, falsified and perverted—on this subject an entire history could be written—but views that rest on dogma are also, of course, not safe from "dogmatic" blinders. The basic thesis of materialism is that men, in the framework of their social production and reproduction, enter into relations, accordingly called production relations, that form a factually existing foundation for corresponding forms of consciousness. In other words, forms of existence are the presupposition for forms of consciousness. Now, since the conception of Marxism embraces not only historical research but also the entire way one perceives the world, the Marxist historian is continually indebted to dialectical materialism, but the adherent of a historical materialism is not necessarily a Marxist. Thus, it is clear that the proposed title of this article was conceptually imprecise; for the Marxist point of view in certain essential questions is less different from materialistic views that are non-Marxist than it is from idealistic views, whereas in other questions it again can stand closer to dialectical idealism. However, the difference in point of view, of course, does not lie in the cataloging of facts, but it can rest only on a very high level of abstraction, which nonetheless causes a different approach to many questions or, in fact, sets up entirely different questions. And that would be my position regarding Josephus.

My task is the treatment of his report of the Jewish War, and I shall attempt to choose several problems that will make such differences clear. It is amazing—for the historian almost horrifying—how few modern scholars, before they turn to the work of Josephus, concern themselves with the author and his world and on that basis attempt to understand him. On the contrary, it is regarded as sufficient to establish the fact that he was a priest and then begin the work of analysis. Thus, for example, W. W. Buehler makes a terribly artificial equation: Josephus' *prōtoi* = aristocracy by birth = Roman senators, *dynatoi* = "capitalistic" aristocracy = Roman equites, *hoi en telei* = magistrates; and this leads him to improbable identifications: *dynatoi* = capitalists = Sadducees, and *prōtoi* = patricians = Pharisees.[2] To manufacture a politico-social situation on the basis of only one source—and that a literary source—seems to me in any case questionable, especially since this procedure, to a certain extent, presupposes the position of the source author over or beyond the situation that then obtained. The nonhistorical confusion that arises with Buehler's treatment proves the imprecision of such a method.

To cite another example, Helgo Lindner wants to base Josephus' concept of history on his *War*.[3] He proceeds from the great orations and comes to the conclusion that Josephus perceived in the collapse of Judea the judgment of God over the entire people because of their sin in regard to the veneration of the Torah. In other words, for him history is a legal process between God and the people who are bound to Him in cultic veneration. Josephus' hostility against the rebels originates in his perceiving that on the basis of this divine judgment the people have become unworthy of freedom, that their striving for freedom therefore is untimely. In Jotapata, Josephus consciously placed himself in the service of the divine plan. Thus Lindner, and that, of course, is precisely what Josephus expresses in the great orations. But to establish this, it is best to read Josephus himself and not some secondary literature, which, in addition, does nothing else than to establish once again what Josephus, in fact, already has said. The historian's task, however, certainly lies in establishing how an ancient author—whether he be historiographer, poet, anthologist, rhetorician, or whatever—came to his opinion and what, as a consequence, he wanted to express and achieve. But how can one do this if he considers only what the author writes and takes absolutely no notice of his origin and social position, the society in which he lived, and all his actual relationships to the history of his time? Consider what would result if one intended to judge today's politicians, philosophers, and historians of their own times—and Josephus was all that—only on the basis of what they said! Such relationships, however, can emerge with sufficient probability only when one uses the entire spectrum of all possible sources. The solitary source remains meager and imprecise, often even false without the context of the others.

Concerning himself, Joseph ben Matthias said that he came from a respectable priestly family that possessed considerable holdings in land around Jerusalem in the first century C.E.[4] This is, of course, a critical point of departure, and it must lead to the question as to how a priestly landowner lived. This is also a question that cannot be answered without considering the other layers, classes, and estates of the period, their interplay and tension, the foundations on which they were based, and the mental powers that they manifested. This is especially important because we have little personal information about a priest from a landowning family. For example, it is not clear whether, as a priest, he was active in the Temple. A priest was a position achieved by birth, and it was independent of the exercise of a clerical office. According to his own indications, Josephus studied the doctrines of the three theological schools in the Mosaic religion of his time and was a scholar while still a child. He seems to have been more prominent as a jurist, but the evidence for this is only his own assertions. No ancient source, in particular no Hebrew source, mentions him or speaks of him.

Let us, therefore, first ask whether Josephus' hostility toward the rebels, as unworthy of freedom because they did not submit to God's judgment, in fact is a personal characteristic of the historiographer, as Lindner appears to think. I have elsewhere expansively treated the situation of Judea in the first century B.C.E.[5] and therefore here can content myself with a summary, without once again going into detail concerning other interpretations.

A characteristic of the economic situation of Judea (and of Galilee) lay in the opposition between the capital, Jerusalem, where trade and commerce had developed to a certain extent, and the rest of the territory, which lived almost entirely on the basis of the land. Apart from portions of the Jordan valley, the areas of Megiddo and the shore of the Sea of Galilee, the land was "barren, without water, and covered with stones,"[6] while in these areas the cultivation of wheat, date palms, olives, figs, and grapes was possible. In the valleys in the highlands of Judah and in the hills of Galilee, barley was grown. In addition, one could herd sheep on the western slopes.

The owners of the best land were the numerous descendants of the royal house, even though this no longer existed as such (the "Herodians"), the priestly families who held the most influential temple offices, and such laymen as had been able to preserve their property after the period of Herod's hegemony. In terms of acreage, the land was primarily divided amongst small private owners. The less fertile areas were in part given up by the large owners and again parcelled out, and only especially suitable plots were cultivated by day laborers, less often by slaves, for their own immediate use. The possessors of the parcels of land (*lessee* is probably an incorrect expression; at least we associate it today with legal relationships that did not obtain in antiquity) were frequently previous owners or their descendants, who had lost their land because of debts and now sat as dependents upon what had been their family's inheritance.

There was a relatively broad layer of free men who no longer possessed any claim to land and eked out their living as wage earners or day laborers. They were far above the slaves, of whom only a few were active in agricultural production or trade. The work that they offered was on demand not only during the season of harvest.[7] In addition there were wage earners who enjoyed a more secure, that is, longer, work contract; and these were to be found in the courts of the larger landowners and, wherever possible, also in the city's workshops (the *bene bajīt* mentioned in talmudic sources).

The concentration of all the good land in the hands of a few reached its high point in the first century c.e. Many small farmers were transformed into propertyless day laborers. The large landowners obtained an absolute monopoly over wages and prices and exploited it recklessly. The money lender flourished in spite of the Old Testament's prohibition of interest. The small farmer was harder hit than the landowner by the ritual taxes due the Temple (if one has to pay one bushel of barley in taxes out of ten, only in terms of bookkeeping is it the same as paying ten bushels out of one hundred!). In addition, there were the taxes and tariffs levied by the Romans. Thus, it is no surprise when in the contemporary Gospel of the Nazarenes Jesus says to a rich man: "Many of your brothers here, sons of Abraham, are covered with filth and are dying of hunger; but your house is filled with many possessions, and nothing comes to them from there."[8]

In Jerusalem, Herod's building activity, on the one hand, had overburdened the people with taxes, but, on the other hand, it led to an increase in certain trades. Stone masonry, arts and crafts, weaving—all these flourished. And yet, regular commissions came only from the Temple, the courts of the tetrarchs, and a few wealthy individuals. Tanners, potters, flax workers, and other tradesmen that worked for a broader circle of the population were held in contempt. On the export lists of Judea were to be found no manufactured products, but instead balsam, oil, resin asphalt; that is, raw products over which a few individuals held a monopolistic control. Since imports, on the other hand, concentrated on luxuries (spices, precious jewels, gold, fabrics, precious woods), foreign trade had produced a small but wealthy class of dealers. In the Temple, there was a high concentration of men who were not productively active. As in the time of the hegemony of the Seleucids, since the days of Herod, there were once again high priests who could pay bribes to the king and later to the Roman procurator. It was said that 7800 priests had distributed among themselves the more or less influential positions in the Temple. There is an appropriate comment in the Talmud about the family of the Phiabi: "They themselves are high priests and their sons treasurers, their sons-in-law are chiefs of the Temple, and their slaves beat the people with clubs."[9] The prevalent, class-conditioned nepotism cannot be unmasked better. The men of small means had to pay for it.

The Sanhedrin as legislature and executive was a census corporation for which wealth and appearance were the prerequisites. Its president was the high priest. Under him stood the land's courts. A pronounced class-based justice resulted from this institutionalization.

Concerning the relationship between the ruling class and those they ruled comes a cry of lamentation from the Book of Enoch: "Woe to you, who acquire your silver and gold unjustly and say: We have become rich, we possess goods and chattels and all that we want. And now we intend to effect what we have devised, for we have amassed silver, and our council chambers are filled as with water, and numerous are the farm laborers of our estates."[10]

In these circumstances, the social movements of the time were played out. Like the circumstances themselves, so, too, did the movements take their beginnings precisely in the special conditions of the founding of a new Jewish community after the so-called Babylonian exile. I have thoroughly analyzed this situation elsewhere[11] and here refer only to the revolt at the time of Nehemiah as a first point of culmination. A second high point of the social movements lay in the so-called Maccabean revolt, which—however important and incalculable the contemporary religious controversies may have been— had its origin in the social sphere.[12] Tcherikover has already noted: "It was not the revolt which came as response to the persecution, but the persecution which came as response to the revolt."[13] As the Hasmonean dynasty had come from the Maccabean demagogues and produced—it could hardly have been otherwise—quite normal oriental despots (note that I do not automatically give this term a pejorative moral character), the disturbances continued primarily in the form of brigandage. The expression *lēistai* that Josephus frequently uses clearly designates, in the majority of cases, those who revolt against the ruling power, under which we are to understand primarily the Jewish upper class as opposed to the foreign rulers established by the invaders (for simple robbery, Josephus uses the expression *harpagē,* without, however, being consistent).

Of course, one can also say, as Martin Noth does, that the resistance at the time of Alexander Jannaeus arose because the devout (whom Noth identifies as the Pharisees) refused to sanction their leader's war policy and hated the kingship, which had degenerated into a completely secular institution.[14] One can see, as does F.-M. Abel, the chief resistance against the power of the state in the Pharisees and the high priests who had been weakened by the Maccabees.[15] Or one can attribute the resistance, as does Aptowitzer, to the people's hatred of the Hasmoneans because of their usurpation of the crown of King David.[16] In spite of apparent contradictions, these views all contain an element of truth.

In the complicated situation all such problems played a role, and this receives confirmation from the sources, especially from Josephus. Thus, our author speaks of Jannaeus' cruelty, on account of which the people hated him;[17] the people hated Hyrcanus, says Josephus, because he had declared the Pharisees' regulations to be invalid and penalized their practice.[18] Here, too, there is an element of truth. But one must not overlook the fact that in this author, who stands so close to the Pharisees, the latter are never represented as supporters of the rebellions or in any case its ringleaders, but rather it is always the *plēthos*, the *ethnos*, the *Ioudaioi* who are so represented.

Here, it seems to me, there lies a deeper root of the historical phenomena that are viewed by Noth, Abel, Aptowitzer, and others simply too one-sidedly and (to borrow from Hegel's concept of "polemical reversal") too dogmatically. If in Josephus there remain only envy of wealth and the people's hatred of King Jannaeus because of his cruelty (which through generalization applies to his successors as well), other sources round off the picture in its essential parts: for example, when the Damascus text (which, of course, no more comes from the time of Jannaeus than does Josephus but describes the same events) speaks of the impure wealth of the sons of the pit, which comes from vows, bans, and Temple properties;[19] when in the Book of Enoch those are condemned who drink the power of the root of the source, oppress the lowly through their power, and are able to drink water at any time (!);[20] or when in the Testaments of the Twelve Patriarchs the present time of the last Hasmoneans is "prophesied," and the rulers are compared with monsters of the sea, who enslave daughters and free sons and rob houses, fields, flocks, and storehouses.[21]

Here, too, hostility against the kingship for religious considerations naturally is not immediately demonstrable, but this hostility rests upon and is nurtured by the quite concrete facts of the suppression and exploitation of the lower classes by the rulers; that is, by the only circumstances under which huge masses of people can be moved to revolt. Here lies the reason for the existence of the *lēistai* in the highlands of Arbela in Galilee, people who for generations—first against the high priests supported by the Seleucids, then against the Hasmoneans and Herod, and now against Josephus and finally the Romans—defended their bare existence against the real robber: the power of the state. To repeat mechanically that these men eked out their living because of their resistance to the "non-Jewry" of the Antipater family[22] has an absurd ring to it.

One cannot find these questions touched upon by Josephus. But the reason for this probably lies less in the fact that these items did not concern him than in the fact that the division of his people into a few wealthy men, who had the power, and many paupers, who had no power, was ordained by God and thus completely obvious and unworthy of literary mention. Just as obvious to him was the fact that he belonged to the first group, who alone merited discussion. Nonetheless, he had to speak of the others, because without them he could not speak of the war that he wanted to describe. This is true both for the introductory chapters on the Maccabees up to the time of Herod and for the chapters on the war proper.

If I write "chapters on the war proper," I would contradict myself if I meant thereby only the period of the Roman attack under Vespasian and Titus. The "war" does not begin until Eleazar's refusal to sacrifice. What we conventionally call the Jewish War was in the final analysis only a long last battle, and in this form it is marked by the intervention of the Romans. This last battle, however, stands in direct contact with the preceding struggles between the Jewish social classes and groups, frequently under religious pretexts, struggles that began in the first century B.C.E. and were no longer broken off. After Herod's death, the revolts, which until then had been uncoordinated, assumed a new form, whereby a significant role, without a doubt, attaches to the achievement of the Galilean Judas. The 2000 former soldiers of Herod who rebelled in Idumea; Judas, son of Ezekias, who together with his troops (*plēthos andrōn aponenoēmenōn*[23]) stormed the royal arsenal in Sepphoris; the royal slave Simon, who set fire to the palace in Jericho; the gang of Perean rebels, who burnt to ashes the king's castle of Betharamatha; the supporters of the shepherd Athrongaios (Athronges), who marched through large parts of Judea—all of these still fought in isolation and for quite different goals, including, of course, personal ambition and also personal enrichment. The fact, however, that such persons as these always found broad popular support clearly is due to the precarious social position of the masses. In those cases where religious motives predominated, as with the removal of the golden eagle from the sanctuary,[24] they clearly retreated before the other movements in terms of significance for the entire development.

Judah (Judas) the Galilean, whom I do not identify as the son of Ezekias with the same name,[25] was probably the first (if not the only) one to give a program to such diverse movements. Since his emergence occurred at the same time as the Roman provincial census, some historians have limited his achievement—in harmony with the scanty remarks of Josephus[26]—entirely to the rebellion against this institution.[27] Others have joined together a series of hypotheses, according to which, for example, Judah was the founder of a "patriotic league of zealots,"[28] who strove to be king,[29] or who even emerged as a messiah.[30] According to Hengel, Judah (together with the Pharisee Saddok) had such a great following because the people saw in the Roman emperor's claim to hegemony "a clear threat to the purity of Jewish belief." They rebelled against the census, because according to II Samuel 24 and Hosea 2:1, God had reserved for Himself the numbering of Israel at the end of times.[31]

Such conclusions presuppose a high degree of erudition on the part of the author but have little to do with historical actuality. Josephus himself made no connection between Judah the Galilean and the Zealots. If one refers the derivation of the verb *zēloō* to the political group of the *zēlōtai*, that may be philological subtlety, but in the writing of history it does not serve the discovery of truth. But even this method leads us here to only one passage, where Judah, the son of Ezekias (not the Galilean), fights against those who are eager for domination![32] Not a single one of the passages in the New Testament that mention *zēlōtēs, zēlos,* or zēleuein—Luke, Acts, Epistles—can convincingly be connected with Judah, not even with the political group. Strivings toward kingship or messianic status are nothing but fantastic inventions; for there is not the slightest evidence for them in any of the sources. But, nonetheless, these hypotheses are made within the framework of contemporary historical possibilities, something that cannot be maintained for Hengel's learned constructions.

Hengel assumes that extensive portions of the Jewish masses held the writings of the Old Testament as their own spiritual property and regarded them as the guiding principle of their actions. That is, to put it mildly, a naive assumption. The fact that the Jewish farmers and day laborers, who formed the bulk of the masses and were thereby also the characteristic power behind the popular revolts, could by no means read Deuteronomy, Hosea, the Sibylline Oracles, or anything else, may not be counter evidence; after all, traditions may be maintained orally. In fact, however, the contemporary historical sources provide us with a massive amount of evidence concerning the lack of knowledge of the laws in all levels of the population, but especially in the lower classes, and concerning the failure to observe the laws among the rich and poor alike. The fact that the concept of *am-haarez,* which once stood for the members of a community, had deteriorated into the designation of those who were ignorant of the laws speaks volumes, as does also the fact that the rabbis designated precisely these *ame-haarez* as continual violators of the laws and thus as impure.[33] As one example of many, I should here like to repeat the characteristic passage from the Babylonian Talmud, according to which the rich man answers the question as to why he does not observe the

Torah: "I am rich and must care for my possessions," while the poor man answers: "I am poor and must concern myself with making a living."[34] Who is left?

By themselves, religious contradictions have never and nowhere led to great popular movements. If, however, social tension is present, they can obtain great significance within the erupting class struggles and can even lead to the kindling of revolts. It is therefore completely "Marxist" to concern oneself with this religious component, if one grasps that it is subordinate to the social component. It would, nevertheless, be a "non-Marxist" view to overlook this relationship. Since theologians and many historians underevaluate the social factor, in part intentionally, the Marxist historians are always in danger (I include myself as well) of overevaluating this factor, in order to reestablish the correct balance and not to repeat what others have already correctly stated. The bourgeois dogmatists then call them Marxist dogmatists. A mutual understanding would certainly be more reasonable and would benefit historical truth.

On the basis of this view of relationships we must now observe and investigate Josephus' behavior during his employment as a military commander and during his imprisonment in the Roman camp. P. Vidal-Naquet, who has given the most penetrating answer to this question, has taken Reinach's picture of Josephus as a man of petty spirit and little character (*"ni un grand esprit ni un grand charactère"*), uniquely composed of "Jewish" patriotism, Hellenistic culture, and vanity, and has supplemented it with the notion of "class hatred" (*"de haine de classe"*).[35] But an indispensable prerequisite for class hatred is not only the existence of classes but also the understanding of this existence, however unconscious it may be. Some modern historians struggle mightily against using the concept "class" in studying antiquity,[36] and it would automatically be an extremely nondialectical (and therefore also "non-Marxist") approach to this question if one intended to overlook the fact that the classes—and thus also class differences, class consciousness, and class conflicts—have developed historically. It therefore would be totally false to measure by the standard of today's phenomena the kind and extent of class contradictions in antiquity and thus to construe primitive main contradictions such as those between slaveholders and slaves, city dwellers and farmers, nobility and bourgeoisie, etc. (unfortunately all this already has happened in the name of Marxism!).

The early societies were of significantly more layers than the modern; the transitions therefore were more fluid; and blood ties played a much greater role, and their boundaries broke through social ties. Likewise, the traditional positions of a professional, cultic, and juridical sort, at times with strict demarcations, did not coincide with class differences. The whole accordingly is broken up in various ways. At the same time, however, the tendency that has endured to today is already clearly present in antiquity, that is, the tendency according to which social contradictions become more and more pronounced and polarized, while the other contradictions continually lose their meaning and finally vanish (I am speaking here only of the development in a class society). If one, therefore, can speak in quite general terms of a primacy of class development, local and temporal conditions can often yield a totally different configuration.

If, consequently, we want to associate Josephus with a class, we must at the same time not forget that he comes from a priestly family, that his family lived in Jerusalem, that, finally, he belonged to the group of Pharisees and possessed all the active and passive rights of a member of that community; nor must we forget that he wrote while he lived a luxurious life in Rome as a freedman of the Flavians. Yet, the primary fact remains that he came from a family of large landowners who had their obviously extensive holdings in the vicinity of Jerusalem. This family sat in the Sanhedrin and took part in the history of Judea. At the time of the war, Josephus was probably his family's highest representative and a member of the gerousia. The situation of the land that we have sketched should have made it sufficiently clear how inopportune for these circles were the rebels' goals, which they summarized under the notion of *neoterismus.*

Though Josephus devotes many more words to such indignations as that against Pilate, who wanted to use Temple funds for building an aqueduct,[37] or that against Petronius, who was said to have set up an image of the Emperor Caligula in the Temple,[38] nonetheless, he clearly shows much greater concern regarding the actions of Judah's sons Jacob and Simon, of Eliezer ben Dinai, and the "brigands" in general, who "plundered the houses of the great and hanged the men,"[39] and especially the *sikarioi.*

Since Josephus once uses the expression *sikarioi* for creatures who committed murders in the service of the Roman procurator Felix,[40] one could assume that he wanted to slander them as collaborators. But only a little later he reports that the procurator Albinus had *sikarioi* killed or imprisoned.[41] Finally, the expression is used for the followers of Menachem and the defenders of Masada.[42] It seems that Josephus first uses *sikarioi* as a general designation for murderers who employ the *sica,* but that he later restricts the term to a definite political group within the rebels (without, however, being consistent). At any rate, a tendency to slander is present, although one need not designate it as a conscious method on the part of the author. As a more narrowly defined group, the *sikarioi* appear at any rate under Menachem, possibly a son of Judah the Galilean, for the first time around the year 64, at about the same time as Herod's palace in Tiberias was destroyed by the "sailors and the poor,"[43] at the same time as King Agrippa II was driven out of Jerusalem because he wanted to make the people believe that the patient endurance of blows nullifies their effects and that "serenity on the part of the mistreated has a beneficent effect on the tormentor."[44] However, the actions of these *sikarioi*, who joined the rebel priests in the Temple, appear to have been the following: the occupation of the Upper City, the burning and plundering of the houses of the high priest Ananias and the palaces of Agrippa and Berenice, the storming of the city archives, the cancellation of debts, and the destruction of the Antonia and the palace of Herod.[45]

If I—together with Josephus!—prefer to see here an act of will on the part "of the poor against the rich,"[46] while Hengel prefers to see an "act of purification of the Temple" (because the Antonia stood next to it), doubtless "ideology" is decisive, but certainly not only in the Marxist exegesis! And, if Lindner uses only the speeches of Josephus in order to determine his conception of historiography, instead of taking into account all of his pronouncements, and then comes to the aforementioned one-sided result, is this not also "ideologically" determined? I pose these questions here only because of the task assigned to me by the editors; the answer I leave to the reader. More important to me is the following.

Josephus actually sees the various origins for the situation in the first century C.E. He cannot, however, explain their complexity. Therefore, depending on the exigencies of his narrative, the reasons that he adduces are now religious, later ethnic (i.e., national), but also social. One must by no means overlook the fact that he is absolutely consistent in making the rebels into devils. He does this in the religious arena by reporting their neglect and even contempt of the worship of God;[47] in the national arena, he intentionally excludes the revolutionaries from the concept of "Judean," although clearly the majority of the population stood behind them; what he thought of them in a social view he shows with the designations that he gives to them: brigands (*lēistai*), cheats (*goētes*), desperadoes (*aponoēthentes*), zealots (*zēlōtai*), a pack of evil (*ponērias stiphos*), worthless (*ponēroi*), etc.

The central concept that embraces all, however, is neither *zēlos* nor *lēistrikon* but *neoterismos*. The masses of the people wanted renewal, that is the elimination of the old apparatus of state headed by the Sanhedrin composed of high priests and large landowners, along with the entire nest of nepotism and enrichment at the expense of the people. Although no special program was present, indeed because of the ideological fragmentation of the rebels could not be present, this movement drove the ruling circles into the arms of the Romans. Josephus was nothing more than an exponent of these circles. He was never a leader of the revolt, but he sought to hinder it at the order of the Sanhedrin. One can glean this expressly in his *Vita*.[48] The rebels were already too strong for him to succeed in accomplishing his order, but he had done his best. Since for him the rebels were not Judeans, in his view he did not betray the Judeans to the Romans. Since in his opinion the social order had been given by God, by his action he did not betray the Judean God either. Since he was a representative of the ruling class, by his battle against *neoterismus* he did not betray his class. In view of the state of affairs, he had to believe that the liberal system of justice in Judea, in which the upper levels were so free that they could use their religiously colored justice to their own advantage against the majority, could only be defended by the Romans. That it did not turn out that way lay likewise in the state of affairs. Josephus' picture of history, however, was quite normal, as was his picture of the enemy, which grew out of it: they were the pictures held by the ruling classes of Judea in the first century of our era.

—Translated by Gerald M. Browne

Notes

1. *Wirtschaft und Gesellschaft im Seleukidenreich* (1978), p. 5.

2. W. W. Buehler, *The Pre-Herodian Civil War and Social Debate* (Diss., Basel 1974); cf. also my review in *DLZ* 96(1975):216–217.

3. H. Lindner, *Die Geschichtsauffassung des Flavius Josephus im Bellum Judaicum* (Leiden 1972); cf. my remarks in *EAZ* 15(1974):368–371.

4. *V* 1ff.

5. H. Kreissig, *Die sozialen Zusammenhänge des Judäischen Krieges* (Berlin 1970), with the most important literature then available. Almost nothing essential on this topic, which could have altered my views, has subsequently appeared except the work of P. Vidal-Naquet (see note 25).

6. Strabo XVI, 2.36.

7. Matthew 20:1–16.

8. Origen, *Commentary on Matthew* XV, 14 on 19.16ff. (Klostermann).

9. b. *Pesaḥim* 57a.

10. Enoch 97.8f.

11. *Die sozialökonomische Situation in Juda zur Achämenidenzeit* (Berlin 1973).

12. Cf. H. Kreissig, "Die Ursachen des 'Makkabäer'-Aufstandes," *Klio* 58(1976):249–253, on M. Hengel, *Judentum und Hellenismus* (Tübingen 1973).

13. V. Tcherikover, *Hellenistic Civilization and the Jews* (Philadelphia 1961), p. 191.

14. M. Noth, *Geschichte Israels* (Göttingen 1961), pp. 343–350.

15. F.-M. Abel, *Histoire de la Palestine depuis la conquête d'Alexandre jusqu'à l'invasion arabe,* vol. 1 (Paris 1952), pp. 216f., 231.

16. V. Aptowitzer, *Parteipolitik der Hasmonäerzeit im rabbinischen und pseudoepigraphischen Schrifttum* (Wien 1927), pp. 15f.

17. *BJ* I, 97.

18. *A* XIII, 296.

19. *CD* VI, 15–17.

20. Enoch 96.4–8.

21. Testament of Judah 21.

22. So M. Hengel, *Die Zeloten* (Leiden 1961), p. 323.

23. *A* XVII, 271.

24. *BJ* I, 648ff.; *A* XVII, 149ff.

25. Cf. Kreissig (*op. cit.*, note 5), pp. 114f.; P. Vidal-Naquet, "Flavius Josèphe ou Du bon usage de la Trahison," preface to *La guerre des Juifs*, trans. P. Savinel (Paris 1977), p. 90.

26. *BJ* II, 118; *A* XVIII, 4.

27. So, e.g., E. Meyer, *Ursprung und Anfänge des Christentums*, vol. 2 (Stuttgart 1921), p. 403; F. J. Foakes-Jackson and K. Lake (eds.), *The Beginnings of Christianity*, vol. 1 (London 1920), p. 422.

28. J. Wellhausen, *Israelitische und jüdische Geschichte* (Leipzig 1958), p. 298.

29. R. Eisler, *Iēsous basileus ou basileusas*, vol. 2, (Heidelberg 1930), p. 69f.

30. P. Alfaric, *Die sozialen Ursprünge des Christentums* (Berlin 1963), p. 1; E. Stauffer, *Jerusalem und Rom* (Bern 1957), p. 81.

31. Hengel, (*op. cit.*, note 22), p. 148.

32. *BJ* II, 56: *tois tēn dynasteian zēlousin.*

33. b. *Pesaḥim* 49a–b; b. *Nedarim* 20a; b. *Gittin* 61b–62a, etc. I here cite only those talmudic sources that can be dated with great certainty to the first century C.E.

34. b. *Yoma* 35b. Cf. on this question the detailed discussion in Kreissig (*op. cit.*, note 5), pp. 88–92.

35. *Ibid.*, p. 33.

36. Cf. especially M. I. Finley, *The Ancient Economy* (London 1973).

37. *BJ* II, 175ff.; *A* XVIII, 60ff.

38. *BJ* II, 184ff.; *A* XVIII, 261ff.

39. *BJ* II, 265: *tas tōn dynatōn oikias.*

40. *BJ* II, 254.

41. *BJ* II, 272ff.

42. *BJ* II, 425, and IV, 400.

43. *V* 66: *tōn nautōn kai tōn aporōn.*

44. *BJ* II, 351ff.

45. *BJ* II, 427ff.

46. *Ibid.*

47. For some of the many examples, see *BJ* V, 518, as well as Josephus' speech in Chapter 2 of Book VI.

48. *V* 22f. Cf. *V* 30f., 77f., 212–215, 381–389; *BJ* II, 570f., III, 193–202.

13 The Forms and Historical Value of Josephus' Suicide Accounts

RAYMOND R. NEWELL

T he self-inflicted deaths of 960 Jewish revolutionaries at Masada two thousand years ago has received much attention in the last two decades. This interest has resulted primarily from Yigael Yadin's book about his archaeological excavation of Masada.[1] Yadin's interpretation of the evidence concerning the events at Masada sparked a debate among Jewish scholars. He was assailed on one side by those who said that he did not take Josephus, our only source for the event, literally enough;[2] on the other side, Yadin was excoriated for trusting Josephus too naively.[3] A controversy even arose over the historicity of the mass suicide itself. Some argued that good Jews would not have killed themselves; others claimed the Masada defenders were justified as Jews in their action.[4]

In many ways, this debate over the Masada event was unsatisfactory. Contrasting views of the archaeological evidence or the truthfulness of Josephus were seldom defended, only asserted. The question whether the Sicarii at Masada were "good Jews" by modern or rabbinic standards was of little help in assessing the historicity and nature of their act in A.D. 73.[5] One of the more helpful aspects of the discussion was the comparison of Masada with other accounts of suicide within the Jewish tradition. The full possibilities of developing a form critical comparison of Josephus' version of the Masada incident with other Jewish suicide stories, however, were not developed. By the late 1970s the debate came to a temporary end with the conclusion that current Jewish perceptions of the mythic nature of Masada had been more at issue than the nature of the historical act itself.[6]

In the early 1980s, David Ladouceur reopened the debate by taking a new direction. He examined Roman attitudes toward suicide roughly contemporary with Josephus' writings. From this analysis, Ladouceur argued that Josephus wrote the Masada episode as a caricature of Stoic-Cynic opposition to the Flavians.[7] Shaye Cohen followed up Ladouceur's helpful turn to the classical materials by comparing Masada with some other mass suicides in classical history. He discovered several stock motifs shared by Josephus' description and the descriptions of similar acts by other ancient historians. Because of these shared motifs, Cohen questioned the historicity of Josephus' account of Masada.[8] Menahem Luz and Michael Bünker continued this line of investigation by reasserting the presence of stock Hellenistic themes in the Masada speeches.[9] These studies showed that Josephus' account of the Masada event could not be understood by examining Jewish records alone. Scholars would also have to examine the forms and concepts used by Hellenistic historians before they could hope to evaluate accurately Josephus' tale about what happened at Masada.

In the attempt to understand Masada, we can see that scholars have spent much time looking at either Jewish or classical comparative materials. One important step, however, still seems to be missing. There has been no attempt to compare the literary form of Josephus' description of Masada with other reports of suicide within his writings. L. D. Hankoff has examined Josephus' suicide stories from a psychoanalytic point of view.[10] His work suffers, however, from the lack of a clear understanding that Josephus belongs within a wider historiographic tradition. Hankoff assumes Josephus to be formulating his suicide stories out of his own individual psychological background. In reality, Josephus merely may be following literary or historiographic *topoi*. As Ladouceur has usefully pointed out, it is dangerous to make claims about Josephus' personal disposition on the basis of what turns out to be a historiographic commonplace.[11]

The present study proposes to examine the formal characteristics of the various suicide accounts in Josephus. From such a basis, we shall be better able both to understand the function of suicide forms within Josephus' writings and to assess the historicity of these forms. Masada does not stand alone within the Josephan corpus, just as it does not stand alone within the Jewish and Graeco-Roman traditions. To understand what happened at Masada, we must first understand the literary form Josephus used to describe this event. As form criticism long ago taught biblical scholars, a unit's form gives us important information concerning its meaning, setting, and possible historicity. A formal anaysis of the suicide accounts in Josephus, therefore, should tell us something about how he—and perhaps the wider Jewish-Hellenistic culture of his day—understood the meaning of suicide. It may also give us the tools necessary to assess the historicity of the Masada event.[12]

Suicide accounts in Josephus can be broken up into two major types: short episodes where only the minimum of information is given and longer narratives that contain some form of speech. The first category can be further subdivided into those episodes where the suicide of a named individual is mentioned and those where the suicide of an anonymous mass is noted. The most common suicide form is what we can call the Individual Suicide Episode. Here a named individual faces capture, death in combat, or a threatened loss of honor and, in response, takes his own life. Only the barest sketch of the situation and act are given. For example, a follower of Simon bar Giora named Eleazar enters Herodion to request its surrender: "The guards, ignorant of the object of his visit, promptly admitted him, but at the first mention of the word 'surrender' drew their swords and pursued him, until, finding escape impossible, he flung himself from the ramparts into the valley below and was killed on the spot" (*BJ* IV, 519–520).[13]

Most examples of the Individual Suicide Episode are found in the context of battle where fear of capture prompts self-murder. For example, "He [Izates] did not take Abias alive; for the latter, being surrounded on all sides, killed himself before he was quite trapped and in the hands of Izates" (*A* XX, 80). One Individual Suicide Episode shows that loss of personal honor was as good a reason for suicide as the threat of capture or death at an enemy's hand. Sabinus, one of Caligula's assassins "was not only released by Claudius from the charge but allowed to retain the office which he held. Nevertheless, deeming it wrong to fail in loyalty to his fellow conspirators, he slew himself, falling upon his sword till the hilt actually reached the wound" (*A* XIX, 273). Sabinus faces no hopeless situation on the battlefield, but to avoid disloyalty to his comrades who have been executed, he takes his own life.[14]

All Individual Suicide Episodes contain at least two elements: a reason for the suicide and the act of suicide. In almost all cases, a description of a hopeless situation precedes the episode. Josephus apparently assumes that his reader accepts unquestionably that an individual who faces a situation such as capture, death at an enemy's hands, or loss of personal honor will voluntarily kill himself. The *necessary* listing of one of these three reasons in the form suggests that these were the only acceptable bases for suicide.

The second category of short suicide episodes, the one describing the suicide of an anonymous mass, is the second most common form found in Josephus' writings. These notices of mass suicide also contain a reason for the act as well as a description of the suicide. However, they do not stand alone as do the Individual Suicide Episodes. Rather, Josephus inserts these notices of mass suicide into a larger description of the various events that can occur in the final moments of battle. We can most properly designate this form the Battle Conclusion with Suicide. For example, Josephus describes the capture of the Temple by Pompey's troops in the following manner:

> They formed a ring round the court of the Temple and slew their victims, some flying to the sanctuary, others offering brief resistance. Then it was that many of the priests, seeing the enemy advancing sword in hand, calmly continued their sacred ministrations, and were butchered in the act of pouring libations and burning incense, putting the worship of the Deity above their own preservation.

Most of the slain perished by the hands of their countrymen of the opposite faction; countless numbers flung themselves over the precipices; some, driven mad by their hopeless plight, set fire to the buildings around the wall and were consumed in the flames. Of the Jews twelve thousand perished; the losses of the Romans in dead were trifling, in wounded considerable. (*BJ* I, 149–151; cf. *A* XIV, 69–70)

Another example of the Battle Conclusion with Suicide is found in Josephus' description of the fall of Jotapata:

The Romans, remembering what they had borne during the siege, showed no quarter or pity for any, but thrust the people down the steep slope from the citadel in a general massacre. Even those still able to fight here found themselves deprived of the means of defence by the difficulties of the ground: crushed in the narrow alleys and slipping down the declivity, they were engulfed in the wave of carnage that streamed from the citadel. The situation even drove many of Josephus' picked men to suicide; seeing themselves powerless to kill a single Roman, they could at least forestall death at Roman hands, and, retiring in a body to the outskirts of the town, they there put an end to themselves. (*BJ* III, 329–331)

This Battle Conclusion continues for several paragraphs with other tales of carnage by the Romans, concluding in *BJ* III, 337 with the report that only twelve hundred prisoners were taken while the total killed for the whole siege was "computed at forty thousand."[15]

In these Battle Conclusions, Josephus draws on several elements that turn out to be stock historiographic themes used by ancient historians:[16] the victor is enraged; the conqueror kills mercilessly; flames are all around; the defeated face imminent death or enslavement; some of the conquered commit suicide to avoid the consequences of defeat; casualty figures complete the unit. We should note, though, that even within the broad form of the Battle Conclusion, the hopelessness of the situation for the vanquished is emphasized as the reason for suicide.

If we reflect on the historical value of these short suicide episodes, we can conclude that the Individual Suicide Episodes are probably historically accurate. The altering of the record of an individual's death would be a relatively difficult task. Josephus himself gives evidence for the truth of this conclusion in his story of the death of Phasael, brother of Herod the Great. Captured by Antigonus, Phasael "courageously forestalled the king's malice by dashing his head upon a rock, being deprived of the use of his hands or steel" (*BJ* I, 271; cf. *A* XIV, 367). Josephus reports that some accounts say "Phasael recovered from his self-inflicted blow, and a physician sent by Antigonus, ostensibly to attend him, injected noxious drugs into the wound and so killed him." Josephus' comment suggests that all accounts agreed that Phasael attempted to kill himself. The accounts differed on the success of his suicidal act. The reports most honoring Phasael said he succeeded; the one trying to discredit him said he failed. The suicidal act, however, could not be denied. This suggests that the historical value of the Individual Suicide Episode is quite high. Suicide was such an honorable act that it was not easily introduced into a description of a person's death without historical justification. As Josephus' tale of Phasael suggests, one's honor was not only retained by the act of suicide, it could be won.

When we ask about the historical value of the anonymous mass suicides reported within the Battle Conclusions, however, we must conclude that it is questionable. These Battle Conclusions contain too many stock historiographic phrases to make one confident that the reported suicides can be believed automatically to have occurred. These suicides are always performed by a nameless mass in the general chaos of battle. One sees no controls on the growth of the tale as would be attached to an individual suicide. Also, these supposed mass suicides often are unwitnessed. How would one know later that any specific group of corpses killed itself or was killed by someone else? With these mass suicides, we appear to be more in the realm of rhetoric than reporting. We may safely conclude that at the end of some historical battles some groups within the vanquished perhaps took their own lives rather than be captured or killed by the enemy. We know that the captured faced enslavement at best and excruciating torture at worst. We have also seen evidence that it was not considered honorable to be killed by an enemy. Consequently, we can easily believe that there were occasions when groups did take their own lives upon defeat; but we cannot declare upon the historicity of *any one specific* mass suicide within a Battle Conclusion.

The validity of such a conclusion can be verified again from within the Josephan corpus. After describing Herod's method of smoking out Galilean bandits, Josephus writes in *BJ,* "Anxious to save some of them, Herod, by word of herald, summoned them to his presence. Not one of them voluntarily surrendered, and of those taken by force many preferred death to captivity" (I, 311). Josephus then appends to this general notice a specific narrative about one old bandit who kills his family and himself. This suicidal refusal to surrender contrasts markedly with its parallel in *A* XIV, 427: "and many, after sending spokesmen with the king's consent, surrendered and made their submission." Josephus retains the story of the old bandit in *A* but alters the impression left by the account in *BJ.* In the latter, the old bandit appears as a fitting climax to the suicidal refusal to surrender by all the bandits; in the former, the old bandit stands honorably in contrast to those who surrendered.

We should probably not too quickly credit this change of description to "inconsistency" or "sloppiness" on Josephus' part. Recent studies have shown that Josephus often draws on stock historiographic phrases, motifs, and forms appropriate to the type of history he is writing at the time.[17] Therefore, Josephus' shift in tone between the accounts of Herod and the bandits found in

BJ and *A* most probably has to do with the change in historiographic form, and thus purpose, between the two works. The anonymity of the bandits allowed Josephus the freedom to clothe their end in literary phrases most appropriate to the specific type of history he was writing. In the end, we cannot judge historically whether the bandits surrendered. We can see only that in one literary work Josephus found it appropriate to say they did not surrender, and in another he found it appropriate to say they did. We see, then, that the literary form of the Battle Conclusion with Suicides tells us only what was possible at the end of any battle; it does not tell us what happened at the end of a *specific* battle. With this form, the cloak of rhetoric too heavily clothes history ever to discern what actually happened.

Rhetorical features also clothe the second major category of suicide accounts in Josephus: the longer independent narratives that contain some form of speech. We can designate these Suicide Narratives. Although the rarest literary form used by Josephus for recording suicides, the dramatic structure of Suicide Narratives makes them stand out prominently. Almost all of them are appended to a Battle Conclusion, although suicide does not have to be mentioned in the latter for a Suicide Narrative to be added. The defeat of a large group provides a backdrop for a specific example of dramatic suicide. These Suicide Narratives are self-contained units and have three necessary elements: the description of a hopeless situation, the reason for suicide given in a speech, and the account of the suicidal act. They appear as a flashback to an incident that occurred during the battle Josephus has just described. For example, upon the refusal by the Galilean bandits to surrender to Herod, Josephus tells us:

> It was then that one old man, the father of seven children, being asked by them and their mother permission to leave under Herod's pledge, killed them in the following manner. Ordering them to come forward one by one, he stood at the entrance and slew each son as he advanced. Herod, watching this spectacle from a conspicuous spot, was profoundly affected and, extending his hand to the old man, implored him to spare his children; but he, unmoved by any word of Herod, and even upbraiding him as a low-born upstart, followed up the slaughter of his sons by that of his wife, and, having flung their corpses down the precipice, finally threw himself over after them (*BJ* I, 312–313; cf. *A* XIV, 429–430).

Another example of a Suicide Narrative, this time containing direct rather than indirect discourse, is added by Josephus to the account of the slaughter of the Scythopolitan Jews after they had joined in the defense of their city against attacking Jewish revolutionaries. After stating that close to 13,000 Jews were killed, Josephus writes:

> Mention (*axion*) may be here made of the tragic fate (*pathos*) of Simon, whose father, Saul, was a man of some distinction. Endowed with exceptional physical strength and audacity, he abused both gifts to the detriment of his countrymen.

Day by day he had marched out and slain large numbers of the Jews who were attacking Scythopolis; often had he put their whole force to flight, his single arm turning the scale in the engagement. But now this slaughter of his kin met with its due (*axia*) penalty. For when the Scythopolitans had surrounded the grove and were shooting down its occupants with their javelins, he drew his sword, and then, instead of rushing upon one of the enemy, whose numbers he saw were endless, he exclaimed in a tone of deep emotion (*ekpathōs*): "Justly (*axia*) am I punished for my crimes, men of Scythopolis, I and all who by such a slaughter of our kinsmen have sealed our loyalty to you. Ah! well, let us who have but naturally experienced the perfidy of foreigners, us who have been guilty of the last degree of impiety towards our own people, let us, I say, die, as cursed wretches, by our own hands; for we are not meet to die at the hands of the enemy. This, God grant, shall be at once the fit (*axia*) retribution for my foul crime and testimony to my courage, that none of my foes shall be able to boast of having slain me or glory over my prostrate body." With these words he cast a glance of mingled pity and rage over his family: he had wife, children, and aged parents. First seizing his father by his hoary hair, he ran his sword through his body; after him his mother, who offered no resistance, and then his wife and children, each victim almost rushing upon the blade, in haste to anticipate the enemy. After slaying every member of his family, he stood conspicuous on the corpses, and with right hand uplifted to attract all eyes, plunged the sword up to the hilt into his own throat. So perished a youth who, in virtue of his strength of body and fortitude of soul, deserves (*axios*) commiseration, but who by reason of his trust in aliens met the consequent fate (*pathesi*). (*BJ* II, 469–476)

This latter tale reveals its rhetorical nature by its artfulness. The use of *pathos* to frame the narrative unit, as well as the intricate and subtle use of *axios*—to frame the narrative, introduce Simon's speech, and frame the speech—all point to the narrative's literary artistry.[18]

The narrative aspect of this form focuses on the speaker, who is usually a father or leader. Although many people may be killed in the course of the story, it is only this leader figure who actually kills himself. These Suicide Narratives often contain familiacides and/or homicides. These killings are carried out by the leader figure, or his representative, and are all suffered passively. The action builds so that the others' deaths are passive while the final death of the leader is passionately active. The true suicide of the patriarchal figure climaxes the whole story. We see then, in these Suicide Narratives, that the climactic suicide takes priority in form and function over all other forms of death experienced passively. From this basis, we would suggest that the final suicide also takes priority in honor. We see that taking one's own life for honor or faith brings greater glory than being captured or killed by the enemy. The whole rhetorical structure of these Suicide Narratives spirals up to that final climactic plunging of "the sword up to the hilt into his own throat" (*BJ* II, 476).

Although the final suicide climaxes the narrative aspect of these forms, the central element of the stories is the speech. The presence of a speech, in either direct or indirect discourse, sets Suicide Narratives apart from other suicide forms used by Josephus. The nature of these speeches, however, has not often been understood. Many scholars, apparently working from an assertion made by H. St. John Thackeray, have assumed that the speeches in Josephus' works are pure inventions that reveal Josephus' intentions.[19] This is too simplistic a view of the place of speeches in Josephus or in any other ancient historian. The free invention of speeches purely to express the point of view of the author does not appear to have been widely acceptable in ancient historiography. Starting with Thucydides, the two basic criteria applied to historiographic speeches were that either they suggest what would have been appropriate to say in the situation or they report basically what was actually said. Thucydides and Polybius appear to have striven most to fulfill this latter criterion of veracity.[20] However, because of the difficulty of reporting the actual words of a speaker, even these historians aimed more at recording the essence of a speech rather than its substance.[21]

Most other ancient historians would come to stress the criterion of the suitability of a speech to its setting. Critics such as Dionysius of Halicarnassus, Lucian, and Quintilian argued that the historian should strive in his speeches to portray "what is fitting" (*to prepon*) to the character and situation.[22] Consequently, in Josephus' day there was a debate between historians in the line of Thucydides and Polybius who emphasized reporting what *was* said as closely as possible and those in the line of Livy and Dionysius who strove to write what *should have been* said. This latter group was the one dominant in Josephus' time. It still may be appropriate to note, however, that whichever canon of historiography one was following in writing speeches, the result should exhibit verisimilitude. In conclusion, then, we see that speeches in ancient histories were not free inventions revealing the author's intentions. Rather, speeches were integral to the narrative as a whole and, therefore, often have to be understood in light of the narrative, not vice versa.[23]

All these are necessary considerations when we examine the speeches found in Josephus' Suicide Narratives. The speeches, if Josephus is indeed following the canons of contemporary historiography, will be at least suitable to the situation *and* the character. They also may be more or less close to the essence of what was said, depending on Josephus' source of information. In fact, the attribute of veracity may be stronger in the speeches of *BJ* than in *A*. Harold Attridge has shown that in *BJ* Josephus was consciously following a Thucydidean-Polybian model of history, while in *A* he shifted more to an Isocratean-Dionysian rhetorical mode.[24] This would lead us to expect that Josephus would depart more from his sources in the matter of speeches in *A* than in *BJ*. This expectation is borne out, for example, in the more fulsome explanation of the reasons for the familiacide and suicide of the old bandit found in the *A* version of this tale compared with that found in *BJ*. A more dramatic example is Josephus' transformation of the succinct biblical account of Ahithophel's suicide (II Samuel 17:23) into a full Suicide Narrative, proper speech and all (A VII, 228–229). This latter example shows that in A, at least, Josephus could freely add a speech to the narrative of his source.[25] Still, he fits the speech both to the narrative and to the character. The speech does not stand apart from the narrative.

The highly rhetorical nature of both the narrative and the speeches must be kept in mind as we approach the issue of the historicity in any given Suicide Narrative. The focus of the Suicide Narrative on the words and climactic action of one usually named individual might suggest truth; but the staged quality of the speeches and the rhetorical crafting of the narrative imply fiction. Consequently, it becomes much more difficult to reach a general conclusion about the historicity of this form. Each individual narrative must be examined and evaluated separately. Therefore, we must develop criteria by which to separate the historical from the unhistorical in the Suicide Narratives.

We can probably make an initial judgment about Josephus' faithfulness to his sources in reporting suicides. He does not appear to create freely Suicide Narratives without some basis in his sources. For instance, in his rewriting of the Bible for a Hellenistic audience Josephus does not spice up his work by adding suicides not already recorded in his source. Although he dramatizes the death of Saul (A VI, 368–73) and reforms the Ahithophel story into a Suicide Narrative (A VII, 228–30), Josephus creates no new suicides merely for dramatic purposes. His restructuring of the Ahithophel story shows that he can take what is comparable to an Individual Suicide Episode in his source and transform it into a Suicide Narrative. This suggests two important points: we should look at the narrative aspect of this form—not the speech—to judge the historicity of the event; and those Suicide Narratives that show evidence of being created from Individual Suicide Episodes might have a greater claim to historical validity, since the latter form bears a high level of historicity.

Another factor that must be brought into the discussion of the historicity of any one Suicide Narrative is the nature of Josephus' source of information. Josephus was clearly an eyewitness to only one of the suicides he reports in this form: the thirty-nine men in the cave at Jotapata.[26] Although he may have been present at the suicide of Longus, the opening phrases of this account suggest that this story originated as an official citation for bravery in Roman military reports. Only one other Suicide Narrative probably had its original source in Roman records: the story of Masada. The source for Josephus' account of the old bandit was probably Nicholas of Damascus. Josephus faithfully borrows the tale from his source but, as noted earlier, shifts its import within its context. Whether Nicholas was truthful in his account is another matter. The fact that the old bandit is nameless lowers the probability of its historicity. The presence of certain traditional motifs in this tale also raises questions concerning its trustworthiness.[27] There is a final factor that condemns this story to the realm of fiction: the purpose it serves in the story of Herod the Great.

The story, as told by Nicholas and followed most closely by Josephus in *BJ*, is related in such a way as to heighten the nobility of Herod's deed by ennobling his opponents. This was a literary and artistic commonplace in Hellenistic times.[28] One stresses the greatness of one's victory by honoring one's defeated opponents. Claiming the suicide of one's enemies upon facing defeat at your hands stressed the magnitude of your victory over such honorable opponents. In narrating the supposed suicidal refusal to surrender by the bandits and the climactic familiacide and suicide by one specific—but still unamed!—old bandit, Nicholas was attempting to increase Herod's fame. We should not too quickly make claims that these bandits were Maccabean supporters or the beginning of a religious revolutionary movement.[29] The purpose of the tale was to honor Herod by depicting the supposed noble end of the bandits. Their ennobling is secondary, not primary, to the ennobling of Herod. Josephus apparently recognized that this was the purpose of the tale. In *A* where, it has been noted, he is less favorable to Herod,[30] Josephus changes the refusal to surrender by the bandits into an act of surrender. This lessens the distinction of Herod's victory, even with the retention of the tale of the old bandit. In the end, we can find little of historical value in this story.

The story of Simon of Scythopolis is also of questionable historicity. A specific name appears, which suggests authenticity, but the problem of the source of the story raises difficulties. If all the Jews were massacred, how did the account of the familiacide and suicide of Simon find its way to Josephus? In wording, it shares some characteristics with the citations for bravery that come from Roman sources.[31] If the opponents of the Jews had been Romans instead of the general citizen body of Scythopolis, this might have suggested authenticity; but they were not. It is difficult to see how this story arose. One is tempted to suggest that Simon was known to the Jewish rebels who attacked the city and who witnessed his mighty feats of arms against them. After word was received of the destruction of the Scythopolitan Jews, this story was developed around the figure of Simon as a fitting depiction of the fate faced by a Jew who betrayed his own people.[32] The story then may have arisen orally during the early stages of the revolt to emphasize the need for loyalty to the Jewish people. Josephus may have heard the tale. Later, he simply recorded it, or more likely, he artistically crafted the story himself. Either way, we cannot historically judge whether a certain Simon killed his family and himself. Simon's speech was written by Josephus on the basis of what would have been fitting for a Jew in Simon's position to say. After all, it is doubtful that Simon would have been allowed the time to make such a speech by the attacking Gentiles. We must emphasize again that we should not too readily try to read

Josephus' own views out of this speech. A good ancient historian could write speeches for both sides of an argument with equal cogency. This must be remembered as we turn to the longest Suicide Narratives in Josephus' works: Jotapata and Masada.

The long stories of the suicides in the cave at Jotapata and on the mountain of Masada can be called Extended Suicide Narratives. It is worth noting, however, that their greater length comes primarily from the extensive speeches imbedded in both pericopes. When one examines the purely narrative part of these two accounts, one discovers that they are not all that much longer than the shorter Suicide Narratives we have already examined. Because of the great importance placed on speeches as avenues into Josephus' purposes, these speeches have undergone much analysis, especially the ones in the Masada story.[33] Unfortunately, the major debate over the speeches has been whether their content is more Jewish or more Hellenistic. A full analysis of these speeches would go well beyond the scope of this article, but we should note in passing that this attempt to find which elements weigh heaviest is probably unproductive. In light of what we have come to know about the Hellenization of Palestine at the turn of the eras, we should realize that supposed Jewish and Hellenistic ideas were so closely interwoven that they cannot always be separated clearly.[34] If we would accept this fact, we would probably make further progress in understanding the full implications of how these speeches would, in the historiographic terms of the day, be considered fitting and proper for their contexts.

As we saw earlier, however, it will not be speeches that help us to decide the historicity of these suicides, it will be aspects of the narrative that reveal probable signs of basic authenticity. When we look at the suicide at Jotapata, we must assert that its historicity is highly probable. Josephus was an eyewitness to the event and participated in it. As has often been noted, his own escape from the suicide pact clashes with the nobility of those who willingly died rather than surrender to the Romans.[35] The purpose of the story, and especially of the speeches, is to explain Josephus' own avoidance of suicide rather than to dramatize the deaths of the others. The fact that Josephus must so thoroughly explain his refusal to commit suicide—which we might note in passing has strong parallels with later rabbinic arguments against suicide[36]—argues strongly for the historicity of the self-chosen death by the others in the cave. Considering the expectations of many Jews and Romans of someone in Josephus' situation, it is doubtful that he would invent suicides that did not happen in order to illuminate so starkly his own surrender. On the basis of source alone, the direct words of an eyewitness, we must accept the historicity of the Jotapata cave suicides.

When we turn to Masada, we face a greater problem in assessing authenticity. Among scholars looking at Masada, only S. Cohen has compared it with other known mass suicides in Hellenistic writings.[37] He concluded that the historicity of the Masada suicides is dubious. While his basic approach is helpful, his conclusions are unsatisfying because they make no allowances for the different forms and consequent different levels of historicity by which suicides were recorded in ancient histories. Most of Cohen's proposed parallels to Masada are not true parallels in form. Many of them are Battle Conclusions with Suicides, which we have already discovered have little historical value. On that point, he is correct in his doubts. But the Masada account does not share this form. It is an Extended Suicide Narrative, a form inherently neither historical or unhistorical. We must assess the historicity of the Masada narrative, like other Suicide Narratives, by the criteria of its use of named individuals, the quality of its sources, and its function within *BJ*. An analysis of the speeches will not help us decide historicity. The speeches depend on the narrative. At the least, they state what Josephus and his audience would consider fitting to the occasion; at the most, they record what Josephus believed Eleazar might have said. For judging the historicity of the Masada event, however, the speeches are useless.

When we apply the criteria for evaluating authenticity to the narrative, we find that the Masada suicides are highly probable. The geographical description of Masada has proven to be highly accurate and probably derives from Roman reports rather than from Josephus' personal observations. Also, the straightforward description of the progression of the siege operations from the Roman point of view argues that Josephus is here dependent on the military reports of Flavius Silva. The *specific* casualty figures—960 dead, 2 women and 5 children captured—suggest a source in an official report rather than Josephus' mind. It was probably through these survivors that the Romans learned the personal name of the Sicarii leader. As we have seen, descriptions of suicides by anonymous groups prove to be questionable historically. The presence of individual names in a suicide account raises the probability of historicity. That Josephus did not invent the character of Eleazar ben Yair is shown by the archaeological evidence. The potsherd discovered by Yadin bearing the name "ben Yair" verifies the report by Josephus that this man was present on Masada.[38] The presence of Eleazar's name in Josephus' narrative along with its archaeological verification heightens the historical probability of this event.

Contrary to what some have claimed, a reported suicide by the Sicarii would not have denigrated them in the eyes of the Romans.[39] Rather, with the Hellenistic tradition of suicide to avoid dishonor, such an act would have raised the stature of the Sicarii in the Roman mind. The honorable enemy does not surrender, he does not die fighting (*unless* he has something or someone still to protect), and he does not allow himself to be captured; he kills himself, maintaining his honor. Although a report that his enemies committed suicide might have heightened Flavius Silva's deed in the eyes of Vespasian, it is doubtful that Silva would have dared to report such a thing if it had not happened. That would have been too great a departure from a proper military report. It is also doubtful that Josephus departed wholesale from his source to fashion this tale of mass suicide. Generally, Josephus has proven to be faithful to the content of his sources, even when he freely rewrites them. Specifically, we have seen that Josephus does not freely invent suicide accounts related to named individuals, although he might be willing to add a detail about suicide to his Battle Conclusions. The generality of his Battle Conclusions with Suicides, however, contrasts with the specificity of details in the Masada narrative. At least in relation to suicides, Josephus appears to be inventing when he generalizes groups and numbers; he appears to be faithfully following his source when he specifies individuals and numbers. A final question could be raised about historicity because the Masada story fits so well Josephus' stated purpose of honoring the Romans by honoring the Jews (*BJ* I, 7–9). The evidence already examined, however, argues strongly that he did not invent the act of suicide by the Sicarii. Rather, Josephus took the basic narrative elements from his source, expanded them primarily by adding the two long speeches, and crafted the Extended Suicide Narrative as an appropriate conclusion to his work. Still, the basic authenticity of the act Josephus describes stands. We must conclude that the familiacide and suicide of 960 Sicarii on Masada did occur historically. Ironically, by their act, the Sicarii showed how strongly they had been influenced by the very Hellenistic views that they had fought against so hard.

In conclusion, we have seen that Josephus used three basic forms for recording suicides: the Individual Suicide Episode, the Battle Conclusion with Suicides, and the Suicide Narrative. We have also seen that the historical value of these forms varies. The Individual Suicide Episode, because of its tie with a specific historical person and its unembellished style, carries a high probability of historicity. The Battle Conclusion with Suicides carries little intrinsic, historical probability. Its clichélike description of anonymous masses suggests a popular historiographic form virtually useless as history. The Suicide Narrative form carries no implicit historicity, but it may contain historical content. There are criteria by which we can evaluate historicity. The presence of a named individual in the narrative suggests historicity since we saw evidence that Suicide Narratives could be developed from Individual Suicide Episodes by the addition of the required speech. Since these speeches appear to be developed out of the narrative elements of the unit and are intended to be fitting to the situation, they are useless for the purpose of historical evaluation.

The ability to trace the basic narrative to some type of trustworthy source, either eyewitnesses or official records of some type, raises the probability factor. Basically, the presence of certain types of specific detail within the narrative frame of the Suicide Narrative helps to argue for authenticity. Finally, an evaluation of the function of the form in both its source setting and Josephan setting helps decide the final probability. A meshing of the function of the form with the purpose of the author, while not automatically counting against historical value, may raise questions about trustworthiness. Each example must be evaluated individually.

This study has argued strongly that the importance of form and function of the various suicide accounts must be addressed before any attempt can be made to assess historical value. Josephus drew upon standard historiographic forms in his writings. Before we can really hope to evaluate either Josephus personally or the historical value of his works, we must first understand these various historiographic forms and how they function both generally in the writing of ancient history and particularly in Josephus' writing of history.

Notes

1. Yigael Yadin, *Masada: Herod's Fortress and the Zealots' Last Stand* (New York: Random House, 1966).

2. Cf. Solomon Zeitlin, "Masada and the Sicarii," *JQR* 55(1964–65):314–315; and "The Sicarii and Masada," *JQR* 57(1966–67):203.

3. Cf. Trude Weiss-Rosmarin, "Josephus' 'Eleazar Speech' and Historical Credibility," *Proceedings of the Sixth World Congress Of Jewish Studies*, vol. 1 (Jerusalem: World Union of Jewish Studies, 1977)1:417–427; and her earlier articles in *Jewish Spectator*, 31(1966):4–7; 32(1967):2–8, 30–32; and 34(1969):3–5, 29–32.

4. See the *Tradition* series on Masada in 10, no. 2(1968):31–34; 11, no. 1(1970):5–43; 11, no. 3 (1970):31–37; 12, no. 1(1971):5–43; 13, no. 2(1972):100–105. Also see Robert Gordis, "The Unsullied Saga of Masada," *Hadassah Magazine* 49, no. 2(December 1967):12–13, 27–28; and Louis H. Feldman, "Masada: A Critique of Recent Scholarship," *Christianity, Judaism and other Greco-Roman Cults: Studies for Morton Smith at Sixty*, ed. Jacob Neusner (Leiden: E. J. Brill, 1975), Part Three, pp. 218–48; *Josephus and Modern Scholarship (1937–1980)* (Berlin: Walter de Gruyter, 1984), pp. 765–789, 964–966.

5. Werner Eck, "Die Eroberung von Masada und eine neue Inschrift des L. Flavius Silva Nonius Bassus," *ZNW* 60(1969):282–289, argued that the fall of Masada should be redated to the spring of 74. This has become widely accepted. However, the basis of his conclusion has been effectively countered by C. P. Jones in a review in *AJP* 95(1974):89–90; and by G. W. Bowersock in a review in *JRS* 65(1975):180–185. The year A.D. 73 still appears to be the best date for the fall of Masada.

6. Cf. B. A. Shargel, "The Evolution of the Masada Myth," *Judaism* 28(1979): 357–371.

7. David Ladouceur, "Masada: A Consideration of the Literary Evidence," *GRBS* 21(1980):245–260.

8. Shaye Cohen, "Masada: Literary Traditions, Archaeological Remains, and the Credibility of Josephus," *JJS* 33(1982):385–405.

9. Menahem Luz, "Eleazar's Second Speech on Masada and Its Literary Precedents," *RhM* 126(1983):25–44; Michael Bünker, "Die rhetorische Disposition der Eleazarreden," *Kairos* 23(1981):100–107.

10. L. D. Hankoff, "The Theme of Suicide in the Works of Flavius Josephus," *CM* 11, no. 1(1976):15–24; "Flavius Josephus. First Century A.D. View of Suicide," *NYSJM* 77(1977): 1986–92; and "Flavius Josephus. Suicide and Transition," *NYSJM* 79(1979):937–942.

11. Cf. David Ladouceur, "The Language of Josephus," *JSJ* 14(1983):25–29.

12. See my article "The Suicide Accounts in Josephus: A Form Critical Study," *SBL 1982 Seminar Papers,* ed. Kent Richards (Chico, Calif.: Scholars Press, 1982), pp. 351–369; and my forthcoming work, "The Suicide Accounts in Josephus" (Ph.D. diss., Vanderbilt University).

13. The English translations used in this paper come from the Loeb Classical Library (*LCL*) version of Josephus' works, translated variously by H. St. J. Thackeray, R. Marcus, and L. H. Feldman (Cambridge, Mass.: Harvard University Press, 1926–1965).

14. Other examples of Individual Suicide Episodes are found in *BJ* I, 271–273a = *A* XIV, 367–369 = *A* XV, 13; *BJ* IV, 493; *BJ* IV, 548; *BJ* VI, 280; *A* XII, 236; *Ap* I, 236 = *Ap* I, 258.

15. Other examples of Battle Conclusions with Suicide are found in *BJ* II, 49–50 = *A* XVII, 261–264; *BJ* III, 422–427; *BJ* IV, 78–81; *BJ* IV, 311–313; *BJ* IV, 433–435; *BJ* VI, 180–182; *BJ* VI, 284; *BJ* VI, 429–430. A special case is *A* XV, 358–359, where Josephus uses the form to describe the end of a court "battle."

16. Cf. Cohen (*op. cit.,* note 8), pp. 386–392.

17. Cf. Horst Moehring, "Novelistic Elements in the Writings of Flavius Josephus" (Ph.D. diss., University of Chicago, 1957), pp. 83–123; Harold Attridge, *The Interpretation of Biblical History in the Antiquitates Judaicae of Flavius Josephus* (Missoula, Mont.: Scholars Press, 1976), pp. 43–61; Ladouceur, *op. cit.,* note 11), pp. 18–38; and David Ladouceur, "The Death of Herod the Great," *CP* 76(1981):25–34. See especially Louis H. Feldman's "Hellenization" series: "Abraham the Greek Philosopher in Josephus," *TAPA* 99(1968):143–156; "Hellenizations in Josephus' Portrayal of Man's Decline," in *Religions in Antiquity: Essays in Memory of Erwin Ramsdell Goodenough,* ed. Jacob Neusner, Studies in The History of Religions, 14 (Leiden: E. J. Brill, 1968), pp. 336–353; "Hellenizations in Josephus' Version of Esther," *TAPA* 101(1970):143–170; "Josephus as an Apologist to the Greco-Roman World: His Portrait of Solomon," *Aspects of Religious Propaganda in Judaism and Early Christianity,* ed. Elizabeth Schüssler Fiorenza, Studies in Judaism and Christianity in Antiquity, 2 (South Bend, Ind.: University of Notre Dame Press, 1976), pp. 69–98; "Josephus' Portrait of Saul," *HUCA* 53 (1982):45–99; and "Abraham the General in Josephus," *Nourished with Peace. Studies in Hellenistic Judaism in Memory of Samuel Sandmel,* eds. F. E. Greenspahn, E. Hilgert, & B. L. Mack, Scholars Press Homage Series (Chico, Calif.: Scholars Press, 1984), pp. 43–49.

18. Other examples of Suicide Narratives are found in *BJ* VI, 186–187; *A* V, 251–253; *A* V, 370–72a; *A* VII, 228–29. The stories of Josephus' surrender at Jotapata in *BJ* III, 340–91 and the suicide of the Sicarii at Masada in *BJ* VII, 304–406 are extended examples of this form.

19. H. St. John Thackeray, *Josephus: The Man and the Historian* (New York: Ktav Publishing House, Inc., 1967), p. 42: "These set speeches are purely imaginary and serve the purpose of propaganda." Cf. Weiss-Rosmarin (*op. cit.,* note 3), p. 418; Donna R. Runnalls, "Hebrew and Greek Sources in the Speeches of Josephus' *Jewish War*" (Ph.D. diss., University of Toronto, 1971), pp. i–ii; Roland G. Bomstad, "Governing Ideas of the Jewish War of Flavius Josephus" (Ph.D. diss., Yale University, 1979), p. 2; Luz (*op. cit.,* note 9), p. 25; Otto Michel, "Die Rettung Israels und die Rolle Rom nach dem Reden im 'Bellum Iudaicum'" *ANRW* II, 21, 2 (Berlin: Walter de Gruyter, 1984), pp. 945–951, 972.

20. F. W. Walbank, *Speeches in Greek Historians* (Oxford: B. H. Blackwell, 1965), pp. 3–4, 8–11.

21. Michael Grant, *The Ancient Historians* (New York: Charles Scribner's Sons, 1970), p. 20; Charles W. Fornara, *The Nature of History in Ancient Greece and Rome* (Berkeley: University of California Press, 1983), pp. 142–168.

22. Cf. Walbank (*op. cit.,* note 20), pp. 4–6, 18–19; Cohen (*op. cit.,* note 8), p. 14; P. G. Walsh, *Livy. His Historical Aims and Methods* (Cambridge: Cambridge University Press, 1961), pp. 219–35.

23. Cf. Hans-Peter Stahl, "Speeches and Course of Events in Books Six and Seven of Thucydides," *The Speeches in Thucydides,* ed. Philip A. Stadter (Chapel Hill: The University of North Carolina Press, 1973), pp. 60–77; and H. D. Westlake, "The Settings of Thucydidean Speeches," in *ibid.,* pp. 90–108.

24. Attridge (*op. cit.,* note 17), pp. 44–50; cf. David Ladouceur, "Studies in the Language and Historiography of Flavius Josephus" (Ph.D., diss. Brown University, 1977), pp. 89–95, 103; Feldman, "Josephus' Portrait of Saul," (*op. cit.,* note 17), pp. 46–52.

25. Cf. Josephus' addition of Phasael's supposed thoughts, prior to his suicide in *A* XIV, 367–369, to the original Individual Suicide Episode in *BJ* I, 271–272. Cf. Westlake (*op. cit.,* note 23), p. 103.

26. He was a witness to the false suicide of Castor and his companions (*BJ* V, 317–330), which he reports in the form of a Suicide Narrative.

27. Cf. Francis Loftus, "The Martyrdom of the Galilean Troglodytes (*BJ* i.312–313; *A* xiv.429–30)," *JQR* 66(1975–1976):212–223.

28. Cf. Ladouceur (*op. cit.,* note 7), p. 247; Christine Havelock, *Hellenistic Art* (Greenwich, Conn.: New York Graphic Society, 1968), p. 146.

29. Cf. the comments of William Farmer, "Judas, Simon and Athrogenes," *NTS* 4 (1957–1958):150–151; Shimon Applebaum, "The Zealots. The Case for Revaluation," *JRS* 61(1971):159; Matthew Black, "Judas of Galilee and Josephus's 'Fourth Philosophy,'" *J-S,* pp. 46–47; and E. Mary Smallwood, *The Jews Under Roman Rule: From Pompey to Diocletian* (Leiden: E. J. Brill, 1976), p. 44. Likewise, we should be cautious about drawing sociological data too quickly from these accounts; cf. Richard Horsley, "Ancient Jewish Banditry and the Revolt Against Rome, A.D. 66–70," *CBQ* 43(1981):413–414, 418. We must understand the form and function of the text *before* we derive historical or sociological data from it.

30. Cf. Thackeray, (*op. cit.,* note 19), pp. 65–67; Richard Laqueur, *Der jüdische Historiker Flavius Josephus* (Darmstadt: Wissentschaftliche Buchgesellschaft, 1970), p. 132; F. J. Foakes Jackson, *Josephus and the Jews* (Grand Rapids: Baker Book House, 1977), p. xiv.

31. The use of *axios* appears to be part of such a citation; cf. *BJ* VI, 186.

32. This was a common theme in Jewish works of the Hellenistic era. Cf. Sandra Berg, *The Book of Esther: Motifs, Themes and Structure* (Missoula, Mont.: Scholars Press, 1979), pp. 98–103.

33. Cf. W. Morel, "Eine Rede bei Josephus," *RhM* 75(1926):106–14; O. Bauernfeind & O. Michel, "Die beiden Eleazarreden in Jos. bell 7,323–336; 7,341–388," *ZNW* 58(1967): 267–272; Runnalls (*op. cit.,* note 19), pp. 198–274; Helgo Lindner, *Die Geschichtsauffassung des Flavius Josephus in Bellum Judaicum* (Leiden: E. J. Brill, 1972), pp. 33–40; Weiss-Rosmarin (*op. cit.,* note 3), pp. 417–427; Ladouceur, (*op. cit.,* note 24), pp. 96–102; Pierre Vidal-Naquet, "Flavius Josèphe et Masada," *RH* 260 (1978):13–21; Bomstad (*op. cit.,* note 19), pp. 90–135; Ladouceur (*op. cit.,* note 7), pp. 245–260; Bünker (*op. cit.,* note 9), pp. 100–107; Luz (*op. cit.,* note 9), pp. 25–43.

34. Cf. Martin Hengel, *Judaism and Hellenism,* 2 vols. (Philadelphia: Fortress Press, 1974); and *Jews, Greeks and Barbarians* (Philadelphia: Fortress Press, 1980).

35. Cf. Norman Bentwich, *Josephus* (Philadelphia: Jewish Publication Society of Amer-

ica, 1914), pp. 54–57; Jackson (*op. cit.*, note 30), pp. 14–17; Thackeray (*op. cit.*, note 19), pp. 13–14.

36. Cf. Newell (*op. cit.*, note 12), pp. 359–362.
37. Cohen (*op. cit.*, note 8), pp. 386–392.
38. Yadin (*op. cit.*, note 1), p. 201.
39. Cf. Martin Hengel, *Die Zeloten* (Leiden: E. J. Brill, 1961), p. 266; Weiss-Rosmarin, (*op. cit.*, note 3), pp. 426–427.

14 The Description of the Land of Israel in Josephus' Works

ZEEV SAFRAI

The writings of Josephus Flavius serve as the major source for the history of the People of Israel and the Land of Israel during the last few generations of the Second Temple period. Many details in these writings, whether mentioned briefly or described at great length, are without parallel reference in other examples of early literature. In other cases, ancient authors preserved only incomplete fragments of information that are understood only within the context of events related in Josephus. Therefore, the examination of the methodology of Josephus' writings takes on paramount importance. The reliability of his compositions, his sources and the manner in which he utilized them, and his objectives and those of his sources are among the most important issues for the study of Jewish history at the end of the Second Temple period.

The information available, however, does not offer easy solutions to the problems raised by these issues. As mentioned earlier, many chapters in Josephus' works are without parallel anywhere else and the scholar must base his conclusions on the integral logic of the material. Other times, the evaluation of an issue may depend upon internal parallels and the examination of details of an event related in different contexts.

One of the best methods for examining some of these issues is through a detailed study of the description of the Land of Israel and various geographic details in Josephus. This provides insight into the degree of exactitude and reliability of Josephus regarding the area in question. Geographic detail can be examined not only in terms of parallels in literary sources, but can especially be studied vis-à-vis the characteristics of the particular area being studied. Josephus' descriptions of Judea can be compared with information from archaeological remains and physical topography that is still evident today. This will allow us not only to establish the extent of Josephus' familiarity with the physical topography of the land, but also the degree of his eye for detail and his recall of events years after their occurrence and after he had left Judea never to return.

The purpose of this article is not to describe the Land of Israel during Josephus' time, for such an undertaking could not be limited to a single article, but rather to examine his sources, his reliability, his eye for detail, and the nature of these descriptions. As stated, the ultimate purpose of all this is to serve as an additional tool to examine Josephus' writings and their worth for modern research. In light of this methodological aim the writings of Josephus can be divided into three categories.

First are works based to a great extent on personal knowledge and acquaintances. This is especially true of the *Jewish War* (*BJ*) (except for Book I and half of Book II), the *Life* (*V*), and *Against Apion* (*Ap*). It is true that in these works Josephus also used external sources or established traditions that were handed down orally. In the formulation of these works, however, Josephus' role is still paramount and particularly in the formulation of the material.

Second are works in which Josephus used a well-known ancient source. This mostly refers to *Antiquities* (*A*) I–XI, which is based almost entirely on the biblical narrative.

Third are works in which Josephus used earlier sources that, unfortunately, have not been preserved and, therefore, it is quite difficult to ascertain how many details were derived from the original source and how many were added by Josephus. *Antiquities* XIV–XVII relates the history of the Herodian dynasty. It is well known that in these chapters, and perhaps in others, Josephus used the works of Nicolaus of Damascus. It is not well known, however, whether Josephus had other sources at his disposal, perhaps oral traditions that would have enabled him to add details and evaluate issues in a manner different from those found in the works of Nicolaus.[1]

Our task, therefore, is to examine the geographic details found in the works of Josephus according to this division and in light of the methodological goals presented earlier.

Josephus himself was born in Judea into an upper-class enlightened family and, it seemed, traveled extensively in the land. For at least six months, he served as commander of the Jewish forces in the Galilee and traveled with the Romans in Judea for an additional two years. It is, therefore, to be expected that he would serve as an excellent and reliable source regarding the study of the Land of Israel. Indeed, generally, Josephus is a trustworthy source for the description of the Land of Israel during his period. Thus, he is able to attack the anti-Semitic allegations of the Egyptian upstart, Apion, by pointing out the geographic errors in Apion's charges. The geographic analysis of Josephus in this case is both exact and correct. Thus, Josephus states that: "Idumaea, in the latitude of Gaza, is conterminous with our territory. It has no city called Dora. There is a town of that name in Phoenicia, near Mount Carmel, but that has nothing in common with Apion's ridiculous story, being at a distance of four days' march from Idumaea."[2]

Dora is indeed near Mount Carmel and at this time did belong to the administrative sphere of Phoenicia, even though, geographically speaking, it could have been included in Judea. Dora is 150 to 160 kilometers from Hebron in Idumaea[3] and this is a distance of a four days' march. Josephus also makes maximum usage of the term "Phoenicia." He especially stresses the information most appropriate for his polemical purposes. Josephus locates Idumaea vis-à-vis the city of Gaza, which was well known as a city that was not included in Judea, even though in Josephus' time, Idumaea was a district of Judea.[4] The information is correct but is presented in a manner in keeping with the purposes of the author. This passage is particularly indicative of Josephus' handling of relevant material and his knowledge of the Land of Israel.

There are numerous examples of correct and exact descriptions of the Land of Israel in Josephus' works. Precisely in light of this background, it is necessary to delve into those cases that represent a lesser degree of exactitude, and as we shall see, these cases prove Josephus' dependence on additional sources.

As we have mentioned, there are hundreds of geographical details in Josephus. For our purposes, the study may best be begun by presenting those sections that represent a more complete description. Eight chapters begin with a description of geographic detail, which is meant to serve as a background for the historical narrative that follows. Many Roman historians also described a region and its history before describing particular historical events. Josephus, therefore, is following accepted practice.[5] In the case of Josephus, the events are usually the conquest of a particular area. The eight sections are

1. A description of the entire land[6]
2. Valley of Gennesar[7]
3. Jerusalem[8]
4. Jericho Valley[9]
5. Jotapata[10]
6. Gamala[11]
7. Machaerus[12]
8. Masada[13]

The Description of the Land of Israel (*BJ* III, 35–58)

This description represents the most important geographic selection vis-à-vis the amount of the material presented and its composition. Furthermore, it is a good summary of the situation during Josephus' time. The description is divided into four parts. At first Josephus describes the Galilee, the northern areas of Judea, their boundaries, and the cities found in these regions. Josephus also provides a short and exaggerated description of the agricultural conditions of the Galilee. As mentioned earlier, Josephus served as military commander of the region and would be especially interested in describing it. Therefore, he begins his description with this region, and this region merits the most detailed description of the entire section. Afterwards, Josephus describes the Perea. The next section deals with Judea, and the description of Samaria is added to it. In these sections, Josephus stresses the boundaries of the regions and the cities found there, and he briefly describes the topography of these areas. In his description of Judea, he adds a detailed description of its administrative units (the toparchies or districts of Judea). Josephus also adds a short and inexact description of the coastal plain to Acco in Phoenicia. The last section deals with the kingdom of Agrippa II, its boundaries and administrative and demographic composition. Throughout the entire description, there seems to be a certain tension between geographic detail and administrative detail. We will deal with this tension in the course of our discussion.

Sources of the Description

It is apparent from first glance that there are contradictions in this passage and that it lacks uniformity and internal balance. According to Josephus, the southern border of the Galilee is the village of Dabaritta (Dabbûriye; under the western slopes of Mount Tabor) and the northern border of Samaria is Ginae (Jenîn). There is no reference whatsoever to the Beisan Valley or that of Esdraelon, which extends from Dabaritta to Ginae. The former may have been part of Decapolis, which belonged to Syria, but the latter certainly was part of Judea.[14] Moreover, Josephus himself states that Samaria bordered on the Galilee from the south and thus we have an evident contradiction, or at least an inconsistency. In describing Judea, he adds with a degree of pride that Judea is not cut off from the amenities of the sea because its sea extends as far as Acco. However, the coast of the Sharon Plain did not belong to the district of Judea, and if it were included in Judea, this certainly would have found some expression in the list of toparchies of that area. (Narbata and Caesarea certainly were worthy of mention as administrative units.) Moreover, the entire coast from Dora northward was not included in Palestine and certainly not in the administrative unit Judea. This, then, represents an additional internal contradiction. There is also a lack of uniformity in the description. In the description of the Galilee, Josephus first delineates the borders of the administrative units and then describes the area itself. This is also the case regarding Judea and the Perea. In the case of Samaria, however, Josephus delineates the borders. Its economic conditions are appended to the description of the economy of Judea. The kingdom of Agrippa is also described in brief, and its borders mentioned, but there is no discussion of its topography and economy.

The Perea appears as an independent unit. The kingdom of Agrippa II, which included the Perea, also received separate treatment. We will deal with the details of these descriptions in the course of our discussion, but it should be quite clear already that both of these descriptions were drawn from different sources. If this is not the case, the descriptions would certainly seem strange and repetitious.

There are other problems as well. Thus, the inclusion of Idumaea in the district of Judea, even though they were separate districts. Moreover, Tiberias is not included in the kingdom of Agrippa, even though this entire district had been added to his realm by 54 c.e.

It is hard to imagine that Josephus simply erred in his presentation of this material. In general, the description appears to be reliable and trustworthy, and the administrative situation described by Josephus fits in with other information on this matter.[15] It is most likely that the solution to the problem can be found in the composition of the component parts of the sources used by Josephus.

In spite of the lack of uniformity and internal contradictions we have just seen, there is a basic framework of the description that is quite uniform and schematic. The basic framework includes the description of the Galilee, Perea, and Judea. Each area is described in a schematic form and the order of details is quite similar. These details include the basic structure of the region, its borders and settlements, and the areas surrounding it. There is also a description of local agriculture in quite superlative terms and the inclusion of a few topographic details. This is the basic framework, and it is most likely that this framework was taken from an earlier source; then the author added the various details that gave the description its lack of uniformity.

The basic division of Palestine into various districts is also found in some of the few non-Jewish works that describe Palestine, but in these cases the stress is usually on the coast, the main region of the Gentile settlement. Both Pliny,[16] a Roman contemporary of Josephus, as well as Ptolemy, who lived some fifty years afterwards,[17] begin their descriptions with the coastal district; and it is clear that as far as they were concerned, this was the most important part of Palestine. Josephus, on the other hand, does not devote a separate discussion to this area and makes do with a short, inexact and misleading reference that attaches the coastal region to the district of Judea. This distinction leads us to the conclusion that Josephus made use of a Jewish source in which the Land of Israel was divided into three regions. This source ignored the coastal area, which was basically non-Jewish.

The division of the Land of Israel into "three lands" (districts)—Galilee,

Perea, and Judea; or if we wish to be more exact, "Judea, Galilee, and Perea"—appears in talmudic literature in various contexts, such as in connection with the laws of possession, marriage, and the sabbatical year.[18] We will not deal here with these laws. For our purposes, it is sufficient to state that the sages were familiar with this geographic division and saw each area as a separate geographic, agricultural, and economic unit. In the case of the sabbatical year, there is a more complicated division of these areas. According to the version restored by scholars from various sources, the Land of Israel was divided into three "lands," which were then subdivided into three: mountainous region, hills, and valley. Boundaries, or various settlements connected with each subdistrict, were then given. It is possible that the agricultural characteristics of each area were included.[19] This detailed and complex division can be discerned through a comparison of the Mishnah, Tosefta, and Palestinian Talmud; and the complete version can be restored only through a comparison of all the sources. It would seem that, originally, there was a basic division into three lands, which were then subdivided for the specific purpose of the sabbatical year, or some other purpose.

The latest stage of the division, which is found in the Mishnah, must be from the end of the Second Temple period, since the Sea of Galilee basin is referred to as the "territory of Tiberias." This name could not have been used before the establishment of Tiberias in 18 B.C.E.[20] However, in the Tosefta, this same basin is called *Ginnosar,* the earlier name of this area. It is difficult to determine when the transition in usage from the "territory of Ginnosar" to the "territory of Tiberias" took place. An old and established name is certainly not replaced immediately. It would seem, however, that in the original form of the division, the "territory of Ginnosar" appeared and that only in the Mishnah was the form changed. It is difficult to assume that the opposite is true, that the original section had "Tiberias" and that the Tosefta later switched to the archaic form.

Thus, it would seem that the original formulation of this division predates the establishment of Tiberias or was formulated very soon after the founding of the city. It is clear, though, that the division could not have been formulated after the Yavneh period (70–132 C.E.), since both Rabban Simeon ben Gamaliel and Rabbi Simeon, sages of the Usha period (135–180 C.E.), discuss and elucidate the Mishnah. As mentioned earlier, the division into three lands predates the subdivision.

Josephus was familiar with and used the division into three lands but not the subdivisions, or in any case he did not use them in his works. This distinction between Josephus and the Mishnah is especially prominent in the description of the division of the Galilee, in which there are similarities between the two. Both sources make note of a division into the Upper and Lower Galilee, but the Mishnah is familiar with the additional subdivision ("the territory of Tiberias"). Moreover, in the Mishnah, the boundary point between the two parts of the Galilee is Kefar Ḥanania, while in Josephus the boundary is the Galilean Beersheba. These sites are near one another, and it is clear that the boundary between the two parts of the Galilee passes through Beth Ha-Cerem and that the two sites were likely to represent the boundary line. The similarity between the sources prove that both were familiar with the geography of the region, while the difference between them proves that each source was independent.

It remains now to determine the date and purpose of this source that divides Palestine into three lands. It would seem that this is a halakhic source, since it appears in three different halakhic contexts. Since this is a halakhic source, it does not deal with those areas inhabited by non-Jews. At the end of the Second Temple period, the Jews represented a marked majority in the Beisan and Esdraelon valleys and the coastal plains, excluding the actual coast itself. This source then represents the period of Jewish settlement after the Jewish expansion into the Galilee and the Transjordan (the beginning of the Hasmonean period, approximately 160 B.C.E.) but before Jewish expansion reached the coastal plain (during the time of Alexander Jannaeus). In any event, after the death of Alexander Jannaeus (76 B.C.E.), the coastal plain was almost entirely Jewish.

However, it is still possible that the division reflects the end of the Second Temple period. It is true that at this time the coastal plain was basically Jewish, but the coastal cities were non-Jewish and thus it is possible that for this reason the sages refrained from dealing with the entire area.[21]

If such is the case, Josephus used a system for the division of Palestine that was known and used in rabbinic literature of the period. Josephus used a similar method in his description of the agriculture of the various regions of Palestine. S. Klein has already shown that Josephus' description of agriculture in the Galilee is very similar to descriptions of the Galilee in talmudic literature.[22] In this case, however, there was no single elaborate source, but rather isolated sayings in talmudic literature. Thus, many component parts of Josephus' description appear also in midrashic sources, such as those describing the large population of the Galilee, the richness of the land, the many orchards, and other such details. Thus, it would appear that the essential framework of the description in *BJ* III is taken from talmudic literature.[23]

The Additions of Josephus

As mentioned earlier, Josephus added details that were meant to complement and update the description of Palestine. We shall cite several examples.

The Description of Samaria

This was lacking in the original source. His description of boundaries seems quite realistic and is not dependent on any source. Proof of this is the fact that citing Ginae as a boundary point contradicts another detail in the original description and that the description of the economic situation in Samaria was appended to the description of Judea. Although the formulation of Josephus' description is similar to the original model (longitudinal and latitudinal boundaries), it is not an exact imitation.

Idumaea

This area appears with Judea as if it were one of the toparchies of Judea. Josephus faced a dilemma. The source that he used did not mention Idumaea at all. Josephus, however, did not wish to ignore the area and thus erred when he described it, indicating that it was part of Judea rather than an independent district.

Coastal Region

This is also the case regarding the description of the important coastal district, which was not mentioned at all in the source that Josephus used. His comment that "nor is Judea cut off from seaside delights" represents an attempt to "praise" the area under discussion. In the Hellenistic world, economic development was associated with trade and port cities. A country that was developed only in terms of agriculture was not considered fully developed. The truth is that the Land of Israel was essentially an agricultural nation. Josephus, however, in seeking to extol and praise the land, added a rather clumsy reference to the coastal cities of Judea. The same approach also appears in the *Letter of Aristeas*.[24]

Administrative Division

The description of the administrative division of Judea and the importance of Jerusalem were added by Josephus based on the following three considerations. First, the section partially repeats material mentioned earlier. In the preceding sentence, Josephus states that Jerusalem is the center of the Land of Israel and now he returns to this same subject and stresses its importance. Second, in the description of the Galilee and Perea, there is no discussion whatsoever of an administrative division. Thus, it would seem that this is not an integral part of the descriptions. Finally, the division reflects the end of the Second Temple period and perhaps some of the steps taken by Vespasian in Judea.[25] The division itself is quite exact and serves as a good basis for the description of administration in Judea at that time.

The Description of Agrippa's Kingdom

This description is shorter than those of other areas. It does not describe the agriculture in this area, as is the case in the other regions. According to this description, Julias (north of the Sea of Galilee) is included in Agrippa's kingdom but not Tiberias. This is not correct since Julias was given to Agrippa in 54 C.E. together with Tiberias and Migdal.[26] It is inconceivable that his kingdom should include Julias and not Tiberias. At this point, it would seem that Josephus diverged from the description reflecting his own time, since this contradicted the description of the Galilee. It is clear that including Tiberias as part of the Galilee did not reflect the administrative situation during the time of Josephus. Josephus wished to avoid a quagmire of contradictions based on the various sources he was using.

Josephus wished to avoid open contradictions based on his sources. The very reference to the kingdom of Agrippa represents a contradiction to the basic division into three lands. Josephus wished to include this kingdom but, in order to avoid open contradictions in his description, distorted somewhat his description of this kingdom, particularly in order to refrain from an over-lap between the kingdom of Agrippa and the Galilee and Perea.[27]

This addition is written in the same style as the descriptions of the other regions, but it is clear that the similarity is only partial. Thus, in the original description, the boundaries are always settlements, even if the topographic line is clear. Thus, Thella on the Jordan, Exaloth and Ginae in Esdraelon, and even Joppa but not the "coast." Only the Jordan River appears as a boundary point between the Perea and Judea. Agrippa's kingdom, however, is related as extending from Mount Lebanon and the sources of the Jordan River and Lake Tiberias (Sea of Galilee).[28] This attempt at times resulted in inconsistencies, but it did prove that Josephus was quite familiar with conditions in Palestine.

Jericho and Gennesar

Both of these descriptions serve as introductions to the description of the military campaigns there. The introductions, however, are much longer than is necessary simply for this purpose. This is especially true in the case of the Jericho region. The capture of Jericho merits a rather laconic description, whereas the description of the Jericho Valley is much longer.

Both of these descriptions are quite good. Most of the information is exact and balanced, although sometimes there is the introduction of local folk traditions, which are usually far from exact. While describing the source of the Jordan, Josephus mentions a scientific "experiment" conducted by Philip, the ruler of the region. He discovered that the waters of the pool called Phiale (Birkat Râm in the northern Golan) flow to the spring of Paneas. Josephus relates that Philip scattered chaff in the Phiale pool and afterwards the chaff-filled water came out from the spring at Paneas (Baniâs) (*BJ* III, 509–513).

This information is certainly not correct, and there is no doubt that this "experiment" could not have yielded such results. It is most likely, however, that rumors of such results abounded in the area and Josephus relates what he had heard. Josephus is somewhat more circumspect in his description of the spring of Capernaum that "some have imagined this to be a branch of the Nile" (*BJ* III, 520). His statement that "some have imagined" reflects his awareness of the popular nature of this tradition. It should also be clear that there is no scientific basis for this theory.

In his description of the Jericho region, Josephus also describes the Dead Sea, which is nearby. The Dead Sea was always considered quite exotic.[29] Almost every non-Jewish author who discusses Palestine describes the Dead Sea, whether briefly or at great length. These authors, as well as Josephus, stressed the fact that it was impossible to drown in this body of water and that chunks of asphalt floated in it. Josephus also mentions the misconceived notion that these chunks may be separated only through the use of menstrual blood or urine. It is somewhat difficult to imagine how someone who certainly had seen the Dead Sea could repeat such tales. Josephus even relates that he had studied with "Bannus," who appears to have been one of the leaders of the Essenes who lived in the Judean desert near the Dead Sea.[30] Although he must have visited the Dead Sea many times, he repeats this unfounded tale. In a similar manner, he tells of the "Sabbatical" River that flows six days of the week and on the seventh day rests.[31] The modern reader may find all of this somewhat strange, but in ancient times authors would cite such folktales as if they were historical truths, and no one thought it necessary to test the authenticity of these "scientific truths."

As we have mentioned, the description contains many correct facts, although at times they became clouded by legendary elements. Thus, for instance, Josephus praises the Gennesar Valley and attributes to it a favorable climate and abundance of water. Water was supplied to this area from the spring of Capernaum (et Tâbgha) and served also for agricultural purposes. Josephus, though, does exaggerate somewhat when he states that the trees bear fruit for nine months of the year. The fruit-bearing season of trees, however, is quite long and fruits ripen earlier than expected. In his description of the Jericho area, Josephus points out the extraordinary nature of the agriculture in this region, while comparing it with the barren mountains of the Perea. These descriptions are basically correct and prove that Josephus had a real understanding of the nature of these areas.

Josephus also provides quantitative information about certain areas, such as the length and width of the Jordan Valley and the dimensions of the Dead Sea and the Jericho Valley. For the sake of clarity, this information appears in

Table 14.1

Comparison of Distances of Gennesar Valley and Jericho Valley in Josephus

	Distance in Josephus	Actual Distance	% Error	Notes
Valley of Gennesar:				
Length of Sea of Galilee	26.25	20	31.25	
Width of Sea of Galilee	7.5	7.5	0	
Panias to Birkat Ram (Phiale)	22.5	7	221	actual distance as the crow flies
Semachonitis Lake to Sea of Galilee	22.5	20–22	4	
Length of Gennesar Valley	5.6	5.5	2	
Width of Gennesar Valley	3.75	1.5–3.5	7	
Jericho Valley:				
Length of Jordan Valley from Sennabris to Dead Sea	225	1061	372	
Width of Jordan Valley	22.5	6–12	87	
Length of Jericho Valley	13.1	13–14	0	the irrigated area
Width of Jericho Valley	3.75	3–4	0	the irrigated area
Jericho to Jerusalem	28.1	22–28	0	22 km. as crow flies; 28 km. in actuality
Jericho to Jordan	11.25	8	41	
Length of Dead Sea	108.7	35	211	
Width of Dead Sea	28.1	15–18	56	

Table 14.1. A quick glance at this table proves to what extent the distances mentioned in Josephus are not exact. In all fairness, however, Josephus may not be the only one at fault here. It is possible that the errors crept into these numbers in the course of the transmission of the text, since they lacked all meaning to the copyist or scribe. Moreover, the techniques of measuring distances were not very refined in the ancient world. Errors are found in numbers and measurements in many works from the Roman-Byzantine period, including works not transcribed or transmitted by copyists.[32] The errors in distances in Josephus' writings are quite great and, if not attributable to errors in transmission, they would seem to prove that at some time Josephus' memory failed him. In any event, it is unlikely that Josephus while in Rome benefited from access to material on the areas with which he was concerned.

A rather short description, but similar in nature to those in Table 14.1, is the description of the Acco Valley,[33] listed in Table 14.2. Josephus provides an

Table 14.2

Distances in the Acco Valley

	Distance in Josephus	Actual Distance	% Error
Acco to Mountains of Galilee	11.25	10–12	0
Acco to Mount Carmel	22.5	14–18	25
Acco to Ladder of Tyre	18.75	18–25	0

Note: The Stadia are computed according to 8 stadia in a mile of 1.5 km. or 187.5 meters.
Source: BJ II, 10, 2(192–94).

excellent description of the plain enclosed on three sides by mountain ranges. The description is both correct and exact, except once again for the distances, as we can see from Table 14.1

Jerusalem, Jotapata, Gamala, Machaerus, and Masada

The descriptions of these five sites are entirely different in nature from those discussed earlier, since they are essentially descriptions of buildings and fortifications and not geographic descriptions of a particular area. To this list of areas, we may add the short descriptions of Caesarea and Sebastê. The most famous description of this type is the description of Jerusalem. This description has been examined quite often, and it provides the best basis for our understanding of late Second Temple period Jerusalem.[34] Although the numbers and figures in this description are also somewhat suspect, the basic description of the city, its walls, and its towers is dependable, although there are some elements of exaggeration.

Gamala, for example, is described as a settlement built on a steep hill, similar to the hump of a camel. This description served as the basis for the theory that Gamala should be located on the slope west of Dir Kerach in the Golan. Archaeological excavations at the site have confirmed this assumption and the identification is accepted by almost all scholars.[35]

In his description of Jotapata, Josephus states that the city is not visible from a distance because it is hidden by the hills that surround it. And Khirbet Shifat, which preserves the ancient name, lies on the spur of a steep hill but is lower than the surrounding ones.

Josephus' description of Masada has received quite extensive treatment[36] as a result of the high state of preservation of the site, which enabled scholars to reconstruct the buildings on the site and to examine the veracity of Josephus' description. Josephus describes especially well the mountain surrounded on all sides by deep ravines. Josephus, however, exaggerates not only when stating the length of the path that ascends to the mountain, 64 stadia (5.74 km.), but also in describing the dangers associated with this path: "The least slip means death; for on either side yawns an abyss so terrifying that it could make the boldest tremble." While it is true that the ascent is dangerous, particularly toward the end, this description is certainly exaggerated. Josephus mentions Herod's palace "on the western slope . . . inclining in a northerly direction." The palace really is on the northern side of the fortress, and perhaps Josephus simply did not notice this since he saw Masada from the east, and from that direction it would appear that the palace was on the western side of the fortress. The rest of the description is correct, including the description of the path that led from the palace to the fortress itself. Josephus relates that there were thirty-seven towers at Masada; but only twenty-seven or thirty have been found to date, and this perhaps would represent another inconsistency. In any event, it is clear that the description contains both exact and inexact details.[37]

It is impossible to encompass and list all of the details in Josephus' writings pertaining to the geography of Judea, and certainly it would be impossible to discuss every such detail. This information is of extreme importance for the study of Judea. As we have mentioned, however, there is a degree of error, inconsistency, and sloppiness in some of these geographic descriptions.[38] Thus, as we have seen, many of the distances recorded by Josephus are incorrect, as can be seen in Table 14.1. All of Josephus' population statistics, figures on casualties during wars, or numbers of prisoners taken certainly bear no relation whatsoever to reality. Certain scholars[39] have claimed that these figures could serve as a reliable basis for the computation of the population of Judea, if the exaggeration factor were taken into account. The figures, however, are not just exaggerated but completely baseless, and thus lack any historical value whatsoever for the purpose of determining the population of Judea.[40]

An interesting example of a combination of reliable historical method and a sloppy formulation is the material regarding the hierarchy of the settlements in the Galilee. In one source, Josephus relates that Tiberias, Sepphoris, and Gabara (Araba) were the largest cities in the Galilee.[41] In another source, he mentions the fortresses that he built and lists Taricheae, Tiberias, and Sepphoris as the cities of the Galilee.[42] Gabara was not fortified and, therefore, not mentioned in this list. From all of Josephus' descriptions it would seem that Tiberias, Sepphoris, Taricheae (Magdala), and Gabara were the major settlements of the Galilee, and perhaps Gischala in the Upper Galilee should be added to this list. This list is based on the many details found in the works of Josephus, but ironically, when Josephus could have summarized some of this information in a systematic and correct manner, he lapsed into inconsistencies.

Josephus often uses the terms *city* (πόλις) and *village* (κώμη), but does not always maintain a distinction between the two terms. In his *Life*, however, a distinction is more or less maintained; and in the list of fortresses mentioned earlier, we find that Josephus stressed the difference between the cities of the Lower Galilee, which were fortified, and the villages of the Golan and Lower and Upper Galilee, which were not. It should be remembered, though, that Tiberias was a polis, and it appears that Sepphoris was also one. Taricheae and Gabara, however, never attained this position, and the use of the term *polis* regarding these settlements is not exact. It is simply to show their general importance in the area and not necessarily their administrative position.

Moreover, Gabara is sometimes referred to as a village;[43] Jotapata,[44] Asochis,[45] and Beth Shearim[46] are at times called cities, even though they are not included in the four "cities" of the Galilee. Thus, in the *Life*, there is a rather free usage of the term *polis*, not always consistent in use and certainly not exact.

In the *Jewish War*, the distinction between city and village is blurred even more. In this work Josephus introduces new terms, such as *township* (πο-λίχνη),[47] *very large village*,[48] and even a village that is falsely called *polis*.[49] In this composition, the use of the term *polis* is less significant and many settlements are referred to as cities with little or no justification. A settlement referred to as a "city" was certainly an important site, but little can be learned from this term regarding administrative status. Moreover, it is certainly possible that large villages need not have been called cities but simply villages, even if they were important. We shall deal later with the use of this term in other writings of Josephus. It is possible already, however, to state that the use of this term in Josephus is quite free. The usage, though, does at times have some limited historical value.

The reader, however, should not be misled by our discussion of discrepancies in Josephus' writings. Even taking into account all of the mistakes, the general geographic picture found in Josephus is acceptable, and there are not really that many mistakes or discrepancies. Thus, for example, the description of Vespasian's campaigns in Palestine seems to be exact and based on correct information. The portrayal of the battles in the Galilee appears reliable and, likewise, the many other geographic details in this context.

The combination of correct and incorrect geographic detail in the same context has led scholars to search for some sort of methodology in this presentation. According to M. Broshi,[50] for instance, the correct material, and particularly the correct distances, is based on archival material from the campaigns of Vespasian and Titus in Judea. The incorrect material derives from lapses in Josephus' memory, which at times seemed to have betrayed him. It would appear to me that this distinction is not valid. Correct distances are sometimes found in descriptions of areas where the Roman army was not active. The distances cited in *Antiquities*, which we shall discuss later, and the exact distances between villages in the Galilee mentioned in relation to Josephus' travels there were in fact in areas where the Roman army was never stationed—which proves this point. On the other hand, mistakes are found as descriptions of areas about which there must have been much Roman archival material, such as the description of Masada, the dimensions of the Sea of Galilee, and the distance between Jericho and Jerusalem, which was traversed by a Roman legion. One might also assume that the Roman army had some sort of records on the number of prisoners taken. Yet, these numbers as cited in Josephus are totally unreliable, as we shall see later. Both exact and inexact numbers appear in other writings of Josephus. Sometimes, this is the case even in the same chapter of *Antiquities,* and on matters which do not pertain to any Roman archival material. It is clear, however, that the combination of excellent and reliable material on Judea, together with faulty and incorrect information, is characteristic of Josephus.

The *Vita* contains many details on the Galilee. It is impossible to say, however, that Josephus knew this area better than the other parts of the Land of Israel. Samaria was inhabited at this time by Samaritans and, thus, it is not of much interest to Josephus. Jewish settlement in the Perea was also not very widespread, and it is impossible to learn anything from the fact that Josephus devoted only a small amount of material to this area. *Antiquities,* which attempts to deal with "earlier" Jewish history, also does not deal very much with these areas, perhaps because the Bible did not devote much discussion to them. However, there is one major difference between the description of Judea and Galilee. In the description of Judea, the administrative term "toparchy" is often used, and thus Josephus has provided us with an administrative map of Judea. However, there is no similar reference to "toparchies" in the Galilee, Perea, or in Samaria.[51] It is likely that the Jewish inhabitants of Palestine were not too much interested in the Roman administrative system, and this system did not serve them as a means for the description of the land of Israel or for the understanding of events or geography of the country. Roman documents, however, must have used this system, and it would seem likely that this served as their point of reference.

If Josephus had used Roman documents, then there would have been some reference to the Roman administration in his description of the Galilee. Since this is not the case, there is then no proof that Josephus used official documents. His repeated usage of Roman administrative detail in his description of Judea is probably the result of his long stay in the Roman camp when this area of Palestine was conquered. While in the Roman camp, Josephus probably learned this system and its implementation for Roman "map" preparation and the study of topography. Although this explanation is quite likely, the issue still requires further clarification.

Much of Josephus' writings deal with the biblical period. In describing this period, Josephus bases himself almost entirely on the Bible, and thus, details of his descriptions in this area for the most part are based either on Scripture or Jewish interpretation of Scriptural passages. This is also mostly true in the case of *Antiquities,* Book XIV, which deals with the Hasmonean period and is based to a great extent on I Maccabees.[52] As it has been said, in these cases, Josephus uses an earlier source.[53] There are times that he adds a word or sentence that is meant to enlighten the reader further, particularly the non-Jewish reader of Greek.[54] In these cases, we can make contact with the author himself and his period. These passages are of extreme importance for the scholar, since they always provide an interesting source of information on Judea during Josephus' time.

A study of these geographic additions requires an examination in two areas. On the one hand is the geographic sphere, that is, the contribution of the particular details added by Josephus to our understanding of Judea in the first century C.E. The other sphere represents an examination of Josephus' credibility as a "historical geographer," that is, his understanding of the biblical period. Did he correctly identify the settlements mentioned in Scripture, and did he understand the geographic background of the biblical account? Both of these spheres are intertwined and it is difficult to distinguish between them. However, they really represent two independent questions, each of which requires an independent discussion.

Two sections of Josephus' writings preserve a more or less continuous geographic description of biblical Judea and Israel. The first is Josephus' description of the tribal allotments,[55] and the second is the description of the provinces of Palestine during Solomon's rule.[56] We shall examine the latter in great detail and briefly describe the former.

The Bible, in I Kings 4:7–17 describes the realms of the provincial governors of Solomon. The term "provincial governor" (*Neẓiv*) was correctly understood by Josephus as an administrative term, and he used the corresponding phrase from his period. He refers to the governors as *stratêgoi* and *hêgemones.* The *stratêgos* had by Josephus' time lost its literal meaning and took on a connotation of a senior functionary, army officer, or governor of a district. The *hêgemon* is, for the most part, the governor of a country, but it seems that Josephus saw the term in this case being limited to a district (hyparchy).[57]

The second province includes the "toparchy" of Beth Shemesh. "Toparchy" is the accepted term for subdistrict in Josephus' time. In the course of his description, Josephus uses two terms. The first is "toparchy" and the second is *chora.* The first is administrative and the second refers to an undefined area.[58] The provinces mentioned by Josephus are as follows:

Josephus	Bible
1. Ures—territory of Ephraim	hill—country of Ephraim
2. Diokleros—toparchy of Beth Shemesh (Bithiemes)	Makaz, Shaalbim, Beth Shemesh, Elon–Beth-Hanan
3. omitted	Son of Hesed in Aruboth
4. Abinadab—(the district of) Dora and the coast	All the region of Dora
5. Banaias, the son of Achilos—the great plain . . . as far as Jordan	Taanach, Megiddo, and all Beth Shean that is beside Zarethan, beneath Jezreel, to Abel-Maholah, as far as beyond Jokmeam
6. Gabares—all of Galaditis and Gaulanitis up to Mount Lebanon and sixty cities	Ramoth-Gilead, to him pertained the villages of Jair . . . the region of Argob which is Bashan, threescore great cities.
7.–8. Achinadab—all of Galilee as far as Sidon	Achinadab in Mahanaim; Ahimaaz in Naphtali
9. Banakates—the coast about Acco	Asher and Bealoth
10. Saphates—Mount Itabyrion and Mount Carmel and all of the Lower Galilee as far as the river Jordan	Issachar
11. Sumius—the territory of Benjamin	Benjamin
12. Gabares—the country across the Jordan	land of Gilead, the country of Sihon . . . and of Og, king of Bashan

For Province 1, Josephus simply cites the biblical account. For Province 2, instead of using biblical names, Josephus cites the toparchy of Beth Shemesh. During Josephus' time this was an independent toparchy, whose headquarters was Betholeptepha. It is possible that Josephus was not familiar with the other settlements and thus interpreted this province as being the equivalent of the toparchy. This might also serve as proof of the importance of Beth Shemesh at the end of the Second Temple period or soon after the destruction. Province 3 is omitted.

For Province 4, Josephus understood the phrase "all the region of Dora" as the coast. In Josephus' time, it was an independent administrative region whose headquarters was Caesarea. It is clear that Josephus understood "all the region of Dora" as referring to this area. The description of Province 5 is Josephus' interpretation, apparently correct, of a difficult biblical verse.[59]

Province 6 is basically the kingdom of Agrippa II as it is described in the *War* III.[60] We saw earlier that this description was not correct, since his kingdom also included part of the Galilee. This represents, then, a combination of the administrative and settlement situation during the time of Josephus, which considered the Sea of the Galilee basin as part of the Galilee.

In Josephus' description of this area, precedence is given to the situation in Josephus' day over details described in the Bible. In the biblical account only Ramoth-Gilead is included in Province 6, while the rest of the Gilead is included in Province 12. Josephus does not accept this distinction. The entire Transjordan is included in his account in Province 6, and Province 12 receives an undefined area referred to as "the country across the Jordan," even though this general term includes Gilead.

In Province 7, Josephus combines two provinces. Perhaps this is a mistake, or perhaps Josephus sought to avoid a possible contradiction, since the region of Mahanaim was included in the previous province.

The term "Galilee" seems to refer only to the Upper Galilee, since the Lower Galilee is included in Province 10. In this section, the territory of Naphtali corresponds to the Jewish Upper Galilee. This is the case despite the fact that in the Bible this area is divided between the tribes of Naphtali and Asher.

Provinces 8–10 include the entire Galilee. According to Josephus, the breakup among the various tribes was as follows. Naphtali ruled the entire Upper Galilee, and Issachar ruled the entire "Lower Galilee" (he mentions Mount Itybarion [Tabor] and Carmel up to the Jordan). Asher controlled only the Acco Valley. This is all based on the situation during Josephus' day.

The administrative situation in the Second Temple period was different. The Lower Galilee was divided into two districts, and the territory of Acco included a rather large tract of the Upper Galilee.[61] The settlement picture, however, was different. Both the Lower Galilee and the Upper Galilee, or the entire mountainous region including the eastern part, were single units. The Upper and Lower Galilee were inhabited by Jews. The Acco Valley, however, was non-Jewish. Jewish population even extended into Southern "Syria," reaching even Sidon. This is hinted at in the description of Province 7.

The breakup of the Galilee into tribal areas also appears, of course, in the description of the portions of the tribes. This description is somewhat different and, likewise, is not based on biblical material. We shall deal with this tribal division in the course of our study.

Province 9 was discussed earlier. It is interesting to note that Acco is called Acco and not Ptolemais, as is usually the case in Josephus. Province 10 also was mentioned earlier. The territory of the tribe of Issachar is identical with the entire Lower Galilee.

The inclusion of Mount Tabor and Mount Carmel is somewhat strange, since they do not appear in the biblical account. These mountains are mentioned, however, in the description of the portions of the tribes in the Book of Joshua, and Josephus mentions them in the description of the tribe of Issachar in the course of his description of the Land of Israel in tribal portions (A V, 84). As stated, Mount Tabor is mentioned in the portion of Issachar in the Bible and the phrase "as far as the river Jordan" also appears in the Bible

(Joshua 19.17–22). However, the description of the portion of Issachar includes sixteen sites, and therefore it would seem that the inclusion of the Tabor region as representing the entire area reflects the choice of the author and not just the biblical text.

This is especially true in the case of Mount Carmel. In the Book of Joshua, Mount Carmel is not included in the territory of Asher nor in that of Issachar, even though it is mentioned as the border of the territory of Asher, which reached Carmel westward[62] (Joshua 19.26). In the description of the portions of the tribes in *Antiquities* V, Josephus states that Zebulon received the area up to the environs of Mount Carmel (*A* V, 84) and that the tribe of Issachar's border extended along the length of the Carmel (*ibid.*). Mount Carmel is ascribed, thus, to both tribes, but essentially to Issachar. This phenomenon may be attributed to the connection between the Jewish settlements of Mount Carmel and the Jewish Galilee during the time of Josephus. A similar phenomenon is found in midrashic literature, and in the descriptions of the tribal portions in Samaritan literature.[63]

The mentioning of Mount Tabor as an integral part of Issachar shows its importance in the settlement history of the area. During the early Hellenistic period, there was a non-Jewish polis on the site. During the Byzantine period, the area was an independent administrative unit and it would appear that the same was also true for the second century (toparchy).[64] It would seem that this also testifies to the importance of the area for Jewish settlement, since the administrative headquarters, most likely, was the major settlement in the area. The description of Josephus fits into this picture and proves the importance of Mount Tabor during the Second Temple period.[65]

For Province 11, Josephus quotes the Bible text. Province 12 was discussed earlier.

The Portions of the Tribes

As mentioned earlier, scholarly research has dealt with this topic.[66] Therefore, we can make do with a summary of the situation.

The tribe of Judah included Ascalon and Gaza. This is based on the interpretation of biblical verses and does not reflect the situation during Josephus' time. The tribe of Benjamin included Jericho and extended from Jericho to the sea. The expansion of Benjamin over northern Judah represents the situation in Josephus' time, when Benjamin was considered to be identical with the entire area of Jewish settlement north of Jerusalem.[67] The mention of Jericho and the Jordan River is likely to be based on the Bible but, perhaps, also on the situation during Second Temple times. For Simeon, Josephus cited the appropriate biblical verses.

According to Josephus, the tribe of Ephraim's area extended to Beth Shean. This contradicts the plain meaning of Scripture and even Josephus himself, who ascribes to Manasseh the northern areas of Samaria. The borders of the tribe of Ephraim, then, are based on the identification of Ephraim with "Samaria" of the Second Temple period. The distinction between Benjamin (all of northern Judah) and Ephraim (Samaria) appears also in talmudic literature. The inclusion of Gezer in the context of the tribe of Ephraim is based on Josephus' understanding of verses and not on the situation in the Second Temple period.

According to Josephus, the area of the tribe of Manasseh included the city of Beth Shean. This has a basis in the Bible and it is not clear whether this, or the situation in the Second Temple, is the source for this statement in Josephus.

The description of the tribe of Issachar's land included Mount Carmel, the river Jordan,[68] and Mount Tabor. As mentioned earlier, there is a biblical basis for all of this, but the choice of these sites is also the result of the situation in Josephus' time.

Josephus states that the portion of the tribe of Zebulon extended from Mount Carmel to the Sea of Gennesar. There is no basis for this in the Bible, and this also contradicts somewhat the description of the portions of Issachar and Asher. The connection between the Sea of Gennesar and Zebulon appears in other sources from the Second Temple period and reflects both the settlement and administrative situation of the time.[69]

The tribe of Asher's portion included the area from Mount Carmel to Sidon. This area is called the *Shephelah* (plain). The rest of the Galilee, including the Iyyon Valley is included in the territory of Naphtali. As mentioned earlier, the boundary between the two tribes represents the ethnic boundaries of the time of Josephus. The cities mentioned in Asher include only Arce, also called Ecdipus. This city was chosen since it was the central site of the area in the Second Temple period.[70] The term *Shephelah* (κοιλάδα) implies either the plain of Acco or the western slopes of the Galilee, which is today part of Lebanon. This area was also called the Shephelah in the Bible, although in a different context.[71]

The portion of the tribe of Dan included "Azotus, Dora, all Jamnia and Gath from Ekron to the mountain range."[72] The entire description in Josephus reflects the biblical verses, but the choice of cities is influenced by two factors. The Bible also mentions Gath Rimmon that is incorrectly identified with Gath, which is mentioned, it would seem, because it is referred to a number of times in the Bible as a Philistine city. Jamnia, Azotus, and Dora were not mentioned in the portion of Dan, but they were the centers of the Gentile population in the Shephelah in Josephus' time and, therefore, were chosen by Josephus to represent the tribe of Dan.[73] As for Ekron, it appears in the list in the Book of Joshua and is mentioned often in the Bible. On the other hand, Ekron was also a small administrative headquarters during the time of Josephus.[74] We shall deal later with Josephus' reasons for including Ekron in Dan.

As mentioned earlier, Josephus includes details from his own time that at times may contradict the biblical account. Moreover, he identifies the portions of certain tribes with areas familiar to him from his own time, even though the identifications may be only partly correct. This is not new, and this has been pointed out often by scholars. It would seem, though, that the matter could be expanded upon somewhat. The question is To what extent is the Second Temple period reflected in these descriptions? Do only details not found in the Bible reflect the Second Temple period? Or, do passages that seemingly only reflect the biblical account also reflect a later period? This would seem to be the case concerning Ekron in the territory of Dan, Mount Tabor in Issachar, Ecdipus in Asher, Jericho in Benjamin, and Beth Shean in Menassah. All of this may be understood in light of the Bible, but these sites might also have been selected because of their particular situations in the Second Temple period.

There might also be another possibility. These sites were chosen not only because they were known to Josephus but because in his opinion they represented the entire area and the settlement picture of his time. Thus, for example, the portion of Dan is considered as part of the coastal region. Therefore, the mention of Ekron in this context refers not only to its importance at the end of the Second Temple period but also to possible connections with the coastal region. Up until now, it is not clear whether this toparchy belonged both administratively and in terms of ethnic settlement to the district of Jewish Idumaea or to the Gentile coastal region.[75] It is possible that mentioning Ekron in this context points to its connection with the coastal cities (Jamnia and Azotus). All of this, however, remains hypothetical. If the basic methodology presented here can be accepted, it will be possible to use these descriptions of Judea during Josephus' time.

However, there are additional questions to be asked. Thus, for example, Ascalon and Gaza were severed from the coast by Josephus and transferred to Judea. This distinction between individual coastal cities is not appropriate for the Second Temple period, but it does have a basis in the Bible. It would seem that, in this case, Josephus was basing himself on the biblical description. On the other hand, it is possible that this case provides an additional hint of the administrative ties between Judea and the coastal cities. A clear-cut decision is difficult, but the first possibility seems more logical.

In addition to these larger descriptions, there are many scattered geographic references in Josephus' discussions of the biblical period. These may be divided into identifications, additions, and descriptions of ancient events with contemporary terminology.

Identifications

In this category Josephus identifies a biblical settlement with a settlement from his own time or gives the Second Temple period form of an earlier and Semitic name, such as Salem and Jerusalem, Goshen and Heroonpolis, Mount Hor and Arce (Rekeme), Petra and Rekeme, Etzion and Geber, Aila and Berenice, Edom and Idumaea, and similar identifications.[76] Some are acceptable, such as those for Salem and Etzion Geber. Others are less acceptable, such as placing Mount Hor in the vicinity of Petra.

Additions

Josephus at times adds details that are not included in the Bible; for example, the sons of Jacob were also buried in Hebron, which is not mentioned in the Bible, but was an accepted tradition in the Second Temple period.[77] Josephus also states that the Philistines assembled at Rega to meet Israel in battle. The Bible does not state where the Philistines assembled,[78] and the identification of Rega is not at all clear. Waters (*Mê*) of Meron mentioned in the Book of Joshua is referred to as *Berothe,* the "city in the Upper Galilee," and Kedese as a "place belonging to the Upper Galilee."[79] In order to illustrate the fact that the tribal division took into account the characteristics of the land, Josephus adds that the area of Jerusalem and Jericho were most fertile.[80] Such additions were also quite numerous in Josephus' parallel passages to the Books of the Maccabees. Thus, for instance, it is stated in I Maccabees that Ekron was given to Jonathan. Josephus states that this also included the toparchy of Ekron.[81] Josephus adds that the Seleucid commander Gorgias, who is referred in Maccabees as the governor of Idumaea, was also a *stratêgos* (commander/ruler) of Jamnia. This would not appear to be accepted tradition but rather Josephus' interpretation, since Jamnia and Azotus are mentioned in connection with the retreat of Gorgias' army.[82] Arbel, which is mentioned in the campaign of Bacchides against Judah Maccabee, is identified by Josephus with Arbel in the Galilee,[83] and "the environs of Samaria" mentioned in Maccabees are described as being in Gofna (a Jewish village in northern Judea and near Samaria).[84]

These details, and especially the additions in the descriptions of the Hasmonean campaigns, misled many scholars who saw them as authentic traditions, whereas they are interpretative additions of Josephus. Sometimes they are correct, other times they are not. The latter is the case, for instance, in the identification of Arbel in the Galilee, which is not correct, or the description of Gorgias as the ruler of Jamnia.[85] In these additions, Josephus serves as a commentator and interpreter of contemporary geography. Mentioning Ekron is indicative, in my opinion, of the administrative status of Ekron in Josephus' time, and the identification of Arbel proves that Josephus was familiar with the site by that name in the Galilee. On the other hand, his statement that

Gorgias was the ruler of Jamnia represents only his (incorrect) interpretation and has no geographic basis.

Descriptions of Ancient Events
with Contemporary Terminology

At times Josephus describes the biblical period in contemporary terminology. For the most part, these are additions to the biblical descriptions that we discussed earlier. The unique nature of these descriptions lies in the use of terms and names from the Second Temple period, such as mentioning the toparchy of Ekron, the description of the Amalekites as residing near Gebal and Petra, or the description of Doeg the Edomite as the Syrian.[86] An interesting example is found in *A* V, 125. In Judges 1.8, it is stated that the tribe of Judah conquered Jerusalem. The city was conquered, however, only during the time of David. This contradiction led Josephus to describe the capture of Jerusalem in the Book of Judges in the following manner: "The Lower Town they mastered in time and slew all the inhabitants; but the Upper Town proved too difficult to carry, due to the solidity of the walls and the nature of the site." Thus the tribe of Judah conquered only the Lower City, while David captured the rest of the city. The problem that Josephus faced in this matter was quite real. The solution that Josephus offered was not based on the Bible but rather on conditions in Jerusalem at the end of the Second Temple period, when the city was quite clearly divided into an Upper and Lower City; thus, for example, Titus conquered the Lower City and only later the Upper City. The biblical city of Jerusalem was on another hill and there was no distinction between the Upper City and the Lower City. Thus, a problem in biblical geography is solved by recourse to the geography of Josephus' times. It is interesting to note that Josephus states that the Upper City was enclosed within a wall. This question has been a matter of scholarly interest for quite some time, and from Josephus it would seem that such a wall existed. This matter, however, still requires further research.

Most of these additions attest to Josephus' understanding of the geographic background of the Bible; and numerous examples can be cited, in addition to the few cited here. Thus, for example, the spies sent by Moses "starting from the Egyptian frontier, traversed Canaan from end to end, reached the city of Amathe and Mount Libanus (Lebanon)."[87] Mount Lebanon is not mentioned in the Bible but its inclusion is quite logical and attests to the biblical route. Likewise, in the case of Beer Sheba as a city on the border of Judah, "in that part of the land of the tribe of Judah which is near the land of the Idumaeans,"[88] or in the case of the description of En Gedi,[89] and many other such geographic details.

However, there are also geographic details that are not correct. Josephus writes that the spies reported to Moses that the Land of Israel was difficult to

Table 14.3

Samples of Distances (in km.) in Josephus' Writings

	Source	Distance in Josephus	Actual Distance	% Error	Notes
Description Dealing with End of Second Temple Period:					
Jerusalem to Herodian	*BJ* I, 13, 4 (265) *A* XIV, 13, 9 (359)	11.25	14.5	29	As the crow flies; actual distance is 17 km.
Aqueduct of Jerusalem to Wells of Solomon or Artas	*BJ* II, 9, 4 (175)	37.5/56.25 7–5	48–40	0	According to a different version
Caesarea to Narbata	*BJ* II, 14, 5 (292)	11.25	11.25	0	According to accepted identification
Jerusalem to Geba	*BJ* II, 19, 1 (516)	4	4	0	See parallel sources
Jerusalem to Mount Scopus	*BJ* II, 19, 4 (528)	1.3	1.5	15	See parallel sources
Jerusalem to Ascalon	*BJ* III, 2, 1 (10)	91.5	75–85	10.8	As the crow flies
Tiberias to Sennabris	*BJ* III, 9, 7 (447)	5.6	8	43	
Mount Tabor (height)	*BJ* IV, 1, 8 (55)	5.6	.350	1500	
Mount Tabor (circumference)	*BJ* IV, 1, 8 (55)	4.9	4.5	9	
Hebron to Elah Valley	*BJ* IV, 9, 7 (55)	1.1	4	264	

conquer because of "rivers impossible to cross, so broad and deep withal were they, mountains impracticable for passage." [90] To the average Greek reader, this description sounded quite logical and perhaps reminded him of similar descriptions of the Alps or the Apennines or areas in Asia Minor that were difficult to traverse. Josephus' description in this case of the Land of Israel, however, is exaggerated and incorrect. The mountain ranges of Judea are not impassable, and there are hardly any rivers in Palestine except for the coastal plain.

Josephus refers to Mount Ebal, near Sichem, by the name of *Counsel.*[91] This etymology is based on the Greek *Boulê,* meaning "counsel." This type of incorrect etymology might be expected of a Greek author, but it is hard to imagine how Josephus could be so confused as to base his etymology on the Greek. Likewise, Josephus refers to Ai as near Jericho,[92] although in reality there is a rather large distance between the two sites. Josephus errs similarly

Table 14.3

	Source	Distance in Josephus	Actual Distance	% Error	Notes
Walls of Jerusalem (circumference)	BJ V, 4, 3 (159)	6.2	7	12.9	Colonia-Mozah
Beth Sheramin to Gaba	V 34	3.75	12.5	233	Based on Gaba to Tel Abu Shaweh
Simonias to Gaba	V 34	11.2	11	1.8	Ibid.
Tiberias to Magdala	V 32	5.6	5.5	.2	
Gabara to Jotapata	V 45	7.5	7–8	0	
Gabara to Sogane (Sikhnin)	V 21	7.7	4.5	71	
Jerusalem to Etam	A VIII, 7, 3 (186)	24–30	11–12	100	
Jordan to Jericho	A V, 1, 4 (20)	11.25	8	40.6	For similar description, see Table 14.1
Bethlehem to Jerusalem	A V, 2, 8 (139)	5.672	5–6	0	
Geba to Jerusalem	A V, 2, 8 (140)	3.75	4	7	
Jerusalem to En Gedi	A IX, 1, 2 (7)	56	57	2	As the crow flies; in actuality the distance is greater
Jerusalem to Bethlehem	A VII, 12, 4 (312)	3.75	4	7	

when he claims that the territory of Sihon "lies between three rivers and is similar in its nature to an island." [93] In terms of a dry reading of the biblical text, Josephus is correct in that the Bible does mention the Arnon, Jabbok, and the Jordan River as the boundaries of the realm of Sihon's land. The similarity to an island, however, is based only on a literal reading of the text. This area includes a vast expanse whose border on the west is the Jordan River and that is enclosed on the north and south by ravines whose waters take on the form of rivers only as they approach the Jordan. Someone who is familiar with the region of Sihon would have avoided such a reading of the biblical text. Someone more familiar with the geography of Europe, however, and interpreting the verses literally might have made such a mistake.

Such a description is in keeping with the genre of Greek and Roman historians whom Josephus sought to imitate. It would seem that Josephus in this description was using this style and not attempting to describe the region.

Such descriptions are found more than once in Josephus' writings, when he describes historical or sociological situations. This literary genre is responsible for Josephus' comment on mountains impracticable for passage and his description that Sihon's land is like an island. Some of the distances listed in *Antiquities* are correct, whereas others are not (see Table 14.3). This is in keeping with what we have seen earlier about distances in Josephus' other writings.

One of the most important consequences of our study of Josephus and the geographic additions in his writings is that it would seem that he used a similar method in those books where his sources remain unknown. If, for example, in his descriptions of Herod's kingdom, Josephus used, among other works, the book of Nicolaus of Damascus, it is likely that Josephus added commentary identifications and the like, based on his understanding of the period. This results in an additional problem. Do these chapters reflect the ability of Josephus and his truthworthiness, or do the mistakes and correct details simply depend, in part or whole, on his source? This question is beyond the scope of our study and requires a separate discussion.

The use in *Antiquities* of the phrases "city" and "village" is rather free. Almost every city referred to in the Bible as "city" is called *polis* by Josephus.[94] The reason for this lies in the Hebrew language. In Hebrew, the word city (*ʿir*) means a rural settlement with tens or even thousands of inhabitants. The Hebrew equivalent of the Greek *polis* is "very large city" or *krkh*. This phrase hardly ever appears in biblical sources. The Bible uses only the term "city," (*ʿir*) for very large settlements such as Jerusalem.[95] Therefore, Josephus mistakenly turned the Hebrew "city" into the Greek *polis*.

Roman and Greek authors use a similar method in their description of villages and events connected to them. This also adds importance to the description of these events when the phrase *polis* is used. This does not reflect the use of inexact detail as much as the desire to conform to a particular genre, as we have seen. This is characteristic not only of Josephus' geographic descriptions but of his writing in general. It is incorrect to call this a faulty method; rather, it reflects an attempt to elaborate upon a literary style, at the expense of individual details.

In summary, it is possible to state that Josephus was very familiar with the geography and topography of the Land of Israel both in his time and during the biblical period. Sometimes there are mistakes resulting from ignorance of certain conditions or from Hebrew sources or from the need to conform to a particular literary style. Josephus was not always consistent in his use of administrative-geographic material and cannot be trusted in such matters. There are many mistakes in distances recorded in Josephus, which may result from copyist's errors or from the lack of consequence given to such matters by ancient authors. Josephus' population figures are totally unreliable. All in all, though, Josephus has proven himself to be generally reliable and of the utmost importance for the study of the Second Temple period.

Notes

1. This study was sponsored by the Dr. Irving and Cherna Moskowitz Chair in the Land of Israel Studies. The issue of Josephus' sources has been discussed quite often in scholarly literature. See H. St. John Thackeray, *Josephus: The Man and the Historian* (New York 1929); L. H. Feldman, *Josephus and Modern Scholarship* (Berlin 1984), 392–419. On Nicolaus of Damascus, see B. Z. Wacholder, *Nicolaus of Damascus* (Berkeley, Los Angeles 1962).

2. *Ap* II, 9 (115–120).

3. The reading Judea, instead of Idumaea, in some manuscripts is certainly corrupt.

4. On the status of the district of Idumaea, see Z. Safrai, *Boundaries and Administration in Eretz-Israel in the Mishnah-Talmud Period* (Tel-Aviv 1980), pp. 1–2, 87–90 [Hebrew]. It should be stated that in Greek literature the corruption of the term *Idumaea* implies all of Judea of the Hebrew sources. See S. Klein, *The Land of Judea* (Tel-Aviv 1939), pp. 249–254 [Hebrew]. In Latin and Greek sources, see Juvenal, *Satires* VIII, 160; Virgil, *Georgics* III, 12; Valerius Flaccus *Argonautica* I, 12; Appian of Alexandria, *Bella Civilia,* V, 75.319; Martial *Epigrams* X, 50.1; Statius, *Silvae* I, 6.13, III, 2.138, V, 2.139; Lucan, *Pharsalia* III, 216; Silius Italicus, *Punica* III, 600, VII, 456; Aelianus, *De Natura Animalium* VI, 17.

5. For example, Caesar, *Bellum Gallicum* I, 1; Tacitus, *Histories* V, 1; Herodotus, *Histories* IV, 1–9; Arrian, *Anabasis* V, 6, VII, 10–12 etc.

6. *BJ* III, 3 (35–38).

7. *BJ* III, 10, 7–8 (506–521).

8. *BJ* V, 4 (136–183).

9. *BJ* IV, 8 (451–476).

10. *BJ* III, 7 (158–160).

11. *BJ* IV, 1 (1–9).

12. *BJ* VII, 6 (163–189).

13. *BJ* VII, 8 (280–294).

14. Although Gaba Hippeum in the Valley is mentioned as a city that bordered on the Galilee.

15. See note 4.

16. Pliny, *Naturalis Historia* V, 4, 68–74.

17. Claudius Ptolemaeus, *Geographia* V, 15.

18. *Baba Bathra* 3, 2; *Kethuboth* 13, 2; *Sheviith* 9, 2. On the entire issue, see Z. Safrai, "The Description of Eretz-Israel in Josephus' Works," in U. Rappaport (ed.), *Josephus Flavius* (Jerusalem 1982), pp. 91–116 [Hebrew].

19. For a complete reconstruction of the Mishnah, see Safrai, *ibid.,* pp. 106–110.

20. M. Avi-Yonah, "The Foundation of Tiberias," in *All the Land of Naphtali* (Jerusalem 1967), pp. 163–169 [Hebrew]).

21. The division into three does not represent the administrative division of Judea from the time that Pompey conquered Palestine (63 B.C.E.) until the reign of Herod (37 B.C.E.). As we have seen, at this time there was a separate district, Idumaea, inhabited by Jews, and therefore, it is not quite clear why this district does not appear in the list. If the list, however, reflects only the geographic situation, Idumaea can be included in Judea, just as Josephus included it in Judea in the description we are studying.

22. S. Klein, "A Chapter in Palestine Research Towards the End of the Second Temple" in F. I. Baer et al., (eds.), *Magnes Anniversary Book* (Jerusalem 1938), pp. 216–223 [Hebrew].

23. For our purposes, it makes no difference whether Josephus draws on a written and established source or formulates the basic outline of his description from material with which he was familiar.

24. This letter is part of the Apocrypha and was written in the Hellenistic period by a Jew who wished to describe Judaism for the Hellenistic world. See Aristeas to Philocrates (*Letter of Aristeas*) 115.

25. See Safrai (*op. cit.*, note 4), pp. 73–80.

26. *A* XX, 8, 3, (159); *BJ* II, 13, 2 (252).

27. Here Josephus uses the phrase "Sea of Tiberias" and not "Gennesareth," used more commonly in his writings. In *BJ* IV, 8, 2 (456), Josephus mentions the Lake of Tiberias. I have no explanation for the use of this unusual term.

28. Likewise, it contains a short description of the population in the kingdom of Agrippa. This detail is not found in the description of the other regions.

29. There are too many descriptions of the Dead Sea in non-Jewish literature to cite in this study.

30. *V* II, 11.

31. *BJ* VII, 5, 1 (97–99). This legend of the river that flows only six days of the week is found in many other Jewish sources, most of them later than Josephus.

32. A prominent example is the itinerary of a high Egyptian official on his journey, which took place during 317–323 C.E. This itinerary was recorded in a papyrus and it is clear that it was not subject to the whims of copyists. The official traveled on major thoroughfares marked with milestones and, even so, there are many errors. See C. H. Roberts & E. G. Turner, *Catalogue of the Greek and Latin Papyri in the John Rylands Library, Manchester* (Manchester 1952), vol. IV, nos. 628, 638.

33. *BJ* II, 10, 2 (188–191). From the description it would appear that Acco is included in the Galilee, and this is not correct.

34. We shall not deal with this matter in our study. See M. Broshi, "The Credibility of Josephus," in G. Vermes and J. Neusner (eds.), *Essays in Honour of Yigael Yadin, JJS*, 33(1982):379–384.

35. S. Gutman, *Gamla* (Tel Aviv 1981), pp. 27–37 [Hebrew].

36. *Ibid.*

37. M. Broshi, "The Credibility of Josephus" in U. Rappaport, *Josephus Flavius* (Jerusalem 1982), pp. 21–22 [Hebrew].

38. A discussion of many details is found in S. J. D. Cohen, *Josephus in Galilee and Rome* (Leiden 1978), pp. 233ff.

39. See most recently A. Byatt, "Josephus and Population Numbers in First Century Palestine," *PEQ* 105(1973):51–60.

40. M. Broshi, "The Population of Western Palestine in the Roman-Byzantine Period," *BASOR* 236 (1980):1–10.

41. *V* 25, 123.

42. *V* 37, 188. The list itself also appears in *BJ*, but there the division between cities and villages is not mentioned.

43. *V* 45, 229; 97, 242. In other instances, it is again referred to as a *city*. See, for example, *V* 124.

44. *V* 64, 332. Jotapata is referred to in other sources as a village, see note 42.

45. *V* 68, 384.

46. *V* 24, 118. The reference to Beth Shearim as a city stems from a desire to stress its importance as the center of Berenice's holdings.

47. *BJ* I, 1, 1 (33).

48. As, for example, *BJ* IV, 8, 1 (447).

49. *BJ* IV, 9, 9 (552).

50. *Op. cit.*, note 34.

51. An exception to the rule is the region of Narbata (coastal plain), which is referred to as a toparchy.

52. H. W. Ettelson, *The Integrity of I Maccabees* (New Haven 1925). For bibliography see p. 225, n.2. See also Cohen (*op. cit.*, note 38).

53. At times, there are long selections that are not dependent on the Bible as, for example, *A* IV, 8, 5 (199ff.), in which the author describes the laws of the Torah. Much of this information is not included in the Torah. There are other such cases, but these are beyond the scope of the present article. However, see H. W. Attridge, *The Interpretation of Biblical History in the Antiquitates Judaicae of Flavius Josephus* (Missoula, Mont. 1976).

54. Josephus often adds a sentence that brings the biblical description closer to a Greek framework. Thus, for example, his mention of the public festival (*A* II, 4, 3, 45) or the Song of Deuteronomy 32.1–43 as written in hexameter verse (*A* IV, 8, 44, 303). We refrain from dealing with such additions in this study since they rarely contain geographic detail.

55. *A* V, 1, 22 (81–87); VIII, 2, 3 (35–38).

56. Safrai (*op. cit.*, note 18); (*op. cit.*, note 4), pp. 178–194.

57. For a discussion of the terms and administrative system in the Land of Israel, see Safrai (*op. cit.*, note 4), pp. 9–28. In the Septuagint, the term "governor" is translated as "appointed officer." This is not an administrative term. The Aramaic translation appears as *'strtg* (*stratêgos*=general). In the continuation of the passage in Josephus, the governor appointed over the other governers is referred to as an *archon*.

58. Another way of describing a region is to cite a name in relation to the area to which it belonged. Thus, for example, the mountain (land) of Dora is referred to as "that of Dora." The administrative term χώρα (*chôra*) refers to the rural territory subject to a city. In certain Palestinian sources, the term lost its exact connotation. We intend to deal with this phenomenon at a future time.

59. See Z. Kallai, *The Tribes of Israel* (Jerusalem 1967), pp. 53–55 [Hebrew].

60. See *ibid.*

61. Safrai (*op. cit.*, note 4), pp. 119–136.

62. Joshua 19.26. See Kallai (*op. cit.*, note 59), pp. 164–190, 355–366.

63. Safrai (*op. cit.*, note 4), pp. 44, 184.

64. *Ibid.*, pp. 125–126.

65. Mount Tabor was also a holy site in the biblical and Byzantine periods. See B. Mazar, " 'They Shall Call Peoples to Their Mountain'," *EI* 14(1978):39–41. I am not able to determine if there is a connection between the holiness of the site and its importance as a settlement. Josephus mentions Sepphoris as the headquarters of the region in his time because it is not mentioned in the Bible. This reflects the connection between his description and the Bible. We shall return to deal with this phenomenon.

66. Z. Kallai, "The Biblical Geography of Flavius Josephus," *EI* 8(1967):269–272 [Hebrew].

67. Safrai (*op. cit.*, note 4), pp. 183–86.

68. This refers to either the Jordan River or Naḥal Kishon.

69. Safrai (*op. cit.*, note 4), pp. 186–190.

70. I do not know the source of the identification Arce-Ecdippa (Akhzib).

71. I. Finklestein, "The Shephelah of Yisrael," Tel Aviv 8(1981):84–94. The boundary of the *shephelah* according to Finklestein is also the boundary of Jewish settlement.

72. Joshua 19.41–46.

73. It is interesting that Josephus refers to Jamnia as a Philistine city, even though this is only hinted at in the Bible (II Chronicles 10:1). Likewise, Epiphanius, *De Mensuris,* and the Mid-

rash state that Ekron is Caesarea, situated in the sandy areas. In all of these instances, there is a desire to identify an important early settlement with an important settlement existing during the days of the author. Josephus did not mention Caesarea since he knew that it was a new city and is not mentioned in the Bible. There were others who did identify Ekron with Caesarea. See Jerome in his translation of the Onomasticon on the entry of Ekron. Joppa was not mentioned since it had a Jewish population and was included in Judea.

74. The toparchy of Ekron was not included in Judea. See Safrai (*op. cit.*, note 4), pp. 162–163, and see *infra*.

75. *Ibid.*, p. 163.

76. *A* I, 8, 2 (181); II, 7, 5 (184); IV, 4, 7 (82); IV, 7, 1 (161); VIII, 6, 4 (163); VIII, 12, 5 (312).

77. *A* II, 8, 2 (200). This tradition also appears at the end of each of the Testaments of the Twelve Patriarchs.

78. I Samuel 28.1; *A* VI, 14, 1 (325).

79. *A* V, 1, 18 (63); V, 1, 22 (92). The difference between Me-Merom and Berothe is dependent on the version of the Bible used by Josephus and, therefore, is not relevant to our discussion here.

80. *A* V, 1, 21 (79). The tradition concerning the fertile lands of the Jericho and Jerusalem regions is often repeated in other literature. This is certainly true regarding the Jericho region but far from the case vis-à-vis Jerusalem.

81. *A* XIII, 4, 4 (102); I Maccabees 10:89.

82. *A* XII, 7, 4 (308); II Maccabees 12:13; I Maccabees 4:15.

83. *A* XII, 9, 1 (421); I Maccabees 9:2. See note 85.

84. *BJ* I, 1, 5 (45); I Maccabees 15:2.

85. B. Bar-Kochva, *The Battles of the Hasmoneans, The Times of Judas Maccabaeus* (Jerusalem 1980), pp. 368 [Hebrew].

86. *A* III, 2, 1 (40); VI, 12, 4 (254).

87. *A* III, 5, 3 (85).

88. *A* VIII, 13, 7 (347); I Kings 19:3.

89. *A* IX, 1, 2 (7).

90. *A* III, 13, 2 (304).

91. *A* IV, 8, 44 (305).

92. *A* V, 1, 12 (35).

93. *A* IV, 5, 2 (95); Numbers 21:24. In another passage, Josephus states that the Transjordan region in the vicinity of the Arnon river was very fertile (*ibid.* 85). It is difficult to determine the exact region to which Josephus refers. In any event, the lands along the Arnon certainly do not fit Josephus' idealized description.

94. The area is referred to as a village only a few times. There are usually textual reasons for such a reference as, for example, *A* VI, 1, 3 (14); VI, 1, 4 (16, 17).

95. As, for example, II Samuel 15:37 and many other verses.

15 Josephus Flavius and the Archaeological Excavations in Jerusalem

BENJAMIN MAZAR

The excavations south and southwest of the Temple Mount, which I carried out for many years beginning February 1968, focused my interest more and more on the works of Josephus Flavius. *The Jewish War* and the *Antiquities of the Jews* are of special significance as an unfailing source of information and as basic handbooks for the study of Jerusalem's history in the Second Temple period, and particularly of its central role as a holy city, the capital of Judea, and a populous megalopolis. In the course of this work, I encountered several problems connected with Josephus' personality as a historian of Jerusalem and especially with the structure of his book, *The Jewish War*. In this short paper, I shall attempt to survey briefly the main tentative conclusions I have reached.

First of all, it should be remembered that Josephus gives prominence to his Jerusalemite origins and emphasizes his descent from an illustrious priestly family on his father's side and from the Hasmonean royal house on his mother's side. His conscious pride in Jerusalem is understandable, for he was devoted to the tradition of the city's great antiquity and exalted sanctity and of the unique importance and splendor of the Temple, invested with divine radiance. Josephus regarded Jerusalem as the hub of the state, the metropolis of the Jewish people, and as a focus for pilgrims from Palestine and the Diaspora. In emphasizing the greatness and fame of Jerusalem, Josephus did not deviate from the expressions found in Hellenistic and Roman literature, which often describe Jerusalem as a famous city, Tacitus' *famosa urbs*.

Instructive in this respect is Menahem Stern's paper on Jerusalem in the *Schalit Memorial Volume*, which presents a wealth of relevant material under the title of a quotation from Pliny the Elder (*Natural History* V, 70): *Hierosolyma longe clarissima urbium orientis*, that is, "Jerusalem, by far the most famous city of East." [1]

Should Josephus' first work, *The Jewish War*, be considered a comprehensive composition about the war of the Jews against the Romans? Or, is it rather a work devoted mainly to Jerusalem, as the focal point of Jewish life and to the description of its growth, flowering, and then suffering the siege, and the total destruction that befell it, all this by means of a shrewd and one-sided analysis of the causes that brought about the disaster? Moreover, is it likely that the first six books of the work form a single, complete, historiographic unit covering the last 240 years of Jerusalem, while the seventh book is a kind of appendix devoted to the results of the war and to the events that occurred after the destruction of Jerusalem, including the tragic chapter of Masada?[2] I believe, in fact, that the seventh book was written by someone else and not by Josephus.

The preamble to the work implies that the opening section, comprising the conquest of Jerusalem by Antiochus Epiphanes and the appearance of the Hasmoneans on the historical scene, is only the introduction to the account of the momentous events during the rule of the Hasmonean and Herodian dynasties and the period leading up to the Revolt. Jerusalem, it is fairly evident, is central to Josephus' interest and personal experience. This is particularly striking in his detailed descriptions of the city and its fortifications, of the Temple (*BJ* V, 136–246), and especially of the siege of Jerusalem and its conquest by the Romans.

No less instructive is the fact that the sixth book ends (*BJ* VI, 435–442) with a succinct summary of the history of Jerusalem. The summary begins with Melchizedek, who is described, perhaps in the spirit of the tradition current in priestly circles, as a remarkable figure, who "as his name is, so is he," who built the sanctuary in Jerusalem and worshipped God there. It ends with the destruction of the Second Temple by the Romans. Thus, according to Josephus' chronology, this summary spans 2177 years. What is surprising here is the glorification of Melchizedek, who is presented as the first to erect the Temple in Jerusalem, and the omission of Solomon's role in building the Temple on Mount Moriah, as well as the fairly elaborate chronology that Josephus took pains to construct for a detailed description of the history of Jerusalem. Most instructive is the last paragraph in this book: "But neither its antiquity, nor its vast wealth, nor its people dispersed through the whole habitable world, nor yet the great glory of its religious rites, could do aught to avert its ruin. Thus ended the siege of Jerusalem" (*BJ* VI, 442).

Can we assume that these were the concluding words of the original work? True, Josephus, who was endowed with great literary and historical sense, knew how to incorporate in his books many important matters relating to his country and to the Diaspora. We can understand his special interest in the war in Galilee, as this episode touched him directly, and he had to defend himself against the accusations brought up by his opponents. However, perhaps the elevation of Jerusalem to such unique greatness should be considered as a clue to a basic quality in Josephus' personality and literary work, and even as a reason for his decision to devote a work to the history of the Jewish war against the Romans.

At the same time, the sheer extent of Josephus' familiarity with Jerusalem revealed in both *War* and *Antiquities* is surprising. This is apparent in his intimate knowledge of the city's quarters, fortifications, palaces, markets, and water supply systems, and of course of the Temple precinct, as well as of all strata of its society, its public figures, and especially of the city's history. Josephus collected his source material from books and documents, from oral traditions, and Midrashim and added to these his personal knowledge and first-hand experiences.

Josephus' detailed descriptions of Jerusalem as well as incidental references to that city have undergone a close critical examination in relation to the archaeological excavations carried out near the Temple Mount, in the Upper City, and in other areas of Jerusalem. The results achieved up to the present show, on the whole, that Josephus' information should be considered trustworthy; though in several cases contradictions, obscurities, and even intentional deviations can be found.

This is especially evident in the excavations I directed south and southwest of the Temple Mount, which revealed a reasonably clear picture of the layout and character of this area during the period of the Herodian dynasty. Josephus' descriptions of the Tyropoeon Valley and the main street running along it, the towering supporting walls of the Temple Mount, the location of the four gates in the Western Wall, and the approach to them have all basically been proved accurate. The same is true of the stairway carried on "Robinson's Arch," which led to the southernmost gate in the Western Wall, that is, the gate of the Royal Stoa. His description of the Royal Stoa in the southern part of the Temple precinct as "a structure more noteworthy than any under the sun" (*A* XV, 411–416) was illuminated by a limited archaeological survey carried out in that area. The place above the Temple chambers, where a priest proclaimed by a trumpet call the approach of the Sabbath (*BJ* IV, 582), was determined by the discovery of a large stone block among the debris on the flagstone paving of the street near the southwest corner of the Temple Mount. This ashlar block had a niche on the inner side and a Hebrew inscription carved in the stone reading: "To the house of trumpeting [to proclaim]." [3] The majority of Josephus' descriptions and many of the details he records have been confirmed by the excavations, but some have remained obscure. [4] In any case, clearly Josephus collected faithfully and diligently a great deal of material concerning Jerusalem and its history, both from written sources and from oral traditions. No doubt, since his boyhood he also had access to the counsel of the Temple priests and the sages and elders of Jerusalem.

The excavations in the Jewish Quarter of the Old City have contributed significantly to our understanding of Josephus' descriptions and sources concerning Jerusalem. This important archaeological undertaking, directed by Professor N. Avigad, has revealed an impressive picture of the Upper City of Jerusalem and its history.[5] In addition, there have been more limited excavations in the Citadel, in the Armenian Quarter, and on Mt. Zion, and of course, the extensive excavations in the City of David directed by Y. Shiloh.[6] First and foremost, it has been established with certainty that, in the latter part of the First Temple period (eighth–seventh centuries B.C.E.), an extensive quarter spread out on the western hill, the Mishne (second quarter) of the Bible (Zephaniah 1:10; II Kings 22:14), which was enclosed by a massive wall, apparently joining up with the wall of the City of David. The line of the Mishne Wall is essentially identical with the line of the later Hasmonean wall, indicating that when the Hasmoneans came to erect a new residential quarter on the ruins of the earlier Mishne, they not only followed the line of the earlier fortifications, but even integrated in the new defensive system parts of the older fortifications, which had lain in ruins for centuries. Thus, in the northern section of the Hasmonean wall, a tower was built against the east face of a tower dating from the end of the First Temple period, which was preserved to a height of eight meters, a fact rightly described by Avigad as "most remarkable." It is now clear that, after the destruction of the Mishne quarter in 586 B.C.E. by the Babylonians, its fortifications lay in ruin and desolation until the advent of the Hasmoneans, who were able to undertake the rebuilding of the Upper City and its strong defenses. We can also assume that the Hasmoneans built their palace in the northeastern part of the Upper City, in an area adjoining the city wall. This palace has not yet been uncovered, but it probably stood on the site of a palace of the later Davidic kings and included in its precinct the "imposing house" Jehoiakim built (Jeremiah 22:13–14). Nearby was probably the house of the prophetess Hulda and her husband Shallum, keeper of the wardrobe (surely, the wardrobe in the king's house, II Kings 22:14, II Chronicles 34:22). These ambitious building projects may well have been connected with the wish to restore the city to its former glory and to renew the Jewish monarchy, with Jerusalem as its chief city.

Finally, I shall discuss only very briefly the complex problems concerning the history of the Upper City arising from Josephus' descriptions (*BJ* V, 137–138; *A* VII, 61ff.), which contain discrepancies and corrupt passages. I believe that opinions were divided among the sources available to Josephus, but it is possible that a tradition current in Jerusalem placed the stronghold of Zion" (II Samuel 5:7) in the Lower City and identified it with the *Akra,* the name Josephus uses to designate the southeastern hill south of the Temple Mount. However, at the same time he seems to agree with the theory that already in David's time there was a fort (*phrourion*) in the Upper City, and that David linked it up with the Akra "so as to form one whole, enclosed it with a wall" and called it after himself the "City of David" (in *A* VII, 66, the variant "the Upper City" must be correct). Obviously, Josephus refers to the first wall, which he believes to be the earliest of the city walls, erected by David, Solomon, and their successors (*BJ* V, 143). In any case, Josephus was acquainted with the Jerusalemite tradition concerning the massive wall that encircled the Upper City, the Mishne, during the Judean monarchy, and that was succeeded by the Hasmonean wall incorporating remains of the earlier fortifications. Excavations have shown that this massive wall was probably first built in the late eighth century, perhaps by Hezekiah before Sennacherib's campaign. However, in the days of the Second Temple, it was customary, and rightly so, to attribute it to the House of David and even, by way of exaggeration, to David himself. Thus, it was possible to include in the Song of Degrees attributed to David the following words: "Our feet have been standing within your gates, O Jerusalem! Jerusalem, built as a city which is bound firmly together" (Psalms 122:2–3).

Notes

1. M. Stern, in *Jerusalem of the Second Temple Period* (*Abraham Schalit Memorial Volume*) (Jerusalem 1980), 257ff. [Hebrew].

2. A similar opinion has been expressed by Shaye J. D. Cohen, *Josephus in Galilee and Rome* (Leiden 1979), pp. 84–90.

3. Cf. A. Demsky, "The Trumpeter's Inscription from the Temple Mount," *EI* 15 (1985):40–42.

4. B. Mazar, "Herodian Jerusalem," *IEJ* 28 (1978):230ff.; *idem*, "The Royal Stoa on the Temple Mount," *PAAJR* 45–47 (1980):381ff.; *idem, The Mountain of the Lord* (New York 1975), pp. 28ff. Cf. also K. M. Kenyon, *Digging Up Jerusalem* (New York 1974), pp. 207ff.

5. N. Avigad, *The Upper City of Jerusalem* (Jerusalem 1980) [Hebrew]; *Discovering Jerusalem* (Jerusalem 1983).

6. Short reports on the excavations of Mazar, Avigad, Ruth Amiran, A. Eitan, M. Broshi, and others can be found in *Jerusalem Revealed*, ed. Y. Yadin (Jerusalem 1975). On the excavations in the City of David see Y. Shiloh, *Excavations at the City of David*, vol. 1 (*Qedem*, 19; Jerusalem 1984).

A Selective Critical Bibliography of Josephus

LOUIS H. FELDMAN

Bibliography

It is fair to say that there is no classical or Jewish author for whom the student has more complete or more fully annotated bibliographies than Josephus. Heinz Schreckenberg, *Bibliographie zu Flavius Josephus* (Leiden 1968), covering the period from the appearance of the *editio princeps* of the Latin translation in 1470 to 1965 (with a few entries for the period 1966–1968), contains 2207 entries. However, there are several problems: the arrangement is by year instead of by subject matter; there are numerous omissions; summaries are missing from a large number of items; and there are many errors, inevitable in this kind of work. Schreckenberg's supplement, *Bibliographie zu Flavius Josephus : Supplementband mit Gesamtregister* (Leiden 1979), arranged alphabetically by author, in which he attempts to be reasonably complete through 1975, has 1453 entries. Though Schreckenberg has corrected many errors of omission and commission of the first volume, many still remain. Morever, the value of Schreckenberg's first volume is greatly enhanced by the indices of citations and of Greek words in Josephus; but these are lacking in the second volume. My own *Josephus: A Supplementary Bibliography* (New York 1986), arranged alphabetically by author, has approximately 3600 entries, of which approximately 900 cover the period from 1976 through 1984, while approximately 1900 are items that Schreckenberg missed, and the remainder contain summaries where Schreckenberg lacked them. My own work also supplies indices of citations and of Greek words in Josephus which are missing from Schrenkenberg's second volume. It also lists approximately 300 corrigenda for Schreckenberg's first volume and approximately 200 for his second volume. My *Josephus and Modern Scholarship* (Berlin 1984), with 5543 entries, arranges the subject matter according to 29 major topics and 428 subtopics and presents not only summaries but, in most cases, criticisms, often at length, of the various items and, for all major problems, an evaluation of the state of the question. It also gives a list of desiderata in the field and the reasons why such works are needed.

For selective bibliographies, we may call attention to Peter Thomsen, ed., *Die Palästina-Literatur: eine internationale Bibliographie in systematischer Ordnung, mit Autoren- und Sachregister*, 6 vols., (Leipzig 1908–1953), vol. 7, Peter Thomsen et al., eds. (Berlin 1972), which lists reviews and (occasionally) brief summaries. It is especially comprehensive in covering literature about the *Testimonium Flavianum*. Ralph Marcus, "Selected Bibliography (1920–1945) of the Jews in the Hellenistic-Roman Period," *PAAJR* 16(1946–1947):97–181 (Josephus, pp. 178–81), is very selective, noting with a single asterisk those works that are useful introductions and with a double asterisk those that are indispensable to the specialist. His work has been continued by Uriel Rappaport "Bibliography of Works on Jewish History in the Hellenistic and Roman periods, 1946–1970" [Hebrew and English], *Meḥkarim* 2(1972): 247–321; (in collaboration with Menahem Mor), *Bibliography of Works on Jewish History in the Hellenistic and Roman Periods: 1971–1975* [Hebrew and English], (Jerusalem 1976); Menahem Mor and Uriel Rappaport, *Bibliography of Works on Jewish History in the Hellenistic and Roman Periods: 1976–1980*, (Jerusalem 1982); Devorah Dimant, Menahem Mor, and Uriel Rappaport, *Bibliography on Works on Jewish History in the Persian, Hellenistic and Roman Periods: 1981–1985* (Jerusalem 1987), on a far more comprehensive scale, with increasingly elaborate subdivisions, detailed indices, and numerous cross-references, and with particularly good coverage for items in Hebrew. My own critical *Scholarship on Philo and Josephus* (1937–1962) (New York 1963), arranged, as is the present article, by subject matter, covers only the years 1937 through 1962, whereas the present work covers all the years of scholarship and is more selective. Gerhard Delling et al., *Bibliographie zur jüdisch-hellenistischen und intertestamentarischen Literatur: 1900–1965* (Berlin 1969), (Josephus, pp. 51–60; 2d ed., 1975 (Josephus, pp. 80–94), in his new and very useful, much enlarged edition has about 1400 items pertaining to Josephus; but he omits many important items, while including numerous works of minor significance. For a very brief, annotated selection of works pertaining to the whole period, I recommend Jonathan Kaplan, ed., *2000 Books and More: An Annotated and Selected Bibliography of Jewish History and Thought*, [Hebrew and English], (Jerusalem 1983); also published as *International Bibliography of Jewish History and Thought* (München 1984); on pp. 119–143, the book lists 44 works in Hebrew and 72 in European languages.

Editions and Translations

The best edition of Josephus remains that of Benedictus Niese, *Flavii Josephi Opera*, 7 vols. (Berlin 1885–1895) (the *editio maior*), which has a much fuller *apparatus criticus* than his *editio minor* (6 vols., Berlin, 1888–

1895). In general, Niese is much more conservative in his *editio maior*. Following the prevailing tendency of his era, he relied unduly on one group of manuscripts to the exclusion of others and thus usually failed to accept individual readings from other manuscripts on a case-by-case basis. Samuel A. Naber's edition, *Flavii Joseph: Opera Omnia post Immanuelem Bekkerum* (Leipzig 1888–1896), appeared almost simultaneously with Niese; and although he often has a smoother and more readable text than Niese, he emends too freely. Moreover, his *apparatus criticus* has numerous errors.

Heinz Schreckenberg, *Die Flavius-Josephus-Tradition in Antike und Mittelalter* (Leiden 1972) has provided an annotated listing of all manuscripts of Josephus, as well as a discussion of ancient translations, together with a list of citations of and borrowings from Josephus, author by author, through the sixteenth century. We may note that of the 133 manuscripts of the Greek text, in whole or in part, described by Schreckenberg, 50 were unknown to Niese, though only 2 of them seem to be of any major significance. Hence, the future improvement of the text of Josephus will most likely come through emendation, based, we may suggest, on the newly completed concordance to Josephus, on a careful study of Josephus' grammar (yet to be done), and on the careful consultation of the Latin translation ascribed to Cassiodorus (a critical edition of which remains to be completed).

We may note that there exists only a single papyrus fragment (*BJ* II, 576–579, 582–584) of Josephus, dating from the late third century, published by Hans Oellacher, *Griechische Literarische Papyri* II (Baden bei Wien, 1939), 61–63. Though it is poorly preserved and contains only 112 words in whole or in part, there are no fewer than nine places where the fragment differs from all the manuscripts collated by Niese. Hence, we are inclined to the view—though, of course, the papyrus is too brief to be definitive and its readings are not necessarily superior to those of the manuscripts— that our text of even the *War,* which seems to be in much better shape than that of the *Antiquities,* is in need of further emendation. This is true especially when we consider that the papyrus agrees now with one group of manuscripts and now with another, thus indicating that we should not rely excessively on one group alone. Schreckenberg's book highlights the fact that often citations of Josephus by later writers may help in reconstituting the text; but he himself missed a number of citations from church fathers and later writers. The text of the *Antiquities,* in particular, is in poor shape, and a new edition is an important desideratum.

Schreckenberg, *Rezeptionsgeschichtliche und Textkritische Untersuchungen zu Flavius Josephus* (Leiden 1977), discusses the transmission of the text of Josephus in various versions and presents many emendations of the Greek text. We may remark, however, that the work of Pines and Dubarle on the *Testimonium Flavianum* and of Buchard on Josephus' passages concerning the Essenes shows how much can be done for the text of Josephus through a study of those who quote or paraphrase him.

Schreckenberg, "Einige Vermutungen zum Josephustext," *Theokratia* 1(1967–1969):64–75, in proposing 34 emendations, and "Neue Beiträge zur Kritik des Josephustextes," *Theokratia* 2(1970–1972):81–106, in suggesting 22 emendations, often through making good use of the translation into Latin and of the newly completed concordance, has almost always improved the sense, grammar, and style; but this presupposes that Josephus wrote better Greek than he apparently did. Of these emendations, few are both necessary and palaeographically probable. We may remark, moreover, that there is a danger in the use of the concordance, in that Josephus wrote over a long period of time and presumably changed his style as he became better acquainted with the Greek language, became less dependent on his assistants, and changed his subject matter.

The standard translation into English is by William Whiston, *The Genuine Works of Flavius Josephus* (London 1737), which has been reprinted at least 217 times, an average of almost once a year. To be sure, the translation has virility, but it is based on Haverkamp's (1726) inferior text, is full of outright errors, and in its notes expresses such strange notions as that Josephus was an Ebionite Christian and a bishop of Jerusalem. The Loeb Classical Library edition, by Henry St. John Thackeray, Ralph Marcus, Allen Wikgren, and myself, 9 vols. (now reprinted in 10 vols.) (London 1926–1965), is based on an eclectic text dependent on Niese and Naber, with relatively few original emendations. The translation itself is sometimes rather free, the commentary (often indebted to Reinach's French edition) is increasingly full, and there are a number of useful appendices, especially of bibliographical material, in the last four volumes. Geoffrey A. Williamson's translation, *Josephus: The Jewish War* (Harmondsworth 1959) (revised by E. Mary Smallwood, London 1981) is popular and readable, though we must express the warning that he has removed passages that interrupt the narrative. Gaalya Cornfeld, general ed.; Benjamin Mazar and Paul L. Maier, consulting editors, *Josephus: The Jewish War* (Grand Rapids 1982), which is often closely related to Thackeray's Loeb version, has an extensive commentary and lavish illustrations but contains many errors.

The standard translation into French, corresponding to Whiston in its great popularity, is by Arnauld d'Andilly, *Histoire des Juifs,* etc. (Paris 1667), though it has been reprinted much less often. It, too, is based upon an inferior Greek text. The translation by Théodore Reinach, et al., *Oeuvres complètes de Flavius Josèphe,* 7 vols. (Paris 1900–1932), is based on Niese's text and is copiously annotated. The one missing work has been translated by André Pelletier, *Flavius Josèphe: Autobiographie* (Paris 1959): it is based on Thackeray's Loeb text. The Greek text has a number of misprints, the translation has a number of errors, and the notes are largely based on Thackeray. Pelletier, *Flavius Josèphe: Guerre des Juifs,* vol. 1: Livre I (Paris 1975); vol. 2: Livres II et III (Paris 1980); vol. 3: Livres IV et V (Paris 1982); vol. 4: Livres VI et VII (Paris 1987), has produced his new version of the *War,* containing Greek text, *apparatus criticus,* translation into French, notes (largely dependent on Thackeray), and an introduction, especially on the transmission of Josephus' text, notably by Eusebius.

The standard translation into German, that by Heinrich Clementz, *Des Flavius Josephus Jüdische Altertümer,* 2 vols. (Halle 1899); *Geschichte des Jüdischen Krieges* (Halle 1900); *Kleinere Schriften* (Halle 1900), is of a lower order of merit than the Loeb or Reinach. It is based on the texts of Haverkamp (1726) and Dindorf (1845), though Niese and Naber were available, and is more of a paraphrase than a translation. Philip Kohout, *Flavius Josephus' Jüdischer Krieg* (Linz 1901), bases himself on Niese and Naber and is precise and literal, though his diction is rhetorical and often antiquated. A great improvement is to be seen in Otto Michel and Otto Bauernfeind, *Flavius Josephus, De Bello Judaico. Der Jüdische Krieg. Zweisprachige Ausgabe der sieben Bücher,* 3 vols. (Bad Hamburg 1959–1969), who have a text based on Niese, *apparatus criticus,* accurate translation into German, brief notes but extended appendices on specific points, and four valuable indices.

The Latin, Syriac, Slavonic, and Hebrew Versions

There are two translations into Latin: the first is a free paraphrase of the *War* dating from the fourth century and ascribed to a certain Hegesippus, and the second is a more literal translation of the works (with the exception of the *Life*) made under the direction of Cassiodorus in the sixth century. Inasmuch as our earliest Greek manuscripts date from the eleventh century, these Latin versions are of considerable value for reconstructing the text.

The standard critical edition of the text of Hegesippus is by Vicentius Ussani, *Corpus Scriptorum Ecclesiasticorum Latinorum,* vol. 66: *Hegesippi qui dicitur historiae libri V. Pars prior: textum criticum continens* (Wien and Leipzig 1932); *pars posterior,* preface by Carolus Mras and indices by Ussani (Wien 1960). In Part 2, Mras discusses the manuscripts, the title, and the unresolved identity of the author. The only thorough analysis of the work is by Albert A. Bell, Jr., "An Historiographical Analysis of the *De Excidio Hierosolymitano* of Pseudo-Hegesippus" (Ph.D. disser., University of North Carolina 1977), who attempts to view Hegesippus as a historian in his own right, since he has thoroughly rewritten Josephus. Hegesippus has consulted several sources in addition to Josephus, has included much Christian material, and above all, has developed a distinct philosophy of history.

As to the Latin version ascribed to Cassiodorus, we have critical editions only for *Against Apion,* by Carolus Boysen, *Flavii Josephi opera ex versione latina antiqua. . . .* Pars VI: *De Judaeorum vetustate sive contra Apionem libri II* (Prag-Wien-Leipzig 1898), and for the first five books of the *Antiquities* by Franz Blatt, *The Latin Josephus,* I: *Introduction and Text. The Antiquities: Books I–V* (Aarhus 1958). The latter is disappointing in that it is based on only a few of the 171 manuscripts, its stemma is less than careful, and manuscripts are cited only to disappear and then reappear without warning. Blatt, on the one hand, has criticized the translator in many places where the latter has rendered the text accurately and, on the other hand, has omitted mention of many places where he has not done so. The work clearly must be done over again; in particular, the stemma should be reconsidered, perhaps with the aid of a computer, since the manuscripts are so numerous. As to the principles that governed the translation, a careful comparison deserves to be made of the principles underlying such contemporary translations as Rufinus, Jerome's Vulgate, the Latin version of Pseudo-Philo's *Biblical Antiquities,* and Cassiodorus' other translations. The value of a critical edition, particularly for such thorny questions as the *Testimonium Flavianum,* is considerable. As to the *War,* Giulano Ussani, *Studi preparatori ad una edizione della traduzione latina in sette libri del 'Bellum Judaicum'* (*Bollettino del Comitato per la Preparazione dell' Edizione nazionale dei Classici greci e latini* N.S. 1, 1945, pp. 86–102), indicates his intention of preparing a scholarly edition, but the work never appeared.

We have a Syriac version of the sixth book of the *War* dating from the fourth or fifth century. Heimann Kottek, *Das sechste Buch des Bellum Judaicum nach der von Ceriani photolithographisch edirten Peschitta-Handschrift übersetzt und kritisch bearbeitet* (Disser. Leipzig) (Berlin 1886), believes that the translator had before him a portion of the Aramaic original; but inasmuch as the Aramaic original is totally lost, it is difficult to substantiate this.

To arrive at a scientific edition of the text of Josippon, the Hebrew paraphrase of the *Jewish War,* is extremely difficult, inasmuch as there are three very different recensions: those of Mantua, Constantinople, and Venice. It was not until David Flusser, *The Josippon* [*Josephus Gorionides*]. *Edited with an Introduction and Notes* [Hebrew], 2 vols. (Jerusalem 1978–1980), that we have managed to obtain such a text, with *apparatus criticus* and with cross-references to Josephus.

An important source for the text of Josippon is the eleventh-century Jerahmeel, which was written about three centuries before the earliest printed version of Josippon (1480) and which closely accords with the Mantua recension, though with some instances of agreement with the Constantinople version (1510), as noted by Jacob Reiner, "The Book of the Hasmonean Kings from the Chronicles of Jerahmeel," 2 vols. (D.H.L. diss., Yeshiva University 1966), and "The Original Hebrew Yosippon in the Chronicle of Jerahmeel,"

JQR 60 (1969–1970):128–146. Haim Schwarzbaum, "Prolegomenon," *The Chronicles of Jerahmeel; or The Hebrew Bible Historiale, being a collection of Apocryphal and Pseudepigraphical Books Dealing with the History of the World from the Creation to the Death of Judas Maccabeus,* Moses Gaster, trans. (New York 1971) 1–124, has emphasized the importance of Jerahmeel as presenting an untampered text of Josippon but notes that Jerahmeel's references to Josippon often are actually to Josephus, especially on Daniel.

The only translation into English has been that of Peter Morvvyne (Morwyng, Morvvyn, Morwyn), *Joseph ben Gorion. A Compendious [and most marveilous] History of the [Latter Tymes of the] Jewes Communeweale* (London 1558), based upon a Latin version (by Sebastian Münster) of Abraham ibn Daud's abstract of Josippon of the twelfth century. The popularity of this translation may be gauged by the fact that, in the century after its appearance, it went through as many reprintings as the translation of Whiston in the century after its appearance. A new translation, long overdue, the first of the complete work, is now being prepared on the basis of Flusser's edition by Steven Bowman of the University of Cincinnati.

Discussion of Josippon has centered on his date, his sources, and the purpose of his work. For a brief survey of the work, marked by judicious comments on the chief questions associated with it, the best treatment is that of Hirsch J. Zimmels, "Aspects of Jewish Culture: Historiography," *WHJP* 2.2 (New Brunswick 1966), pp. 277–281, who correctly remarks that the effrontery of certain scholars in ascribing historical significance to certain passages in the work has met with little success.

Yitzhak Baer, "The Book of Josippon the Jew," [Hebrew] *Sefer Benzion Dinaburg,* Yitzhak Baer et al., eds. (Jerusalem 1949), pp. 178–205, insists that the author had an outstanding knowledge of both Latin and talmudic literature, but that since he shows selectivity in his use of sources, his views are his own, and that he exemplifies two opposite trends: submission to the Romans and willingness to suffer martyrdom. Abraham A. Neuman, "Josippon: History and Pietism" (*Alexander Marx Jubilee Volume,* Saul Lieberman, ed., [New York 1950], pp. 637–667; reprinted in his *Landmarks and Goals: Historical Studies and Addresses* [Philadelphia 1953], pp. 1–34), concludes that Josippon was familiar with the II and IV Maccabees and did not know the later talmudic account of the miracle of Hanukkah and that, in contrast to Josephus, he stresses the struggle to preserve from Gentile defilement the land of Israel and the Temple. Hence, the date of Josippon, usually assigned to the middle of the tenth century, may be even earlier than that of the third or early fourth century assigned by Solomon Zeitlin, "Josippon," *JQR* 53 (1962–1963):277–297, who suggests that Josippon shows familiarity with tannaitic and early patristic but not with amoraic material. However, the references to the Apocrypha may be accounted for by the fact that the translator knew Latin and thus may well have known the Books of Maccabees in the Vulgate version. Neuman, "Josippon and the Apocrypha," *JQR* 43 (1952–1953):1–26 (reprinted in his *Landmarks and Goals: Historical Studies and Addresses* [Philadelphia 1953], pp. 35–57), argues that the omission of the Prayer of Azariah and the Song of the Three Children from Josippon can be readily explained as due to the fact that they were not extant in the text available to Josippon, thus indicating an extremely early date for Josippon. But this is an *argumentum ex silentio;* and, moreover, Ariel Toaff, "La storia di Ester nella letteratura ebraica medievale," *ASE* (1968–1969):25–45, has suggested that the differences between Josippon and the Apocrypha may be explained by the hypothesis that Josippon was also acquainted with an oral Apocryphal tradition. Neuman contends that Josippon's statement, in his version of the Story of the Three Pages, that the king is strongest, compared with his source, I Esdras, that wine is strongest, is further evidence of an early date for Josippon; but, we may counter, this may indicate only that the author sought to avoid offending the emperor. In addition, if Josippon was composed as early as the tannaitic period, we may well ask why it is never cited before the tenth century. Indeed, David Flusser, "The Author of the Book of Josippon, His Personality and His Age" [Hebrew], *Zion* 18 (1953):109–126, and "Der lateinische Josephus und der hebräische Josippon," *Festschrift Otto Michel* (Göttingen 1974), pp. 122–132, dates the author in the first half of the tenth century and cites evidence that he came from southern Italy and that his chief sources were the so-called Hegisippus, a Latin Bible, and the first sixteen books of the *Antiquities* in a Latin version. In *Josephus and Modern Scholarship* (Berlin 1984), pp. 64–66, I noted thirteen points of evidence that support such a dating.

That Josippon's chief source is Hegesippus has been demonstrated by Esther Sorscher, "A Comparison of Three Texts: The Wars, the Hegesippus, and the Yosippon" (M.A. diss., Yeshiva University 1973), who shows that for Book 3 he never includes anything omitted by Hegesippus. This, we may comment, does not hold true for the rest of Josippon, especially Book 1. The chief difference separating Josephus, Hegesippus, and Josippon is that the purpose of the first is political, of the second is religious (to prove that the war was God's punishment inflicted upon the Jews), and of the third is religious (to counteract Hegesippus' prejudice against the Jews).

Luitpold Wallach, "Quellenkritische Studien zum hebräischen Josippon: I: Josippon und der Alexanderroman," *MGWJ* 82 (1938):190–198, concludes that the first part of Josippon's story of Alexander the Great is a twelfth-century interpolation in a medieval folkbook. This conclusion, we may note, is supported by the fact that the passage appears in a Parma manuscript but not in the Constantinople or Mantua version. Wallach, "Quellenkritische Studien zum hebräischen Josippon," *MGWJ* 83 (1939; did not appear until 1963):

288–301; translated into English as "Yosippon and the Alexander Romance," *JQR* 37 (1946–1947):407–422, constructs a stemma indicating the relationship among the Arabic, Ethiopic, and Hebrew versions and shows that there are two distinct versions of the Alexander romance preserved in Josippon.

As to the sources of the passages on John and Jesus in Josippon, Abraham A. Neuman, "A Note on John the Baptist and Jesus in 'Josippon'," *HUCA* 23.2 (1950–1951):137–149, argues that the references to Jesus are interpolated but that those referring to John are authentic. He postulates a common Jewish source for the references to John in Josephus, Josippon, and the New Testament. We may suggest that a most likely source is Hegesippus, inasmuch as there is no indication that such a Jewish source was available to Josippon.

As to the purpose of Josippon, Sara R. Duker, "Political Ideas in the Sefer Josippon" (M.A. diss. Columbia University 1969) comments that Josippon was influenced by classical Christian *Romanitas* both in his theory of history and in his enumeration of the qualities of a good ruler, that his idea of kingship reflects a response to the memory of the brutal outbursts against the Jews in ninth- and tenth-century Italy and that, by advocating acquiescence in the divinely sanctioned legitimate ruling power of Rome, Josippon attempts to demonstrate that the Jews do not constitute a threat to the eastern Roman Empire. We may reply, however, that the motif of the qualities of a good ruler is a broad one and that Josippon's mention of the common ancestry of the Romans and the Jews may reflect merely the fact that the Maccabees formed an alliance with the Romans or the rabbinic idea that the two peoples were related, inasmuch as the Romans were traced back by the rabbis to Esau, the twin brother of Jacob, the ancestor of the Jews. Jacob Reiner, "The Jewish War: Variations in the Historical Narratives in the Texts of Josephus and the Yosippon" (Ph.D. diss., Dropsie University 1972), more convincingly remarks that the chief difference between Josephus and Josippon is that the former views the confrontation between the Jews and the Romans as a war for national liberty, whereas the latter looks upon it as a holy war.

The fact that a translation of Josippon was made into Arabic so soon after its composition in the tenth century would indicate its importance for the constitution of the original Hebrew text; but, thus far, we lack a critical edition of this Arabic version. Julius Wellhausen, *Der arabische Josippus (Abhandlungen der königlichen Gesellschaft der Wissenschaften zu Göttingen. Philologisch-historische Klasse*, Folge 1, Nr. 4; Berlin 1897), has merely an abridged translation into German of an inferior fourteenth-century manuscript. M. Sanders and H. Nahmad, "A Judeo-Arabic Epitome of the Yosippon," *Essays in Honor of Solomon B. Freehof*, Walter Jacob et al., eds. (Pittsburgh 1964), pp. 275–299, have the text and translation of a twelfth-century manuscript summarizing the period from the end of Herod's reign to the destruction of the Temple and including a passage about John the Baptist.

Murad Kamil, *Des Josef Ben Gorion (Josippon) Geschichte der Juden (Zêna Aïhūd) nach den Handschriften* (Diss., Tübingen 1937) (Glückstadt–Hamburg–New York 1938), is a critical edition, based on all twelve known manuscripts of the translation into Ethiopic that was made from the Arabic version some time between the twelfth and the fourteenth centuries.

The definitive edition of the eleventh-century Slavonic version of the *Jewish War* has been issued by N. A. Meščerskij, *History of the Jewish War by Josephus Flavius in the Old Russian Translation* [Russian] (Moscow 1958). In it, he joins Solomon Zeitlin, "The Slavonic Josephus and Its Relation to Josippon and Hegesippus," *JQR* 20(1929–1930):1–50, 281, in arguing against the theory of Robert Eisler, *Iesous Basileus ou Basileusas* (Heidelberg 1929) I, 221–226, and James Rendel Harris, *Josephus and His Testimony* (Cambridge 1931), that the Slavonic version is based, at least in part, on Josephus' original Aramaic. The definitive answer to Eisler's theory is by Alfons Hocherl, *Zur Übersetzungstechnik des altrussischen 'Jüdischen Krieges' des Josephus Flavius* (München 1970), who shows, on the basis of the use of such constructions as the articular infinitive, that the Slavonic version only occasionally deviates from Niese's Greek text.

We have translations into French (Viktor M. Istrin and André Vaillant, *La prise de Jérusalem de Josèphe le Juif;* trans. by Pierre Pascal, 2 vols.; Paris 1934–1938) and into German by Alexander Berendts and Konrad Grass, *Flavius Josephus, Von Jüdischen Kriege Buch I–IV, nach der slavischen Übersetzung deutsch herausgegeben und mit dem griechischen Text verglichen,* Part 1 (Dorpat 1924–1926); Part 2 (1927), but no translation into English. According to Arthur B. Posner's review (*Gnomon* 2[1926]:677–681), the German version is close to the Slavonic text but is also obscure.

As to the question whether Josephus is the author of the additions and modifications in the Slavonic version, this has usually been answered in the negative; but Gustave Bardy, "Le témoignage de Josèphe slave sur Jésus," *RA* 43(1926):344–353, declines to commit himself. Paul-Louis Couchoud, "Les textes relatifs à Jésus dans la version slave de Josèphe," *RHR* 93(1926):44–64, argues that it contains Christian interpolations, dating from the third century; and this is the view, though without commitment as to date, of John M. Creed, "The Slavonic Version of Josephus' History of the Jewish War," *HTR* 25(1932):277–319, and Nikolay K. Gudzij, "The History of the Jewish War in Old Russian Translation," *Collection of Russian Tales. Essays and Investigations* [Russian] (Moscow and Leningrad 1941), pp. 38–47. Creed says that Josephus could not possibly have composed the additions in the Slavonic version without ceasing to be a Jew (a questionable assumption in view of the great diversity of views held by various Jewish sects at the time). J. Spencer Kennard, Jr., "Gleanings from the Slavonic Josephus Controversy," *JQR* 39(1948–1949):161–170, concludes that there may be in it some elements of genuine historical tradition, and that the account of the arrest of Jesus—reconstructed by Eisler from Slavonic materials—qualifies for the kind of description found in the Jewish books known to Augustine. Indeed, there seem to have been such Jewish works, perhaps the antecedents of the *Toledoth Jeshu*, that sought to prove that the Gospels were fabricated. Kennard, "Slavonic Josephus: A Retraction," *JQR* 39(1948–1949):281–283, later recanted and admitted that if the author had been a Jew he would have written "according to the law of our fathers" not "according to the law of their fathers." We may add that a Jew could hardly have written "They [i.e., the Jews] crucified him," whereas crucifixion is a Roman, not a Jewish, mode of punishment. Indeed, Nikita A. Meščerskij, "The Importance of Old Slavic Translations for the Reconstruction of Their Archetypes (Based on the Material of Old-Russian Translation of the History of the Jewish War by Josephus Flavius)" [Russian], *Issledovaniia po slavianskomu literaturavodiia i folkloristike (= Studies in Slavonic History of Literatures and Folk-Lore;* Andrei N. Robinson, ed. [Moscow 1960], pp. 61–94), stresses that because of significant differences in style, the changes must be regarded as the original work of the translator and argues that the work was used in the ideological struggle against the Khazars, who had earlier been converted to Judaism. The stylistic basis for such a view is found in the analysis of figures of speech in the Slavonic version in relation to those in Old Russian literature generally, as has been shown by Eva Krull, "Zur Bildsprache des altrussischen Josephus Flavius" (Diss., Bonn 1959).

Josephus' Life

Uriel Rappaport, "Josephus Flavius: Notes on His Personality and His Work" [Hebrew], *Ha-Ummah* 15 (1977):89–95, has presented what amounts to almost a psychoanalysis of Josephus as a man full of contradictions. David Daube, "Typologie im Werk des Flavius Josephus" (*Bayerische Akademie der Wissenschaften. Philosophisch-historische Klasse, Sitzungsberichte*, Jahrgang 1977, Heft 6; München 1977; reprinted in *FR* 31 [1979]:59–69; translated into English as "Typology in Josephus," *JJS* 31 [1980]:18–36), has presented a very suggestive theory that Josephus' treatment of such biblical characters as Joseph, Jeremiah, Daniel, Esther, and Mordecai is affected by his self-identification with them. We may add to this list his self-identification with Saul, the defeated general.

Solomon Zeitlin, "A Survey of Jewish Historiography: From the Biblical Books to the *Sefer Ha-Kabbalah* with Special Emphasis on Josephus," *JQR* 59 (1968–1969):171–214; 60 (1969–1970):37–68, 375–406, conjectures that Josephus, because of his distinguished ancestry, had high hopes of becoming both high priest and king; but, we may comment, if this were so we would guess that his opponents would have accused him of excessive ambition and he nowhere feels the need to answer such a charge in his *Life.*

As to Josephus' boast (*V* 9) that at the age of fourteen the chief priests and leaders of the city of Jerusalem constantly consulted him with regard to the laws, Abraham Wasserstein, ed., *Flavius Josephus: Selections from His Works* (New York 1974), has noted that this is paralleled in the case of Jesus (Luke 2:46–47), who similarly, at the age of twelve, amazed onlookers with his understanding in learned discourse with the teachers in the Temple. This is indeed a traditional motif in the biographies of Moses, Homer, Aeschines, Alexander the Great, Apollonius of Rhodes, Augustus, Ovid, Nicolaus of Damascus, and Apollonius of Tyana. Léon Herrmann, "Bannoun ou Ioannoun. Félix ou Festus? (Flavius Josèphe, Vie, 11 et 13)," *REJ* 135 (1976):151–155, suggests that Luke may have been inspired by an earlier edition of Josephus' *Life;* but the earliest date that we can suggest for any version of the *Life* is 93, and Luke seems to have been written somewhat before then.

As to experiencing the three sects before selecting the best (*Life* 10–12), this, too, is a common motif, as we see in the cases of Nicolaus of Damascus, Apollonius of Tyana, Justin, and Galen. As to the discrepancy between Josephus' statement that he began his experimentation of three years with the three sects at the age of sixteen and that he completed his three years with Bannus the hermit by the time that he was nineteen, Robert J. H. Shutt, *Studies in Josephus* (London 1961) 2, n. 3, suggests emending the text in *Life* 12 and reading that Josephus spent three years with them (αὐτοῖς), that is, the three sects rather than with him (αὐτῷ) [Bannus] alone. However, this emendation seems unnecessary, since Josephus had presumably already lived as a Pharisee and as a Sadducee, and hence spent most of his time with Essenes, with whom Bannus seems to have had a close relationship.

As to the reason why Josephus, inexperienced in war and definitely not a hothead, should have been chosen by the revolutionary council in Jerusalem to be the general in Galilee, where the Romans were almost certain to attack first in their descent from Syria, Shaye J. D. Cohen, *Josephus in Galilee and Rome: His Vita and Development as a Historian* (Leiden 1979), counter to the modern trend after Richard Laqueur, *Der jüdische Historiker Flavius Josephus. Ein biographischer Versuch auf neuer quellenkritischer Grundlage* (Giessen 1920), follows Hans Drexler, "Untersuchungen zu Josephus und zur Geschichte des jüdischen Aufstandes 66–70", *Klio* 19 (1925):277–312, in regarding Josephus as a revolutionary, as he, indeed, appears in the *War*. Cohen asserts that the narrative in the *War* covering Josephus' generalship is structured not chronologically but thematically. He declares that Josephus invented a moderate faction in order to make it seem that he was not alone in his eventual defection. But, ingenious as he is, Cohen suffers from the flaw of choosing where to believe Josephus and where not to believe him. Moreover,

Josephus' letter to Jerusalem from Jotapata requesting military aid or instructions to surrender shows that Josephus was actually prepared to surrender. Cohen is followed by Sean Freyne, *Galilee from Alexander the Great to Hadrian, 323 B.C.E. to 135 C.E.: A Study of Second Temple Judaism* (South Bend, Ind. 1980), pp. 77–97, 208–255, who concludes that Josephus actively fought the Romans, though he was not outstanding in bravery or foresight. As to Josephus' lack of experience for the position of general, we may note that in antiquity, even among the Romans, generals were elected rather than trained for the position.

On the other hand, there are those, such as Aharon Kaminka, "The Work of Josephus in Galilee" [Hebrew], *Mozenaim* 13 (1941):170–176; reprinted in his *Critical Writings* (New York 1944), pp. 66–75, who justify Josephus, comparing him with Polybius (though Polybius, we should note, did not voluntarily surrender to the Romans). Isaac H. Herzog, "Something on Josephus" [Hebrew], *Sinai* 25 (1949):8–11, chief rabbi of Israel at the time, magnanimously adopts the point of view that Josephus redeemed himself in part through writing the history of the period and through defending the Jews in his *Against Apion*. Similarly, Joseph Klausner, *History of the Second Temple* [Hebrew], 5 vols. (Jerusalem 1949), despite his fervent nationalism, feels that we should not look upon Josephus as an utter traitor, that he was not a soldier but a writer, and that he saved himself in order to devote his life to the task of writing the history of his people.

The prevalent point of view, however, is that Josephus was an outright traitor. Aron Baerwald, "Flavius Josephus in Galiläa, sein Verhältniss zu den Parteien insbesondere zu Justus von Tiberias und König Agrippa II" (Diss., Breslau 1877), for example, says that there was a secret understanding between Josephus and Agrippa II whereby they both played a double game, initially hoping for a Jewish victory and the restoration of an autonomous Jewish state, but later realizing that this was impossible to attain, they turned to the Romans. Heinrich Graetz, *Geschichte der Juden,* vol. 3 (Leipzig 1856), pp. 391–419 and Pinkhos Churgin, *Studies in the time of the Second Temple* [Hebrew] (New York 1949), berate him sharply for his surrender. Ephraim E. Urbach, "The Personality of Flavius Josephus in the Light of His Account of the Burning of the Temple" [Hebrew], *Bitzaron* 7 (1942–1943):290–299, attacks Kaminka for attempting to absolve Josephus of blame in the revolt against Rome. As Roger E. Herst, "The Treachery of Josephus Flavius," *CCARJ* 19, no. 1 (1972):82–88, expresses it, Josephus' mission in Galilee was not to fight but to defuse the war. We may remark that we have every right to be suspicious of one who received such rewards from Titus as a tract of land outside Jerusalem, some sacred books (presumably Torah scrolls), the liberation of some friends, Roman citizenship, lodging in the former palace of Vespasian, and a pension. Especially damning is Josephus' remark (*V* 72) that he refused to give grain to John of Gischala since he intended to keep it either for the Romans or for his own use.

One incident in Josephus' life that has aroused much comment is his prediction (*BJ* III, 400–402) to the then-general Vespasian that he would become emperor. As a prophet, he is compared to Jeremiah by Reinhold Mayer and Christa Möller, "Josephus—Politiker und Prophet," *J-S*, pp. 271–284. Abraham Schalit, "Die Erhebung Vespasians nach Flavius Josephus, Talmud und Midrasch. Zur Geschichte einer messianischen Prophetie," *ANRW* 2.2 (1975), pp. 208–327, contends that Josephus' motive was cowardice, for without the pardon of Vespasian he would have been imprisoned after marching in the Roman triumph. Horst R. Moehring, "Joseph ben Matthia and Flavius Josephus: The Jewish Prophet and Roman Historian," *ANRW* 2.21.2 (1984), pp. 864–944, sharply attacks Schalit as arbitrary and apologetic in rejecting the evidence of Josephus and in preferring the late, tendentious account of the Talmud about Johanan ben Zakkai. The Talmud, we may remark, is a work that has the advantage of presenting divergent points of view, whereas Josephus quite obviously presents a single viewpoint.

We would be very grateful if we had the account of Josephus' great opponent, Justus of Tiberias; but unfortunately we have not a single fragment and only a few references to the latter's work. Heinrich Luther, "Josephus und Justus von Tiberias. Ein Beitrag zur Geschichte des jüdischen Aufstandes" (Diss., Halle 1910), suggests that Josephus falsely presented Justus as a supporter of the rebellion against Rome. Franz Ruhl, "Justus von Tiberias," *RhM* 71 (1916):289–308, concludes from the brief notice in Photius that if the work of Justus had come down to us we would have preferred it to that of Josephus. He finds utterly incredible Josephus' statement (*V* 355) that Agrippa II twice imprisoned him and once even ordered him to be executed. In answer, we may remark that Josephus himself (*V* 364), shortly after this passage, declares that Agrippa wrote sixty-two letters testifying to the truth of his account. Ruhl argues that the reason why Justus' work could not have been published in Titus' lifetime was that Justus had told the truth concerning the Romans and, in particular, about Titus, in contrast to Josephus, who distorted the facts in order to placate his Roman hosts. But we may remark that Justus could hardly have been court secretary to Agrippa for as many years as he was, unless he, too, had been a lackey of the Romans. Abraham Schalit, "Josephus und Justus. Studien zur Vita des Josephus," *Klio* 26 (1933):67–95, in contradiction to Richard Laqueur, *Der jüdische Historiker Flavius Josephus. Ein biographischer Versuch auf neuer quellenkritischer Grundlage* (Giessen 1920), argues that Josephus' refutation of Justus is not an interpolation in an earlier text but part of an organic whole, inasmuch as all the differences between the *Life* and the *War* can be explained by the attacks of Justus. He remarks that the repeated attempts of Justus to demean Josephus in the eyes of the Romans balance the violence of Josephus' response, but we must remark that we know Justus' views only as they have been filtered through the prism of Josephus' venom. Tessa Rajak, "Justus of Tiberias," *CQ* 23 (1973):345–368, has a balanced survey of Justus, in which she notes that the reason why his work is lost is that it lacked the great asset of Josephus, a testimonium concerning Jesus. Ben Zion Wacholder, *Eupolemus: A Study of Judaeo-Greek Literature* (Cincinnati 1974), pp. 288–306, implies that Justus' work is preferable to that of Josephus and suggests that the third-century Sextus Julius Africanus followed Justus in treating Herod more fairly than did Josephus and that Justus was more objective in treating Agrippa II; but these are mere conjectures, since we have no fragments of his work. Shaye J. D. Cohen, *Josephus in Galilee and Rome: His Vita and Devlopment as a Historian* (Leiden 1979), suggests that Justus wrote his history to support Tiberias' appeal for autonomy and for meaningful territories, but there is no concrete evidence in Josephus to support this. Indeed, the latest treatment by Yaron Dan, "Josephus Flavius and Justus of Tiberias" [Hebrews], *CP* (1982):57–78, plausibly concludes that Josephus and Justus were actually similar both in their attitudes to the Romans and in their conceptions of historiography. They were rivals, we may suggest, precisely because they were so similar in their outlooks.

Book-Length Studies on Josephus

Though he did not write a work on Josephus as such, Heinrich Graetz, *Geschichte der Juden von den ältesten Zeiten bis auf die Gegenwart,* 11 vols. Leipzig 1853–1875), especially vol. 3.2, deals at length with Josephus. See particularly pp. 483–500 on Josephus' life, character, and role in the war against Rome; pp. 553–558 on Josephus' writings; and pp. 559–844 containing thirty appendices on various specific topics, mostly dealing with Josephus. In view of Graetz's strong nationalistic feeling it is not surprising that he has a vehement personal attack on Josephus as a traitor devoid of conscience, though he does distinguish between Josephus the man and Josephus the writer and defender of Judaism in *Against Apion*. Because of the author's exhaustive scholarship and lively style, this work has had a more profound impact on Jewish readers than any other history of the Jews and has been published in numerous translations and editions, despite its inconsistencies, sentimentalism, apologetics, and disregard of social and economic factors.

The monumental work of Emil Schürer, *Geschichte des jüdischen Volkes im Zeitalter Jesu Christi,* 3 vols. (Leipzig 1886–1901; 3d–4th ed., Leipzig 1901–1909); new English version revised and edited by Geza Vermes, Fergus Millar, and Martin Goodman (vol. 3), *The History of the Jewish People in the Age of Jesus of Christ (175 B.C.–A.D.,135),* 3 vols. Edinburgh 1973–1986), in the revised English version, has been modified especially with regard to the divergent sects of Judaism and is more charitable toward the Talmud vis-à-vis Josephus. This is really a new work, which takes full account of the latest archaeological and epigraphical discoveries, as well as of all principal secondary scholarship.

Bernhard Brüne, *Josephus der Geschichtsschreiber des heiligen Krieges und seine Vaterstadt Jerusalem. Mit Angabe der Quellen dargestellt und untersucht* (Wiesbaden 1912), commenting on Josephus' life, works, theology, philosophy, and language, attempts, in particular, to show statistically which words Josephus took from Herodotus, Thucydides, and Polybius, and which New Testament authors might have known the works of Josephus. He fails to realize, however, that agreement in familiar words does not prove literary influence. In a second book that suffers from bad arrangement, *Flavius Josephus und seine Schriften in ihrem Verhältnis zum Judentume, zur griechisch-römischer Welt und zum Christentume mit griechischer Wortkonkordanz zum Neuen Testamente und I. Clemensbriefe nebst Sach- und Namen-Verzeichnis* (Gütersloh 1913), Brüne surveys Josephus' life, theology, relation to the Graeco-Roman world of ideas, and relation to Christianity. The work emphasizes the resemblances in diction between Josephus and Polybius and, to a lesser degree, Herodotus, Thucydides, Xenophon, Plato, Aristotle, and the Stoics, but is uncritical in listing words that are hardly distinctive to those authors. As to his religious views, Josephus emerges as an advocate of both faith and reason, a quasi-Pharisee whose rationalism is Platonic-Pythagorean.

Norman Bentwich, *Josephus* (Philadelphia 1914), has a popular survey of Josephus' life and works, including especially his relationship to his predecessors.

Gustav Hölscher, "Josephus," *RE* (1916), vol. 9, pp. 1934–2000, in what remains the most influential general survey of Josephus, deals especially with Josephus' sources, contending, in particular, that for the *Antiquities* Josephus made uncritical use of an intermediate lost Hellenistic Midrash. This reflects the prevalent tendency in scholarship of that era, largely discredited today, to regard it as unlikely that an ancient author would have used more than one source at a time because of the difficulty in consulting several manuscripts at once.

The most original and most challenging book on Josephus remains that by Richard Laqueur, *Der jüdische Historiker Flavius Josephus. Ein biographischer Versuch auf neuer quellenkritischer Grundlage* (Giessen 1920), who concludes that Josephus' works reflect the circumstances of the time when he wrote them, a point developed by Seth Schwartz, *Josephus and Judaism from 70 to 100 of the Common Era* (diss., Columbia Univ., 1985). Laqueur postulates, in particular, that the *Life*, his administrative report, is reliable but that the *War* is a tendentious version. His contention that various portions of the

Life were written more than thirty years apart can surely be challenged on the ground that, from the point of view of vocabulary and style, the work has unity. As to the places where the *Antiquities* parallels the *War,* Laqueur contends, for example, that Josephus rewrote his account of Herod because, with the passage of time, he became more nationalistic; however, we may suggest that a factor of at least equal significance may have been that he had an additional source, which was more negative toward Herod. Laqueur's most famous and most controversial theory is that Josephus revised his *Antiquities* in order to win a following among the Christians by inserting a highly complimentary passage about Jesus. However, we may comment, there is no evidence that Josephus was in need of such a market, since he had a very comfortable pension and probably would have further antagonized his much larger potential Jewish audience.

Frederick J. Foakes-Jackson, *Josephus and the Jews: The Religion and History of the Jews as Explained by Flavius Josephus* (London 1930), in a popular handbook, summarizes for seminary students Josephus' remarks about the Jewish history and religion.

Leon Bernstein, *Flavius Josephus: His Time and His Critics* (New York 1938), in a popular work written with utmost passion in defense of Josephus and with venom against those who attack him, is an amateur who admits his incompetence in handling texts in the ancient languages.

Yitzhak I. Halevy (Rabinowitz), *Dorot Ha-rishonim* [Hebrew] (*Generations of Old*), vol. 4, part 1: *The Last Period of the Second Temple: The Time of the Roman Procurators and the War,* Moshe Auerbach, ed. (Benei Beraq 1964), in a posthumous work by a great rabbinic scholar, is highly critical of Josephus as a source.

Edward R. Levenson, "New Tendentious Motifs in Antiquities: A Study of Development in Josephus' Historical Thought" (M.A. diss., Columbia University 1966), in effect, continues Laqueur's approach, contending that the discrepancies between *War* I–II and *Antiquities* 12–20, which parallel each other, are largely due to the different circumstances in which Josephus found himself when he wrote the two works.

In what remains the fairest and most comprehensive survey in English, Henry St. John Thackeray, *Josephus: The Man and the Historian* (New York 1929, 1967), in a semipopular work, surveys the life and works of Josephus. His most original theory, that Josephus employed an assistant particularly well versed in Sophocles for Books 15 and 16 of the *Antiquities* and an assistant particularly well versed in Thucydides for Books 17 to 19 is highly questionable, now that we see, from the completion of the concordance to Josephus, that Sophoclean and Thucydidean words and motifs appear throughout his works. Thackeray, moreover, was unduly influenced by Eisler in accepting the view as to how the *Testimonium Flavianum* was interpolated by Christians.

Robert J. H. Shutt, *Studies in Josphus* (London 1961), is concerned primarily with the relationship between Josephus' language and style and those of Nicolaus of Damascus, Dionysius of Halicarnassus, Polybius, and Strabo. The book is methodologically flawed, since many of the words cited are hardly unique with those authors.

Solomon Zeitlin, *The Rise and Fall of the Judean State: A Political, Social and Religious History of the Second Commonwealth*, 3 vols. (Philadelphia 1962–1978), the culmination of his life's work, in effect, is an extended commentary on Josephus. Volume 3, pp. 385–417, has a biographical essay on Josephus, surveying his life and works, in which he concludes that Josephus was motivated by a genuine desire to save his people. The work, marked by frequent stimulating, original insights, however, is marred by the idiosyncratic views of the author.

Geoffrey A. Williamson, *The World of Josephus* (London 1964), is a popular lively account that attacks Josephus as a self-righteous traitor. The attention given to Josephus' attitude to Christianity is clearly out of line with the interest which Josephus himself shows.

Abraham Schalit, *Zur Josephusforschung* (Darmstadt 1973), is a collection of essays (in some cases, chapters of books), originally published between 1900 and 1965 by Willrich (2), Norden, Laqueur, Thackeray, Moore, Schlatter, Bickerman (2), Collomp, Grintz, and Schalit (2). The essays, with the exception of that by Grintz, are highly significant, though one would have expected a portion of Hölscher's essay in Pauly-Wissowa.

I have seen only a portion of Tessa Rajak, "Flavius Josephus: Jewish History and the Greek World" (Ph.D. diss., University of Oxford 1974, 2 vols.). In it, she discusses Josephus' education and formation; Josephus and the Greek language; Josephus' writings on the Jewish revolt; the two accounts of the campaign in Galilee; the setting of the *Antiquities;* Josephus and the Greek Bible; Josephus' Moses; and the three conquests of Jerusalem. Also, there are appendices on the native language of Josephus; correspondences and contrasts between Josephus' *Life* and *War;* evidence of Josephus' dependence on the Greek *Esther;* the chronology of the return of the Jews from Babylon: connections by Josephus of the biblical versions; *Antiquities* 2–3, and the Septuagint version of Exodus; Posidonius' view of Judaism: the evidence of *Against Apion;* and an emendation of the text of *Antiquities* 13, 262, and the interpretation of the Roman decree in favor of John Hyrcanus.

Otto Betz et al., *Josephus-Studien: Untersuchungen zu Josephus, dem antiken Judentum und dem Neuen Testament Otto Michel zum 70. Geburtstag gewidmet* (Göttingen 1974) is a collection of twenty-three essays particularly concerned with Josephus' religious views and his relationship to the thought of his time.

Shaye J. D. Cohen, *Josephus in Galilee and Rome: His Vita and Devel-*

opment as a Historian (Leiden 1979), has written the most challenging and most controversial book since Laqueur, to whom he is much indebted in approach. In it, he suggests that Josephus used a preliminary draft for both the *War* and the *Life*, but that he modified it less in the *Life*. However, we may object, first, that the whole theory is speculative since we have not a single fragment of the memoir, and second, that if so, Josephus might have been expected to use the document for all the material common to the *War* and the *Life*. Cohen contends that Josephus, in writing his *Life*, followed standard Greek practice in seeking a thematic narrative rather than adhering to strict chronology, that he has a predilection for *topoi*, that in his works we may see the development of Josephus from a Roman apologist to a religious nationalist who sought to conciliate the Pharisaic leaders in Yavneh, and that Josephus is a sloppy writer who is frequently confused, obscure, and contradictory. We may object that even if Josephus has frequent *topoi* (yet he is much more than a cento, we must add, of the motifs later noted by Lucian), this does not necessarily prove that the facts behind them are invented, and that closer attention to Josephus' narrative, particularly in the earlier books of the *Antiquities*, where we can check him against his biblical and midrashic sources, indicates a consistency of approach and a deeply personalized imprint, as I have tried to show in a number of essays listed later. As to Josephus' catering to Pharisaic influence in the *Antiquities*, Cohen himself is forced to admit that there are several passages (e.g., *A* XIII, 41ff.) that are very negative toward the Pharisees.

Uriel Rappaport, ed., *Collected Papers: Josephus Flavius—Historian of Eretz-Israel in the Hellenistic-Roman Period* [Hebrew] (Jerusalem 1982), contains a series of essays on Josephus, the general theme of which seems to be the question of how reliable Josephus is as a historian. There is also an unannotated bibliography of Josephus for the years 1976–1981 compiled by Menahem Mor and Rappaport.

Tessa Rajak, *Josephus: The Historian and His Society* (London 1983), interprets Josephus' social, educational, and linguistic background in the light of what can be known about his contemporaries and their attitudes. Examining the character of the first century as a social and intellectual phenomenon, she seeks to cast light on the cultural and social history of the Roman Empire. The book focuses on the Jewish revolt against the Romans, which the author interprets in the comparative light of other revolutions. It is a useful, if much less challenging, corrective to Cohen's book.

My own "Flavius Josephus Revisited: the Man, His Writings, and His Significance," *ANRW* 2.21.2 (1984):763–862, in effect, is a comprehensive update of Thackeray's volume. I conclude that the most important achievements in Josephan scholarship since the middle of this century have been Schreckenberg's bibliographies, Flusser's edition of Josippon, the laying of the groundwork for a new edition of the Greek text by Schreckenberg, various interpretative articles on Josephus' version of the Bible, Pines' monograph on Agapius' and Michael the Syrian's versions of the *Testimonium Flavianum*, the findings by archaeologists (notably by Yadin at Masada) that enable us to check up on Josephus' statements, and Rengstorf's concordance.

A comprehensive collection of fifty-two essays by various scholars, some of them reprinted from previous publications but most commissioned especially for this work, plus a long, selected, and critical bibliography of Josephus (from the beginning of scholarship to the present) by me and critical discussions of the various essays by Gohei Hata, has appeared in Japanese, edited by Hata and me, *Josephan Studies*, 4 vols. (Tokyo 1985–1986). The following twenty-one essays from this collection, all of them original, have been published in English in *Josephus, Judaism, and Christianity*, edited by me and Hata (Detroit 1987), with a lengthy introductory essay discussing each of the essays. The essays include Menahem Stern, "Josephus and the Roman Empire as Reflected in The Jewish War"; Tessa Rajak, "Josephus and Justus of Tiberias"; David J. Ladouceur, "Josephus and Masada"; E. Mary Smallwood, "Philo and Josephus as Historians of the Same Events"; Louis H. Feldman, "Hellenizations in Josephus' *Jewish Antiquities:* The Portrait of Abraham"; James L. Bailey, "Josephus' Portrayal of the Matriarchs"; Gohei Hata, "The Story of Moses Interpreted Within the Context of Anti-Semitism"; David M. Goldenberg, "*Antiquities* IV, 277 and 288 Compared with Early Rabbinic Law"; Otto Betz, "Miracles in the Writings of Josephus"; Morton Smith, "The Occult in Josephus"; R. J. Coggins, "The Samaritans in Josephus"; Jacob Neusner, "Josephus' Pharisees: A Complete Repertoire"; Lawrence H. Schiffman, "The Conversion of the Royal House of Adiabene in Josephus and Rabbinic Sources"; Heinz Schreckenberg, "The Works of Josephus and the Early Christian Church"; Wataru Mizugaki, "Origen and Josephus"; Zvi Baras, "The *Testimonium Flavianum* and the Martyrdom of James"; Albert A. Bell, Jr., "Josephus and Pseudo-Hegesippus"; Steven Bowman, "Josephus in Byzantium"; David Flusser, "Josippon: A Medieval Hebrew Version of Josephus"; Guy N. Deutsch, "The Illustration of Josephus' Manuscripts"; and Betsy H. Amaru, "Martin Luther and Josephus."

Shorter General Accounts of Josephus' Life and Works

The best of the short accounts of Josephus, especially in its views on Josephus' sources for the biblical period, on Josephus' religious views, and on Josephus' standing as a historian and on the manuscript tradition is Benedictus Niese, "Der jüdische Historiker Josephus," *HZ* 40 (1896):193–237; translated into English as "Josephus," *HERE* 7 (1914):569–579; the English version includes an extensive note by Louis H. Gray on the *Testimonium Flavianum*.

Pinkhos Churgin, *Studies in the Time of the Second Temple* [Hebrew] (New York 1949) pp. 274–370, is a systematic treatment of Josephus, especially of his relation to the Bible in the *Antiquities*. He is particularly valuable for his notice of midrashic parallels.

Salo W. Baron, *A Social and Religious History of the Jews,* 2d ed., vols. 1 and 2 (New York 1952), is a very judicious survey, thoroughly annotated with reference to primary and secondary sources, which very often refers to Josephus.

Tobias (Tubiah) J. Tavyomi (Tavyoemy), "Josephus Flavius" [Hebrew], *Memorial Volume to Yitzhak Isaac Halevy,* Moshe Auerbach, ed., Part 1 (Benei Beraq 1964), pp. 306–334, is a survey with an intemperate attack on Josephus.

Among articles in encyclopedias, the best are those by Abraham Schalit, "Josephus Flavius" [Hebrew], *Encyclopaedia Hebraica* (1968), vol. 19, pp. 681–690, and "Josephus Flavius," *EJ* (1971), vol. 10, pp. 251–263, 265. Both are comprehensive critical surveys and are especially concerned with Josephus' documentary and literary sources, with the principles professed by Josephus and defects in his works, and with Josephus' importance as a writer and a historian.

Pierre Vidal-Naquet, *Flavius Josephus ou du bon Usage de la Trahison* (Preface à 'La guerre des Juifs') (Paris 1977), pp. 9–115, summarizes the historical period of the war against the Romans, the life and personality of Josephus, and especially the episode at Jotapata.

Horst R. Moehring, "Joseph ben Matthia and Flavius Josephus: The Jewish Prophet and Roman Historian," *ANRW* 2.21.2 (1984), pp. 864–944, attempts to rehabilitate Josephus by contending that the attitude toward Rome of Josephus, like that of the rabbis of Yavneh, in principle, was positive, and that this political realism places Josephus in closer proximity to such prophetic figures as Jeremiah than to the apocalyptic dreamers, such as the fanatics of 66. We may reply, however, by noting that although the rabbis were realistic in their attitude toward Rome they generally despised the government and the society and their immorality and excessiveness, whereas Josephus avoided such expression.

Josephus' Conception of Historiography

In an important article, Isaak Heinemann, "Josephus' Method in the Presentation of Jewish Antiquities" [Hebrew], *Zion* 5 (1940):180–203, aims to set forth the method of Josephus in describing the antiquities of his people, to indicate the nature of this method by comparison with other Palestinian and

Hellenistic haggadists, and to determine the extent of his originality. Josephus, he says, employs the methods used by the great Greek historians, especially Dionysius of Halicarnassus, and also follows the Hellenistic Jewish authors who preceded him, especially as regards the objects of the precepts. Josephus, he concludes, spoke to the Greeks as a Greek more than did the Apostle Paul, as seen particularly in the Hellenization of his biblical portraits.

Paul Collomp, "La place de Josèphe dans la technique de l'historiographie helleñistique, *Publications de la Faculté des Lettres de l'Université Strasbourg* 106 (Mélanges 1945, 3: *Études historiques;* Paris 1947), pp. 81–92, concludes that Josephus, though resembling Dionysius of Halicarnassus in his conception of historiography, is closer to Polybius in his condemnation of those who diverge from the truth, but that Josephus' theory is better than his practice. We may remark that Collomp takes too seriously Josephus' attacks on Greek historiography in *Against Apion,* which is an apologetic work.

In a significant work, Gert Avenarius, *Lukians Schrift zur Geschichtsschreibung* (Meisenheim 1956), notes that the historiographical commonplaces in Lucian, *Quomodo Historia Conscribenda Sit,* are paralleled in many historians, including Josephus, and that many of them originate in Isocratean rhetoric.

Solomon Zeitlin, "A Survey of Jewish Historiography: From the Biblical Books to the *Sefer ha-Kabbalah* with Special Emphasis on Josephus," *JQR* 59 (1968–1969):171–214; 60 (1969–1970):37–68, 375–406, concludes that Josephus' statement of facts is reliable but that his interpretation of facts is subjective.

Willem C. van Unnik, *Flavius Josephus als historischer Schriftsteller: Franz Delitzsch-Vorlesungen 1972* (Heidelberg 1978), contains essays assessing research on Josephus, interpreting the phrase that Josephus has neither added nor subtracted anything in his account of the biblical period, exploring the meaning of prophecy in Josephus (he saw his own prototype in Jeremiah), and noting the significance of Josephus for the exposition of the New Testament. In his review, David Goldenberg, "Josephus Flavius or Joseph ben Mattithiah," *JQR* 70 (1979–1980):178–182, remarks that van Unnik cites only Hellenistic authors and neglects Josephus' rabbinic sources. This is a valid comment, though we should note that Josephus almost never cites the names of the rabbis of his time.

Daniel R. Schwartz, "Josephus on Jewish Constitutions and Community," *SCI* 7 (1983–1984):30–52, suggests that Josephus' terminology to designate the Jewish constitution at various stages of the nation's history reflects a well-thought-out, consistent theory regarding the political situation of the Jewish nation. However, as Schwartz himself admits, Josephus contradicts himself, designating the period of the Judges at one point an aristocracy (*A* VI, 36, 84–85, 268) and at another point a monarchy (*A* XX, 229), and the period between the return from Babylonian Captivity until the Hasmoneans at one point an aristocracy (*A* XI, 11) and at another point a democracy (*A* XX, 234). These may reflect different sources, but more likely, as Schwartz suggests, they reflect a gap in time between the period when he composed the earlier part of the *Antiquities* and a later period, perhaps due to a change in historical circumstances.

Pere Villalba i Varneda, *The Historical Method of Flavius Josephus* (Leiden 1986), a revised version in English of his dissertation in Spanish, *El metode historico de Flavi Josep* (University of Barcelona 1981), is largely a study based on Josephus' vocabulary for causality and an analysis of his art of narration. Unfortunately, the author does relatively little to set Josephus within the framework of the historiographical theories of his time; in particular, we should like to know how his paraphrase of the Bible compares in style with that of the Septuagint and to what extent Josephus lives up to the historiographical theory enunciated at such length by Dionysius of Halicarnassus and somewhat later by Lucian, topics that the author deals with only in passing. One can hardly isolate those elements that are peculiarly Josephan, as the author attempts to do, unless one has first made a thorough preliminary study of his antecedents, as he does not do. Nor does the author do much to explain the wide variation in style in the various parts of Josephus' corpus.

Josephus' Biblical Text and Canon

No systematic study of Josephus's biblical *Vorlage* has yet been made. Assertions range from the statement of Gustav Tachauer, *Das Verhältniss von Flavius Josephus zur Bibel und Tradition* (Erlangen 1871), that Josephus employed only a Hebrew text, and that of Abraham Schalit, *Namenwörterbuch zu Flavius Josephus,* in *A Complete Concordance to Flavius Josephus,* Karl-Heinrich Rengstorf, ed. Supplement 1 (Leiden 1968), that Josephus used only a Greek Bible. To complicate the matter, apparently, at the time of Josephus, there were a number of divergent Hebrew and Greek texts of the Bible, as the Dead Sea fragments show.

The only attempt to study the question for even a portion of the Pentateuch is Robert J. H. Shutt, "Biblical Names and Their Meanings in Josephus, Jewish Antiquities, Books I and II, 1–200," *JSJ* 2 (1971):167–182, who notes that in four cases Josephus' names follow the Hebrew text rather than the Septuagint, in twenty-five cases he follows the Septuagint rather than the Hebrew, in six cases his discussions or interpretations of names follow the Hebrew rather than the Septuagint, in fourteen cases his discussions follow the Septuagint rather than the Hebrew, in twenty cases he is independent of both, and in sixteen other cases he is apparently independent. But Shutt does not consider systematically the various manuscripts of the Septuagint or the possibility that the gap between the Septuagint and the Hebrew text may not, to judge from the Dead Sea fragments, have been as great in Josephus' day as in our own. Furthermore, we may suggest that a Greek form in proper names may reflect the fact that Josephus is writing in Greek or that he or his alleged literary assistants Hellenized the form of Hebrew proper names.

In his paraphrase of Joshua, according to Adam Mez, *Die Bibel des Josephus untersucht für Buch V–VII der Archäologie* (Basel 1895), Josephus stands very close to the Masoretic text, in Judges his text is mixed, but for Samuel Josephus follows the Lucianic text, including Lucian's errors. But Sebastian P. Brock, *The Recensions of the Septuagint Version of I Samuel* (Ph.D. diss., Oxford University 1966), argues that Mez made vastly exaggerated claims for the Ur-Lucianic character of Josephus' text and notes that of the thirty examples adduced by Mez in support of his theory only nine are actually valid and that, when Josephus agrees with Lucian against the Septuagint, his changes may often be explained as conforming to sense. The fact, we may add, that most of Mez's evidence is from Josephus' spelling of proper names and from the numbers that he cites weakens his case because it is precisely in such details that copyists are most likely to make corrections to bring a text into accord with preconceived data. Mez, moreover, does not note the degree to which Josephus disagrees with Lucian, agrees with the Masoretic text, or is unique in agreeing with no text.

A crucial new element in the equation has been introduced by Eugene C. Ulrich, *The Qumran Text of Samuel and Josephus* (Missoula 1978), who offers a number of examples from the Dead Sea fragments of Samuel to prove that Josephus used a Greek rather than a Hebrew text for I and II Samuel. This Greek text, he suggests, following his teacher Cross, was revised so as to conform to the Hebrew text as found in the Dead Sea fragments, the so-called Palestinian text found also in the Chronicler, in Pseudo-Philo's *Biblical Antiquities*, in Lucian, and in the sixth column of Origen's Hexapla. We may remark, however, that Ulrich does not include in his study the more fragmentary manuscripts, 4QSam[b] and 4QSam[c], but only the segment 4QSam[a]. Emanuel Tov, "The Textual Affiliations of 4QSam[a]," *JSOT* 14 (1979):37–53, concludes that the Dead Sea manuscript of Samuel and the Septuagint version are independent of each other but that the former is close to the Septuagint and to Josephus' biblical text. T. Muraoka, "The Greek Text of 2 Samuel 11 in the Lucianic Manuscripts," *Abr-Nahrain* 20 (1981–1982):37–59, cites at least one case (II Samuel 11:8) when Josephus is evidently not dependent on the Greek. Others, notably Alessandro Catastini, "Su alcune varianti qumraniche nel testo di Samuele," *Henoch* 2 (1980):267–284, and Julio Trebolle, "El estudio de 4QSam[a]: Implicationes exegaticas e historicas," *EB* 39 (1981):5–18, have shown appreciation of the importance of Ulrich's work, the former noting that some of the readings of the Samuel scroll are earlier than the priestly version (P) of the Masoretic text, and the latter remarking that, in the light of the Dead Sea manuscript of Samuel, the discrepancies between the Masoretic text and the Septuagint cannot be explained by positing a Palestinian *Vorlage* of a non-Masoretic type rather than by postulating that the Septuagint shows targumic-midrashic elements. We may remark that it seems hard to believe that Josephus would have ceased to consult the Hebrew text so suddenly and so utterly, especially since he must have heard portions of Samuel, seven selections from which are included in the annual cycle, in the synagogue on Sabbaths and holy days during readings of the Haftaroth, a practice going back to Temple times.

George E. Howard, "Kaige Readings in Josephus," *Textus* 8 (1973):45– 54, shows that in fifteen places Josephus agrees with manuscripts boc$_2$e$_2$, which, according to Dominique Barthélemy, *Les Devanciers d'Aquila* (Leiden 1963), are not a Lucianic recension but the old Septuagint, and concludes that Josephus relies upon at least two types of Greek manuscripts, those of boc$_2$e$_2$ and *Kaige*. We may equally well suggest, however, that Josephus had before him both a Hebrew text and a Greek text. Furthermore, the Hebrew text was close to the present Masoretic text, whereas the Greek text was of the boc$_2$e$_2$ type, since of the sixteen passages where Josephus agrees with the *Kaige* type he agrees with the Masoretic text in thirteen places.

For his account of Solomon, Harry E. Faber van der Meulen, "Das Salomo-Bild im hellenistisch–jüdischen Schrifttum" (Diss., Kampen 1978), concludes that Josephus used a Greek translation of the Bible that was close to the Masoretic text, though he may have used more than one such translation, checking them against the Hebrew text.

Frederick F. Bruce, "Josephus and Daniel," *ASTI* 4 (1965):148–162, declares that Josephus' version of Daniel is based almost entirely on the contents of the Hebrew-Aramaic text and that he did not know at all the additions found in the Septuagint.

Nisan Ararat, "Ezra and His Deeds in the Sources" [Hebrew] (Diss., Yeshiva University 1971), postulates a "Comprehensive Chronicle" as the source of Josephus' account of Ezra, as well as the Hebrew and Greek Ezra, the apocryphal I Esdras, and the rabbinic legends pertaining to this era. We may reply, however, that there is not a single fragment in existence from such a work. It seems more reasonable to assume that Josephus proceeded here as elsewhere with texts in Hebrew, Aramaic, and Greek before him that are not before us.

For the book of Esther, Josephus clearly used a Greek text, presumably because he found it stylistically on a more polished level than the rest of the

Greek Bible. Bacchisio R. Motzo, "Il testo di Ester in Giuseppe," *Studi e Materiali di Storia delle Religioni* 4 (1928):84–105, cites evidence, in Josephus' text, of kinship (though not of identity) with the major groups of manuscripts of the Septuagint.

As to the canon, Rudolf Meyer, "Bemerkungen zum literargeschichtlichen Hintergrund der Kanontheorie des Josephus," *J-S*, pp. 285–299, says that the Qumran discoveries show that it was still fluid at the time. We may reply, however, that the Qumran community was sectarian and consequently may have had a different canon.

In a definitive work, Sid Z. Leiman, *The Canonization of Hebrew Scripture: The Talmudic and Midrashic Evidence* (Hamden 1976), pp. 31–34, comments that *Against Apion* I, 37–43 is the first evidence of a closed canon of Hebrew Scripture and contends that Josephus' reference to twenty-two books corresponds precisely to the twenty-four books of the talmudic canon (Judges and Ruth are a single book, as are Jeremiah and Lamentations), and that Josephus implies that the canon had been closed for a long time. He suggests that Josephus' actual arrangement of the biblical books is ad hoc and was designed specifically for the readers of *Against Apion;* but we may reply that in an apologetic work one must be especially careful about one's facts, lest one be open to one's opponents' charge of misrepresentation.

Josephus' Treatment of the
Biblical Period: General

Louis Ginzberg, *Legends of the Jews,* 7 volumes (Philadelphia 1909–1938), frequently cites Josephus in his notes as paralleling rabbinic Midrashim, Philo, Pseudo-Philo's *Biblical Antiquities,* and the church fathers. Bernhard Heller, "Ginzberg's Legends of the Jews," *JQR* 24 (1933–1934): 175–184, has an extensive summary of Ginzberg's use of Josephus. However, despite the excellent beginning that Ginzberg made, he missed far more than he noted and, moreover, usually failed to indicate the differences between Josephus and the rabbinic Midrashim.

Salomo Rappaport, *Agada und Exegese bei Flavius Josephus* (Wien 1930), has attempted to be exhaustive in noting rabbinic parallels, but although he has far more than Ginzberg, he also has missed many; and, moreover, he suffers from having tried too hard to find parallels where none exist. Rappaport explains differences by noting that Josephus had lost contact with the country of his origin, Palestine, for twenty-five years; but we may suggest that Josephus may well have had some contact, because of his closeness to the emperors and to the various rabbinic delegates who came to Rome and who hence may have refreshed his memory. He argues against Hölscher's theory of an intermediate Hellenistic Midrash as a source and suggests, rather, that Josephus had a targum at his disposal. We may remark, however, that Rappaport fails to consider that many of the modifications of Josephus, as well as his decision on whether to include Midrashim at any given point, may be due to a conscious appeal to his audience of Greek-speaking Jews and non-Jews.

Bernhard Heller, "Grundzüge der Aggada des Flavius Josephus," *MGWJ* 80 (1936):237–246, 363, suggests that Josephus' haggadic remarks are based on his personal background and that he portrays his biblical heroes from the standpoint of his own time.

In two significant works, Martin Braun, *Grieschische Roman und hellenistische Geschichtsschreibung* (Frankfurt am Main 1934) and *History and Romance in Graeco-Oriental Literature* (Oxford 1938), discusses, though with some exaggeration, the erotic-novelistic elements in Josephus' paraphrase of the Bible against the background of Hellenistic historiography. In particular, he compares Josephus' treatment of the story of Joseph and Potiphar's wife with the similar motif in Euripides' play *Hippolytus* and in later Greek novels. He concludes that whereas Josephus Hellenizes the biblical narrative, the testament of Joseph, which treats the same episode, Judaizes alien elements.

Abraham Schalit, "Hellenistic Literary and Apologetic Motifs in Josephus' *Jewish Antiquities*" [Hebrew], *Moznaim,* o. s. 16 (1943):205–210, on the other hand, concludes that in Josephus' paraphrase of the Bible the shell is Hellenistic but the inner core is Jewish. Similarly, Aaron Mirsky, "Biblical Explanations in the *Jewish Antiquities* of Flavius Josephus" [Hebrew], *Sinai* 22 (1948):282–287, attempts to show that passages in Josephus that apparently contradict the Bible really do not.

We should like to have a complete inventory of the places where Josephus differs from the Bible or, at least, from the Pentateuch; but the one attempt to do this, Ronald B. Sobel, *Josephus' Conception of History in Relationship to the Pentateuch as a Source of Historical Data* (M.A. rabbinical thesis, Hebrew Union College 1962), is far from complete, is based on an English translation of Josephus, does little to explain the differences, and fails to consider Greek influences working upon Josephus.

Naomi G. Cohen, "Josephus and Scripture: Is Josephus' Treatment of the Scriptural Narrative Similar throughout the Antiquities I–XI?" *JQR* 54 (1963–1964):311–332, on the basis of an examination of a brief selection of from one to three paragraphs in each of the first eleven books of the *Antiquities,* concludes that Josephus is much freer in vocabulary, style, order, and content in Books 1 through 5 than he is in Books 6 through 11 in paraphrasing the Bible. She concludes that Josephus' source is a Hellenistic Midrash that is more elaborate for the Pentateuch than for the other books of the Bible and that Josephus is answering anti-Semites who drew chiefly upon the Pentateuch.

We may suggest, as an alternative explanation, however, that Josephus may have drawn upon a targum or Midrashim, which were much fuller for the Pentateuch than for the rest of the Bible, inasmuch as this portion of the Bible was read and expounded each week in the synagogue.

Carl R. Holladay, *'Theios Aner' in Hellenistic Judaism: A Critique of the Use of This Category in New Testament Christology* (Missoula 1977), pp. 47–62, commenting on Josephus' treatment of Abraham, Joseph, Moses, David, and Solomon, concludes that Josephus' treatment of these figures is strikingly uniform, that their characteristics are those of Stoic sages, and that Josephus is particularly indebted in his portrayal of them to popular, semiphilosophical ethics.

Harold W. Attridge, *The Interpretation of Biblical History in the Antiquitates Judaicae of Flavius Josephus* (Missoula 1976), through an examination of Josephus' paraphrase of Scripture, attempts to present him as a theological thinker. Josephus, he says, deliberately followed Greek historiographical models, notably Dionysius of Halicarnassus, in producing an apologetic and propagandistic type of history; but he added the themes of the reality of God's retributive providence and of the moral relevance of the Jewish truth. He contends that Josephus' personal experience in the Jewish revolt and in the life of the Diaspora was chiefly responsible for his particular brand of covenant theology. But, we may reply, theology was of no particular concern to the talmudic rabbis in whose midst Josephus was raised; and Josephus himself (*A* I, 25) asserts that he is postponing a profound philosophical work that will explain the reasons for Jewish beliefs; hence, that work is not the *Antiquities*. We may note, moreover, that in his paraphrase of Aristeas, Esdras, and I Maccabees, Josephus does not generally add theologizing. Finally, his relationship to his Roman patrons may explain why he avoids discussions of eschatology and other theological issues.

Judith R. Baskin, *Pharaoh's Counsellors: Job, Jethro, and Balaam in Rabbinic and Patristic Tradition* (Chico 1983), notes that the identification of Jethro and Balaam as Gentiles did not play an important part in either Philo's or Josephus' discussions of the passages in which they appear. Since Josephus is writing for a predominantly Gentile audience, he is more concerned with presenting Jewish history and belief in a favorable light and, unlike the rabbis, does not reflect the practices and attitudes of an established religious community.

David Daube, "Typology in Josephus," *JJS* 31 (1980):18–36, explains Josephus' modifications of the Bible by stressing that he identified himself with such figures as Joseph, Jeremiah, Daniel, Esther, and Mordecai as one with prophetic powers who had suffered for his people. We may also add that his very deep interest in Saul, to whose encomium he devotes approximately three times as much space (*A* VI, 343–350) as to the encomium of Moses, may be due to the fact that Josephus, too, had been a general and had been confronted with the spectre of suicide.

Betsy H. Amaru, "Land Theology in Josephus' Jewish Antiquities," *JQR* 71 (1980–1981), pp. 201–229, comments that Josephus was influenced by his aversion to the contemporary revolt of the revolutionaries against Rome and consequently shifted the stress, in his paraphrase of the Bible, from the covenanted land of Israel, which was so central to the revolutionaries, to the biblical personalities themselves, to the role of the Diaspora, and to the great increase in Jewish population due to proselytism. His moral is that disobedience of the law leads to expulsion or dispersion without a covenant-rooted ingathering of exiles; and there is no link with, or even mention of, a messiah out of the house of David.

Tessa Rajak, "Josephus and the 'Archaeology' of the Jews," *JJS* 33 (1982):465–477, comments on the meaning of the title of Josephus' *Antiquities,* which differs from other works with such a title in that Josephus' goal is not to rearrange and criticize ancient memories but to transmit the texts unaltered. The justification for Josephus' rewriting of biblical history, in contrast with the goal of pagan histories, was that it had been ignored by others. We may comment that in distinguishing the goals and methods of the *War* and the *Antiquities,* it might have been useful to consider the distinction drawn in Cicero's *Ad Familiares* 5.12 between a monograph and a history: in the former, the tradition permitted latitude with the truth.

One problem on which much has been written is the apparent contradiction between *Antiquities* I, 17, in which Josephus says that he will set forth the "precise details of what is written in the Scriptures, neither adding nor omitting anything," and the fact that he adds and subtracts on practically every page. Avenarius, Attridge, and S. Cohen all declare that the formula is a stock way of affirming one's claim to accuracy and need not be taken too seriously. Bertil Albrektson, "Josephus, Rabbi Akiba and Qumran: Three Arguments in the Discussion of the Date of the Standardization of the Consonantal Text of the Old Testament" [Swedish], *Teologinen Aikakauskirja* 73 (1968):201–215, says that the phrase implies merely that it is prohibited to add to the content of the Bible rather than that it is forbidden to modify the actual consonantal text. But, we may reply, if so, this would make it difficult to understand the statement in the *Letter of Aristeas* (30) that the Torah had been committed to writing somewhat carelessly and would certainly go against the very stringent laws embodied in the talmudic literature pertaining to the writing of a Torah scroll. Indeed, we may add, Rabbi Akiba, Josephus' great contemporary, stressed that every spelling, every apparent error had significance. Gustav Tachauer, *Das Verhältniss von Flavius Josephus zur Bibel und Tradition* (Erlangen 1871), pp. 45–46, and I, "Hellenizations in Josephus' Portrayal of

Man's Decline," *Studies in the History of Religion* 14 (*Religions in Antiquity: Essays in Memory of Erwin Ramsdell Goodenough,* Jacob Neusner, ed. [Leiden 1968], pp. 336–353), have suggested that Josephus included in "Scriptures" not only the written Bible but Jewish tradition generally. Another possibility, we may suggest, is that Josephus understood the phrase to mean that one was not permitted to modify halakhah but that this did not apply to haggadah. W. C. van Unnik, "De la règle Μήτε προσθεῖναι μήτε ἀφελεῖν dans l'histoire du canon," *VC* 3 (1949):1–36, and *Flavius Josephus als historischer Schriftsteller* (Heidelberg 1978), says that it means merely that nothing has been changed for the sake of adulation or enmity.

Josephus' Treatment of the Biblical Period: Individual Episodes

Thomas W. Franxman, *Genesis and the 'Jewish Antiquities' of Flavius Josephus* (Rome 1979), systematically compares Josephus' treatment of Genesis with parallels in Jubilees, Philo, and Pseudo-Philo's *Biblical Antiquities.* He concludes that Josephus noticeably expands ten segments, contracts twelve, and does not appreciably alter twelve others. He declares that Josephus is a far more careful author than has been previously thought and that his alterations may represent exegetical traditions much better thought out than has been heretofore supposed. He does not indicate, however, the relative frequency of the various techniques employed by Josephus, nor does he treat the nature of Josephus' biblical text, whether Hebrew or Greek, and the nature of his deviations from that text. In "Josephus' Commentary on Genesis," *JQR* 72 (1981–1982):121–131. I have noted many omissions in Franxman's work and try to explain the reasons for Josephus' modifications.

In "Hellenizations in Josephus' Portrayal of Man's Decline," *Studies in the History of Religions,* 14 (*Religions in Antiquity: Essays in Memory of Erwin Ramsdell Goodenough,* Jacob Neusner, ed. [Leiden 1968], pp. 336–353), I have suggested that, in his developed picture of the original bliss of mankind, Josephus follows a Greek tradition found in many authors from Hesiod on. In his elaboration of Cain's wickedness after the murder of Abel, Josephus' language is highly reminiscent of Greek and Roman descriptions of the decline and fall of man from the age of primitive simplicity.

André Paul, "Le récit de la Chute par Flavius Josèphe," *Foi et Vie* 80 (December 1981):41–47, concludes that Josephus' account of the fall (*A* I, 40–43) is that of a subversion of equilibrium, that in his view of φρόνησις, he inclines totally to Greek culture and concepts, but that in his view of speech (φωνή), he is totally in accord with Jewish belief and traditions.

Jack P. Lewis, *A Study of the Interpretation of Noah and the Flood in Jewish and Christian Literature* (Leiden 1968), pp. 77–81, merely summarizes Josephus and concludes that Josephus' treatment of the flood is a simple paraphrase of the Septuagint. He alludes only once to a pagan parallel and only twice to rabbinic parallels and attempts no specific comparison with Philo or with Pseudo-Philo's *Biblical Antiquities*. A further examination will, I believe, show that Josephus' version is much less concentrated than the biblical narrative, that he makes careful and deliberate modifications largely motivated by apologetic concerns. In particular, Josephus felt obliged to defend the historicity of the Bible, upon which Jewish history rested, not merely by appealing to the evidence of non-Jewish writers such as Berossus but also by employing language that would clearly identify the flood with the flood of the Greek mythical figure Deucalion. Parallels with Plato and with Herodotus, as well as with Apollodorus and with motifs later found in Lucian, likewise would serve to make the narrative more readily intelligible and more acceptable to a Greek audience.

André Paul, "Flavius Josephus' 'Antiquities of the Jews': An Anti-Christian Manifesto," *NTS* 31 (1985):473–480, commenting on Josephus' version of the flood (*A* I, 103), explains the complete absence of any reference to a covenant between God and man and his emphasis on the mythical character of the ark as due to his attempt to answer the Christian challenge as seen in the New Testament (the "New Covenant"). We may add that Josephus' diminution of the importance of David, especially as compared with Saul, likewise may be due to David's importance for Christianity, as the ancestor of the Messiah. Nevertheless, it seems hard to believe, as Paul suggests, that the major objective of the *Antiquities* was to readjust the equilibrium between the Jews and the Christians, since the Christians in the latter half of the first century were surely still a minuscule group and were hardly perceived as a threat to Judaism.

A thesis similar to that of André Paul had been presented by Pierpaolo Fornaro, "Il Cristianesimo Oggetto di Polemica Indiretta in Flavio Giuseppe (Ant. Jud. IV 326)," *RSC* 27 (1979):431–446, who suggests that Josephus, in his depictions of the deaths of Enoch (*A* I, 85), Moses (*A* IV, 326), and Elijah (*A* IX, 28), was carrying on an indirect polemic against the views of the early church about the death and resurrection of Jesus. If so, we may counter, none of the church fathers, who so admired Josephus, perceived this. We may add that Christianity in Josephus' day seems to have been too unimportant for such a polemic. If he were interested in carrying on a polemic, it seems more likely that Josephus would have done so against the Samaritans, whom he hated with a passion and who, indeed, did elevate the personality of Moses beyond the status that he held among the Jews.

James R. Lord, "Abraham: A Study in Ancient Jewish and Christian Interpretation" (Ph.D. diss., Duke University 1968), pp. 162–163, presents a general survey in which he concludes that Josephus' paraphrase shows Hellenization. In "Abraham the Greek Philosopher in Josephus," *TAPA* 99 (1968): 143–156, I concluded that Josephus' Abraham, in contrast to rabbinic and other portrayals, is presented as distinctly original in his sophisticated inversion of the teleological argument for the existence of God, in his broadmindedness, including a willingness to be converted if defeated in argument, and in his usefulness in sharing his scientific knowledge with Egyptian philosophers and scientists. Nikolaus Walter, *Fragmente jüdisch-hellenistischer Historiker (Schriften aus hellenistisch-römischer Zeit,* Band 1, Lfg. 2 [Werner G. Kummel, ed.]; Gütersloh 1976; 2d ed. 1980), pp. 144–160, concludes that certain features in the portrait of Abraham (*A* I, 154–168) may be derived from Pseudo-Hecataeus II. In "Josephus as a Biblical Interpreter: The 'Aqedah," *JQR* 75 (1984–1985):212–152, I conclude that Josephus (*A* I, 222–236) has Hellenized the Aqedah (Gen. 22.1–19) by giving it clarity and depth and by removing suspense. Josephus seeks to show the superiority of Judaism to pagan mythology by the implied comparison with the parallel sacrifice of Iphigenia. He builds up the character of Abraham and Isaac, as he does with his other biblical heroes, and plays down the aspects of theology and theodicy.

Martin Braun, *Griechischer Roman und hellenistische Geschichtsschreibung* (Frankfurt 1934), analyzes the erotic and novelistic motifs in Josephus' account of Joseph and Potiphar's wife, comparing them with the Hippolytus-Phaedra story as treated by Euripides, though, as noted previously, pressing too far. He returns to this theme in his *History and Romance in Graeco-Oriental Literature* (Oxford 1938), noting, especially, the parallels with the treatment in the Testament of Joseph in the Pseudepigrapha. Hans Sprödowsky, *Die Hellenisierung der Geschichte von Joseph in Aegypten bei Flavius Josephus* (Ph.D. diss., Greifswald 1937), sees Josephus' source as being the Alexandrian Jewish tradition and stresses that the Hellenization found in him occurred in the centuries before Josephus. He has neglected to consider the extent of Josephus' debt to Hellenistic historians generally, however, and to the Graeco-Jewish historians in particular. Edgar W. Smith, "Joseph Materials in Joseph and Asenath and Josephus Relating to the Testament of Joseph," *Studies on the Testament of Joseph,* George W. E. Nickelsburg, ed. (Septuagint and Cognate Studies 5; Missoula 1975), pp. 133–137, concludes that Josephus has more parallels than Joseph and Asenath with the Testament of Joseph. Smith, however, has neglected to consider the lovesickness of Asenath as a Hellenization reminiscent of the story of Hippolytus and Phaedra and of Greek novels, nor does he examine midrashic parallels.

Meyer A. Halévy, *Moïse dans l'histoire et dans la légende* (Paris 1927), pp. 103–117, presents a general, uncritical survey of Josephus' modifications of the biblical narrative about Moses, particularly the episode of Moses' campaign in Ethiopia. Géza Vermès, "La figure de Moïse au tournant des deux Testaments," in Henri Cazelles et al., *Moïse, L'Homme de l'Alliance* (Paris

1955), pp. 86–92, surveying the portrayal of Moses in Josephus and in Pseudo-Philo's *Biblical Antiquities,* suggests that here we may trace the historical development of the haggadic tradition, just as we may discern the development of the halakhic tradition. We may comment, however, that there is no definitive way to discern the antiquity of the traditions implied in each of our sources and, hence, such a theory is difficult to prove. Wayne Meeks, *The Prophet-King Moses Traditions and the Johannine Christology* (Leiden 1967), pp. 131–146, concludes that Josephus' models in portraying Moses as a Hellenistic θεῖος ἀνήρ, were the Hellenistic historians and that his major sources were all Greek; but this seems extreme, since Josephus also drew upon haggadic traditions, which have survived in the Midrashim and in the targumim, and also apparently introduced themes of his own. David L. Tiede, *The Charismatic Figure as Miracle Worker* (Missoula 1972), pp. 207–240, in reaction to the effort to see in Josephus' portrait the θεῖος ἀνήρ, stresses Josephus' attempt to ascribe to Moses those qualities that would make him as appealing as possible to his audience by making him a paradigm of the virtues of the ideal sage so highly prized in Roman society. As a lawgiver, Moses approaches divine status, since Josephus calls him θεῖος ἀνήρ (*A* III, 180), but, we may note, Josephus is here merely repeating the statement of the Bible (Exodus 4:16 and 7:1). Mary R. Graf, "The Hellenization of Moses" (Ph.D. diss., Hebrew Union College 1977), pp. 131–144, in her general survey of Josephus' version of Moses, concludes that Josephus has gone beyond the biblical narrative by including legendary and romantic motifs and that he has represented Moses primarily as a lawgiver who was well skilled in the practical virtues. Gohei Hata, "On Josephus' Portrayal of Moses" [Japanese], *Kiristokyogaku Kenkyu* 7 (December 1983):82–96, shows how Josephus, in answer to the anti-Semitic distortions of Moses, has rewritten the biblical description of him by presenting him to his readers as an ideal figure.

The question of the sources of the episode of Moses' campaign in Ethiopia (*A* II, 238–257), the most dramatic of all of Josephus' additions to the biblical narrative, has attracted particular attention. Daniel J. Silver, "Moses and the Hungry Birds" *JQR* 64 (1973):123–153, concludes that Josephus is answering the anti-Semitic portrayal of Moses as a traitor-priest who served the devil Typhon-Seth. In particular, since the ibis was a symbol of Egyptian loyalty, he uses it to stress Moses' patriotism and asserts that it reflects memories of a syncretistic cult of the Egyptian Diaspora that focused on Moses as leader and intercessor. Tessa Rajak, "Moses in Ethiopia: Legend and Literature," *JJS* 29 (1978):111–122, considers it probable that Josephus' source was an Alexandrian Jewish work written prior to Artapanus, who has a somewhat similar account, since some of the material does not suit him well. We may comment that there is no evidence here or anywhere else in his long narrative that Josephus was dependent upon an Alexandrian source. Furthermore, in view of the emphasis during this period on oral transmission, it is more likely that this was Josephus' source, as we may guess from the fact that some elements of the story appear in targumim, which often reflect such oral traditions. Finally, we may suggest that Josephus introduced elements of his own for apologetic reasons. Donna Runnalls, "Moses' Ethiopian Campaign," *JSJ* 14 (1983):135–156, argues that Josephus' version is a polemic against Artapanus, that the core of the story is even older than the Hellenistic period, but that Josephus has changed the role of the ibis from an indispensable and divinely sent bird to a merely useful bird, but that Josephus sought to avoid a direct attack on Alexandrian Jewish tradition.

Larry Moscovitz, "Josephus' Treatment of the Biblical Balaam Episode" (M.A. diss., Yeshiva University 1979), concludes that Josephus (*A* IV, 102–130), most probably out of apologetic considerations, gives a straightforward and relatively unbiased portrait of Balaam, that his emphasis is not on Balaam's personality but on the political and military conflict between Israel and her adversaries, and that he avoids theological elements and real Hellenizations but presents instead a study in rhetoric. Willem C. van Unnik, "Josephus' Account of the Story of Israel's Sin with Alien Women in the Country of Midian (Num. 25:1 ff)," *Travels in the World of the Old Testament: Studies Presented to M. A. Beek,* M.S.H.G. Heerma van Voss, ed. (Assen 1974), pp. 241–261, remarks that whereas Josephus does not expand the story of Phinehas, he does so greatly in the case of the Israelites' harlotry with the Midianite women, presumably in order to warn his contemporaries against the evils of intermarriage.

Klaus Haaker and Peter Schäfer, "Nachbiblische Traditionen vom Tod des Moses," J-S, pp. 147–174, comparing Josephus' account of the death of Moses with that of Pseudo-Philo, the Pseudepigraphic *Assumption of Moses,* the Samaritan *Memar Marqah,* and rabbinic tradition, stress the Stoic influence, and note, in particular, parallels with the deaths of such pagan heroes as Hercules and Romulus.

F. Gerald Downing, "Redaction Criticism: Josephus' *Antiquities* and the Synoptic Gospels," *JSNT* 8 (1980):46–65; 9 (1980):29–48, illustrates how, in his version of Joshua and Judges, Josephus strives to avoid discrepancies, duplications, interruptions in the narrative, miracles and magic, inappropriate theology, and apologetically awkward passages. We may remark that Downing stresses but fails to demonstrate precisely the influence of Dionysius of Halicarnassus on Josephus and that he does not consider the influence that rabbinic tradition may have had on Josephus in his modifications.

In "Josephus' Portrait of Saul," *HUCA* 53 (1982):45–99, I conclude that in his portrait of Saul, Josephus has combined the historiographic ideals of the schools of Isocrates and Aristotle and that he has Hellenized his portrait of Saul, stressing those qualities that would appeal to his Greek audience, namely the four cardinal virtues, as well as good birth, handsomeness, and piety. I suggest that the close connection between tragedy and history that we see in his version may be due to their common source: epic.

Jan Wojcik, "Discriminations against David's Tragedy in Ancient Jewish and Christian Literature," *The David Myth in Western Literature,* Raymond-Jean Frontain and Jan Wojcik, eds. (West Lafayette 1980), pp. 22–25, comments that Josephus' version of David is marked by a sense of decorum, which is related to his view of history as the unraveling of a divine plan, and that he subtly manipulated the chain of causality so as to emphasize the divine role.

We may add that it is particularly striking that Josephus ascribes to God achievements that are imputed in the Bible to David himself, whereas elsewhere in his treatment of the sacrifice of Isaac, Joseph and Potiphar's wife, Samson, Ruth, and Saul, he diminishes the role of God. To be sure, where Josephus is eager to answer anti-Semitic charges, he amplifies the portrayal of David. However, his diminution of the importance of David as king, especially as compared with Saul, perhaps may be explained by the fact that since David was traditionally regarded as the ancestor of the Messiah, who as a political figure would seek to reestablish an independent Jewish state, Josephus' Roman patrons would presumably have objected to such an emphasis. Perhaps the deemphasis may also have been occasioned by Josephus' reaction to the importance that David had for Christianity as the ancestor of the Messiah.

Alberto R. Green, "David's Relations with Hiram: Biblical and Josephan Evidence for Tyrian Chronology," in Carol L. Meyers and M. O'Connor, *The Word of the Lord Shall Go Forth* (Winona Lake 1983), pp. 373–397, concludes that Josephus offers a bewildering variety of chronological schemes and that, in particular, there is no historical basis for Josephus' synchronism between the eleventh and twelfth years of Hiram's reign and the fourth year of the reign of Solomon. He notes that although Josephus has preserved relatively well the names of the Tyrian kings, his figures for their regnal years are open to serious question. We may comment that Josephus is spotty when it comes to such details, especially in matters of arithmetic. An example is his error (*BJ* VI, 425) in adding up the number of pilgrims in Jerusalem for Passover. On the other hand, Green's suggestion that Josephus transferred to the construction of Solomon's Temple the data concerning the construction of the temple of Heracles and Astarte in Tyre seems hard to believe, since Josephus could hardly have dared to make such a transfer when there were certainly readers who could and presumably would check up on him.

In "Josephus as an Apologist to the Greco-Roman World; His Portrait of Solomon," in *Aspects of Religious Propaganda in Judaism and Early Christianity,* Elisabeth S. Fiorenza, ed. (South Bend 1976), pp. 69–98, I conclude that Josephus, seeking to raise the stature of Solomon, consciously colors his portrait with Stoic phraseology and that he may have had the character of Oedipus in mind, to judge from some of his phraseology. Harry E. Faber van der Meulen, *Das Salomo-Bild im hellenistisch-judischen Schrifttum* (Diss., Kampen 1978), concludes that Josephus' Solomon is the typical righteous ruler who is transformed into a tyrant under the influence of his foreign wives.

Dennis C. Duling, "The Eleazar Miracle and Solomon's Magical Wisdom in Flavius Josephus's *Antiquitates Judaicae* 8.42–49," *HTR* 78 (1985):1–25, suggests that despite his general aversion to the irrational, Josephus was willing in this one instance to describe the legend of Solomon, since this was an instance of white magic, which in his era was growing in attraction. We may suggest that in this respect Josephus was in accord not only with the Graeco-Roman but also rabbinic interest in magic; and that the depiction of Jews as experts in magic is acknowledged by such writers as Pompeius Trogus (*ap.* Justin, *Historiae Philippicae* 36, *Epitoma* 2.7) and Pliny (*Naturalis Historia* 30.2.11) in the first century and Apuleius (*Apology* 90) in the second century, all of whom mention Moses as a master magician. This may help to account for the attraction of pagans to Judaism, as indicated by the apparently large-scale conversions to Judaism which took place in this period.

André Paul, "Le concept de prophétie biblique. Flavius Josèphe et Daniel," *RSR* 63 (1975):367–384, in a detailed examination of Josephus' treatment of Daniel (*A* X, 266–281), concludes that it encapsulates the entire book, since in summarizing Daniel Josephus presented himself as the authentic representative of a defeated Jewish nation. His version is prophetic because it is historical and is biblical because it is readable.

Bacchisio Motzo, *Saggi di storia e letteratura giudeo-ellenistica.* (*Contributi alla Scienza dell' Antichità,* 5) (Firenze 1924), postulates that Josephus employed an anti-Samaritan chronicle for most of Books XI through XIII, which itself was based on the books of Ezra and Nehemiah, on certain apocryphal books, and on a narrative about the Tobiads. We may reply, however, that at least for the events narrated in the Bible it seems more likely that Josephus, with his knowledge of the Bible, used it directly or that he used both the Bible and an expansion thereof. Moreover, many passages, often at length, in these books are hardly anti-Samaritan, as one would expect from an anti-Samaritan chronicle.

C. G. Tuland, "Josephus, *Antiquities,* Book XI: Correction or Confirmation of Biblical Post-Exilic Records?", *AUSS* 4 (1966):176–192, explains Josephus' deviation from both Ezra and III Esdras by noting that they are thematically arranged, whereas Josephus sought to write a continuous historical narrative, and by asserting that Josephus' inaccuracies are due to his preconceived notion as to the model that a history must follow.

Karl-Friedrich Pohlmann, *Studien zum dritten Esra. Ein Beitrag zur Frage nach dem ursprünglichen Schluss des chronistischen Geschichtswerkes* (Göttingen 1970), pp. 74–126, argues that Josephus did not use the books of Ezra and Nehemiah but rather only III Esdras (apparently, we may suggest, because of its superior Greek style, its elimination of chronological difficulties, and its heightening of romantic elements), as we can see from the way he reproduces the accounts about Nehemiah. The very fact, however, that Pohlmann is forced to admit that Josephus is sometimes far from the text of III Esdras should make us skeptical of this thesis.

Nisan Ararat, "Ezra and His Deeds in the Sources" [Hebrew] (Diss., Yeshiva University 1971), as we have noted, postulates that Josephus' source for the period of Ezra was a fourth-century comprehensive chronicle, since Josephus does not refer to the biblical book of Ezra but rather to a version of III Esdras. Inasmuch as, however, we have not a single fragment of this chronicle, it seems more likely that he employed both III Esdras and Ezra.

As to the book of Esther, Josephus may have had access to an Aramaic targum, inasmuch as the second edict of King Ahasuerus is found only in Josephus (*A* XI, 273–283) and in the Targum Sheni (8.12). Rose-Marie Seyberlich, "Esther in der Septuaginta und bei Flavius Josephus," *Neue Beiträge zur Geschichte der Alter Welt,* Band 1: *Alter Orient und Griechenland* (II. Internationale Tagung der Fachgruppe Alte Geschichte der Deutschen Historiker-Gesellschaft vom 4.–8. Sept. 1962 in Stralsund; Charlotte Welskopf, ed.; Berlin 1964), pp. 363–366, dismisses this theory as improbable, however, because Josephus had been living in Rome for twenty years at the time of the completion of the *Antiquities* and had presumably lost contact with targumim. Instead, she postulates that Josephus had recalled some details of Pharisaic Midrashim that he had heard in his earlier years. We may remark, however, that inasmuch as Josephus was thirty-three years old when he came to Rome it seems unlikely that he would have forgotten his native Aramaic at that age. In any case, if Josephus had lost contact with his Aramaic mother tongue it seems even more farfetched that he would remember Midrashim that he had heard decades before.

In "Hellenizations in Josephus' Version of Esther," *TAPA* 101 (1970): 143–170, I describe how Josephus has converted the biblical narrative into a Hellenistic novel, noting such touches as his concern with the beauty of women, with cosmetics, with the elaborate description of royal banquets, with elimination of difficult names, with the build-up of suspense and irony, and with expansion of the romantic element generally. I cite many touches in Josephus that aim to combat anti-Semitic propaganda, such as the charge that Jews are intolerant of other religions and that the Bible contains contradictions and discrepancies in chronology, as well as other details that would tax a reader's credulity.

Josephus as Historian of the Postbiblical Period

For the postbiblical period Joseph Klausner's *History of the Second Temple* [Hebrew], 5 vols. (Jerusalem 1949; 6th ed., 1954), is comprehensive but often betrays nationalistic bias. In his magisterial *Judentum und Hellenismus. Studien zu ihrer Begegnung unter besonderer Berücksichtigung Palästinas bis zur Mitte des 2. Jh. v. Chr.* (Tübingen 1969); English translation *Judaism and Hellenism; Studies in Their Encounter in Palestine during the Early Hellenistic Period,* 2 vols., (Philadelphia 1974), relying heavily on the evidence of Josephus, Martin Hengel argues that Judaism in the land of Israel was already deeply Hellenized by the middle of the third century B.C.E., long before the decrees of Antiochus Epiphanes, and that the distinction between the Diaspora and Palestinian Judaism, so far as Hellenization is concerned, should be eliminated. In "Hengel's *Judaism and Hellenism* in Retrospect," *JBL* 96 (1977):371–382, I challenge him on twenty-two counts, contending that the question is not so much how greatly Jews and Judaism in the land of Israel were Hellenized as how strongly they resisted Hellenization, and that the answer may lie in Judaism's paradoxical self-confidence and defensiveness, its unity and diversity, its stubbornness and flexibility. Hengel himself drew in his sails somewhat in *Juden, Griechen und Barbaren. Aspekte der Hellenisierung des Judentums in vorchristlicher Zeit* (Stuttgart 1976); translated by John Bowden as *Jews, Greeks and Barbarians: Aspects of the Hellenization of Judaism in the Pre-Christian Period* (Philadelphia 1980). In "How Much Hellenism in Jewish Palestine?" *HUCA* 57 (1986):83–111, I emphasize that in Upper Galilee, in particular, to judge from the inscriptions, there was little Hellenization, perhaps because the Jews lived in townlets similar to those of the Jews in Eastern Europe in modern times. The fact that even Josephus admits (*Ap* I, 50) that he needed assistants in writing the *Jewish War* shows that Greek was not well known even by intellectuals. Hellenization could not have been profound, since we hear of few apostates; on the contrary, far more pagans were attracted to Judaism either as proselytes or as "sympathizers." We know of no rabbi who wrote in Greek, and there is little if any indication of rabbinic knowledge of Greek literature, let alone of Greek philosophy.

Ido Hampel, "The Historiography of Josephus Flavius for the Period 'Shivat Zion'—The Return of Zion" [Hebrew] (M.A. diss., Tel-Aviv University 1969), concludes that Josephus is unreliable for the chronology of the Persian kings, and that for Ezra and Nehemiah he used an unknown Jewish and anti-Samaritan source. H. G. M. Williamson, "The Historical Value of Josephus' *Jewish Antiquities* XI, 297–301," *JTS* 28 (1977):49–66, using form-critical analysis, concludes that Josephus has imposed his own interpretation upon his source for the story of the murder by the high priest of his brother Jesus and that he has reduced the Persian period by at least two generations.

Inasmuch as we have some very different accounts of Alexander the

Great, we are presumably in a good situation to evaluate the credibility of Josephus. Adolphe Buchler [sic], "La relation de Josèphe concernant Alexandre le Grand," REJ 36 (1898):1–26, concludes that Josephus' account of Alexander's sojourn in Palestine is composed of three parts, two of Jewish and one of Samaritan origin, which are easily separable because they have been juxtaposed rather than combined. Ralph Marcus, "Alexander the Great and the Jews," Appendix C in his translation of Josephus, vol. 6 (Loeb Classical Library: London 1937), pp. 512–532, adopts Büchler's theory and argues against the historicity of Alexander's visit to Jerusalem (though with some diffidence) on the ground that the oldest Greek and Latin sources do not mention it. Jerusalem, he claims, was hardly worth visiting, since the Jews were comparatively unimportant to the Greeks at the time; and Josephus' sources may be suspected of having brought Alexander into connection with Jerusalem for apologetic reasons. Frederick Pfister, Alexander der Grosse in den Offenbarungen der Griechen, Juden, Mohammedaner und Christen (Berlin 1956), pp. 24–35, concludes that both Josephus and the Talmud go back to a common late Hellenistic-Jewish source. The fact that Moses' crossing of the Red Sea (A II, 345) is compared with Alexander's of the Pamphylian Sea shows that Alexander was firmly fixed in the religious writings of the Jews. Aryeh Kasher, "Some Suggestions and Comments Concerning Alexander Macedon's Campaign in Palestine" [Hebrew], BM 62 (1975):187–208, in opposition to Büchler, argues that Josephus' account of Alexander is a single organic composition rather than one composed from three separate strands. Josephus' account is credible because there is evidence that the conquest of Syria and Palestine was achieved through a well-planned military scheme, one that was important to Alexander. Arnaldo Momigliano, "Flavius Josephus and Alexander's Visit to Jerusalem," Athenaeum 57 (1979):442–448, concludes that the account of Alexander is apocryphal and that it dates from the Maccabean period, since Alexander is shown the Book of Daniel. The account, he conjectures, may have been invented in Egypt. He suggests that the idea that the two versions (by Samaritans and by Jews) of Alexander's visit of Jerusalem arose in Egypt in the middle of the second century B.C.E. is confirmed by the detail that the book of Daniel was consulted by Alexander in Jerusalem. We may comment, however, that the very fact that the rabbinic texts that mention Alexander also involve the Samaritans should make one realize that Josephus' account has at least a substratum of truth. David Golan, "Josephus, Alexander's Visit to Jerusalem and Modern Historiography" [Hebrew], in Uriel Rappaport, ed., CP (1982), pp. 29–55, contends that Josephus' account of Alexander's visit is in accord with other sources. Shaye J. D. Cohen, "Alexander the Great and Jaddus the High Priest according to Josephus," AJSR 7–8 (1982–1983):41–68, denies the historicity of Alexander's visit to Jerusalem and suggests that the Alexander story is a combination of two popular genres in Hellenistic-Jewish literature: an adventus story (the high priest and the Jews greet Alexander) and an epiphany story (the Temple and the Jews are rescued from Alexander by divine manifestation). We may comment, however, that to deny, as does Cohen, an Alexandrian source for the Jaddus story and to ascribe to Josephus the reference to Daniel, the change in Alexander's dream, the addition of the reference to Babylonia and Media, as well as the chronological setting and the juxtaposition of the material about the Samaritans, is to indicate that Josephus knew traditions of which we know nothing. It seems more likely that Alexandria, which prided itself on its name and its privileges given by Alexander, was the main source of Josephus' narrative.

In an extremely thorough work, André Pelletier, *Flavius Josèphe adaptateur de la Lettre d'Aristée. Une reaction atticisante contre la koiné* (Paris 1962), comparing Josephus (*A* XII, 11–118) with his source, the Letter of Aristeas, notes that there is only one sequence of as many as twelve words, as well as another of ten, that are identical in both. Most of Josephus' changes are for change's sake. Printing Josephus and Aristeas in parallel columns, Pelletier stresses Josephus' vocabulary, grammar, word order, metrical clausulae, prose rhythms, and his concern for making his style uniform so as to attain literary unity. Since this is one of the very few places where we definitely know Josephus' source, the work is of very great importance in illustrating Josephus' method in indicating the Atticizing reaction against the *koiné*. Pelletier, however, is unacquainted with anything written after Norden on the subject of clausulae, and he omits consideration of Josephus' Hellenistic predecessors.

In a survey of Seleucid rule in Palestine from 200 to 162 B.C.E., James E. Taylor, *Seleucid Rule in Palestine* (Ph.D. diss., Duke University 1979), concludes that the chief factor leading the high priest to favor Antiochus was the Ptolemies' policy toward the Jews of Jerusalem.

Elias Bickermann, "La Charte Séleucide de Jérusalem," *REJ* 100 (1935): 4–35, in a careful study of the formulas and of the chronological order of the decrees of Antiochus III cited by Josephus (*A* XII, 138–153), concludes that they are authentic. Bikerman (Bickermann), "Une proclamation séleucide relative au temple de Jérusalem," *Syria* 25 (1946–1948):67–85, has an extensive commentary on the decree of Antiochus III (*A* XII, 145–146) designed to preserve the purity of Jerusalem. Abraham Schalit, "The Letter of Antiochus III to Zeuxis Regarding the Establishment of Jewish Military Colonies in Phrygia and Lydia," *JQR* 50 (1959–1960):289–318, through a careful analysis of the style and content of Antiochus III's letter to Zeuxis, governor of Lydia (*A* XII, 148–153), concludes that it is genuine. Jörg-Dieter Gauger, *Beiträge zur jüdischen Apologetik. Untersuchungen zur Authentizität von Urkunden bei Flavius Josephus und im I. Makkabäerbuch* (Köln-Bonn 1977), however, contends that it is spurious, having been falsified, he suggests, in the course of the disputes between Greeks and Jews in Asia Minor in the first century B.C.E., though he admits that it may contain historically correct elements.

In a bold essay, Jonathan A. Goldstein, "The Tales of the Tobiads," *Festschrift Morton Smith*, 3 (Leiden 1975), pp. 85–123, postulates as Josephus' source for his account of the Tobiads (*A* XII, 158–236) a propagandist who was pro-Ptolemaic and anti-Seleucid, namely an account written by Onias IV, the founder of the Jewish temple at Leontopolis, whom Josephus attacked elsewhere. But, we may remark, there is no evidence that Onias IV wrote anything or that Josephus attacked him; and, indeed, it seems unlikely that Josephus would have used as a major source the work of a renegade priest, especially since he himself was a priest of the first order. Susan Niditch, "Father–Son Folktale Patterns and Tyrant Typologies in Josephus' Ant. 12.160–222," *JJS* 32 (1981):47–55, contends that in his Tobiad narrative Josephus follows a typical folktale pattern closely resembling the tale of the biblical Joseph.

I Maccabees is one of the few works that we can be reasonably sure Josephus used; and, as with his adaptation of the Letter of Aristeas, the manner in which he paraphrases the book is of great value in assessing Josephus' method. Hans Drüner, "Untersuchungen über Josephus" (Diss., Marburg 1896), pp. 35–50, effectively refutes the theory that Josephus' source was an anonymous work and explains the additional manner, including precise figures that are not in the original of I Maccabees, by noting that Josephus characteristically introduces such data to enliven his narrative. Ezra Z. Melamed, "Josephus and Maccabees I: A Comparison" [Hebrew], *EI* 1 (1951):122–130, through a comparison of nineteen passages in Josephus and in I Maccabees, shows that Josephus employed both a Hebrew original and a Greek translation and that the latter was more accurate than ours. Menahem Stern, "The Books of the Maccabees and 'Jewish Antiquities' as Sources for the Hasmonean Revolt and the Hasmonean State" [Hebrew], in *The Documents on the History of the Hasmonean Revolt,* Menahem Stern, ed., (Tel-Aviv 1965), pp. 7–11, notes that in addition to I Maccabees, Josephus used Nicolaus of Damascus as a major source for the Hasmonean period. Jonathan A. Goldstein, *I Maccabees: A New Translation with Introduction and Commentary* (Garden City 1976), pp. 558–568, analyzes Josephus' rewriting of I Maccabees 1:20–64 and concludes that three factors will account for Josephus' changes: his belief in the veracity of Daniel 7–12, his belief in the efficacy of martyrdom, and his intention to write his work in good Greek rhetorical style. Goldstein, however, does not recognize that Josephus, as indicated by his deliberate modifications of almost every phrase in the Letter of Aristeas merely for the sake of variation, modifies his source even where there is no specific difficulty. Moreover, while there will be few who will subscribe to the theory, popular earlier in this century, that an ancient writer could not be expected to consult more than one source at a time because of the inaccessibility of manuscripts and because of the difficulty in consulting them without indices, it seems that Goldstein has gone too far in the other direction in indicating that he simultaneously consulted I and II Maccabees, Jason of Cyrene, the Book of Daniel, the Testament of Moses, and the work of Onias IV. Isaiah Gafni, "On the Use of I Maccabees by Josephus Flavius" [Hebrew], *Zion* 45 (1980):81–95, contrasts Josephus, who ascribes the victory of the Jews over the Syrian Greeks to their piety, with I Maccabees, where God guarantees them victory; but he rightly confirms that Josephus' major source was I Maccabees.

As to the background of the Maccabean revolt, Elias Bickermann, *Der Gott der Makkabäer. Untersuchungen über Sinn und Ursprung der makkabäischen Erhebung* (Berlin 1937), argues with great effectiveness that it was the Jewish reformers rather than Antiochus Epiphanes who originated the persecution. Otto Mørkholm, *Antiochus IV of Syria* (Copenhagen 1966), looks upon Antiochus Epiphanes as a politican and statesman rather than as a mystic or missionary. He stresses, in particular, that in 164 B.C.E. Antiochus was realistic enough to attempt to correct his mistakes. We may note, furthermore, that if Antiochus were really anti-Jewish we would expect similar decrees against the Jews in Syria and in Asia Minor; and we hear of none such. Fergus Millar, "The Background to the Maccabean Revolution: Reflections on Martin Hengel's 'Judaism and Hellenism'," *JJS* 29 (1978):1–21, on the other hand, arguing that there is little evidence that a Hellenizing party instigated the imposition of paganism upon the Jews, contends that Diodorus (24.5.1), Tacitus (*Histories* 5.8), and II Maccabees all indicate that Antiochus proceeded not to continue a development that was in motion and to effect a syncretism but to abolish Jewish observance completely. The fact, moreover, that the attempt forcibly to convert the Jews to paganism was abandoned so abruptly tends to indicate, though admittedly it does not prove, that the original decision of Antiochus was a whim rather than the climax of a gradual movement.

Thomas Fischer, *Untersuchungen zum Partherkrieg Antiochos' VII. im Rahmen der Seleukidengeschichte* (Tübingen 1970), pp. 1–27, in his discussion of our sources for Antiochus VII, concludes that Josephus' major source was a lost Syrian history. Tessa Rajak, "Roman Intervention in a Seleucid Siege of Jerusalem?" *GRBS* 22 (1981):65–81, contends that the Antiochus mentioned in the decree of the Roman Senate (*A* XIII, 261) was Antiochus VII and that the Romans had expressed ambiguous support for him prior to their forming an alliance with the Hasmoneans.

As to Egypt during this period, John G. Gager, *The Origins of Anti-Semitism: Attitudes Toward Judaism in Pagan and Christian Antiquity* (New York 1983), concludes that Josephus' statement (*BJ* II, 487) that there had been incessant strife between the native inhabitants and the Jewish settlers of Alexandria since the time of Alexander, while overstated for the Hellenistic period, is not inaccurate for the remainder of the first century and for the early decades of the second.

Joseph Sievers, "The Hasmoneans and Their Supporters from Mattathias to John Hyrcanus I" (Ph.D. diss., Columbia University 1981), identifies the classes of people who supported the Hasmoneans at various stages. The picture, however, is hardly clear-cut, and the role of the Pharisees and the Sadducees in such "parties" is hardly clear.

With regard to Jonathan the Hasmonean, Bezalel Bar-Kochva, "Hellenistic Warfare in Jonathan's Campaign near Azotos," *SCI* 2 (1975):83–96, commenting on Josephus (*A* XIII, 86–119), concludes that Josephus derived his information from a source (or sources) well acquainted with Syrian events.

As to King Alexander Jannaeus, Abraham Schalit, "Die Eroberungen des Alexander Jannäus in Moab," *Theokratia* 1 (1967–1969):3–50, concludes that Josephus' source is a Greek translation of a history originally written in Hebrew that was favorable to the Hasmoneans. Comparing the list of places controlled by Jannaeus (*A* XIII, 397 and XIV, 18) with the names in the Septuagint version of Isaiah (15.4–9) and Jeremiah (31.3–5, 8, 34, 36), he notes that Josephus' source was a poem lauding Jannaeus' achievements in biblical language and attempting to show that the prophecies were fulfilled by Jannaeus. Though there are discrepancies between the list in *Antiquities* XIII, 397, and that in XIV, 18, and though the lists cannot be used as a source without qualifications, he argues that the apparently different names are actually variant forms and that the lists consequently cannot be used as a historical source. Ben-Zion Lurie, *King Jannaeus* [Hebrew] (Jerusalem 1960) and "The Fate of the Followers of Alexander Jannaeus" [Hebrew], *BM* 22 (1965):33–39, charges that Josephus' account of Jannaeus is highly prejudiced and that he presents the Sadducean point of view, though, we must comment, it is hard to believe this in view of Josephus' extremely negative statements about the Sadducees. Michael Krupp, "Der Konflikt Alexander Jannais mit den Pharisäern: Das Ringen um des Verständnis der Thora im Spiegel einer antiken jüdischen Münzprägung," *Festschrift Günther Harder,* 3 (Berlin 1977), pp. 30–35, concludes that Jannaeus did not succumb to Hellenism. M. J. Geller, "Alexander Jannaeus and the Pharisee Rift," *JJS* 30 (1979):202–211, commenting on the discrepancy between Josephus (*A* XIII, 288–297), who declares that John Hyrcanus fought the Pharisees, and the Talmud (*Kiddushin* 66a), that ascribes this attitude to Jannaeus, favors the Talmud, since the reign of the latter is a more likely setting and since the language is archaic; but the archaism in the talmudic passage, we may suggest, may be deliberate and consequently may have little import for the dating of the document.

Most recently, Jacob Neusner, *The Peripatetic Saying: The Problem of the Thrice-Told Tale in Talmudic Literature* (Chico 1985), pp. 27–29, noting the remarkable affinities in theme, development, and detail, especially in the antiquity of the language attributed to the heavenly echo, suggests that a single, brief *logion* in Aramaic was available to both Josephus and the rabbis and that the rabbis may have known Josephus' writings in the original Aramaic. We may respond, however, that there is no indication that Josephus composed his *Antiquities* originally in Aramaic, though he may have used Aramaic sources for his accounts of Asinaeus and Anilaeus (*A* XVIII, 310–379) and of the conversion of Izates (*A* XX, 17–96), and that the fact that this incident does not appear in the parallel passage in the *War*, which, to be sure, was originally written in Aramaic, may be an indication that Josephus did not have an Aramaic source for this tale; a more likely source would appear to be Nicolaus of Damascus. Gideon Fuks, "On the Reliability of a Reference in Josephus" [Hebrew] *CP* (1982):131–137, concludes that Josephus cannot be relied upon, inasmuch as Jannaeus and the people of Gaza were hostile to each other at the beginning of his reign. Menahem Stern, "Judaea and Her Neighbors in the Days of Alexander Jannaeus," in *The Jerusalem Cathedra*, Lee I. Levine, ed. (Jerusalem 1981), pp. 22–46, analyzes the political and military activities of Jannaeus within the larger context of the Hellenistic east of his time.

As to the reign of Aristobulus I and his alleged use of force to convert the Ituraeans, according to Aryeh Kaplan, "Relations of the Jews and the Ituraeans in the Hellenistic and Roman Period" [Hebrew], *Cathedra* 33 (1984):18–41, Josephus is guilty of tendentiousness in portraying the Hasmoneans as tyrants in order to please his Roman patrons, who despised them as enemies of Hellenistic civilization.

For the period when Judea was under Roman domination, E. Mary Smallwood, *The Jews under Roman Rule: From Pompey to Diocletian* (Leiden 1976), relying on Josephus and rejecting the evidence of the Talmud, stresses the tolerance shown to the Jews by the Romans; but she places undue credence on official documents and not enough on the actual administration by corrupt and prejudiced magistrates. Richard D. Sullivan, "The Dynasty of Judea in the First Century," *ANRW* 2.8 (1977), pp. 296–354, focuses on the figures of Alexander son of Herod, Herod Antipas, Herod Archelaus, Herod of Chalcis, Berenice, Antipater, Aristobulus, Agrippa I, and, above all, Agrippa II. Josephus, he concludes, approved of the pervasive Greek influence upon these rulers. He stresses the extensive intermarrying by which dynasties tended to strengthen themselves and the methods used to reach accommodations with both the Romans and the Parthians. Lucio Troiani, "Gli Ebrei e lo stato pagano in Filone e in Giuseppe," *RSA* 2 (1980):193–218, contends that Josephus seeks, especially in his *Antiquities,* to reestablish the coexistence of Jews and Romans by stressing the special privileges given them by the Romans and to further the goals of Jewish missionaries. We may remark, however, that Josephus generally carefully avoids mention of missionary activity by Jews in the *Antiquities* and that where he does mention such activity it is in negative terms, presumably because he realized what a sensitive issue this was to the Romans. The one exception is the account of the conversion of the royal family of Adiabene, and this may be explained by the fact that Adiabene was outside the Roman Empire. As to unusual interest by Josephus in the Diaspora, Lea Roth-Gerson (Roth-Garson), "The Contribution of Josephus Flavius to the Study of the Jewish Diaspora in the Hellenistic-Roman Period" [Hebrew], *CP* (1982):185–201, says this can be explained very simply as arising from his residence in Rome, his visit to Alexandria, and his marriages with a woman from Alexandria and with a woman from Crete. Uwe Baumann, *Rom und die Juden. Die Römisch-Jüdischen Beziehungen von Pompeius bis zum Tode des Herodes (63 v. Chr.–4 v. Chr.)* (Frankfurt am Main 1983), distinguishes three phases in the relationship of Rome with the Jews during the period from 63 B.C.E. to 4 B.C.E.: (1) the period of Antipater, during which there was voluntary cooperation without loss of independence; (2) the period from the death of Antipater in 43 B.C.E. to the battle of Actium in 31 B.C.E., during which problems arose that ultimately led to the revolt against Rome; (3) the reign of Herod, whose chief problem was reconciling his duties as a Roman client with the precepts of the Jewish religion.

Ludwig Korach, *Über den Wert des Josephus als Quelle für die römische Geschichte*, Teil 1: *Bis zum Tode des Augustus* (Breslau 1895), expresses his gratitude to Josephus for using excellent sources for many events that are unknown or very imperfectly known elsewhere.

Baruch Kanael, "The Partition of Judea by Gabinius" [Hebrew], *BJPES* 18 (1954):168–175; translated into English in *IEJ* 7 (1957):98–106, concludes that Gabinius' reorganization of Palestine helped consolidate the situation in Judea. E. Mary Smallwood, "Gabinius' Organization of Palestine," *JJS* 18 (1967):89–92, concludes that Gadara (*BJ* I, 170; *A* XIV, 91) is the city in Perea and not in the Decapolis. This identification, however, we may object, requires that we admit that Josephus erred in stating (*A* XIII, 356, 374) that Jannaeus conquered Gadara in the Decapolis. Smallwood's statement that such a position makes little military sense disregards the fact that small pockets of territory such as Pella existed frequently during this period.

There has long been an intensive debate as to the authenticity of Josephus' documents, especially those in Book XIV. Jean Juster, *Les Juifs dans l'empire Romain* (Paris 1914), vol. 1, pp. 132–158, cites the decrees consecutively, discusses their nature and date, the reason why Josephus reproduces them, the criteria he uses in their reproduction, the source of these acts, and the order followed by Josephus in his classification. Alfredo M. Rabello, "The Legal Condition of the Jews in the Roman Empire," *ANRW* 2.13 (1980), pp. 662–766, has a summary, appreciation, and updating of Juster's great work. He lists (pp. 682–685) the documents cited by Josephus and concludes that there is no reason to doubt their authenticity. Otto Roth, *Rom und die Hasmonäer. Untersuchungen zu den jüdisch-römischen Urkunden im ersten Makkabäerbuch und in Josephus' Jüdischen Altertümern XIV* (Leipzig 1914), concludes that the documents in *Antiquities* XIV, 145–155, 190–212, and 217–222, were apparently taken by Josephus from Nicolaus. Hugo Willrich, *Urkundenfälschung in der hellenistisch-jüdischen Literatur* (Göttingen 1924), declares that the pro-Jewish decrees in Josephus are false. Arnaldo Momigliano, "Ricerche sull' organizzazione della Giudea sotto il dominio romano (63 A.C.–70 D.C.)," *ASNSP*, Series 2, vol. 3 (1934), pp. 183–221, 347–396, attempts to date the decrees (*A* XIV, 145–148, 149–155). He argues that the destruction of the Temple in 70 did not bring about any major change in the juridical status of the Jews. Daniela Piattelli, "Ricerche intorno alle relazioni politiche tra Roma e l'ἔθνος τῶν 'Ιουδαίων dal 161 a. C. al 4 a. C.," *BIDR* 74 (1971):219–340, reconstructs the history of the relations between Rome and Judea from the beginning of the Roman control of the Mediterranean through Herod, using the decrees as a major source. In *Concezioni giuridiche e metodi construttivi dei giuristi orientali* (Milano 1981), she concludes that Josephus' work is based on documents of the greatest value coming from both Rome and Judea. Jörg-Dieter Gauger, *Beiträge zur jüdischen Apologetik. Untersuchungen zur Authentizität von Urkunden bei Flavius Josephus und im I. Makkabäerbuch* (Köln-Bonn 1977), contends that Josephus modified the Roman decrees in the context of the bitter dispute between Greeks and Jews in Asia Minor in the middle of the first century B.C.E., but that he did so in form but not in content. Horst R. Moehring, "The 'Acta Pro Judaeis' in the *Antiquities* of Flavius Josephus: A Study in Hellenistic and Modern Apologetic Historiography," *Festschrift Morton Smith*, 3 (Leiden 1975), pp. 124–158, very cynically contends that if Josephus did include forged documents he would illustrate thereby how well he had learned the methods of historians. He asserts that the fire of 69 destroyed about 3000 documents in the Roman archives, and that some of these must have pertained to Jewish rights. He concludes that in antiquity historians did not bother to check original documents and that the invitation to the reader to check his accuracy is a matter of literary courtesy. Christiane Saulnier, "Lois romaines sur les Juifs selon Flavius Josèphe," *RB* 88 (1981):161–198, analyzing the privileges granted by the Romans to the Jews, concludes that they greatly enhanced the vitality of Diaspora Judaism. Uwe Baumann, *Rom und die Juden. Die Römisch-Jüdischen Beziehungen von Pompeius bis zum Tode des Herodes (63 v. Chr.–4 v. Chr.)* (Frankfurt am Main 1983), pp. 69–87, concludes that the documents are introduced by Josephus primarily for apologetic reasons. Tessa Rajak, "Was There a Roman Charter for the Jews?", *JRS* 74 (1984):107–123, regards the decrees as part of a political process and not merely as the bare, ambiguous, and unsatisfactory legal statements that they appear to be. To Josephus, she declares, the worth of the texts is not that they uphold precise privileges that might be under threat but rather that through a reminder of the attitudes underlying earlier grants, they make a compelling case for the acceptance by the pagans of the practice of Judaism.

Tessa Rajak, "Jewish Rights in the Greek Cities under Roman Rule," in W. S. Green, ed., *Approaches to Ancient Judaism*, vol. 5: *Studies in Judaism and Its Greco-Roman Context* (Brown Judaic Studies, 32; Atlanta 1985), pp. 19–35, rejects Moehring's view that the documents quoted by Josephus are apologetic Jewish forgeries. Josephus, she says, deployed the documents as part of his literary design and for apologetic purposes to contribute to mutual understanding between Jews and Greeks. She stresses the religious background of the tension between Jews and non-Jews; but, we may suggest, she might have done more to differentiate governmental and popular anti-Semitism; indeed, the very fact that the Roman government kept reaffirming Jewish rights was a source of tension with non-Jewish groups, who resented the granting of these special privileges to Jews.

Akiva Gilboa, "L'octroi de la citoyenneté romaine et de l'immunité à Antipater, père d'Hérode," *RHDFE* 4 (1972):609–614, concludes that the privileges granted by Caesar to Antipater were similar to those given to Seleucus of Rhosus by Octavian at about the same time.

Herod has long been a subject of peculiar fascination to scholars—and psychiatrists. Apparently this was true for Josephus himself, inasmuch as we have more information about Herod than any other figure in antiquity. The standard article, that by Walter Otto, "Herodes I," *RE,* Supplement 2 (1913), pp. 1–205, assumes an anonymous "middle source" between Nicolaus of Damascus and Josephus. This, we may remark, reflects the fashion of the time, which found it difficult to suppose that Josephus might have used personal discretion in his use of sources. Otto, moreover, had no real understanding of the internal religious, economic, and social dynamics of the Jews in Palestine.

Hugo Willrich, *Das Haus des Herodes zwischen Jerusalem und Rom* (Heidelberg 1929), in a work marked by anti-Semitism, seeks to show that Herod was really an enlightened ruler who tried to bridge the two worlds of Judaism and paganism and genuinely to improve the condition of the Jews but failed because of Jewish stubbornness. In a popular work, Arnold H. M. Jones, *The Herods of Judea* (Oxford 1938), defends Herod for establishing law and order and approves of his (and Josephus') pro-Roman bias.

In a magisterial work, Abraham Schalit, *King Herod, the Man and His Work* [Hebrew] (Jerusalem 1960); translated in expanded form, into German as *König Herodes. Der Mann und sein Werk* (Berlin 1969), attempts to rehabilitate Herod as one who deserved the title *the Great* by pointing, in particular, to his achievement in improving the economic status of Judea, and especially the lot of the peasants. Schalit analyzes the constitutionally ambiguous political position of Herod within the Roman Empire and his almost religious faith in Rome's mission to rule. Herod sought to produce a spiritual metamorphosis of the Jewish people. Indeed, he regarded himself as the Messiah and was so regarded by some others, perhaps the Herodians of the New Testament, to judge from Epiphanius (*Panarion,* Heresy 20.1). If Herod was such a friend of the Roman Empire, however, we may well ask why Josephus, who, though he was a descendant of Herod's rivals, the Hasmoneans, surely shared Herod's appraisal, is so negative toward him. In "Herodes und seine Nachfolger," *Kontexte* 3 (1966):34–42; translated into English as "Herod and His Successors," in *Jesus in His Time,* Hans-J. Schulz, ed. (Philadelphia 1971), pp. 36–46, Schalit has a brief summary defending Herod and his successors. But we may well ask why the Romans would have had such a high opinion of him if he looked upon himself as a messiah, since the standard portrait of a messiah is that of a political leader who will establish a truly independent and theocratic state. To be sure, Wolf Wirgin, "Bemerkungen zu dem Artikel über 'Die Herkunft des Herodes'," *ASTI* 3 (1964):151–154, argues that Herod's coins have non-Jewish symbols, thus showing that his messianism was different from that of the prophets; but we may reply that the average follower of Herod as the Messiah would most likely have had the traditional portrait of a messiah in mind. Moreover, we may remark, Herod seems to have been aware of Jewish sensibilities in not putting his image on his coins. Finally, if Josephus is so unfavorably disposed toward Herod, we may well ask why he did not highlight this claim to messianism, inasmuch as this would have made him a forerunner of the Fourth Philosophy and hence would have blackened him completely.

Ben-Zion Lurie, "King Herod" [Hebrew], in *Sepher Shemuel Yeivin* Samuel Abramsky et al., eds. (Jerusalem 1970), pp. 501–538, vehemently objects to Schalit's portrayal and contends that Herod was a mere vassal of Rome, who had no independence of action and whose fabled achievements as a builder were actually only for his personal security rather than for the benefit of his people. He disdained the Sanhedrin and preferred Hellenistic culture. But, we may remark, so far as the Romans were concerned, Herod must have been an effective ruler to have found favor in the eyes of such diverse judges as Julius Caesar, Crassus, Cassius, Antony, Agrippa, and Augustus.

Among other full-length, more popular portraits of Herod we may single out Samuel Sandmel, *Herod: Profile of a Tyrant* (Philadelphia 1967); Michael Grant, *Herod the Great* (New York 1971); and Gerhard Prause, *Herodes der Grosse. König der Juden* (Hamburg 1977). The first counteracts Schalit's excessive nationalism and concludes that the mightiest corrupter of all for Herod was the fear of the loss of power. The second is in line with Schalit's appreciation of Herod and concludes that Josephus' attitude toward Herod changed in the *Antiquities* because he had done more research after he wrote his *War;* and the third likewise follows Schalit in accusing Josephus of falsely maligning Herod, whose political, economic, and building activities showed real genius.

Among the articles, we may point to Abraham Schalit, "Herod and Mariamne: Josephus' Description in the Light of Greek Historiography" [Hebrew], *Molad* 14 (1956):95–102, who demonstrates that Josephus' description of Mariamne shows motifs typical of Greek tragedy and Hellenistic historiography. In "The Family of Herod in the Christian Tradition—A Chapter in the History of Party Accusation in the Period of the Second Temple" [Hebrew], *Ha-Ummah* 1 (1963):579–598, Schalit notes that Josephus' version, which describes Herod as an Edomite, will better explain the origin of the hatred toward Herod's family than does that of the Christian Justin Martyr, who states that he came from Ashkelon. Solomon Zeitlin, "Herod a Malevolent Maniac," *JQR* 54 (1963–1964):1–27, concludes that, in his portrait of Herod, Josephus used material that was both favorable and unfavorable to Herod but that he did not blend his sources well. He contests Schalit's view that Herod regarded himself as the Messiah since, he declares, Jews at the time of Herod did not believe in a messiah; but, we may object, the belief in a messiah is at least as old as the prophets. Menahem Stern, "The Reign of Herod and the Herodian Dynasty," *JPFC* (1974):216–307, and "The Reign of Herod," *WHJP* 7 (1975):71–123, 351–354, 388, conjectures that Josephus tempered Nicolaus of Damascus' encomium of Herod with information from the circle of Agrippa I and II, but that he is original in his criticism of Herod. In "Social and Political Realignments in Herodian Judaea," *JC* 2 (1982):40–62, Stern finds that the Talmud confirms Josephus in noting that Herod's reign was marked not by compromise with formerly pro-Hasmonean factions but rather by the emergence of entirely new groups unrelated to the Hasmoneans, such as immigrants from Babylonia. In "The Politics of Herod and Jewish Society towards the End of the Second Commonwealth" [Hebrew], *Tarbiz* 35 (1965–1966): 235–253, Stern notes this trend in particular in Herod's appointments to the priesthood.

On legal matters, we may note Akiva Gilboa, "The Intervention of Sextus Julius Caesar, Governor of Syria, in the Affair of Herod's Trial," *SCI* 5 (1979–1980):185–194, who stresses that, according to Josephus (*BJ* I, 211; *A* XIV, 170), Sextus Julius Caesar, the governor of Syria, sought to clear Herod not of the charge of homicide but of the need of a trial. Alfred M. Rabello, *"Hausgericht in the House of Herod the Great?"* [Hebrew], *Schalit Memorial Volume* (Jerusalem 1980), pp. 119–135, concludes that Herod, in the trials of his wife Mariamne (*A* XV, 228–231) and of his sons (*A* XVI, 367–372; XVII, 89–145, 182–187), acted not with *patria potestas* but as a Hellenistic king, and that the court before which these trials were held was not a *Hausgericht* (domestic tribunal).

David Braund, "Four Notes on the Herods," *CQ* 33 (1983):239–242, challenges my identification, "Asinius Pollio and His Jewish Interests," *TAPA* 84 (1953):73–80, of the Pollio (*A* XV, 343) at whose home in Rome Herod's sons Alexander and Aristobulus stayed. He contends that, if the Pollio were a man of the stature of Asinius Pollio, we would expect Josephus to make his identity clear and not to describe him solely in terms of the fact that he was one of Herod's most devoted friends. Moreover, Josephus' reference merely to Pollio here is different from the reference to Asinius (*A* XIV, 138) or to Gaius Asinius Pollio (*A* XIV, 389); furthermore, in this latter passage, his name is spelled with a single lambda, whereas the name of the host of Herod's sons has a double lambda. Finally, since when Herod sent his other two sons to Rome they stayed with "a certain Jew" (*A* XVII, 20), it seems likely that the first two also stayed with a Jew. My reply in "Asinius Pollio and Herod's Sons," *CQ* 35 (1985):240–243, notes that in accordance with Josephus' normal practice, since Josephus does not identify him further, Pollio was known to the reader; and the only Pollios previously mentioned are Pollio the Pharisee (*A* XV, 3), who was living in Jerusalem, and Asinius Pollio (*A* XIV, 389); that, if Josephus refers to Pollio previously (*A* XIV, 138) as Asinius, it is because he is quoting Strabo, who thus refers to him; and that there are numerous instances where Josephus refers to a person alternately by his *nomen gentile* and by his *cognomen.* Five of the major manuscripts of Josephus (*A* XIV, 389) have a double lambda and elsewhere when Josephus refers to a person named Pollio the spelling varies. Finally, the statement (*A* XVII, 20) that Herod's sons stayed with "a certain Jew" rests upon an emendation. In any case, it makes better sense for the ambitious Herod, as later in the case of Herod's grandson Agrippa I and his great-grandson Agrippa II, to have sent his sons to a prominent Roman.

A. T. Sandison, "The Last Illness of Herod the Great, King of Judaea," *Medical History* 11 (1967):381–388, on the basis of Josephus' detailed description (*BJ* I, 656ff., *A* XVII, 168ff.), presents a medical diagnosis of the cause of Herod's death as due to cerebral arteriosclerosis. David J. Ladouceur, "The Death of Herod the Great," *CPh* 76 (1981):25–34, denies the validity of such a diagnosis, since he notes that Josephus' description is modeled on Thucydides' account of the plague; this parallelism, in turn, leads to the resolution of a textual difficulty (*A* XVII, 168–169). However, we may reply that although the Thucydidean language is clear, this does not necessarily refute the validity of Josephus' description, inasmuch as it seems unlikely that such precise detail as is found in Josephus is without a reliable source.

Eliezer Paltiel, "War in Judea—After Herod's Death," *RBPH* 59 (1981):

107–136, argues that the major disturbances in Jerusalem after Herod's death were anti-Herodian rather than anti-Roman and that the smaller messianic disturbances, which were anti-Roman, were of lesser significance.

As to Herod's sons, Frederick F. Bruce, "Herod Antipas, Tetrarch of Galilee and Peraea," *ALUOS* 5 (1963–1965):6–23, in a general survey, concludes that Josephus' account (*A* XVIII, 101–105) may be relied upon since his personal interests were not involved. We may object, however, that since Josephus, who is so proud of his Hasmonean origins, blackens his portrait of the Hasmonean's great rival, Herod, to such a degree, we may expect him to extend his bitterness to Herod's son by Malthace, who, we may conjecture, was additionally despised as a Samaritan. Harold W. Hoehner, *Herod Antipas* (Cambridge 1972), is more credible when he concludes that Josephus is prejudiced against Antipas because of his favoritism toward the latter's opponent Agrippa I and his son Agrippa II. Shimon Applebaum, "The Question of Josephus' Historical Reliability in the Two Test Cases: Antipatris of Kefar-Saba and Antipatris of Caesarea" [Hebrew], *CP* (1982):13–19, likewise casts doubt on Josephus' reliability when he notes that Josephus significantly does not mention the real reason why Antipas was removed from office, namely that he had attempted to develop Jewish cities in Judea in direct confrontation with Roman policy. We may remark, however, that in view of Josephus' antagonism to Antipas, one would have expected him to note such a disobedience to Roman policy. As to the place of Antipas' exile, Josephus contradicts himself, stating once (*BJ* II, 183), that it was Spain and later (*A* XVIII, 252) that it was Lugdunum in Gaul. D. Braund, "Four Notes on the Herods," *CQ* 33 (1983):239–242, favors the latter and asserts that Josephus has thus corrected himself. Christiane Saulnier, "Hérode Antipas et Jean le Baptiste. Quelques remarques sur les confusions chronologiques de Flavius Josèphe," *RB* 88 (1984):362–376, concludes that Josephus had only meager information on Antipas, that to make up for it he must have received oral information from Agrippa II, and that chronological discrepancies in Josephus' account may be explained by referring to Roman history and to the nature of Josephus' account.

Josephus is a most important source for our knowledge of Roman relations with the Parthians. Eugen Täubler, *Die Parthernachrichten bei Josephus* (Berlin 1904), concludes that Josephus used not a Roman source but, in part, a Graeco-Parthian author with hostility to Rome who wrote a chronicle of the Parthian wars and, in part, the memoirs of Herod Antipas, and that his account is confirmed by coins. We may comment that we have neither any mention of nor fragments from either of these accounts. In view of the extraordinary length of the episodes of Anilaeus and Asinaeus (*A* XVIII, 314–379) and of Izates (XX, 17–96), both of whom successfully fought against the Parthians, it seems at least as likely that Josephus had a source, perhaps in Aramaic, the language of the Jews of Babylonia, dealing with the Parthians generally.

Nelson C. Debevoise, *A Political History of Parthia* (Chicago 1938), likewise notes that Josephus is confirmed by numismatics and comments that, when Josephus and Tacitus cover the same ground, Josephus is to be preferred—a most likely hypothesis in view of the fact that Josephus' source may well have been a Jewish narrative that was independent of both the Romans and the Parthians, whereas Tacitus, despite his protestations of impartiality, was a patriotic Roman senator.

Carsten Colpe, "Die Arsakiden bei Josephus," *J-S*, pp. 97–108, notes that, beginning with the reign of Augustus, Josephus becomes more objective in his treatment of Parthian history, inasmuch as the Romans had made treaties with the Parthians. Marina Pucci, "On the Tendentiousness of Josephus' Historical Writing" [Hebrew], *CP* (1982):117–129, however, remarks that Josephus' tendentiousness is seen in his omission of the alliances between Hyrcanus I and the Parthian Phraates II and between Aristobulus II and Mithridates of Pontus. In "Jewish–Parthian Relations in Josephus," *JC* 3 (1983):13–25, she suggests, however, that Josephus' omissions may be due to the fact that otherwise the Jews would have been laid open to the charge of having collaborated with Rome's archenemies, the Parthians.

As to the Roman administration of Judea under the procurators, Eliezer Paltiel, "From Protectorate To Empire: A Study of Roman Policy in Judaea and Other Ethnic States in the Eastern Provinces of the Empire from ca. 14 to ca. 73 C.E." (Ph.D. diss., University of Pennsylvania 1976), argues that the Roman attitude was in accord with their policy in other parts of the empire and depended upon overall political factors rather than upon administrators' personal whims, and that initially the rebels in the provinces, including Judea, sought only autonomy rather than independence. We may respond by admitting that the rapid turnover of procurators indicates that there was a consistent policy, but it also shows that this policy was consistently breached.

As to the procurator Pontius Pilate, we now have an extremely comprehensive account by Jean-Pierre Lémonon, *Pilate et le gouvernement de la Judée. Textes et monuments* (Paris 1981), which, however, tends to prefer Josephus' account in the *War* to that of the *Antiquities*, despite the fact that the latter is generally fuller for the period before the war and presumably more reliable, especially in chronological questions. As to Josephus' account, Daniel R. Schwartz, "Pontius Pilate's Appointment to Office and the Chronology of Josephus' *Jewish Antiquities*, Books XVIII–XX" [Hebrew], *Zion* 48 (1983):325–345, contends that it is not at all confused, and that in the specific matter of the date of Pilate's appointment, the fact that the expulsion of the Jews from Rome in 19 is narrated in the midst of Josephus' discussion of Pilate shows that the procurator Gratus ruled only until 18/19.

Paul L. Maier, "The Episode of the Golden Roman Shields at Jerusalem," *HTR* 62 (1969):109–121, and Gideon Fuks, "Again on the Episode of the Gilded Roman Shields at Jerusalem," *HTR* 75 (1982):503–507, conclude that the episode described by Josephus (*BJ* II, 169–174; *A* XVIII, 55–59) is distinct from that mentioned by Philo (*Legatio ad Gaium* 299–305). Daniel R. Schwartz, "Josephus and Philo on Pontius Pilate" [Hebrew], *CP* (1982):217–236; translated into English in *JC* 3 (1983):26–45, however, argues that they represent a single event, that the discrepancies may be explained by Philo's (and/or Agrippa's) apologetic bias, and that the account in Josephus is simpler and more convincing. The discrepancies, however, we may react, cannot so easily be dismissed, since the episode of the standards, as described by Josephus, occurred at the beginning of Pilate's administration, whereas that of the shields, as delineated by Philo, occurred much later. Moreover, the standards bore images, while the shields did not. Finally, in Josephus the people appeal successfully to Pilate at Caesarea, whereas in Philo they appeal unsuccessfully to Pilate, apparently in Jerusalem. As to two accounts that seemingly duplicate each other, we may suggest a parallel in the case of the edict of Claudius (*A* XIX, 280–285) and his letter in a papyrus with regard to the rights of Jews of Alexandria, the latter of which Josephus neglects to mention, but which, to judge from details in language, does appear to be a separate document.

In "Pontius Pilate's Suspension from Office: Chronology and Sources" [Hebrew], *Tarbiz* 51 (1982):383–398, Schwartz declares that Josephus errs in stating that the Roman governor of Syria, Lucius Vitellius, visited Jerusalem twice (*A* XVIII, 90–95, 122–126) and that actually these are two accounts of a single visit, drawn from two different sources, the first a Jewish priest and the other one dealing with Herod Antipas. We may remark, however, that in view of Josephus' residence in the palace of the Flavians and the presumed accessibility to him of official records, such an error seems unlikely.

Moses Aberbach, "The Conflicting Accounts of Josephus and Tacitus Concerning Cumanus' and Felix' Terms of Office," *JQR* 40 (1949–1950): 1–14, attempts to reconcile Tacitus (*Annals* 12.54), who says that Palestine was ruled by Cumanus, who was in charge of Galilee, and by Felix, who governed Samaria, with Josephus (*A* XX, 137), who declares that Felix succeeded Cumanus, by theorizing that Cumanus was in charge of Judea and Samaria, while Felix ruled Galilee, in which Josephus was less interested at the time. We may reply that this theory presupposes that Tacitus was guilty of the gross error of confusing who was in charge of Galilee; moreover, in view of the fact that not long afterwards Josephus was general in Galilee, it seems unlikely that he would not have ascertained the recent history of the rule of the area.

There has been much speculation as to Josephus' sources for his extraordinarily detailed account of the assassination of Caligula and the accession of

Claudius. Theodor Mommsen, "Cornelius Tacitus und Cluvius Rufus," *Hermes* 4 (1870):295–325, noting that Josephus (*A* XIX, 91–92) refers to a certain Cluitus, a man of consular rank, adopts the emendation to Cluvius and suggests that Josephus' source was Cluvius Rufus the historian. Justin von Destinon, *Untersuchungen zu Flavius Josephus* (Kiel, Programm 1904), suggests instead that Josephus' source was a pamphlet that praised the merit of the conspirator Chaerea. Dieter Timpe, "Römische Geschichte bei Flavius Josephus," *Historia* 9 (1960):474–502, asserts that both Josephus and Tacitus, who are senatorial in their sympathies, are dependent on the same source. In "The Sources of Josephus' Antiquities, Book 19," *Latomus* 21 (1962):320–333, I object that the fact that Agrippa's role in the accession of Claudius is built up to such a degree can hardly be due to Cluvius Rufus but rather depends on Agrippa II, with whom Josephus was so friendly and who sent him (*V* 364) no fewer than sixty-two letters testifying to the truth of Josephus' history of the Jewish War.

In an extremely suggestive article, Thomas R. Martin, "Quintus Curtius' Presentation of Philip Arrhidaeus and Josephus' Accounts of the Accession of Claudius," *AJAH* 8 (1983, published 1987):161–190, notes a curious parallel between Quintus Curtius' account (10.7.1–2) of the role of an unknown soldier in the accession of Philip Arrhidaeus, the half-brother of Alexander the Great, and the role of an unnamed soldier in Josephus' account (*BJ* II, 211–212) of the accession of the Roman Emperor Claudius. The fact that neither Diodorus (18.2) nor Justin (13.2.1–4.4), in their accounts of the aftermath of Alexander's death, refer to this incident leads Martin to postulate that this is a fictitious episode which Curtius drew from first-hand knowledge of Claudius' accession. This would confirm the historicity of Josephus' account, despite the fact that neither Suetonius (*Claudius* 10) nor Dio Cassius (60.1.1–4) refers to the episode of the unknown soldier. We may suggest that the reason why Josephus omits this episode in his otherwise much longer version of the accession of Claudius in the *Antiquities*, Book XIX, is that he wished to put more emphasis there upon the role of Agrippa I in Claudius' rise to power. To his credit, Martin is careful to admit that the other parallels between Curtius and Josephus in their accounts of the respective accessions of Arrhidaeus and Claudius are not sufficiently unique to be conclusive. But his suggestion ultimately rests on the silence of the other two sources with regard to the role of the unknown soldier; and, we may suggest, such an *argumentum ex silentio* is dangerous, especially since one of these sources, Diodorus, is very brief and the other, Justin, is only an abridgment of the lost work of Pompeius Trogus; and either Pompeius or Justin may have omitted the incident out of antidemocratic bias. Nevertheless, we may suggest that a search of other writers of the period covered by Josephus' lifetime may reveal further examples to corroborate Josephus' account. They may also reopen the question as to whether Josephus knew Latin sufficiently well to utilize works written in that language.

As to Claudius' achievements, Arié Kasher, "Les circonstances de la promulgation de l'édit de l'Empereur Claude et de sa letter aux Alexandrins 41 ap. J.-C.," *Semitica* 26 (1976):99–108, and *The Jews in Hellenistic and Roman Egypt* [Hebrew] (Tel-Aviv 1978), carefully differentiates between the edict cited by Josephus (*A* XIX, 280–285) after riots by Jews against Greeks and the letter sent to the Alexandrians (London Papyrus 1912), which was issued later and in response to different circumstances, namely riots by Greeks against Jews. He concludes that ἰσοπολιτεία as seen in Caesarea, Antioch, and Alexandria, does not signify equal civic rights for the Jews, but rather an equality between the Jewish *politeuma* and the Hellenic *polis*. On Antioch see Kasher, "The Rights of the Jews of Antioch on the Orontes," *PAAJR* 49 (1982):69–85, who cites *War* VII, 44, and *Antiquities* XII, 119, to substantiate his claim that the Jews there had the right to organize as a *politeuma* rather than that they were citizens. In "The Status and Rights of the Alexandrian Jews According to Josephus and the Term *Politeia* in Philo and Josephus," in *The Jews in Hellenistic and Roman Egypt: The Struggle for Equal Rights* (Tübingen 1985), pp. 226–309, 358–364, Kasher reiterates his view that the Jews struggled against the Alexandrians to affirm their own *politeuma* and not to gain the rights of citizenship in the *polis*. The fact, however, we may remark, that both Josephus (*A* XIV, 188) and Philo (In *Flaccum* 47) refer to the Jews as citizens makes it hard to believe that they used the term in an imprecise sense, even though Josephus is often less than accurate in his technical terminology, especially since Josephus had to be particularly careful not to commit errors of fact lest he be pounced upon by the anti-Semitic writers whom he was trying to refute.

Per Bilde, "The Roman Emperor Gaius (Caligula's) Attempt to Erect his Statue in the Temple of Jerusalem," *ST* 32 (1978):67–93, asserts that Josephus is more reliable as a historian than has previously been supposed, since he resisted the temptation to theologize. We may wonder, however, about such alleged impartiality in view of the extraordinary attention given to Agrippa in the account in the *Antiquities* of the accession of Claudius, whereas his role is much less important in Josephus' parallel account in the Jewish War. In *Josefus som historieskriver, En undersøgelse af Gaius Caligulas konflikt med jøderne i Palaestina (Bell 2, 184–203) og Ant 18, 261–309) med saerligt henblik på forfatterens tendens og historisk pålidelighed (Josephus as an Historical Writer. An Investigation of Josephus' Account of Gaius Caligula's Conflict with the Jews in Palestine (Bell 2, 184–203 and Ant 18, 261–309 with Special Reference to the Tendency and the Historical Reliability of the Author) (Copenhagen 1983), a work that I have not seen but a summary of which the author has graciously sent to me, Bilde apparently gives a full ac-

count of previous scholarship on the subject, comparing Josephus' two accounts in the light of his writings as a whole, and concludes that Josephus
based his account in the *Antiquities* on his previous version in the *War* and
that he seems to have been both cautious and loyal in his use of sources.

Wolf Wirgin, *Harod Agrippa I. King of the Jews* (Leeds 1968), comparing the accounts of Josephus, Philo, and the Mishnah, accuses Josephus of
concealing facts, just as he, in turn, had accused Nicolaus of Damascus. We
may comment that, though Josephus' glorification of Agrippa accords with
that of the rabbis, we may suspect that Josephus is biased, since he had such
close connections with Agrippa's son (*V* 362–367) and since, after all, he was
a puppet of the Romans, whose staunch defender he was. Wirgin's suggestion
that Agrippa regarded himself as the Messiah seems unlikely, since Josephus
would hardly have praised him if that were so, inasmuch as a messiah by definition would have been a political rebel against the ruling power of Rome.
Menahem Stern, "The Kingdom of Agrippa the First" [Hebrew], *Memorial
Volume to Joseph Amorai* (Tel-Aviv 1973), pp. 117–135, in a survey, generally follows Josephus, even when he disagrees with Roman sources, such
as Suetonius. He disagrees with the generally accepted view that Agrippa
showed a pro-Pharisaic policy in his attitude toward the high priests.

In a brilliant article, Daniel R. Schwartz, "Κατὰ τοῦτον τὸν καιρόν;
Josephus' Source on Agrippa II," *JQR* 72 (1981–1982):241–268, notes seventeen passages that interrupt Josephus' main source. He notes that of the six
passages in *Antiquities* XX that contain slurs on Agrippa or his family, all
show Agrippa in clashes with the priesthood, all are absent from the *War*'s
parallel account, and three begin with the phrase "about this time." He thus
concludes that all six were copied from some other source. Schwartz has now
given us a definitive account in his *Agrippa I: The Last King of Judea* [He-
brew] (Jerusalem 1987).

Josephus as Historian of the Jewish War
Against the Romans

Wilhelm Weber, *Josephus und Vespasian. Untersuchungen zu dem jüdischen Krieg des Flavius Josephus* (Stuttgart 1921), seeks to demonstrate that
Josephus' *Life* is based on an apologetic work that Josephus wrote to win the
support of Titus' Jewish courtiers; but there is no evidence to support such a
theory. Weber's view that Josephus used Vespasian's commentaries extensively is more likely, though in the absence of any fragments from that work
it is difficult to determine the extent of Josephus' indebtedness. Adolf Schlatter, *Der Bericht über das Ende Jerusalems. Ein Dialog mit Wilhelm Weber*
(Gütersloh 1923), agrees with Weber that Josephus had a Roman source for
the *War* and insists that that source was Antonius Julianus, the Roman pro-

curator of Judea, who participated in the council of war convened by Titus to decide the fate of the Temple in 70 (Minucius Felix, *Octavius* 33.4).

Hans Drexler, "Untersuchungen zu Josephus und zur Geschichte des jüdischen Aufstandes 66–70," *Klio* 19 (1925):277–312, concludes that the *War* is just as biased as the *Life* in that it apologetically asserts that the priests and the aristocrats, with whom Josephus identified himself, had, in general, opposed the war. He asserts that Josephus' omissions and his arrangement of material may be explained by his relations with Agrippa II and by his treason. We may respond that, although it is true that Josephus is biased in both the *War* and the *Life,* the latter may be a more reliable account since he apparently had more and better sources for it.

Joseph Klausner, "The Great Revolt and the Second Destruction in the Days of the Second Commonwealth" [Hebrew], in his *In the Days of the Second Temple: Studies in the History of the Second Temple* 3d ed. (Jerusalem 1954), pp. 54–81, in a discussion, marked by his strong nationalism, of the political, economic, social, and religious causes of the war, contends that the revolt and the consequent destruction of the Temple were inevitable.

Alan Lettofsky, *The Jewish War against the Romans according to Josephus Flavius and Talmudic Sources* [Hebrew] (Senior Honors Thesis, Brandeis University 1959), in a systematic comparison of Josephus with all references to the war in rabbinic literature, notes that the chief difference is that the rabbis placed the blame for the defeat upon all the people, whereas Josephus castigates only the extremists, and that Josephus omits mention of the courage of the Jewish captives. He explains these differences by remarking that whereas Josephus was writing for the Romans, the rabbis sought to inspire the Jewish masses. We may remark that Josephus himself, in the proemium to the *War,* declares that he is writing his work for the benefit of the Jews of the "upper country," that is, Mesopotamia, presumably to deter them from later revolt. Furthermore, it is misleading to compare Josephus and the rabbis, since the rabbis range over a great period of time and most of them report statements in the name of other, earlier rabbis. In any case, there is no systematic discussion in the talmudic or midrashic literature of the war. Moreover, in the most important source in rabbinic literature about the revolt (*Gittin* 56a), the rabbis specifically blame only the extremists among the people.

Moses Aberbauch, *The Roman–Jewish War (66–70* A.D.*): Its Origin and Consequences* (London 1966), contends that the fundamental causes of the war were not social, economic, or political but rather the rise to power in Rome of anti-Jewish freedmen of Greek origin and, above all, the tremendous success of Jewish proselytizing activities, which alarmed the conservative Graeco-Roman world. We may comment that neither Josephus, the rabbis, nor Tacitus, though writing from sharply different points of view, present such an analysis; and, in any case, though the Jewish success in proselytism is noted by all of these, as well as by other sources, none of them indicate any connection between this and the outbreak of the war.

In Marxist analyses, Heinz Kreissig, "Die landwirtschaftliche Situation in Palästina vor dem judäischen Krieg," *AA* 17 (1969):223–254, and in an expanded form in *Die sozialen Zusammenhänge des judäischen Krieges* (Berlin 1970), concludes that Josephus is not objective and that the chief causes of the war were social and economic, as seen particularly in the class warfare of the Judean-Galilean peasantry against the priests and landowners of the upper class, rather than nationalistic or religious. He is particularly critical of the theory that the chief cause of the revolt was the messianic movement. Shimon Applebaum, "The Struggle for the Soil and the Revolt of 66–73 C.E." [Hebrew], *EI* (1975):125–128, likewise emphasizes the economic factor but is critical of Kreissig for not giving sufficient emphasis to the problems of overpopulation, the restriction of the average Jewish peasant's holding, and the struggle for land to be cultivated. In "Judaea as a Roman Province; the Countryside as a Political and Economic Factor," *ANRW* 2.8 (1977), pp. 355–396, Applebaum berates Josephus for underestimating the shortage of land and the oppressive taxation as factors accounting for the uprising against Rome. He criticizes, however, the view of Kreissig that a major cause was that the large landowners had undersold the small landowners. A view similar to Kreissig's is that of Peter A. Brunt, "Josephus on Social Conflicts in Roman Judaea," *Klio* 59 (1977): 149–153, that the revolt was almost as much directed against the native landlords and usurers as against the Romans. A similar emphasis on the economic factor is found in Martin Goodman, "The First Jewish Revolt: Social Conflict and the Problem of Debt," *JJS* 33 (1982): 417–427, who concludes that the main cause was the rotting away from within of Judean society due to social imbalance resulting from excessive wealth attracted to the city of Jerusalem during the Pax Romana. Consequently, both the small, independent farmers and the craftsmen and urban plebs of Jerusalem fell heavily into debt and turned to banditry or slavery. Josephus, he asserts, may be assumed to be reliable unless there is good reason to conclude otherwise. We may remark that the burning of the records of debts (*BJ* II, 427) at the beginning of the war by the revolutionaries would seem to confirm the importance of the economic factor.

Uriel Rappaport, "The Relations between Jews and Non-Jews and the Great War against Rome" [Hebrew], *Tarbiz* 47 (1977–1978):1–14, translated into English in "Jewish-Pagan Relations and the Revolt against Rome in 66–70 C.E.," in *The Jerusalem Cathedra*, Lee I. Levine, ed. (Jerusalem 1981), pp. 81–95, and "Notes on the Great Revolt against Rome" [Hebrew], *Cathedra* 8 (1978):42–46, finds the chief cause of the revolt in the confrontation between the Jewish and non-Jewish inhabitants of Palestine and the fact that the Romans favored the latter. In the latter article, he remarks that the war followed the pattern of revolution outlined by Crane Brinton in *The Anatomy of Revolution* (New York 1938). We may venture to guess that Rappaport's analysis may have been influenced by the analogy with the present position of Israel vis-à-vis the "Palestinians."

Rafael Yankelevitch, "The Auxiliary Troops from Caesarea and Sebaste—A Decisive Factor in the Rebellion against Rome" [Hebrew], *Tarbiz* 49 (1979–1980):33–42, notes that the procurators favored non-Jews because their troops were derived primarily from the local non-Jewish population, who were viciously anti-Semitic, and that if these auxiliaries had been recruited from Jews or from non-Jews from other countries a major cause of the revolt would have been eliminated.

Per Bilde, "The Causes of the Jewish War According to Josephus," *JSJ* 10 (1979):179–202, seeks to rehabilitate Josephus as a careful historian who, though he emphasizes the guilt of the revolutionaries, saw the complexity of the causes of the war and possessed a purely historical interest in the sequence of events. He notes that there are no significant differences between the *War* and the *Antiquities* as to the causes of the war. He acknowledges, however, that Josephus did view the war and its results in theological terms, as divine punishment for the people's sins. We may remark, nevertheless, that statements such as *Antiquities* XVIII, 6, that the revolutionaries "sowed the seed of every kind of misery" and *Antiquities* XVIII, 10, that Josephus' reason for including an account of the rise of the Fourth Philosophy is that the zeal that their founders aroused "meant the ruin of our cause," seem to underline the responsibility of the revolutionaries.

John G. Gager, *Kingdom and Community: The Social World of Early Christianity* (Englewood Cliffs 1975), evaluates the revolutionary movement in Judea as reflecting a premillenarian mood of political alienation and economic discontent with Pilate, as paralleled in Melanesia and in other cultures. He suggests, though with no hard evidence, that those priests who were discontented and attracted to early Christianity probably came from a large number of poor and powerless priests of the lower order who, according to Josephus (*A* XX, 179–181), engaged in open conflict with the high priest in Jerusalem.

Richard A. Horsley, "Josephus and the Bandits," *JSJ* 10 (1979):37–63, and "Ancient Jewish Banditry and the Revolt Against Rome, A.D. 66–70," *CBQ* 43 (1981):409–432, emphasizes social banditry as a major cause of the revolt and remarks on the close relationship between the brigands and the people.

Aryeh Kasher, ed., *The Great Jewish Revolt: Factors and Circumstances Leading to Its Outbreak* [Hebrew] (Jerusalem 1983), has gathered together eighteen previously published articles dealing with the causes of the revolt. The authors include Menahem Stern (3), Peter A. Brunt, Solomon Zeitlin,

Shimon Applebaum, Uriel Rappaport (2), Lee I. Levine (2), Gedaliah Alon (2), E. Mary Smallwood, H. Paul Kingdon, Morton Smith, Martin Hengel, Joseph Klausner, and Kasher himself. Kasher, in his introduction (pp. 9–92), views the war as the climax of 130 years of Roman domination.

David M. Rhoads, *Israel in Revolution: 6–74 C.E.: A Political History Based on the Writings of Josephus* (Philadelphia 1976), presents a balanced picture of the many causes for the fighting among the revolutionary groups: political, economic, social, and religious. He argues that there is little evidence for the presence or activity of a Jewish revolutionary sect in the prewar history. He stresses that Josephus may be correct in indicating that the civil war among the revolutionary groups was a more important factor in the defeat of the Jews than the Roman military might.

Clemens Thoma, "Die Weltanschauung des Josephus Flavius. Dargestellt anhand seiner Schilderung des jüdischen Aufstandes gegen Rom (66–73 n. Chr.)," *Kairos* 11 (1969):39–52, contrasts the *War* as pro-Roman propaganda with the *Antiquities* as pro-Jewish apology. Josephus, he says, is motivated in the *War* by a theological tendency; and, moreover, there are Hellenistic tendencies in his portrayal of Jewish religious parties and in his idealization of the future of Israel. We may remark, however, that it is in the proem to the *Antiquities* (I, 14) rather than in the proem to the *War* that Josephus speaks of the theological import of his work.

Yitzhak Baer, "Jerusalem in the Times of the Great Revolt. Based on the Source Criticism of Josephus and Talmudic-Midrashic Legends of the Temple's Destruction" [Hebrew], *Zion* 36 (1971):127–190 and 37 (1972):120, contends that Josephus' account of the revolution is utterly unreliable since it is plagiarized from classical Greek writers; but we may reply that the mention of passages definitely showing the influence of Thucydides or Polybius is very small. In any case, even if such influence could be shown, this would indicate merely that Josephus had turned to classical writers as a model for style and would not prove that the facts themselves had been tampered with, any more than the several phrases in Eleazar ben Jair's speeches at Masada that have been lifted from Plato's *Phaedo* disprove the substance of those speeches. Furthermore, Baer argues that the talmudic account of the destruction of the Temple goes back to Josephus and to Christian legends, and that Josephus and Tacitus used the same sources. We may reply that it seems unlikely that the rabbis, in view of their strong opposition to Christianity, would have used Christian sources, and that, in any case, neither the rabbis nor Christian writers mention one another when they discuss the war. It is certainly possible that Josephus and Tacitus (in *Histories* 5) used each other's accounts, inasmuch as they are almost exact contemporaries and, as intimates of emperors, presumably had access to the same official archives; but neither mentions the other, and there are numerous contradictions between them. Baer is hypercritical in his approach to Josephus. For example, he denies Josephus' statement (*BJ* II, 652) that Simon bar Giora confiscated the property of the rich and maltreated them and liberated slaves (*BJ* IV, 508). We may further comment, however, that Baer is right in noting Josephus' many inaccuracies and contradictions in his account of the war and in stressing that the fact that he is generally accurate in describing buildings and topography hardly warrants our having confidence in his historical account as a whole.

In a more recent account comparing Josephus and the rabbis, Mireille Hadas-Lebel, "La Tradition rabbinique sur la première Revolte contre Rome à la Lumière du De Bello Judaico de Flavius Josèphe," *Sileno* 9 (1983):155–173, argues that Josephus and the rabbis are of mutual benefit in enabling the reader to discern their respective ideologies, though their theology of history is fundamentally similar. We may comment that the rabbinic comments are particularly useful precisely because they represent so many different points of view and because they present comments only in passing, since their work deals with history only rarely.

Shaye J. D. Cohen, "Parallel Historical Tradition in Josephus and Rabbinic Literature," *Proceedings of the Ninth World Congress of Jewish Studies, Jerusalem, August 4–12, 1985, Division B, Vol. 1: The History of the Jewish People (From the Second Temple Period Until the Middle Ages)* (Jerusalem 1986), pp. 7–14, asserts that Josephan traditions are older and more "original" than those of the rabbis, that in not a single case is there a compelling reason to assume the contrary, and that hence Josephus provides a "control" for the study of the rabbinic texts. We may comment that, in view of the distrust that Cohen has expressed elsewhere for Josephus' account of the Jewish War and in view of the sloppiness that he ascribes to Josephus' paraphrase of the Bible, his general preference for Josephus in episodes that parallel the rabbinic accounts seems surprising. As to the places where Josephus and the rabbis agree against Dio Cassius, and where Cohen prefers Dio, this may be due to a common theological position, but it may also be due to the fact that they reflect events accurately.

Pierre Vidal-Naquet, *Flavius Josèphe ou du bon Usage de la Trahison (Preface à 'La guerre des Juifs')* (Paris 1977), pp. 9–115, stresses the apocalyptic element in the revolt and the relation with the Qumran sect. He seeks to explain the emergence of the various revolutionary parties by positing their relation to the divisions of Judaism generally in that period. We may remark that, despite the fact that Josephus mentions the Essenes, in particular, at great length in the *War,* he nowhere indicates that they bore any relation to the revolt.

Paul W. Barnett, "The Jewish Eschatological Prophets A.D. 40–70 in Their Theological and Political Setting" (Ph.D. diss., University of London 1977), contends that the Jewish prophets whom Josephus mentions in his account of the events immediately preceding the war were eschatological rather than revolutionary or messianic. In "The Jewish Sign Prophets—A.D. 40–70—Their Intentions and Origin," *NTS* 27 (1981):679–697, Barnett remarks that the prophets prior to the outbreak of the war were "sign prophets" similar to those who led the exodus and the conquest of Palestine and that Jesus was of this type.

As for the events of the war, Mordechai Gichon, "Cestius Gallus' March on Jerusalem, 66 C.E." [Hebrew], *Abraham Schalit Memorial Volume* (Jerusalem 1980), pp. 283–319; translated (revised) into English in "Cestius Gallus' Campaign in Judaea," *PEQ* 113 (1981):39–62, 140, concludes that Josephus' account of the campaign of Gallus is credible and that, from a military point of view, Gallus' chief mistake was to allow himself to be diverted from his main objective.

Abraham Schalit, "Destruction of Jerusalem" [Hebrew], in *The Book of Jerusalem,* Michael Avi-Yonah, ed. (Jerusalem 1956), pp. 252–263, in tracing the history of the attack on Jerusalem, concludes that Josephus' figures are exaggerated.

As to military aspects of the war, D. B. Saddington, "The Roman *Auxilia* in Tacitus, Josephus and Other Early Imperial Writers," *AC* 13 (1970):89–124, remarks that Josephus cannot be depended upon in his military terminology since we cannot be sure that he is using terms in a technical sense. Indeed, when Josephus and Tacitus refer to the same auxiliaries, in one case Josephus (*BJ* II, 236) is more precise than Tacitus (*Annals* 12.54.3), whereas in the other Tacitus (*Histories* 5.1.2) is more exact than Josephus (*BJ* V, 47ff). We may remark that in view of the fact that Josephus served as a general in Galilee and later had a close association with Titus, we may expect that he would be knowledgeable in military matters, perhaps more so than Tacitus, who apparently had no such experience. If, we may suggest, Tacitus is more reliable in the *Histories,* Book 5, this may be because at this point he presumably had the detailed archives of the Roman generals at his disposal. Indeed, D. L. Kennedy, "Military Cohorts: The Evidence of Josephus BJ III 4.2 (67) and of Epigraphy," *ZPE* 50 (1983):253–263, comments that Josephus' description (*BJ* III, 67) of the military organization of Vespasian's invading forces is trustworthy, despite his disagreement with Tacitus and with Suetonius, since his figures are based on imperial commentaries and because he had no reason to exaggerate the size of the Roman forces. We may remark, however, that Josephus did have something to gain from exaggerating the size of the Roman forces, since his chief aim in the *War* was to deter future revolutions; and an important argument to this end was that the Roman forces were huge and invincible.

One of the most controversial points in Josephus' narrative is his account of the burning of the Temple (*BJ* VI, 236 ff). In an extremely influential monograph, Jakob Bernays, *Ueber die Chronik des Sulpicius Severus* (Breslau 1861), argues that Sulpicius Severus' version (*Chronica* 2.30.36), which asserts that Titus argued that the Temple be burnt, is preferable to Josephus', which indicates that Titus opposed this act. Bernays argues that Sulpicius would have had no motive for modifying Josephus' account; but we may reply that Sulpicius did in that he insists that the real motive of the Romans in attacking the Jews was to destroy the roots of Christianity. Sulpicius' source may well have been Tacitus, according to Bernays and Timothy D. Barnes, "The Fragments of Tacitus' Histories," *CPh* 72 (1977):224–231, since in the preceding chapter he had used Tacitus' account in the *Annals* of Nero, though we may remark that the fact that he had used the *Annals* of Tacitus does not prove that he also had the *Histories*.

Gedaliah Allon, "The Burning of the Temple" [Hebrew], *Yavneh* 1 (1939):85–106, translated into English in his *Jews, Judaism, and the Classical World: Studies in Jewish History in the Times of the Second Temple and Talmud* (Jerusalem 1977), pp. 252–268, noting that the Talmud is unanimous in condemning Titus, is convinced that Titus gave the order to destroy the Temple. Johanan (Hans) Lewy, "The Motives of Titus to Destroy the Temple according to Tacitus" [Hebrew], *Zion* 8 (1942–1943):81–83, agrees with Bernays that Josephus' account is deliberately falsified and cites Josephus' own statement (*BJ* VI, 339) in which Titus hints at the need to extirpate the worship in Jerusalem. On the other hand, Sulpicius' statement that Titus favored the destruction of the Temple agrees with Tacitus' view (*Histories* 5.3–5) that the destruction of the Temple, with its opposition to the representation of the divinity, was an appropriate punishment for those who had their beginnings through a show of hatred to the gods. We may comment that the passage in Josephus (*BJ* VI, 339) states that if Vespasian had come to extirpate the entire worship his goal would have been to sack the city of Jerusalem immediately, but the clear implication is that this was not his intention. Abraham Schalit, "Destruction of Jerusalem" [Hebrew], in *The Book of Jerusalem,* Michael Avi-Yonah, ed. (Jerusalem 1956), pp. 252–263, likewise prefers Sulpicius' version to that of Josephus, whose figures, he remarks, are exaggerated.

Hugh Montefiore, "Sulpicius Severus and Titus' Council of War," *Historia* 11 (1962):156–170, adopts an intermediate position, positing that Josephus has more accurately reproduced Titus' actual words but that Sulpicius has more accurately represented the real intent behind his words. He suggests that Antonius Julianus, who was present at the council Titus convened to decide the fate of Jerusalem, is most likely the source for the view that Titus favored the destruction of the Temple. We may remark that the fact that Sulpicius gives Josephus' and not Tacitus' figures for those killed and captured during the siege indicates that Josephus was his main source; but the fact that he gives a different version of Titus' view shows that he had another source as well.

Ingomar Weiler, "Titus und die Zerstörung des Tempels von Jerusalem— Absicht oder Zufall?" *Klio* 50 (1968):139–158, likewise prefers Sulpicius' version, pointing, in particular, to the proem of Valerius Flaccus, a contemporary of Josephus, who refers to Titus' conquest of Jerusalem "as he hurls the brands and spreads havoc in every tower." Although this does not necessarily refer to the burning of the Temple, the fact that Titus is alleged to have done so "in every tower" implies that this includes the Temple, surely the most famous building in Jerusalem.

G. K. van Andel, *The Christian Concept of History in the Chronicle of Sulpicius Severus* (Amsterdam 1976), argues that Sulpicius' source for his account of the destruction of Jerusalem was not Josephus but the lost account of Tacitus' *Histories,* Book 5. In answer to the objection that Sulpicius gives Josephus' figures for the number of Jews present in Jerusalem before the destruction (*BJ* VI, 420), he asserts that Sulpicius may have known them through indirect knowledge via Eusebius/Jerome. We may suggest, however, that it may better be explained by the hypothesis that Sulpicius knew both Josephus and Tacitus.

In general, Josephus' account of Titus is less than trustworthy, since, as Zvi Yavetz, "Reflections on Titus and Josephus," *GRBS* 16 (1975):411–432, has remarked, during the period when Josephus wrote the *War,* Titus needed favorable publicity to counteract the rumors implicating him in his father's death. Brian W. Jones, *The Emperor Titus* (London 1984), pp. 34–76, has shown how Josephus exaggerates Titus' military achievements, since actually Titus had shown immaturity and recklessness, and seeks to bring his account into line with the official Flavian version, omitting, significantly, all mention of his embarrassing relationship with Berenice, the sister of Agrippa II.

Studies of Josephus' Individual Works

There have been no fewer than seven recent dissertations concentrating on Josephus' *Jewish War* and especially on the speeches therein. Helgo Lindner, *Die Geschichtsauffassung des Flavius Josephus im Bellum Judaicum. Gleichzeitig ein Beitrag zur Quellenfrage* (Leiden 1972), stresses the biblical and theological basis of the speeches as a vehicle for Josephus' own thoughts, and the conception of history as an encounter between God and His people, a *Heilsgeschichte.* Yet, we may comment that he does not take into sufficient account the extent to which they are exercises in Greek rhetoric fashioned in Josephus' scriptorium in Rome. In any case, Lindner oversimplifies the nature of the Hellenistic historiographical tradition that influenced Josephus.

Donna R. Runnalls, "Hebrew and Greek Sources in the Speeches of

Josephus' 'Jewish War'" (Ph.D. diss., University of Toronto 1971), analyzes eight speeches in the *War* in the light of Aristotle's *Art of Rhetoric* and Demetrius' *On Style* and notes that six of these follow the general rules of Greek rhetoric, while two of them, in effect, are Jewish sermons in the manner of Cynic-Stoic diatribes. Like Lindner, she concludes that the speeches are not in the form in which they were originally delivered but, rather, that they are vehicles for expressing the theological and ideological views of Josephus himself and not his literary assistants.

Gohei Hata, "The Jewish War of Josephus: A Semantic and Historiographic Study" (Ph.D. diss., Dropsie University 1975), supplemented by his "Is the Greek Version of Josephus' 'Jewish War' a Translation or a Rewriting of the First Version?" *JQR* 66 (1975):89–108, has commented at length on the question of the relationship between the present Greek version of the *War* and the Aramaic original. He argues that Josephus' statement (*BJ* I, 3) that he had translated (μεταβαλών), the original into Greek is to be understood in the sense of new, utterly transformed creation. Although it is true that Josephus himself (*Ap* I, 50) admits that he had assistants who helped him with the Greek of the *War,* the fact that there are so few Semiticisms in the work supports this thesis. We may comment that Josephus' use of this word in connection with the translation known as the Septuagint (*A* I, 10; XII, 14, 15, 107) is an indication that he viewed himself as carrying on the tradition of the Septuagint in not merely translating but also interpreting, though he claims (*A* I, 17) that he has neither added to nor subtracted from the precise details of the Scriptures.

Roland G. Bomstad, "Governing Ideas of the Jewish War of Flavius Josephus" (Ph.D. diss., Yale University 1979), commenting on the speeches of Eleazar ben Jair, Agrippa II, and Josephus, similarly stresses their biblical and theological elements. Bernard Thérond, "Le discourse de l'histoire dans 'La guerre des Juifs' de Flavius Josèphe" (Thèse de doctorat de 3 Cycle [Études grecques], University of Paris 1979), goes even further in concluding that Josephus is a veritable philosopher or, more precisely, a theologian of history, who only incidentally adopted the genre of history. Thérond, "Les Flaviens dans 'La Guerre des Juifs' de Flavius Josèphe," *DHA* 7 (1981): 235–245, states that in alluding to the messianiclike role of the Flavians, Josephus showed that he was capable of stepping beyond the historical point of view in order to stress a theology of history.

Shaye J. D. Cohen, *Josephus in Galilee and Rome: His Vita and Development as a Historian* (Leiden 1979), commenting on the relationship between the *War* and the *Life,* remarks that while writing the latter, following standard Greek practice, Josephus sought a thematic rather than a chronological narrative. As to Cohen's theory, however, that Josephus' memoir (*hypomnema*) is his source for both the *War* and the *Life,* this hardly tells us much about the accuracy of any data taken from the memoir, since we have not a single fragment thereof.

In an unusually challenging thesis, Seth Schwartz, "Josephus and Judaism from 70 to 100 of the Common Era" (Ph.D. diss., Columbia University 1985), has made the striking observation that, with few exceptions, the passages in the *War* in which Josephus refers to the Bible diverge from and even contradict our biblical texts and the version found his later *Antiquities*. He conjectures that this is because Josephus was working for the most part from memory, and what he remembered may often have been popular storytelling or priestly practice. However, we may suggest that, at least in part, Josephus may have used midrashic or midrashiclike sources for the *War* that were different from those that he employed for the *Antiquities*. In any case, there is ample rabbinic precedent that permits liberty to be taken when giving illustrations in a sermon; and the biblical references in the *War* appear in the context of speeches, notably Josephus' speech to the rebels in Book V. Schwartz, moreover, makes much of the fact that in the *War* we hear nothing of the prophets (except for Jeremiah and Haggai) or of the Hagiographa, and concludes that this shows Josephus' ignorance of these books; but we may object that we should hardly expect such references in a work dealing with the Jewish war against the Romans. According to Schwartz, Josephus increased his biblical knowledge while he was in Rome, as seen in his *Antiquities;* but we may wonder whether it is not more likely that he acquired his knowledge of the Bible during the first half of his life, spent in Jerusalem, where, according to his own account, he received such an excellent Jewish education, in which the Bible surely was the cornerstone. Since most of the passages allegedly revealing Josephus' ignorance of the Bible are to be found in one speech in the *War* (*V*, 362–419), we may suggest that they reflect Josephus' source or sources at that point. In general, Schwartz's theory that Josephus improved his education drastically while in Rome seems hard to substantiate, since the *Life* and the treatise *Against Apion,* both dating from approximately the same time, are so utterly different in style by Schwartz's own admission: the *Life* being the worst and the *Against Apion* being the best, the most sophisticated, and the most learned of Josephus' works. A more likely theory is that Josephus had better sources or better assistants for the *Against Apion.*

Much attention has recently been given to the date of the composition of the *War.* Menahem Stern, "The Date of the Composition of *Bellum Judaicum*" [Hebrew], *PSWCJS* (Jerusalem 1975), 2, pp. 29–34, concludes that the *War* was published toward the end of Vespasian's life or at the beginning of Titus' reign, since it has a negative attitude toward Alienus Caecina (*BJ* IV, 634–644)—who after originally deserting to Vespasian, was killed as a conspirator against the Flavian dynasty at the behest of Titus at the very end of Vespasian's reign—whereas the *War* has such a positive attitude toward Titus.

Shaye Cohen, *Josephus in Galilee and Rome: His Vita and Development as a Historian* (Leiden 1979), pp. 87–90, while concurring in a post-Vespasianic date for the first six books of the *War,* contends that the adulation for Domitian in VII, 85–88, as compared with the almost total disregard of him in the first six books, is an indication that this book was composed in Domitian's reign. This view is supported by Andrew Q. Morton and Sidney Michaelson, "Elision as an Indication of Authorship in Greek Writers," *ROIELAO* no. 3 (1973):33–56, who note that when it comes to elision there is a marked difference between Book VII and the first six books of the *War.*

Most recently, Seth Schwartz, "Josephus and Judaism from 70 to 100 of the Common Era" (Ph.D. diss., Columbia University 1985) and "The Composition and Publication of Josephus's *Bellum Iudaicum* Book 7," *HTR* 79 (1986):373–386, has argued that Book VII is the product of two revisions: an early version composed under Titus and revised under Domitian, probably early in his reign, and a final revision made under Nerva or early in Trajan's reign. He notes that this book is marked by great formal incoherence in contrast to Books I through VI. Hence, he concludes that Book VII, in its present form, was composed at the earliest in the mid-nineties, since it describes the death of Catullus (VII, 451–453), whom Schwartz identifies as Valerius Catullus Messalinus. Indeed, we may remark that the account of the *War* proper does seem to end with the destruction of the Temple at the close of Book VI, and that Book VII does appear to be added as a kind of appendix.

The question of the relationship of the *War* to the *Life* has been much debated. Richard Laqueur, *Der jüdische Historiker Flavius Josephus. Ein biographischer Versuch auf neuer quellenkritischer Grundlage* (Giessen 1920), believes that the source of the *Life* must be earlier than the *War* because it is more reliable. Hans Drexler, "Untersuchungen zu Josephus und zur Geschichte des jüdischen Aufstandes 66–70," *Klio* 19 (1925):277–312, as noted, asserts that the *War* is no less tendentious that the *Life,* and that this tendentiousness may be explained by Josephus' close relationship with Agrippa II. Matthias Gelzer, "Die Vita des Josephus," *Hermes* 80 (1952):67–90, concludes that the *Life* is more trustworthy than the *War* and that it closely follows not an administrative report but a personal memoir of Josephus. Yitzhak Baer, "Jerusalem in the Times of the Great Revolt. Based on the Source Criticism of Josephus and Talmudic-Midrashic Legends of the Temple's Destruction" [Hebrew], *Zion* 36 (1971):127–190 and 37 (1972):120, regards this memoir as notes jotted down during the war and flatly asserts that the *Life* is based on this, whereas the *War* is not. Shaye Cohen, *Josephus in Galilee and Rome: His Vita and Development as a Historian* (Leiden 1979), as noted, suggests that Josephus used this preliminary draft for both the *War* and the *Life* but that he modified it less in the *Life.* He then concludes that originally Josephus had backed the revolt but that after he had surrendered he invented a moderate faction to make it appear that he had not been alone in his defection. Here we have the phenomenon of the believing skeptic, for whereas Cohen looks upon much of Josephus as historical fiction, he is ready to believe Josephus' version of his mission in the *War.*

As to the date of the composition of the *Life,* this depends, as Abraham Schalit, "When Did Josephus Write His *Vita?"* [Hebrew], *Zion* 5 (1933): 174–187, indicates, on the date of the death of Agrippa II, since Josephus (*V* 359) clearly indicates that Agrippa is no longer alive. The statement of Photius (*Bibliotheca,* p. 33), citing Justus of Tiberias, that Agrippa died in the third year of Trajan's reign (i.e., 100) would appear to be decisive. However, as Schalit remarks, we have no numismatic evidence to support the view that Agrippa reigned after 95/96, though we must add, this is the *argumentum ex silentio,* which is hardly conclusive. Thérèse Frankfort, "La date de l'Autobiographie de Flavius Josèphe et des oeuvres de Justus de Tibériade," *RBPH* 39 (1961):52–58, likewise disputes this date, remarking that, if Agrippa were not already dead, Josephus could hardly have mentioned the rumor that he had had relations with his sister Berenice and that, if Domitian were emperor when Josephus completed his work, he would hardly have been likely to avoid flattering him. We may reply, however, that Josephus, writing the *Antiquities* in Rome, had hardly anything to fear from a petty prince thousands of miles away and that, if Josephus was really such a flatterer, he could hardly have presented such a positive picture of Titus, Domitian's hated brother. Indeed, Cohen (*Josephus in Galilee and Rome,* pp. 170–180) suggests that Josephus might well have spoken negatively of Agrippa II in the *Antiquities* in view of his new nationalistic religious bias; but the simplest explanation is that Agrippa was now dead.

Emil Schürer, *The History of the Jewish People in the Age of Jesus Christ,* rev. ed. by Geza Vermes and Fergus Millar, vol. 1 (Edinburgh 1973), pp. 481–483, likewise contests Photius' date for Agrippa's death. We may comment that it hardly seems justified to put such faith in the comments of a ninth-century antiquarian, especially since, as Schürer (p. 482) remarks, the confusion may be explained by the fact that the entry on Justus immediately precedes that on Clemens, who, according to Jerome, died in the third year of Trajan's reign.

Another question is the relation of the *Life* to the *Antiquities.* David A. Barish, "The *Autobiography* of Josephus and the Hypothesis of a Second Edition of His *Antiquities,"* *HTR* 71 (1978):61–75, regards the *Life* as the conclusion of the *Antiquities.* If so, however, we may ask why Josephus does not give us the number of lines at the end of the *Life* as he does at the end of the *Antiquities* (XX, 267). Moreover, he says (XX, 267) that in the concluding work (the *Life,* according to Barish), he will discuss the war and the later events of Jewish history up to his own day, whereas such events do not belong in an autobiography. Barish claims that there is a paraphrase of *Antiquities* XX, 266–267, in the conclusion of the *Life;* but the only parallel, we may remark is the word καταπαύω, which means "close" and has no special significance.

As to the purpose of the *Life,* Cohen (pp. 101–170) notes that its style and content are in the Graeco-Roman, especially the Roman, tradition; that it partakes of both apologetic and polemic, being directed against Justus of Tiberias and against attacks from other fellow Jews in Rome; and that, since the chords are not unique with the *Life* but are found also in the *Antiquities,* they are not due to Justus. Elvira Migliario, "Per l'interpretazione dell' Autobiografia di Flavio Giuseppe," *Athenaeum* 59 (1981):92–137, views the *Life* as an apologetic work seeking to impress Josephus' countrymen with the urgent need for peaceful coexistence with Rome and desiring to buttress his standing with the Jews of the Diaspora. We may comment, however, that there is little direct evidence to support the latter as a motive, unless we regard Josephus' boast that he is in the good graces of the emperor as one that deserves to be taken at face value.

As to the treatise *Against Apion,* several writers, notably Arnaldo Momigliano, "Intorno al 'Contro Apione'," *RF* 59 (1931):485–503; Samuel Belkin, "The Alexandrian Source for Contra Apionem II," *JQR* 27 (1936–1937): 1–32 (who suggests that Josephus merely gave the material a popular expression); and F. H. Colson, *Philo,* vol. 9 (Loeb Classical Library: London 1941), pp. 409, 540 and passim, have independently suggested its dependence, direct or indirect, upon Philo's *Hypothetica.* Although it is true that the similarities in law of the two works are also paralleled in rabbinic sources, the rabbinic parallels are not quite as precise as those in Philo. In particular, we may note the striking parallel in language between Philo (*Hypothetica* 7.9) and Josephus (*Ap* II, 213) in connection with the animal that has taken refuge in one's house as a suppliant. We may suggest that this dependence is particularly likely in view of the similarity between Philo and Josephus in their symbolic explanation of the Temple and its accoutrements. Indeed, Jacob Freudenthal, *Hellenistische Studien. Alexander Polyhistor und die von ihm erhaltenen Reste jüdischer und samaritanischer Geschichtswerke* (Breslau 1874–1875), long before had argued that Josephus used Philo's writings. More recently, David M. Hay, "What is Proof? Rhetorical Verification in Philo, Josephus, and Quintilian," *SBL 1979 Seminar Papers,* Paul J. Achtemeier, ed., vol. 2 (Missoula 1979), pp. 87–100, notes that Philo's *In Flaccum* and Josephus' *Against Apion* show major similarities not only in fundamental religious ideas but also in types of apologetic argument, since both writers are indebted to a long-standing tradition of Hellenistic rhetoric, as summarized in Quintilian's later *Institutio Oratoria,* and to Hellenistic Jewish apologetic. Moreover, in particular, Arnaldo Momigliano, "Un' apologia del Guidaismo. Il Contro

Apione di Flavio Giuseppe," *RMI* 6 (1931–1932):33–41, adds that Josephus has imposed a Hellenistic mentality upon Jewish theology. Erhard Kamlah, "Frömmigkeit und Tugend. Die Gesetzesapologie des Josephus in c Ap 2, 145–295," *J-S* (1974), pp. 220–232, though admitting that *Against Apion* shows some dependence on Diaspora apologetic, stresses Josephus' orientation toward Palestinian Judaism. Christoph Schäublin, "Josephus und die Griechen," *Hermes* 110 (1982):316–341, stresses, in particular, Josephus' debt to Plato, notably for the basis of his idea of theocracy. We may remark, however, that while there is much evidence for Josephus' indebtedness to Plato (see my "Josephus as a Biblical Interpreter; the 'Aqedah'," *JQR* 75 [1984–1985] 225, n. 39), Josephus was hardly indebted to Plato for the idea of theocracy, since Plato himself in the *Republic* (4.427b–c) assigns only a very incidental role to the gods in his ideal state.

In "'Let Wives Be Submissive . . .' The Origin, Form and Apologetic Function of the Household Duty Code (*Haustafel*) in I Peter" (Diss., Yale University 1974); "Josephus, 'Against Apion' II. 145–296. A Preliminary Report," *SBL 1975 Seminar Papers*, George MacRae, ed., vol. 1 (Missoula 1975), pp. 187–192; and "Two Apologetic Encomia: Dionysius on Rome and Josephus on the Jews," *JSJ* 13 (1982):102–122, David L. Balch notes that in his defense of the Jewish constitution, Josephus (*Ap* II, 145–295), despite his denial that he is writing an encomium, follows the handbook rhetorical pattern for praising a city or a people in response to prior invectives, found, for example, in Dionysius of Halicarnassus (*Roman Antiquities* 1.9–2.29) and in the third-century Menander of Laodicea. In doing so, Josephus thus fits into the international atmosphere of the Roman Empire, where it was common for historians and rhetoricians to compare, contrast, and apologize for various peoples. We may add that Josephus follows the guidance of rhetorical handbooks not merely here but also in his praise of biblical heroes in the *Antiquities,* as seen, for example, in his paraphrase of the ʿAqedah.

As to Josephus' projected works, Hans Petersen, "Real and Alleged Literary Projects of Josephus," *AJP* 79 (1958):259–274, argues that Josephus wrote all the works that he had planned and that most of the references in the *Antiquities* to contemplated works are to the *Against Apion,* which, when finally written, however, differed from the original plan of the work. We may reply that the *Against Apion* can hardly be the projected discussion of theology and halakhah, since it is merely incidental to that treatise. As to the projected running account of the Jewish War (*A* XX, 267), this can hardly be the *Life,* which seems too personal and too spotty and which has no account of the causes of the war or especially the climactic destruction of the Temple. David Altschuler, "The Treatise ΠΕΡΙ ΕΘΩΝ ΚΑΙ ΑΙΤΙΩΝ 'On Customs and Causes' by Flavius Josephus," *JQR* 69 (1978–1979):226–232, suggests that instead of writing a separate treatise on Jewish law, Josephus revised Book III of the *Antiquities*. This, however, seems unlikely in view of the promise (*A* XX, 268) that Josephus makes that the projected work will be a separate one in four books.

Josephus' Sources

Much of the earlier scholarship on Josephus was concerned with an attempt to isolate his sources. In line with the fashion of German scholarship at the end of the nineteenth and beginning of the twentieth century, the assumption, based primarily on the difficulty that the ancients had in consulting manuscripts, was generally made that Josephus did not use more than one source at any given time. Heinrich Bloch, *Die Quellen des Flavius Josephus in seiner Archäologie* (Leipzig 1879), who was the pioneer in this search, concludes that the greatest part of the last books of the *Antiquities* depended on oral sources. Friedrich Schemann, *Die Quellen des Flavius Josephus in der jüdischen Archäologie, Buch XVIII–XX—Polemos II, cap. VII–XIV, 3* (Hagen 1887), explicitly disagrees and declares that Josephus is dependent on a very detailed Roman universal history—he says that the unfulfilled cross references in Books XIX and XX have been lifted bodily from that source—and only to a minor degree on an oral source. But we remain skeptical about Josephus' use of a universal history of which not a single fragment has survived. He asserts that, for the years of Josephus' own lifetime, he used the works of his predecessors; but again we have not a single fragment of these. All of this, we may comment, presupposes that Josephus did not have a mind of his own. Justus von Destinon, *Die Quellen des Flavius Josephus in der Jüd. Arch. Buch XII–XVII—Jüd. Krieg Buch I* (Kiel 1882), concludes that Josephus used an anonymous source without great modifications and declares that when he uses the phrase ὡς καὶ ἐν ἄλλοις δεδήλωται, that is found so often in Books XII and XIII of the *Antiquities,* he is simply copying what he found in his source. Inasmuch as not a single fragment of this anonymous "middle" source has survived, we may be pardoned for remaining skeptical about its existence.

Adolphe Buchler [*sic*] "Les sources de Flavius Josèphe dans ses *Antiquités* (XII, 5–XIII, 1)," *REJ* 32 (1896):179–199; 34 (1897):69–93, asserts Josephus' dependence in *Antiquities* XIII, 236–244 on an anonymous author and on Nicolaus, who, in turn, are indebted to Polybius and Poseidonius, and in *Antiquities* XII, 242–256 on I Maccabees and Nicolaus.

Gustav Hölscher, *Die Quellen des Josephus für die Zeit vom Exil bis zum jüdischen Kriege* (Leipzig 1904), concludes that Josephus' sources for *Antiquities,* Books XI to XX, were, successively, Alexander Polyhistor (for Ezra and Nehemiah), the Greek Esther, Pseudo-Aristeas, I Maccabees, Strabo, Nicolaus, a historian of the Herodians, and an oral rabbinic source. He, however, assumes a "middle" source between Nicolaus and Josephus, as he does a Hellenistic Midrash between the Bible and Josephus for the first half of the *Antiquities*. A useful correction to the hypothesis of von Destinon and his followers is Eugen Täubler, "Die nicht bestimmbaren Hinweise bei Josephus und die Anonymushypothese," *Hermes* 51 (1916):211–232, and Richard Laqueur, "Nikolaos von Damaskos," *RE* 17.1 (1936), pp. 362–424, who convincingly argue that Josephus was not a mindless copier of an intermediate source. Heinrich Guttmann, *Die Darstellung der jüdischen Religion bei Flavius Josephus* (Breslau 1928), contends that Josephus knew some Jewish writings that we no longer possess as well as some Hellenistic sources; but, arguing against Hölscher, he concludes that he put his own personal imprint on the traditional material before him.

As to Josephus' indebtedness to specific authors, Sven Ek, "Herodotismen in der jüdischen Archäologie des Josephos und ihre textkritische Bedeutung," *Skrifter utgivna av Kungl. Humanistiska Vetenskapssamfundet i Lund. Acta Regiae Societatis Humaniorum Litterarum Lundensis*, vol. 2 (Lund 1945–1956), pp. 27–62, 213, finds Herodotean phraseology throughout the *Antiquities* and thus argues against Thackeray's theory that Josephus had assistants for certain parts alone of the work.

David Flusser, "Josephus on the Sadducees and Menander," *Immanuel* 7 (1977):61–67, finds a parallel with Menander's *Epitrepontes* but deems it improbable that Josephus was directly influenced by Menander. We may note, however, that in view of Menander's great popularity during the Hellenistic period this is hardly unlikely.

Menahem Luz, "Clearchus of Soli as a Source of Eleazar's Deuterosis" [Hebrew], *CP* (1982):79–90, noting parallels between Eleazar ben Jair's second speech at Masada (*BJ* VII, 341–388) and Clearchus of Soli, as well as with other Hellenistic writers, concludes that Josephus modeled himself upon these works.

Ehrhard Kamlah, "Frömmigkeit und Tugend. Die Gesetzapologie des Josephus in c *Ap*. 2, 145–295," *J-S*, pp. 220–232, postulates that the source for many of Josephus' comments about Jewish piety and virtue is Hecataeus. We may object, however, that since the phraseology of Josephus is seldom similar to that of Hecataeus, it is more likely that both are dependent on a common source, which contained *topoi* that are common in encomia.

Jörg-Dieter Gauger, "Zitate in der jüdischen Apologetik und die Authentizität der Hekataois-Passagen bei Flavius Josephus und im Ps. Aristeas-Brief," *JSJ* 13 (1982):6–46, concludes that Josephus had Hecataeus' original before him and did not merely consult an intermediary.

Jacob Freudenthal, *Hellenistiche Studen. Alexander Polyhistor und die von ihm erhaltenen Reste jüdischer und samaritanischer Geschichtswerke* (Breslau 1874–1875), argues that Josephus knew the Graeco-Jewish writers, particularly through Alexander Polyhistor's compilation. We may remark, however, that Josephus refers only once to Alexander, and that in the treatise *Against Apion* he cites several Graeco-Jewish writers as if they were pagans. Indeed, Nikolaus Walter, "Zur Überlieferung einiger Rester früher jüdisch-hellenistischer Literatur bei Josephus, Clemens und Euseb," *SP* 7 (1966): 314–320, asserts that Josephus did not use the treatise of Alexander in the *Antiquities,* though, as he admits, on the one occasion when he refers (*A* I, 239) to the work of Cleodemus-Malchus he cites him from a treatise of Alexander.

Ben Zion Wacholder, *Eupolemus. A Study of Judaeo-Greek Literature* (Cincinnati 1974), pp. 52–57, remarks that since Josephus (*A* XII, 415–419, *Ap* I, 218) looked upon Eupolemus as a non-Jew, his knowledge of his work must have been very limited. We may object, however, that Josephus elsewhere especially favors evidence from non-Jewish historians, for example, Dius (*A* VIII, 147, 149; *Ap* I, 112–115) and Menander of Ephesus (*A* VIII, 144–146; *Ap* I, 116–120), inasmuch as they would be regarded as more impartial than Jews.

Howard Jacobson, *The Exagoge of Ezekiel* (Cambridge 1983), though noting the absence of Ezekiel the tragedian from Josephus' literary review (*Ap* I, 218) nevertheless postulates that Josephus was influenced by Ezekiel's work, most likely in the excerpts in Alexander Polyhistor, for example in his account of the crossing of the Red Sea.

Several writers have stressed Josephus' indebtedness to Nicolaus of Damascus. Menahem Stern, "Flavius Josephus' Method of Writing History" [Hebrew], *HHS* (1962):22–28, agrees with Gustav Hölscher, "Josephus," *RE* 9 (1916):1934–2000, in postulating Nicolaus as the source for the account in the *Antiquities* of John Hyrcanus and his successors. As a partisan of Herod, Nicolaus, he says, was probably anti-Hasmonean, as we see in Josephus' treatment of Alexander Jannaeus, whereas the version of Maccabean history in the *War* is fairly positive. In "Nicolaus of Damascus as a Source for Jewish History in the Herodian and Hasmonean Periods" [Hebrew], *BJH* (1972): 375–394, Stern explains Josephus' unsympathetic portrait of the Hasmonean dynasty by postulating that he was heavily dependent on Nicolaus. However, he admits that, with regard to Herod, Josephus also derived some information from descendants of Herod and Mariamne who were highly critical of him.

Ben Zion Wacholder, *Nicolaus of Damascus* (Berkeley 1962), goes even further and argues that Nicolaus was Josephus' source not only for the Maccabean and Herodian periods but for earlier Jewish history as well. Despite Wacholder's remark that in the *Antiquities* Josephus followed Nicolaus more closely than in the *War,* we may remark that it is in the *Antiquities* that Josephus consciously tried to free himself from the panegyrical approach of Nicolaus to Herod and endeavored to approach his subject more critically.

Jonathan A. Goldsten, *I Maccabees* (Garden City 1976), pp. 60–61, objects to the common view that Josephus' source for the Hasmonean revolt was Nicolaus because he doubts that the praise of Judas would have been found in a pagan historian, particularly one who was the chief courtier of Herod, who so hated the Hasmoneans. But, we may counter, the fact that Herod married Mariamne, a Hasmonean princess, shows that he wished to gain legitimacy by allying himself with the Hasmoneans and, in any case, that Nicolaus would certainly have approved of the earliest Hasmoneans, at least so far as their alliance with Rome against Antiochus Epiphanes.

In presenting the arguments used by the Jews when they appealed to Pompey to replace the Hasmonean rule with their traditional theocratic form of government, Jürgen C. H. Lebram, "Der Idealstaat der Juden," *J-S*, pp. 233–253, argues that Josephus (*A* XIV, 41) was echoing pagan views, such as are found in Diodorus Siculus and Strabo, more than biblical ideas. We may object that, from the point of view of language at least, Diodorus and Strabo can be regarded as Josephus' source only by a considerable stretch of imagination.

A number of writers, notably Henry St. J. Thackeray, *Josephus the Man and the Historian* (New York 1929), pp. 56–58, and Robert J. H. Shutt, *Studies in Josephus* (London 1961), pp. 91–101, have stressed the parallels between Josephus and Dionysius of Halicarnassus. But David J. Ladouceur, "The Language of Josephus," *JSJ* 14 (1983):18–38, has noted that many of the verbal parallels alleged by Shutt may actually be found in Greek writers of the fourth century B.C.E. or even earlier. Seth Schwartz, "Josephus and Judaism from 70 to 100 of the Common Era" (Ph.D. diss., Columbia University 1985), p. 158, has made the revealing observation that whereas Josephus (*Ap* I, 66) says that though the Romans were a significant power in the fifth century B.C.E., neither Herodotus nor Thucydides nor any of their contemporaries mention the Romans, the fact is that Dionysius (*Roman Antiquities* 1.72.2–4) mentions several fifth century writers who did; hence, Josephus could not have known at least this passage in Dionysius. We may add that our own attempts to find parallels in vocabulary, grammar, and style between the two writers have almost invariably led to negative results.

Most recently Schwartz (pp. 138–143) made an extended attempt to deny Josephus' familiarity with Philo. He argues that the similarities in biblical material can be explained as arising from a common apologetic concern resorting to commonplaces expressed in common constructions or common correct understanding of the biblical text. He stresses that except for the description of the Tabernacle and the priestly vestments, Josephus never resorts to allegory, the hallmark of Philonic exegesis, to explain biblical laws. We may remark that the very fact that he does so in these cases is itself rather remarkable, inasmuch as we should hardly expect Josephus, as a historian, to be interested in such philosophical exegesis, particularly since he says (*A* IV, 198 and XX, 268) that he will reserve for a separate work a discussion of the reasons for the commandments. Moreover, even Schwartz (pp. 172–180) admits Philo's strong influence upon the summary of the laws in Book II of *Against Apion*, which was written shortly after the *Antiquities*. To be sure, David M. Hay, "What Is Proof? Rhetorical Verification in Philo, Josephus, and Quintilian," *SBL 1979 Seminar Papers*, Paul J. Achtemeier, ed., vol. 2 (Missoula 1979), pp. 87–100, has stressed the similarities both in religious ideas and in types of apologetic argument between Philo's *In Flaccum* and Josephus' *Against Apion;* but this may be due, as he suggests, either to the fact that both drew on a long-standing tradition of Hellenistic Jewish apologetic or to the pagan rhetorical tradition.

In my "Prolegomenon," in the reprint of M. R. James, *The Biblical Antiquities of Philo* (New York 1971), pp. lviii–lxvi, and "Epilegomenon to Pseudo-Philo's *Liber Antiquitatum Biblicarum (LAB)*," *JJS* 25 (1974):305–312, I have noted thirty instances where parallels between Josephus and Pseudo-Philo's *Biblical Antiquities* are to be found in no other extant work. I have also noted, however, thirty-six instances where they disagree. Hence, it would be a mistake, I conclude, to regard Josephus as Pseudo-Philo's source or vice versa; the most likely hypothesis is that they have a common source or sources.

One of the most puzzling questions with regard to Josephus' sources is his possible use of Latin writers. Theodor Mommsen, "Cornelius Tacitus und Cluvius Rufus," *Hermes* 4 (1870):295–325, noting that Josephus (*A* XIX, 91–92) refers to a conversation between a certain very prominent person named Cluitus and a senator named Bathybius, adopts Hudson's emendation of the former name to Cluvius, and concludes, as we have remarked, that Josephus' source of the anecdote and, indeed, of the whole lengthy account of the assassination of Caligula and of the accession of Claudius must be the historical work of Cluvius Rufus. Justus von Destinon, *Untersuchungen zu Flavius Josephus* (Kiel 1904), however, suggests that Josephus' source was a pamphlet that praised the merit of Cassius Chaerea, the conspirator against Caligula. Since, we may comment, nothing remains of this pamphlet it is hard to substantiate such a theory. Dieter Timpe, "Römische Geschichte bei Flavius Josephus," *Historia* 9 (1960):474–502, asserts that both Josephus and Tacitus are dependent on the same source, since both are senatorial in their sympathies; but in "The Source of Josephus' *Antiquities* Book 19," *Latomus* 21 (1962):320–333, I suggest that the build-up of the role of the Jewish king Agrippa I in the accession of Claudius can hardly have come from a Roman source but more likely came from Agrippa II, with whom Josephus (*V* 366) says that he had close relations. If, moreover, we adopt the suggestion of Hans W. Ritter, "Cluvius Rufus bei Josephus? Bemerkungen zu Ios. ant. 19, 91f.," *RhM* 115 (1972):85–91, that Bathybius (*A* XIX, 91) be emended to Talthybius, the name of Agamemnon's herald, this would refer to the decline of the status of heralds under Nero. Hence, it would hardly be likely that Josephus' source was Cluvius Rufus, who was a herald under Nero.

Josephus on Jewish Beliefs

Several writers have recognized the value of Josephus as a source for the Jewish beliefs of his time, especially as compared with the Mishnah, which is not recorded until a full century later. A. Lewinsky, *Beiträge zur Kenntnis der religionsphilosophischen Anschauungen des Flavius Josephus* (Breslau 1887), discusses Josephus' comments on God, His existence, His attributes, and His relations to the world, angels, demons, and man. Adolf Poznanski, "Über die religionsphilosophischen Anschauungen des Flavius Josephus" (Ph.D. diss., Halle 1887), covers practically the same ground, concentrating on Josephus' teachings concerning God, providence, the relationship of God to Israel, fate, angels, demons, prophecy, anthropology, the Messiah, allegory, and ethics. Paul Krüger, *Philo und Josephus als Apologeten des Judentums* (Leipzig 1906), who insists that all of Josephus' works are clearly apologetic, argues that Josephus' views on theology, cosmology, anthropology, eschatology, allegory, and ethics are truly Jewish, and that only the outer appearance shows similarity to Greek philosophy. A like view is expressed by James A. Montgomery, "The Religion of Flavius Josephus," *JQR* 11 (1920–1921):277–305, who concludes that Josephus is a philosopher of religion rather than a theologian; that his chief aim was to be an apologist for his people and for his religion; that he is a genuine believer, even if he appears to be an un-Pharisaic Hellenizer; and that his views represent a conception of Pharisaic thought broader than that to be found in such other Jewish sources as the Talmud. We may comment that in this Montgomery anticipated the prevalent present-day view challenging the picture of normative Judaism painted by George Foot Moore's *Judaism,* 3 vols. (Cambridge, Mass. 1927–1930).

Erhard Kamlah, "Frömmigkeit und Tugend. Die Gesetzesapologie des Josephus in c *Ap* I, 145–295," *J-S,* pp. 220–232, asserts that Josephus combines a thoroughgoing Hellenism with Judaism in his view of piety and virtue.

Jacob Bos, "Josephus' Presentation of First-Century Judaism" (Ph.D. diss., University of Chicago 1922), views Josephus' picture of Judaism as a forerunner of Christianity and emphasizes that the religious interest of Josephus, as a priest, centered around the Temple. Josephus, he adds, is everywhere tendentious, but he is to be judged by the standards of his day.

Henrich Guttmann, *Die Darstellung der jüdischen Religion bei Flavius Josephus* (Breslau 1928), arguing against the view of Gustav Hölscher, "Josephus," *RE* (1916):1934–2000, that Josephus had slavishly copied from an intermediate source, postulates that Josephus has put his personal imprint upon the traditional material before him. He concludes that Josephus was definitely not genuinely religious.

Adolf Schlatter, *Die Theologie des Judentums nach dem Bericht des Josefus* (Gütersloh 1932), though he suffers from having approached his topic as a student of the origins of Christianity, presents Josephus as a Pharisee, albeit a somewhat disillusioned and diffident one. He admits, nevertheless, that Josephus had the capacity to step back from Pharisaism and to regard his group as a sect parallel to the Sadducees and the Essenes. As to his personal beliefs, Josephus never regarded the priest as being particularly bound in his inner life to God and instead viewed the priesthood as being of value only because it conferred political power and prestige. We may remark, however, that Josephus is often critical of the Pharisees; that his technique of interpretation is not simply Pharisaic; that, whereas the Pharisees were wary toward the government, Josephus tried to win the regime's approval; that Josephus' education was broad enough to include experience with all the sects; and finally, that he devotes far more space to the Essenes in the *War* than to the Pharisees or the Sadducees.

Jerry T. Daniel, "Apologetics in Josephus" (Ph.D. diss., Rutgers University 1981), contends that Josephus neglects, even in *Against Apion*, the great theological concepts of covenant and election to a point that is equal to denial and that thus Josephus ceases to speak for orthodox Judaism. We may remark, however, that Josephus' failure to address these tenets is not necessarily relevant, since he is writing history and since he significantly indicates that he will deal with theology in a separate work—one that was never published. As to not speaking for Orthodox Judaism, this presupposes a monolithic view of Orthodox Judaism, whereas the most likely view is of a wide spectrum of views within the orbit of the Orthodox Judaism of that time.

As to Josephus' theology, Adolf Schlatter, *Wie sprach Josephus von Gott?* (Gütersloh 1910), deals with various aspects of God and His attributes, as viewed by Josephus, especially as compared with Philo, the New Testament, and rabbinic literature.

Jacob Jervell, "Imagines und Imago Dei. Aus der Genesis-Exegese der Josephus," *J-S*, pp. 197–204, argues that Josephus' omission of the statement that man was created in the image of God is due to his view that God Himself is not describable rather than to his strictness about images.

Robert J. H. Shutt, "The Concept of God in the Works of Flavius Josephus," *JJS* 31 (1980):171–189, concludes that though Josephus' views about God are generally consonant with the Bible, he also employs non-Jewish, especially Stoic, language and that today he would consequently be described as a liberal Jew. We may suggest that, to some degree at least, this may be explained as due to Josephus' apologetic aim and to the fact that he is addressing primarily a non-Jewish intellectual audience in Greek.

Much speculation as to Josephus' source has come from his differentia-tion (*A* XIII, 172–173) of the three sects of Judaism on the basis of their atti-tude toward fate, whereas, in fact, this is hardly the major point that separates the two major groups, the Pharisees and the Sadducees, at least, if we are to use the Talmud as our basis. George F. Moore, "Fate and Free Will in the Jewish Philosophies according to Josephus," *HTR* 22 (1929):371–389, notes that there is no equivalent in Hebrew for Josephus' word for fate, εἱμαρμένη (though we may suggest *goral*), indicates that Josephus is seriously mislead-ing his reader, and declares that the classification of the Jewish sects on this basis may well have come from Nicolaus of Damascus. We may remark that, aside from the fact that we have no fragments of Nicolaus dealing with fate, this theory seems unlikely, since Nicolaus was a Peripatetic rather than a Stoic and hence was hardly obsessed with fate. Ludwig Wächter, "Die unter-schiedliche Haltung der Pharisäer, Sadduzäer und Essener zur Heimarmene nach dem Bericht des Josephus," *ZRGG* 21 (1969):97–114, plausibly conjec-tures that the reason why Josephus differentiates the sects on this basis is that such a concept was of interest to the Hellenistic audience he was addressing. We may add that the fact that Josephus (*A* XIII, 171) states that the sects held different opinions "concerning human affairs" is an indication that he felt that his non-Jewish audience would not be particularly interested in theological matters, to which he promises (*A* XX, 268) he will devote a separate treatise, presumably for a primarily Jewish audience. Gerhard Maier, "Die jüdischen Lehrer bei Josephus: Einige Beobachtungen," *J-S*, pp. 260–270, contends that Josephus' philosophical statements concerning sectarian doctrines actu-ally reflect current Jewish discussions rather than Hellenistic influence. On the other hand, Gustav Stählin, "Das Schicksal im Neuen Testament und bei Josephus," *J-S*, pp. 319–343, noting the ambivalence in Josephus' use of the terms for fate in contrast to the unambiguous usage in the New Testament, concludes that Josephus was influenced by Hellenistic ideas, though, we may comment, his assumption that Josephus does not distinguish between πρόνοια and εἱμαρμένη merely adds to the confusion. Luther H. Martin, "Josephus' Use of *Heimarmene* in the *Jewish Antiquities* XIII, 171–73," *Numen* 28 (1981):127–137, concludes that in his use of εἱμαρμένη Josephus was influ-enced by nontechnical casual Stoicism and by the astrological tradition, where the word refers to the determined governance of the human condition, in contrast with πρόνοια or divine providence. We may further comment that Stoic influence seems likely in view of Josephus' striking and totally unex-pected comparison (*V* 12) of the Pharisees, the party with which he identified himself, and the Stoics, and in view of Josephus' use of Stoic terminology in connection with Abraham's proof for the existence of God (*A* I, 156), the use of a typical Stoic phrase in Solomon's dedicatory prayer for the Temple (*A* VIII, 108), and King Jeroboam's use of Stoic terminology (*A* VIII, 227). Indeed, Otto Michel, " 'Ich komme' (Jos. Bell. III, 400)," *TZ* 24 (1968):123–124, has noted that Josephus' portrayal of himself as a harbinger of greater destinies marks a Hellenistic interpretation of political history that differentiates him from Pharisaism and concludes that the roots of his historical thought do not lie in Pharisaism despite his professed adherence to this sect. We may comment that such a contradiction would hardly have bothered Josephus or any other Pharisee, since the roots of Pharisaism lay not in theological theory but in adherence in practice to the Oral Law as eventually codified in the Talmud.

Willem C. von Unnik, "An Attack on the Epicureans by Flavius Josephus," *Festschrift J. H. Waszink* (Amsterdam 1973), pp. 341–355, has noted original elements in Josephus' views (*A* X, 277–281) of providence and concludes that this originality refutes those who assert that Josephus was merely copying handbooks. We may reply, however, that in this case, at least, the argument is inconclusive, since almost all of our primary sources for Epicureanism are lost.

Noting a significant similarity in vocabulary and style between Josephus' version of the Pharisaic teaching (*BJ* II, 162–163; *A* XIII, 172) concerning providence and that of Apuleius (*De Platone et eius Dogmate* 1.12.205–206, 1.584–586) in the second century, Shlomo Pines, "A Platonistic Model for Two of Josephus' Accounts of the Doctrine of the Pharisees Concerning Providence and Man's Freedom of Action" [Hebrew], *Iyyun* 24 (1973):227–232; translated into English in *Immanuel* 7 (1977):38–43, postulates that Josephus' source was a good Platonist, possibly the first century B.C.E. Antiochus of Ascalon, whose views were similar to Apuleius'.

A question similarly arises as to how much Jewish and how much Greek content there is in Josephus' interpretation of prayer. S. (= Istvan) Hahn, "Josephus on prayer in c. Ap. II. 197," *Études orientales à la memoire de Paul Hirschler,* Otto Komlos, ed. (Budapest 1950), pp. 111–115, remarks that the unique aspect in Josephus' conception is that it is centered on man rather than on God and notes the view (*Ap* II, 197) that we should beseech God not to give us blessings but to give us the capacity to receive them, a view that closely parallels a motif found in Cynic diatribes, as reflected in Horace, *Odes* 1.31. We may remark, however, that the parallels are to be found in rabbinic literature.

Willem C. van Unnik, "Eine merkwürdige liturgische Aussage bei Josephus: Jos Ant 8, 111–113," *J-S,* pp. 362–369, comments that Solomon's prayer of thanksgiving, like Philo's remarks in *De Plantatione* (130–131), is derived from popular thought as transmitted through the Hellenistic synagogue; but a more likely source, as indicated by the terminology (*A* VIII, 111), is Stoicism.

One problem that has exercised a number of scholars is the discrepancy between Josephus and the Mishnah's description (*Middoth*) of the Temple. Israel (Azriel) Hildesheimer, *Die Beschreibung des Herodianischen Tempels im Tractate Middoth und bei Flavius Josephus* (Berlin 1877), translated into English (with omission of notes) in *PEFQS* 18 (1886):92–113, reduces these differences, which appear so vast, to comparatively minor dimensions and concludes that the Mishnah furnishes the means for correcting Josephus. Friedrich Spiess, *Der Temple zu Jerusalem während des letzten Jahrhunderts seines Bestandes nach Josephus* (Berlin 1880), on the other hand, prefers Josephus and finds confirmation in archaeological discoveries. Yitzhak Magen, "The Gates of the Temple Mount According to Josephus and the Tractate Middoth" [Hebrew], *Cathedra* 14 (1980):41–53, explains the discrepancies, so far as the descriptions of the gates of the Temple Mount are concerned, by the hypothesis that the Mishnah represents the period before Herod, whereas Josephus depicts the period after him. Ben Zion Wacholder, *Messianism and Mishnah. Time and Place in Early Halakhah* (Cincinnati 1979), presents the revolutionary suggestion that the Mishnah does not delineate the halakhah current in the Second Temple period but rather the law that would take effect when the Messiah would come and rebuild the Temple. If so, this would likewise explain the discrepancies in the description of the Temple itself. We may comment, however, that this would explain basic but hardly minor differences. More likely, the Mishnah represents the Solomonic temple, and Josephus depicts the Herodian temple, based on his own participation in it as a priest.

Gustav Hölscher, *Die Hohenpriesterliste bei Josephus und die evangelische Chronologie* (Heidelberg 1940), commenting on the discrepancies between the list of high priests in Books XV through XX of the *Antiquities* with the summary in *Antiquities* XX, 224–251, suggests that the latter list is based not on the earlier list but upon the Temple archives. We may ask how these archives were available to Josephus writing in Rome and, in any case, why they were available only while he was writing Book XX and not while he was writing the earlier books of the *Antiquities*. Moreover, Hölscher, here as elsewhere, attributes independence only to Josephus' anonymous sources, none of which are intact, while denying such independence to Josephus himself.

As to the temple at Leontopolis, Robert Hayward, "The Jewish Temple at Leontopolis: A Reconsideration," *JJS* 33 (1982):429–443, notes the curious fact that Josephus both begins (*BJ* I, 22) and ends (*BJ* XII, 421–432) his account of the Jewish War against the Romans with his version of the establishment of the Jewish temple at Leontopolis. The temple thus is the symbol of the fruit of party strife. We may comment that the lack of any mention of the temple by Philo, who lived much closer to it than Josephus, would appear to indicate its lack of importance; and, hence, this supports the view that its significance was largely symbolic, as Josephus portrays it.

As to prophecy, we are confronted with the apparent discrepancy between the generally accepted tradition that Malachi was the last of the prophets and Josephus' claim to possess the prophetic gift. Adolf Poznanski, "Über die religionsphilosophischen Anschauungen des Flavius Josephus" (Ph.D. diss., Halle 1887), however, has noted that, long after Malachi, Josephus notes the existence of such prophets as Jesus son of Ananias, John Hyrcanus, and the Essene prophets. Otto Michel, "Spätjüdische Prophetentum," *Festschrift Rudolf Bultmann* (Berlin 1954), pp. 60–66, however, insists that Josephus' account of his revelation and prayer at Jotapata is wholly unprophetic. Ernest Best, "The Use and Non-Use of Pneuma by Josephus," *NT* 3 (1959):218–225, notes that Josephus restricts the term θεῖον πνεῦμα to prophecy within the biblical period.

Azriel Shochat, "On the 'Ambiguous Oracle' in the Words of Josephus" [Hebrew], *Sefer Yosef Shiloh,* Michael Handel, ed. (Tel-Aviv 1960), pp. 163–165, concludes that the ambiguous oracle in *War* VI, 312, refers to the prophecy in Isaiah 10:33, 34; but this seem unlikely, inasmuch as the prophecy in the *War* predicts that "at that time" someone would become ruler of the world, whereas in Isaiah there is no prediction for a specific time. A more likely explanation is given by Istvan Hahn, "Josephus és a Bellum Judaicum eschatológiai háttere" [Hungarian] ("Josephus and the Eschatological Background of the Bellum Judaicum"), *AT* 8 (1961):199–220, who refers the prophecy of the coming of a world-ruler to Daniel 9:24–27, which indicates that the Messiah will come 490 years after the destruction of the First Temple, a chronology based on priestly records that Josephus presumably knew. Basing himself on *War* VI, 291, Otto Michel, "Studien zu Josephus. Apokalyptische Heilsansagen im Bericht des Josephus (*BJ* 6, 290f., 293–95); ihre Umdeutung bei Josephus," in *Festschrift Matthew Black,* Edward E. Ellis and Max Wilcox, eds. (Edinburgh 1969), pp. 240–244, concludes that Josephus adhered to the priestly rather than to the prophetic, apocalyptic tradition; but we may remark that Josephus regarded those who misinterpret portents as inexperienced, whereas those who currently interpret them are sacred scribes, with no indication that the latter group are necessarily priests.

Marianus de Jonge, "Josephus und die Zukunftserwartungen seines Volkes," *J-S,* pp. 205–219, concludes that Josephus did not give the oracle a messianic interpretation and that he did not regard Vespasian as a messianic figure. We may remark that Josephus could hardly have viewed Vespasian as a messianic figure, inasmuch as the Messiah must be Jewish and Vespasian was not.

Francesco Lucrezi, "Un' 'ambigua profezia' in Flavio Giuseppe," *AAN*

90 (1979):589–631, theorizes that Josephus invented the ambiguous oracle in order to thwart the Jewish messianic movement, which was so hostile to the priestly class to which he adhered; but it is hard to see how such an oracle would hinder the messianic movement. Hans G. Kippenberg, "'Dann Wird der Orient Herrschen und der Okzident Dienen': Zur Begründung eines gesamtvorderasiatischen Standpunktes im Kampf gegen Rom," *Festschrift Jacob Taubes*, W. W. Bolz and W. Hübener, eds. (Würzburg 1983), pp. 40–48, remarks that the ambiguous oracle is a Jewish interpretation of the prophecy of which Tacitus' version (*Histories* 5.13.2) is primary, while that of Josephus is secondary.

As to false prophecy, J. Reiling, "The Use of ΨΕΥΔΟΠΡΟΦΗΤΗΣ in the Septuagint, Philo and Josephus," *NT* 13 (1971):147–156, notes that, whereas in the Septuagint and Philo false prophecy is associated with pagan divination, in Josephus such terms of divination as μάντις no longer have this connotation. We may suggest that since Josephus' usage is paralleled in the Talmud, the difference is one between Alexandrian and Palestinian usage.

Otto Betz, "Das Problem des Wunders bei Flavius Josephus im Vergleich zum Wunderproblem bei den Rabbinen und im Johannesevangelium," *J-S*, pp. 23–44, suggests that Josephus at Jotapata acted as a prophet of the Essene type, who addressed himself to rulers and thus gave oracles of political significance. We may remark that, just because there are Essenes in Josephus who give prophecies to rulers, this does not prove that Essenes generally were political prophets, since in Josephus, writing a political history, his mention of the Essene prophecies would naturally be in connection with political events.

Joseph Blenkinsopp, "Prophecy and Priesthood in Josephus," *JJS* 25 (1974):239–262, notes that Josephus stresses the close relationship between prophecy and the priesthood. He is surprised that Josephus devotes so little space to the prophets in his version of the Bible; but we may remark that it is precisely because Josephus is writing a history rather than a work of theology that he does so. Moreover, his rationalistic pagan readers might have found the concept of prophecy difficult to accept.

D. E. Aune, "The Use of προφήτης in Josephus," *JBL* 101 (1982):419–421, insists that, despite the general view of Reiling and Blenkinsopp, there are passages, notably *War* VI, 286, and *Antiquities* I, 240–241, in which Josephus does apply the term *prophet* to postbiblical figures.

Richard A. Horsley, "'Like One of the Prophets of Old': Two Types of Popular Prophets at the Time of Jesus," *CBQ* 47 (1985):435–463, doubts that there were eschatological prophets in Judaism during the first century. Instead, there were oracular prophets, as well as prophets who led movements and performed actions of deliverance as agents of God following the model of Moses. He suggests that the whole scholarly construct of the Zealots would best be abandoned so that we may discern more clearly the several distinctive social forms that social unrest assumed historically. But, we may reply, Josephus is not a good source for the fine distinctions within the revolutionary groups, since he condemned them all so violently.

In "Popular Prophetic Movements at the Time of Jesus. Their Principal Features and Social Origins," *JSNT* 26 (1986):3–27, Horsley emphasizes the contrast between the popular prophetic movements in the first century and the Sicarii and the Zealots. The former looked forward to some liberating act of God, whereas the latter were oriented to liberating acts by men. Both sought to overcome the oppression of the Jewish peasants. Such a distinction, we may remark, seems artificial in view of the central theological orientation of all such movements.

As to Josephus' ambiguous attitude toward miracles, Gerhard Delling, "Josephus and das Wunderbare," *NT* 2 (1957–1958):291–309, remarks that Josephus' belief in miraculous divine intervention was commonplace in the Hellenistic-Roman world, whereas George W. MacRae, "Miracle in *The Antiquities* of Josephus," in *Miracles: Cambridge Studies in Their Philosophy and History,* Charles F. D. Moule, ed. (London 1965), pp. 127–147, notes that Josephus' skepticism is an expression of courtesy to his pagan readers. Horst R. Moehring, "Rationalization of Miracles in the Writings of Flavius Josephus," *TU* 112 (1973) (=*SE* 6):376–383, goes further and remarks that even when Josephus chooses to stress a miracle, this, too, is a rationalization and that whereas Philo allegorizes Josephus rationalizes.

As to land theology, Azriel Shochat, "The Views of Josephus on the Future of Israel and Its Land" [Hebrew], in *Jerusalem,* Michael Ish-Shalom et al., eds. (Jerusalem 1953), pp. 43–50, has noted that Josephus stresses not political independence but the Jewish religious beliefs as being most vital and that he emphasizes that the Jews were dispersed in order to facilitate proselytism, such as was so successfully being pursued during his lifetime. Betsy H. Amaru, "Land Theology in Josephus' *Jewish Antiquities,*" *JQR* 71 (1980–1981):201–229, notes that, in his biblical paraphrase, Josephus deliberately omits stress on the covenanted land of Israel and shifts the center of gravity to the Diaspora. This shift, to some degree, we may comment, is a move from the centrality of a theological concept, the idea of the covenant, to the centrality of political history, which, in the wake of the destruction of the Temple, had shifted the center of gravity to the Jewish diaspora.

As to eschatology, Otto Böcher, "Die heilige Stadt in Völkerkrieg. Wandlungen eines apokalyptischen Schemas," *J-S,* pp. 55–76, notes the especially close relationship between Josephus and the Apocalypse of Baruch in looking upon the Romans as servants of the God of judgment. Dean Charles Kallander, "The Defense of Jerusalem in the Roman Siege of 70 C.E.: A Study of First Century Apocalyptic Ideas" (Ph.D. diss., Miami University

1980), concludes that a major source of conflict among the various revolutionary groups during the war against Rome was their divergence in apocalyptic and eschatological views. Betsy H. Amaru, "Land Theology in Josephus' *Jewish Antiquities*," *JQR* 71 (1980–1981):201–229, remarks that Josephus replaces the classical messianic eschatology with his own version of future divine blessings, one that reflects the Hellenistic world, a motherland with an extensive string of colonies. T. Middendorp, "Het geheim van de Messias bij Josephus" ("The Secret of the Messiah According to Josephus"), *Skrif en Kerk* 4 (1983):41–58, notes that Josephus deliberately omitted statements about messianic expectations and that the Christians took his incidental reference to Jesus and converted it into a statement about Jesus as the Messiah. Richard A. Horsley, "Popular Messianic Movements around the Time of Jesus," *CBQ* 46 (1984):471–495, discusses the popular messianic movements following the death of Herod and during the revolt of 66–70 and notes that the leaders were all men of humble origins. The figures who "claimed the kingship," according to Josephus, were apparently messianic pretenders.

Finally, we may comment on Josephus' remarks about proselytes and "sympathizers," the so-called semi-proselytes. In "Jewish 'Sympathizers' in Classical Literature and Inscriptions," *TAPA* 81 (1950):200–208, I stress the eagerness with which Josephus says that the Jews welcomed proselytes. If the estimate of Salo W. Baron, *A Social and Religious History of the Jews*, vol. 1 (New York 1952), pp. 370–372, is at all accurate, the world Jewish population had risen to about 8 million by the first century C.E. from about 150,000 in 586 B.C.E. Since there was apparently no increase in the birth rate or improvement in health conditions during this period, only proselytism can account for this vast change. The expulsion of 4000 Jews from Rome in 19 C.E. in the aftermath of the swindling by Jewish embezzlers of the noble proselyte Fulvia (*A* XVIII, 81–84), as corroborated by Tacitus (*Annals* 2.85), Suetonius (*Tiberius* 36), and Dio Cassius (57.18.5a), indicates that the success of proselytism was the factor involved.

Josephus' account (*A* XX, 17–96) of the conversion of King Izates to Judaism, on the whole, is confirmed by the talmudic and midrashnic sources, as noted by Bernard J. Bamberger, *Proselytism in the Talmudic Period* (Cincinnati 1939), pp. 225–228. Jacob Neusner, "The Conversion of Adiabene to Judaism," *JBL* 83 (1964):60–66, presents the interesting suggestion that the conversions of Queen Helena and King Izates were motivated not only religiously but also politically, and that Izates hoped thereby to gain the throne of Judea; but, we may remark, while it is tempting to ascribe pragmatic motives in the cases of conversions, such as that of Constantine in the fourth century and the king of the Khazars in the eighth century, Izates could not have hoped to be crowned king of a Jewish state, inasmuch as the Bible (Deuteronomy

17:15) specifically says that the king must be "one from your brethren," which the Talmud interprets to mean one born a Jew.

Abraham Schalit, "Evidence of an Aramaic Source in Josephus' 'Antiquities of the Jews'," *ASTI* 4 (1985):163–188, finds evidence that Josephus' source was an Aramaic account that attempted to defend the conversion by noting that divine favor descended upon the kingdom thereafter, despite its apparently vulnerable location between the Roman and Parthian Empires. This theory, however, rests upon the fact that in Izates' prayer (*A* XX, 90), he uses the word μεγαλορρήμονα, which is found in Daniel 7:8 and 20, the original of which is in Aramaic. We may respond that it seems extravagant to build a theory upon the evidence of a single word, which, in any case, might well have been taken from the Septuagint version of Daniel. Lawrence H. Schiffman, "Proselytism in the Writings of Josephus: Izates of Adiabene in Light of the Halakah" [Hebrew], *CP* (1982):247–265, likewise has noted that the beginning of the passage in Josephus is typical of his deviation from one source to a second that supplies additional material. He concludes that Josephus' source had a firm grasp of the history of Adiabene and of its international relations. Despite his use of legendary sources, he understood the chronology of events, as well as the process of conversion. When his account differs from that of the rabbis, it is to be preferred. Schiffman correctly notes, in contradiction to Menahem Stern, "The Jewish Diaspora," in *The Jewish People in the First Century,* Samuel Safrai and Menahem Stern, eds., vol. 1 (Assen 1974), pp. 170–178, that there is no evidence that the population of Adiabene as a whole converted. He suggests that the chief reasons why Josephus includes such a long account were that the royal house of Adiabene played a prominent role in the revolt against Rome and that their conversion disproved the allegation that Jews hated non-Jews. We may comment that the role of the Adiabenians in the revolt against Rome must have been extremely embarrassing to Josephus, who never refers in the *War* to the fact that they were converts. Moreover, the Adiabenians are the only instance of converts to Judaism that Josephus dwells upon in the *Antiquities,* presumably because the subject of proselytism by Jews was a sore point in relations with the Romans; and if he does mention the incident, he can explain the conversion as one of a people in the Parthian, not the Roman, Empire.

Jacob Bernays, "Die Gottesfürchtigen bei Juvenal," *Commentationes philologae in honorem Theodori Mommseni* (Berlin 1877), pp. 563–569, interprets the eleven references in Acts to οἱ φοβούμενοι τὸν θεόν and οἱ σεβόμενοι τὸν θεόν, as well as the references in Josephus (*A* XIV, 110) to the σεβομένων τὸν θεόν, who contribute to the Temple, and to Poppaea Sabina, the wife of Nero, as θεοσεβής (*A* XX, 195) and in Juvenal (14.96) to *metuentem sabbata,* as references to "semi-proselytes" or "sympathizers" with

Judaism, who observed certain Jewish practices and held certain Jewish beliefs without actually embracing Judaism. In "Jewish 'Sympathizers' in Classical Literature and Inscriptions," I argue that the references in Josephus and elsewhere are to people who are religious, whether Jewish or pagan. Ralph Marcus, "The *Sebomenoi* in Josephus," *JSS* 14 (1952):247–250, disputes this on grammatical grounds; but the very facts that Acts has two different expressions for the alleged sympathizers and that an inscription from Miletus speaks of the place of the Jews "who are also θεοσεβεῖς" would indicate that the terms are hardly technical ones for "sympathizers." Baruch Lifshitz, "Du nouveau sur les 'Sympathisants'," *JSJ* 1 (1970):77–84, argues that Josephus, the New Testament, and inscriptions do indicate the existence of sympathizers, but that each case must be judged on its own merits. Folker Siegert, "Gottesfürchtige und Sympathisanten," *JSJ* 4 (1973):109–164, after systematically examining all passages referring to the sympathizers, distinguishes between those who were seriously interested in the Jewish religion but who were not members of synagogue communities and those who adopted some Jewish practices and who were politically sympathetic to the Jews. He argues that the existence of sympathizers was due to the impossibility of changing one's religion completely and to the willingness of Jewish missionaries to compromise. In reply, we may note that there are many cases of conversions to other religions and quasi-religions or philosophies; and, as far as the willingness to compromise, the case of Ananias in Adiabene is hardly evidence, since there was good reason to believe that conversion would have brought dire consequences to the king from the nobles.

A. Thomas Kraabel, "The Disappearance of the 'God Fearers'," *Numen* 28 (1981):113–126, notes that from the six synagogues of the Roman Diaspora that have thus far been excavated not a single inscription ever uses the term φοβούμενοι or σεβόμενοι, and that the term θεοσεβής, which is used perhaps ten times, is an adjective describing Jews. In reply, Thomas M. Finn, "The God-Fearers Reconsidered," *CBQ* 47 (1985):75–84, points to a recently discovered inscription from Aphrodisias in Asia Minor (published with an extensive commentary by Joyce Reynolds and Robert Tannenbaum, *Jews and God-fearers at Aphrodisias* [Cambridge Philological Society, Supplementary Vol. 12; Cambridge 1987]) giving a list of θεοσεβεῖς in contradistinction to Jews. He notes, in particular, Josephus' statement (*BJ* VII, 45) that the Jews of Antioch were constantly attracting to their religious ceremonies multitudes of Greeks and that they had in some measure (τρόπῳ τινὶ) incorporated them with themselves. We may comment that the inscription from Aphrodisias, to judge from the form of the letters, is probably to be dated in the third century; hence it cannot be given as evidence as to whether θεοσεβεῖς was a technical term in the first century. The Jerusalem Talmud (*Megillah* 3.2.74a) likewise supports the view that by the third century the term *God-fearer* was a technical one, since the third-century Rabbi Eleazar remarks that *even* "fearers of Heaven" (*yirei shamayim*) wear sandals on the Day of Atonement.

Robert S. MacLennan and A. Thomas Kraabel, "The God-Fearers—A Literary and Theological Invention," *BAR* 12, no. 5 (September–October 1986):46–53, suggest that the inscription from Aphrodisias refers to pious Gentiles who contributed to a synagogue rather than to "sympathizers" and that the God-Fearers disappear from Luke's narrative as soon as he no longer needs them for theological purposes. In "The Omnipresence of the God-Fearers," *BAR* 12, no. 5 (September–October 1986): 58–69, I argue that evidence from pagan writers, Philo, Josephus, rabbinic literature, Christian church fathers, papyri, and inscriptions, especially from Aphrodisias, indicate a class of "sympathizers," at least for the first century and especially for the third century. The fact that one of the inscriptions from Aphrodisias actually refers to Jews, proselytes, and "sympathizers" and that another refers to "complete Hebrews," presumably in contrast with "sympathizers," would seem to settle the matter at least for the third century.

Josephus' Views on Jewish Law

The importance of Josephus for our knowledge of Jewish law is great, inasmuch as the first rabbinic codification, the Mishnah, dates from a full century after him. Gustav Tachauer, "Das Verhältniss von Flavius Josephus zur Bibel und Tradition" (Ph.D. diss., Erlangen 1871), in a dissertation that is often uncritical and inaccurate, attempts to show that Josephus was acquainted with the oral law as later codified by the rabbis and that, when he deviates from it, he does so because of apologetic reasons. Marcus Olitzki, "Flavius Josephus und die Halacha. I. Einleitung, die Opfer" (Ph.D. diss., Leipzig 1885); II. "Die Einkünfte der Leviten und Priester," *MWJ* 16 (1889):169–182; "Rituelle und judicielle Fälle bei Flavius Josephus," *IM* nos. 3, 4, 7 (1886 and 1887), grants Josephus neither a precise knowledge nor an impartial presentation of Jewish law. He theorizes that discrepancies between Josephus and the rabbinic codification are due to the fact that the latter was unwritten and that Josephus, who had learned it orally as a youth, had forgotten much in the course of the many years after his departure from Palestine. When Josephus deviates from halakhah (Jewish law), he is simply wrong, according to Olitzki. A more likely explanation, we may suggest, would seem to be that Josephus represents the actual practice in his circle of his own days, whereas the Mishnah represents the later practice or that Josephus represents a minority or sectarian point of view.

Heinrich Weyl, *Die jüdischen Strafgesetze bei Flavius Josephus in ihrem*

Verhältnis zu Schrift und Halacha (Mit einer Einleitung: Flavius Josephus über die jüdischen Gerichtshofe und Richter) (Berlin 1900), commenting on offenses against God, the social order, morality, and property, warns that we must not be misled into thinking that because Josephus was a priest he was an expert in religious law. He suggests that where Josephus departs from halakhah the influence of Roman law is often to be seen. We may remark, however, that the very fact, mentioned in several places and notably at the very end of the *Antiquities* (XX, 268), that Josephus announces his plan to write a work on the laws, obviously more extensive than his summary treatment in Books III and IV of the *Antiquities* or his succinct resumé in *Against Apion* (II, 190–219), is an indication that he regarded himself as eminently qualified to write such a work. As to Josephus' indebtedness to Roman law, Josephus nowhere indicates that he had studied or admired Roman law—modesty is not one of his virtues and, moreover, he did seek to ingratiate himself with the Roman imperial family, at least—and, on the contrary, he insists on the unique excellence of Jewish law (*A* I, 22–23; *Ap* II, 163).

Kaufmann Kohler, "The Halakik Portions in Josephus' Antiquities (IV, 8, 5–43)," *HUC Monthly* 3, no. 4 (February 1917):109–122; reprinted in his *Studies, Addresses, and Personal Papers* (New York 1931), pp. 69–85, dogmatically postulates a priestly document, such as the Damascus Covenant of the Dead Sea sect, as Josephus' source for his halakhic material, and declares that Josephus' legal material actually represents an older stage of halakhah, midway between Sadduceeism and Pharisaism; but it would seem unlikely that Josephus, a Pharisee, would have turned to such an extremist group as the Dead Sea sect or, in view of his very negative comments about the Sadducees, that he would have been influenced by them.

Heinrich Guttmann, *Die Darstellung der jüdischen Religion bei Flavius Josephus* (Breslau 1928), like Weyl, correctly emphasizes that we must not be misled into thinking that Josephus was an expert in religious law merely because he was a priest.

Harry O. H. Levine, "Halakah in Josephus: Public and Criminal Law" (Ph.D. diss., Dropsie College 1935), deals with Josephus' statement of the laws pertaining to kings, executive and judicial administration, trial procedure, capital crimes, damages and injuries, misdemeanors against private property, commercial misdemeanors, social obligations, retention and inheritance of property, idolatry, and witchcraft. He attempts to be systematic but generally is content merely to cite the respective passages in Josephus and rabbinic sources with a bare minimum of interpretation.

Steven Riskin, "The Halakhah in Josephus as Reflected in *Against Apion* and *The Life*" (M.A. diss., Yeshiva University 1970), notes that Josephus agrees with rabbinic interpretation of the law in twelve cases and agrees in eleven other cases with a rabbinic interpretation that had not yet been fixed. In the five cases where he disagrees, this is due to Josephus' appeal to a non-Jewish audience or to his confusion of good advice with law. David Altshuler, "Descriptions in Josephus' Antiquities of the Mosaic Constitution" (Ph.D. diss., Hebrew Union College 1977), contends that Josephus' only source for law was the Bible and that his deviations from Scripture, as well as his selection from and organization of the laws, may all be ascribed to his desire to defend Judaism. David Goldenberg, "The Halakah in Josephus and in Tannaitic Literature: A Comparative Study" (Ph.D. diss., Dropsie University 1978), however has systematically challenged this thesis by noting, for example, that Josephus' omission of child sacrifice to Molech (Leviticus 18.21) was hardly for apologetic reasons, especially since, we may add, the rabbis saw fit to make this part of the Torah reading on the Day of Atonement; but, we may counter, perhaps the matter was obsolete or perhaps Josephus read *melech,* as did the Septuagint, which renders it as ἄρχοντι, and it would have been embarrassing to say that "Thou shalt not give of thy seed to serve a ruler." Moreover, Josephus has not omitted (A IV, 266) what would seem to be the embarrassing law (Deuteronomy 23.21) that one may charge interest from a non-Jew but not from a Jew, though here, too, we may remark, Josephus may be making an appeal to would-be proselytes.

As to Josephus' confusion of command with advice, an example would be his statement (*Ap* II, 200) that the law commands (κελεύει) that in taking a wife one should not be influenced by a dowry. Here the verb κελεύει, we may suggest, is used in the sense of Latin *iubet,* which may mean "bids" rather than "orders," just as it does in *Life* 414, as noted by David Daube, "Three Legal Notes on Josephus after His Surrender," *Law Quarterly* 93 (1977):191–194, an indication perhaps that Josephus knew some Latin.

In "The Halakah in Josephus and in Tannaitic Literature: A Comparative Study" (Ph.D. diss., Dropsie University 1978), and "The Halakha in Josephus and in Tannaitic Literature. A Comparative Study," *JQR* 67 (1976):30–43, Goldenberg has by far the most thorough analysis of Josephus' relation to rabbinic law, though he, too, realizes that he has dealt with a restricted number of legal areas (the rebellious elder, the rebellious son and honor to parents, execution and burial of criminals, usury, loans and pledges, the housebreaker, restitution of lost property, assistance to beasts in distress, directions on the road, reviling the deaf, quarrels and resulting injuries, withholding wages, burial and funeral rites, mourning rites, respect for the aged, martyrdom, and false prophecy). He insists that Josephus' deviations from the Bible pertaining to Jewish law are paralleled in tannaitic sources, Ben Sira, Philo, the New Testament, and targumim. He suggests that Josephus possessed written sources for his interpretation of laws, noting that a newly discovered manuscript of the

Talmud (*Avodah Zarah* 8b, Ms. Marx-Abramson) declares that Rabbi Judah ben Bava, a contemporary of Josephus, recorded laws of fines. We may comment that the very fact that Philo (*On the Special Laws*) as well as the Dead Sea *Damascus Covenant* and the *Temple Scroll* and Josephus, all record the laws, including much oral law, in a systematic way should lead us to think that perhaps such a written compendium was available to Josephus. If Josephus differs in some points from the rabbinic code, we would comment, in the first place, that Josephus, who was under constant attack from his fellow Jews, would hardly have dared to present such deviations unless he had solid ground for his interpretations. We may explain his deviations by noting that he reflects the law in force in his own day—in which case Josephus, like Philo presumably, would be very important as a stage in halakhic development prior to the codification of halakhah by Rabbi Judah the Prince in the Mishnah at the end of the second century—in contrast to the law that prevailed at the time when the Mishnah was reduced to writing; or that he is more strict than the rabbinic law; or that he is presenting good advice, as noted earlier, rather than legal prescription.

Yigael Yadin, ed., *The Temple Scroll*, vol. 1 (Jerusalem 1977), pp. 62, 93–94, 305, notes parallels between the Dead Sea sect's *Temple Scroll* and Josephus in classification of subjects and suggests that Josephus' sojourn with the Essenes (*V* 9–12) may thus have influenced him. If this is so, it may suggest a possible explanation of Josephus' divergences from Pharisaic rabbinic understanding of the law. David Altshuler, "On the Classification of Judaic Laws in the *Antiquities* of Josephus and the *Temple Scroll* of Qumran," *AJSR* 7–8 (1982–1983):1–14, however, concludes that there is little concrete evidence to support this suggestion and notes that, whereas the Temple Scroll seeks to emphasize the particularity of Israel, the *Antiquities* tones down this exclusivity and emphasizes instead universalistic and ethical law.

Geza Vermes, "A Summary of the Law by Flavius Josephus," *NT* 24 (1982):289–303, remarks that Josephus' lack of concern with ritual matters in his summary of the Law (*Ap* II, 164–219) implies that they were the work not of God but of Moses. Indeed, since his work is clearly apologetic, we should not be surprised if he toned down the divine element, inasmuch as Josephus' intellectual readers would have been skeptical of this, as we see, for example, in the way that even someone as relatively sympathetic to the Jews as Strabo (16 2.36–37) looked at revelation.

As to particular laws, Paul Grünbaum, "Die Priestergesetze bei Flavius Josephus. Eine Parallele zu Bibel und Tradition" (Ph.D. diss., Halle 1887), declares that Josephus was not inexperienced in priestly tradition and hence is reliable in marriage laws, age specifications, and other requirements of priests. In the matter of divorce, Alfredo M. Rabello, "Divorce in Josephus" [Hebrew], *CP* (1982):149–164, notes that in the cases of both Salome (*A* XV, 259–260) and Herodias (*A* XVIII, 136) the procedure violated Jewish tradition, though, of course, Josephus himself did not deviate.

Josephus on Religious Movements:
Samaritans, Pharisees, Sadducees,
Essenes, Zealots, Sicarii, and Galileans

There can be little doubt of Josephus' prejudice against the Samaritans. In this, he reflects the general Jewish attitude of bitterness and contempt, as seen in rabbinic writings. Abram Spiro, "Samaritans, Tobiads, and Judaites in Pseudo-Philo," *PAAJR* 20 (1951):279–355, notes a bias against the Samaritans even in Josephus' account of the patriarchs, remarking, for example, that he conveniently manages to forget Abram's stay in Shechem, the city especially associated with the Samaritans. Spiro even goes so far as to postulate that Josephus' source was a Hellenistic Midrash that was biased against the Samaritans. We may comment that Pseudo-Philo's agreement with Josephus in several of the omissions concerning the Samaritans would argue against such a theory, since Pseudo-Philo, who clearly knew no Greek, would hardly have employed a Hellenistic Midrash.

Morton Smith, *Palestinian Parties and Politics that Shaped the Old Testament* (New York 1971), especially pp. 182–190, regards Josephus as practically worthless as a source for Samaritan affairs for the period from Nehemiah to Antiochus Epiphanes, inasmuch as he is guilty of blatant anachronisms in projecting onto earlier periods the Pharisaic hostility against the Samaritans of his own day.

Stanley J. Isser, *The Dositheans: A Samaritan Sect in Late Antiquity* (Leiden 1976), pp. 5–11, likewise disputes the value of Josephus as a source for the Samaritans, noting that the dispute (*A* XIII, 74–79) involving Ptolemy Philadelphus in Josephus smacks of propaganda and literary motif.

Rita Egged, *Josephus Flavius und die Samaritaner: eine terminologische Untersuchung zur Identitätsklärung der Samaritaner* (Göttingen 1986), concludes that there is no ground for asserting that Josephus was an anti-Samaritan writer, but that he failed to differentiate among the terms for Samaritans, and suggests that it was his assistants who had confused the terms. We may respond, however, that the major references to the Samaritans are in the *Antiquities,* and that it is in the *War* and not in the *Antiquities,* as we learn from Josephus himself (*Ap* I, 50), that Josephus had assistants. As for the assertion that Josephus was not anti-Samaritan, if, indeed, as he asserts (*V* 12), after experimenting with the other sects, he chose to identify with the Pharisees, we would certainly expect that he would adopt the strong anti-Samaritan stance that marked the Pharisaic attitude, based on their refusal to accept the Oral

Law, as we find it delineated in a number of passages, though admittedly not unanimously, in rabbinic literature (e.g., *Kiddushin* 75b).

As to the Pharisees, Hans-Friedrich Weiss, "Pharisäismus und Hellenismus: Zur Darstellung des Judentums im Geschichtswerk des jüdischen Historikers Flavius Josephus," *OLZ* 74 (1979):421–433, concludes that Josephus cannot be regarded simply as a Pharisee or as a Hellenist; he is to be viewed in the first instance as a historian of the Jewish people.

Morton Smith, "Palestinian Judaism in the First Century," in *Israel: Its Role in Civilization,* Moshe Davis, ed. (New York 1956), pp. 67–81, has presented the challenging thesis that, whereas the Pharisees hardly figure in Josephus' *Jewish War,* they take first place in the discussion of sects in the *Antiquities* because Josephus desired to win support from the Romans for the Pharisees against the Sadducees. This thesis is upheld by Jacob Neusner, "Josephus' Pharisees," *Geo Widengren Festschrift* (Leiden 1972), pp. 224–244, who stresses that Josephus' aim in emphasizing the power of the Pharisees is to point out to the Romans that they cannot rule Judea without the Pharisees' support. Hence, he remarks, we must discount all of Josephus' references to the influence and power of the Pharisees. But Shaye J. D. Cohen, *Josephus in Galilee and Rome: His Vita and Development as a Historian* (Leiden 1979), who accepts the theory, is forced to admit that there are several passages in the *Antiquities* (e.g., *A* XIII, 410ff.) that are very unfavorable to the Pharisees and that of all the pious behavior approved of in the *Antiquities* nothing is specifically Pharisaic. Moreover, we may add, there was hardly any point in winning support against the Sadducees, since, so far as we can tell, the Sadducees had lost power with the destruction of the Temple, and we hear nothing of them thereafter. We may also add that the fact that Josephus differentiates the sects on the basis of their attitude toward fate would hardly support the theory that the distinguishing factor was the power and influence of the respective groups. Hugo Mantel, "The Sadducees and Pharisees," *Society and Religion in the Second Temple Period,* Michael Avi-Yonah and Zvi Baras, eds., *WHJP* 1.8 (Jerusalem 1977), pp. 99–123, 346–351, suggests that the distinction in the treatment of the Pharisees between the *War* and the *Antiquities* may be explained by noting the diverse classes of readers for whom the works were intended: the *War* for the Jews and the *Antiquities* for the Romans. Daniel R. Schwartz, "Josephus and Nicolaus on the Pharisees," *JSJ* 14 (1983):157–171, explains the difference as due to divergent sources: the negative passages about the Pharisees can be attributed to Nicolaus of Damascus and probably reflect Herod's experience with the Pharisaic political opposition. He concludes that the *War* reflects Josephus' attempt to portray the Pharisees, incorrectly but safely, as uninvolved in politics and in rebellion, while the *Antiquities* is less cautious due to inattention.

Albert I. Baumgarten, "Josephus and Hippolytus on the Pharisees,"

HUCA 55 (1984):1–25, notes that the third-century Christian Hippolytus used a version of Josephus' account of the Jewish sects that was more pro-Pharisaic than the extant version of Josephus. We may remark, however, that though some, such as Laqueur, have posited a second edition of Josephus, so far as the end of Book XX of the *Antiquities* is concerned, there is no evidence for such an alternative version for any other part of this work. Moreover, even if the Josephus text that Hippolytus had before him was more pro-Pharisaic, Hippolytus shows elsewhere that he can and does revise Josephus to accord with his Christian point of view vis-à-vis the Jews.

As to the Sadducees, Günther Baumbach, "Das Sudduzäerverständnis bei Josephus Flavius und im Neuen Testament," *Kairos* 13 (1971):17–37, contends that Josephus is biased against them even though they were politically and religiously in control of Judea. David Flusser, "Josephus on the Sadducees and Menander," *Immanuel* 7 (1977):61–67, cannot believe that they, as one of the three representative groups of ancient Judea, actually rejected all involvement of providence in human life. But we may remark that to the Jews theological beliefs, in contrast to practice, at this time were not of major concern and, hence, extreme positions were possible.

Josephus' extended comments (especially *BJ* II, 119–161) about the Essenes have been the subject of much discussion, especially since the discoveries of the manuscripts of the Dead Sea sect, which has generally been identified with them—or, at least, as being akin to them. For the establishment of the text Christoph Burchard, "Zur Nebenüberlieferung von Josephus' Bericht über die Essener Bell 2, 119–161 bei Hippolyt, Porphyrius, Josippus, Niketas Choniates und anderen," *J-S*, pp. 77–96, notes the importance of the quotations of this passage (*BJ* I, 119–161) by later writers. He concludes that most extant texts go back to either Hippolytus or Porphyry.

For the bibliography on the Essenes, we may call attention to Siegfried Wagner, *Die Essener in der wissenschaftlichen Diskussion vom Ausgang des 18. bis zum Beginn des 20. Jahrhunderts. Eine wissenschaftliche Studie* (Berlin 1960), who notes exhaustively the trends in scholarship until 1947, the year when the Dead Sea Scrolls were first discovered, and Georges Ory, *A la recherche des Esséniens. Essai critique* (Paris 1975), who summarizes scholarship of both before and after 1947.

A good deal of this scholarship has been concerned with comparing the account of the Essenes given by Philo with that by Josephus. Abbé A. Regeffe, "La secte des Esséniens, Essai critique sur son organisation, sa doctrine, son origine" (Diss., Lyon 1898), concludes that, whereas Philo deals primarily with the intellectual and moral life of the Essenes, Josephus is concerned principally with their exterior life. Josephus' evidence, he concludes, deserves our entire confidence, even though elsewhere Josephus is more an apologist than a true historian.

Todd S. Beall, "Josephus' Description of the Essenes Illustrated by the Dead Sea Scrolls" (Diss., Catholic University of America, 1984), has a very full commentary on the major passages. He insists that the identification of the Essenes with the Qumran sect is valid and that there are only a handful of apparent discrepancies. Josephus, he concludes, is a trustworthy historian so far as the Essenes are concerned.

Solomon Zeitlin, "The Account of the Essenes in Josephus and the Philosophumena," *JQR* 49 (1958–1959):292–300, insists that Josephus could not have used an outside source for his account of the Essenes, since no one in Judea could have written about the Essenes in Greek at this time. Yet, we may reply, the fact that we have found Greek fragments at Qumran and numerous Greek words in talmudic writings is an indication that Greek was widely known. Moreover, Philo had written about the Essenes; and there seems good reason to believe, as noted, that Josephus knew his works. Morton Smith, "The Description of the Essenes in Josephus and the Philosophumena," *HUCA* 29 (1958):273–313, suggests that Josephus and Hippolytus have a common Greek, originally Aramaic, source.

Abbé J. Leytens, "Les Esséniens dans l'oeuvre de Flavius Josèphe et dans les Philosophoumena d'Hippolyte de Rome" (Diss., Louvain 1962), asserts that Josephus' statement (*V* 10) that he had joined the Essenes cannot be taken seriously. His comments are due to sources that he copied, though with additions of his own. Despite the fact that Hippolytus is later, he is more precise. On the other hand, Christoph Burchard, "Die Essener bei Hippolyt. Hippolyt, Ref. IX 18, 2–28, 2 und Josephus, Bell 2, 119–161," *JSJ* 8 (1977): 1–41, regards it as probable that Hippolytus derived his account directly from Josephus, rather than that both utilized a common source, though he admits that there are two instances in Hippolytus of novel material. We may comment that despite the chronological discrepancy between the number of years that Josephus spent with the Essenes and his age upon his emergence from his trial of the sects (*V* 12), his statement must be taken seriously, since he had to be careful in recounting autobiographical details due to the tremendous enmity against him on the part of his fellow-Jews.

One of the key questions concerning the Essenes is their attitude toward the sacrifices in the Temple. Here the manuscripts (*A* XVIII, 19) read that the Essenes do send votive offerings to the Temple but perform their sacrifices employing a different ritual of purification. The epitome of the Greek text, as well as the Latin version, however, reads that the Essenes do not send offerings. Joseph M. Baumgarten, "Sacrifice and Worship among the Jewish Sectarians of the Dead Sea (Qumran) Scrolls," *HTR* 46 (1953):141–159, suggests that the passage refers to the spiritualized sacrifices; but the phrase, we must say, is never found elsewhere in this sense. John Strugnell, "Flavius Josephus and the Essenes; Antiquities XVIII, 18–22," *JBL* 77 (1958):106–115, identifying the Essenes and the Dead Sea sect and noting that the Qumran texts and archaeological evidence suggest that sacrifice was practiced, concludes that the Essenes did send sacrifices but used a different method of purification. John Nolland, "A Misleading Statement of the Essene Attitude to the Temple (Josephus, *Antiquities* XVIII, 1, 5, 19)," *RQ* 9 (1978):555–562, arguing against Strugnell, says that Josephus deliberately gives a misleading description of the Essenes as having been expelled by the Temple authorities rather than that they separated themselves; but we may reply that as a leading priest Josephus was surely aware of the Essene attitude toward the Temple. Moreover, in view of his great praise of the sect in the *War,* it seems hard to believe that he would have presented a negative attitude toward them here unless it was indeed warranted. We may further remark that if the Essenes had sacrificed elsewhere than in the Temple, it is unlikely that Josephus would have included them as one of the four sects of the Jews, since in that case they would have been a heretical group such as the Samaritans, who had their own place of sacrifice on Mount Gerizim. We may note, furthermore, that the Latin version reads "sacrificia vel hostias cum populo non celebrant" and would indicate that they did not celebrate their sacrifices together with the people but rather by themselves, since they had a different and more stringent standard of purity.

A number of writers have challenged various details in Josephus' lengthy account of the Essenes (*BJ* II, 119–161). In particular, Ernst Kutsch, "Der Eid der Essener, ein Beitrag zu dem Problem des Textes von Josephus Bell. Jud. 2, 8, 7 (142)," *TLZ* 81 (1956):495–498, argues that the Dead Sea Scrolls show that Josephus is mistaken in his view that the Essenes swore to abstain from robbery; but, we may remark, this rests on the assumption that the Essenes are the sect of the Dead Sea Scrolls, whereas, in view of several differences between them, such an assumption seems questionable.

Another such disputed question is the relationship between the Essenes and the other sects. Istvan Hahn, "Zwei dunkle Stellen in Josephus" (Bellum Judaicum VI, 311 und II, 142) *AOASH* 14 (1962):131–138, says that the Essene oath to refrain from brigandage (λῃστεία) actually refers to the prohibition of revolting against Rome and that near the end of their history the Essenes actually moved closer in ideology to the Zealots. However, we may respond that it would seem hard to believe that Josephus would look with such admiration upon the Essenes if, indeed, they ultimately moved closer in ideology to the revolutionary Zealots. Joseph D. Amoussine, "Observatiunculae Qumraneae," *RQ* 7 (1971):535–545, noting that the immediate context of the oath speaks of transmitting the rules and the lore of the sect with absolute accuracy, suggests that λῃστεία is the equivalent of the Hebrew *hamas,* a word that in the Dead Sea Scrolls refers to violence to the text, that is, incorrect interpretation. If so, we may wonder that Josephus' assistants, who helped him with the style of the *War,* did not catch such a Semiticism and correct it. There is certainly very little indication in our present Greek text that betrays that it has been translated from an Aramaic original.

Literature on the Zealots has generally been marked by bias, either for or against them because of their extreme nationalism, as demonstrated by Israel L. Levine, "The Zealots at the End of the Second Temple Period as a Historiographical Problem" [Hebrew], *Cathedra* 1 (1976):39–60.

William R. Farmer, *Maccabees, Zealots, and Josephus: An Inquiry into Jewish Nationalism in the Greco-Roman Period* (New York 1956), regards the Zealots as spiritual followers of the Maccabees and asserts that Josephus deliberately obscured their connection because he himself was descended from the Hasmoneans, who had been allies of the Romans. However, we may note that Josephus praises the Hasmoneans but is bitterly critical of the Zealots. Moreover, the origin of the Maccabean revolution was allegedly the suppression of religious freedom, whereas at the time of the Zealot revolt the Jews had religious freedom and were now seeking political liberty. In addition, the Zealots had a strong eschatological strain, whereas the Maccabees did not.

There is an enormous literature on the question of the relationship of the Zealots to the Sicarii. Kirsopp Lake, "The Zealots," in Frederick J. Foakes-Jackson and Kirsopp Lake, *The Beginning of Christianity,* Part 1, vol. 1 (London 1920), pp. 421ff., notes that Josephus never uses the term *Zealots* to refer to a political party before 66, and that there is no justification for identifying the party with the Fourth Philosophy, which, according to Josephus (*A* XVIII, 9), arose in the year 6 C.E. in connection with the census of Quirinius. However, inasmuch as the Talmud connects the *Sikarin* (presumably the Sicarii) with the last siege of Jerusalem, whereas according to Josephus the Zealots defended Jerusalem, it is tempting to identify the two. Samuel G. F. Brandon, *The Fall of Jerusalem and the Christian Church* (London 1951), argues that the fact that one of Jesus' disciples is Simon the Zealot is evidence that the Zealots existed before 66; but this epithet, we may reply, is merely an indication that he was zealous in the tradition of Phinehas of the book of Numbers.

Cecil Roth, "The Zealots in the War of 66–73," *JSeS* 4 (1959):332–335, regards the Zealots and the Sicarii as two wings of the same party. But we may reply that the fact that Josephus himself (*BJ* VII, 259–274) lists the Sicarii and the Zealots separately, as two of the five groups of revolutionaries, would argue against this. Roth, *The Historical Background of the Dead Sea Scrolls* (Oxford 1958), identifies the Zealots (Sicarii) with the Dead Sea sect, and this would seem to be confirmed by the discovery at Masada, a stronghold of the Sicarii, of documents also found at Qumran; but the fact that Josephus (*A* XVIII, 23) says that the Fourth Philosophy (if they are identical with the

Sicarii) agreed with the Pharisees in all respects except that they had an unconquerable passion for liberty, argues against this, since the sect at Qumran had a different calendar from that of the Pharisees.

H. P. Kingdon, "Who Were the Zealots and Their Leaders in A.D. 66?" *NTS* 17 (1970):68–72, concludes that the first use of the term *Zealots* is with reference to the armed followers of Menahem, but he neglects to consider that there the term is referring to "zealous" followers of Menahem rather than Zealots; and indeed the Latin version renders it thus.

Shimon Applebaum, "The Zealots: The Case for Revaluation," *JRS* 61 (1971):155–170, concludes that Josephus' own independent observations are influenced by his family and social derivation, which was Sadducean, so that he was therefore out of sympathy with the masses, and by the fact that he was in conflict with the revolutionaries in Galilee. The Zealots, he stresses, are to be viewed as an organic growth of Judaism in response to the critical situation created by the relations of Judea to the Roman Empire as a whole. He insists that Judah of Galilee's group, the Fourth Philosophy, was the creator of the Zealot ideology and the most consistent and most successful in action against the Romans. We may comment that Josephus nowhere in his autobiography indicates that his family had Sadducean ties; such a view is based upon the assumption that the upper-class priests had such an affiliation. If, indeed, his family had had such ties we may assume that he would have been attacked by his opponents on such grounds; and he mentions no such charge in his *Life*.

In a sharply worded article, Morton Smith, "Zealots and Sicarii: Their Origins and Relation," *HTR* 64 (1971):1–19, insists that the Sicarii must be distinguished from the Zealots in date of origin, locale, leadership, and philosophy. We may suggest, however, that the fact that the name *Sicarii* is Latin while the name *Zealots* is of Greek origin is an indication that the names were given to these groups by their opponents. Moreover, the fact that the names *Sicarii* and *Zealots* do not occur in the *Antiquities* and that the strange name *Fourth Philosophy* does not occur in the *War,* even in the enumeration of the five revolutionary groups (*BJ* VII, 259–274), may be an indication that the latter is a term for an umbrella organization that embraced the various revolutionary groups. Finally, the fact that Josephus (*A* XVIII, 4) singles out Saddok the Pharisee, whose name has distinct priestly associations, as a colleague of Judas the Gaulanite (the founder of the Fourth Philosophy), may be a point of contact with the Zealots, who were apparently directed by a group of priests in Jerusalem and who centered their attention on the Temple. We may note that the almost universal assumption that the Sicarii are the same as the Fourth Philosophy rests on the statement (*BJ* VII, 253) that the leader of the Sicarii at Masada was Eleazar ben Jair, who was a relative of Judas of Galilee; but, we may object, kinship historically hardly proves adherence to the same point of view. Moreover, Menahem, the son of Judas of Galilee (the founder of the

Fourth Philosophy, whom most identify with the Sicarii, as noted earlier), was an enemy of the Zealots, according to those who refuse to regard this as a reference to zealous individuals. Indeed, Menahem Stern, "Zealots," *EJ Year Book 1973* (Jerusalem 1973), pp. 135–152, correctly concludes that only a hypothesis connecting the Fourth Philosophy, the Sicarii, and the Zealots can explain the significance that Josephus assigns to the first. Martin Hengel, "Zeloten und Sikarier: Zur Frage nach der Einheit und Vielfalt der jüdischen Befreiungsbewegung 6–74 nach Christus," *Festschrift Otto Michel* (Göttingen 1974), pp. 175–176, in reply to Morton Smith, minimizes the differences in ideology and maximizes the differences in leadership among the five revolutionary groups and concludes that their differences were as much religious as political. We may comment that the one common denominator of these revolutionary groups was apparently that they made their political platform into a matter of religious principle.

Günther Baumbach, "Einheit und Vielfalt der jüdischen Freiheitsbewegung im 1. Jh. n. Chr.," *EvT* 45 (1985):93–107, follows Josephus in stressing that it was the Sicarii who played a leading role in the Jewish resistance against the Romans. But he insists that any attempt at eliminating the differences among the various revolutionary groups should be rejected.

Richard A. Horsley, "Sicarii: Ancient Jewish Terrorists," *JR* 59 (1979): 435–458, maintains that the Zealots, the Sicarii, and the λῃσταί are three distinct groups. He notes the parallels between the tactics of the Sicarii and those of modern terrorists: selective assassinations, general assassinations, and kidnapping. In "Menahem in Jerusalem: A Brief Messianic Episode among the Sicarii—Not Zealot Messianism," *NT* 27 (1985):334–348, emphasizing the difference between the Zealots and the Sicarii, Horsley concludes that the messianic excitement centered around Menahem in 66 was a passing episode connected with the Sicarii rather than a movement of broader scope. But, one may reflect, it is hard to believe that any such personality, in view of the messianic beliefs of the world at that time, would not have looked upon himself as a universal figure who would bring about massive changes for all Jewry. In "'Like One of the Prophets of Old': Two Types of Popular Prophets at the Time of Jesus," *CBQ* 47 (1985):435–463, Horsley stresses the distinctions among the several popular movements that opposed the Romans. But, as we have suggested, most likely the very term *Fourth Philosophy*, which Josephus employs in the *Antiquities* (XVIII, 23), refers to an "umbrella" group that embraced the views of various revolutionary movements. In "The Zealots. Their Origin, Relationships and Importance in the Jewish Revolt," *NT* 28 (1986):159–192, Horsley stresses the economic motives of the Zealots in seeking an egalitarian theocracy. Their presence in Jerusalem, he contends, blocked the mediating strategy of the high priests in seeking a negotiated settlement with the Romans and gave other groups time to consolidate their resistance against the Romans. W. Stenger, "Bemerkungen zum Begriff 'Räuber' im Neuen Testament und bei Flavius Josephus," *BK* 37 (1982):89–97, insists that we should distinguish between social banditry, which has an economic and political background, and a revolutionary movement based on ideology. The Fourth Philosophy, he notes, started with the former but developed into the latter.

Uriel Rappaport, "John of Galilee: From Galilee to Jerusalem," *JJS* 33 (1982):479–493, objects to the theory connecting the Sicarii and the Zealots in view of the sharp antagonism between the two groups; but we may reply that the history of radical movements is usually one of splits between erstwhile allies.

David M. Rhoads, "Some Jewish Revolutionaries in Palestine from 6 A.D. to 73 A.D. According to Josephus" (Ph.D. diss., Duke University 1973), argues that, despite Josephus, the five revolutionary groups represent a geographical cross-section of Palestine and suggest widespread and spontaneous, if disorganized, support of the war.

Considerable dispute has arisen as to whether the Galileans as such constituted a specific revolutionary group. Solomon Zeithlin, "Who Were the Galileans? New Light on Josephus' Activities in Galilee," *JQR* 64 (1973–1974): 189–203, and Francis Loftus, "The Galileans in Josephus and Jewish Tradition: A Study in Jewish Nationalism" (B. Phil. diss., St. Andrews 1975), cite as evidence that the Galileans were a revolutionary group the statement in *Life* 381 that Tiberias narrowly escaped being sacked by the Galileans, and that since Tiberias is in Galilee the name *Galileans* cannot be a geographical name. However, Sean Freyne, "The Galileans in the Light of Josephus' *Vita*," *NTS* 26 (1980):397–413; Joseph R. Armenti, "On the Use of the Term 'Galileans' in the Writings of Josephus Flavius: A Brief Note," *JQR* 72 (1981–1982):45–49; and I, "The Term 'Galileans' in Josephus," *JQR* 72 (1981–1982):50–52, have argued that inasmuch as Josephus (*A* XVIII, 37) declares that the new settlers of Tiberias were a promiscuous rabble, "no small contingent being Galilean," the term must be geographical, since it would make no sense for Herod the Tetrarch to settle revolutionaries in his newly established city. Likewise, Josephus' statement (*Ap* I, 48) that he had been in command of "those whom we call Galileans" could hardly refer to a group of revolutionaries. In addition, if they had been a distinct revolutionary group, they should have been included in what appears to be an exhaustive list of such groups (*BJ* VII, 259–274). Finally, the reference in *Life* 381 is not to "the" Galileans but to Galileans, and hence not to a party. Moreover, Francis X. Malinowski, "Galilean Judaism in the Writings of Flavius Josephus" (Ph.D. diss., Duke University 1973), has noted that neither the Zealots nor the Sicarii are mentioned by Josephus as being present in Galilee. Most recently, Giorgio Jossa, "Chi sono i Galilei nella Vita di Flavio Giuseppe?" *RiBi* 31

(1983):329–339, has refined the hypothesis of Freyne in concluding that the Galileans were not revolutionaries but that it is too rigid to identify them with the rural against the urban element. Rather, the hostility is of a religious and social order.

Among those who came from Galilee, none were of greater importance for the period of the war against Rome than John of Gischala. Henry St. J. Thackeray, *Josephus the Man and the Historian* (New York 1929), p. 119, has suggested that Josephus' portrait of John is indebted to that of Sallust's *Catiline;* but in view of the fact that Josephus' knowledge of Latin is doubtful, this seems unlikely. This thesis is indeed rejected by Yitzhak Baer, "Jerusalem in the Times of the Great Revolt. Based on the Source Criticism of Josephus and Talmudic-Midrashic Legends of the Temple's Destruction" [Hebrew], *Zion* 36 (1971):127–190, who argues that Josephus' model is the Athenian Cleon as portrayed by Thucydides and Aristophanes. But, we may respond, the influence of Thucydides is more manifest in the *Antiquities,* especially in the latter books, than in the *War.*

Uriel Rappaport, in a series of articles, "John of Gischala" [Hebrew], *CP* (1982):203–215; "John of Galilee: From Galilee to Jerusalem," *JJS* 33 (1982):479–493; "John of Gischala in Galilee," *JC* 3 (1983):46–57; and "John of Gischala in Jerusalem" [Hebrew], *NH* (1983):97–115, notes the important facts that both John and Justus of Tiberias, like Josephus, came from the same moderate party and that, like the Zealots, John could not identify with the social goals of the Sicarii and of Simon bar Giora. He traces the evolution of John from his status as a local politician who avoided open confrontation with the Romans into his status as one of the outstanding leaders of the revolt. Josephus' portrait, especially in the light of the coins issued by the rebels, turns out to be biased.

Josephus on John the Baptist, Jesus, and Christianity

There can be little doubt as to the genuineness of Josephus' passage about John the Baptist (*A* XVIII, 116–119), since, as pointed out by Henry St. J. Thackeray, *Josephus the Man and the Historian* (New York 1929), pp. 131–133, it contains a number of phrases, brief though it is, that are characteristic of this part of the *Antiquities* and not of the rest of the work. Charles H. H. Scobie, *John the Baptist* (London 1964), pp. 17–22, notes, quite plausibly, that if the passage had been interpolated by a Christian we would have expected some reference to John's connection with Jesus. We may add that an interpolator would probably have removed the discrepancy between the Gospel account of the reason for John's condemnation, namely his denunciation of Herod Antipas' immorality, and Josephus' version, which stresses his success in attracting crowds and hence the fear that he was fomenting a revolution. Furthermore, we may add, belief in the genuineness of this passage is corroborated by Origen, who explicitly states that Josephus did not believe in Jesus as the Christ (*Contra Celsum* 1.47 and *Commentary on Matthew* 10.17) and hence did not have the so-called *Testimonium Flavianum*, and cites (*Contra Celsum* 1.47) the passage about John. In addition, the fact that Josephus has two different words (βαπτισμῷ, βάπτισιν) for baptism in consecutive sentences would again argue against the theory of interpolation, since an interpolator would almost surely have been consistent in his choice of language. Moreover, it is hard to believe that a Christian interpolator would have assigned almost twice as much space (163 words) to John as to Jesus (89 words). Finally, Josephus' account seems to be historically valid, since we should have expected Josephus to agree with the Gospels in giving the cause of John's death, inasmuch as he praises John, whereas the political charge against him was clearly embarrassing to Josephus, who so fiercely opposed all revolutionary stirrings.

Roland Schütz, *Johannes der Täufer* (Zürich 1967), pp. 13–27, suggests that Josephus suppressed John's messianic claims for the sake of his Roman readers; but we may comment that if, indeed, John claimed to be the Messiah and, therefore, was a political rebel against Rome, Josephus could hardly have called him a "good" man.

The literature on Josephus' passage about Jesus, the *Testimonium Flavianum* (*A* XVIII, 63–64) is enormous. For the period 1937–1980 alone, in *Josephus and Modern Scholarship* (Berlin 1984), pp. 680–684, 957–958, I have listed eighty-seven discussions, the overwhelming majority of which question its authenticity in whole or in part.

The chief arguments usually given for authenticity are (1) that it is found in all the Greek manuscripts and in all the manuscripts of the Latin translation of Josephus; (2) that the language seems generally consistent with Josephus in this portion of his work; and (3) that Josephus refers elsewhere (*A* XX, 200), in a passage whose authenticity is generally accepted, to the "so-called" or "aforementioned" Christ. To be sure, Per Bilde, "Josefus' beretning om Jesus" ("Josephus' Text about Jesus"), *DTT* 44 (1981):99–135, contends that the reference to Jesus in *Antiquities* XX, 200, is intended merely to distinguish him from other persons named Jesus and does not presuppose a text about him; but we may reply that it would hardly be in character for Josephus to mention someone as *Messiah* without describing the implications of this word or giving an anecdote to illustrate it. To these arguments, we may add that, aside from this passage, and possibly those about John and James, there are no other passages in Josephus whose authenticity has been questioned; hence, the burden of proof rests upon anyone who argues for interpolation.

Louis Préchac, "Réflexions sur le 'Testimonium Flavianum'," *BAGB*

(1969):101–111, asks how an interpolator could have tampered with the passage in all copies of Josephus then circulating; but we may explain this by noting that our earliest manuscript containing this part of the *Antiquities* dates from the eleventh century and indeed may be derived from such an interpolated manuscript.

The case for interpolation has been most carefully stated by Eduard Norden, "Josephus und Tacitus über Jesus Christus und eine messianische Prophetie," *NJKA* 16 (1973):637–666. The chief arguments for interpolation, as I have discussed in *"The Testimonium Flavianum:* The State of the Question," in *Christological Perspectives: Essays in Honor of Harvey K. McArthur,* Robert F. Berkey and Sarah A. Edwards, eds. (New York 1982), pp. 179–199, 288–293, are (1) that Origen in the third century, who certainly knew Book XVIII of the *Antiquities* since he cites the passage about John, specifically (*Contra Celsum* 1.47 and *Commentary on Matthew* 10.17) states that Josephus disbelieved in Jesus as Christ; and (2) the fact that the passage, despite its obvious usefulness in debates with Jews, is not found in any writer before Eusebius in the fourth century. If the passage had existed in Josephus' original text, we would have expected the passage to be cited by Justin Martyr in his dialogue with the Jew Trypho, since it would have been an extremely effective answer to Trypho's charge that Christianity is based upon a rumor and that if Jesus was born and lived somewhere he is entirely unknown. On this point I note that no fewer than eleven church fathers prior to or contemporary with Eusebius cite various passages from Josephus (including the *Antiquities*) but not the *Testimonium*. Moreover, it is a full century—and five other church fathers, most notably Augustine, who had many an occasion to find it useful—before we have another reference to the *Testimonium* in Jerome *(De Viris Illustribus* 13.14); and it seems remarkable that Jerome, who knows Josephus so well, cites him ninety times, and admires him so much that he refers to him as a second Livy (*Epistula ad Eustochium* 22), cites the *Testimonium* only once. We may add that the fact that in the passage in the *War* parallel to the one in the *Antiquities* about Pilate there is no mention of Jesus, despite the fact that the account of Pilate in the *War* is almost as full as the version in the *Antiquities,* corroborates our suspicion that there was either no passage about Jesus in the original text of the *Antiquities* or that it had a different form. We may also note that Josephus' great contemporary and rival, Justus of Tiberias, apparently made no mention of Jesus (Photius, *Bibliotheca* 33). As to the argument, frequently stated, that Josephus, as a believing Jew, could not have acknowledged Jesus as the Messiah, the fact that Rabbi Akiva in the following century acknowledged Bar Kochba as the Messiah, even though the majority of the other rabbis and time seem to have disproved his belief, would indicate that such a declaration in and of itself was not impossible for a good Jew, though time should prove him wrong. Moreover,

Jerome's notice reads *credebatur esse Christus;* and the Arabic version, as noted later, avers that "he was perhaps the Messiah."

David S. Wallace-Hadrill, "Eusebius of Caesarea and the Testimonium Flavianum (Josephus 'Antiquities', XVIII, 63f.)," *JEH* 25 (1974):353–362, commenting on the contradictory citations of the *Testimonium* in the three places where Eusebius quotes it, concludes that already in his time there existed various versions of the *Testimonium.* He concludes that it is improbable that Eusebius himself interpolated the text, since if so we would have to explain why he quoted his own interpolation differently on three separate occasions. The latter argument seems convincing but, as to divergent quotations of the same text, there are a number of other instances of this sort (in Clement and Jerome, for example), due to the fact that it was difficult to consult original texts and consequently authors relied much more upon memory.

The most ingenious, though hardly convincing, attempt to restore Josephus' original text has been made by Robert Eisler, *IHCOYC BACIΛEYC OY BACIΛEYCAC,* 2 vols. (Heidelberg 1929–1930). A number of writers, such as Paul Winter, "Josephus on Jesus," *JHS* 1 (1968):289–302, have noted that inasmuch as in the passage immediately preceding the *Testimonium* Josephus gives two instances of Pilate's maladministration, this should have been a third, whereas actually it blames the Jews and not Pilate for the condemnation of Jesus. Ernst Bammel, "Zum Testimonium Flavianum (Jos Ant 18, 63–64)," *J-S*, pp. 9–22, and Albert A. Bell, "Josephus the Satirist? A Clue to the Original Form of the 'Testimonium Flavianum'," *JQR* (1976):16–22, suggest that inasmuch as the passage that follows tells of a seduction of a noble Roman lady, the original version of the *Testimonium* may similarly have described the seduction of Mary in a manner such as is described in the *Toledoth Yeshu.*

If the passage was inserted by Josephus, we may ask what the motives for this insertion were. Richard Laqueur, *Der jüdische Historiker Flavius Josephus. Ein biographischer Versuch auf neuer quellenkritischer Grundlage* (Giessen 1920), pp. 274–278, suggests that Justus of Tiberias had charged that Josephus had misinterpreted the Bible and had taken the Septuagint rather than the Hebrew text as his basis, at a time when the movement against the Septuagint was becoming strong in the rabbinical schools. Josephus now turned to the Christians to gain their small but devoted support, since they regarded the Septuagint as divinely inspired. We may reply, however, that though we have in the *Life* Josephus' answer to many of Justus' charges, there is no claim that he had misinterpreted the Bible. As to seeking a market among the Christians, Josephus hardly needed the money, since he was living in comfortable quarters under royal protection and with a pension. Moreover, why should Josephus have sought to gain the very small Christian audience, when it would have probably meant alienating his much larger potential Hellenistic

Jewish audience? Finally, Josephus, at least in the manuscripts of his work that we have, often diverges from the Septuagint.

The most striking development on the subject of the *Testimonium* in recent years has been the publication of Shlomo Pines' *An Arabic Version of the Testimonium Flavianum and Its Implications* (Jerusalem 1971), which cites a text of the *Testimonium* by a tenth-century Arab Christian named Agapius that omits Josephus' statement "if indeed we ought to call him a man," as well as the reference to Jesus' miracles and to the role of Jewish leaders in accusing Jesus. It states not that Jesus appeared to his disciples on the third day but that his disciples reported this and, most significantly, that "he was perhaps the Messiah" rather than that he was the Messiah. Pines shows that Agapius' text is essentially based upon Eusebius' *Historia Ecclesiastica,* and he suggests that it is an attempt at Christianization of the original version, which was unfavorable to Christians. We may comment that, on the messiahship of Jesus, Agapius seems to be close to Jerome's version that "he was believed to be the Messiah"—the version of Michael the Syrian in the twelfth century is directly in line with Jerome in declaring that "he was thought to be the Messiah"—though one wonders how a believing Christian could have cited a text stating that Jesus was perhaps the Messiah without recording a strong reaction. However, the fact that the order of statements in Agapius differs from that in Josephus would seem to indicate that we are dealing here with a paraphrase. The fact, furthermore, that Agapius declares that according to Josephus, Herod burned the genealogies of the tribes, whereas there is no such passage in Josephus but there is in Eusebius (*Historia Ecclesiastica* 1.7.13), is further indication that Agapius did not consult Josephus directly.

A recent discussion of the passage by J. Neville Birdsall, "The Continuing Enigma of Josephus's Testimony about Jesus," *BJRL* 67 (1985):609–622, concludes, on the basis of its vocabulary, that it is the work of a forger who knew the favorite phrases of Josephus but who used these phrases in senses that are not customary in the rest of Josephus' work. We may comment, however, that if the forger had such a profound knowledge of Josephus' vocabulary it seems likely that he would also know how Josephus used these words. Moreover, in view of Josephus' propensity for using certain words in particular parts of his work (perhaps under the influence of his reading at the time or as a result of help from "assistants"), we cannot draw conclusions, especially in so short a passage.

Geza Vermes, "The Jesus Notice of Josephus Re-Examined," *JJS* 38 (1987):1–10, concludes, in particular, that the phrases describing Jesus as a wise man ($\sigma o \phi \grave{o} \varsigma$ $\mathring{a} v \mathring{\eta} \rho$) and a performer of astonishing deeds ($\pi a \rho a \delta \acute{o} \xi \omega v$ $\mathring{\epsilon} \rho \gamma \omega v$ $\pi o \iota \eta \tau \mathring{\eta} \varsigma$) are consonant with Josephus' style and that they are unlikely to be Christian fabrications. The second phrase, notably, echoes a positive popular representation of Jesus which accords with the description of him in the New Testament and in rabbinic literature. Vermes appositely notes that the same phrase is used of Elisha by Josephus (*A* IX, 182); we may add that the fact that this phrase is a Josephan addition in connection with Elisha adds to the likelihood that it is a Josephan expression in the *Testimonium*. Likewise, Celsus' reference (*ap*. Origen, *Contra Celsum* 1.6.17–18) to Jesus' performance of παράδοξα is a further indication that Origen had the phrase in his copy of Josephus, especially since the word occurs only once in the New Testament (Luke 5:26). Thus the notice is actually impartial. We may remark that the rabbis (Tosefta, *Ḥullin* 2.22–23) do, indeed, acknowledge the possibility of performing miraculous cures in the name of Jesus, without endorsing his religious views; but to speak of someone as "wise" is hardly impartial, since this is almost the ultimate compliment for a Jew. Vermes says that if Josephus had written an anti-Christian statement the Christians, who are responsible for the preservation of his work, would never have permitted his writings to survive. We may remark, however, that the *Jewish War* would most likely have been preserved in any case because it depicts so vividly the sufferings of the Jews, and especially the destruction of the Temple.

The passage about James (*A* XX, 197–203) has generally been accepted as authentic. Most recently, however, Tessa Rajak, *Josephus: The Historian and His Society* (London 1983), p. 131, has argued that the case for the whole account being a Christian interpolation is very strong, particularly because it sharply diverges from Josephus' view of Ananus the high priest in the *War* IV, 319–321, and because it so harshly criticizes the Sadducees and the Sanhedrin. We may comment, however, that Josephus is hardly averse to harsh criticism of the Sadducees and even, to some degree, of the Sanhedrin (it was probably not a Sanhedrin but a special court appointed *ad hoc* by the Sadducean high priest). But, in particular, we would suggest that a forger, presumably someone who knew the works of Josephus well, would have been careful not to contradict another text of Josephus. Moreover, Origen (*Commentary on Matthew* 10.17) explicitly says that Josephus gave witness to so much righteousness in James, while expressing wonder that he did not admit Jesus to be the Messiah.

The contradiction between Josephus (*A* XVIII, 1–2) and Luke (2:1–5) with regard to the date of the census of Quirinius has occasioned a very considerable literature. Luke speaks of "the first enrollment, when Quirinius was governor of Syria," at the time of the birth of Jesus, near the end of the reign of Herod (4 B.C.E.), whereas Josephus speaks of the census when Archelaus was removed from his kingship in 6 or 7 C.E. William M. Ramsay, *Was Christ Born at Bethlehem? A Study on the Credibility of St. Luke* (London 1898), pp. 229–283, attempts to vindicate Luke by suggesting that Quirinius was governor of Syria before 4 B.C.E. as well as in 6 C.E. However, Lily R. Taylor,

"Quirinius and the Census of Judaea," *AJP* 54 (1953):120–133, argues convincingly that, at the time of the Homanadensian War, Quirinius was more probably governor of Galatia. In any case, the list of governors of Syria for the period before the birth of Jesus, which seems complete, does not contain the name of Quirinius. Moreover, if Quirinius had been governor of Syria previously, we should have expected Josephus, in accordance with his usual habit and in view of the importance of this province and of this position for events in Palestine, to have indicated such. Finally, Josephus mentions the census (*A* XVIII, 3) as having shocked the Jews, presumably because it was unprecedented.

Willem Lodder, *Die Schätzung des Quirinius bei Flavius Josephus. Eine Untersuchung: Hat sich Josephus in der Datierung der bekannten Schätzung (Luk. 2,2) geirrt?* (Leipzig 1930), concludes that Luke is right and that Josephus has erred in confusing KZ and LZ and that he has thus read that the census took place in the thirty-seventh rather than in the twenty-seventh year after the battle of Actium (31 B.C.E.). But, we may reply, it seems very unlikely that there was a Roman census under Herod in view of Herod's relationship to the Roman princeps and Senate.

Josephus and Archaeology

How accurate is Josephus in his description of the land of Israel and of buildings therein? There is no land that has been excavated more extensively than Israel, where archaeology has become almost the national hobby; and, hence, it would seem, we should be in a good position to answer this question.

Isaiah Press, *Eretz Israel: A Topographical-Historical Encyclopaedia of Palestine* [Hebrew], 4 vols. (Jerusalem 1946–1955); translated into English, 4 vols. (Jerusalem 1948–1955), concludes that Josephus is an excellent source for the geography of Palestine, inasmuch as he had been born there. Christa Möller and Götz Schmitt, *Siedlungen Palästinas nach Flavius Josephus* (Wiesbaden 1976), superseding the outdated work of Gustav Böttger, *Topographisch-historisches Lexikon zu den Schriften des Flavius Josephus. Compilatorisch zusammengestellt* (Leipzig 1879), give modern place names of sites mentioned by Josephus, references to the Hebrew Bible and to the Septuagint (except for references in the first half of Josephus' *Antiquities*), the Talmud, and the church fathers, and to discussions in present-day scholarship.

Magen Broshi, "The Credibility of Josephus" [Hebrew], *CP* (1982):21–27; translated into English in *JJS* 33 (1982):379–384, expresses admiration for Josephus' precision when checked against archaeological data. This accuracy, he suggests, is due to Josephus' access to Roman imperial commentaries, such as those of Vespasian and Titus; but, we may remark, the fact that Josephus had errors in distances where we know the Roman army (which was noted for its precision in such matters) was active seems to challenge such a theory.

Though commending Josephus for his general accuracy, Zeev Safrai, "The Description of Eretz-Israel in Josephus' Works" [Hebrew] *CP* (1982): 91–115, notes a number of inconsistencies in Josephus, particularly in his description of the land of Israel (*BJ* III, 35–58) and in his indication of certain (though only a minority of) distances: for example, the length of the Dead Sea is described as only one-third of what it actually is; and the width of the Jordan valley is only half of what it really is; and the distance between towns, though usually accurate, is sometimes mistaken, as for example between Jerusalem and Etam. Josephus shows considerable independence in his description of the land itself and of its divisions, presumably basing himself on first-hand knowledge. Even in his description of Galilee, where Josephus served as general and which he knew well, there is a mixture of accuracy and inconsistency—a conclusion that confirms the view of Eric M. Meyers, "The Cultural Setting of Galilee: The Case of Regionalism and Early Judaism," *ANRW* 2.19.1 (1979), pp. 686–702.

The three sites most carefully explored by archaeologists are Caesarea, Jerusalem, and Masada; and in each case Josephus has emerged with a good, though hardly a perfect, score.

In the case of Caesarea, Lee I. Levine, *Caesarea under Roman Rule* (Leiden 1975), criticizes Josephus' statement that there existed a port between Dor and Jaffa, noting that this reflects a situation of the fourth century B.C.E. rather than that of Josephus' own lifetime. Moreover, Josephus' suggestion that Caesarea was established to add an additional step along the trade route from Egypt to Phoenicia is not in accord with the crucial role it later played. But Josephus' actual description of Caesarea is substantially vindicated by the archaeological discoveries of the last few years, according to Avner Raban, "Josephus and the Herodian Harbour of Caesarea" [Hebrew], *CP* (1982): 165–184.

Benjamin Mazar, the present-day dean of Israeli archaeologists, "Josephus Flavius—The Historian of Jerusalem" [Hebrew], *CP* (1982):1–5, concludes that Josephus, drawing upon written and oral sources, as well as on personal observation, on the whole, is accurate in his description of Jerusalem, despite the discrepancies and obscurities and even intentional deviations on occasion. When the elaborate excavations of the city of David, currently in progress under the direction of Y. Shiloh, will be completed, we shall be further able to see how precise Josephus is in his description.

As to Masada, the most celebrated of all archaeological sites in Israel, Yigael Yadin, *Masada—in Those Days, in This Time* [Hebrew]; translated into English *Masada: Herod's Fortress and the Zealots' Last Stand* (New York 1966), was amazed at the degree to which his finds confirm Josephus' description, despite the fact that Josephus was in Rome at the time the fort was besieged in 74 C.E. There are some errors in detail, however: (1) Josephus (*BJ* VII, 289) says that Herod's palace was on the western slope, whereas actually it is on the north, but this may be due to the fact that when seen from the west, where the view is best, the palace appears to be on the west; (2) Josephus (*BJ* VII, 290) says that the pillars of Herod's palace were cut from a single block, whereas actually they are made up of several sections, but we may note that the sections have been covered with stucco so carefully that the joints cannot be seen; (3) Josephus (*BJ* VII, 394) says that the possessions of the defenders were burnt, whereas actually some of them were found preserved; but this may be explained by the fact that the fire that the defenders set did not completely consume the food; (4) Josephus (*BJ* VII, 394) says that all the possessions were gathered together in one large pile and set on fire, whereas archaeology shows many piles and many fires; (5) Josephus (*BJ* VII, 336) says that Eleazar ordered his men to destroy everything except the foodstuffs and (*BJ* VII, 297) that when the Romans entered the fortress they found what remained of Herod's original fruits undecayed, but archaeology shows that many storerooms that contained provisions were burnt—this, however, may be explained by the fact that the original fire spread and consumed some of the food as well; (6) Josephus (*BJ* VII, 395) says that ten were chosen by lot to dispatch the rest, whereas Yadin found eleven ostraca, but the fact that one of them contains the name of the leader, Ben Jair, would corroborate Josephus' account, and we may suggest that Ben Jair may not have been counted or that one of the lots may have been erroneously inscribed; (7) Josephus (*BJ* VII, 397) says that the last survivor of the defenders set fire to the palace, but archaeology shows that all the public buildings had been set ablaze; (8) Josephus (*BJ* VII, 399, 404) says that a woman who had survived by concealing herself in a subterranean aqueduct lucidly reported to the Romans the speeches of Eleazar ben Jair, but the aqueduct is at the other end of the fortress from the place where the grisly deed was done; (9) it would seem poor strategy for the Romans to delay their assault on Masada until the morning (*BJ* VII, 407) after fire had taken hold of the inner wall (*BJ* VII, 315–319); (10) Josephus (*BJ* VII, 405) clearly implies that all the murder-suicides had taken place in the palace, but the palace is too small for 960 people; (11) only 25 skeletons were found, whereas Josephus (*BJ* VII, 400) says that the number of victims was 960 (one manuscript has 560, and Zonaras 6.29 has 260), but while it is tempting to conclude that here, as probably elsewhere, Josephus has been guilty of exaggeration, the fact that pigs' bones were found together with those of the defenders and that elsewhere on the site remains from the Byzantine period were found would cast doubt on the identity of these 25 skeletons, and it is possible that the defenders were later buried elsewhere or that the Romans had disposed of their bodies in some other way.

Shaye J. D. Cohen, "Masada: Literary Tradition, Archaeological Remains, and the Credibility of Josephus," *JJS* 33 (1982):385–405, has contended that ancient historians often exaggerated the truth when narrating collective suicides, and that Josephus has done likewise, being accurate in matters that were verifiable by the Roman general at Masada, Flavius Silva, and by the Romans generally, but improving on the story by seeking to foist on Ben Jair the full responsibility for the war. He declares, for example, that the lots discovered by Yadin verify, at best, a Roman conjecture; but we may ask why the name of Ben Jair appears on one of them.

As to Eleazar ben Jair's two speeches, most scholars have raised the question as to how much genuine Jewish traditional material there is beneath the Hellenistic veneer. Otto Bauernfeind and Otto Michel, "Die beiden Eleazarreden in Jos. bell. 7, 323–336; 7, 341–388," *ZNW* 58 (1967):267–272, have answered positively, noting their rhetorical connection with each other: the first being a homogeneous, sermonic, historical review, while the second adds rhetorical elements taken from Hellenistic diatribe, together with didactic and eschatological motifs. Trude Weiss-Rosmarin, "Josephus' 'Eleazar Speech' and Historical Credibility," *PSWCJS*, vol. 1 (Jerusalem 1975), pp. 417–427, has expressed thoroughgoing skepticism that a guerrilla of Eleazar's type could have composed the philosophical-theological speeches ascribed to him by Josephus. Michael Bünker, "Die rhetorische Disposition der Eleazarreden (Josephus, Bell. 7, 323–388)," *Kairos* 23 (1981):100–107, and Menahem Luz, "Eleazar's Second Speech on Masada and Its Literary Precedents," *RhM* 126 (1983):25–43, have analyzed the speeches and concluded that they show all the earmarks of the Hellenistic rhetorical techniques and motifs of the time. David J. Ladouceur, "Masada: A Consideration of the Literary Evidence," *GRBS* 21 (1980):245–260, views the speeches against the backdrop of the time, when the question of the propriety of suicide was much debated. He says that Josephus actually intended to heap opprobrium upon the defenders of Masada but that he spoke ironically in noting that the Romans expressed amazement at their fortitude. We may comment, however, that Josephus almost never alludes to contemporary events and that this is perhaps one major reason why he managed to remain on good terms with all the Flavian emperors. Moreover, the remark (*BJ* VII, 405), that the Romans upon entering Masada did not find it easy to listen to the surviving woman's account of the suicide, since they were "incredulous of such amazing boldness" (τῷ μεγέθει τοῦ τολμήματος ἀπιστοῦντες), hardly smacks of irony.

Shaye J. D. Cohen, "Masada: Literary Tradition, Archaeological Remains, and the Credibility of Josephus," *JJS* 33 (1982):385–405, noting the presence in Josephus' account of the suicide of a number of stock motifs found in descriptions of suicides in other ancient historians, expresses doubt as to the historicity of Josephus' version. The parallels, however, are hardly as uniform as Cohen contends and, in any case, Cohen fails to explain why Josephus would want to glorify the Sicarii at Masada when he condemns them so strongly (*BJ* VII, 262) in the passage just before the account of Masada.

I. Jacobs, "Eleazar ben Yair's Sanction for Martyrdom," *JSJ* 13 (1982): 183–186, wondering, as have many others, as to the basis of Ben Jair's statement (*BJ* VII, 387) that Jewish law commands suicide if it is impossible to live as free people, finds the source in the Scriptural verse (Deuteronomy 6:5), which is part of the Shema, that one should love God with all one's soul, which the rabbis (*Berakhoth* 61b) interpreted to mean, as Rabbi Akiva declares, "even if He takes away your soul," that is, your life. We may reply, however, that at the time when the rabbis issued this interpretation they declared (*Sanhedrin* 74a) that one should allow one's life to be taken only if one is required to commit incest (or adultery) or murder or to worship idols. There is no indication that the Romans would have required any of these from the defenders of Masada, and the fact that the Romans might well have wanted to teach the Jews a lesson of what happens to those who in haughtiness defy the Roman might (*debellare superbos,* Virgil, *Aeneid* 6.853) would still not have justified their suicide. In any case, we may comment that there is no evidence that the rules pertaining to permissibility of suicide that the rabbis adopted in the second century during the Hadrianic persecutions were in effect during the first century at the time of the Masada episode. Moreover, the rules do not permit the kind of mutual suicide which was practiced at Masada. Finally, we may suggest that the suicide was perhaps justified not according to Pharisaic law but according to the sectarian law of the Sicarii, just as was their raid on En Gedi on Passover (*BJ* IV, 402), when such an attack would surely be prohibited according to Pharisaic law. Yet, we may note the suicides of the old man and his family at Arbela to escape surrendering to Herod's troops (*BJ* I, 312–313; *A* XIV, 429–430), of thirty-nine of Josephus' men at Jotapata (*BJ* III, 387–391) to avoid surrendering to the Romans, the mass suicide at Gamala (*BJ* IV, 79–81) again to avoid surrendering to the Romans, and the suicide (*BJ* VI, 280) of two distinguished men who plunged into the flames of the burning Temple rather than surrender. In none of these cases, so far as we can tell, were those who committed suicide sectarians.

Trude Weiss-Rosmarian, "Masada, Josephus and Yadin," *JS* 32, no. 8 (October 1967):2–8, 30–32, has charged that Josephus' account is a deliberate falsification, that there was no mass suicide, and that Yadin was too involved emotionally to evaluate his archaeological discoveries impartially. In "Masada: A Critique of Recent Scholarship," *Morton Smith Festschrift* 3 (Leiden 1975), pp. 218–248, I have defended Josephus against this charge. David J. Ladouceur, "Masada: A Consideration of the Literary Evidence," *GRBS* 21 (1980):245–260, contends that Josephus' account reflects the contemporary philosophic, especially Stoic, environment in which he composed the *War* far more than the actual events, and that Eleazar's speeches have much in common with the so-called Stoic-Cynic diatribes.

The Language of Josephus

A good example of needless duplication in scholarship is to be seen in the making of concordances to Josephus. The first, Johann B. Ott, *Thesaurus Flavianus,* 7 vols., remains in manuscript in the Zentralbibliothek in Zürich; it is very incomplete. The second, likewise unpublished, by Adolf Schlatter and in the hands of Karl H. Rengstorf of Münster, was composed with a view toward finding parallels to the Gospels. The third, Henry St. J. Thackeray and Ralph Marcus, *A Lexicon to Josephus,* 4 fascicles (Paris 1930–1955), going through ἐμφιλοχωρεῖν was in the hands of the late Horst Moehring of Brown University, Providence. The last, Karl H. Rengstorf, ed., *A Complete Concordance to Flavius Josephus,* 4 vols. (Leiden 1973–1983), is now complete, except for the small portion of *Against Apion* (II, 51–133), which is extant only in the Latin translation.

In comparing Thackeray-Marcus and Rengstorf, we may note that the chief advantages of the latter are that (1) it is complete; (2) it lists every occurrence of every word (with the exception of a very few common words), whereas Thackeray-Marcus lists most but not all occurrences; (3) it has a very high degree of accuracy; (4) it is generous in quoting lemmata; (5) it lists noteworthy textual variants; and (6) it often cites the Latin translation of Josephus. Its chief deficiencies are that (1) unlike Thackeray-Marcus, it usually does not give the meaning of the word in a given passage but merely lists all the meanings at the beginning of the entry; (2) it omits the context for prepositions, conjunctions, pronouns, numbers, and particles, though precisely such words are often the key to the appreciation of the author's style; and (3) it is less analytical of Josephus' grammar than Thackeray-Marcus.

For proper names Adolf Schlatter, *Die hebräischen Namen bei Josephus* (Gütersloh 1913), basing himself on the index to Niese's edition of Josephus' text, gives the Hebrew and Aramaic equivalents. He attempts to reconstruct Josephus' original spelling by making his rendering harmonize with the Masoretic text; but we may remark that, beginning especially with the book of Judges, Josephus becomes quite free in rendering his biblical text and appears to draw increasingly on the Septuagint. Abraham Schalit, *Namenwörterbuch zu Flavius Josephus,* in *A Complete Concordance to Flavius Josephus,* Karl H. Rengstorf, ed., Supplement 1 (Leiden 1968), supersedes Schlatter, giving for all proper names in Josephus the Greek form with its variants, the Hebrew equivalent according to the Masoretic text, and the spelling in the Septuagint. Moreover, he has a valuable Hebrew-Greek index of the proper names. We should note, however, that almost no aspect of the text of Josephus has been subject to more corruption than proper names, since scribes were forever tempted to have the names conform to the spelling of the Septuagint.

For extended discussions of the meanings in the Septuagint, Philo, Josephus, and the New Testament of individual key words, the masterwork is Gerhard Kittel and Gerhard Friedrich, *Theologisches Wörterbuch zum Neuen Testament* (Stuttgart 1933–1973), 9 vols.; translated into English (Grand Rapids 1964–1974), 9 vols. Some of the articles, however, as noted by James Barr, *The Semantics of Biblical Language* (Oxford 1961), do not perceive that the special meaning can be seen only in the context rather than as isolated words.

As to Josephus' vocabulary and grammar, the indispensable work, remarkable for its carefulness and critical insights, remains Guilelmus Schmidt, *De Flavii Josephi elocutione observationes criticae. Pars prior* (Leipzig 1893; complete version in *JCP,* Supplement 20 [Leipzig 1894], pp. 341–550), who seeks to determine the value of various textual readings. For a study of prepositions, an excellent indication of style and authorship, we may turn to Robert Helbing, *Die Präpositionen bei Herodot und anderen Historikern* (Würzburg 1904), who compares Josephus' use of prepositions and the cases following them with the usage of fourteen other Greek historians.

The grammatical and lexical study of Josephus has been continued by David J. Ladouceur, "Studies in the Language and Historiography of Flavius Josephus" (Ph.D. diss., Brown University 1977), and "The Language of Josephus," *JSJ* 14 (1983):18–38, who notes that in declensional and conjugational forms Josephus, far from being dependent upon any single author such as Dionysius of Halicarnassus, fluctuates freely between classical and post-classical usage. Moreover, his usage of ἴδιος in place of the reflexive pronoun, of periphrases such as διά τινος ἔχειν, and of compound verbs with two prepositional prefixes, alleged by Robert J. H. Shutt, *Studies in Josephus* (London 1961), to be derived from Dionysius, may be found in Polybius and in Attic inscriptions of the first century B.C.E. What would be helpful would be a thorough study of the language and style of Dionysius, as well as of other Hellenistic writers, to determine precisely how much Josephus owes to them. Ladouceur is continuing this important work, and we may expect significant further results.

As to Josephus' vocabulary, Bernhard Brüne, *Flavius Josephus und seine Schriften in ihrem Verhältnis zum Judentume, zur griechischen-römischen Welt und zum Christentume mit griechischer Wortkonkordanz zum Neuen Testamente und I. Clemensbriefe nebst Sach- und Namen-Verzeichnis* (Gütersloh 1913), falls far short of being systematic in his examination of Josephus' indebtedness to Herodotus, Thucydides, Xenophon, and Polybius. Elchanan Stein, *De Woordenkeuze in het Bellum Judaicum van Flavius Josephus* (Amsterdam 1937), has a more thorough investigation and concludes that

Josephus was well versed, especially, in his knowledge of these historians, as well as of Homer, the tragedians, and Demosthenes. In particular, he shows that Sophoclean elements are hardly restricted to Books XV and XVI and that Thucydidean elements are hardly restricted to Books XVII through XIX of the *Antiquities,* where, according to Henry St. J. Thackeray, *Josephus the Man and the Historian* (New York 1929), pp. 107–118, assistants with a particular love of these authors helped Josephus stylistically. In my review of the reprint of Thackeray, *JAOS* 90 (1970):545–546, I have noted the irony of the fact that neither Thackeray nor anyone else has been able to pinpoint the influence of assistants in the *War,* where Josephus himself (*Ap* I, 50) says he received such help, whereas Josephus says nothing of receiving such assistance in the *Antiquities.* Moreover, there is no indication of the work of assistants in the essay *Against Apion,* clearly Josephus' most polished work. I have also remarked that there are Sophoclean and Thucydidean phrases in other Greek works of the period, notably in Dionysius of Halicarnassus, thus indicating that such language is characteristic of first-century Greek rather than that it is the work of assistants. Moreover, the fact that Josephus used Strabo as a major source in Books XIII through XV shows that there is no sharp dividing line at the beginning of Book XV, as alleged by Thackeray. Finally, the Sophoclean element may be due to Josephus' use of Nicolaus of Damascus, who was Josephus' main source for Books XIV through XVII and who was steeped in that author. The fact that, as shown by Horst R. Moehring, "Novelistic Elements in the Writings of Flavius Josephus" (Diss., University of Chicago 1957), novelistic and erotic elements are found throughout Josephus' writings is another indication that Thackeray's theory is untenable. Moreover, Sidney Michaelson and Andrew Q. Morton, "The New Stylometry: A One-Word Test of Authorship for Greek Writers," *CQ* 22 (1972):89–102, have cast further doubt on this theory by showing that there is no statistically significant difference in the occurrence of the genitive of αὐτός in representative samples of various works of Josephus: Books I and V of the *War,* the *Life,* and *Against Apion,* Book I, though one should have liked to see this study extended to Book VII of the *War,* the style of which seems to be rather different from the rest, and to representative books of the *Antiquities,* especially Book XVIII, which contains the *Testimonium Flavianum.* Thus, the likelihood of a single author for all of them is indicated, though we must note that Michaelson and Morton have not applied their test to the books of the *Antiquities* where, according to Thackeray, Josephus had "Sophoclean" and "Thucydidean" assistants. Heinz Schreckenberg, *Rezeptionsgeschichtliche und Textkritische Untersuchungen zu Flavius Josephus* (Leiden 1977), who has been so intimately connected with the compilation of the concordance of Josephus, likewise has concluded that the works of Josephus show a stylistic and linguistic unity. A further warning has been issued by David J. Ladouceur, "The Language of Josephus," *JSJ* 14 (1983):18–38, that poetic words and Ionic prose forms may simply represent a non-Attic dialectical contribution to the *koine*, as seen in the papyri, and should not be used as unambiguous evidence of the writer's literary attainments. And yet, we may suggest that there may be some significance in the fact that, for example, in the case of the common pronoun ὅδε, which occurs 191 times in Josephus, over half (107) of these are in Books XVII through XIX, which Thackeray assigned to the "Thucydidean hack." Likewise, more than half (11) of the 21 occurrences of the common word πα-ράδειγμα, appear in the "Thucydidean" books of the *Antiquities*.

John G. Gibbs and I, "Josephus' Vocabulary for Slavery," *JQR* 76 (1986):281–310, conclude that Josephus demonstrates no precise verbal distinctions between various kinds of slaves or between other subservients; thus he does not distinguish in his terminology between Jewish and non-Jewish slaves or between one who becomes a slave through inability to pay for his theft and one who becomes a slave in war or between a household slave (οἰκέτης) and a slave in general (δοῦλος). One striking result of the inquiry is the fact that there is a major shift in vocabulary in *Antiquities*, Books XV through XIX; thus the word θεράπων (attendant," "servant"), which occurs 23 times in Books I through XIV, occurs nowhere in Books XV through XIX; this is especially striking when we note that the ratio in the use of the most common word for slave, δοῦλος, is 41:15 as between these parts of Josephus' work. This would seem to be in line with other evidence of the peculiar nature of these later books. Similarly, we may note that the word εὐχαριστεῖν is found 26 times in the *Antiquities* but nowhere in Books XVII through XIX.

As to style, Alfredus Wolff, "De Flavii Iosephi Belli Iudaici scriptoris studiis rhetoricis" (Diss., Halle 1908), has studied, though very selectively and hardly exhaustively, effects such as hiatus, juxtaposition of words, and figures of speech. Wilhelm Hornbostel, "De Flavii Josephi Studiis Rhetoricis Quaestiones Selectae" (Diss., Halle 1912), has collected many examples of rhetorical figures in Josephus. Edmundus Stein, "De Flavii Iosephi arte narrandi," *Eos* 33 (1930–1931):641–659, has brief analyses of Josephus' dramatic descriptions, his use of philosophical "colors," and his rhetoric in speeches. Horst R. Moehring, "Novelistic Elements in the Writings of Flavius Josephus" (Diss., University of Chicago 1957), has argued that the erotic elements in Josephus' treatment of such episodes in the life and loves of Herod are Josephus' own invention. However, we may reply, they may be due to Nicolaus of Damascus, who, we know, was Josephus' major source and whose writings are almost completely lost; the fact is that similar novelistic-erotic elements are found throughout Josephus' works, notably in Josephus' retelling of the Bible, especially in his adaptation of Esther, and in his version of such events as the persecution of the Jews in Rome (*A* XVIII, 66–84)—all of which would appear to substantiate Moehring's case. In connection with the last passage, Bernhard Justus, "Zur Erzählkunst des Flavius Josephus," *Theokratia* 2 (1970–1972):107–136, has commented on Josephus' use of double narrative (*A* XVIII, 66–80; XVIII, 81–84); that is, two stories on the same theme. In this, he appears to be following the literary technique of the tragic school of Hellenistic historians. Similarly, as shown by Raymond R. Newell, "The Suicide Accounts in Josephus: A Form Critical Study," *SBL 1982 Seminar Papers,* Kent H. Richards, ed. (Chicago 1982), pp. 351–369, Josephus follows closely the pattern found in many Greek and Latin writers of suicide narrations, and this would impugn the historical value of such accounts.

A special problem is the question of the composition and authorship of Book VII of the *War,* to which we have alluded above. Yitzhak Baer, "Jerusalem in the Times of the Great Revolt. Based on the Source Criticism of Josephus and Talmudic-Midrashic Legends of the Temple's Destruction" [Hebrew], *Zion* 36 (1971):127–190, who has argued, though hardly convincingly, that almost all of Books II through VI consist of a fiction composed by Josephus' helpers from classical Greek sources to replace Josephus' original Aramaic draft, puts Book VII into a separate category stylistically. Andrew Q. Morton and Sidney Michaelson, "Elision as an Indicator of Authorship in Greek Writers," *ROIELAO* 3 (1973):33–56, have concluded, on the basis of a study of crasis and elision, that Book VII differs from the other books of the *War,* though, we may suggest, this may indicate merely that it did not benefit from the careful mechanical editing that the other books received. Moreover, one wonders how useful such a test is when it indicates different rates of elision for various parts of *Against Apion,* whereas no one has seriously doubted the unity of that work. In the most recent study of Book VII, Seth Schwartz, "The Composition and Publication of Josephus' *Bellum Iudaicum* Book 7," *HTR* 79 (1986):373–386, concludes, on the basis of content rather than of style, that the book consists of three strands: the first composed in 79–81, the second in 82–83, and the third added early in Trajan's reign (ca. 100).

On the question of the Aramaic version of the *War,* Tessa Rajak, *Josephus: The Historian and His Society* (London 1983), pp. 178–184, has expressed doubt that Josephus really composed such a version at all and suggests that the Aramaic version was merely a short booklet that was not intended to be used by the Roman emperors as a form of propaganda, since at this time there was hardly much of a military threat from the Parthians; and, in any case, the Jews of Babylonia would have had difficulty in understanding Josephus' western Aramaic. We may reply, however, that there was a long history of tension between the Parthian and Roman Empires; that Josephus would hardly have undertaken to write such a pamphlet if he knew that it would be understood only with difficulty; and that the fact, as seems likely, that Josephus had an Aramaic source (presumably in the Babylonian dialect) for the extended account of Asinaeus and Anilaeus, as indicated by Abraham Schalit, "Evidence of an Aramaic Source in Josephus' 'Antiquities of the Jews'," *ASTI* 4 (1965): 163–188, makes it likely that the difference between the two dialects was not so great. Support for Schalit's thesis, we may add, has been given by Naomi G. Cohen, "Asinaeus and Anilaeus: Additional Comments to Josephus' Antiquities of the Jews," *ASTI* 10 (1975–1976):30–37, who notes several unusual Greek expressions that can be best understood as Aramaic.

Another question that has been raised is Josephus' knowledge of Latin. The only Roman writer Josephus mentions by name is Livy (*A* XIV, 69); and Gustav Hölscher, "Josephus," *RE* 9 (1916), pp. 1977ff., does, indeed, claim that he was one of Josephus' chief sources. But, since there is only this one reference, it may have come from another source or from a collection of excerpts. If, however, Theodor Mommsen, "Cornelius Tacitus und Cluvius Rufus," *Hermes* 4 (1870):295–325, is correct in postulating that Josephus' source for the lengthy account of the assassination of Caligula and of the accession of Claudius is Cluvius Rufus, a thesis that, as noted earlier, I have disputed in "The Sources of Josephus' *Antiquities*, Book 19," *Latomus* 21 (1962):320–333, this would certainly answer the question in the affirmative.

Beniamin Nadel, "Quid Flavius Josephus sermoni atque colori dicendi invectivarum Romanorum debuerit" ("Josephus Flavius and the Terminology of Roman Political Invective") [Polish with Latin summary], *Eos* 56 (1966): 256–272, asserts, though hardly with conclusive proof, that Josephus' polemical vocabulary against the Zealots and the Sicarii is indebted to the invectives of Sallust and Cicero. David Daube, "Three Legal Notes on Josephus after His Surrender," *LQR* 93 (1977):191–194, finds Latinisms in Josephus' use of κελεύσαντος (*V* 414) in the sense of *iubeo,* as employed in the normal Roman marriage ceremony; but, even if Josephus did use this single word in this sense, it hardly proves his ability to read and to be influenced by Latin literature. If we ask how Josephus could have lived in Rome for three decades without learning Latin, the answer may be that there were so many Greek-speaking inhabitants in Rome (including especially the Jews, as we may see from the predominant use of Greek in tombstone inscriptions) that he may hardly have felt a need to learn Latin.

The Influence of Josephus

In view of the influence of Josephus both during the Middle Ages—that there are 171 manuscripts of the Latin version of the *Antiquities* is one indication of his popularity—and modern times, it is surprising that there is no systematic study of this topic. Eva M. Sanford, "Propaganda and Censorship in the Transmission of Josephus," *TAPA* 66 (1935):127–145, has discussed briefly the motives of the interpolations and changes in the text of Josephus in the course of its transmission, though, we may remark, the only passage in

Josephus the authenticity of which has been seriously contested is the *Testimonium Flavianum* (*A* XVIII, 63–64); and one wonders why an interpolator should not have sought to effect further changes in Josephus' text, especially in his discussion of John the Baptist (*A* XVIII, 116–119), which contradicts the Gospels. Heinz Schreckenberg, *Die Flavius-Josephus-Tradition in Antike und Mittelalter* (Leiden 1972) lists systematically all citations, direct or indirect, from Josephus in authors from antiquity through the sixteenth century, with bibliography and very brief discussions for each author; but he has missed a number of writers who show the influence of Josephus, such as Prosper of Aquitaine's *Chronicum Integrum* of the fifth century, the *Palaea Historia* of the ninth century, Albarus of Cordova in the ninth century, Baudri of Bourgueil in the eleventh century, Alchrine in the twelfth century, and Frutolf in the twelfth century.

In "Josephus und die christliche Wirkungsgeschichte seines 'Bellum Judaicum'," *ANRW* 2.21.2 (1984), pp. 1106–1217, Schreckenberg has emphasized that the church fathers found in Josephus' *War* a strong affinity with New Testament themes, especially the significance of the destruction of the Temple and its connection with the passion of Jesus. We may cite, in particular, the influence of Josephus upon the twelfth-century Peter Comestor, noted, though hardly exhaustively, by Sandra R. Karp, "Peter Comestor's Historia Scholastica: A Study in the Development of Literal Scriptural Exegesis" (Ph.D. diss., Tulane University 1978). The fact that Comestor's work soon became the most popular book in Europe is a gauge of Josephus' influence, since Comestor used Josephus to such a degree that he is often a clue to restoring the original text of the Latin translation of Josephus and vice versa.

Josephus' influence may also be seen in the popularity of the legend of Josephus the physician who cured Titus of a swollen leg, as commented upon by Hans Lewy, "Josephus the Physician: A Mediaeval Legend of the Destruction of Jerusalem," *JWI* 1 (1937–1938):221–242, and Guido Kisch, "A Talmudic Legend as the Source for the Josephus Passage in the Sachsenspiegel," *HJ* 1 (1938–1939):105–118. Lewy suggests that the author of the legend was a converted Jew who drew upon both Josephus and the Talmud (*Gittin* 56b); but we may remark that the talmudic version speaks only of a brain disease from which Titus died. The idea that Josephus was a physician may have arisen, as Lewy suggests, from the fact that so many medieval rabbis were famous as physicians.

The influence of Josephus upon Byzantine writers, which was likewise profound, remains to be examined in detail. Rivkah Fishman-Duker (Duker-Fishman), "The Second Temple Period in Byzantine Chronicles," *Byzantion* 47 (1977):126–156, and "The Works of Josephus as a Source for Byzantine Chronicles" [Hebrew], *CP* (1982):139–148, has noted that his influence on Byzantine chroniclers varies from writer to writer.

The only systematic study of the influence of Josephus on a modern literature is Maria Rosa Lida de Malkiel's unfinished and unpublished study of his influence on Spanish literature, which reaches 1000 pages in typescript, as described by Yakov Malkiel, "El libro infinido de M.R.L. de M.: Josefo y su influencia en la literera española," *Filologia* 13 (1968–1969):205–226. Similar studies on Josephus' influence on English, French, German, Italian, and other modern literatures are very much needed.

A study of illustrations of the works of Josephus has been made by Guy N. Deutsch, "Iconographie de l'illustration de Flavius Josèphe au temps de Jean Fouquet" (Ph.D. diss., Hebrew University 1978), who, though he concentrates on the period of Fouquet in the fifteenth century, also discusses his predecessors at length. The study of the influence upon music of themes drawn from Josephus remains to be made.

Brief studies of the influence of the Slavonic version of the *War* may be found in Dmitrij Tschiżewskij, *Geschichte der altrussischen Literatur im 11., 12., und 13. Jahrhundert, Kiever Epoche* (Frankfurt 1948), pp. 313–314, 355–358; Nikolai K. Gudzii, *History of Early Russian Literature*, translated from the 2d Russian ed. (New York 1949), pp. 57–63, 222–224; and Adolf Stender-Petersen, *Den russiske litteraturs historie I–III* (Copenhagen 1952); translated into German as *Geschichte der russischen Literatur*, vol. 1, (München 1957), pp. 91–96; but an exhaustive study remains a desideratum.

The influence of Josippon likewise deserves a comprehensive treatment. Y. Lainer, "On Josephus [i.e., Josippon] and His Books in Rabbinic Literature" [Hebrew], in *Sura*, Samuel K. Mirsky, ed. (Jerusalem 1953–1954), pp. 428–438, traces uncritically this influence upon the great rabbis of medieval and modern times. Jacob Reiner, "The English Yosippon," *JQR* 58 (1967–1968):126–142, concludes that Morvvyng's translation of Josippon into English should be classified with the anti-Jewish literature of the seventeenth century that opposed Cromwell's move to permit the Jews to resettle in England. However, the fact that the translation was published in 1558, a century before Cromwell, would argue against this theory, though, of course, it was used by those who opposed the reentry of the Jews.

The Future of Josephan Studies

Shaye J. D. Cohen, "Josephus, Jeremiah, and Polybius," HT 21 (1982): 380, n. 41, lists the following as important topics awaiting investigation: (1) Roman sources of Josephus' thought; (2) a detailed comparison of Josephus' views with those of Dionysius of Halicarnassus, Dio Chrysostom, Plutarch, and Aelius Aristides; (3) other biblical typologies that might have affected Josephus' self-perception; (4) Jeremianic and Polybian themes in the *Jewish Antiquities;* and (5) Josephus' views on the future of Rome and Israel.

To these we may add the following: (1) a new edition of the Greek text, taking into account the advances in scholarship on the subject of textual criticism generally and availing itself of the newly completed concordance to determine Josephus' word usage; (2) a scientific edition of the Latin translation of Josephus, which is of importance since it antedates the earliest Greek manuscripts by approximately five hundred years; (3) the compilation of a grammar of Josephus, which will be of great help to the next editor of Josephus' Greek text; (4) a systematic analysis of the places where archaeology confirms or refutes Josephus' geographical and other descriptive comments; (5) the completion of David Goldenberg's study comparing Josephus' views on the spectrum of Jewish law with those of Philo, the Dead Sea sect, and the talmudic rabbis; (6) the completion of systematic studies of Josephus' version of the biblical text and content, especially as compared with Philo, Pseudo-Philo's *Biblical Antiquities,* and rabbinic Midrashim; and (7) a systematic study of the influence of Josephus, Josippon, and the Slavonic version upon literature, art, and music, and the correlation of this influence with historical movements, such as the Crusades, the Renaissance, the Reformation, the Enlightenment, and the rise of modern Zionism.

Index of References to Josephus

Antiquitates Judaicae

IV.140: 66
IV.153: 36
IV.180–83: 199
IV.189: 67
IV.198: 403
IV.201: 202
IV.219: 27
IV.223–24: 200
IV.266: 418
IV.326: 360
V.1: 324
V.21: 324
V.84: 312, 313
V.125: 317
V.182: 67
V.200: 67
V.234: 68
V.235–39: 67
V.251–53: 292
V.265: 68
V.276: 69
V.277: 69
V.279: 69
V.280: 70
V.281: 70
V.282: 70
V.284: 70
V.285: 83
V.286 ff: 70
V.298: 68
V.305: 70
V.306: 70
V.309: 71
V.313: 71
V.314 ff: 71
V.316: 71
V.318 ff: 54
V.344–45: 71
V.370–72: 292
VI.1: 324
VI.3: 324
VI.4: 324
VI.36: 351
VI.45: 73
VI.49: 72
VI.50: 73
VI.68–69: 82
VI.84–85: 351
VI.104–5: 85
VI.137: 73

VI.173: 85
VI.186–87: 292
VI.262–68: 72
VI.263–64: 72
VI.268: 351
VI.296: 87
VI.325: 87
VI.343: 72
VI.343–50: 72, 358
VI.348: 72
VI.349: 73
VI.368–73: 286
VII.61 ff: 328
VII.66: 329
VII.78: 86
VII.85: 88
VII.100: 166
VII.103: 166
VII.121: 88
VII.174: 86
VII.228–29: 286, 292
VII.228–30: 286
VII.328: 86
VIII.4: 324
VIII.6: 324
VIII.7: 324
VIII.12: 324
VIII.13: 324
VIII.108: 407
VIII.111: 408
VIII.131: 83
VIII.142: 47
VIII.144–46: 402
VIII.147: 402
VIII.149: 402
VIII.227: 407
VIII.280: 202
VIII.363: 166
VIII.363–80: 166
VIII.392: 166
VIII.401: 166
IX.1: 324
IX.2: 324
IX.28: 360
IX.182: 434
X.35: 55, 57, 58
X.37: 206
X.78–79: 54, 57
X.79: 57
X.149: 205

X.149–53: 205
X.152–53: 33
X.210: 37, 57
X.266–81: 365
X.267: 57
X.276: 57
X.277–81: 408
X.278: 175
XI.5: 57
XI.11: 352
XI.85: 198
XI.86: 205
XI.111: 201, 205
XI.184: 54, 57
XI.229: 57
XI.273–83: 366
XI.296: 54
XI.297–301: 367
XI.299–300: 203
XI.304: 504
XI.309–10: 200
XI.317–47: 202, 206
XII.4: 324
XII.7: 324
XII.11ff: 57
XII.11–18: 22, 369
XII.12: 104
XII.14: 394
XII.15: 394
XII.17: 394
XII.20: 25, 104
XII.22: 207
XII.48: 25
XII.56–57: 98
XII.57: 23
XII.107: 394
XII.108b: 104
XII.119: 384
XII.136: 34
XII.138–53: 369
XII.145–46: 369
XII.148–53: 369
XII.158–236: 370
XII.184: 54
XII.237: 191
XII.240ff: 57
XII.241ff: 116
XII.248: 131
XII.252: 46
XII.255–56: 130

XII.267: 122, 124
XII.281–82: 124
XII.285: 123
XII.286: 123
XII.289–91: 119, 120
XII.292: 120
XII.302: 127
XII.303: 123
XII.304: 124
XII.307: 121
XII.314: 123
XII.315: 125
XII.316: 122
XII.318: 118
XII.319: 131
XII.321: 131
XII.352: 119
XII.387f: 191
XII.408–9: 121
XII.411: 128
XII.412: 131
XII.415–19: 402
XII.433: 123
XIII.1: 324
XIII.4: 324
XIII.5: 119
XIII.5–6: 125
XIII.9: 324
XIII.12ff: 187
XIII.41ff: 348
XIII.62–73: 191
XIII.74–79: 420
XIII.86–119: 372
XIII.115–17: 198
XIII.126: 141
XIII.145–83: 181
XIII.171ff: 176, 187
XIII.171: 30, 174, 178, 189, 407
XIII.171–73: 173, 176, 177, 181, 407
XIII.172: 189, 190, 408
XIII.172–73: 407
XIII.173: 174, 176
XIII.197–99: 207
XIII.228–35: 133
XIII.240–50: 207
XIII.245: 171
XIII.249: 182
XIII.253: 167
XIII.254ff: 182
XIII.257: 193

XIII.257–58: 33
XIII.261: 371
XIII.282: 198
XIII.288: 178, 181, 193
XIII.288 ff: 170, 174
XIII.288–96: 180
XIII.288–97: 372
XIII.288–98: 176
XIII.290–99: 202, 208
XIII.291: 135, 192, 208
XIII.292: 208
XIII.293: 174
XIII.293–96: 32
XIII.294: 194, 208
XIII.296: 180, 276
XIII.297 f: 177
XIII.297–298: 32
XIII.298: 174, 176, 191
XIII.299–300: 31, 208
XIII.299 f: 182
XIII.302–404: 193
XIII.308: 135
XIII.318: 33
XIII.320: 135
XIII.344: 168
XIII.345–47: 168
XIII.372: 208
XIII.372 ff: 193
XIII.395–97: 33
XIII.397: 372
XIII.398: 137
XIII.399–404: 136
XIII.404: 136
XIII.405–32: 137
XIII.406: 136, 137
XIII.407: 136, 137
XIII.408: 209
XIII.408 ff: 182
XIII.409: 32
XIII.410 ff: 421
XIII.418: 137
XIII.424: 140
XIII.430: 27
XIII.432: 138
XIV.2: 170
XIV.2–3: 118
XIV.5: 140
XIV.8: 155, 168
XIV.9: 28
XIV.18: 372

XIV.20: 260
XIV.24: 260
XIV.43: 260
XIV.43–47: 260
XIV.66: 209
XIV.69–70: 281
XIV.72: 209
XIV.77: 139
XIV.78: 182
XIV.79: 141
XIV.90: 140
XIV.97: 140, 141
XIV.110: 414
XIV.124–25: 141
XIV.126: 141
XIV.127: 210
XIV.128–32: 210
XIV.138: 379
XIV.141–42: 171
XIV.142: 35
XIV.145–48: 375
XIV.145–55: 375
XIV.149–55: 375
XIV.159: 260
XIV.159 ff: 193
XIV.175: 183
XIV.188: 384
XIV.190–212: 375
XIV.202: 260
XIV.208: 260
XIV.217–22: 375
XIV.297: 141
XIV.330 ff: 141
XIV.353–62: 142
XIV.367: 281
XIV.367–69: 292
XIV.385: 193
XIV.389: 379
XIV.403: 184
XIV.427: 282
XIV.429–30: 283, 439
XIV.467: 144
XV.3: 379
XV.6: 183
XV.11–15: 210
XV.13: 292
XV.22: 183
XV.24: 142
XV.25–30: 171
XV.26–27: 142

XV.40: 211
XV.46: 143
XV.46–48: 143
XV.50–56: 143
XV.55–56: 143
XV.58: 143
XV.62–63: 143
XV.71–73: 143
XV.87: 143
XV.174: 210
XV.179–81: 209
XV.179–82: 209
XV.181: 210
XV.183–86: 143
XV.216–17: 27
XV.228–29: 144
XV.228–31: 378
XV.232–36: 144
XV.247–51: 143
XV.259–60: 420
XV.264: 262
XV.320ff: 183
XV.343: 379
XV.358–59: 292
XV.365: 260
XV.371–79: 170
XV.373–78: 29, 58
XV.380: 260, 263
XV.389: 379
XV.410: 46
XV.411–16: 327
XVI.26: 169
XVI.90ff: 171
XVI.154: 260
XVI.179–85: 172
XVI.184: 172
XVI.225: 224
XVI.271: 17
XVI.291: 262
XVI.299: 171
XVI.335–55: 169
XVI.367–72: 378
XVII.20: 379
XVII.41–45: 170
XVII.41–46: 226
XVII.54ff: 169
XVII.89–145: 378
XVII.149ff: 276
XVII.152: 130
XVII.168–69: 379

XVII.182–87: 378
XVII.228–49: 169
XVII.230–47: 169
XVII.271: 260, 276
XVII.289: 260
XVII.301–23: 169
XVII.308: 260
XVII.309: 171
XVII.315: 171
XVII.323: 168
XVII.339: 184
XVIII.1: 424
XVIII.1–2: 434
XVIII.3: 184, 226, 435
XVIII.4: 179, 260, 277, 426
XVIII.4–9: 230
XVIII.5: 260, 424
XVIII.6: 388
XVIII.6–7: 226
XVIII.9: 126, 425
XVIII.10: 388
XVIII.11: 30, 174, 176
XVIII.11–22: 173, 176
XVIII.12: 189
XVIII.17: 32, 181, 187
XVIII.18: 190
XVIII.18–22: 170, 190, 423
XVIII.19: 31, 35, 423, 424
XVIII.20–21: 170
XVIII.21: 170
XVIII.22: 170
XVIII.23: 187, 425, 427
XVIII.26: 184
XVIII.34: 184
XVIII.37: 428
XVIII.55–59: 382
XVIII.60ff: 277
XVIII.63: 37
XVIII.63–64: 430, 446
XVIII.66–84: 443
XVIII.81–84: 413
XVIII.90–95: 382
XVIII.101–105: 380
XVIII.116–19: 429, 446
XVIII.122–26: 382
XVIII.136: 420
XVIII.147: 262
XVIII.252: 380
XVIII.269–71: 26
XVIII.272–74: 38

XVIII.274: 263
XVIII.293–98: 173
XVIII.310–79: 373
XVIII.314–15: 263
XVIII.314–79: 380
XIX.91–92: 383, 404
XIX.186: 68
XIX.273: 280
XIX.280–85: 382, 384
XIX.326–27: 46
XX.2: 260
XX.3: 322
XX.5: 260
XX.8: 322
XX.17–96: 373, 380
XX.80: 280
XX.90: 414
XX.113–17: 263
XX.121: 37
XX.137: 382

XX.161: 37
XX.161–64: 194
XX.168–72: 233
XX.179–81: 388
XX.195: 414
XX.197–203: 203, 212, 211, 434
XX.198: 211
XX.199: 31, 34, 184, 194
XX.199f: 173, 174, 183, 185
XX.200: 37, 185, 430
XX.201: 185
XX.201–3: 185
XX.205–6: 262
XX.206–7: 263
XX.216–17: 263
XX.222: 263
XX.224–51: 33, 409
XX.229: 351
XX.231: 33, 205
XX.234: 352

Bellum Judaicum

I.1: 322, 324
I.3: 186, 196, 394
I.5: 324
I.7–9: 290
I.13ff: 170
I.22: 409
I.33: 191
I.34–35: 130
I.54–60: 133
I.56: 207
I.63: 193
I.67f: 173
I.67–69: 31
I.68–69: 58, 205, 208
I.76: 135
I.85: 135
I.86: 168
I.97: 276
I.107: 135, 138
I.107–12: 182
I.107–19: 137
I.109: 136
I.111: 32
I.111–12: 27
I.118: 174

I.121: 140
I.122: 174
I.137: 174
I.142: 174
I.148: 36
I.149–51: 281
I.150: 260
I.158: 141
I.162: 177
I.168: 140
I.169: 201
I.174: 140, 141
I.184–85: 141
I.186: 141
I.197: 171
I.204ff: 193, 260
I.204: 225
I.239: 141
I.248: 141
I.256: 225
I.263–67: 142
I.271: 281
I.271–73: 292
I.282: 193
I.303: 232

VII.253: 426
VII.254: 232, 260
VII.259–74: 425, 426
VII.262: 36, 439
VII.289: 437
VII.290: 437
VII.297: 437
VII.304–406: 292
VII.315–19: 437
VII.324: 232
VII.336: 437
VII.341–88: 401
VII.379: 36
VII.387: 439
VII.394: 437
VII.395: 437

VII.397: 437
VII.399: 27, 41, 437
VII.400: 437
VII.404: 437
VII.405: 36, 437, 438
VII.405–6: 43
VII.407: 437
VII.410ff: 231
VII.417: 36
VII.417–19: 125, 219
VII.437: 263
VII.437ff: 231
VII.438: 45
VII.440: 232
XII.421–32: 409

Contra Apionem

I.29: 205
I.29–30: 206
I.36: 206
I.37–43: 18–19, 50–51
I.38–41: 113
I.41: 57
I.42: 125
I.48: 428
I.50: 21, 394, 420
I.54: 47, 187, 206
I.66: 403
I.116–20: 402
I.145–295: 405
I.167: 47
I.218: 104, 402
II.9: 321
II.91–96: 34
II.106: 34, 199
II.145–295: 399, 401

II.158: 193
II.163: 417
II.164–219: 419
II.167: 202
II.185: 190, 193, 202
II.190–219: 417
II.190: 203
II.193: 202
II.194: 200
II.197: 408
II.200: 418
II.213: 125
II.218: 125
II.223–24: 40
II.235: 130
II.256–57: 40
II.272: 125
II.279: 193
II.292: 130

Vita

1f: 187
1: 178
2: 187
2–4: 196
7: 40
7–9: 99

7–12: 208
9: 341
9–12: 419
10–12: 187, 341
12: 27, 32, 100, 174, 420, 423
22f: 277

Index

Jephthah's daughter, 68
Jerahmeel, 335–36
Jeremiah, Book of, 52
Jericho, description of, 303–4, 305
Jerome, 24, 98–99, 111, 112, 113, 431, 433
Jerusalem: Alexander's visit to, 368–69; archaeological excavations in, 46, 327–29; Jewish population of, 41; Josephus' description of, 44–45, 46, 302, 306, 317, 326, 327–29; Josephus' familiarity with, 46, 325, 327; Josephus' history of, 45–46, 326; radical activists in, 255; siege of, 153, 201, 202, 206, 230–31, 233; Titus' conquest of, 392–93; walls of, 116, 329. *See also* Palestine; Priesthood, high; Temple
Jervell, Jacob, 406
Jesus, 18, 24, 42, 64, 224, 227, 252, 340, 346, 360, 413. *See also Testimonium Flavianum*
Jesus ben Damnaeus, 211
Jewish Antiquities (Josephus). *See Antiquitates Judaicae* (Josephus)
Jewish law in Josephus, 18, 416–20
Jewish Temple State, 203
Jewish War: Adiabenian role in, 414; attitude of sects toward, 228–29; comparison of Josephus and rabbinic accounts of, 386, 390; comparison with Contestado Rebellion, 257–58; economic causes of, 37–38, 40–41, 237–59, 387, 427–28; and fall of Jotapata, 42, 281; Jewish proselytism as cause of, 386–87; Josephus' contributions on economic causes of, 38, 40, 258–59; Marxist view of causes of, 39–41, 265–76, 387; preceding struggles to, 269–71; religious factors in, 35, 41, 216–23, 237–38, 257, 272–73; and revolutionary movements (*see* Revolutionary parties); size of Roman forces in, 391; stages of, 229–31
Jewish War (Josephus). *See Bellum Judaicum* (Josephus)
Joazar, 184
Johanan (high priest), 203
John of Gischala, 227, 230, 231, 233–35, 243, 244, 343, 429
John the Baptist, 18, 429–30, 446

Jonathan Aristobulus III (high priest), 142, 143, 180, 210, 211
Jones, Arnold H. M., 376
Jones, Brian W., 393
Josephson of Gorion, 230
Josephus, Flavius: accused of treason, 342, 344, 386; attack on tyranny by, 68; attitude toward rebels, 231–33, 274–76, 388, 396–97; attitude toward women, 26–28, 32, 43, 145n; belief in messiah, 37; belief in miracles, 412; bibliography of (*see* Bibliography of Josephus); biographical approach to history, 29; as characterized by Reinach, 273; charged as propagandist, 17; Christianity in work of, 429–30 (*see also Testimonium Flavianum*); education in Jewish tradition, 19–20, 21, 395; as exponent of ruling class, 273–76; future studies of, 447–48; as general in Galilee, 40, 296, 341–43, 344, 436; geographical details in work of, 295–321, 327–29, 435–40; Hasmonean descent of, 32, 33, 35, 46, 182, 187–88, 325; high priests as reported by (*see* Priesthood, high); importance as historical source, 17–18; importance for Christianity, 18; indictment of Nicolaus, 163, 164; influence of, 445–47; at Jotapata, 42, 266, 281, 410, 411; justification of war, 26, 119–20, 125–27; and Justus of Tiberias, 343–44; knowledge of Greek, 36–37; knowledge of Latin, 445; language in work of, 440–45; member of priestly/landowning family, 33, 39–40, 186–87, 196, 267, 274; Nicolaus as source for, 28–29, 30, 34, 133, 143, 147, 150–51, 152, 153–55, 156, 158–59, 176, 370, 400, 402–3, 421, 442; Palestine described by, 435–40; personal knowledge of Palestine, 44, 296, 325, 327; praise of martyrdom, 25–26, 124–25, 129n, 130n; projected work of, 399–400; refutation of anti-Semitism by, 17, 26, 296, 366, 384; reliability as historical source, 46–47; religious beliefs of, 405–16; and sects, 30, 174–78, 341, 407, 420–29 (*see also* Essenes; Pharisees;

Morton, Andrew Q., 45, 396, 442, 444
Morvvyne, Peter, 336
Moscovitz, Larry, 363
Moses, 24, 34, 56, 74, 200, 224, 225, 227,
317–18, 361–62; birth of, 64–65;
campaign against Ethiopians, 152, 361,
362–63; farewell address of, 67; treat-
ment by Nicolaus, 151, 152
Moses, Books of, 54, 55
Motzo, Bacchisio R., 355, 365
Mount Carmel, 312, 313, 314
Mount Gerizim, 182, 227, 424
Mount Tabor, 312–13, 314
Mras, Carolus, 334
Müller, Joel, 23
Muraoka, T., 90, 91, 92, 353

Naber, Samuel A., 332, 334
Nadel, Benjamin, 445
Nero, 220
Neuman, Abraham A., 336, 338
Neusner, Jacob, 132, 136, 359, 372–73,
413, 421
Newell, Raymond R., 42–43, 44
Nicetas, 112
Nickelsburg, George W. E., 361
Nicolaus of Damascus, 21, 139, 407; as
agent of Herod, 147, 161, 162; description of Jewish customs and practice, 159–60; description of Jewish
sects, 160–61; life and works of, 147;
reliability of contemporary account,
161–64; scope of biblical histories,
148–50; as source for Josephus,
28–29, 30, 34, 133, 143, 147, 151,
152, 153–55, 156, 158–59, 176, 370,
400, 402–3, 421, 442, 443; sources
for biblical histories of, 147, 151–52;
suicide account of, 286–87; treatment
of Abraham, 150, 151, 152; treatment
of Herod, 29, 30, 155–58, 161–63;
treatment of Jewish Hellenistic history,
152–59; treatment of Judean and Syrian prowess, 150; treatment of Moses,
152; treatment of Noah's ark, 151, 152
Niditch, Susan, 370
Niese, Benedictus, 331–32, 333, 334,
349–50
Nikiprowetzky, Valentin, 35–37
Nimrod, 78 n

Noah's ark, 28, 150–51, 152
Norden, Eduard, 431
North, Martin, 270

Oellacher, Hans, 332
Olitzki, Marcus, 416
Olympias (mother of Alexander the Great),
134
Olympiodorus, 111
Onias IV, 370
Origen, 98, 430, 431, 434
Othniel, 61, 67
Ott, Johann B., 440
Otto, Walter, 376
Ovid, 78 n

Palestine: census of Quirinius in, 184, 226,
242, 434–35; coinage of, 252–53;
cultivator class in, 246–47, 250–52,
254; day laborer in, 258; expansion of
Jewish settlement in, 37, 301; Gabinius' organization of, 374; geographical
description of, 44–45, 295–321,
435–40; geographical divisions of,
299–300; Hellenization of, 36–37,
41, 238–39, 288, 367; Jewish coexistence with Rome, 41, 373–76;
Jewish-Greek conflict in, 39, 41, 387–
88; Josephus' personal knowledge of,
44, 296, 325, 327; Josephus' views on
future of, 412, 413; land distribution
in, 238–39, 244–46, 267–68, 387;
national consciousness in, 256, 257;
overpopulation in, 39, 40, 251; problems of indebtedness in, 351–52, 387;
relations with frontier populations in,
256; revolts at death of Herod in,
158–59, 225, 271, 380; rise of zealous
theology in, 220–21; under Roman
procurators, 381–82; social/agrarian
change in, 37–38, 40, 247–50; taxation in, 241, 242–43, 255, 268;
tradesmen/craftsmen in, 255, 268–69;
tribes in, 313–15; upper class in, 38,
238–39, 244, 246, 267–68, 387;
urban-rural cleavage in, 254–55. See
also Hasmonean dynasty; Herod; Jerusalem; Jewish War; Priesthood, high;
Revolutionary parties; Temple

Louis H. Feldman received his B.A. and M.A. degrees from Trinity College and his Ph.D. from Harvard University. A professor of classics at Yeshiva University, Dr. Feldman has also taught at Trinity College and Hobart and William Smith Colleges.

Gohei Hata received his B.A. at the International Christian University, his M.A. at Kyoto University, and his Ph.D. at Dropsie University. A professor at Tama Bijutsu University, he previously taught at Kyoto Sangyo University and the Graduate School of Kyoto University.

The manuscript was edited by Gnomi Schrift Gouldin. The book was designed by Joanne Elkin Kinney. The typeface for the text and the display is Times Roman with American Uncial used as an additional display face. The book is printed on 60-lb. Arbor text paper. The cloth edition is bound in Kivar 9 Chrome over binders boards. The paper cover is 12 pt. Carolina ClS.

Manufactured in the United States of America.